*An Economic History*

*of Medieval Europe*

# An
# Economic History
# of Medieval Europe

*N.J.G. Pounds*

LONGMAN

# Longman
# 1724-1974

LONGMAN GROUP LIMITED
London
and LONGMAN INC., NEW YORK
*Associated companies, branches and representatives
throughout the world*

First published 1974

ISBN 0 582 48266 6
Library of Congress Catalog Card Number: 73–93716
Phototypeset in Apollo by Filmtype Services Limited, Scarborough
and printed in Great Britain
by Whitstable Litho (Straker Brothers Limited)

ISBN 0 582 48680·7
Paperback Edition

# Contents

# List of Figures

ix

# Foreword

This book is the first of two which will cover the economic history of Europe from the time of the Romans until the recent past. The divide between them comes at about 1500, though there will inevitably be a small overlap. This particular volume had its origin and its basic organisation in a course of lectures given in the Department of History of Indiana University, though in scope and detail it has grown far beyond this original format.

An attempt has been made to present the economic history of continental Europe as a whole, giving as much attention to Eastern Europe and the Balkans as considerations of space and balance would permit. References to Great Britain are incidental, and are made only when British developments – the wool trade, for example – impinged directly on those of continental Europe. Russia, similarly, receives scant attention, since, for much of the period covered, it lay remote from the affairs of 'peninsular' Europe. The method has been to begin (Chapters 1–3) and end (Chapter 10) with chapters which deal broadly with the changing economy, and to sandwich between them six topical or systematic chapters, which each deal with one of the salient sectors of the economy. Such an organisation leads inevitably to a certain repetitiveness, and for this the author apologises.

The author is greatly indebted to his friends and colleagues at Indiana University for their help and encouragement, especially to Professors Glanville Downey, A. R. Hogue, and Maureen F. Mazzaoui (now of the University of Wisconsin), each of whom read much of the manuscript; to Dr Edward Miller, Master of Fitzwilliam College of the University of Cambridge; to Dr John

Hatcher of the Department of History of the University of Kent at Canterbury, who also read and commented on it; and to numerous students, especially Miss Annette Koren, whose 'feedback' did much to soften some of its asperities.

He also wishes to express his gratitude to Professor E. M. Carus-Wilson for permission to use her graph of English cloth and wool exports; to Mr R. A. G. Carson of the Department of Coins of the British Museum for authorising him to make the drawing in Figure 9.2 from illustrations in his study of the coinage systems of the world.

*Department of History,*
*Indiana University,*
*Bloomington,*
*Ind., U.S.A.*

# 1

# The later Roman Empire

In the middle years of the second century A.D. the Roman Empire stood at the height of its power and prosperity. Eulogised by contemporaries and praised by posterity, the Empire was peaceful, happy and affluent. From this high level under the Antonine emperors the fortunes of the Empire declined – so it is commonly held – to the nadir of its fortunes in the fifth century, when power fell from the hands of the last feeble emperor in the West, and imperial soil was occupied by barbarian invaders and ruled by their tribal leaders.

The reasons for this reversal of fortunes have been a subject of controversy and debate for fifteen centuries, and every possible argument, from racial degeneration to climatic change, has been advanced. The decline of Rome still arouses interest, even though no one today would dare to explain it in terms of a single decisive factor. The phenomenon of Rome's fall was complex, and no simple explanation can ever be admissible.

All was not well with the empire of Antoninus Pius and Marcus Aurelius. The legend of the golden age of the Antonines is unquestionably exaggerated, and by this time the seeds of Rome's decay had already been sown. Fighting was increasing in intensity along the frontiers of the Empire, and Marcus Aurelius was obliged to spend much of his later years campaigning along the Danube. The army was increased in size and heavier taxes were levied to support it. The soldiery, once recruited from among the peasants of Italy, was more and more drawn from provincials and even from those barbarian peoples whom it was its purpose to resist. Heavy and all too often inequitable taxation depressed the

1

peasant and increased the gulf between rich and poor. The well-to-do broadened their estates while the descendants of a once free peasantry become in the course of time *coloni*, bound to the soil of their masters.

The needs of defence explained and in some measure excused the strengthening of imperial control over the provinces and over the cities (*civitates*) of which they were composed. The imperial bureaucracy grew in size and power, and the social structure became increasingly rigid. Imperial edicts bound the craftsman to his trade and the farmer to his land. Such occupations, and even membership of the city councils, were made hereditary, restricting social mobility and destroying initiative.

The cities, the principal bearers of Roman civilisation and culture, had grown steadily in number, as well as in size and splendour during the later years of the Republic and under the Principate. But few were founded after the first century A.D. and almost none after the middle of the second. The erection of vast public buildings and the construction of public works such as aqueducts and baths, diminished in importance during the second century, except in Rome itself, and, during the third, the building of defensive walls against barbarian raids came to be of greater urgency and importance.

The age of the Antonines was a watershed between the period of territorial expansion and economic growth which had, in general, characterised the Principate, and that of invasion and economic recession which followed. The economic change which took place in these centuries is difficult to trace and impossible to express in any quantitative manner. The decline was not continuous or consistent; there were periods when the fortunes of the Empire appear to have taken an upward turn; when the military commanders met with success on the frontiers and the Emperors, through their edicts, tried courageously, if in the end vainly, to stem the spreading social evils of the times.

Nor was the decline common to the whole Empire. The Middle East and eastern Mediterranean did not in all respects share the fortunes of the western Mediterranean and of the European provinces. If the Roman Empire in the West 'fell' in the fifth century, one must always remember that the Eastern Empire, with its focus in Constantinople, continued for another thousand years.

The 'fall' of the Roman Empire, politically considered, meant the termination of a succession of emperors who had ruled it from Rome or Milan or Ravenna. At the same time the provinces of the Empire were transformed into kingdoms ruled by barbarian leaders and dominated by a non-Roman élite. This transition, however, was not matched by any comparable event in the economic field. The urbanised society of the second century passed slowly and gradually into the non-urbanised society of the early Middle Ages. Trade, which had characterised the former, dried up, and the interdependence of town and country and of one province with another by and large gave way to local self-sufficiency and isolation. This was not a sudden and revolutionary change. It took centuries to accomplish, just as, during the Middle Ages, it took centuries to restore towns, manufacturing and trade to the European economy.

This economic change was not an even and continuous process. It was strongly marked in the third century, but in the fourth there was a recovery in the West, followed by a golden autumn of the ancient world, before the winter of the Dark Ages. The fortunes of the Western Empire were not reflected in those of the Eastern. The latter did not fall. Its territory was restricted by invading Persians and Slavs and later by Arabs, but its capital city of Constantinople remained inviolate and its ships continued to ply the seas, bearing its trade and maintaining the food supply of its cities.

There were many reasons for this contrast. The eastern provinces were wealthier and more populous by far than the western, and in this way could more easily support both the burden of defence expenditure and the bureaucratic superstructure of the Empire. The eastern provinces had an exportable surplus of grain and of manufactured goods. The West had very little with which to requite its imports from the East, and, except when these represented the proceeds of imperial taxation of the eastern provinces, they were presumably paid for by an outflow of gold from West to East.[1]

The Western Empire, despite the lower level of wealth and the very much sparser population, seems to have been exposed to greater dangers than the Eastern. The Persians, it is true, represented a threat, especially after the accession of the Sassanids (A.D. 224). One emperor – Valerian (A.D. 253–260) – was even captured by the Persians, but the latter showed no desire to occupy more than the territories to which they could show some historic claim and to maintain a defensible boundary against the Roman Empire.

The West, however, was exposed to the pressure of the Germanic peoples and, in the fifth century, of the Mongol Huns. Their invasion routes impinged most readily on the Rhine and Danube frontiers, and, at least from the mid-second century A.D., there was almost continuous war. Most of the legions were stationed along the line of the two rivers, and the supply both of recruits and of supplies taxed the resources of the Western Empire to the uttermost. The eastern provinces, from Egypt to Asia Minor, were in no great danger, at least until the seventh century, of invasion and destruction. In the West such fears were ever present. In the later years of the third century Germanic tribes raided deep into Gaul, and the hastily contrived defences of the towns show how the provincials attempted to meet the danger.

The social problems facing the Western Empire were more serious and more deeply rooted than those in the East. In part they were the consequence of the military danger and of the need to maintain a large army; in part, they date from the Principate and even from the Republic. In short, there was a widening gap between rich and poor, with the rich increasingly successful in evading their social responsibilities. The burden of taxation was borne by an increasingly impoverished tax-base, while the technological backwardness of the Empire – itself in some degree a consequence of the institution of slavery – prevented any significant increase in production.

### THE FRONTIERS

The Empire had reached its greatest territorial extent under Trajan, with the subjugation of the province of Dacia. Antoninus Pius advanced the frontier in northern Britain to the Scottish Lowlands, but this was shortlived and unsuccessful. For the rest, the boundary between the Empire and the Germanic and Celtic tribes, between civilisation and barbarism, followed the course of the lower Rhine (Fig. 1.1); then from near Coblenz (*Confluentes*) it cut across to the Danube, which it met near its great bend at Regensburg (*Regnum*) and followed, except for the inclusion of Dacia, to its mouth in the Black Sea. The river boundary was clearly defined and readily defensible. It, furthermore, made the

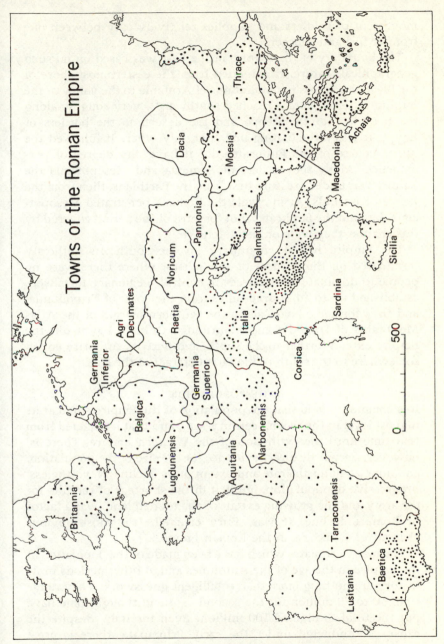

## Towns of the Roman Empire

Fig. 1.1 Towns and provinces of the Roman Empire.

movement of soldiers and supplies relatively easy between one frontier fort and another.

The boundary of the Empire in the East was based on no such geographical feature. It extended from the easternmost shore of the Black Sea across the mountains of Armenia to the valley of the Euphrates. From here it reached southwards, very roughly along the boundary of the steppe and the desert, to the borders of Egypt. It was a fluctuating line, and only where it followed the upper course of the Euphrates did it have any degree of permanence. Along the borders of Armenia and Mesopotamia the Empire was under pressure first from the Parthians, then from the Persian Sassanids. At intervals the Romans penetrated Mesopotamia, beyond the Euphrates, but for most of the period covered by this chapter they were on the defensive.

The Empire had no boundary on the south. Its authority terminated on the borders of the Sahara, where there were no people to dominate or resources to control. Legionary forts were established up to a hundred miles from the coast of Tripolitania, and they formed a chain along the southern margin of the Atlas Mountains of Numidia and Mauritania. Only in Egypt did the Empire extend farther to the south, and here its authority ended somewhere to the south of the First Cataract of the Nile.

### THE POPULATION

It is commonly held that the population of the Empire stood at its highest level in the second century A.D., and that it declined from that time until the extinction of the Western Empire. There is, however, very little direct evidence for the size of the population, and none at all for the rate and extent of its decline. Nevertheless, progressive depopulation, implicit in the shortage of recruits for the army and the growing extent of abandoned land, was a factor in Rome's decline. It was, Bury claimed, 'the most obvious element of weakness in the Roman Empire'.[2]

The many estimates which have been made of the population of the Empire in the age of the Antonines and at other periods in its history are nothing more than intelligent guesswork. They range from 50 to 70 million for the second century, though some have put the total as high as 100 million. Even for Italy, despite the censuses conducted under the early Principate, there is great uncertainty because children and slaves were omitted. The most recent, and also the most scholarly examination of the data, that of Brunt, puts the Italian total in the early years of the first century A.D. at about 7·5 million.[3]

If the total population of the Empire was, in the mid-second century, about 60 million, this would suggest an average density of about 16 persons to the square kilometre.

Population was not only sparse; it was also very unevenly distributed. The most densely populated provinces were in the Middle East, but, since large areas here were desert and mountain, the oases of population were by the standards of the ancient world very densely peopled. Foremost was the valley of the Nile; next in all probability came the coastlands and irrigated valleys of Asia Minor and Syria, and the Tigris-Euphrates basin.

The population of Italy, in all probability the most densely settled of the European provinces, did not exceed 6 or 8 million. In Spain and Gaul, the overall density was very much less, though the 'cities' of the Mediterranean coastland appear to have been fairly populous. Britain, the Germanies and the Danubian and Balkan provinces can have had between them no more than a few million. The present trend, it should be added, is to raise these estimates somewhat, as more and more evidence for inhabited sites of the Roman period is discovered by the spade.

Much of the imperial territory, especially that within the European provinces, must have presented the appearance of an uninhabited wilderness, broken by islands of cultivation. The latter were all too often widely spaced and linked together only by the imperial system of roads and perhaps by local trackways. In consequence the provision of transport and the maintenance of communications between them was difficult and costly.

The death rate was high and the expectation of life very short. The evidence is scanty and derived in the main from funeral inscriptions and *stelae*. The sample of the Roman population for which we have information is very far from random, and is, by and large, composed of those who were wealthy enough to record their lifespan. The average age at death for adults appears to have been between thirty and thirty-five years. One assumes that there was a high rate of infant mortality, and the average expectation of life at birth was probably not a great deal more than twenty years.

By far the greater part of the population of the Empire lived in rural areas and worked on the land. All their lives they were at a subsistence level, and after paying taxes and rent they had no reserves. The depredations of invaders from beyond the Rhine and Danube or the scarcely less damaging actions of Roman legionaries could reduce them to starvation. Disease was rife among this undernourished population. In the time of Marcus Aurelius, the bubonic plague swept through the Empire, and, as was usual with the plague, sporadic outbreaks occurred through the following century. Again in the sixth century (542–3) the plague spread westwards, and again claimed an immense toll of life. If the Black Death of 1348–51 provides any analogy, the death role must have been enormous and the recovery of the population very slow. Perhaps it never fully recovered from these earlier outbreaks. In addition, malnutrition must always have exposed the population to other, if less lethal, diseases.

The evidence for a chronic shortage of labour in the later Empire is overwhelming. Agricultural workers were tied to the soil – *adscripti glebae*, and, if they should escape, were savagely pursued. To the landlord they were a precious commodity that could not easily be replaced. Much land lay uncultivated (see below, page 19). From the third century onwards imperial edicts encouraged and required the reoccupation of abandoned lands (*agri deserti*), and their very number shows both how ineffective they must have been and how urgent the problem had become.

The Roman citizens of the Italian provinces had long since ceased to supply the bulk of the legionaries. Recruits were obtained increasingly from the provincials, and from the time of Diocletian a species of conscription was initiated. Military service was unpopular, and it took men from the land whom agriculture could not easily spare. No doubt it was the continuing labour shortage that chiefly led to the increasing use of barbarians – mainly Germans – in the armies. These were mostly absorbed into regular units, and served under Roman officers. Jones is of the opinion that they were in general loyal and reliable soldiers.[4] The same cannot be said of the *foederati*, the federated troops, who served under their own leaders and arranged with the Roman authorities for a lump sum payment for their services. They were not subject to Roman discipline and seem in general to have been unreliable. Indeed, they seem to have produced in the Romans a feeling of consternation not unlike that aroused in the Duke of

Wellington by a certain contingent of motley recruits to his Peninsular army.

The boundary of the Roman Empire in Europe separated civilisation from barbarism. This does not by any means imply that Roman civilisation was all-pervasive within the Empire. Though it might be said that no provincial could have been wholly immune to the cultural influences of Rome, there were certainly many areas where the local Celtic, Iberian, Illyrian or Thracian cultures endured through the imperial period little influenced by it. In the same way, the local languages and cultures – Aramaic, Syriac, Coptic – were perpetuated in the Middle East, just as Celtic and other languages survived in the European provinces.

'There were always barbarians within the Roman Empire,' wrote Ramsay MacMullen,[5] 'left to themselves in remote mountains and deserts.' Added to these native peoples, whose veneer of Roman culture was at best superficial, were the large numbers of Germanic peoples who were settled on imperial soil. Every barbarian intrusion within the frontiers of the Empire must have left some legacy to the imperial population. In the first century A.D. large bodies of barbarians were ferried across the Danube and given land near the southern bank. A governor of Moesia under Nero claimed to have settled 100,000 in this way, a total which seems improbably large, and Augustus himself gave lands on the left bank of the Rhine to German tribes whom he had defeated in war. The practice grew, and in the third and fourth centuries there must have been immense numbers of half-assimilated barbarians living not only in the frontier provinces but also deep within imperial territory.

Mobility within the Empire was less marked. During the early Empire there was a migration of people from the eastern provinces to Rome. Juvenal condemned it and declared, probably with some exaggeration, that the Syrian Orontes was flowing into the Tiber.[6] Such a movement from the densely populated East to the less populous West was to be expected. That it did not assume larger proportions and was largely restricted to the cities was probably due to the simple fact that in most such migrations people migrate to areas of greater wealth and higher standards, not into areas of lower. Germans came to settle in the European provinces, not middle easterners.

Rome, nevertheless, did serve to attract such peoples, and Syrians, by which term we must probably understand almost any commercial peoples from the Levant, became very active in the trade of the West. If middle easterners moved to the western provinces it was to the towns, never to the thinly peopled rural areas, except as itinerant merchants. Christianity, it must be remembered, was an eastern sect, and in the West it became an urban religion.

### THE LAND AND RURAL CONDITIONS

By far the larger part of the population of the Empire lived in villages and hamlets (*vici*) and gained its livelihood from the cultivation of the soil. How large a proportion it was one cannot say. It would be surprising if it were less than 80 per cent, and in all probability it was a good deal more. On the shoulders of some four-fifths of the population lay the burden of supporting a large and growing army, a venal and oppressive bureaucracy, and the frivolous and idle rich. The land tax, which bore chiefly on the small proprietor, was the principal source of government revenue. Invasion by the enemies of Rome, destruction in the course of civil conflict, the vagaries of the weather and the uncertainty of the harvest all threatened the wellbeing of the peasant. He was liable to be conscripted to help defend the Empire, and a great landowner was ever ready to seize his lands if his debts should force him to relinquish them. Who can wonder, wrote Dill, 'that people exposed to such brutality, in the name of civilised government, should welcome the rude justice of the Gothic chief?'[7]

Throughout the Empire the principal crops were the cereals from which bread was made. In the Mediterranean region, with its mild winters and hot and generally dry summers, wheat in its several varieties was grown as well as barley. Wheat was the dominant crop in Egypt and Syria. In the European provinces remote from the Mediterranean, wheat was also cultivated, but other cereals were generally more important. Spelt, a variant of wheat, was grown in Gaul. Rye was a major crop amongst the Germans and was being cultivated, perhaps by German settlers, within the Empire. Oats were still of slight importance, perhaps because, with the low population pressure, there was no need to cultivate the poor and acid soils on which their superior qualities could be demonstrated. Millet was cultivated in parts of the

Mediterranean region, and rice was known though the general lack of heavy summer rain in the most southerly provinces made it very difficult to cultivate.

The pattern of cropping was changing under the Empire, and the relative ease of long-distance commerce by sea facilitated local specialisation. Within Italy itself grain-growing was diminishing in importance. Extensive areas were given over to flocks and herds, and on the rich soils of Campania and of parts of Latium, olive-growing and viticulture became more extensive and important. There is abundant evidence from excavated villas for oil mills which crushed the olives and prepared the oil for the market. Southern Spain also became an important olive-growing region, sending much of its output to Rome in millions of amphorae, whose broken fragments still today comprise the *Monte Testaccio* beside the Tiber on the southern edge of the city.

One of the most important examples of agricultural specialisation was that of wheat growing in Sicily, North Africa and, above all, in Egypt. From the grain fields of these regions the population of Rome and later also of Constantinople was in large measure fed. In the summer months a procession of ships brought the wheat to Ostia, in whose docks it was unloaded, stored, and eventually transported in small boats up the Tiber to the city.

The populace could not live by bread alone. Peas and beans were important field crops; vegetables and herbs were grown, and industrial crops – flax and hemp – were cultivated for the manufacture of linen, canvas, ropes and cordage. In addition there were the exotic foods which made their appearance at orgies and in the pages of Athenaeus, Petronius and Martial.

The rich had sophisticated tastes in wine and oil. The good vineyards were no less well known under the early Empire than they are today, though the difficulty and high cost of transport (see p. 28) made their products very expensive when they at last reached the feast of a Trimalchio. The spread of the olive was restricted to the frost-free lowlands which bordered the Mediterranean Sea. The grape-vine had no such limitations, and its cultivation was diffused almost to the limits of the Empire. It spread as a part of the culture of Rome. Under the early Principate the grape-vine was not grown in all probability farther north than the lowlands of Languedoc and Provence. In the fourth century the emperor Julian described vineyards in the Paris suburbs and Ausonius those around Bordeaux and over the steep hillsides along the Moselle. The vine was grown on the villa farms of Noricum and Pannonia, and there is evidence for it in parts of the Balkans. This wide diffusion of the grape-vine is an aspect of Roman civilisation which has survived (see p. 201–3).

Animal rearing was of little importance in the Mediterranean regions of the Empire. The summer drought, when grass withers, and the shortage of meadow and lack of fodder crops combined to restrict pastoral activities. A ploughing ox was the most that the peasant could usually maintain. Transhumance, however, permitted some animals – principally sheep and goats – to survive the summer. In spring they migrated to the mountains and returned again in autumn. The practice appears to have been of increasing importance in Italy under the Empire, perhaps because, with the decay of peasant farming, lowland areas became available for winter grazing. Nomadic shepherds twice a year led their flocks along the *calles*, or migration routes, which, according to Roman Law, had to be kept open for them. They were an unruly group, little distinguishable from bandits. They were forbidden the use of horses by imperial decree, since this would increase their mobility and thus the danger they posed to settled Roman society. Their flocks nonetheless provided the wool which was the only real alternative to flax in the weaving of cloth. The chief meat supply of Rome probably came from the pigs which were fattened in the forests of the Apennines and driven down to the city. There were complaints of their loss of weight on the journey.

Outside the Mediterranean region climatic conditions were more favourable to animal rearing, and cattle, in particular, were numerous and important. Meat entered into the human diet on a large scale, and Julius Caesar commended his Italian troops who were serving in Gaul for their readiness to accept an unaccustomed meat diet. Draught animals were more readily available and far greater use was made of them than in the Mediterranean provinces. It was no accident that the heavy plough (see p. 194), drawn by a team of oxen, made its first appearance in northern Europe. The pig, which could be left to fatten in the forests with a minimum of supervision, was an important source of meat, as it remained throughout the Middle Ages.

From the technical point of view Roman agriculture was unprogressive. The institution of slavery may have been a factor inhibiting innovation, but it cannot be claimed that an abundance of labour made labour-saving devices unnecessary. Indeed, the reverse is the case; there was an acute shortage of rural labour under the later Empire. It is more probable that the educated classes failed to involve themselves in the day-to-day activities on their lands. The kind of education they had received predisposed them to ignore technical matters. It is symptomatic that neither Varro nor Columella in their treatises on agriculture tell us anything about the construction of the plough, and in the work of Palladius the description is short and ambiguous.

Over most of the Mediterranean region the land appears to have been cropped in alternate years. This was, of course, a concession to the lack of fertiliser, but it was no less due to the inadequacy of the rainfall. If weeds could be eradicated by ploughing – Columella recommended that the land be ploughed three times for each crop – and a fine tilth maintained over the fields, the rainwater could be conserved and a two years supply be made available for each crop. Only in areas where irrigation was regularly practised, and this in effect meant Egypt, was the land cropped every year.

The plough was a light wooden instrument, which could be carried to the fields by the ploughman and drawn by a single beast (Fig. 5.4). It had not changed in its essentials since it had been described by Hesiod about 800 B.C. It only disturbed the surface of the soil; it did not undercut the sod and turn it over, as the later mouldboard plough was to do. Fields, which must have been square or oblong in plan, were commonly cross-ploughed. Manure was spread if it was available, but the shortage of farm-stock meant that the small farmer had very little. The stubble seems sometimes to have been burned so that the ashes might enrich the soil, and there is an obscure passage in Silius Italicus,[8] which implies that the stubble and the fallow may have been grazed by transhumant animals in winter.

Outside the region of Mediterranean climate a different pattern of agriculture was dictated by the differing climatic conditions. The Roman agronomists, however, wrote for an Italian public, and they tell us nothing of agricultural practice north of the Alps. That pastoralism was more important than to the south is implicit in the bone finds at excavated sites. It is probable, also, that a heavier plough, drawn by a team of oxen, was used at least sporadically. Pliny referred to such a plough, fitted with wheels and equipped with a coulter, or knife, which cut vertically through the soil. Whether it also had a mouldboard, like the medieval and modern plough, to turn over the soil and bury the weeds, is far from clear. It would, however, have been a simple matter to add one as soon as the wheeled plough had been developed.

Coulters, made of iron, have been found at a number of sites in northern Europe, suggesting that the heavy plough was fairly widespread. It is generally assumed (see p. 55) that the plough with its team of oxen was difficult to turn at the end of the furrow, and that this consideration dictated a long furrow, with a minimum number of turns in a day's ploughing. A field consisting of a number of long narrow strips would appear to be the logical consequence of using the heavy plough. It was so during the Middle Ages and early modern times. Such a field pattern may have begun to emerge in northern Europe during the later Empire, but the evidence is inconclusive.[9]

The productivity of agriculture was low and its demands on human labour were heavy. Cicero considered an eightfold yield to be normal in Sicily, and a tenfold the highest that could be expected. Columella noted that it was a very rare occurrence if most of Italy yielded fourfold. It has been argued[10] that Columella was unduly pessimistic, and that yields were in general higher than this. Harvests fluctuated greatly with the weather, and in bad years – so medieval practice shows us – yields could be a great deal less than fourfold.

No less important to the peasant than the yield which he received on the grain sown was the amount of labour expended to achieve it. It has been demonstrated, on the basis of the evidence of Columella, that a *iugerum* of corn land required about ten days' labour in ploughing and preparing the soil, sowing and harvesting.[11] This is equivalent to about fifteen man-days per acre. Given that the working year was effectively about 250 days, a peasant might be expected to cultivate about 16 acres, or somewhat less since work tended to pile up at certain seasons of the year.

Grain would have been sown at from four to six modii to the iugerum, or six to nine modii, or 850 to 1300 litres to the hectare. A fourfold yield would have given the farmer from 24 to 36 modii. A quarter would have been set aside as seed, leaving from

18 to 27 modii, or 160 to 240 litres for consumption or sale. An active man was thought to need up to 8 modii a year. It is easy to see that the labours of a single husbandman, even if he had sufficient land to keep fully occupied, could yield only a poor living for himself and his family.

Of course he may, and probably did, have other sources of income and of food; his crops may have yielded appreciably better; he had possibly an olive tree and a few vines, like Aristophanes' peasant whose ambition it was to have:

> First a row of vinelets . . .
> Next the little fig-tree shoots beside them growing lustily
> Thirdly the domestic vine . . .
> Round them all shall olives grow to form a pleasant boundary.

Whether or not the poverty of the cultivator is exaggerated, he had little enough income to pay his taxes and often enough his rent. It was by these outgoings that the husbandman supported the imperial and social superstructure.

The rural population of Italy had at one time been made up largely of free peasants who cultivated farms which they either owned or rented. Toynbee[12] has argued persuasively that a mortal blow was dealt the Roman peasantry by the Punic Wars, in particular by the devastation wrought by Hannibal's campaign in the Second. Much of Italy, he claims, never recovered. The peasant abandoned his lands, which passed out of cultivation. So originated the vast estates – *latifundia* – of the rich, and also the footloose masses which crowded into Rome or provided the manpower to fight the civil wars of the Republic. To some extent this trend was offset by the establishment of colonies of veterans and by attempts to attract city dwellers back to the land by favourable tenancies, as was done by the Gracchi, but the trend was never really reversed.

Under the Empire the number of peasants continued to decline. There were no military campaigns to drive them from the land or to force them into debt, but high taxation performed the same role. The principal tax under the Empire was on cultivated land. It was a fixed amount, which did not change in nominal value with circumstances. The harvest might be ruined by the weather or by human enemies; the land tax was payable nonetheless. Inflation, it might be supposed, would have reduced the real value of a fixed tax. But the inflation in the second and third centuries was in the smaller silver coinage, which was increasingly debased. The taxes were assessed in the gold *aureus*, which retained its value. The peasants were thus obliged to pay increasing amounts, as measured in *denarii* or *nummi* in order to contribute the same amount in terms of gold *aurei*. Payment was, however, sometimes made in kind: foodstuffs for the provisioning of the army and for the grain supply of Rome, but this was dependent on the availability of transport. At the same time many, perhaps most peasants owed a rent, the payment of which took precedence after the land tax.

The burden of payment had been increasing during the first century. Hadrian remitted a very large sum in taxes, a step which it is very unlikely that he would have taken if there was ever the slightest chance of collecting it. The land tax, it has been said, commonly amounted to a third of the crop on a peasant farm. Add to this the rent, which could have been at least as much again, and the peasant was left with very little on which to live. There are instances of peasants selling what bread crops they had left and purchasing with the proceeds enough inferior and less palatable food such as beans to keep themselves alive.

In the last resort the peasant sold his holding in order to pay his taxes and lived on someone else's land as a tenant, paying a rent in money or in kind or performing some form of service.[13] In the second century the size of the army was increased, and this placed an added burden on the imperial treasury. Defaulting taxpayers were pursued with the full vigour of officialdom. In the anarchy which characterised much of the third century, the peasant stood to lose yet more. To oppression by tax-gatherer was added the danger of looting and destruction by campaigning armies.

The free peasantry, owning its own land and paying rent to no one, never entirely disappeared, and there is good evidence that it remained more numerous and prosperous in the eastern provinces than in the European. But most peasants appear to have been reduced to the status of *coloni* on the lands of others. Under Diocletian their position deteriorated yet more. They were tied to their land and forbidden to move to another tenancy or to abandon agriculture, unless they joined the legions. The purpose of the edict was to secure the payment of the capitation tax and to maintain land in cultivation. It also served the interests of the landowners at a time when the shortage of farm labour was becoming a problem for them.

The *coloni* were thus *adscripti glebae*, and their descendants who inherited the tenancy inherited also the same restrictions on movement. It is true that some escaped from the land to which the law had bound them, but for the most the new status was permanent and increasingly oppressive. The unhappy position of the *coloni* is implicit in the edicts of the emperors and explicit in writers such as Salvian of Marseilles, who condemned the acquisitiveness and cruelty of landowners. In extreme cases the landlord built a gaol and used soldiers to intimidate and discipline his tenants. At a time when the status of the slave was beginning to improve, that of the *coloni* was being further depressed, and the gap between them was narrowed almost to the vanishing point. 'What difference can be understood,' said Justinian in the sixth century, 'between slaves and *adscripticii*, when both are placed in their master's power and he can manumit a slave with his *peculium* and alienate an *adscripticius* with the land?'[14] Society was moving inexorably towards the medieval system of serfdom.

The converse of the *coloni* was the great landowner, whose broad estate had been pieced together over a period of perhaps centuries from the holdings of independent peasants. Such estates had been known under the Republic. The Younger Pliny owned perhaps 8000 iugera, scattered over central Italy.[15] From the second century the number as well as the size of the great estates grew steadily. Land was acquired by grants of the emperor, as well as from peasants who could no longer discharge their obligations. Some estates were consolidated by marriage and inheritance, as in medieval Europe. The largest were in all probability owned by members of the senatorial class, but the emperor, the municipalities, the temples and gilds and, in the closing years of the Empire, the Christian Church all owned wide estates and derived an income from them.

The rich acquired land both because it conferred prestige and because the purchase of real estate was the only way in which they could invest. They boasted of their possessions, as Trimalchio did of his estate which was so large that he had no idea of what it embraced.[16] This, of course, was satire. Most large estates, even that of Trimalchio, bore the evidence of their piecemeal origin.

They were made up of scattered fragments. No doubt their owners tried to round them out by acquiring intermediate lands. Occasionally, also, estates would be broken up and divided between heirs. Statistics unhappily are lacking of the number and size of estates. We know, however, the Apion estates in Egypt must have covered some 120 square miles. Symmachus, a senator of the later fourth century, possessed 'at least three great houses in Rome or the suburbs, and fifteen country seats in various districts of Italy. He had large estates in Samnium, Apulia and Mauretania.'[17] The income from such lands was immense. That of Symmachus, wrote Dill at the end of the last century, amounted to £60,000 a year, or perhaps £300,000 in terms of present purchasing power. Many senators were far richer than this. The very dispersal of their holdings gave them some protection against bad harvests and misfortune.

Clearly such wealth could not have been acquired honestly, and much of it must surely have come from what, in modern jargon, we would call protection and extortion rackets. The victims in most instances were the peasants. The greed and acquisitiveness of the landowners was matched only by their indifference to political and social issues. Their lives were frivolous; they rarely assumed public office, and these playboys of the ancient world displayed energy and ingenuity only in acquiring more land and evading the taxes on it.

They normally lived in villas; sometimes they possessed several between which they made the rounds in the manner of a medieval baron moving from one castle to another. There were many ways of managing an estate. No doubt on most a part was retained for the direct supply of the villa. It was, in effect, a demesne, managed by a bailiff (*procurator*) and worked in all probability by slaves. Part might be leased to a contractor, who thus intervened between the peasants and the owner and drew his profit from his exploitation of the former. Much of the land, in all probability, was leased on short or long terms to *coloni*, who paid both rent and land tax. The officials of the estate, often enough men of humble or even servile origin, had no hesitation in exploiting the poor in the service of their master. Salvian declared in his passionate condemnation of Roman society, that there was more humanity and justice under the rule of the Goths than could be found within the Empire.

18

It is easy to overdraw this picture of the extravagant rich battening on the masses of the poor. There were in the fifth century many estates of modest dimensions owned by the *curiales* of the towns or by corporations. There were also free peasants who had not been obliged to pledge their lands to pay their debts and thus to become the *adscripticii* of the rich. It is probable that these were more numerous in Macedonia and Thrace and in the Levantine provinces and Egypt than in the West. The evidence, however, is entirely qualitative, and no firm judgments can be made. Nevertheless, in this small difference in the course of social development may lie in some degree the reason for the survival of the Eastern Empire and the disappearance of the Western.

It is certain that agricultural land came to be abandoned during the third and succeeding centuries in all parts of the Empire. Emperors tried to check the trend, not only by binding peasants to the soil, but by continuing to exact the land tax from fields which had passed out of cultivation, by settling veterans on abandoned lands, and by leasing it on very favourable conditions.

Jones estimated[18] that by the fifth century the situation had become alarming in North Africa, where from a third to a half of the cropland had passed out of cultivation. Elsewhere it was much less serious, and was perhaps least dangerous in Egypt and the Middle East. The fact that land was being abandoned did not make the great landowners less eager to acquire more, and real estate seems to have continued to be a favoured and generally profitable form of investment. In fact, it is unlikely that more than a fifth of the land passed out of cultivation in most areas,[19] and much of this was land of marginal quality. It is possible that land abandoned for cereals nevertheless continued to nourish sheep and other animals.

One reason for the decline in the extent of cropland must have been the decline in the total population of the Empire, though it can, of course, be argued that abandonment of cropland with the consequent reduction in food supply was itself a factor in depopulation. It is likely, also, that agricultural installations, such as irrigation works, which had been built up over a long period of time, were destroyed by invasion or civil war, leading to the abandonment of the lands they served. Even the loss of ploughing oxen and the destruction of farm tools might have the same effect. The insecurity of the times, exposure to bandits or to peasant risings, might also have led to the abandonment, in particular, of outlying and isolated farms. Lastly the land tax itself, weighing equally on good soil and bad, may well have amounted in some cases to more than the land could be made to yield. It was more profitable to abandon the cultivation of marginal land than to continue the unequal fight against both poor soil and the tax-collector.

What resistance, one may ask, was there to the oppression of the lower classes? It was difficult to oppose a system in which the forces of the army and of the courts were enlisted on the side of the landowners. Nevertheless, there were risings. There were violent outbreaks of the peasants of North Africa in the fourth century, linked with the heretical sect of the Donatists. In Gaul, from the late third century there were revolts by the *Bacaudae*, prompted by peasant discontent but having overtones of Celtic resistance to the Romans. They spread to Spain and continued intermittently through the fourth century.

## THE TOWNS[20]

Roman civilisation, it is often claimed, was essentially urban. It was through towns, founded or refounded by them, that the Romans sought to impress the provincials with the might and majesty of the Roman Empire. Cities, however, were more than this. They were the cells of which the imperial body politic was built. Colonies (*coloniae*) had been established throughout Italy in the course of the expansion of the Republic, and occupied by veterans after the expiration of their military service. The process was continued beyond the confines of Italy. The hilltop forts of the Gauls were in many instances replaced, usually on a nearby valley site, by a planned town of the Romans, which perpetuated the name of the tribe which it served.

Other towns were founded *de novo* at the meeting point of routes, at river crossings and at strategic points along the frontier. Their number is not easy to assess. Thomsen considers[21] that there were no less than about 300 in Italy, and there were certainly 78 in the Po valley.[22] The *Notitia Galliarum* lists 122 in Gaul, of which 114 were cities (*civitates*) in the formal sense. Gildas wrote of the 28 cities of Britain, though it is not easy to discover which settlements he had in mind, and Pliny enumerated 175 in the south Spanish province of Baetica.[23] The Danubian and

Balkan provinces were much less intensively urbanised, but in Greece the number of poleis ran to hundreds, and Pausanias listed no less than about 140 in the southern districts of peninsular Greece. Jones has estimated that there were about 900 cities in the eastern provinces. The map in Fig. 1.1 is an attempt to show the urban settlements of the Empire in the second century.

These towns – some 500 are shown on the map – varied greatly in their form and function. Most of those in Greece and many in Italy antedated the Roman conquest. With a few conspicuous exceptions they were unplanned, and many were merely villages writ large. Most others were of Roman foundation. They were laid out according to a regular plan, with streets crossing at right angles, and around most in the second century was a defensive wall, itself very often of rectangular plan. To this Rome itself was an exception. It was without plan, and the Servian Wall had long since disappeared before its spreading suburbs. The Aurelian Wall which yet survives was not built until about 275.

Near the centre of all towns, whether planned or not, was a forum or market place. Nearby were public buildings: the temple of the imperial cult, the baths, and the basilica in which public business was conducted. On the edge of the city was, at least in the larger of them, a theatre or stadium. Many cities, in the spirit of competition which prevailed in the early Empire, gave more than they could afford and ran themselves into debt. Old tribal rivalries had been transmuted into intercity competition.

The town was the central place of its district, and the term *civitas*, commonly translated as city, denoted in fact both central place and surrounding region. The region was, wherever possible, a tribal area, recognised as such before the Roman conquest. This is particularly clear in Roman Britain and in parts of Gaul. The *civitas* was in most respects self-governing, and in this it resembled the πόλις of the Greeks. A fundamental difference, however, lay in the fact that the *civitas* in much of the Empire derived from a tribal territory and transmitted a tribal name: *Corinium Dubonorum* (Cirencester) and *Venta Belgarum* (Winchester); *Durocortorum Remorum* (Reims) and *Augusta Treverorum* (Trier). The Greek polis, by contrast, had no such associations.

The *civitas* was governed by its council or *curia*, consisting of a variable number of members – five or six hundred in the larger *civitates* – who served for life and in practice transmitted the office to their descendants. From the *curia* were elected the magistrates who administered the *civitas*, performed its religious ceremonies and provided entertainment for the urban masses. No doubt in the early days of the Empire there was some competition for office, but the burdens soon came to outweigh the advantages. The *curiales*, or decurions, who were elected to city office were expected to organise gladiatorial displays and other shows, to maintain the baths, city walls and public utilities, and to erect public buildings to the honour of the city. On their small and local scale it was hoped that they would do what the emperors were themselves able to do in Rome.

The tasks of both emperors and *curiales* may in these respects have been beyond their means. Cases are known of members of the *curia* who were bankrupted by the financial burdens of office. Add to this the fact that on the *curiales* rested the obligation to collect the taxes owed by the *civitas* and that they were collectively responsible for them to the Emperor. On the other hand there was a property qualification for membership of the *curia*, and most *curiales* were not poor. During the third century all citizens of the *civitas* possessing the minimum financial qualification were conscripted to the *curia*, and it became impossible for them to contract out or withdraw from the city. At the same time exemptions from the obligation to take up public office were made more difficult to secure.

Thus the decurion was tied to his city's administration no less closely than the peasant to his land. A rigidity is seen spreading through the social structure of the Empire. The question has been raised whether the curial class was dealt with as harshly as the *coloni*. Jones thinks that it was not; that few suffered serious financial loss, and that as a class they continued, however unwillingly and inadequately, to discharge their curial functions in the sixth century. The fact is that they were more articulate than the *coloni*; they complained more loudly and have been heard more widely. Indeed, there is good evidence that the misfortunes of the *coloni* stemmed in part from the oppression of the curial tax-collectors. Salvian, not perhaps one of the less biased witnesses, was able to write that there were as many tyrants as there were *curiales*.

A second feature of city government under the later Empire was the increasing injection of imperial authority into the local affairs of the *civitas*. If the Empire had been, in Rostovtzeff's words, 'a vast federation of city-states',[24] the governmental system was nevertheless becoming increasingly unitary. The emperors were more and more preoccupied with financial matters, and it was this that led them to designate *curatores* to oversee the city's finances and *exactores* to collect taxes. These officials came in time to be chosen from the decurions themselves, thus making the *curia* itself more dependent on the imperial administration.

The foremost function of the urban central place within each *civitas* was to provide a seat of local government and centre for the imperial cult. But there could be no such concentration of people without certain other functions. Of necessity the town acquired a market at which the produce of the surrounding countryside could be sold. At the same time crafts developed to supply the surrounding villages with simple manufactured goods. Some towns acquired a military function at an early date. They did not house a garrison, but they might provide the services needed in a nearby legionary fort. In all towns, with the exception of the largest, agriculture was an important function. It has been noted that villas are notably absent from the neighbourhood of towns. Those who might otherwise have built themselves villas now erected elaborate town houses where they lived on their rents just as if they had been deep in the countryside. The decurions, who formed the élite of the *civitas*, owed their status in large measure to their rural landed possessions.

A large part of the town's population, furthermore, consisted in all probability of rural workers. Many of the towns of the Empire can have been nothing more than elaborate villages, upon which had been fastened the apparatus of city government. There was little else in their function that distinguished them from *vici* or villages.

This suggests that most towns were small. There was little in them to require the presence of more than a thousand or two thousand persons. Nor in many instances could the surplus production of the *civitas* support many more than this. If we may assume that the population of the European provinces did not exceed 30 million, and if there were about 500 *civitates*, then their average size cannot have been more than about 60,000. A large town could not have been supported by a total population of this size. Conversely, if 10 per cent of the population was urban and, in the main, not engaged directly in agriculture, this suggests that the average size of towns was no more than 6,000. There was one very large town – Rome itself – and a number of large towns, so that most are likely to have had a great deal less than 6,000 inhabitants. Of course, the data are too uncertain for anything more than very tentative suggestions to be made; but at least they indicate an order of magnitude.

Another line of argument uses the area and ground plan of the towns. By the third century most had been fortified with walls, whose outline is in many cases known today with a considerable degree of precision. The question is, then, whether there was any simple relationship between the walled enclosure of a town and its population. Except in a very few cases, where the house plans of some part of a town have been uncovered by excavation, it is not known how closely the town area was built up. Two familiar instances, the British towns of *Calleva Atrebatum* (Silchester) and *Isca Silurum* (Caerwent), had a very low density and were made up largely of spacious homes of a landowning class. Was their low density normal, or may not their failure to survive have been due to the fact that they were exceptional?

On the other hand, in the Italian towns of Pompeii, Herculaneum and Ostia, all of which have been in some degree exposed by excavation, the density was very much greater. They *may* have had about 150 persons to the hectare, whereas *Isca Silurum* had only about forty-five, and *Calleva* about ten. A further problem lies in the fact that many towns did not build walls until they were threatened by the Germanic invasions of the third century, and some which had possessed walls from a much earlier date, contracted their area at this time. At *Augustodunum* (Autun, in Burgundy), an extreme case, the walled area was reduced from about 200 hectares to only 10. One might expect a very high density in these contracted towns, which had, in effect, become a kind of *Fluchtburgen*.

If, for the sake of argument, it can be postulated that the provincial towns of the Empire in the prosperous days of the second century had about 125 persons to the hectare – and this figure is in line both with the little concrete evidence and with the later medieval experience – we can at least arrive at an order of magnitude of Roman towns. The largest in Gaul would have had about 35,000 and the smallest around 600. In Britain the size would have ranged downwards from London, with under 20,000, to less than 500 for a few of the smallest. Fig. 1.2 represents the *area* of the Gallic towns, ordered by rank-size. It is apparent that the majority were very small, with – if our formula can be accepted – less than about 2500 in each. This throws some light on the

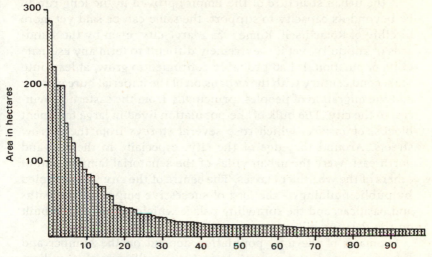

Fig. 1.2   Rank-size graph of the towns of Roman Gaul. Size is measured by the area enclosed within the walls of the town.

position of the *curiales*. There never were enough of them, except in the few large towns, to discharge the obligations placed on them. After the enthusiasm of the first century had worn off they must have found their curial duties oppressive in the extreme. It is not surprising that whenever they were able, they found refuge from civil responsibilities in the seclusion of their rural estates.

Classical urbanism was a fragile growth. It was supported by the rents and taxes of the agricultural population, and it never generated on an important scale the essentially urban functions of manufacturing and commerce. A further difficulty was that many towns had in the early years of the Empire been overbuilt. The rivalries between cities and among the curial class had led to the creation of a costly superstructure of public buildings, baths, aqueducts, and the like. Their construction may have impoverished their builders and donors; their maintenance certainly represented a burden which the towns of the later Empire could not afford. The impoverishment of the peasantry and the drift of the rentier class from the towns to their rural villas destroyed the basis of the provincial town. Some contracted in area; others were abandoned; all decayed.

If the urban structure of the Empire proved in the long run to be beyond its capacity to support, the same can be said yet more forcibly of Rome itself. Rome was a large city, even by the standards of antiquity, yet it is extremely difficult to form any estimate of its population. It had probably continued to grow, at least into the second century with the expansion of the imperial bureaucracy and the migration of peoples, principally from the eastern provinces, to the city. The bulk of the population lived in large tenement blocks, or *insulae*, which rose several storeys from the narrow streets. Around the edge of the city, especially to the east and north-east, were the urban villas of the senatorial families and of others of the wealthier classes. The centre of the city was occupied by public buildings – the *fora* of successive emperors, the baths and basilicas, and the sprawling palace which Augustus had built on the Palatine hill.

Estimates of the total population depend on the number and size of the *insulae*, and range from half a million to two million. The balance of probability is against the higher figure, and it is probable that the total varied from a million down to half this total. Never before, and in all probability not since has so large a city had so little economic activity to support it. It could not be fed from the farms of the Campagna; local crafts may, on balance, have satisfied most local needs for simple manufactured goods, but there was no significant export of goods from the city, and the import of grain, oil and wine had, in effect, to be paid for by a levy on the Empire. There was a highly organised movement of grain, chiefly from Egypt, to the port of Ostia, from which a fleet of barges carried it up the Tiber to the city.

A significant part of the population was underemployed, or unemployed, entertained by the emperors and fed by a dole of bread and oil. A technologically advanced civilisation can support such a burden, and regularly does so in its welfare, social security and unemployment payments. But the Roman Empire was technically backward, living always on the edge of starvation. Rome was a luxury which it could not afford; a symbol of imperial unity and power, and its cost was borne by every overtaxed and underfed peasant.

## MANUFACTURING AND TRADE

One of the most widely known and at one time most generally accepted explanations of the decline of the Roman Empire (see p. 71), represented it as the result of the destruction of its trade. The Empire, it was said, was held together by its roads and above all, by its sea routes, along which there was a steady flow of commodities. It was the movement of trade through the arteries of the Empire that gave it life and prosperity. The Empire, it is true, seemed designed to encourage internal trade. An elaborate system of well engineered roads, many navigable rivers, and above all the Mediterranean Sea across which the provinces could exchange their products, all encouraged movement, communication and trade. Aristides, in his eulogy of the Empire in the mid-second century, claimed that 'there are always ships putting into or sailing out of the harbour [of Rome], and the whole world's products could be seen in Rome'.

Aristides had clearly not visited Ostia in winter, and if he had looked into the holds of ships as they left the port he would have found only ballast. It was a seasonal trade, as the voyage of St Paul so forcibly demonstrates, and it was also a oneway trade. It is very easy to exaggerate both the volume of commerce and also its role in holding the Empire together. In fact the volume was, in relation to the size, variety and population of the Empire, quite small, and the movement of commodities was very expensive. A subsistence economy, such as prevailed over much of the Empire, cannot generate a large volume of trade and aside from the supply of Rome it was largely geared to satisfying the extravagent tastes of the rich and the demands of the army.

The Empire had developed a complex system of roads which could be used at all seasons of the year, but they were built by the military and were designed to serve military ends. Merchants were allowed to use them, sometimes on payment of a toll, but the *cursus publicus*, the transport system maintained by the provincial government was, in theory at least, not available to them. Furthermore, a duty or octroi – in general quite small – was payable by private citizens on the commodities which they transported. Movement of goods was both slow and costly. A harness that would have permitted horses to pull wagons had not yet been devised. Oxen were generally used, but there were instances of the use of mules. Diocletian's price edict prescribed 20 denarii a mile for a wagon carrying about half a ton; eight denarii a mile for a camel and four for a donkey. In a journey of about 300 miles, it is claimed, the price of wheat was approximately doubled. The movement of grain to relieve a local famine was, in fact, impossible unless it could be sent by ship. Under these conditions road transport was effectively restricted to lightweight goods of high value and to the priority requirements of the army.

Rivers appear to have been used wherever possible, because of the lower cost of transport by water. Other than the Po, the Nile and the lower Tiber, however, few Mediterranean rivers were navigable. In Gaul, the Rhône and Moselle were important, if the surviving bas reliefs are any guide, for the transport of wine (Fig. 1.3), and in Spain the Guadalquivir was used. The frontier rivers, the Rhine and Danube, were important for the movement of goods between the legionary forts which lay along their banks. A towpath, for example, was cut into the steep rock-face of the Iron Gate on the river Danube. It has now been submerged by the lake which has formed behind the new dam.

There are no statistics of any kind which might give an idea of the volume of trade within the Empire. Seaborne shipping was the most important, and if it could be expressed in ton/miles its importance would be seen to be overwhelming. Yet navigation was seasonal. For a third of the year all ships were laid up in harbour, and for a further third navigation was considered dangerous. Most of the voyaging was therefore concentrated into the four months of summer weather. Ships were small; few exceeded 200 tons capacity. Most harbours were merely open roadsteads, with little protection, and the elaborate docks at Ostia were quite exceptional, justified only by the volume and importance of Rome's grain trade which was handled there. Nor was shipping a prosperous and profitable business. Under the early Empire rich men had to be cajoled into the business. Later the shipowners were organised in gilds or corporations of *navicularii*. Their members were accorded various privileges, which included exemption

Fig. 1.3 Transport within the Roman Empire; (*a*) from Neumegen, (*b*) from Trajan's Column, (*c*), (*d*) and (*e*) from the Igel monument.

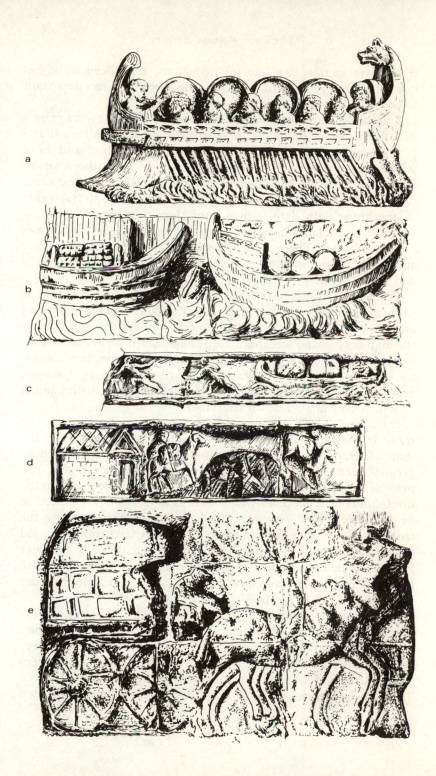

from curial duties, but, like the decurions, their occupation became hereditary. The task of supplying Rome was too important to be left to the whim of private speculators.

The chief commodities in Mediterranean commerce were grain – in volume by far the most important, followed by olive oil and perhaps wine. Egypt and North Africa were the chief sources of wheat. The oil seems to have come mainly from southern Spain. In the third century the volume of Spanish oil imported by Rome began to decline, and the Monte Testaccio contains no fragments of amphorae with date stamps later than this period. Building materials, especially the more decorative marbles, were sometimes imported by sea. There were also small quantities of high quality and relatively valuable consumers' goods, including spices, cloth and metal goods.

Trade by land was restricted to the more valuable commodities. Among them were pottery and glass, the better qualities of wool and a variety of small decorative objects which were able to bear the high cost of land transport. Large amounts of timber must have been transported not only for building construction, but also for use as fuel. The bathing establishments of the larger towns, especially of Rome, must have required immense quantities, much of which was floated down the Tiber.[25]

Prominent in the commerce of all parts of the Empire was the trade in slaves. They had been obtained in the course of the imperial wars of conquest, but after the Empire had reached its greatest territorial extent the supply became less abundant. The price of slaves rose, and numbers were kept up by breeding in the households of their rich owners. But new slaves never ceased to be available. They were most numerous and cheapest along the frontiers where wars and trade with the barbarian peoples beyond yielded a continuing supply. There is some evidence in the later Empire of the enslavement of freemen, despite imperial edicts to the contrary, as impoverished peasants sold or abandoned their children in order to pay their rents and taxes.

Slaves provided much of the labour on the large estates, especially on the 'demesnes' which were managed directly by their owners. The imperial administration itself used slaves on a very considerable scale in the workshops which supplied equipment for the army and in the services maintained by the administration. The rich had immense numbers of slaves, and often acted as if their prestige was directly related to the number of their retainers, however unnecessary many of them may have been. There must have been a high level of underemployment amongst these swarms of domestic slaves.

Most of the manufacturing activities which were carried on in the Empire were, however, in the hands of free craftsmen. There is no evidence for any large-scale organisation of industry, apart from the imperial weapon and uniform factories. In every town there were craftsmen, many of them working up the products of the surrounding countryside. There were millers, tanners and weavers; there were craftsmen who made goods for the citizens of the *civitas*; carpenters, blacksmiths and builders. Some had a slave or an apprentice; all operated on a very small scale, had little capital and sold their products directly to a local market. In larger towns groups of similar craftsmen were organised into gilds or *collegia*, membership of which was made permanent and hereditary in the third century. In the smallest towns there can have been little specialisation as between craftsmen. Xenophon's description of urban crafts, written in the fourth century B.C., was probably no less applicable to conditions half a millennium later:

> In large cities . . . one trade alone and very often even less than a whole trade, is enough to support a man; one man, for instance, makes shoes for men, and another for women, and there are places even where one man earns a living only by stitching shoes, another by cutting them out, another by sewing the uppers together, while there is another who performs none of these operations but only assembles the parts . . .

In small towns, on the other hand:

> the same workman makes chairs and doors and ploughs and tables, and often this same artisan builds houses, and even so he is thankful if he can only find employment enough to support him.[26]

Most towns of the Roman Empire were small.

Nor was there any high degree of specialisation between one region and another. In most respects all areas were self-sufficing, and only in a few quality products was there any significant interregional trade. A few areas were noted for the excellence of their cloth. Gallic cloth was known in Rome; Athenian in Asia Minor, and fabrics woven in Alexandria, Laodicea and Tarsus seem to have been widely known in the Middle East. There must have been numerous cloth merchants, some of them wealthy, if one may judge from the Igel monument which was raised in the fourth century near Trier to the memory of one of them.[27]

Pottery was a prominent article of trade, though it must be remembered that as potsherds are almost indestructible, the finds may tend to exaggerate its importance. Most abundant was the smooth, brown Arettine ware, which came originally from Arezzo in Italy, but was imitated first in southern Gaul (La Graufesenque and Lezoux) and in the second century in the Rhineland. Lamps, made of baked clay were also traded widely, as also were glass objects and small metal goods. Bricks and tiles were mostly made where they were needed and there seems to have been a brickyard at most legionary forts and in the vicinity of at least the larger towns.

Iron and the nonferrous metals – lead for pipes and cisterns, copper and tin for bronze-making, gold and silver for currency and works of art – were mined. The most important sources of metals were Spain and the Alpine region, though some tin and lead came from Britain, and silver and lead from the Balkans. Metals must have entered into long-distance trade on a not inconsiderable scale.

Taken together the evidence for trade within the Empire suggests that its scale was very small. One might go as far as to say that the vast majority of the peasants who, in turn, made up most of the imperial population, never possessed or used any artifact that was not made in their own neighbourhood and, in all probability by a craftsman known to them. Even the excavations of *Calleva* (Silchester) a town which was abandoned without any extensive destruction, revealed a pitifully short list of articles which had not been produced locally.

It has been argued[28] that the focus of manufacturing activity tended under the Empire to move away from Italy and towards the newer provinces of the Empire. Such a shift was inevitable. The provinces came in time to demand luxuries and necessities similar to those long available in Italy. The high cost of transport, however, dictated that they should make their own. This is very conspicuous in the adoption of Arettine styles in the potteries of Gaul and the Germanies. There is some evidence, also, that the quality of cloth production in Gaul was improved to the point at which

Gallic fabrics were in demand in Rome. The instance of the pack-ing-case of Gallic pottery overwhelmed at Pompeii by the erup-tion of Vesuvius in A.D. 79 before it could be opened, is well known. Can one argue that wares produced in the European provinces were now underselling those of Italy in the 'home' market? If so, this is another instance of the now familiar fate of Empires.

It seems clear that the manufactures of Italy declined relatively as those of the provinces developed. Whether there was an abso-lute decline is not clear. It seems certain, however, that the Middle Eastern provinces retained their pre-eminence, and that their merchants, generally referred to as Syrians, became active throughout the Mediterranean basin and were to be found deep within Gaul.

The imperial authority never encouraged trade between the Empire and its barbarian neighbours. A number of commodities, deemed to have some military or strategic value, might not be sent out of the Empire, and most of the Roman exports were of a luxury nature.[29] Pottery and bronzes appear to have been amongst the goods most often traded, perhaps because they have survived most easily. Unlike much of the internal trade of the Empire, that which crossed its borders was paid for by imports from the bar-barian world. These appear in the main to have consisted of cattle, of forest products including honey and amber, and, most valuable of them all, slaves. There can be little doubt that Germanic leaders hunted slaves for sale to the Romans in much the same way as African chiefs procured them for sale to white slavetraders in the seventeenth and eighteenth centuries. A bronze crater among the grave furniture of a German king might well have been his reward for passing on to the Romans those captured in a successful foray.

The points of commercial contact between the Empire and its neighbours were few. This was in part due to the fact that the Rhine and Danube were wide rivers and difficult to cross. Most of the trade radiated into the German lands from no more than ten or a dozen crossing points. The most important of these are likely to have been on the lower Rhine, where they gave access to the Frankish lands of north-west Germany, and on the middle Danube, from which the routes into the hinterland followed approximately those established by the prehistoric amber trade. There was, in addition, a seaborne trade, not only with Britain but also along the coast and up the rivers of Germany. Ships also carried on trade between the towns – first and foremost Constantinople after its refoundation by Constantine (A.D. 330) – of the eastern provinces and the barbarian peoples who bordered the Black Sea.

Finds of Roman artifacts show a strangely clustered pattern within central and eastern Europe (Fig. 1.4).[30] They are most common in the regions of loess soil in the northern plain, especially in Westphalia, Saxony and Thuringia, in the lowlands of Bohemia and in the plain of Moravia. These, one assumes, were the richest

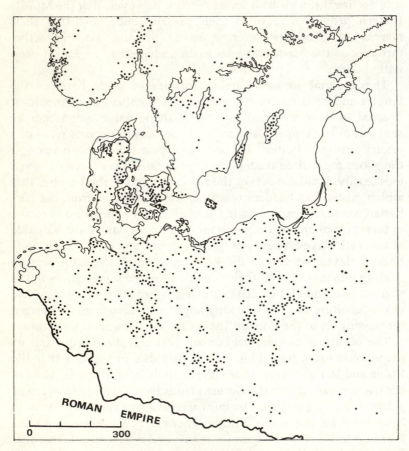

Fig. 1.4 Distribution of finds of goods exported from the Roman Empire: after H. J. Eggers, *Der römische Import im freien Germanien*, Hamburg, 1951, map 6.

and most densely settled areas of Germany. Finds are, however, very far from rare in Silesia and central Poland, on the Danish islands, and around the shores of the southern Baltic Sea.

### THE ECONOMIC FORTUNES OF THE EMPIRE

The territorial expansion of the Roman Empire came to an end in A.D. 106 with Trajan's conquest of Dacia. Henceforward the Empire stood on the defensive against the barbarian world. For a period of several centuries victorious armies had overrun one territory after another. They had amassed vast stores of booty, of bullion and, above all, of slaves, and had transmitted them back to the older provinces of the Empire. After a victorious campaign able-bodied slaves were cheap in the markets of Rome. Not only were the fortunes of senatorial families founded on the profits of conquest and administration; the Empire also was made to supply at small cost the means for elaborate spectacles and triumphs and for more enduring monuments and buildings.

There are no statistics of the profits of imperialism, but one must assume from such evidence as Cicero presented in his prosecution of Verres for the abuses of his administration of Sicily, that they must have been considerable. This income in bullion and above all in labour must have been a factor of no small importance in Rome's programme of building towns, roads and monuments during the first and second centuries A.D. Thereafter the profits of the Empire continued to be large, but the windfalls of new conquests ceased to replenish the treasury and stimulate the economy. Instead, the Empire was faced with the large and mounting costs both of administering a vast territory and of defending it from renewed pressure from beyond its borders.

The Empire, nevertheless, did have very great resources for meeting the new dangers, though these were very unevenly spread over its territories. The eastern provinces were by far the richer. They had a denser population and a longer and richer tradition both of urban living and of manufacturing than the west, and their focus extended from Egypt to Syria and Bithynia. By contrast, most of the European provinces were a pioneering fringe, the objective of speculative ventures by Syrian merchants, waiting to be opened up and developed.

The formal income of the emperors derived from a variety of sources which they never succeeded in consolidating and administering effectively. First were the private lands and properties of the emperors, which formed the nucleus of a very large imperial estate. It continued to grow as the lands of conquered princes, of condemned criminals, and of attainted senators were added to it. This complex of possessions, known under the later Empire as the *res privata*, was of immense size, and was administered by an elaborately organised bureaucracy. In some parts of the eastern provinces it *may* have amounted to a fifth of all agricultural land. There is no evidence for its extent in the Western Empire.

In general, the lands of the *res publica* were leased or rented. Conditions of tenure varied, but a steady income accrued to the imperial treasury from them. On the other hand, in the difficult times of the fourth century, emperors sometimes sold parts of their patrimony in order to raise cash. There were always wealthy senatorial families ready to buy them.

By far the larger part of the imperial income, however, derived from taxes. There was a bewildering variety of taxes and a yet more confusing system of exemptions from them. The largest yield came from the land tax, from which the province of Italy was exempt. We do not know how much it yielded. It is certain that the assessment was in many areas inequitable, and that periodic revisions were never made. It came to be, under the later Empire, a crushing burden on the peasantry, and it has been estimated that in Egypt the land tax amounted to about a third of the value of the crop.

There was a poll tax, from which Roman citizens were exempt until 212, no less inequitably assessed. Since the liability of unit areas does not appear to have been based on any form of periodic census, the amount tended to become yet another assessment on the land. There were tolls – small it is true – on goods moving from one part of the Empire to another; there were heavier duties on goods crossing the imperial frontier. In some provinces there was a species of sales tax. The estates of senators were subjected to a small levy which they could easily pay but nevertheless resisted. Merchants – a term used in its widest connotation to include every kind of craftsman – paid yet another, and the cities made a contribution at the accession of each new emperor.

The overriding needs of the military dictated a wide range of impositions. The legions had to be fed and clothed, and this in turn led to levies of food and clothing, usually, however, only in areas from which they could without much difficulty be conveyed to the troops. Taxes in grain and wine, in charcoal and in woven garments, tended to be commuted for money payments, and, small as they generally were, nevertheless added to the burdens of the peasantry. Even the obligation to provide recruits for the army could be commuted for money.

The tax system was very complex and costly and required a vast bureaucracy for its management. There are even instances of the costs of collection being added to the taxes themselves and thus being extracted from the peasantry. Furthermore, it was regressive and inflexible, making no allowance either for the greater capacity of the rich to pay or the variations in agricultural yields from which, in the last resort, most of the tax came. Above all, those supported by this mountainous tax structure – the bureaucracy, the army and, Gibbon would have added, the Church – were non-productive, contributing nothing to the gross product or to the capital investment of the Empire.

Heavy as the burden of taxation was, it was never enough for the needs of government. It is probable that more rational organisation of the tax system might have yielded more at a lower cost. In the event, the emperors from the time of Septimius Severus (A.D. 193–211) resorted increasingly to the debasement of the currency. They added a proportion of base-metal to the silver from which the *denarii* were minted, so that they had a greater volume of coins with which to discharge their obligations. This process continued through the third century, until the *denarius* was essentially a copper coin.

The minting of a larger supply of coins, without any commensurate increase in productivity, combined with the reduced intrinsic value of each, led inevitably to a rise in prices. It is said that by the end of the third century the purchasing power of the *denarius* was less than one per cent of its value before the inflation began.

The *denarius* was far from being the only coin in circulation. There were copper coins, smaller in value than the *denarius*, which passed out of circulation with the depreciation of the latter. There were also gold pieces, the *aurei*, worth originally 25 *denarii*. These were not debased, and it seems to have been hoped that they would hold up the value of the *denarii*. Instead, the latter, following the universal rule of currency, drove the better coinage out of existence. The *aureus* was hoarded or melted down. No one exchanged it for *denarii*, at least not at par, unless he was compelled to do so.

Such was the chaotic condition of currency and prices at the accession of Diocletian (A.D. 284). He attempted to remedy the situation by fixing maximum prices and wage rates and by issuing a new currency. In both respects he failed. The Edict of Prices of 302 was an immense catalogue of rates and prices which might not be exceeded. It was published throughout the Empire, and generally ignored. The inflationary trend was too strong to be halted by such means.

The issue of a new currency met with no less difficulty. The precious metals were in short supply, and one emperor's currency could be minted only by melting down that of his predecessors. Most of the coinage in circulation was so debased that it consisted largely of copper, and sufficient metal was not available for a regular gold and silver currency. It was not until the reign of Constantine that a gold and silver currency again became generally available. He was able to use the hoards which had been accumulated by the temples and, with the adoption of Christianity, had passed to the state. He also, by means of levies on towns and the land, coaxed a quantity of gold and silver out of private hoards. Thus a gold *solidus* was minted and kept a fairly stable value, but the evils of bimetallism were all too apparent. Copper *denarii* remained in circulation and, in fact, were minted on a lavish scale. The legionaries were paid in *denarii*, which thus passed into general circulation. The inflation of the copper currency continued unabated until it became almost valueless, and very little continued to be minted at the end of the fourth century.

The Empire was thus left with a gold currency, the *solidus*, and smaller gold coins which were fractions of the *solidus*. Taxes were paid in *solidi*. Copper *nummi* continued to pass in the everyday transactions of ordinary people, but the need was keenly felt for a stable coin smaller than the gold currency. This was supplied under Anastasius at the end of the fifth century by the issue of large copper *nummi* in several denominations. Not dissimilar coins were also issued in Italy and North Africa. Some control seems to have been maintained over the issue. Their value did not vary greatly, and a relatively stable relationship was maintained to the gold *solidus*. Thus, in its declining years the Empire had at last come to grips with one of its major problems – inflation and the debasement of the coinage. It is symptomatic of the problem that a *modus vivendi* was achieved in the richer East. In the West the availability of a currency was becoming less important as the economy moved slowly towards the self-sufficing manor.

The contrast between the East and the poorer West was apparent long before Diocletian formally separated them. His dividing line ran from the Danube near Sirmium, southwards across the mountains of Illyria to the Dalmatian coast near the old Greek settlement of Epidaurus. From the southern shore of the Mediterranean Sea it ran into the desert between Tripolitania and Egypt. It did not, with any degree of precision, separate the rich provinces from the relatively poor, and in this respect much of Greece belonged with the West. It is nevertheless developments to the west of this line which must in the main engage our attention.

In the European provinces a small élite, attuned from the early years of the Empire to a life of luxury, continued to demand and to exact more than the western economy could afford. Grain was brought from Egypt for the supply of Rome, and Syrian – later Jewish – merchants made available to their western clientèle the sophisticated products of the East. The European provinces, however, generated no exportable surplus of significance, except perhaps in metals, and their imports must have been paid for out of taxes and rents which accrued in the East and by the export of the precious metals. It is likely that many of the hoards of *aurei*, tapped so successfully by Constantine, were in the eastern provinces.

The façade of Roman civilisation in the West, its towns, villas and roads, was created mainly in the first two centuries of the Empire, when the profits of imperialism made it possible to do so. It constituted, however, a superstructure which the later Empire found it increasingly difficult to support. The barbarians did not overthrow the Empire in the West; they merely caused it to expend its scanty resources in ways which it could not really afford. In other words they made necessary a high taxation for military ends.

Tax burdens contributed to the reduction in the number of free peasants, and thereby increased the wealth in the hands of the Senatorial class. The latter, as we have seen, became adept at avoiding or at least minimising its taxes and shirking its social obligations. This did not happen, or it happened only to a smaller degree, in the eastern provinces. In the West, the rich formed a leisured class of literary dilettantes; their lives revolved around their estates; their letters were filled with trivia; their desire to serve the Empire in its years of crisis was non-existent. For the barbarians they had no more thought, provided they kept their distance, than for the emperor in distant Rome or Constantinople.

# 2

# The early Middle Ages

The Roman Empire in the West came to an end and the Middle Ages began during the period of the Germanic invasions of the fifth century. The emperor Romulus Augustulus was deposed in 476, and, though the Eastern emperors continued to rule in Constantinople in unbroken succession until the coming of the Crusaders in 1204, an era had nevertheless ended.

The termination of imperial rule was matched by no comparable change in society or in the economy. The evolution in these respects from classical to medieval times was slow and gradual. Barbarian kings had long ruled within the territory of the Empire, and Germanic settlers had cultivated its soil. The medieval manor was in many respects foreshadowed in the *villa* of the later Empire. Imperial social and legal institutions were perpetuated into the Middle Ages, and the Merovingian period in Gaul reflected the pale, fading afterglow of Roman civilisation. Yet change there was during the fifth century and the invaders of the Roman Empire were its most significant instrument.

THE INVASIONS OF THE FIFTH CENTURY

Barbarians had been filtering into the Roman Empire for centuries before the last of the Western emperors ended his rule. They had come in war bands, like those which Marius had defeated at *Aquae Sextiae* in 102 B.C., or those against which the walls of Gallic towns were hastily improvised in the later years of the third century. They had come as traders, as settlers in search of land to cultivate, as recruits for the legions or as federated allies to fight the wars of the Empire. The barbarians were familiar with the

41

civilisation of Rome. They had long been accustomed to purchasing the products of the Empire and to selling their agricultural and forest products in its frontier settlements. They knew what lay ahead of them when they crossed the Rhine or the Danube. They wanted land to cultivate, a greater abundance of consumers' goods and, above all perhaps, security from those enemies of their own who had been driving them forward against the ramparts of the Empire.

The first of the Germanic tribes to emerge in strength from east-central Europe had been the Goths. They had left their Scandinavian homeland perhaps in the first century B.C. and had settled in the plains of eastern Europe. Here they had divided into the western, or Visigothic people and the eastern, or Ostrogothic, before the threat of the Huns again set them in motion. The Visigoths crossed the lower Danube and entered the Balkans more as panic-stricken refugees than as triumphant warriors. Only the cruel and vacillating policy of the Romans led them to turn against their oppressors and to humiliate them, killing the emperor Valens, at the battle of Adrianople (378).

The Visigoths lingered in the Balkans for a number of years, and for much of this time their soldiers were in the pay of the Empire. They then moved into Italy, where, in 410, they captured and sacked the city of Rome – a destruction which appears to have been far less severe than that by the soldiers of Charles V in 1527. From here they moved into Gaul, where their kingdom extended from Aquitaine and Auvergne into central Spain.

The Visigoths were followed by their former neighbours, the Ostrogoths, who also moved through the Balkans and into Italy, in turn the exploiters and the servants of the Empire. In the meanwhile other Germanic peoples had been shaken loose from their traditional homes in the northern plains. The Vandal people moved first towards the Danube and then westwards, in alliance with the Alans and the Suevi, to the Rhine, across Gaul and into Spain. They lingered in southern Spain long enough to leave their name in that of the region of Andalusia, before crossing the sea to North Africa.

Other Germanic peoples migrated over shorter distances: the Alamanni from south-western Germany into eastern Gaul, and the Burgundians from the northern plain into the valley of the middle Rhine, whence those who survived the onslaught of the Huns migrated into the French province which today bears their name. The Franks, the only one amongst these Germanic peoples to acquire a lasting importance, were an association of tribes in north-west Germany. In the fifth century they crossed the Rhine and diffused slowly through Gaul until they mingled with the Burgundians and the Visigoths. At about the same time peoples from the coastlands of the North Sea, collectively known as Anglo-Saxons, crossed the sea to Britain.

These tribes, whose impact on the history of Europe has been so profound, were each made up of relatively small groups of people. It is unlikely that the largest of them – the Visigoths or the Franks – greatly exceeded 100,000 men, women and children. The smallest, such, for example, as the Alans, the Suevi and the Burgundians, were probably not much more than 20,000. It is unlikely that the total number of Germanic settlers in Gaul in the course of the fifth century made up more than three or four per cent of the total population, certainly not more than five per cent. The Ostrogothic and later the Lombard settlers in Italy and the Visigothic, Suevic and Vandalic peoples in Spain made up, in all probability, an even smaller fraction of the total population.

The population of the Empire had unquestionably declined since the second century. The extent of this decline is unknown, but contemporary references to labour shortage and to abandoned fields and depopulated towns imply that it was considerable. It is unlikely, therefore, that the injection of barbarian peoples served to raise the total population to the level at which it had stood under the Antonines. In other words, none of the invading peoples *needed* either to dispossess the Romans or to engage in the arduous business of clearing forest and tilling virgin land, and there is no evidence, except on a small and local scale, that they ever did so during the period of the invasions.

The detailed studies that have been made on the basis of place-names and archaeological finds show the early medieval settlers filling out the area formerly occupied by the Romans, and only rarely going beyond it.[1] They established their homesteads most often close to those of the latter, and they must have shared with them in the cultivation of the same fields. Continuity rather than revolution was the keynote of the Germanic settlement in western Europe.

The invaders, of course, did not settle evenly or uniformly

throughout the lands which they occupied. Most appear to have been good judges of the quality of the soil, and to have taken that which they could cultivate most easily and profitably. Those who crossed the Rhine settled densely within a short distance of the former imperial frontier. Here they constituted a great deal more than the hypothetical five per cent of the population that has been postulated above. Deep within Gaul, where their settlements were a great deal less numerous, their contribution to the total population must have been a great deal less than five per cent.[2]

The Germanic invaders of the Western Empire inherited social and political institutions and legal codes no less than fields, farms and villages. They may have only half understood the former and have misused the latter, but their own contribution in these respects was small. The background of the Salian Law of the Franks, wrote Wallace-Hadrill, 'Is Vulgar, not Classical Law, but it is still inescapably Roman. . . . Their rule was Roman-derivative'.[3] The level of Roman civilisation may in their hands have been lowered or degraded; it was not destroyed.

This cannot, however, be said also of the invaders of the sixth and subsequent centuries. They originated in areas more remote from Roman civilisation and power. Most had been much less influenced by it, and some, notably the Muslim Arab-Berber peoples, were hostile to it.

The Lombards, who began to enter Italy in 568, had lived for a time along the Danube, and before that had come southwards from the Baltic region. More than any other invading people they had retained an organisation of tribes, which came together for war and conquest and broke up again in peace. The Lombard state of Italy was centred in Pavia, but it quickly disintegrated into autonomous 'duchies', two of which, Spoleto and Benevento, remained as Lombard enclaves in central and southern Italy. The Lombards 'were as little familiar with the law as with the language of Rome'.[4] Whereas the Ostrogothic code of Theodoric had been in effect an abstract of late Roman law, made applicable to both Goth and Roman, the Lombard code showed a primitive society in which warfare and hunting were the principal occupations. It was concerned primarily with such primitive matters as the *wergild*, or blood price of injured parties, and is thus closer to the early Anglo-Saxon laws than to the codes of the Goths and Franks.

While the Lombards were occupying northern Italy, the Slavs

were spreading southwards into the Balkans. Little is known either of their numbers or of the routes they followed. They probably found only a very thin population in the interior of the peninsula, and they can themselves have added but little to the overall density. 'Living apart one man from another,' wrote Procopius, 'they inhabit their country in a sporadic fashion . . . in consequence . . . they hold a great amount of land.'[5]

Last among the invaders of the sixth century were the Avars and the Bulgars. The former held the north-western part of the Hungarian Plain until they were destroyed by Charlemagne. The latter settled the plains bordering the Black Sea, but were quickly absorbed by the Slav peoples who were already there.

Over most of the eastern European provinces there was little continuity of institutions or of economic life from the Roman Empire to the societies which succeeded it. The coastal towns of the Byzantine Empire retained their corporate life, and their citizens carried on a maritime trade, but Monemvasia in southern Greece was described in the eighth century as *in slavonica terra*. Slavs had destroyed the coastal towns of Dalmatia, and Thessaloniki had been saved from them, it was said, only by a miracle wrought by St Demetrius. The interior of the Balkan peninsula saw only the destruction of the heritage of Rome.

The period of the barbarian invasions was undoubtedly one of immense destruction and loss of life. Towns were ravaged, villages burned and crops destroyed, yet life went on almost as usual under shadow of war. Villas continued to be built and there continued to be a market in land. If the town of Trier was destroyed four times,[6] it is evident that there must have been some degree of recovery between each act of destruction. Sidonius described the destruction of *Augustonemetum* (Clermont), but added that it was restored and reoccupied.[7] He noted that the Goths had destroyed the crops in the Rhône valley, but was able to commend his friend Patiens, bishop of Lyons, on importing grain to feed the destitute.

The barbarian invaders of the West were very far from being the enemies of the Roman order. There was collaboration, even friendship, between the opposing peoples in the intervals between periods of war. The invaders respected and learned from the Roman social and political system, and the Roman provincials came to tolerate, if not also to respect their new masters. Dopsch is absolutely right in his insistence on continuity of institutions and ideas through the period of the invasions. Syagrius, who was killed resisting the Frankish invasion, nevertheless found it worth his while to learn the German tongue,[8] and, if we may believe the dyspeptic Salvian, the poor of southern Gaul sought refuge under the rule of the barbarians, 'since they cannot endure the barbarous mercilessness they find among the Romans'.[9]

In Italy, despite the destruction of the Gothic wars and the incursion and settlement of the Lombards, the continuity of economic and social institutions was probably more clearly marked than in Gaul. A few towns were destroyed by the Lombards; others were sacked by the Goths, but in most urban life went on unhindered, though on a reduced scale. In Spain, also, rule passed from Hispano-Romans to the Visigothic leaders, but the invaders can have made up no more than five per cent of the population,[10] and most were settled in the region later known as Old Castile. Elsewhere life continued little changed from that under the Empire. The invaders had received a fraction of the land as *hospites* of the Roman Empire, but they inherited the agricultural technique of the Romans.

### VILLA AND MANOR

The three centuries which elapsed between the end of the Western Empire and the accession of Charlemagne are amongst the darkest in the whole history of western civilisation. Sources are few, and raise as many questions as they solve. How extensive was the *villa*, and to what extent was it topographically the heir to the estate of the later Romans? What was the status of those who worked the lands of the *villae*, and what was their relationship to a free and independent peasantry; lastly, to what extent was there a market for farm produce, and conversely how dependent were the peasants and the villa owners on the products of urban and other craftsmen?

To none of these questions is there a clearcut answer. The extreme romanist view, now in large measure discredited, regarded the structure of rural estates in the ninth century as essentially the same as that which existed before the invasions. Gaul is pictured by this school as made up of estates, not unlike that which Sidonius Appollinaris owned near Clermont in the Auvergne. It consisted of a residence which may have borne a certain resemblance to the villa built by the younger Pliny in

Tuscany. The estate itself embraced 'spreading woods and flowery meadows, pastures rich in cattle and a wealth of hardy peasants', but the old Roman aristocrat disdained to write any description of its exploitation. He and his friends lived 'in terror of a sea of tribes',[11] but even in these troubled times they continued to lay acre to acre; to become the protectors of the poor, and to depress free men to the status of *coloni*. The poor, wrote Salvian, 'put themselves under the care and protection of the powerful, make themselves the surrendered captives of the rich and so pass under their jurisdiction',[12] losing their small tenements in the process.

Villa estates were probably increasing in both number and size throughout these centuries, but the villages (*vici*) of free tenants had by no means disappeared even by the ninth century. Largest of all estates were those of the barbarian rulers. These derived from imperial estates and from forfeited and expropriated lands. They were the source of the wealth and power of the Frankish and Gothic kings, yielding an income for the support of their courts and the maintenance of their armies, but also providing a means by which they could reward the services of dependants and purchase the prayers of the Church. The strength of the early Merovingian rulers sprang, in part, from their control of land. The weakness of their late Merovingian successors was due more than anything to their reckless dispersal of these estates.

The Church was probably the foremost recipient of royal largesse during these centuries. The Merovingian period was the most active period for the foundation and endowment of monasteries west of the Rhine and in Italy, as the Carolingian was to be in central Europe. Large estates were built up through the generosity of both kings and laymen, as the polyptyques of the ninth century were to show. The kings also made grants of land and even of groups of serfs[13] to their followers, so that the lay estates were growing from below by the commendation of peasants (see p. 52) and at the same time from above by concessions by the kings.

Such grants, however, were usually for a term of years, the grantee commonly receiving the usufruct during the period of his life. In return he performed a service, discharged the obligations of an office, or perhaps, only pledged his loyalty. Doubtless one concern of the grantee was to make the concession hereditary in his family, and, though we hear of many estates being returned to the king, far more were probably lost to the royal fisc. The early Carolingians, notably Charles Martel, were successful in securing the return of alienated lands, including some which had passed to the Church, but many were again lost, notably under Louis the Pious when imperial generosity reached dangerous proportions.

The grant of land – *beneficium* or benefice – was conceived as a salary for services, even if these consisted only of the eleemosynary services of a community of monks. The Merovingian and Gothic kings, lacking any regular tax income, had no other means of repaying their faithful servants. The tendency, however, grew for the grant of a benefice to be coupled both with that of immunity for the grantee and the commendation of the latter to his lord. Immunity was an exemption of the lands in question from all other jurisdiction; commendation was the act whereby the grantee swore homage and became the 'man' of his lord. A charter of Louis the Pious of 815:

> A certain faithful man of ours, named John has come before us and has asked our permission to occupy and take possession of whatever our father and we ourselves have granted to him (presumably *in beneficio*), together with possession of whatever he or his sons have occupied and possessed in the past. And he has shown us the charter which our father gave to him; but we have ordered another for him, and we have improved upon the old one. We concede to our faithful man John in the district of Narbonne . . . with land both cultivated and uncultivated and whatsoever he and his sons have occupied in other places; and all these things he and his sons shall hold as a gift from us; they and their posterity shall hold them from us free from rent and free from all molestation. No count, vicar, steward, nor other official shall presume to distrain or judge any of their men who shall live there; but only John, his sons and posterity shall do these things. . . . And in order that this charter may have permanence we have sealed it with our seal.[14]

Here we have exemplified not only the reckless generosity of Louis himself, but also the combination of the grant of *beneficium*, the commendation of John in respect of *all* his lands, and the concession to him of *immunitas* from all other jurisdiction for the totality of his possessions. Most of the elements of later feudalism are here.

Estates, the only significant source of income and influence for kingship, were managed with considerable care. In this Charlemagne set an example. His capitulary known as the *Brevium exempla* was a catalogue of three groups of estates, in respectively Swabia, Alsace and Artois,[15] only one of which, the last named, was in fact an imperial possession. The other two belonged to the bishop of Augsburg and the abbey of Weissembourg. The *Brevium exempla* was, as its name suggests, probably intended to serve as a model upon which other such inventories might be based. No doubt the reason for their compilation was to keep a check on alienations of land *in beneficio*, and to secure their ultimate return to the lord who had granted them. The successive partitions of the Carolingian empire between the descendants of Charlemagne, though outwardly divisions of sovereignty, were in fact attempts to secure the equitable sharing of the imperial estates.

No inventory of imperial estates has survived, but a good deal is known of the possessions during the ninth century of no less than seven monasteries in western Europe. The oldest and by far the most detailed of these is the polyptyque which Abbot Irminon caused to be prepared of the lands of the Abbey of Saint-Germain, near Paris.[16] Only half the original text survives, the rest having disappeared in a fire in the eighteenth century (see p. 127). The text describes twenty-five villas belonging to the abbey, extending geographically from near Château Thierry in the east to the vicinity of Nogent le Rotrou 120 kilometres to the west of Paris, with outlying possessions south of the Loire and at the mouth of the Seine (Fig. 2.1). Most units appear to have been compact bodies of land, grouped round a manor house. About half were divided between demesne cultivated on behalf of the abbey and peasant-held lands. West of Paris, however, no less than four villas were largely made up of small, scattered possessions, some of which cannot be identified with certainty today. It is possible that each of these villas represented a group of ill-assorted bequests and commendations to the monastery.[17]

Another monastery which had acquired extensive possessions was that of Saint-Rémi at Reims. An inventory of its lands was compiled by abbot Hincmar in 861, but survives only in an eighteenth-century copy.[18] Its possessions, which lay mostly around the town of Reims, were largely made up of compact blocks of land, with a few small and scattered possessions.

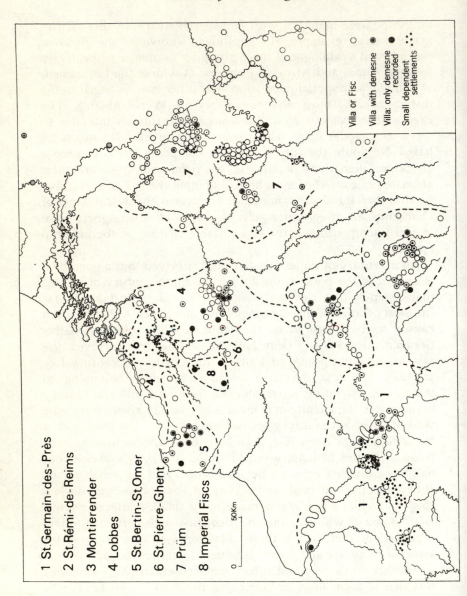

1 St.Germain-des-Près
2 St.Rémi-de-Reims
3 Montierender
4 Lobbes
5 St.Bertin-St.Omer
6 St.Pierre-Ghent
7 Prüm
8 Imperial Fiscs

○ Villa or Fisc
◉ Villa with demesne
● Villa: only demesne recorded
∵ Small dependent settlements

50Km

Fig. 2.1   The fiscs recorded in the surviving ninth century polyptyques.

The polyptyque of Montierender, near St Dizier, on the borders of Champagne and Burgundy was compiled between 832 and 845. It lists some thirty villas, almost half of them divided between demesne and the lands of dependent cultivators. Lobbes in the Sambre valley of Belgium and Saint-Bertin, near St Omer in western Flanders also held a number of compact villas, most of them similarly divided between tenant *mansi* and demesne.

The monastery of Prüm, situated in a valley of the Eifel to the north of Trier, possessed a very large number of widely scattered possessions. The monastery had been burned in the course of a Viking inroad, and in 893 an inventory of its possessions was made while ownership could still be established.[19] It held at this time over a hundred possessions, individually very small, and scattered over an area which extended from Lorraine to the Ruhr and from the Ardennes of Belgium to the middle Rhineland. The lands of Prüm spanned a wider area than those of any other known estate, but most of the units of which it was comprised had no demesne and yielded only a rent, in money or in kind, to the abbey.

Saint-Pierre at Ghent produced an inventory in the first half of the ninth century. The example of Charlemagne's *Brevium exempla* was not followed and, indeed, may not have been known. The list, which survives in an eleventh-century catalogue of bequests to the monastery,[20] is of small settlements, of separate *mansi*, and even of isolated parcels of land. There is no suggestion here of an organisation of lands into villas.

About a quarter of the total number of villas recorded in these seven polyptyques was bipartite, that is, each consisted on the one hand of demesne land – *mansus indominicatus* – cultivated for the monastery which received the produce from it into its granges, and, on the other, of the small tenements which the peasants cultivated on their own behalf. A very small number of villas – eighteen out of about 275 – consisted exclusively of demesne. They, were in effect, slave-run estates like those of late antiquity. About eighty had no demesne. They were divided into peasant holdings, or *mansi*, and held by peasants who commonly paid a rent in kind. A few of these were free men, but most had some form or other of unfree status. They resembled the colonate of the later Roman Empire, and indeed were often called *coloni*.

The tenants of the bipartite manors, which made up almost two-

51

thirds of the total, held their *mansi* in virtue, first and foremost, of the services which they performed on the demesne. Without their services the demesne would not have been cultivated. They commonly owed, in addition, carting duties which might necessitate absence from the villa for several days, as well as such items as chicken, eggs, and woven cloth. Only very rarely did they owe any money payment. The following extract from the short and fragmentary polyptyque of the abbey of Saint-Amand, which lay near Lille in northern France, illustrates this relationship:

> In the villa of Businiacas is a demesne mansus, with a house and other buildings, as well as a garden, an orchard and a chapel. Sixteen bonniers [about 20 hectares] of cropland belong to the demesne. Of these 5 bonniers are sown in autumn with 20 modii, and 6 are sown in spring with 36 modii. There are 4 bonniers of meadow, from which 30 loads of hay can be taken. There are 3 bonniers of copse. There is a mill which yields 20 modii a year.
>
> There are 11 mansi, each paying 10 modii of malt and 2 modii of hops; and-as a relief [*pro levamine*] a denarius, and also a pig. They journey to the vineyards in every other year, or pay a solidus instead. Every seventh year they each pay a solidus for military service [*pro hostelicio*]. They each provide a pound of flax, a chicken and five eggs. They make [*wagtas*]. They work two days a week with an ox, and for a third day they provide manual labour.[21]

There were ten other mansi whose labour services and dues in kind differed in minor respects from those of the eleven mansi previously mentioned. There were as well twenty-eight female slaves who each owed a *solidus* – clearly their servile status was less than absolute. Lastly there was enough woodland to support ten pigs.

Here, by the early years of the ninth century, the fundamental aspects of the medieval manor are already present. How, we may ask, did the bipartite villa originate? Such an estate would, under the early Roman Empire, have been cultivated as a unit by slave labour. The supply of slaves diminished during the later Empire, and it ceased to be practicable to run an estate in this way. On the other hand the insecurity of the times led increasing numbers of free men to commend themselves, together with their land, to a local potentate who had the power to protect them. This practice had developed long before the end of the Western Empire; it grew in scale during the following centuries. The commended peasant was no longer wholly free; he owed something in return for the protection he received, and what was easier than to place upon his shoulders some at least of the obligations formerly borne by the *familia rustica* of farm slaves?

The *coloni* had ceased to own their lands, but these, as a general rule, were not absorbed into the demesne. To do so would have placed upon the lord the obligation to feed his *coloni*. It was easier by far to demand from the latter whatever services were necessary to manage the estate and, for the rest, to leave them to fend for themselves, to cultivate their small holdings in whatever time they had after discharging their obligations to their lord.

The bipartite villa was, therefore, the simplest way of getting the land cultivated. Each *colonus* was endowed with a *mansus* or *hufe*. There seems to have been no pretence at a real equality amongst them, though the average *mansus* on the lands of Saint-Germain was of the order of 9·5 bonniers, or about nine hectares. A *mansus* was, as a general rule, what it took to support a peasant family. It varied greatly in area. The diagram (Fig. 2.2) shows the size in bonniers of the 936·5 recorded *mansi* of Saint-Germain. The *mode* was between 7 and 9 bonniers (9–11 hectares); the range, from less than three to more than thirty-three. The *mansi* of Saint-Rémi of Reims, to the number of 248½, had an average size of a little over twelve bonniers (15 hectares). The records show the existence of half-*mansi*, as if pressure of population were beginning to necessitate the division of farm holdings between heirs. It is possible that the smaller *mansi* enumerated on the lands of Saint-Germain and Saint-Rémi had originated in this way.

The majority of villas for which ninth-century evidence survives, had no demesne. Their *coloni* may have provided labour services, but these cannot have included ploughing the fields of their lords, since there were none. Cutting timber in the forests, preparing vine poles and trimming roofing shingles were amongst their obligations. The wives made woollen and linen cloth, and other payments in kind were poultry, eggs and young pigs. Villas without demesne were in general appreciably smaller than the bipartite villas, so that the organisation of a *mansus indominicatus* would have been difficult, if not impossible. Villas without demesne, furthermore, tended to lie at a considerable distance from the monastery (Fig. 2.1). In all probability such villas represented *vici* whose free peasants had commended themselves,

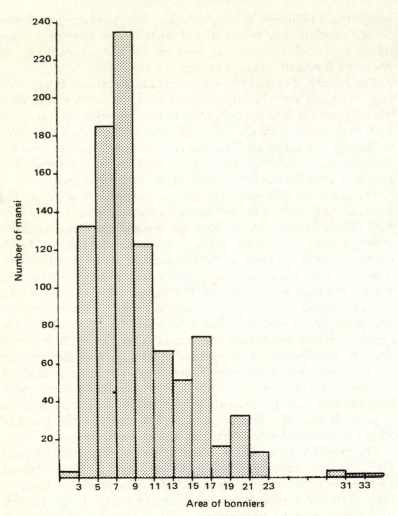

Fig. 2.2   Size of the *mansi* of the Abbey of Saint-Germain, about 810.

leading to the 'incorporation of the village into the sphere of action of a great land owner'.[22] A number of villas, furthermore, subsumed small and remote settlements, consisting each of a single *mansus* or even a fractional *mansus*. Were these clearings newly made in the forest, or were they merely the possessions of a peasant who, in his search for security, had commended himself to the monastery? We shall never know the answer.

Alongside the villas of the king, the monasteries and the lay landlords were the communities of free men, who cultivated their own fields. How numerous they were we have no means of knowing. The use of the term *vicus* appears to have implied such a settlement, and it was used frequently in the sixth and seventh century. Gregory of Tours is said[23] to have mentioned about seventy. Their number was declining, but they had not all, even in the ninth century, given place to communities of half-free *coloni*.

Little is known of the systems of agriculture favoured under the later Empire, and even less of the changes that took place with the invasions of the barbarians. It is assumed that in most parts of the Roman Empire fields were sown in alternate years, and that they were ploughed with the light or Mediterranean plough (Fig. 5.4), which only stirred the surface layers of the soil. This necessitated repeated ploughing, so that fields were in fact cross-ploughed. Their most convenient shape under these circumstances. was roughly square, and small, compact fields, cultivated with the light plough, have remained the rule in southern Europe into modern times.

The light plough was also used in northern and north-western Europe. Specimens have been dug from the Danish bogs, and the scratch marks left by cross-ploughing with such a tool have survived in some clay soils. In the Celtic north-west a similar practice prevailed and the Life of St Breock describes how a company of monks cleared forested land, laid out small fields, and cross-ploughed them with light ploughs.[24]

At some unknown date the practice of using a heavy plough spread through parts of Germany, the Low Countries and northern France. This instrument was drawn by a team of animals. Its coulter made a vertical cut through the soil, while its share cut horizontally, and the mouldboard turned the sod over, burying the weeds (see p. 194). A pair of wheels usually supported its weight and controlled the depth to which it ploughed. It was a clumsy instrument; the team which pulled it called for the services of two men at least, and the whole was difficult to turn at the end of its furrow. In consequence, land tended to be ploughed in strips or furlongs, each representing a day's ploughing, and the strips were themselves grouped into fields.

A team adequate to pull a heavy plough could have been maintained on the demesne, but was far beyond the capacity of a peasant family to provide. Those who owed ploughing service on the lands of Saint-Amand were required to come with an ox; only the community could furnish a team. In areas where the heavy plough was adopted ploughing was a communal undertaking, and imposed its own regime upon the land. The bundle of strips which were ploughed by the same community effort came to be a single field, and such it may have remained until enclosure or *remembrement* changed its form in modern times. It is highly improbable that small communities, such as those recorded in the Saint-Germain polyptyque in the west of the Paris basin, could have maintained a heavy plough.

The polyptyque of Saint-Rémi actually gave the dimensions of a number of these strips which lay on the demesne of the abbey. Each was, in theory at least, a tenth of a bonnier in area, and its length was ten times its breadth. In reality the size of the strip, or *mappa*, varied within wide limits (Table 2.3). Considerations of economy both of time and effort suggested that the demesne strips should be interspersed with or alongside those of the *coloni*.

The introduction of the heavy plough was an important innovation because it permitted the cultivation of the heavy and intractable, but potentially fertile soils. Its use probably spread from south Germany, but whether it was widely adopted before the end of the Western Empire, or was dispersed by the Alamannic and Frankish invaders is unknown. There is some evidence, in the forms of coulters, that the Romans were aware of it.[25] It appears to have been widely, though not universally adopted in the area between the Loire and the Rhine, but was probably used little if at all to the south of the Loire. Gregory of Tours described the lands around Dijon as fertile 'and so productive that the fields are sown after a single ploughing, whereupon follows a great and rich harvest'.[26] Can this mean that the heavy plough had reached the Saône valley, while Gregory, more familiar with Touraine and Auvergne, had not previously seen it?

The *coloni* and the *servi* on the villa lands were called upon to perform ploughing duties and, on occasion, to furnish an ox, but never did they provide a plough. One tends to assume that a piece of equipment as large and complex as a heavy, wheeled plough could have been provided only by the lord, and that it was used

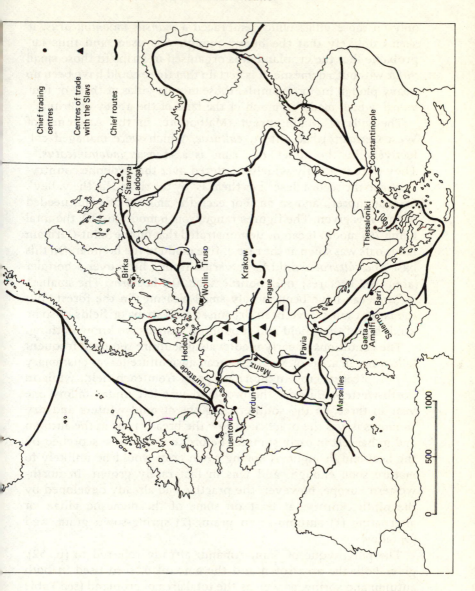

**Fig. 2.3   Trade routes of the Carolingian Empire.**

only on those villas which embraced a *mansus indominicatus*. It seems unlikely that the heavy plough was used, and thus improbable that the cropland was organised in strips in those small *villae* without a demesne. It is certain that there could have been no heavy plough in, for example, those minute villas of three or four *mansi*, which made up much of the land of the abbey of Prüm.

The villa of Malbunpreyt (Malbonpré, in the Ardennes of West Germany) had fifteen *culturae*, which were managed collectively by the abbey of Prüm as a *mansus indominicatus*.[27] They were evidently widely scattered over the Ardenne countryside, and the record describes them as 'by the river', 'in the valley', 'in longunpret', and so on. For each the amount of grain needed to sow it is given. The figures range from 6 modii to 110, the total being 767 modii. It can be demonstrated that on the Saint-Germain lands oats was sown at the rate of five modii to the bonnier. On this basis the *culturae* would have varied from a little over a bonnier (about 1·2 hectares) to 22 bonniers, or 20·2 hectares. The smallest *culturae* can have been merely small clearings in the forest; but the largest must have been organised into strips or fields of some kind, but of their field and ploughing systems we know nothing.

The conditions of early medieval agriculture required frequent fallowing. In areas of Mediterranean agriculture it was customary to take a cereal crop in alternate years from each field, while in north-western Europe, the cropland was left under fallow one year in three. In the southern regions of mild winters and dry summers it was the practice to sow the bread crops in the autumn and to harvest in early summer before they could be scorched by the heat and drought. A spring sown crop would be unlikely to mature soon enough, and was in fact rarely grown. In north-western Europe, however, the practice had already developed by the ninth century, at least on some of the demesne *villae*, of alternating (1) autumn-sown grain, (2) spring-sown grain, and (3) fallow.

The polyptyque of Saint-Amand, already referred to (p. 52), gives both the area sown and the amount of seed used in both autumn and spring, as well as the total area of cropland (see Table 2.1).

Table 2.1 Saint-Amand – areas under autumn and spring sown crops (in bonniers)

| Villa | Autumn sown | Spring sown | Fallow | Total |
|---|---|---|---|---|
| Businiacus | 5 | 6 | [ 5] | 16 |
| Madria | 10 | 10 | [10] | 30 |
| ——* | 16 | 16 | [16] | 48 |
| Millio | 5 | 5 | [ 5] | 15 |

* name obliterated in the MS.

Here we clearly have three great fields, or at least three areas of approximately equal size, which were cropped in turn. The Saint-Amand case has often been cited as if it were typical of estates in the Carolingian period. In fact, such elegant simplicity was very rare, and cropping systems were extremely untidy. In general, however, we can estimate the area of cropland sown respectively in spring and autumn from the amount of seed used or of corn harvested. The cereal crops grown were:

*Autumn sown* – wheat, spelt,[28] rye.
*Spring sown* – barley, oats, occasionally spelt.

Almost every record from this period shows a disharmony between autumn-sown and spring-sown grain. The amount of grain *sown* on the lands of the abbey of Saint-Rémi or received as dues from its tenants is shown in Table 2.2.

Table 2.2 Saint-Remi: grain sown or received as dues (in modii)

| Crop | Sown on the demesne | Per-centage | Received from tenants | Per-centage |
|---|---|---|---|---|
| Wheat (frumentum) | 150 | 1·7 | 55·5 | 2·3 |
| Rye (sigilum) | 586·5 | 6·5 | 53·5 | 2·2 |
| Barley (ordeum) | 6 | 0·1 | 271·5 | 10·9 |
| Spelt (spelta) | 7,256 | 80·7 | 2,024 | 81·6 |
| Oats (avena) | — | — | 15·5 | 0·6 |
| Variety not specified (*annona*) | 988 | 11 | 60 | 2·4 |
| | 8,986·5 | 100 | 2,480 | 100 |

Table 2.3 The size of Mappae on the lands of Saint-Remi

| Size of Mappa in square perches | Number of Mappae | Total area in square perches |
|---:|:---:|---:|
| 120 | 1 | 120 |
| 160 | 6 | 960 |
| 200 | 3 | 600 |
| 240 | 1 | 240 |
| 250 | 1 | 250 |
| 280 | 1 | 280 |
| 300 | 1 | 300 |
| 360 | 3 | 1,080 |
| 400 | 6 | 2,400 |
| 440 | 1 | 440 |
| 500 | 1 | 500 |
| 3,250 | 25 | 7,170 |

Average: 286·8 square perches

Source: Calculated by author.

It is very difficult to reconcile these figures with any simple three-field system; the predominance of spelt, generally an autumn sown crop, was overwhelming. A not dissimilar situation is found on the lands of Lobbes. One must assume that in these instances a two-field Mediterranean rotation of autumn-sown grain and fallow was used, suggesting the interesting speculation that such a system may have been introduced by the Romans and have survived unaltered. East of the Rhine, in the few instances where statistics of crops are available, it is spring-sown grains which predominate. At Duisburg, the abbey of Prüm received from its tenants: barley, 70 modii; oats, 34 modii; rye, 60 modii. Seigneurial exactions always leaned in favour of wheat, spelt and rye, which made a light bread, rather than of oats and barley, which, when used as a food for human beings, were usually consumed as a gruel or porridge. The Duisburg pattern shows 104 modii of spring grain as against 60 of autumn.

There were, lastly, some areas where no attempt was made to

grow autumn-sown grains. The *culturae* at Malbunpret, and also at other small, upland villas of the abbey of Prüm bore only oats, and at Aldenselen in the Netherlands was a tract of land which took oats 'whenever it was sown',[29] and another, near Ghent, which was sown with oats every third year.[30]

The field systems of the Carolingian period defy analysis. In the fragmentary evidence one can discern the later medieval organisation of fields and crops, but only on the larger bipartite villas. Elsewhere the constraints of villa agriculture seem not to have been imposed, and peasants may have been free to lay out their fields as they wished and grow what best suited the soil and climate. There are many questions which we would wish to ask of the records. To what extent was the heavy plough associated both with a three-field cropping system and with the large, bipartite manors; how many of the latter derived from the villas of the later Roman Empire? Alternatively, to what extent did monastic or seigneurial control aim to systematise and regulate the business of holding and cultivating the soil? There is at least a presumption that the later manorial system was a product of efficient estate management in the Merovingian and Carolingian period.

Charlemagne himself set an example in the careful running of his estates. His *Capitulare de Villis*[31] is made up of minute instructions to his stewards and others regarding the maintenance of buildings, the proper care of farm animals and tools, and the conduct of officials and of the men who worked the fields. The keeping of bees, the tending of vineyards and making of wine, the storing of food and the planting of trees were all regulated. At the end of this ill-organised set of injunctions is a requirement that certain plants be grown in the gardens of the imperial villas. There follows an extraordinary list of vegetables, herbs and fruit trees, which could not all have been grown successfully at any single villa. Doubtless the emperor was ruminating on what he would like to have available for his use and enjoyment.

Full as this document is of detailed instructions for the management of an estate, it nowhere tells us anything about the disposition of fields, the varieties of farming tools or the rotation of crops. The stewards who managed the villas might be expected to know more of such matters than the emperor. Their only instruction touching field crops was to see to it that there is 'good seed well prepared and from another place'. If there was any general effort to standardise the cropping and field systems, it is not apparent in the *Capitulare de Villis*.

In addition to the cereals which were grown on most of the cropland, and the garden crops of which Charlemagne has left so detailed a list, there was also a considerable production of flax in the Low Countries and Rhineland. Flax, retted and scutched, was prominent amongst the dues paid by the peasants. Linen cloth was woven in the *gynaecea*, the place in which women worked for the monastery.

Vineyards were no less important in the eighth and ninth centuries than in the later years of the Roman Empire. Indeed, they were more widespread, and had been established as far north as Flanders and the region of the Ardennes. The monasteries created a heavy demand for wine. Gregory of Tours commented on the noble 'Falernian' obtained from the hills above Dijon,[32] and Fredegar described how the vineyards of Aquitaine, from which churches and monasteries had obtained their wine, were destroyed.[33]

The vineyards in northern France and the Low Countries were small in extent, and yielded only a poor and sour vintage. Northern monasteries and even secular villas accordingly acquired possession of small, vine-growing estates far to the south and held them in demesne. Lobbes (near Namur, in Belgium) thus owned vineyards near Reims, and some of its tenants were required, amongst their multifarious duties, to go to the vineyards at the feast of St Remigius.[34] The imperial villas in Artois, named in the *Brevium exempla*, also had a small vineyard estate near Paris. Prüm owned vineyards along the steep slopes of the Moselle valley – Ausonius had described them almost five centuries earlier – as well as along the Rhine near Bonn and Remagen.

Most villas, especially the largest of them, owned meadowland, and in Flanders some of the meadows were of very great extent. Their area was most often estimated in terms of the loads of hay which they could provide, thus showing that they were valued chiefly for their ability to provide winter fodder for the farm animals. The water-meadows of Flanders (*watris-campi*) supported sheep, and on one such meadow, belonging to Saint-Pierre of Ghent, they could be pastured throughout the year, clearly an unusual circumstance.

This account of rural economy of north-western Europe is based mainly on the polyptyques prepared for some half-dozen monasteries. They give a distorted picture, because they necessarily relate only to lands which had passed into the possession of a monastery. We have no comparable evidence for the surviving communities of free tenants. Nor, with the exception of northern Italy, are there inventories of land and peasants for other parts of Europe.

In Italy the insecurity of the times and the practice of commendation had led to the formation of estates comparable with those of northern France. It appears – the evidence is too scanty for one to be certain – that the slave-run demesne was to be found more frequently than in France. In general, however, large bipartite manors prevailed, a great many of which derived from the estates of the later Roman Empire. The estates of the monasteries of Bobbio and of St Giulia of Brescia, the only examples for which we have much data, were each made up of a large number of widely scattered units. Bobbio possessed no less than 650 dependent tenants, some of whom provided, as in northern France, the labour required by the demesne. Many, however, discharged their obligations in kind – wheat, wine, oil, poultry and eggs, and there was a marked tendency towards a system of métayage, or share-cropping, by which the tenant contributed a certain fraction of his total product.[35]

St Giulia had about sixty separate villas or manors, most in the northern plain of Italy near Brescia, some within the mountains which overlook the town.[36] Again, one finds the system prevailing by which the unfree and part-free tenants provided not only labour on the demesne, but also rents in cash and in kind. In particular there were *liberi homines* who performed weekly labour dues in respect of their land because they had handed it over to the monastery (*qui illorum proprium ad illam curtem – Porzano – traditerunt*); in short they were *coloni* similar in all respects to those of the later Empire (see p. 16). The largest body of landholders, however, were the *manentes*, in effect share-croppers, who owed the third bushel of grain (*qui reddit de grano modium tertium*), as well as certain services. The monastery still owned a small and probably diminishing number of slaves, and it had a larger number of *prebendarii* who worked for the monastery but held no land.

The possessions of St Giulia were immense. As part of its

demesnes it owned more than 3500 head of livestock. In its barns large but unspecified amounts of grain and wine by its *manentes*. Its tenants performed 54,200 *opera*, or separate services, many of which would have taken the form of ploughing, sowing and harvesting duties, and, as on so many monastic estates at this time, chicken, eggs and cheese were prominent amongst payments in kind. The monastery owned a fishery (*dominica piscatione*) which could be expected to yield 1200 fish, and amongst the annual receipts of the monastery were 610 pounds of iron as well as substantial amounts of wool, of roofing shingles and of many other non-edible goods.

Clearly the income in kind was far more than the monastery could consume, and even admitting that the building materials could have been used in the fabric of the monastery, and that the wool was probably spun and woven in its own *gynaeceum*, much must have been sold into the market and doubtless used in the provisioning of the towns of the region. Furthermore, St Giulia received the not inconsiderable sum of 320 solidi as money rent from its tenants.

The legacy of Rome was less conspicuous in the Spanish peninsula than in Italy or even France. The Roman imprint had been strong only in Baetica and along the Mediterranean coast, and one looks in vain for villa estates in much of the Meseta and most of northern Spain. It is impossible to say with any degree of assurance how much of the Roman rural structure survived the Vandalic and Gothic invasions, because it eventually succumbed in the eighth century to that of the Muslims. The mountainous regions of northern Spain – the Cantabrians and the Pyrenees – resisted Muslim control as they had Roman. When the Carolingian conquest of northern Spain began in the late eighth century there was to be found, living in the mountain valleys, a highly compartmentalised and stratified society, on which incipient feudalism had had little influence. Basically it was a society of freeholders, who cultivated their lands with the help of servile labour. But war and insecurity were having their inevitable result, commendation and the creation of benefice and immunity. Already in the ninth century extensive estates had been put together in this way, especially in Catalonia, and the churches were as active here in laying farm to farm as they were in Italy and

France, though the scale of their operations remained small beside the gigantic estates of St Giulia or Saint-Germain.

The classical villa was not found east of the Rhine or north of the belt of open country which extends from Artois through Hainault and Brabant towards the Rhine. Beyond these limits there is evidence of large estates in the possession of wealthy monasteries, but they were as a general rule made up of small and widely scattered holdings of land (*Streubesitz*). Their organization was looser than in the Paris basin. Though labour services were demanded, the obligations of the peasants were largely discharged in kind. Both Saint-Pierre and Saint-Bavon, at Ghent, owned such estates. In general the desmesne was small, and only rarely were labour services required on it. It is to be presumed that the lands directly cultivated by the abbeys were worked by servile labour. A not dissimilar situation is found in the Rhineland possessions of Prüm.

We find, however, that the proprietors of such estates tried to impose on them some regularity and order, disposing of the more remote and less manageable holdings, consolidating those nearer home, and organising all into compact and administratively convenient units. The Ghent abbeys were doing this when their work was interrupted by the Norse invasions.[37] The tendency generally in Germany was to integrate the demesne with the peasants' *hobae*, as *mansi* were more often called in Germany, the latter being made to provide the ploughing and other services required on the former.

Few German estates equalled in extent those of France which have already been discussed, though the bishop of Augsburg possessed in all 1427 *mansi* occupied by tenants (*vestiti*) and eighty which, at the time when the *Brevium exempla* was compiled, were without occupants (*absi*). The lands of Fulda, of Gandersheim and perhaps of some others exceeded 10,000 *hobae* or *mansi* and must have been spread over very large areas. During the Carolingian period these estates were growing in size with commendations and bequests to monasteries, and also with the extension of the settled and cultivated land at the expense of the forest and the waste. The *Brevium exempla* described a bipartite manor at Staffelsee, on Lake Constance, belonging to the bishop of Augsburg; it had a demesne of 740 ploughlands (*iurnales*), enough meadow to yield 610 loads of hay, and was owed ploughing and other obligations by twenty-three free *mansi* (*mansi ingenuiles*) and nineteen servile. The demesne included a relatively large number of animals, including twenty-six ploughing oxen (*boves*). It is difficult to see how the demesne could have been tilled, even if a third of it was fallow, by the labours of so few tenants; one tends to assume that there must also have been slaves who, since they were not *casati*, 'hutted', were not recorded.

The lands of St Emmeram of Regensburg were made up of fifty-one small, scattered units of land.[38] Each consisted of a few *mansi* or *hobae*; none owed ploughing services, and there is no mention of such obligations at any of them. Instead each owed a few measures of rye, oats, malt or beer, pigs, poultry and, above all, pieces of woollen and linen cloth. Many of the peasants owed a money payment to the monastery. The evidence of other polyptyques and censiers suggests that throughout most of Germany the estates, both monastic and lay, were composed more of small units like those of St Emmeram, than of large, like the manor of Staffelsee.

The Roman villa had become, towards the end of the Empire, not only an agricultural estate but also a self-sufficing centre of manufacturing production. Cloth was woven and finished, leather was tanned and fabricated, even iron was smelted. The Carolingian villa inherited these activities. It did not need a market to supply it with the products of craft industries. Some villas made blooms of iron, others malted grain and brewed beer, fabricated wood and even prepared dyestuffs. The manufacturing activities which had once been carried on in towns had, with the partial exception of those of Italy, been transferred to the country-side. It was the achievement of the towns during the two or three succeeding centuries to attract them back again to an urban environment.

The spread of the estates, grouped for administrative purposes into villas or manors, carried with it the ultimate disappearance of the free peasants, living in their village communities. It is likely that their numbers had declined most in those parts of northern France where the bipartite villa was most firmly established. But there were many areas where communities of free cultivators continued through the ninth century. Latouche has found evidence for their survival in Maine.[39] They survived also in some parts of

Germany and in the Alpine region, where the development of the seigneurie was less marked.

### THE TOWNS

Town life, like the life of the villa, survived through the centuries which followed the fall of the Western Empire, but always in an attenuated form. Towns suffered severely at the hands of the invaders of the fifth century. Many, as contemporary writers tell us, were burned; others were abandoned and fell to ruin. An Anglo-Saxon poem, commonly referred to as *The Ruin*, gives us the impression made upon an invading people by the decayed monuments of a Roman city:

> The work of giants moldreth away. Its roofs are breaking and falling; its towers crumble in ruin. Plundered those walls with grated doors – their mortar white with frost. Its battered ramparts are shorn away and ruined, all undermined by eating age . . .

Comparatively few Roman towns, however, were destroyed and never reoccupied. Wroxeter, Caerleon and Silchester are examples from Britain, and in Gaul several were abandoned by their bishops – amongst them Jublains, Tongres and Javols – and reduced to mere villages. In most others there was either an uninterrupted history of settlement, or some form of urban life was resumed after only a short intermission. Trier was sacked no less than four times, but after each occasion it was reoccupied. Sidonius wrote from Clermont to his friend Graecus 'from within the narrow enclosure of half-burned and ruined walls, with terror of war at the gates'.[40] Yet he continued to live here, and the town survived the Visigothic wars. So, too, did many other towns in the Roman West. Gregory of Tours records an anecdote which shows that in one of the Roman towns the system of aqueducts remained in use and that an engineer continued to be appointed to look after it. At Vienne, on the Rhône, which was under attack 'the artificer who had charge of the aqueduct was driven from the city'. He offered his services to the attackers and led a company of armed men 'along the aqueduct, preceded by men with iron crow-bars. For there was an outlet covered by a great stone, which was moved away by the crow-bars under the direction of the artificer, and so they entered the city.'[41] The narrative of Gregory of Tours is, indeed, filled with references to towns and to town life. The plague ravaged Narbonne and Albi; Orleans was filled with Jewish and Syrian merchants, and along the streets of Tours were merchants' houses with precious ornaments and articles of silver.[42] Lyons, Paris, Toulouse, Verdun and others appear to have remained populous through the Merovingian and Carolingian periods. But not all towns enjoyed such good fortune. For every town praised for its vigour and commercial activity by Gregory, Sidonius or Fredegar there were at least half a dozen which disappeared from the records. Some vanished also from the face of the land, abandoned and never again inhabited. Most, however, deserted by imperial officials and well-to-do *rentiers*, became merely substantial villages, from which the peasants made their daily journey to the fields.

The survival of towns in Gaul was highly selective. It was even more so in Spain, where even fewer can show a continuity of urban life from Roman times to the later Middle Ages. In Italy, however, the situation was different. Towns had deeper roots in the economic life of the country. Trade with the Byzantine Empire and with other parts of the Mediterranean world was maintained on a more intensive scale. Ports continued to be centres of trade, and their activity communicated itself through their hinterlands. Apart from those, such as Aquileia and Concordia, which were destroyed in the course of the Lombard invasions, most Italian towns retained some economic activity, other than the practice of agriculture, through the early Middle Ages. It was the plague, not the Lombard invaders or the economic depression which depopulated Pavia (*Ticinum*) 'so that all the citizens fled to the mountain ranges and to other places and grass and bushes grew in the market place and throughout the streets of the city'.[43]

One should not be surprised at the decay of urban life outside Italy. The astonishing fact is that it survived at all. Towns of the Empire were, in the words of Latouche, 'centres not of production, but of expenditure . . . sources not of wealth but of impoverishment'.[44] They did not diffuse economic life through the surrounding countryside; they were supported by it. The retreat of landowners to their estates, together with the emergence of the self-sufficing villa economy, threatened the end of the town as an economic entity.

It was saved from extinction by two factors: its own defensive walls and the institutions of the Christian Church. Few things in the Roman towns impressed the invaders more than their defences. Built of masonry, they were almost indestructible, and in this dangerous age they gave some degree of security against roving bands of marauders. To Isidore of Seville a town was essentially a place *quo esse vita tutior*.[45] Gregory of Tours wrote of *Dibio* (Dijon): 'Four gates face the four quarters of the world, and thirty-three towers guard the circuit of the walls, which are of squared stones, the total height being 30 feet with a thickness of 15. Why the place is not styled a city I cannot say.'[46] The defences of many towns of the Western Empire survived through the Middle Ages and, patched, repaired and occasionally enlarged (see p. 228) continued even in modern times to form a protective ring around them. Walled towns, therefore, provided shelter for people who might have lived more conveniently beyond their walls. Merchants made them the base of their operations, where they could accumulate their wares and offer them for sale in relative security, and the institutions of the Christian Church found protection within them.

It was the Church which, more than any other institution, gave continuity to the life of the town. Christianity was, in origin, an urban cult, and its organisation reflected that of the state. Its basilicas were built alongside those of the deified emperors, and its bishops lived in towns and administered dioceses which corresponded closely with the *civitates* of the Roman administration. Dijon was not a *civitas* capital; nor was it the seat of a bishop; hence Gregory's apparent surprise at the elaboration of its defences. Sidonius's Clermont was both, and here, as a dutiful bishop, he continued to live amid the ruins of the Roman town.

The cathedral of the bishop stood in most instances beside the market-place, heir to the forum of the Romans. It was not a monastic institution, except in Britain, and it probably did not give permanent employment to more than a handful of people. But it attracted the pilgrim and the merchant and did something towards guaranteeing the peace and security of the market-place itself. In the sixth and seventh centuries monasticism spread through the provinces of the Western Empire. The Rule of St Benedict, by which it was organised, had enjoined field labour on its followers, but had never called for the abandonment of the busy world of people and escape to the desert. In fact it called for the creation of communities which were quasi-urban.

Fredegar describes how Guntram in 584 'built in the suburb of Chalon-sur-Saône – *suburbanum Cabilonninsim* – the sumptuous church of Saint-Marcel'.[47] Many other foundations were located outside the line of the Roman walls, but close to a town; St Remigius at Reims, St Sernin at Toulouse, St Victor at Marseilles, St Vaast at Arras, and St Germain and St Denis at Paris are examples. In Italy, the Lombards founded, amongst others, the church of St Peter outside the walls of Beneventum, and another with the same dedication outside those of Pavia.[48] More familiar, perhaps, are the monasteries of St Augustine at Canterbury, St Botolph at Colchester and St Mary at York. This situation, near but not within the town, has given rise to much speculation. Were their founders reluctant to intrude within the bishop's urban sphere of action; was it even possible for them to acquire title to enough urban land for their needs? Or can one assume that the towns were so built up that monastic foundations were forced into the suburbs beyond their walls? When monastic foundations were established within the line of the Roman walls, as at Bath,[49] Gloucester and Chester, there is good reason to suppose that the towns had themselves been abandoned. The suburban location of so many monasteries suggests that the walled towns continued to be well populated.

The foundation of a monastery beyond the limit of an existing town created a second nucleus, a further pole of attraction for pilgrims, merchants and travellers, and one, furthermore, which could compete on favourable terms with the older institutions of the town. The monasteries – at least the larger amongst them – became great centres of production; they had surpluses of grain and, in many instances, of wine, animal products and cloth, and these they were obliged to sell into the market. Serfs of the northern French monastery of Lobbes had to make the journey to the vineyards at the feast of St Remigius (1 October), probably to a wine fair at the monastery of St Remigius at Reims. There is other evidence of a monastery establishing a market or a fair before its gates.[50] The Lendit fair, one of the earliest of international fairs, was established on the land of the abbey of Saint Denis at Paris.[51] Saint-Vaast and Saint-Sernin became rich on the profits of trade, until their suburbs were built up with shops, workshops and warehouses, and, finally, the city wall was extended to include them within its fortified perimeter (see p. 231).

In many a town of France one can distinguish still the twin nuclei around which it has developed, and in some instances, as at Arras and Toulouse, the two are distinguished from one another as 'la cité', heir to the Roman *civitas*, and 'la ville', the centre of later trade and commerce, developed around the Benedictine monastery (see pp. 238–41).

Ennen, in describing the early history of the European town, has distinguished three zones of urban history.[52] The first was the Mediterranean region in which there was contraction, but no interruption in urban life. In the second zone, which covered much of Spain, most of Gaul and the whole of Roman Britain, the Rhineland, and the Danubian and Balkan provinces, some towns were abandoned; in many there was some continuity of settlement, but in all of them, forms of government inherited from the Romans disappeared. Continuity was in many cases maintained by the institutions of the Church. New needs had, however, brought a new category of settlement into existence. This was the merchants' town, or *wik*. The commercial suburbs of Reims, Cologne, Verdun, Bonn and Regensburg, whether they had formed around a monastic foundation or not, were early examples. But trade did not necessarily focus on ancient Roman sites. New commerical centres were formed, like Quentovic on the coast of Picardy, from which trade was conducted with Britain.

The third zone of European urban history lay outside the boundary of the former Roman Empire. Here there were no towns as the Romans understood them, though numerous forts, defended by palisade, bank and ditch, provided places of refuge and may have had a small number of permanent inhabitants. But here too were to be found embryo merchants' settlements, or *wiks*. These would have included Duurstede in the Rhine estuary, and the bases from which the Franks carried on their trade with the Slavs, the embryos from which Magdeburg, Erfurt and Bamberg were to develop.

## TRADE AND MANUFACTURING

Commerce during the centuries following the end of the Western Empire has been the subject of a more strenuous controversy than any other aspect of the period. This debate centres in the so-called Pirenne thesis, and concerns essentially the fortunes of trade in the Mediterranean basin. Pirenne argued – and in this he cannot be contradicted – that during the period of the Roman Empire there was an important seaborne trade. He claimed, further, that the vitality of this commerce communicated itself to the surrounding provinces of the Empire. The barbarian invasions, he claimed, 'destroyed . . . not the Empire, but the Imperial Government in *partibus occidentis'*. They disturbed, but they did not disrupt the trade of the Mediterranean basin. 'In other words, the Mediterranean unity which was the essential feature of this ancient world was maintained in all its various manifestations.'[53] The Vandals took to the sea after their conquest of North Africa in 430, but their piratical attacks were halted, and under Justinian the balance was restored.

This unity of the Mediterranean basin was terminated, Pirenne claimed, by the Muslim conquest of much of its littoral and the domination of its surface by Arab fleets. This happened in the seventh century. In 640 the Arabs occupied Egypt. Between 642 and the beginning of the eighth century they spread through North Africa; in 711 they invaded Spain, and in 732 made a foray deep into France. They established piratical bases on the Mediterranean islands, and in the ninth century, even settled at Garde Freinet on the coast of Provence, from which they not only obstructed movement and trade, but even raided far into the Alps.

The 'sudden thrust' of Islam

> had put an end to the Mediterranean commonwealth. . . . The familiar and almost 'family' sea which once united all the parts of this commonwealth was to become a barrier between them. On all its shores, for centuries, social life, in all its fundamental characteristics, had been the same; religion, the same; customs and ideas, the same or very nearly so. . . . But now, all of a sudden, the very lands where civilization had been born were torn away. . . . The Mediterranean had been a Roman lake; it now became, for the most part, a Moslem lake.[54]

Trade dried up in Mediterranean ports, and the routes leading to them were abandoned.

> Of a regular and normal commercial activity, of steady trading carried on by a class of professional merchants, in short, of all that constitutes the very essence of an economy of exchange worthy of the name, no traces are to be found after the closing off of the Mediterranean by the Islamic invasion.

Commerce became of negligible importance. The gold currency of the Merovingians gave place to the debased silver of the Carolingians. Estates and communities, *villae* and *vici*, turned in upon themselves.

> For an economy of exchange was substituted an economy of consumption. Each demesne, in place of continuing to deal with the outside, constituted from this time on a little world of its own. . . . The ninth century is the golden age of what we have called the closed domestic economy and which we might call, with more exactitude, the economy of no markets.[55]

The clarity and elegance of Pirenne's expression of his ideas were impressive, and for many years they seemed to carry conviction. But for some thirty years now the Pirenne thesis has been subjected to increasingly rigorous criticism. It is realised that he ignored some and exaggerated the importance of other evidence. He postulated an antithesis between the economic systems of Merovingians and Carolingians, and invented a revolution to explain the transition from the one to the other. His case was overdrawn, yet it cannot be denied that there was a contrast between the economies of the sixth and seventh centuries on the one hand and of the eighth and ninth on the other. The transition however was a long slow process of decay in some areas, of growth in others. It was marked by the emergence of local and regional economies, which cannot be painted with the broad brush and contrasted colours of a Pirenne.

The Mediterranean basin under the later Roman Empire was not the scene of as vigorous a commerce as Pirenne suggested. Wheat and oil were transported in quantity, primarily to provision the city of Rome, but its population was declining and – certainly after the Gothic wars of the mid-sixth century – made few calls on the grain of Africa or the oil of Spain. There was a westward movement of goods from the Levant, but these were mainly luxury wares and their volume was small, even if their value was not inconsiderable. This trade continued after the end of the Western Empire. It consisted of spices and herbs, silks, ivories and papyrus, goods for which demand in the west must have been infinitesimal. It is even possible that trade on the Atlantic, around the coasts of France, and between France and the British Isles was as great as that within the Mediterranean basin itself. That there was some trade between the Mediterranean and the Atlantic is shown by a well-known anecdote in the Life of St John the Almsgiver about a merchant of Alexandria who 'ventured' a cargo of corn to Cornwall, and returned with a load of tin.

Trade seems to have been largely in the hands of Syrians and Jews, and there is little certain evidence of Frankish, Gothic or Roman merchants. Most traders appear to have operated with little capital and on a small scale. They were, in fact, petty hucksters, and Latouche has aptly compared them with North Africans and middle easterners who sometimes hawk carpets and other wares from house to house in France.[56] Sidonius wrote to his friend Graecus, commending the bearer of the letter as

> one who ekes out a bare living by commerce; he gains no profit or other advantage from any handicraft or employment, nor does he make anything from the cultivation of land. . . . Though his means are small, the general confidence in him is so great that if he wants to raise money for the purchase of a cargo, people are confiding enough to trust him on no greater security than their experience of his good faith.[57]

In the event the good bishop proved too trusting; the merchant was an imposter who absconded with the money he had borrowed.[58]

Gregory of Tours makes frequent mention of Syrians and Jews, usually in a context which suggests that they bought and sold on behalf of someone else. Priscus the Jew, for example, was a familiar of King Chilperic, 'whom he helped . . . in the purchase of precious things'.[59] Others had their *negociatores*, who made purchases and procured goods on their behalf. At Tours (see p. 68) there were streets of merchants' houses, but there is no evidence, at least in Gaul and Spain, for shops in which business was regularly carried on. Purchases were in all probability made at periodic markets and fairs.

Merchants penetrated far into Germany and, even beyond, into the Slav lands. Fredegar repeats the story of Samo, probably a Frank, who travelled eastwards, probably in search of slaves; became involved in the defensive wars of the Slavic 'Wends' against the Avars, and became in time their king. Slaves were amongst the leading exports to the west. They were the product, and perhaps the cause of the wars between Germans and Slavs, and the town of Verdun on the Meuse in eastern France, appears to have become a focus of the slave trade.

The evidence, entirely qualitative though it is, suggests that the volume of trade declined in most of the west during the Merovingian period, though there was probably an intensification of commerce in the area of the Low Countries, the Austrasian homeland of the Carolingians. In the Carolingian period the volume of trade diminished yet more, especially in areas bordering the Mediterranean Sea, but there is no evidence that it ever ceased, even in areas most exposed to Arab raids. An incident, reported by the Monk of St Gall, tells how Charlemagne happened to be 'at a certain town . . . on the seashore in southern Gaul' when a band of pirates approached the harbour. 'As their ships came in sight, some said that they were Jewish merchants, others that they were Africans or traders from Britain.'[60] Charlemagne alone knew better, for he recognised from the cut of their ships that they were Norse pirates. The story is certainly apocryphal, but it nevertheless suggests that traders, whether Jewish or North African, were not unknown on the coast of Languedoc or Provence at this time.

No doubt the Arab pirates did make the western Mediterranean unsafe for commercial shipping, especially after they had established themselves at Garde Freinet and occupied the Mediterranean islands about 890. The old route from France to Rome, which was by sea from a Provençal port to Ostia, probably ceased to be used, but there is evidence for an increasing traffic across the passes of the French Alps. The Mont Cenis and the two St Bernard passes appear to have been the most used, and Charlemagne established toll places at the 'cluses', or narrows, where the Alpine valleys crossed the mountain foothills. Oriental goods continued to reach the Frankish empire by this route. The St Gall chronicle described how people who 'had just come from Pavia, to which city the Venetians had of late brought from their lands beyond the sea all the riches of the East' decked themselves out at carnival time 'in ribbons of Tyrian purple and of lemon colour; others were wrapped around with skins of ermine'.[61] Possibly the gifts of the Persian envoys, which included 'balsam, nard, unguents of various sorts, spices, scents and a wide variety of medicaments', also came by this route. Charlemagne repaid the compliment with Spanish horses, mules and hunting dogs, as well as 'cloaks from Frisia, white, grey, crimson and sapphire-blue, for these . . . were in short supply in those parts and extremely expensive'.[62] When Charlemagne was building his cathedral at Aachen, so Einhard tells us, 'he was unable to find marble columns for his construction anywhere else, and so he had them brought from Rome and Ravenna'.[63] How they were transported, whether across the Alps, by sea to Provence, or by sea all the way to the Rhine mouth, we do not know. Whatever the route, his achievement suggests that long-distance commerce was far from dead.

The Muslim conquest of much of the Mediterranean basin unquestionably hastened a change in the principal *locale* of economic activity. For the western provinces of the Roman Empire the focus of trade and the most active centres of manufacture had been in Languedoc, Provence and the Rhône valley. This region could not expect to retain its primacy after the Frankish conquest. The centres of power of the Franks lay in northern France and the Low Countries. Here lay most of the imperial fiscs;[64] and here the Carolingians spent much of their time, travelling from one imperial villa to another. The presence of the emperor and his court brought trade to the region. The numerous richly endowed monasteries not only created a demand for building materials, *objets d'art* and foodstuffs, but also generated a surplus of wine and cloth which passed into the market.

In this trade the Frisians played an important role. They seem to have lived in the coastal regions of the Netherlands and Flanders. They traded with England, and their merchants used the river Rhine to transport goods to south Germany and perhaps as far as the trans-Alpine routes to Italy.[65] They appear to have engaged primarily in the cloth trade. They supplied Frisian cloth (*pallia fresonica*) to the monks of Saint Gall, one of whom had a low regard for their commercial honesty. Notker recorded that Charlemagne allowed them to sell short cloaks, which seem to have become fashionable until he 'caught them selling these little short cloaks at the same price as the large ones' and ordered their sale to cease.[66]

The source of Frisian cloth, which clearly was widely sold in the Carolingian period and, dyed in a variety of colours, was even sent to the Caliph of Baghdad, has been hotly disputed. It was not English cloth, and it is unlikely that it was woven by the Frisians themselves. On the other hand the monasteries of Austrasia were receiving immense quantities of woollen and linen cloth (*sarciles* and *camsiles*) as dues from their peasants. The abbey of Lobbes was owed by its tenants each year no less than 17,000 bundles of flax together with other unspecified amounts, and Prüm received flax from forty-six of its villas and linen cloth from twenty-one. It is difficult, if not impossible, to express this in terms of pieces of cloth. The amount, however, must very greatly have exceeded the personal requirements of the monks, and one must assume that the surplus was bought and marketed by travelling merchants; in short by the so-called Frisians.

A number of ports had been developed in north-western Europe, and through them passed much of the seaborne trade of the Carolingian empire with Britain and northern Europe. Foremost were Quentovic, or Wicus, at the mouth of the river Canche, and Duurstede, lying on the Lek, one of the branches of the Rhine delta. At the same time trade with the Slav peoples was increasing. Charlemagne sought to regulate it by forbidding the export of weapons and restricting it to nine places between the lower Elbe river and the Danube. Amongst them were Magdeburg, Halberstadt, Bamberg, Regensburg and Lorch. Jews appear to have been prominent in this eastern commerce, and were particularly active in the slave trade. Indeed, the word 'slave' itself derived from the Slavs from amongst whom most were obtained.

Within the Frankish empire there was a small but significant movement of commodities. Salt, essential both in the human diet and also for preserving food was obtained from coastal saltpans and inland salt springs. The abbey of Prüm had six men at its villa of Moyenvic, in Lorraine who managed four small holdings, but gave most of their time to making salt from brine springs. The water was evaporated in pans from April to December, but, if the monastery wished, the salt could also be obtained *in canlo* (by boiling?) during the rest of the year.[67] The monastery of Bobbio obtained salt from the lagoons of Commachio, and the salt trade was one of the earliest commercial activities of the Venetians. Salt was also carried by boat up the river Loire from the salt-pans along the Biscay coast, where again some of the monasteries had the right to make salt. There were salt works on the flat coast of Languedoc, though it is unlikely that they survived the raids of the Saracens.

The lands of the wealthier monasteries, as well as the imperial fisc itself, were widely scattered, and this imposed upon their tenants a heavy transport burden. Grain, wool, woven cloth, wine, building timber, roofing shingles and vine-poles were sometimes carted immense distances. Water transport was used wherever possible, but the carting obligations of the peasants, involving absence from home for as much as fifteen *noctes*, is evidence of the difficulties in gathering in the profits of a monastic estate.

The currency is an index of the economy. It is not only the medium by which trade is conducted, but is also, in its volume and quantity, an indicator of the amount and extent of this trade. Pirenne contrasted – and this was an essential part of his argument – the strong currency of the Merovingians with the weak coinage of their successors. In this, as in other respects, the antithesis was presented in terms which were too strong. The Merovingians, indeed, inherited the coinage of the later Roman Empire (see page 38). The coins were the gold *solidus*, first minted by Constantine I; the *trimissis* or *triens*, also of gold and amounting in value to a third of a *solidus*, and the silver *denarius*, or penny. The coins continued, even under the Frankish kings, to bear the image of the emperor, and few were bold or arrogant enough to replace it with their own.

The gold currency of the Merovingians gradually declined in importance and ultimately disappeared from circulation. According to Pirenne, this reflected the collapse of the western economy under the blows of Islam. It could as easily have reflected a Frankish preference for silver as a metal and a need for purposes of trade of smaller units than *solidus* and *triens*. The *solidus* may have disappeared because it became progressively debased until it was unacceptable outside Merovingian France. Long before the Muslim conquest of the Mediterranean the silver *denarius*, worth a fortieth of the gold *solidus*, had come to make up most of the coinage in circulation.

This was the situation when Charlemagne introduced his much discussed currency reform. It had been preceded by efforts on the part of Pepin the Short to regulate the value of the coinage. About 780, Charlemagne established new monetary values: a livre of twenty *solidi*, and a *solidus* of twelve *denarii*, thus initiating a system which remained in use until the British abandoned it in February 1971. Since Charlemagne minted only a silver *denarius*, the higher denominations served only as a money of account (see p. 119). There were no gold coins except for the few *solidi* that were minted for trade with the East.[68] These represented an outward flow of bullion, indicative of an adverse trade balance, not unlike that which took place during the later centuries of the

Roman Empire. For internal transactions the silver penny was adequate, especially as the Carolingians saw to it that it retained its intrinsic value. The capitularies, however, make it clear that there was considerable resistance to Charlemagne's currency reforms. His insistence that only he or his deputies could mint coins struck at one of the privileges which had been granted to or usurped by the growing feudal immunities of the empire. Added to this there was a widespread reluctance to accept new and unfamiliar coins. The frequent iteration of injunctions against illicit moneyers and against those who rejected the official currency shows how difficult it was to get the laws enforced. As late as 864 Charles the Bald found it necessary to enact that:

> Following the practice of our ancestors. . . . we have ordained that money shall be made in no other place in all our kingdom, except in our palace, at Quentovic and Rouen which money belongs from ancient custom to Quentovic, and in Reims, Sens, Paris, Orleans, Chalons sur Saône, Melle [in Poitou] and Narbonne.[69]

He further enjoined the severe punishment of those who refused to accept the legal tender of the land.

Far from implying the collapse of commerce, the currency reforms of Charlemagne suggest surely that there was a not inconsiderable volume of trade and that it could best be supported by the issue of sound money. It was the Merovingians who lacked a monetary policy, and, indeed, could probably not have conceived of one. The gold coinage which they inherited was probably unsuited to the needs of Merovingian society. It went uncontrolled and degenerated into an issue of ill-formed tokens of silver gilt. It was from this that Charlemagne rescued the Frankish currency.

What happened to the gold of which the early Merovingian coins were made? It is generally assumed that Frankish trade with the Byzantine Empire and the Levant was unbalanced, and that luxury imports had in part to be requited by an outflow of gold. No doubt this is true, but it is unlikely that gold was lost from circulation entirely by this means. Carolingian inventories of church goods, of which that of the church of Staffelsee is an example, suggest a not inconsiderable treasure in gold ornaments and other sacred bric-à-brac. Western Europe produced no gold, or produced it only in minute quantities, so that it is at least probable that much of the gold used for the adornment of newly founded churches and monasteries was in fact abstracted from current circulation, where the diminishing volume of business no longer justified its continued use. If Paul the Deacon is to be believed a gold canopy 'of wonderful size and great weight' was placed over the body of Saint Marcel at Chalons-sur Saône.[70] Is it not probable that the gold was cast from coins contributed by those who came to the saint's shrine?

Charlemagne and his successors did not limit their economic policy to currency matters. They attempted to regulate the whole of the economy, though what they produced was a series of *ad hoc* pronouncements, difficult to enforce and possibly ineffective. Some attempt appears to have been made to control the establishment of markets and to eliminate those which served no useful purpose. At times of crop failure, tables of prices were promulgated, though it seems highly improbable that Charlemagne achieved any greater success in this field than Diocletian had done five centuries earlier. The practice of usury was condemned with more than usual vehemence, but the practices against which the capitulary of 806 fulminated appear to have been little more than lending money at a high rate of interest in time of famine and engrossing grain supplies in anticipation of rising prices. The capitulary of Nijmegen of 806 stated that:

> Anyone who at the time of the grain harvest or of the vintage stores up grain or wine not from necessity but from greed – for example buying a modius for two denarii and holding it until he can sell it again for four denarii, or six or even more – we consider to be making a dishonest profit. If, on the other hand, he obtains it because he needs it, to keep for himself or to give to others, this we regard as a business transaction (*negotium*).[71]

All the economic regulations of the time were appropriate to the small scale transactions of a largely agricultural and predominantly self-sufficing society. The provision of capital for business enterprises on a large scale or for trade over a great distance was, it would appear, too unimportant to engage the attention of the emperor.

### THE BYZANTINE EMPIRE

The Eastern Empire had for political purposes been separated from the Western since the final division between the sons of

Theodosius I in 395. The Western Empire was, as we have seen, invaded and overrun by barbarian peoples who in varying degrees inherited the culture and institutions of Rome. The Eastern Empire was both more resistant and more resilient than the Western. Its central organisation remained inviolate in the city of Constantinople, while the territory which it controlled in turn expanded and contracted with the success or failure of its armies. It was invaded from the north first by Slavs from eastern Europe and then by Bulgars from the Steppe of southern Russia. From the southeast in the seventh century came the armies of the Prophet, overrunning the Levant, invading Anatolia and threatening Constantinople. Within the Balkan peninsula, as in western Europe, barbarian kingdoms emerged within the limits of the Empire: the kingdom of Serbia, the First Bulgarian Empire, and, on its borders, the Avar state.

The barbarian kingdoms of the Balkans inherited little from the civilisation of the ancient world. There was, indeed, little to inherit. Urban development north of the Greek lands was insignificant; the road system had been developed almost exclusively for the convenience of the military, and over much of the area a sparse population continued to live, isolated and self-contained, in its villages. The few towns of the interior of the Balkan peninsula, wrote Procopius, 'which were captured by the Slavs, now stand uninhabited and deserted, and nobody lives in them'.[72] The citizens of Salona found refuge within the walls of the palace which Diocletian had built beside the Adriatic Sea; those of Epidaurus fled to the offshore island of Ragusa, and Narona and Dioclea were abandoned in favour of coastal settlements accessible to Byzantine sea power. Procopius also described how Justinian subsequently attempted to secure the southern Balkans by founding towns, fortified with strong walls. His account closely parallels the description given by Strabo[73] of the processes of urbanisation and civilisation – to Strabo they were identical – in north-western Spain.

Justinian's success in the Balkans was no greater than that of the Romans in Turditania (north-west Spain). Of a total of about 140 places in Macedonia and Epirus thus 'urbanised' little more than a dozen have survived as towns, and even the sites of most of the others have been lost. One lost town of Justinian, Stobi, lying in the Vardar valley of Macedonia, near Titov Veles, has been excavated.[74] It was a walled enclosure of about twenty hectares, with paved streets, shops and masonry-built houses. It was, like most others, the artificial creation of the emperor. It may have shown some feeble, economic life as late as the ninth century, but was then abandoned and vanished. These evanescent Balkan towns never became the seats of bishops or centres of the institutions of the Church. They had no real economic importance, nothing to perpetuate their existence once the protective hand of the emperor was removed and his soldiers withdrawn.

On the coast, however, things were different. Constantinople, unlike Rome, was a maritime city. It was no great distance from the imperial palace, overlooking the Bosporus, to the Golden Horn, where ships unloaded. Constantinople grew under Justinian to be a city of perhaps a quarter of a million people, and it required an import of grain almost as large as that of Rome. It was easier, however, to handle the grain supply of Constaninople, since the Byzantine Empire had retained effective control of its seas. The barbarian peoples who surged around the shores of the Black Sea remained land-based, and never disputed the supremacy of the Byzantine fleet. To the south, the Aegean Sea was enclosed by a barrier of islands which extended from southern Greece to southwestern Asia Minor. It was thus partially cut off from the Mediterranean Sea and remained under Byzantine control. Grain moved to supply the city of Constantinople from Thessaly, Macedonia, Thrace and Asia Minor, as well as from the coastal lands of the Black Sea. Other towns of the Aegean, particularly Corinth, Thebes and Thessaloníki, retained some degree of prosperity, perhaps because they handled much of this trade with Constantinople.

The similarity between the New Rome, Constantinople, and the Old, is not complete. The former developed manufactures on a scale which allowed it, in part at least, to requite its imports. The *Book of the Eparch*[75] was compiled in the city at about the same time that Charles the Bald was throwing together his *Capitulary of Pistres* (see p. 79). The latter related to a rural society; the former to an urban. The latter regulated petty markets and the price of grain; the former prescribed the ways in which craftsmen might organise and the silk weavers, linen manufacturers, leather workers and the makers of a host of other items, both luxury goods and necessities, might manage their affairs. It was a rigid and inflexible system, but at least it bore witness to a large body of specialised, urban craftsmen who made goods for distant markets.

In the rural areas of the Eastern Empire the formation of great estates appears to have been less advanced than in the West, and it is even possible that the opposite process, the break-up of estates had been taking place. The *Farmer's Law*[76] of the late seventh century presents a picture of village communities, the free peasants, with perhaps the help of slave labour, cultivating both enclosed garden plots and also strips in some form of open field. The Law regulated disputes over boundaries and straying animals, the use of water for irrigation and the clearing of the forest for cultivation. The importance of the *Farmer's Law* is difficult to assess, and it is not even clear to what part of the Empire it was intended to apply. Agricultural conditions portrayed in it would be most likely to have occurred in Macedonia or Thrace. Nor is it certain that the social conditions which it shows were to be found at all widely at this time. Indeed, the agricultural history of the Byzantine Empire is one of the darkest corners of medieval economic history.

Eastwards, beyond the indefinite limits of the Frankish empire, lived the free Germans and the Slavs. Much has been written on the social structure and economic level of the peoples of central and eastern Europe. One thing we can be sure of; it was not an egalitarian society practising a primitive communism in its *Markgenossenschaften*. Society was as stratified in Germany as it was in the Frankish lands, and Dopsch claims to find there 'great "manorial" estates' as well as nobles who could command the services both of half-free *adscripti* and of unfree peasants.[77] Nor can it be assumed that the description of Germanic society given by Tacitus was still applicable. In all probability people lived in small, compact villages or hamlets and cultivated the surrounding fields according to some form of infield—outfield system (see p. 180). In some parts of central and eastern Europe there were fortified places – the Burgwalls of the Germans and the *grody* or *hrady* of the Slavs, to which they could retreat in times of invasion. Helmold wrote of the Nordalbingians, living in the present-day Holstein, that, after such a disturbance 'the . . . people came out of the stronghold in which they were keeping themselves shut up for fear of the wars. And they returned each one to his own village or holding, and they rebuilt houses and churches long in ruins because of the storms of the wars.'[78]

THE INVASIONS OF THE NINTH CENTURY

The period covered by this chapter ended, as it had begun, with widespread and destructive invasions. The most important and widespread of these were from the north, but the Muslims continued to threaten the southern coastal regions of Europe and Magyars occupied the plains of the middle Danube, from which they raided deep into central and even western Europe.

One does not know what prompted the Scandinavian peoples to break out of their northern homes and to raid and, locally at least, to settle parts of eastern, western and even southern Europe. A possible explanation is to be found in a climatic fluctuation which may have made their marginal lands incultivable. More likely, population pressed hard against their limited resources, and they succumbed to the attractions of plundering and settling the richer lands which lay to the south. One must remember that the numbers involved in the Viking migrations were small, and that the largest of their ships could carry at most a hundred people. They relied in their forays more on the element of surprise than on weight of numbers. Possibly their forces, in the aggregate, never amounted to more than those who took the eastward route to the Levant at the call of the Crusades.

The damage and disruption which they occasioned, however, was at least as great as that caused by the Germanic invaders of the Roman Empire. The area they covered was immense. Danes from the Jutland peninsula sailed up the Frisian, Frankish and British rivers, looting, pillaging and destroying. The Norwegians, who could never be clearly distinguished from the Danes, sailed to Scotland and Ireland, where there was little booty to be had, and to Iceland, where there was none. Only acute overpopulation could have driven the Norse to migrate to Iceland, whose harsh conditions have been recorded for us in the pages of the Sagas. The Norse from southern Sweden crossed the Baltic Sea, sailed up the Russian rivers, and, crossing the low divide, sailed down the Dnepr, Dnestr and Don to the Black Sea. They reached the court of the Byzantine emperor, from which some even made their way back to Scandinavia by way of France.[79]

They spread fear wherever they went. At best they could be bought off by heavy payments of gold, as they were by Ethelred from southern Britain. The French chronicler Ermentaire described in sombre terms the destruction which they wrought:

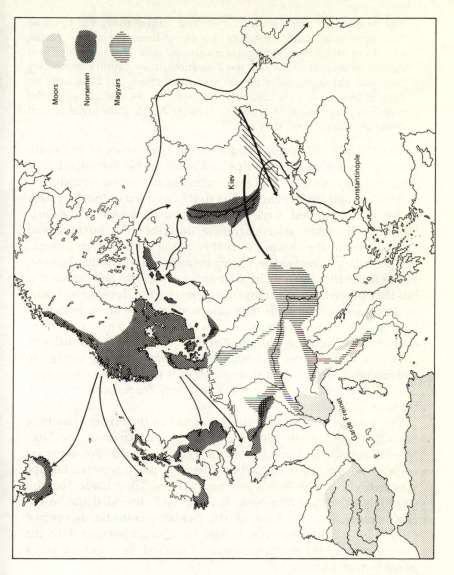

Fig. 2.4   The invasions of the ninth century.

The number of ships grows larger and larger, the great hosts of Northmen continually increases; on every hand Christians are the victims of massacres, looting, incendiarism, clear proof of which will remain as long as the world itself endures; they capture every city they pass through, and none can withstand them. . . . Thus little by little is coming to pass that threat spoken by the Lord through the mouth of his prophet: 'A scourge out of the North shall spread abroad over the inhabitants of the earth.'[80]

The Vikings, becoming bolder in the later years of the ninth century, abandoned their ships and made forays far inland. The Prüm polyptyque describes settlements as destroyed *a paganis*,[81] or Vikings, and the document was itself compiled in the aftermath of the incursion lest some of the monastic property be lost. Monastic chronicle after chronicle describes the burning and looting around the shores of north-western and western Europe. Yet the balance sheet of the Viking inroads is not wholly negative. Not only did they open up new lands for settlement and commerce, but they played an important role themselves in developing trade. In the course of their raids they acquired far more booty than they needed or, indeed, were able to carry away. They sold it or exchanged it for other things. They acquired large quantities of gold and silver, some of which even made the long voyage to Iceland with them. But in time much of it returned to circulation as the Vikings purchased goods which they needed and could pay for in no other way.

The Vikings also bridged the gap between the Frisian traders of the eighth and ninth centuries and the Hansards of the later Middle Ages. The former they entirely displaced. For a period trade along the coasts and up the rivers of north-western Europe was entirely in the hands of the Vikings. They made Hedeby (Haithabu) their western base. It was a well defended site on the river Schlei near the base of the Danish peninsula. It opened towards the Baltic, but was linked by a short portage with the river Eider and the North Sea coast of Jutland. In a sense, it was a precursor of Lübeck.

The commercial sphere of the Vikings extended over much of the Baltic Sea. The Swedes had trading settlements at Birka and Sigtuna, both of them replaced in time by Stockholm. They also settled Wollin – the Jumna of the chroniclers, near the mouth of the Oder, and occupied the islands of Gotland and Bornholm, and numerous sites from southern Finland to the mouth of the Vistula. From here their bands moved up the valleys of the Niemen, Dvina and Lovat, and down the Dnepr and Volga. It was a trading empire which they established. They bought furs from Lappland, Finland and the forested regions of Russia. Their forays netted slaves, which they sold or took with them as serf labour to help clear and settle new land or as an item of trade.

The Norse may have penetrated Russia as early as the seventh century; as is suggested by the Primary Russian Chronicle.[82] Thereafter the coin hoards of Scandinavia help to provide a rough chronology of Norse expansion and trade in Russia and beyond. The earliest coins of this period to be found in Scandinavia are Sassanid (Persian) dirhems of the seventh century.[83] These are followed by an immense number of Muslim coins of the eighth. These are mainly Ommayad silver pieces, and suggest some close contact with the Caliphate of Baghdad. A run of Abbasid coins extending to the middle years of the ninth century follows, but the Muslim coins come to an end in the mid-ninth century. Most of these coins were minted in Mesopotamia or western Persia, and they show conclusively that early Norse trade was not with Byzantium, but, by way of the river Volga, with the Caspian region and western Persia. Nevertheless, it is difficult to explain how so much currency accumulated in Scandinavia. Unless it was acquired as loot, as indeed it may have been, it presupposes a positive trade balance, with the Vikings exporting more commodities than they imported; and this is improbable.

The Volga trade with Persia was cut off in the middle years of the ninth century, probably by the westward incursions of the Pechenegs; but also by a rising against the Norse Varangians of the Lettish people of the Baltic region. Within a period of a few years the Norse again advanced into Russia. This was the movement associated with the name of Rurik. It took a different route from the earlier expansion, following the Baltic rivers and the Dnepr to the Black Sea, and reaching Constantinople by 860. The resulting trade was with the Byzantine rather than the Abbasid empire.

Constantine Porphyrogenitus thus described the Varangian trading expeditions in the later ninth century:

The single-straked ships (Μονόξυλα – probably dug-out canoes) which come down from outer Russia to Constantinople are from Novgorod, where Sviatoslav, son of Igor, prince of Russia, had his seat, and others from the city of Smolensk and from Teliutza and Chernigov and from Busegrad. All these come down the river Dnieper, and are collected together at the city of Kiev. . . . [The Slavs] cut the single-strakers on their mountains in time of winter, and when they have fastened them together, as spring approaches, and the ice melts, they bring them . . . into the river Dnieper . . . and come down to Kiev. . . . The Russians buy these bottoms only, furnishing them with oars and rowlocks and other tackle . . . and so they fit them out.[84]

From Kiev the fleets of small boats made the difficult voyage down the Dnepr, portaging around the more dangerous of the rapids, until they reached the Black Sea. Here they followed the coast, watched by the Tatar Pechenegs, until they reached the Danube mouth and the confines of the Empire, with their cargoes of slaves, furs and forest products.

Along the middle reaches of the Dnepr the Vikings established the 'state' of Kiev. It was not a unitary state in any modern sense; rather a jurisdiction exercised by the Vikings, or Rus,[85] over a group of towns: Smolensk, Chernigov, Vitebsk, Pereyaslav, and Kiev itself. The Rus doubtless predominated in the towns, but their surrounding areas were inhabited by Slavs and Tatars, who appear in turn to have traded with the Rus and to have threatened their commerce across the Steppe.

The Magyar inroads into eastern Europe probably involved a larger movement of people than the total Viking migration, but their impact was less. This was because they fitted into a physical setting which had, as it were, been prepared for them by the Avars. They moved out of the South Russian Steppe in the ninth century, across the Carpathian Mountains and into the Hungarian plain (c. 895). They embraced from the start both agricultural and pastoral peoples, and as they settled their new homeland, the former came gradually to prevail.[86] Their raids into Germany were contained by Otto I; those into Italy and the Alpine region came to nothing, and they were thus restricted to the area which, with only minor changes, has remained theirs for a thousand years.

Southern Europe was no less threatened by invaders than northern. In the ninth century the Muslims fastened their grip yet more firmly on the Mediterranean basin. They occupied most of the islands, including Crete (827), which guarded the entrance to the Aegean, Corsica, Sardinia (760) and the Balearic Islands (798), from which they could watch the coasts of Catalonia, France and northern Italy. The Byzantine Empire had continued to exercise a feeble authority over Sicily and southern Italy, and also over the area around the mouth of the Po. The former fell to the Muslims after 827 and the Byzantine Empire in the western Mediterranean was effectively terminated. In Spain, the Muslim emirate of Cordoba, under its Omayyad rulers, extended northwards approximately to the line of the Duero and Ebro rivers. The Muslims occupied Garde Freinet on the coast of Provence, near St Tropez, from 888 to 975, and from this base they raided the Rhône valley as far as Lyons; they disrupted traffic across the Alpine passes, and devastated ports and coastal settlements from the Pyrenees to southern Italy. Large areas were depopulated, and the economy was reduced everywhere to a subsistence level.

The inroads of the Muslims, like those of the Vikings, were not wholly negative. Out of the ruined towns and wasted fields there developed within a relatively short period of time a new vitality. When, in the later tenth and the eleventh centuries trade re-emerged, it was a Mediterranean trade, in which the Muslims played a conspicuous and important role.

# 3

# The expansion of the medieval economy

The pressures to which Europe was exposed from the Norse, the Magyars and the Saracens culminated in the later years of the ninth century and the earlier decades of the tenth. Thereafter they began slowly to relax. The Norsemen in 885 besieged Paris, ravaging the countryside, massacring its inhabitants, and raiding deep into Burgundy. Twenty-five years later the Danes were making their homes along the Seine valley, and within a few decades had joined with the local Frankish population to build one of the most progressive states in early medieval Europe. The Magyars raided far into Germany and Italy. They overwhelmed the Great Moravian state; reached Bremen and Apulia, and in 926 destroyed the Swiss monastery of St Gall. But in 955 their army was met near Augsburg by the German host under Otto I, and utterly defeated. Thereafter their activities were restricted to the Hungarian plain in the middle Danube valley. In the western Mediterranean the Muslim danger continued longer. Raids were made on coastal towns; Genoa was captured by an African band in 935, and, as late as 972, raiders from Garde Freinet penetrated the Alps of Dauphiné, and actually captured abbot Maiolus of Cluny and held him to ransom.

In 915, the Muslim base on the Garigliano in southern Italy was destroyed, but the Arab occupation of Garde Freinet was not terminated until 973. At the end of the century the ports of northern Italy, especially Pisa and Venice, were building up a sufficient sea power to give protection both to themselves and also to neighbouring coastlands. The dangers threatening Europe were gradually reduced. Moorish pirates continued to molest shipping on the Mediterranean Sea, as, indeed, they continued to do until the nineteenth century. Trade between the Christian states and Islam began to replace the earlier condition of continuous hostility, and the Mediterranean ceased to be a barrier, as for a period it had been, between the European west and the lands of North Africa and the Middle East.

A profound change took place in Europe in the later decades of the tenth century and the early years of the eleventh. There was a popular superstition that the Christian era would last for a thousand years. There is no evidence that such pious folklore inhibited economic life,[1] but there was nevertheless a burst of activity in the years which followed the year one thousand. Raoul Glaber described the new spirit:

> So on the threshold of the aforesaid thousandth year ... it befell almost throughout the world, but especially in Italy and Gaul, that the fabrics of churches were rebuilt, although many of these were seemly and needed no such care; but every nation of Christendom rivalled with the other, which should worship in the seemliest buildings. So it was as though the very world had shaken herself and cast off her old age, and were clothing herself everywhere in a white garment of churches.[2]

No such spiritual revival can occur without an economic base. Churches were built from the profits of agriculture and trade, and monks were supported by the slender surplus produced by the peasant. The tenth century had seen the recovery of western and central Europe from the depredations of successive waves of invaders and the rebuilding of the decimated population. During the eleventh a surplus began to accrue. This was, in part, invested in stones and mortar; in part in the building of social and political institutions, and in part in an outward thrust of Europe, driving the Muslims from Spain and Italy, conquering parts of the Levant, building commercial societies along its coast, and establishing an expanding frontier of European settlements in central and eastern Europe.

The turning point in the European economy came at different times in different parts of the continent, and was earlier in Italy than in France, and earlier in much of France and the Rhineland than in the rest of Germany. The last areas to be touched by the expansive economy of the high Middle Ages were Scandinavia, east-central Europe and the interior of the Balkans. Almost everywhere, however, economic growth, whatever indices and measures we use, was apparent well before the year 1000. It was at this time that it became visible in the landscape of Burgundy, where the monk Glaber lived the greater part of his life.

### THE MEASURES OF ECONOMIC GROWTH

It has come to be accepted that a period of economic stagnation followed the ending of the Empire in the west. This gave place in the tenth or eleventh century to one of expansion or growth, which lasted until the end of the thirteenth or early fourteenth century. On this there is complete agreement. There was some kind of economic decline in the middle years of the fourteenth century, associated in the common view with the spread of the Black Death. Some time in the fourteenth century – the date is a matter of conjecture – the European economy again took an upward turn.

One looks for indicators of economic trends during the Middle Ages. In modern times such indicators assume statistical form; they are indices of employment, investment, bank lending and business turnover, all of which are relatively easy to obtain. For the Middle Ages there are no statistical indicators, and very few that lend themselves to any form of quantitative expression. One can point to five trends, none of them susceptible of precise measurement, which, nonetheless, in their own qualitative fashion, do point to sustained economic growth. They are the formation of a system of states with fixed seats of government and institutions of administration; secondly, the growth of population; thirdly, the bringing of new land under cultivation and the creation of new rural settlements; fourthly, the expansion of the volume of trade and the increase in its variety, and lastly, the process of urbanization.

### The European states system

One of the first fruits of the economic revival was the development of the system of medieval states. The Carolingians had dissipated their landed inheritance, and within a generation or two had themselves disappeared from the political scene. Their place was taken by princes who ruled less extensive lands, but in many instances controlled them more firmly. *Francia* remained a vague concept; within its limits, however, there evolved smaller, more tightly organised political units. The Duchy of Normandy and the County of Flanders became models of efficient and effective territorial organisation. The Capetian lands which focused on the County of Paris, the Duchies of Burgundy and of Savoy and the Kingdom of Arles each evolved organs of central administration. Beyond the river Rhine the fertile lowlands of the Main valley and middle Rhineland became the focus of a Franconian duchy. East of the Black Forest, a Swabian duchy extended over the valleys of the Neckar and upper Danube. Farther to the east was Bavaria, already beginning to extend its authority down the Danube valley, where its protective eastern march – the Ostmark or Austria – began to take shape about 1000. In the north of Germany, Saxony, which had strenuously resisted conquest by Charlemagne at the end of the eighth century, began at the beginning of the tenth to support the first German imperial dynasty.

The tenth century also saw the emergence of the Bohemian or Czech state and of the kingdom of Poland. The Magyars consolidated their power in the Hungarian plain; a Croat state emerged in the north-west of the Balkan peninsula; the first Bulgarian empire spread to the south of the Danube, and between them lay the embryonic kingdom of the Serbs. Even in Scandinavia, the foci of political power began to appear. On the island of Sjaelland there appeared the nucleus of the Danish state. In Norway, around Trondheim and in the lowlands about the head of Oslo Fjord, similar political organisations appeared, and in the tenth century merged to make the kingdom of Norway. Political organisation in Sweden first took shape among the Svea tribes of Uppland, the area lying to the north of Lake Mälaren and centring in the earliest Swedish capital city of Uppsala.

The emerging political entities of the tenth and eleventh centuries centred each in its own discrete area of relatively fertile and productive lowland. None ever emerged without an agricultural base. Trade quickly became an ancillary source of wealth and prosperity, but it was always the surplus engendered by agriculture which made possible an effective and broadly based political organisation. A comparison, for central and east-central Europe, of Schlüter's map[3] of areas of early forest clearance and settlement, with the nuclear areas of political power in the tenth, eleventh and twelfth centuries shows a remarkable coincidence between them. Or take a map of the known perambulations of the earlier German emperors, such as those prepared by Theodor Mayer;[4] they show clearly that the rulers spent most of their time in those territories which were both the bases of their political power and the sources of their daily sustenance.

The nucleus of the Bohemian state was the fertile lowland which lay around and to the north of Prague. Here in the late tenth century came Ibrāhim Ibn Ja'kub, a travelling Jewish trader:[5]

> The town of Prague, he wrote, is built of stone and lime and is the richest of towns in trade. There come to it Russians and Slavs from Krakow with merchandise, and from the lands of the Turks [i.e. Muslims] come Mohammedans, Jews and Turks, also with merchandise and with mitkal [Arabic currency], and they export thence flour, tin and various furs. Their country is the best of the northern countries and the richest in food provision. They sell for a small coin so much wheat that it suffices a man for a month, and barley is sold for a small coin enough to feed a horse forty days.[5]

Ja'kub went on to describe the country of Mieszko I, the earliest authentic king of Poland, who died in 992.

> The country of Mieszko is the greatest of all the Slav countries. It is rich in bread and meat and honey and fish. The taxes which are collected by him are paid in mitkal. They also form the salary of his men. . . . And he has 3000 men in armour. . . . And he gives to these men dress, horses, armament and everything they need.[6]

Evidently these rudimentary states of east-central Europe had the beginnings of a political organisation; they were able to maintain a regular military force, and their capitals were graced with handsome buildings of stone several decades before the year 1000. The evidence of Ibn Ja'kub is confirmed both by archaeological discoveries and by surviving monuments from this period. The wealth of romanesque architecture in the Gniezno-Poznań district of Poland, around Prague in Czechoslovakia, near Goslar and Brunswick in Saxony, and about Speyer, Wörms and Mainz in the Rhineland is an impressive memorial to the early prosperity of these regions. A similar richness was formerly to be found in Normandy and the Paris region of France, but was in large measure destroyed to make way for the Gothic flowering of the thirteenth century.

No doubt the more prolonged periods of peace and the greater sense of security of the later tenth and eleventh centuries encouraged the accumulation of wealth. Population was also permitted to grow, and with it came the clearing of new land for agriculture and the foundation of new settlements. It is difficult to date the beginnings of these processes. There are references to the clearing of new land in the polyptyque of Abbot Irminon, but the scale of reclamation must at this time have been very small, and the cleared land was more than offset by the number of settlements described as vacant or ruined. No doubt there is an element of exaggeration in the accounts left by the chroniclers of the devastation wrought by the invaders, but the conditions which they described were certainly not calculated to stimulate the growth of population or the clearing and settling of the waste.[7]

Conditions had, however, changed in some favoured areas perhaps by the mid-tenth century, and by the early eleventh there was probably evidence of an expanding economy almost everywhere. It is likely that economic growth was first apparent in those areas which were protected by distance from the raids by the Norse, the Magyars and the Saracens. Latouche has suggested[7] that the long period of tranquillity enjoyed by Burgundy was a factor in the early spread of settlement and the establishment here of monastic foundations. The nuclear area of Poland, the region enclosed by the Warta and Noteć rivers, seems also to have enjoyed an immunity from invasions. When a German army did reach the central area of the Polish state, the chronicler Otto of Bamberg described[8] the barrier of protective forest and marsh which held up the invaders. Bohemia, Swabia, Franconia and, in all probability, the nuclear area of the Ottonian state in Saxony also enjoyed conditions of relative peace.

## Population growth

The period of economic expansion was also one of population growth. The human species responds very quickly to the stimulus provided by immunity from attack and unlimited land to cultivate. The opportunity to take over a clearing newly made in the forest or waste leads to earlier marriage and a larger family. Small improvements in the technique of agriculture have the effect of extending the margin of cultivation and thus of broadening the area of settlement. Mortality remained high and the expectation of life short, but the marginal increase in the average size of the family had a cumulative effect. From its slow beginnings in the tenth or early eleventh century population increased with growing rapidity until, locally at least, a Malthusian situation had been created by the early years of the fourteenth. For several centuries there was no shortage of land. Cartularies and rent rolls show how the area of cultivated land was broadened until, some time in the late thirteenth or early fourteenth century, there remained in much of western Europe little uncultivated land that was worth the trouble of breaking up and bringing under the plough.

The abundance of land, at least during the earlier part of the period of growth, combined with a steadily rising population, yielded an increasing surplus of production to the landholding classes. From this came the means to build the great churches of the twelfth and thirteenth centuries. It was no accident that Suger, abbot of Saint-Denis from 1122 to 1151, founded new villages and was also able to rebuild his monastic church in the newly developing gothic style. Surplus agricultural production went to feed the growing urban population, and the latter paid for the rural products which it used or consumed by means of the artifacts of its craftsmen and the services of its traders and middlemen.

The vital revolution of the Middle Ages lies at the root of medieval economic growth. It contributed no less to the economic decline of the later Middle Ages, because, as is commonly the result of unrestricted population increase, without any parallel technological developments, it led directly to overpopulation. The Malthusian checks on a population which had grown too large for its resource base : malnutrition, disease, famine, operated inexorably during the fourteenth century, and the population of Europe was reduced for a period to the level which the resources of the continent could support.

*Expansion of agriculture*
The population could not have grown as it did without the stimulus of new land. The village community grew during the twelfth and thirteenth centuries until it had reached its largest practicable size. In this process of growth groups of men hived off, made new clearings and founded new hamlets, sometimes within the same parish, and within sight and sound of the parent village; sometimes at so great a distance that they must, when they set out, have bid their native village goodbye, with no expecta-

tion of ever seeing it again. The journey of the Flemish peasants to colonise the wastes of Holstein, described in the Slavic Chronicle of Helmold, was as formidable an undertaking as that of the earliest migrants to the New World. The clearing of the forest and the cultivation of the waste of much of western and central Europe was one of the greatest creative achievements of medieval man.

## The growth of trade

There had always been trade in Europe. It was reduced to small proportions during the period of invasion in the ninth and tenth centuries, but, restricted though it may have been to objects of a luxury or religious character, it continued. Kingship was inconceivable without trade, because the outward symbols of royalty and authority were invariably esoteric objects of high value and distant origin. The silks of Constantinople were the marks of rank; so also were ermine and other furs, objects of gold and silver, jewellery and the religious ornaments and stained glass of the barbaric rulers of northern Europe. The clerical nobility, no less than the lay, demanded their own symbols of rank, both vestments and books for their liturgy and ornaments for their churches.

In the tenth or eleventh century the volume of trade and the range of goods which entered into it began to increase. This commercial revolution came first to Italy and then to northern Europe. It was a revival, not a new creation, but it was a revival with considerable differences. The volume of European imports from beyond the Mediterranean began to increase. More bulky goods, including raw wool from North Africa and alum and dyestuffs from the Middle East, began to arrive at the ports of Italy and southern France. In the twelfth century the balance of this trade underwent a fundamental change. Europe had hitherto had little to export – little, that is, that the Muslim world and Byzantine Empire were willing to buy. By and large, Europe's import of oriental goods was requited by the export of slaves and bullion, whereas the Levant had manufactured goods in demand amongst the élite of the west. Europe was the colonial, the underdeveloped region. From the twelfth century, however, Europe had other goods to sell. The gold drain diminished to small proportions as the export of cloth and of metal goods began to be used increasingly to pay for the import of wood, alum, silks and spices.

Trade developed also in the northern seas during the early Middle Ages. It differed fundamentally from that of the Mediterranean. The latter was a trade between a developing Europe and the more highly developed Byzantine and Muslim world. It consisted of an import into Europe of refined and sophisticated goods and an export of whatever Europe had and the Levant and Byzantine worlds could use. In the northern trade it was Europe, or at least the former imperial lands of Charlemagne, which was the more developed region, and Scandinavia and the Baltic, the developing. Trade in these areas may have begun with the looting of towns and monasteries by the Vikings and the disposal of stolen goods in markets and fairs. This was followed by a demand in the less developed north for manufactured goods like cloth, and luxuries such as wine. North-western Europe received in exchange the products of the northern lands – salt fish from the seas and furs and skins from the forests – and at a later date grain, timber and bar iron. The volume of this northern trade appears to have increased continuously through the Middle Ages, but its character changed little. The north remained the 'colonial' sphere, exporting raw materials in return for the manufactures of the developing west.

Mediterranean trade, however, changed in character. Europe gradually lost its 'colonial' role. Its exports came to consist very largely of processed or manufactured goods, and the Muslim world began to supply it, along with silks and spices, with raw alum from Asia Minor and raw wool and grain from North Africa.

There are no commercial statistics to give us an idea of the changing volume and composition of Europe's external trade. There can, however, be no question that it increased many times between the tenth century and the thirteenth. The growth of the port cities, which were overwhelmingly dependent upon seaborne trade, is in itself evidence of this. Amalfi, the pre-eminent Italian port of the eleventh century in the minds of contemporaries, was replaced by the larger port of Pisa, and then by the immeasurably more important ports of Venice and Genoa. The slender evidence for the movement of commodities from the Italian ports across the Alps or up the Rhône valley to central Europe suggests a steadily expanding volume of trade.

While the evidence for the nature and volume of European

overseas trade in these centuries is scanty, that for the movement of commodities within Europe is almost non-existent. It is indirectly – through the establishment of fairs and markets, the growth and prosperity of towns in which commerce played a significant role, the development, in short, of what the social scientists term the infrastructure of commerce – that one becomes conscious of its expansion during these years.

The growth of trade is demonstrated no less by the increasing elaboration of the media by which payments were made and debts settled. There was a money economy throughout the period. Money was used to express the value of goods and to store or hoard wealth. But the amount of money in circulation was unquestionably small. Mints were widespread. They were licensed or authorised by the king; they struck coins bearing his head or insignia from silver brought to them for the purpose, and they were responsible for the quality of the metal used. Yet the moneyers operated in small workshops and their turnover was minute. Lopez has attempted the extremely difficult task of estimating the output of the mints of north-Italy;[9] he found the totals 'almost unbelievably small', and tended to assume that foreign coins circulated along with those from the local mints. The quality of the coinage during the early part of the period of medieval growth was poor; coins were unevenly struck, often in metal that was debased. The volume of coin in circulation in Europe was probably small, at least in comparison with that in use a century or two later. The coinage of the later Middle Ages, in its design, in the care with which coins were struck, in the denominations in use, and in the volume which circulated, is clear evidence of a vast expansion of trade.

In addition to coin the merchants of the later Middle Ages evolved instruments of exchange which obviated the need for coin. If they had not done so, it is very doubtful whether the store of the precious metals could have sufficed for commercial needs. The use of bills of exchange began in Italy by 1300 and became the general practice in long-distance trade by the mid-fourteenth century. It greatly simplified the payment of accounts and to a large degree rendered unnecessary the movement of coin over great distances. At the same time the business of the merchant was greatly simplified by the use of double-entry bookkeeping, though it is probable that this method of accounting was not widely adopted outside Italy (see p. 422). The expanding volume of trade and the growing sophistication of commercial methods constitute one of the most eloquent pieces of evidence for economic expansion between the eleventh century and the thirteenth.

## The urbanisation of Europe

A final index of economic growth was the increase in the number and size of cities and towns. At the beginning of the period there could not have been more than a hundred places which one could call towns, and almost half of these would have been in Italy. When the period of growth drew to a close there were at least 4000, and possibly nearer 5000 places which claimed the

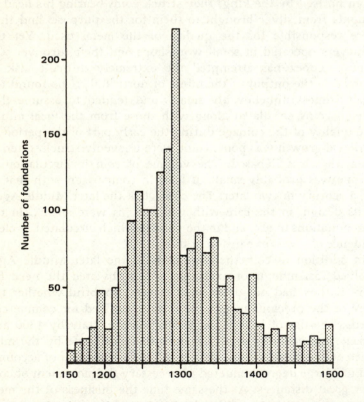

Fig. 3.1 The dates of town foundation in Central Europe (after Heinz Stoob). The number of foundations is shown by decennial periods.

status of town. Not all had strongly developed urban functions; some, indeed, were largely agrarian. But some two thousand must have been centres of local or regional trade and places where craftsmen carried on specialised functions and made goods for the market. The period when most towns were founded was the later half of the twelfth and the thirteenth century. Fig. 3.1 shows the frequency with which towns were incorporated in central Europe. It is in some degree misleading. In most instances we can only know when a town was incorporated or received a charter, and was thus authorised to act as a legal and privileged body. In very many instances the town, as a functional entity, was already in existence and its traders and craftsmen had already demonstrated their ability to manage their affairs even before they received the legal right to do so (see p. 226). Some towns, on the other hand, were, when they received their grants of privileges, nothing more than small agricultural communities and their charters were intended to attract potential citizens to come and settle there. A few never proved sufficiently attractive. They remained in terms of function largely agricultural, even though for a time they masqueraded as towns. Even with these qualifications, the diagram still demonstrates how strong was the urge to establish towns, how strong was the conviction that trade was expanding.

Not only were hundreds of towns founded in western and central Europe, many of the existing towns grew rapidly in size during these years. The evidence for growth consists principally in the extension of town walls to enclose ever more extensive areas, the creation of urban parishes, and the migration to the towns – as shown by the patronymics of many of the citizens – from surrounding villages.

Towns served many functions. There was in all of them an agricultural sector, and in the smallest of them this must have employed the greater part of their population. In many, perhaps most, there was some kind of organisation embracing merchants and craftsmen. At first this was highly generalised, as if there were too few in each category of producers and traders to constitute a separate corporate body. Gradually an initial, all-embracing merchant gild gave place, at least in northern Europe, to more specialised gilds. This change can be documented in the larger towns; in the smaller it is more obscure, and one cannot say with any degree of certainty what gilds were ultimately formed. In any event the trend demonstrates a very great increase in the number of craftsmen and in the degree of specialisation which they achieved. In Italy, the merchant gild continued to exist as an association of merchant capitalists, while the lesser gilds, formed of manual workers, gradually took shape (see p. 290).

These five indicators together provide a kind of measure of economic growth. Unfortunately they cannot, with the possible exception of the growth of towns, be expressed in quantitative terms. This means that one cannot say when growth became apparent and when it ended, nor can one know the rate of growth between these dates. One thing is certain; Europe was too large and too varied for generalisation to be possible. Today an economic crisis can be diffused from some critical manufacturing, consuming or business area to places which merely produce

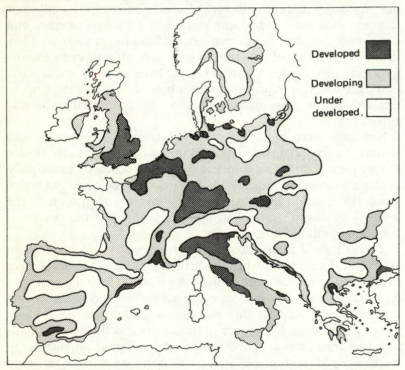

Developed

Developing

Under
developed.

Fig. 3.2 Europe's developed, developing and backward areas during the later Middle Ages.

primary commodities for others to use. The diffusion may take a year or two, but eventually contraction of demand in London or New York will be reflected in a diminished market for the cocoa-growers of Ghana or the producers of cloves in Zanzibar. Such changes occurred in medieval Europe, but they were incomparably slower. If economic growth began in Italy in the tenth century, as, in fact, it probably did, it was many decades before it was reflected in increased demand beyond the Alps, and centuries before the upsurge in the Mediterranean communicated itself to Scandinavia and Poland. During the medieval period, the idea of a European market gained ground. By the fourteenth century, dealers in the more important commercial towns bought and sold the products, cloth for example, from many parts of the continent. The market which Pegolotti knew extended from Scotland to the Levant, and the more important of the international fairs were serving the needs of an ever widening area and attracting traders from an ever increasing number of countries. But there were always areas which stood outside the system, as indeed they continued to do until the revolution in transport and communication in the early nineteenth century forced them at last to become part of a European economy.

## ECONOMIC REVIVAL IN ITALY

The economic revolution of the Middle Ages began in Italy. There were many reasons for this. Italy had been the most highly urbanised province of the Roman Empire, and the recession of the late imperial period and the Dark Ages had probably been less profound here than in Gaul and Spain. Here was a highly literate population, a good network of roads and a more strongly developed tradition of urban crafts than was to be found in other parts of the Empire. The Gothic wars and the invasion of the Lombards marked a severe recession. Some towns were destroyed, never to recover, but over most of the peninsula recovery was not long delayed. Italy had one important advantage over the rest of the former empire of Rome. The villa system, with its near self-sufficing economy and its population of slaves and serfs, bound to the soil, was never developed on the scale to be found in other parts of the Empire. In consequence the landowning classes never wholly forsook the town for their rural villas. Enough of them remained in the towns to provide an urban élite. They created a demand for the products of the countryside, as well as for the more exotic goods offered for sale by merchants. The Italian town never ceased, except perhaps for short periods in time of war, to be a market centre and a focus of an exchange economy.

Another advantage enjoyed by Italy was that part of its periphery remained within the Byzantine Empire until the ninth or tenth century. Constantinople may have been distant and ineffective, but the ports over which it exercised its nominal rule nevertheless had trading privileges in the Aegean and the Levant. It was no accident that the ports which emerged in the ninth and tenth centuries – Amalfi, Gaeta, Bari and, above all, Venice – owed at least a nominal loyalty to the eastern emperor. It was through these ports that the silks and spices and exotic goods from the east reached the lands of western Europe.

Italy thus lay within the commercial orbit of Constantinople. Byzantine coins circulated, especially the gold solidus or nomisma, the most stable and respected currency known to medieval man. Indeed, when a gold coin came to be used as a heraldic charge it was known as a 'bezant'. The European merchants who carried on trade in Italy and the Mediterranean were at first subjects of the Eastern emperor. They were, first and foremost, Syrians and Jews. The former disappeared from western commerce by 800 or soon after. The Jews remained active for a longer period; then they too gradually left the Italian scene, transferring their activities apparently to Germany and east-central Europe, where they met with less competition. They thus left the field clear for the Italians, who were to remain the dominant commercial people of Europe throughout the Middle Ages.

> They were not irretrievably discriminated against as the Jews, [wrote Lopez[9]], nor irretrievably distant from the Mediterranean centre of Oriental trade as the Scandinavians, nor irretrievably tied to the economic systems of antiquity as the Byzantine. Soon they will break loose from the strained bonds which connect them to conflicting overlords, and they will organize free communes – that is, governments of the merchants, by the merchants and for the merchants. The future is theirs.[10]

The earliest commercial cities of Italy grew in the stony soil of the south. They were precocious, but they failed to survive as centres of international trade. If they had not been conquered by the Normans they would inevitably have lost in competition with those of northern Italy, which grew more slowly in an incomparably richer soil. Their hinterland was poor and mountainous, a depressed area, in the judgment of Toynbee,[11] since the time of the wars of Hannibal. Venice and Genoa had behind them the populous Plain of Lombardy and, beyond the encircling line of the Alps, a potential market of unlimited size in the frontier regions of north-western and central Europe. So Bari, Amalfi and Gaeta yielded at the end of the eleventh and in the twelfth century to Pisa, Genoa and Venice.

The trade of the north Italian ports consisted at first of the import of manufactured and luxury goods from the east, paid for by the export of slaves, shipbuilding timber, and enough bullion from accumulated hoards to achieve a balanced trade. But Italy quickly lost this colonial status. In the twelfth century, if not earlier, its own manufactures began to develop, and, by stages which one cannot document, industrial raw materials such as wool, cotton, dyestuffs and alum, began to play an ever greater role in Italian imports. Venice and Genoa never ceased during the Middle Ages to import spices and silks, and 'the glitter and the glamour' of oriental trade were always present, but the economic role of Italy, at least of northern Italy as far south as Tuscany and Umbria, became predominantly that of manufacturer and exporter of manufactured goods.

The thirteenth century was in Italy a period of rapid economic growth. Towns achieved their maximum size. There was extensive land reclamation in the Plain of Lombardy and the marshes of Tuscany, but population outran the productive capacity of the Italian countryside to feed it, and perhaps also of the markets to absorb its manufactures. Well before the Black Death there were signs of economic depression. There was a high level of unemployment, as is shown by the vast horde of paupers in Villani's Florence. The population had ceased to expand, locally at least, before the end of the thirteenth century, and had probably taken a downward turn well before it was struck by the Black Death. The period of medieval growth had come to an end.

ECONOMIC GROWTH IN NORTH-WEST EUROPE

Northern France and the southern Low Countries together formed a second focus of economic growth. Northern Italy had possessed all the advantages, and its economic revival was, in a sense, inevitable. This cannot be said of the Low Countries and northern France. Indeed it is difficult to discern any positive advantages which this area possessed. It had no strong legacy of Roman urbanism. With the exception of Arras, none of the commercial and industrial cities of the Middle Ages derived from Roman origins. Nor was there a dense population or a good network of Roman roads.

Yet the Flemings had their predecessors, the Frisians. Their bases lay on the fringes of the Carolingian empire, but looked out across the northern seas to Britain and Scandinavia. They lived on the border of two worlds. Their hinterland was made up of the lands of Charlemagne, while their ships commanded Europe's pioneer fringe. In this they resembled the merchant pioneers of Italy. They too lived on the border between two worlds, the splendid world of Byzantium and the Levant and the developing world of western Europe. If trade there was to be between such contrasted spheres, then those who lived in the borderlands between them, in southern Italy and the Low Countries, were best placed to develop it.

By the time of Charlemagne the Low Countries and northern France had a commodity for export: cloth, much of it, in all probability, woven by the tenants of the monasteries of the area. The merchants and peasants followed the sound principle of concentrating on those branches of industry for which they had already acquired a certain repute. How the cloth industry passed from the monastic weaving sheds to urban workshops we do not know. But the shift in location, organisation and control of the cloth manufacture was surely related to the good government of the Counts of Flanders. The castles of the counts were scattered over the province, each providing some degree of security within its own castellany. Evidently, there was a need for market centres, for towns grew quickly in the shadow of their walls as soon as the counts gave them any encouragement.

It is often emphasised that certain changes in the physical environment helped the development of the Low Countries as a manufacturing and commercial area. Early in the twelfth century (the date is uncertain) the level of the sea rose a little, broadening and deepening estuaries and opening the Zwin, the river of Bruges, for shipping, and making navigation easier in the ports and waterways of the region. No doubt these events influenced in detail the course of economic development in the Low Countries; they did not bring about the growth of Bruges.

The trading activities of the Frisians took them up the Rhine to Switzerland. They were active in Mainz and in others of the Roman cities of the Rhineland; it is not impossible that their commerce may have reached Italy. In the tenth century their trading activities began to extend eastwards into Germany. The Saxon emperors, especially Otto I, established markets and encouraged trade. Everywhere in the broad Austrasian and Saxon lands there were signs of an economic revival in the tenth century. A peculiar eleventh century poem,[12] in which the sheep and the flax plant disputed which was the more valuable to man, claimed that Flemish woollen cloth sold widely in France. The Frisians meanwhile had disappeared; their role had passed to the Flemings, and by the year 1100 the Flemings were themselves active in the cities of the Rhineland and within a few years were to carry their cloth to the fairs of Champagne.

Thus the people of the Low Countries profited from the slight advantages which location had given them to build up the foremost concentration of cloth-making in medieval Europe. Unlike the comparable economic development in northern Italy, that in the Low Countries was founded essentially on the manufacture of a single commodity. Italian prosperity was more broadly based on oriental trade. But the two regions were in a sense complementary. Inevitably commercial links were established between them. Frisian traders along the Rhine or Meuse prepared the way for the Flemings who sold their cloth in Cologne, Paris and the fair towns of Champagne to other merchants who transported it to Italy. A commercial axis was thus forged between southern and north-western Europe. From the eleventh century until the commercial revolution of the sixteenth it continued to dominate the trading pattern of Europe and to stimulate business along the routes which diverged from it.

This stimulus was felt deep into Germany. The principal routes between Italy and north-western Europe had run at first by way of the valley of the Rhône and thence across either Champagne or Lorraine. Gradually they came to be displaced towards the east, following first the Rhine valley and crossing the more westerly of the Alpine passes. Then, with the opening up of the central and eastern passes, traffic moved across south Germany to Augsburg, Nuremberg and Frankfurt, with branches to Vienna, Prague and Saxony. Throughout these areas a market economy developed. The volume of production – agricultural and industrial – increased and the surplus was sold into the market. Much of it was transported to Italy, the Rhineland or the Low Countries.

Economic growth in the Rhineland and to the east of it contrasts with a relative degree of stagnation in western France. Here, if we except the port cities of Rouen and Bordeaux, there was no comparable wave of urban expansion. Relatively few new towns were founded, and a high proportion of these failed to develop urban functions on any significant scale. Much of the Spanish peninsula also was little influenced by the urban revolution. Scarcely any town in the whole of Spain and western France ever had occasion to extend its walls and to incorporate populous suburbs. Growth was too slow for this to have been necessary.

## The nature of economic growth

The economy can grow only when some part of total production is not consumed (or destroyed), but invested in a productive manner, so that it will contribute to an increased production in the future. Medieval man was not much given to investing for a future on earth. If he had money to spare he would more readily put it into a monastery, a church or a chantry chapel. Nevertheless there was investment and, locally at least, it was on a not inconsiderable scale. The improvement of the waterwheel and its use in flour-milling and cloth-fulling is a case in point. Its primary role was to cut down on labour needs and thus to make labour available for other purposes. There is no doubt that during the period of medieval growth there was an increasing use of waterpower for the small number of purposes for which medieval man had learned to use it.

The evidence for land reclamation from the eleventh century or even earlier is overwhelming. It consisted not only in the clearing of the forest and the ploughing up of the heath but also in the technically more difficult tasks of dyking polders and draining the damp lowlands of the valleys. Investments were made in reclaiming the wet, but fertile plains of the Po valley in northern Italy, and, above all, in creating the polders of Flanders. The Acts of the Counts of Flanders show, with their repeated references to land newly won from the sea, how rigorously the practice was pursued.[13] The monasteries were particularly active in land reclamation and colonisation, and there can be no doubt that it was the profits from this which allowed many of them to engage in ambitious building programmes. Suger founded new villages; he also rebuilt the church of Saint-Denis.

The feudal classes, both ecclesiastical and lay, thus acquired a greater income from their lands, and created a greater demand for goods. Not only did their expenditure on building increase; they also consumed more cloth, leather and exotic foods, and their demand increased for weapons and armour and what, in current terminology, is known as durable consumers' goods. The peasant class must have shared in this increased consumption, if only to a small degree. The expansion of the area of cultivation, in so far as it kept ahead of the rising population, brought about some increase in the average size of the farm holding, and the small increment in the volume of farm production allowed the peasant to make sales in the market and thus to purchase goods. Doubtless, in the case of the peasantry, the increment in the level of consumption was marginal, but in a population running to millions the increased demand for coarse textiles and simple tools could have been very large. Where the peasant's labour dues and other obligations had been commuted for a fixed money rent he was often enough in a strong position, as inflation gradually increased the value of his surplus and left him with a margin of profit.

It was characteristic of the period of expanding agricultural production that the area under cultivation was increased, while the intensity of production changed little. Investment went to cutting down forest and ploughing the waste; very little attention was given to improving the breed of farm stock or selecting grain for seed. In the words of Rodney Hilton,[14] 'an attitude favourable to investment in improvement would lay stress on the expenditure of profits from rents and production in new buildings, drainage, fertilisers and livestock with the object of increasing yields. Instead, all of the treatises are pervaded by an atmosphere of careful parsimony.' This is true, but land *was* reclaimed; manure was carted and spread, marl pits dug, and in many small ways the quality of the land was improved. This was reflected in the very slow improvement in yield ratios (see p. 198).

This is, of course, in line with the generally low level of medieval technology and the reluctance to innovate. There were, of course, exceptions. The lands of Thierry d'Hireçon in Artois yielded so well that one can perhaps assume that their owner (see pp. 198–9) managed his estates in an unusually competent and far-sighted manner. The land reclamation, already mentioned, in the polders of Flanders and the floodplain of the Po also represented very substantial investments in the land. But these took place in areas where people had grown accustomed to investing for the future. It might seem natural for a merchant in Milan or Venice, or a burgess in Bruges or Ypres to conceive of land as a commodity which one could acquire, improve, and turn to profit. Such an enterprise was very far indeed from the thoughts of the petty feudal lord in Normandy, Burgundy or Westphalia.

The growing population in the twelfth and thirteenth centuries was thus paralleled, not by an intensification of agricultural production except in a few significant areas, but by the broadening of the area under cultivation. Inevitably farming spread from the areas of fertile soil which were, in general, amongst the earliest to be cultivated, to marginal lands, which a wiser husbandry would have left under forest or grazing. The result was both a steady diminution in the average size of a peasant's holding and a reduction in the average quality of its soil. This was not offset by an improvement in agricultural technology. The crisis of the four-teenth century can be ascribed in some degree at least to the failure to invest in improving the land. The glory of Chartres and Amiens, the town walls, and the gild halls are the obverse of a coin which has on its reverse a backward and unprogressive agriculture and a lack of investment in agriculture.

Europe during the 'high' Middle Ages had its backward and underdeveloped areas, just as it had under the Roman Empire and as it does in the present age. They were areas where the process of economic growth gained little momentum or, indeed, never started. In the almost complete absence of statistics it is very difficult to define these areas of backwardness. They would, however, have included most of the hilly and mountainous areas in which mining had not stimulated progress in other fields of activity, and many areas of poor soil, like the heathlands of north Germany, and of harsh climate, such as much of Scandinavia. If the absence of urban growth can be regarded as an index of under-development, then Europe's backward areas would be very

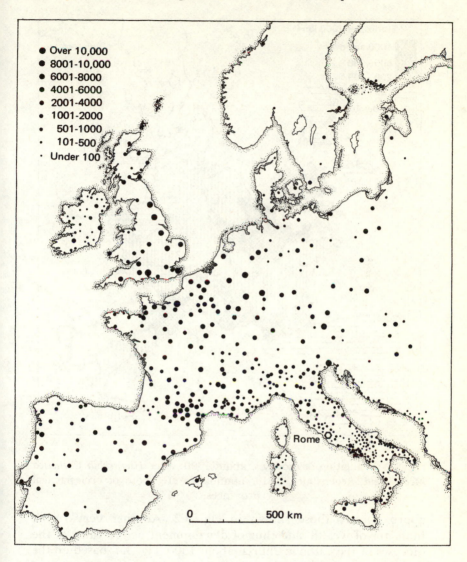

Fig. 3.3   Valuation of dioceses, in florentine florins for Papal taxation, about 1300: after *Hierarchia Catholica Medii Aevi*, Regensburg, 1913.

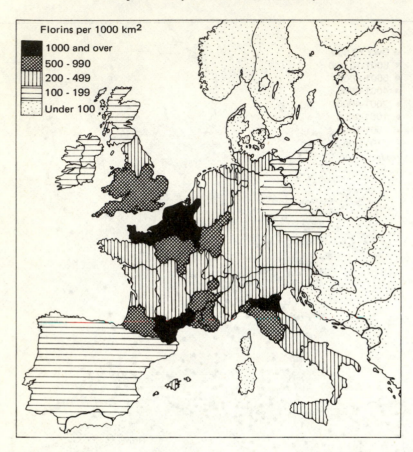

Florins per 1000 km²

1000 and over
500 - 990
200 - 499
100 - 199
Under 100

Fig. 3.4 Valuation of dioceses, about 1300: after *Hierarchia Catholica Medii Aevi,* Regensburg, 1913. Boundaries are those of ecclesiastical provinces.

approximately those shown in Fig. 3.2. Another very rough indicator of wealth, and thus of development, is the value of the dioceses of the Catholic Church about 1300. Fig. 3.4, based on the returns preserved in the papal archives, shows a concentration of wealth along and on each side of the commercial axis which ran from Italy north-westwards to the Low Countries. Western France was relatively undeveloped, and the level of development fell off eastwards across Germany, Bohemia and Poland, and more sharply northwards in Scandinavia.

The period of prosperity and of economic growth appears to have come to an end in much of 'developed' Europe in the late thirteenth and early fourteenth centuries. But the cyclical decline which followed appears to have had little influence on certain of the underdeveloped areas. Underdevelopment implies a high degree of local isolation and economic self-sufficiency with the local economy responding only to external factors like the weather and other such influences on crop yields. Such would appear to have been the case in much of eastern Europe. Bohemia, Moravia and Austria, however, except in the mountains, were relatively developed. They tended to approximate the west European model in which expanding population exerted a strong pressure on agricultural resources, and the margin for investment, whether productive or otherwise, was diminishing. The same was broadly the case in neighbouring areas of Saxony, Silesia and southern Poland. Elsewhere in eastern Europe there remained room for the expansion of agriculture and even for its improvement within the limits set by medieval technology. Over the plain of Poland and north-eastwards into the Baltic region, population was relatively sparse and agricultural techniques primitive. The heavy plough, with its coulter and mouldboard (see p. 194), so desirable if the heavy clays of the Polish plain were to be cultivated, had, before the thirteenth century, been adopted only in a few areas where German influence was strong. Elsewhere a simpler and less effective tool was in use. At a time when western and even central Europe were overpopulated, and their agriculture at the limit of its medieval technological development, there was still room in eastern Europe for expansion. The wider adoption, commonly under German influence, of the heavy mouldboard plough permitted both an extension of the area under cultivation and also an improvement in its effectiveness. There was a growth of market centres and of small towns at a time when contraction was more characteristic of the west. A surplus agricultural production was generated and used in part to supply the markets of western Europe. The period of east European economic growth, with its concurrent development of the Hanseatic trade, spanned the later Middle Ages, and is examined in the final chapter of this book. It began, however, before 1300, at a time of growing economic stringency in western Europe.

To summarise: the expansion of the European economy between the eleventh century and the fourteenth was due, in so far as it can be attributed to any single group of factors, to a spread of human settlement and an increase of the area under cultivation. This led directly to an increase in population and, perhaps, also to increasing returns as more and more people turned to exploit the virgin resources of newly settled land. This investment in land clearance was not accompanied by any significant improvement in the quality of farming or increase in the investment per unit area of land. Apart from a more widespread adoption of the heavy plough and of more effective types of horse harness, and the introduction of certain iron tools and of the waterwheel in some rural activities, there were no important technological advances in agriculture. The result was a Malthusian situation which became apparent in much of western and central Europe by the early years of the fourteenth century.

In areas marginal to western and central Europe there remained, however, scope for increased agricultural production. Here there was no Malthusian situation, and economic growth, stimulated perhaps by the wider diffusion of the heavy plough, continued with little serious interruption throughout the later Middle Ages.

### THE MEDIEVAL MONETARY SYSTEM

The period of medieval growth saw the emergence of a market-based economy in the developed areas of Europe. Both the peasant and his lord sold their agricultural surpluses, and they used the proceeds to buy consumers' goods and to discharge their several obligations towards their superiors. It was an economy which required money, and without an adequate circulation of coin it would slow down and ultimately reduce itself to small-scale barter. Towards the end of the period of medieval growth credit instruments, such as bills of exchange (see p. 415), were used increasingly, thus allowing the volume of commerce to expand without a commensurate increase in that of circulating currency.

The function of a coinage is threefold, to provide a measure of value and a means of comparing commodities; to provide a medium of exchange, and to serve as a means of accumulating and storing wealth. A coinage should be sufficiently abundant to serve the needs of commerce; it should be available in denominations small enough for use in small-scale transactions in the rural market, and it should be stable. Charlemagne had bequeathed to his empire a silver denarius, or penny, weighing about 1·7 grammes and with a fineness of about 95 per cent silver. This coin was imitated in England and became a generally accepted and widely respected medium of exchange throughout the Carolingian Empire.

Its fate, however, illustrates all too well the fortunes of even the best currency. The metal from which it was struck was often scarce. There was therefore a readiness to strike coins of less than the legal weight and to use metal in which the proportion of silver was below that in the original Carolingian pennies. The temptation was also present to profit from the issue of such debased coinage. It never took long for those who used the coins to become aware of their gradual depreciation, and to demand more of them in return for the goods they sold. The penny was in circulation in most of Europe throughout the later Middle Ages. It was minted in most countries, but in all of them it was severely debased. The rate of depreciation varied very greatly from one country to another. It was least in England, where the intrinsic value of the silver penny had been reduced to about half by 1250. In France the silver content of the penny was at the same time worth little more than a twentieth of what it had been under Charlemagne, and in Italy its value sank even lower. The downward trend in the value of the coinage was most marked during the twelfth century, when the need for more currency to match the expanding volume of commerce was felt particularly strongly.

The issue of coins, in origin a royal prerogative, passed into the hands of the greater feudatories in France. There ceased to be any consistency between issues of the same nominal value. From the thirteenth century the French kings gradually concentrated the minting of coins in their own hands. From the early thirteenth century France had two issues, those from the royal mints of Paris and of Tours. The Parisian penny was, however, larger than the 'Tournois,' and served as the basis of a separate system of money and accounting. In Germany the Saxon emperors and their immediate successors were able to maintain an effective control over the coinage, but there too the right to strike coins passed to the territorial princes, never to be resumed into the hands of the emperors. Only in England did the crown maintain a firm and generally effective control over its currency.

Clearly the steadily depreciating value of the small currency at a time of expanding trade made it desirable to introduce a currency of higher value. There was, in fact, even in the Carolingian period, a dominant coinage, minted in units that were too large for the petty business of the market-place. Before the Carolingian reforms the Byzantine *solidus* or *nomisma*, a gold coin, was in the words of Cosmas Indicopleustes,[15] 'accepted everywhere . . . because no kingdom has a currency that can be compared to it'. The *nomisma*, or bezant, was in all respects the outstanding coinage of the earlier Middle Ages. Byzantium had a sufficient supply of gold during much of its history to maintain the gold content of its coinage. There were times when a lightweight bezant, known as a *hyperperon*, was minted, but always the authorities reverted to the full gold content of their coinage. The maintenance of a stable currency was a matter of pride to the Byzantine state, costly though it was to the taxpayer. The *nomisma* circulated in Italy, where it even continued to be minted as long as the Byzantine emperors retained control of parts of the south, but it was rarely seen to the north of the Alps. It represented too large a value for the feeble commerce then carried on in northern Europe.

The *nomisma*, termed by Lopez[16] 'the dollar of the Middle Ages,' was not the only currency of international repute. It had a humbler rival in the *dînar*, sometimes called the *mancus*, of the Moslem world. This also was a gold coin, though it did not enjoy the stability and repute of the *nomisma*. It was brought into Europe from North Africa and Moorish Spain, where it had probably been minted from Sudanese gold. European traders welcomed it in payment for their customary exports from the ninth to the eleventh century: timber, cloth and above all slaves. The role of the *dînar* in the economy of western Europe has unquestionably been greatly exaggerated.[17] It has been represented as a major factor in Europe's economic revival and is said to have been used to requite imports of luxury goods from Byzantium. In reality, the *dînar* reached western Europe in only small quantities, and in stability and general repute was no match for the *nomisma*.

There was, however, a drain of gold from western Europe to the Byzantine Empire, as there had been (p. 79) in the later years of the Roman Empire to the Levant. The trade between the eastern Mediterranean and western Europe was an unbalanced one. Swords were the only manufactured export of Europe, an 'illustration', wrote Lopez, 'of the inferiority of the west in every craft except those of war'.[18] The balance was made good in bullion. The Byzantine Empire was always willing to receive gold; it was used to sustain its excellent currency, to conduct its tortuous foreign policy in the Middle East, and to carry on its own unbalanced trade with the Muslim world. Lombard's view was essentially that western Europe imported gold from the Muslim world, particularly North Africa, and used it to import goods from Byzantium; there is much evidence to support this view.

Europe probably did not need to import African gold. Its hoards, accumulated in the main during the period of the Roman Empire and representing the loot of its eastern provinces, were probably adequate. The volume of trade was very restricted and the dimensions of the west's trading deficit probably small. All the evidence points to the existence of very large hoards of bullion, much of it in the hands of the Church and a great deal in the form of religious objects. When in the later tenth century, a vigorous land market developed in northern Italy, objects of gold and silver, as well as jewellery, furs, fine cloth and even books were used in the financial transactions.[19] This may imply both a serious shortage of coin in circulation and at the same time an abundance of hoarded wealth, ready to come into the market in a time of commercial expansion.

A medium of exchange, adequate in both quality and quantity, is clearly a prerequisite of a developing commerce. If the volume of circulating currency is too small, people will resort to the less flexible and more cumbersome process of barter, and this in turn will reduce the total volume of exchange. If the currency is seriously depreciated, this will also reduce the total volume of transactions, because people will be reluctant to accept it. The Italian commercial manuals of the fourteenth century, of which that of Pegolotti is the most familiar, repeatedly noted the coinages which were debased, and therefore to be avoided.

The economic revival was accomplished, by and large, without a sound and generally respected currency, and its absence probably was a restrictive influence on trade. It is not difficult to understand why the monetary situation in Europe was not as favourable as it might have been. The Byzantine *nomisma* could occasionally be met with in western Europe; attempts were made there to imitate it, but it did not normally circulate. The gold hoards were possibly sufficient, especially when supplemented by the import from Africa, to support a gold currency. But business required coins of low denominations; not large and prestigious coins like the *nomisma*. The coinage was of silver, even though silver was in chronically short supply. There were few silver mines in Europe, and none of them were large. Carolingian silver had probably come mainly from Melle in Poitou, a source of no great magnitude. It is probable that western Europe had no important source of silver before the reserves in the Harz Mountains, above Goslar, were opened up in the later years of the tenth century.

Thus the increasing demand for currency, coupled with the willingness of governments to profit by using smaller quantities of inferior metal, led to its progressive devaluation. As was noted above, the rate of devaluation varied very greatly from one political unit to another. A fundamental reason, apart from the shortage of metal, was the failure of government to maintain proper control over the moneyers whom it authorised. The depreciation of the currency led, on the one hand, to price inflation and, on the other, to the institution of coins of higher denominations. The first of the latter to be adopted was the *grosso*, *groschen* or groat. It appeared first in the trading cities of Italy, where the need for a larger denomination was acutely felt. The Venetian *grosso* of 1202 was quickly followed by other large silver coins minted in other Italian cities. A half century later a *grosso* or *gros tournois* began to be minted in France, and soon afterwards in the Low Countries.

This, however, did nothing to stop the trend towards the debasement of the coinage. The groat became lighter and less fine, while the silver pennies, which in some degree it had superseded, became reduced to small pieces made up mainly of base metal. Even the Byzantine *nomisma* lost value in the twelfth century and declined sharply after the Crusaders had occupied Constantinople in 1204. At the same time the need for a stable currency of high value was increasing. Within about a half century western Europe was itself minting its own élite currency from gold. In 1252, Genoa, which had been accustomed to using the gold *nomisma* and *dînars* of the Mediterranean world, began to issue its own gold *genovino*. The minting of the Florentine florin and the Venetian gold ducat or *zecchino* quickly followed. The need for a gold currency began to be felt outside Italy. Before the end of the thirteenth century the French king introduced a gold coinage which evolved into the very durable *écu* or crown. In the fourteenth century England produced its gold noble, or half-mark, which was imitated in the Low Countries.

Nothing, unfortunately, is known of the volume of currency that was minted. Studies that have been made of the dies used suggest that these were, in general, very few and for some issues even unique. They could not possibly have yielded a large volume of circulating currency, even if the metal had been available from which to strike it. The history of European coinages parallels very closely that of commerce and of general economic growth. The degeneration of the north European Carolingian penny and the maintenance of the élite Mediterranean *nomisma* and *dînar* reflected their contrasted economic roles from the ninth to the eleventh century. The progressive debasement of the penny at a time of commercial revival led both to the introduction of forms of paper transactions and also to the creation of larger denominations both of silver and gold. It was no accident that these occurred in the thirteenth and early fourteenth centuries, and were initiated in those Italian cities which stood foremost in the commerce of the continent.

*Moneys of account*
Only in the years immediately following the currency reform of Charlemagne did a common currency circulate over wide areas of western Europe. Thereafter, as the minting of coins passed into private hands, the penny ceased to mean the same thing even in neighbouring areas. In the local market, where commodities were sold for cash and no records were kept, this made little difference. In long-distance trade, in which some form of book-keeping or accounting was desirable, it mattered a great deal. In a system of bimetallism, intrinsic values of gold and silver coins fluctuated against one another. New coins were introduced which were not necessarily simple multiples of the local penny, and foreign coins, quite unrelated to the local currency except in using the same names, made their appearance. Furthermore, the penny was a coin of low value, and to use it to express all values was to intro-duce totals that were truly astronomical. It was therefore neces-sary to relate the varying local currencies to some widely accepted

but theoretical standard. This was a money of account. There were many such systems of reckoning, none of which was common to all of western Europe. Clearly what was needed was one based upon the gold content of the élite coinage, which could be used to measure all currencies against one another. This was never achieved. Instead each local region had its own money of account, and the merchant was left to work out as best he might the relative values of, for example, the *grosso* or *gros* of France, and of several German states and Italian cities. Some of the Italian cities, with their greater commercial expertise, did try to make their respective élite gold currencies approximately equal in value to one another.

In origin the money of account arose from the need for a term to express a large number of deniers. The term *soldo, sou* or shilling thus came to mean a dozen pennies, and the *libra* or pound, a score of sous. The pound was in origin a unit of weight and was thought of as representing the amount of silver from which a pound's worth of pennies – commonly, though not always, 240 of them – could be minted. The pound and the shilling were for a long period after they first came to be used in twelfth-century Italy, only 'ghost' moneys. One could not see or handle them; they were units used in accounting. The very smallness of the prevailing coins necessitated some such practice. When larger denominations came to be minted an attempt, in general unsuccessful, was made to make the new coins fit into the scheme of moneys of account. The *grosso*, for example, was at first conceived as a *soldo* in the system of ghost moneys.

Unfortunately, as coins of new denominations were devised it was not always possible to fit them into the existing system, and a new money of account had to be devised to represent them. In Venice, for example, there came to be two moneys of account, and the real value of the pound in the one was different from that in the other. The problem of expressing local moneys in terms of money of account and of establishing ratios for the conversion of one money of account into another was always present. Writers, such as Pegolotti, who had great experience of the system, nevertheless found it almost as difficult to explain as it is in this present age to comprehend.

The silver coinage, the deniers and even the *grossi*, rarely circulated far beyond the areas where they had been minted, and the lesser currency, mostly of copper and representing fractions of a penny, probably never. In some areas, such as England, foreign moneys were excluded by law. In general, however, the gold currency minted from the mid-thirteenth century circulated widely. The gold coins of the Italian cities were current throughout most of Europe. They were carried in the wallets of merchants and travellers and in the baggage of ambassadors. They were used by governments to balance trade, by governments to subsidise allies, and generally in the conduct of foreign policy.

As a general rule, however, money entered little into long-distance trade. A significant amount represented a heavy burden and would have added very greatly to the risks normally run by travellers. Each of the Champagne fairs ended with several days which were given over to settling accounts (see p. 356). The Flemish merchant was, at the end of the fair, owed money for his cloth, while he himself owed money for his purchases. The final settlement thus consisted, in effect, of comparing statements which by and large offset one another. In the end, the amount of money which changed hands might have been very small, a minute fraction of the total value of all transactions.

Even after the decline of the Champagne fairs, there continued to be periodic meetings of merchants for the purposes of balancing their books and offsetting their mutual debts against one another. The fairs of Lyons continued to serve this purpose until well into the sixteenth century. The growing complexity of European commerce in the thirteenth century called for yet another device for the discharge of debts. With the decline of fairs, merchants ceased to meet face to face. They placed orders by means of a courier, and paid for them after they had been delivered by means of a notarial act or a bill of exchange. The earliest known use of the bill of exchange was in the first half of the fourteenth century. As a means of discharging financial obligations, however, its use did not become widespread until after the Black Death (see p. 415). The later years of the fourteenth century may in some respects have been a period of economic decline; but in the sphere of commerce they were marked by experiment and innovation.

## CONCLUSION

The period of medieval economic growth culminated in the later years of the thirteenth century or early in the fourteenth. The economy ceased to expand, because, it is generally held, a situation had been reached in which population pressed heavily against resources and the *average* level of welfare had begun to decline. One cannot, however, represent these changes in population and welfare by a smooth graph because an erratic and random factor was introduced by warfare, variations in the soil and, above all, the vagaries of the weather. The real Malthusian situation could be obscured for many years by a sequence of good harvests, and then revealed in its stark reality by a few bad years (see page 134). The cool, wet summers and the winter floods of 1315–1317 are well documented and, thanks to H. S. Lucas,[20] generally familiar. It is easy to say, as some have done, that the late medieval economic decline began with the poor harvests, the famines and epidemics of these years. The statistical probability was very high indeed that most of the continent would at some time or other be affected by such conditions. Herlihy has found evidence for a slight drop in population well before 1300 in some of the densely populated areas of Tuscany,[21] and Postan has argued[22] that in England the depression began long before the Black Death.

In western and southern Europe, as well as in much of central Europe, the population had ceased to grow by the early decades of the fourteenth century. The volume of both production and of demand was reduced. After the initial price rise, occasioned by the food shortages, prices took a downward trend. Yet the dawn of the European Renaissance was not wholly clouded. There was no interruption in the development of business methods. Large fortunes continued to be made and to be invested in land, in buildings and in commercial enterprises. But it was a new Europe that emerged from the pestilence and famine of the fourteenth century. It was smaller in population, but it was more specialised. There was much structural unemployment, but there was also growth in new directions. Above all, there was a contraction in the amount of religious building, and an increasing amount of investment capital went into productive enterprises, into ships, mines, land improvements, and the infrastructure of trade. It was this investment in the later Middle Ages which led to economic growth in the sixteenth century.

# 4

# The population of medieval Europe

The previous chapter traced the ways in which the medieval economy, conceived in its broadest outlines, developed between the ninth century and the thirteenth. This development was closely paralleled by the history of the growth and decline of Europe's population – so closely, indeed, that one may be excused for assuming that there existed a close connection between them. That the volume of production and the level of welfare were linked with the size of the population is obvious. The relationship, however, was very far from being as simple as some scholars have suggested. An examination of the relationship of demographic movements and the long-term trends of the economy is exceedingly difficult. For the latter the indicators are few and imprecise, and for the former no statistics exist that are not susceptible of a variety of interpretations. The economic indicators have already been examined. This chapter examines the evidence relating to the size and the cyclical changes in the population.

SOURCES FOR THE HISTORY OF POPULATION

Medieval man, like classical man before him, was little interested in figures. Neither showed any desire to formulate a precise estimate of population, and when figures were called for they hazarded only the wildest guesses. Indeed, in a society that was by and large rural and self-contained, in which long-term changes in the numbers of people or the volume of their production were not really conceived as possible, there was no need for a census. It was not until the eighteenth century, when the reality of change

123

in economic conditions at last forced itself on the minds of European man, that the first attempts were made on a national scale to count the heads of the people. This is not to say that there is no documentary basis for an estimate of population at different periods during the Middle Ages. The evidence, however, was accumulated for other purposes, and can be manipulated only with difficulty and with a high probability of error in order to yield evidence of total population.

This evidence is, in part, documentary, but it consists also of material drawn from the face of the land. Changes in the area under cultivation, of the number and walled area of towns, and of the size of churches have all been made to contribute evidence. Information drawn from such sources is, however, at best imprecise and at worst misleading. The least uncertain of the many guides to medieval population is probably that provided by the lists of specific categories of people: heads of families, tax-payers, fighting men, communicants, butchers or bakers. If it can be assumed that for a given period and place these totals are approximately accurate, then it remains only to relate them to the total population. Unfortunately this relationship must have varied greatly, not only through the period as a whole, but also from one area to another. The proportion of craftsmen must, in general, have increased in the course of the Middle Ages; the number of fighting men is likely to have varied with the seriousness of the crises which they were called on to face. The number of households, or 'hearths' as they were more often called, provides the most useful form of evidence. Patterns of human behaviour did not differ in place and time so fundamentally that the family group was deprived of all value as a unit of measurement.

With very few exceptions medieval records of hearths and families were compiled for one purpose only. Their object was to enable taxes to be assessed and collected. Of necessity they reflect a struggle, on the part of the seigneur or king to see that no household was omitted from his list; on that of the peasant or craftsman to escape being enrolled. It is reasonable to suppose that some succeeded in excluding themselves. Indeed, the seventeenth-century English hearth tax records are strewn with the evidence of households which had been overlooked when the first lists were compiled. There is no reason to suppose that medieval assessors were more competent, or the peasants less self-effacing.

It is therefore in terms of hearths – *feux, foca* or *fuoghi* – that we must measure medieval population. The most extensive hearth survey in the medieval period is the well known list known as *les paroisses et les feuz des baillies et seneschaucées de France*, compiled in 1328.[1] For thirty-three territorial units, not all of them clearly definable, the numbers of parishes and of hearths is given. In most respects the document is credible, and its evidence is corroborated by other sources. More detailed hearth lists also exist for many of the provinces of France. There is a roll for Rouergue for the year 1341, which lists the hearths by parish

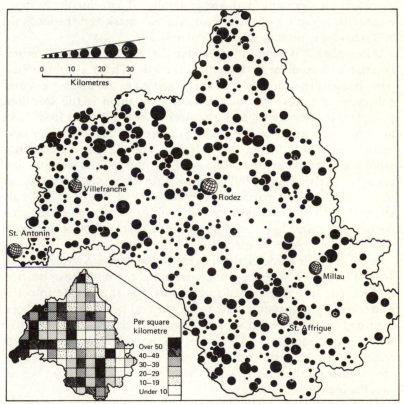

Fig. 4.1 Distribution of population in Rouergue; based on hearth list in A. Molinier, La Sénéchausée de Rouergue en 1341, *Bibl. Ec. Chartes*, xliv (1883), 452–88. The solid symbols represent the towns. Their population was: Rodez, about 11 500; Millau, about 7000; Saint-Afrique, about 4750; Villefranche, about 4000; Saint-Antonin, about 8500.

(Fig. 4.1). Several lists survive for Provence and Languedoc, and short lists are also available for parts of Normandy and the county of Porcien (Champagne). The Low Countries, northern France and the Duchy of Burgundy were surveyed – some provinces on several occasions – in the late fourteenth and the fifteenth centuries. In Switzerland, hearth surveys were made for the cantons of Zurich and Basel.[2]

There were errors, inconsistencies and omissions, but taken together these records provide an invaluable sampling of population densities in much of western Europe. Such records are less abundant in Germany and are generally of late medieval date. Hearth lists exist for Mecklenburg, the Neumark and the lordship of Sorau (Żary, now in western Poland).[3]

Altogether, it is a not unimpressive list, and it can, furthermore, be supplemented by ecclesiastical records. These are more suspect, because they are less obviously geared to the assessment and collection of taxes. One of the earliest of them is the so-called polyptyque of Eudes Rigaud, the Archbishop of Rouen from 1248 to 1276.[4] It consists of the *pouillés* or surveys made when a new incumbent was inducted into a living. The records are thus not wholly contemporary and there are no data – presumably because the parishes never fell vacant within the period – for 100 out of the total of 1341 parishes in the diocese of Rouen. The totals submitted to the archbishop were of the adult males in each parish, but many have been so rounded that one must assume a considerable margin of error.

A survey was made of the diocese of Lausanne, Switzerland in 1416–17 by the bishop's agents, who noted the number of hearths in each parish.[5] A series of excursions was thus made into the hinterland of Lausanne. The parishes appear to have been recorded in the order in which they were visited. It is doubtful whether any parish was omitted in the more densely settled parts of the diocese, but this cannot be said of the thinly peopled Jura mountains to the north-west; here the estimated number of hearths is probably too low.

Manorial records suffer, in general, from the disadvantage that they make no attempt to list all the households, only those which owed services, rents or other obligations to the lord of the manor. They rarely mentioned the landless, labouring population which owned little and owed nothing. Nevertheless, they sometimes contain valuable evidence for the size of families and households, and occasionally allow one to calculate a minimum size for the population of a manor or district.[6]

Abbot Irminon's polyptyque is the most valuable of such sources for the earlier Middle Ages. It is a record, compiled about 810, of the lands of the Parisian monastery of Saint-Germain des Prés (see p. 49). The demographic value of Irminon's polyptyque lies in the fact that it not only lists the tenants of the abbey by name and status, but also gives their family relationships. In many instances the names and, if the parents were of unequal standing, the status of their children were also given. Quite apart from the importance of this evidence in determining the sex ratio and the average size of the family, the document allows one to list most of the inhabitants of the communities which belonged to Saint-Germain.[7] This, combined with the fact that there is at least a possibility that we can calculate the areas of some of the manors, or fiscs, allows an approximate density of population to be obtained.

Urban population is in general better understood than rural. Towns kept better records and have preserved them more carefully, and their rulers had all too often good reason to know how many mouths there were to be fed, since none except the smallest were ever able to produce their own food supply. All towns gave thought to their food needs, and some appointed an official whose function it was to purchase grain and maintain an adequate store within the walls. An estimate of the number of 'mouths' was thus necessary for the proper discharge of these obligations. This is the principal reason for the large number of estimates of Italian urban population. At Nuremberg a count was made of the able-bodied men in 1431 in anticipation of an attack by the Hussites.

Other evidence for the growth or decline of population is even less susceptible of precise interpretation than that which has already been reviewed. The area of cultivated land unquestionably contracted during the later years of the Roman Empire. It is no less certain that it began to expand again from the tenth or eleventh century – and perhaps earlier. This could not have happened without an increase in population, but there is no formula by which one can relate new rural settlements, even if one could list them, to demographic growth.

The upsurge in urban life, the growth of large cities and the proliferation of small towns could not have taken place without an increase in the rural population which grew the food for the city and bought the products of its craftsmen. Most of the larger cities increased their walled area during the thirteenth and early fourteenth centuries, some doing so in two or more stages. The purpose was to permit the growth of urban population and the intensification of urban crafts. Indeed, the transformation of urban life which took place in the twelfth and thirteenth centuries was predicated upon an overall increase in population.

It is no less apparent that in extending their walls and building large parochial churches medieval townspeople were unduly optimistic. Even before the latest curtain walls had been complated their builders were overtaken by a crisis. Population ceased to expand everywhere except in eastern and perhaps northern Europe, and is generally thought to have contracted in most areas (see p. 156). The evidence is both documentary and archaeological. Direct comparison of hearth tax records can be made in only a few cases, but where this is possible, as it is in Burgundy, Provence and Languedoc, a contraction of population is indicated. The evidence drawn from the hearth lists finds support in that provided by field work. The abandonment of villages and the contraction of cropland is well substantiated from England, France and Germany. Indeed the cult of the lost village has become an interesting, if no longer particularly profitable field for muscular young historians. Such, then, is the evidence from which the historian has to establish the size of the medieval population, its variation through time, and its spatial distribution.

### BIRTH AND DEATH IN MEDIEVAL EUROPE

The student of the history of population in modern times has the inestimable advantage of the parish registers of baptisms, marriages and burials. They allow him to analyse, with only a small margin of error, the range of age at marriage, the number and spacing of children, the size of the completed family and the expectation of life from birth to senility. The structure of pre-industrial population in Europe is becoming known. The medievalist has no such aids. It is possible to reconstruct the families of only a minute fraction of the total population, and that a far from representative sample. Royal and princely families are well known, and the vital statistics of the landed aristocracy can in many instances be derived from the public records. Professor Russell has used the evidence of the English *inquisitiones post mortem* for this purpose,[8] and has argued – not altogether convincingly – that his findings for the landed classes can be extended to the rest of the population.

For the mass of the medieval population no true insight can be obtained into its family structure, and one can only use the evidence of modern, but pre-industrial societies as analogues. The birth rates were high, perhaps of the order of 30, 40 or even more per thousand of population per year. It was not, however, the general practice for women to produce a child every year during the fertile period of their married life. Families of ten or a dozen were very much the exception. Parish registers for the pre-industrial period suggest that the intergenesic period – the time which elapsed between conceptions – was on average about thirty months. There is no reason to suppose that such an interval was not also normal during the Middle Ages.

It follows that, in considering the degree to which each generation replaced itself, the age at marriage, and thus of the first conception, is of vital importance. Postponement of marriage by three years might be expected to reduce the potential family by one birth. This, however, is not all. The fertility of women diminishes with increasing age until at the age of forty or somewhat more it ceases altogether. A woman marrying in her late twenties is less fertile than one who marries in her late 'teens or early twenties. Late marriages are thus seen to influence the legitimate birth rate in two ways – by the reduction of the total period during which conceptions could occur and by eliminating from consideration that period of a woman's life when the probability of conception was at its highest.

Any discussion of population growth or decline must thus consider, as one of its most significant factors, the customary age at marriage. Evidence drawn from the records of the upper classes suggests that women were commonly married at a very early age. It does not follow that the same held good for the mass of the peasantry, and Russell suggests that it was as a general rule higher than amongst the landowning classes.[9]

For this there was in all probability a very simple reason. The peasant married only when he had a tenement, a fraction of a *mansus* or of a *hoba*, to support himself, his wife and his future family. This he might acquire through assarting, or breaking in new land; he might also obtain it by inheritance, and this appears to have been the normal course. The peasant all too often married only when his father died or gave up the cultivation of his holding. It seems that few peasants can have lived to see their own grandchildren. It is unwise to generalise from the very little hard evidence that is available, but it does appear that the peasant married late, and it is to be presumed that his wife was not a great deal younger than himself. In the towns the institution of apprenticeship similarly postponed the age of marriage for men, who were usually forbidden to marry until their period of training had ended.

It is, of course, quite impossible to calculate the extent to which late marriage may have reduced fertility and thus set limits to the rate of growth of the population. It is certain, however, that it must have been a restrictive factor. And yet, as will be shown later, the centuries from the eleventh to the thirteenth were a period of sharply rising population. Russell has estimated[10] that it rose from 34·2 million for the whole of Europe about the year 1000 to 68·3 million about 1300. An increase of less than one per cent a year, accompanied as it was by a high mortality rate and a low expectation of life, hardly seems consistent with a high average age at marriage for the mass of the population.

The rise in population which occurred in much of Europe in the middle decades of the eighteenth century influenced though it may have been by better diet and improved health, seems nevertheless to have resulted in the main from a lowering to the extent of a year or two of the average age at marriage. Could the medieval growth of population have been influenced by similar factors? There were technical advances in agriculture which had the effect of both increasing the area under cultivation and also of improving the quality of the farming. A three-field system began to displace a system of biennial cultivation, and improved harness allowed the horse to be used on a larger scale for traction. These advances would have increased the food supply, improved the diet and presumably reduced mortality. But it hardly seems possible that these changes alone could have had the results described. It seems more likely that the birth rate was increased by a downward trend in the average age at marriage. The only factor which could over a broad area of western and central Europe have made this possible was the opening up of new lands to colonisation by the medieval peasant. We must suppose that a proportion of the young men who had learned their craft of farming, sought and obtained permission to make an assart in their lord's waste land or even to migrate beyond his jurisdiction. They thus came into the possession of a tenement before their father's death and were enabled to marry at an earlier age than they could otherwise have done.

Doubtless their decision was influenced by local customs regarding inheritance. Where primogeniture was generally observed, as it was in most of the open-field region of northern France, younger sons had the alternatives of remaining in their communities as cottagers or wage-earners, or of moving out to new lands. It could thus happen that a younger son might have a tenement and wife before his elder brother who waited to inherit his father's holding. In some restricted areas the peculiar inheritance system, known as 'borough English', prevailed, by which the paternal inheritance passed to the youngest rather than the oldest son. Is it not possible that this may have been an attempt to remedy this condition by getting the older sons out of the way and leaving the field clear for the youngest, who might thus be ready to take over the holding by the time his father died?

The argument thus leads to the conclusion that it was not the population explosion which led to the colonisation of the waste, but rather the availability of the latter which encouraged earlier marriage and larger families. The question at once arises why, since the waste had always been there, surrounding the village communities and insulating them from one another, it had not been used in this way before. It is not an easy question to answer. One might perhaps assume that areas left under forest or heath were those least suited to early medieval conditions of agriculture; that they were wet lands in need of drainage, heavy clays difficult to plough, or sandy wastes which yielded very poorly without the addition of manure. There is, indeed, abundant evidence for the drainage and reclamation of marshland early in the twelfth century, and the heavy wheeled plough had long been known. It could till the heavy soils, but it was difficult to construct and demanded a large team. What we do not know is the chronology of its diffusion through western and central Europe. It could have been the crucial factor in the opening up of the heavy land. The wider acceptance of a three-field system, instead of a simple alternation of grain crop and fallow, may also have contributed to the opening up of new lands. A three-field system required a spring sown crop, usually oats or barley. Oats, at least, were suited to light and thin soils and were often used alone in breaking in newly cleared land (see p. 191). They also allowed larger numbers of animals to be kept, and this in turn not only provided more power for the heavy plough, but also more manure for the light soils.

Such advances in the field of agricultural technology may have made it easier to cultivate soils which had previously tended to be neglected. It is doubtful whether they alone could have brought about this agricultural expansion. The contrast between good soils and poor is nowhere absolute and clearcut, and the medieval peasant, empiricist though he was, could not always be relied on to perceive it. His choice of land to cultivate was influenced as much by institutional considerations – demesne land, hunting and commoning rights – as it was by the natural conditions of soil. The expansion of cultivation was not a simple movement from good soils to less good, though this was no doubt an element in it.

One must, then look for a release, perhaps more or less sudden, of the restraints imposed by the manorial system on its dependent peasants. The polyptyques of the ninth century suggest a strengthening control by the monastery over its lands and tenants, who were by and large *adscripti glebae*. There is evidence in Irminon's polyptyque, however, that the status of the peasant was beginning to rise as his value in land development came to be realised. People came to be regarded as a form of wealth, and their proper employment as a source of income to their lords. Irminon, early in the ninth century, took pride in having cleared land and brought it under cultivation, and his successors both at Saint-Germain and at countless other houses encouraged settlers to create new villages and expand the frontier of settlement. The example of Abbot Suger of Saint-Denis is well known (see p. 168). He established the village of Vaucresson not because there were swarms of land-hungry peasants, but because there was land waiting to be developed for the glory of Saint-Denis and the profit of his monastery. The foundation of new villages was very far from being a monopoly of the religious houses. The lay landowners were no less active. Helmold's Slavic Chronicle tells how the lords of Wagria (approximately Holstein) sent messengers to the Low Countries and western Germany to advertise the fact that here was good land awaiting the peasant's plough. When the European frontier of settlement was opened there were no masses of peasants waiting to overflow the boundaries of their native settlements. It was necessary, in a sense, to advertise for them. But new land allowed the younger sons and the co-parceners to set up homes at an earlier age and to have families in the secure knowledge that there was land enough for all.

It can thus be argued that the 'vital revolution' from the tenth or eleventh century to the end of the thirteenth was stimulated by an earlier age at marriage and larger completed families. But earlier marriage would not in itself lead to an increasing population if mortality were heavy. Marriage at the age of twenty and death before thirty would not necessarily have led to any conspicuous increase in population. One needs to know how many families were 'completed' or in how many cases the death of one or other of the partners occurred before the woman reached the end of her child-bearing period. One would also want to know what proportion of the children of such early marriages actually survived and grew up to have families of their own. In other words, one needs to discover the 'net reproduction rate'. These facts about a society can be found only if registers of births, marriages and deaths are available, and these are almost non-existent for the period before 1600.

Such vital data are, however, known for some members of the feudal classes. Their lives are in certain cases well documented; they made wills, and their own lords sometimes conducted inquiries at their deaths into their fortunes and heirs in order to insure that all obligations had been properly discharged. Russell has used such sources to work out for England tables of life expectancy and family size. The error in using such sources – apart from the fact that they do not always present a full picture of the classes which they claim to represent – is that they relate only to a small segment, perhaps two or three per cent of the total population, quite unrepresentative of the masses. It is, in statistical terms, a non-random sample from which it would be very unwise to generalise for the population at large.

The question of life expectancy in the period of medieval population growth has to be looked at from a different angle.

Granted that we cannot know, except for an unrepresentative few, what were the mortality rates, can we discover the relative frequency of abnormal causes of death: war, famine and disease? The sources allow us to do this for the period under discussion only in the broadest sense. In considering mortality amongst any people and at any time, one can distinguish between those causes of death which are always present, the ailments and afflictions to which the whole of mankind is heir: diseases of heart and lung, respiratory ailments, influenza, cancer. These may fluctuate, but in general they do not increase to epidemic proportions. In a large population they can be thought of as yielding a steady death rate of perhaps thirty or more per thousand each year. Superimposed on this 'normal' mortality was the abnormal mortality induced by 'crises' – war, famine and epidemic disease. These produced extreme fluctuations in the death rate, sending it perhaps from a mere thirty in the thousand to several hundreds.

Famine was an ever-present danger. Man lived close to the earth, dependent on what his own fields supplied, and at the mercy of bad weather and poor crops. Not until the end of the Middle Ages did an international trade in foodstuffs, capable of resolving such problems, even begin to develop. Every four or five years there was a poor harvest resulting from events and conditions entirely beyond the control or even the understanding of the peasant.

> Ere five years be fulfilled such famine shall arise
> Through floods and through foul weather fruits shall fail

wrote Langland in the *Vision of Piers the Ploughman*. An ever present condition of undernourishment was, as it were, written into the high mortality rate of the Middle Ages. But at intervals a succession of bad harvests led to famine, as distinct from under-nourishment, and to death rates far above the thirty to forty per thousand that was normal. As in all simple societies, the consequences of food shortages were intensified by the behaviour of society. The idea of rationing was wholly foreign. At the first suggestion of scarcity there was usually a run on food supplies. The rich bought for the purpose of hoarding, and prices soared. Scarcities were artificially intensified, and the poorer classes suffered more acutely than was necessary. Van Werveke has shown[11] how the consequences of the bad harvests of 1315–17 were magnified by the speculations of dealers in the cities of the Low Countries.

Epidemic disease was a second major cause of crises of mortality. To some extent it was a consequence of food shortages; the Reformation litany of the English Church prayed for deliverance from 'plague, pestilence and famine', showing how in men's minds the two were linked. Pestilence could occur without a preceding famine, but its spread was hastened by the fact that people were fundamentally undernourished. Severe mortality through epidemic disease was likely to be followed by famine because it disturbed the routine of ploughing, sowing and harvesting, and thus increased the probability of future epidemic diseases.

The role of warfare is more difficult to assess. That it was destructive of life and property is all too clear; that medieval armies lived off the land in which they were campaigning is well known. The destruction of houses, farm stock and equipment represented the loss of fixed capital which was necessary for the conduct of the business of farming. If they could not be replaced at short notice – and usually they could not – farming, at least under the pre-existing conditions, could no longer be carried on. The destruction of seed grain must have been particularly disastrous, and yet one cannot doubt that the small store of grain which was being held until the next seed time was particularly sought after by marauding soldiers.

Muslim, Viking and Magyar invaders of Europe were immensely destructive, but after these waves of invasions had passed it is likely that for a century or two warfare was less destructive than it had been and was to be again during the later Middle Ages. Armies were small; such obligations as knight service were for short periods, and kings and princes did not have the resources to recruit and pay large armies for prolonged periods of service. Warfare during this period was more static than it subsequently became. It consisted to a considerable extent in building and besieging castles. The immediate vicinity of such fortresses might be devastated and impoverished, but the country at large did not perhaps suffer unduly.

In the later Middle Ages, after very approximately the mid-thirteenth century, all this was altered. The character of warfare changed. Armies grew larger; mercenaries were employed on an increasing scale, and campaigns, instead of being over in a few weeks, now lasted months or even years. It was in the interests of the mercenaries, who were employed increasingly in the four-teenth and fifteenth centuries, to maintain warfare as a contin-uous pursuit. When peace came these bands were thrown loose upon the countryside to rob, destroy and murder. In parts of western Europe, the intervals of nominal peace were more disastrous than the years of formal war. The *Cerche des feux*,[12] the hearth lists which were compiled in the Duchy of Burgundy between 1375 and 1470, show in its depopulated villages what could happen. Settlement after settlement is described in 1431 and 1442 as burned or devastated by the *'gens d'armes'* or by the *écorcheurs*. The chroniclers of the later Middle Ages describe, sometimes in horrifying terms, the destruction wrought by the armies of mercenaries which were at this time let loose on Europe.

What changes, one may ask, occurred during the Middle Ages in these factors which so powerfully influenced population and mortality? It has already been noted that the character of warfare changed during the later Middle Ages, and that it became more destructive of life and property. It is less easy to define the changes that occurred in weather and climate and in the incidence of plague and other epidemics. Weikinn has compiled an immense catalogue of references to weather conditions during the Middle Ages and later centuries[13]. References to bad weather – heavy rainfall, cool and wet summers, severe floods – became very much more frequent during the last two centuries of the Middle Ages, and suggest that, at least in north-western Europe, climatic disasters were in fact more numerous and severe than they had been earlier. This is supported by other evidence:[14] the extension of glaciers in the Alps; the lowering of the upward limits of culti-vation and of tree growth in hilly areas; the inundation of the coastal lowlands in the Netherlands, and the increasing soil moisture in the valleys of central Europe where, in some instances, cultivation had to be abandoned. The North Atlantic became more stormy; contact with the Norse colony in Greenland was lost, and voyages to Iceland became less frequent.

The earliest clearly documented climatic crisis was from 1315 to 1317. During these years wet winters were succeeded by cool and rainy summers. Those crops which were able to germinate and grow failed to ripen properly. Harvests were poor and it became difficult to hold back the seed that would yield the next year's harvest. For three successive years the weather was bad and harvests poor, and famine conditions occurred widely in north-western Europe. No doubt the crisis of 1315–17 was the worst to occur in the later Middle Ages, but other crises, more localised and of lesser magnitude, occurred repeatedly.

Epidemics had been known long before the Black Death of 1347–51. There had been an outbreak of plague under Justinian. It began in 541 in Egypt and spread to much of the Byzantine Empire, though not, it would appear, to most of western Europe. It may have been less virulent than the better known outbreak of the fourteenth century, but nevertheless greatly reduced the population. It was followed by no less than fifteen subsequent outbreaks before it appeared, apparently for the last time, in 767. This illustrates a feature of the bubonic plague; its tendency to remain endemic in the population for long periods and then to break out in epidemic proportions. The plague does not seem to have shown itself again in the west for nearly six hundred years, surprisingly in view of the fact that it remained endemic in Asia. There were, however, outbreaks of other diseases. In 1312–17 a major epidemic, but clearly not the plague, spread westwards across Germany. Many diseases which have long since disappeared from most of Europe were prevalent, such as leprosy and ergotism, a disease which resulted from eating diseased rye. Pneumonia, pleurisy and a great variety of complaints referred to in the writings of a later generation as fevers and catarrhs were also rife, but medieval man was spared one scourge of later generations; smallpox had not yet made its appearance in Europe.[15].

After 1350 epidemics were more frequent and many can be attributed to the bubonic plague. There were local outbreaks in the 1350s, a widespread epidemic in 1363–66 and again in 1393–99.[16] In the course of the fifteenth century the outbreaks are almost too numerous to count. Most were localised, but there can have been few places in Europe which wholly escaped the plague and many were visited by it several times. In the city of Göttingen no less than twenty years between 1350 and 1500 were described as plague years.[17] The plague was itself propagated by the flea and its host the black rat. It spread rapidly through communities which lived crowded into a small space. Whole monasteries were wiped out. It appears to have been most virulent in cities, and thinly peopled areas sometimes escaped lightly. Its association with malnutrition may have been indirect. The poor, who were, almost by definition, undernourished were those most likely to be crowded into the alleys and slums of the medieval town. The burial records of a poorhouse at Cambrai not only show the cyclical nature of periods of very high mortality but also demonstrate their close association with periods of high grain prices[18] Arnould has demonstrated[19] for Hainault in the seventeenth and eighteenth centuries how closely epidemics follow on the heels of crop failure and famine. There is no reason whatever to suppose that the situation was in any way different in the fourteenth and fifteenth. Indeed Favreau on the basis of a study of the population of Poitiers in the fifteenth century, has shown[20] the closest possible association between crop failure and war on the one hand and the spread of epidemics on the other.

The argument of the last few pages is that there was a change in the incidence of those factors: war, crop failure and epidemic disease – which were chiefly responsible for increased mortality. It is suggested that they became more frequent and intensive in the fourteenth and fifteenth centuries than they had been during at least the previous three centuries, and that they were the principal cause of the late medieval decline in population. One must, however, examine the ways in which a high mortality, resulting from epidemic disease, could have influenced population. Much depends on the age group which succumbed most readily. If the older people died, this could in the long run have had little influence on the total population, since the women would have concluded or be near the end of their fertile period. Heavy mortality amongst the young would be far more serious, since society would lose a large part of the next generation of parents, and the diminished number of births would perpetuate itself for a very long period of time. In the absence of parish registers, it is very difficult to discover whether any particular age groups suffered more than others. Russell has claimed[21] that the death rate was greater during the Black Death amongst the higher age groups than in the younger. This is not however borne out by the evidence. The French chronicler, Jean de Venette, wrote of the plague that *fuit tant mortalitas hominum utriusque sexus et magis juvenum quam senum*[22] (mortality was so great amongst men and women, but more in the young than the old), and the present writer in examining the evidence in the parish registers for the local outbreaks of plague in England in 1591–92, found that up to 60 per cent of those who died were children, or at least minors.

It has been argued by Ohlin [23] that a severe mortality, by reducing the number of peasant landholders, would allow the younger persons to inherit the land, marry and raise families at an earlier age than might otherwise have been possible. It is even possible, he added, that 'a rise in mortality would touch off steady growth'. If it could be demonstrated that mortality was higher in the older age group than in the younger this would unquestionably have been the case. No doubt if pneumonia and respiratory complaints became a great deal more prevalent, as they certainly did in some periods, then one might expect older people to suffer more than the young. But in the great 'killer' epidemics this was not the case. It was perhaps more likely that a peasant would have no sons to succeed him than that his premature death would allow one or all of them to inherit or share his holding at an early age.

To summarise: it is suggested that the vital revolution of the period from the eleventh to thirteenth centuries was in large measure due to the coincidence of two factors. These were, in the first place, a lower age at marriage, resulting from the opening up of new land for settlement. The second was the relatively low incidence of famine and epidemic diseases. This situation was reversed in the last two centuries of the Middle Ages. The frontier of settlement was in large measure exhausted. At the same time entirely independent factors increased the probability of famine and war, and thus of the spread of epidemic diseases. Furthermore, the very incidence of mortality – the greater vulnerability of the young – made recovery from the demographic crises of the later Middle Ages more difficult and longer delayed.

### THE MEDIEVAL HOUSEHOLD

The most important medieval sources for the study of population are the hearth lists. In most of western Europe it was the practice to levy extraordinary taxation on the household or hearth. The resulting tax rolls thus consisted of lists of places, with the number of hearths in each. Leaving aside the question of the accuracy of the lists, the problem becomes one of determining the average size of the household. It has usually been assumed that in England the hearth represented as a general rule what we understand as the 'nuclear' family, made up of parents and unmarried children. 'The normal household', wrote Hallam, 'consisted . . . of man, wife and offspring, and both large households of three generations or with unmarried brothers and sisters were uncommon.' From his study of the families of the feudal classes, Russell concluded that the average size of a nuclear family was less than four persons. Very few scholars have been able to accept so low a figure. Hallam himself has found that on certain Lincolnshire manors the average ranged from 4·37 to 4·81.[24]

On the other hand, some households consisted of an extended or 'stem' family, which embraced, in addition to the man, his wife and children, perhaps an elderly parent or a married son. It was not uncommon in pre-industrial societies to find that the extended family included also a servant or a lodger. The practice was for the head of the family, at the age of perhaps sixty, to retire from active farming and give place to his son, who married, if he had not already done so, and set up his family in the parental home. The parents would continue to live there, perhaps with the family, perhaps in a room added for the purpose. The son sometimes contracted to allow his parents grain, fuel, a small garden patch for peas and beans, and even the facilities for keeping an animal. Unmarried brothers and sisters would probably, but by no means certainly, have moved out. There would thus for a time be an extended family of three generations. The death of the parents reduced the household to a nuclear family, but this might be extended by housing a lodger or a servant. Servants – the *famuli* of certain medieval records – were in all probability the younger sons of neighbouring peasants. Normally the nuclear family relied on the labour of its own children to supplement that of the head of the family. There was likely to be a period when this source of manpower was unavailable, with only young children, or none. It was in such circumstances that a servant was employed, only to be discharged as soon as the children could themselves provide labour on the holding. Too many children, conversely, would simply mean that the household provided servants for other peasants.

This picture of the alternation of nuclear and extended households has been drawn from pre-industrial, but not necessarily medieval societies.[25] It is supported by the evidence of medieval manorial court rolls, which sometimes record the agreements between sons, about to take over the family holding, and their parents. The extended family of three generations could not possibly last for more than a fraction of the total time, perhaps a quarter or a third, but it might have been followed by a period when a servant or a lodger was also a member of the household. The sources are too fragmentary and discontinuous to show what fraction of the households embraced extended families, but there must have been enough to raise the *average* family size appreciably above that of the nuclear family.

The point of this discussion is to show that any multiplier, to convert hearths into total population, must take the extended family into account. There is a great deal of evidence for rural communities in which the average size of households exceeded five. It appears that as a general rule the households of well-to-do peasants were larger than those of the poor, perhaps because they were more likely to include a servant or two, perhaps also because space could more easily be found in their larger cottages for parents and other relatives.[26] Urban households appear in general to have been larger than rural, Bautier has shown[27] that at Carpentras, in Provence, the average household was 5·2, but that the size

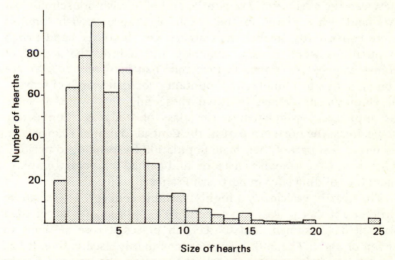

Fig. 4.2   Graph of hearth size at Carpentras; after R.-H. Bautier, 'Feux, population et structure sociale au milieu de XVe siécle: l'exemple de Carpentras', *Ann. E.S.C.*, xiv (1959), 255–268.

ranged from one to twenty-five (Fig. 4.2). In some of the towns of southern France the average size of the hearth was from seven to 8·5. The reason for the greater size of the urban hearth probably lies in the tendency in all ages for the underemployed rural poor to move to the towns in search of employment; in the greater cost of new building within the town's walls, and in a larger number of servants and lodgers.

Over and above the alternation of nuclear and extended family, which in a large community should have made little difference to the *average* size of the household, certain long-term trends are faintly discernible in the size of the nuclear family itself. The evidence for the large family comes, in the main, from the period before the Black Death. In the fifteenth century families appear to have been appreciably smaller. There was a lesser degree of crowding after the plague. If we can assume, furthermore, that the Black Death took a greater toll of the young than of the middle-aged and elderly, we should expect families to have fewer children. This is borne out by, for example, the fifteenth-century registers of Clairvaux, in Burgundy. Here an unusually large number of childless couples was recorded.

It seems likely that there was a significant difference also between the average size of gentile and of Jewish households. At Aix and other places in the south of France Jewish families were consistently smaller than others. On the other hand urban populations were in some instances inflated by the arrival of transient peoples. Orange in Provence had in winter to give accommodation to a number of mountain people in search of seasonal employment. When in town these migrants were, it is to be supposed, assimilated to the class of 'lodgers'. Conversely some areas, the northern part of the Central Massif of France is an example, lost part of their male population for prolonged periods. They were well known as masons, and gained temporary employment on building sites in northern France.

The hearth was clearly a highly variable concept. There can be little doubt that it was, as a general rule, appreciably larger than Russell has assumed, and for certain places it rose at times to seven or eight. The multiplier most commonly used is five. It has the merit of being approximately the mode in the range of family size known to us, but, as Fig. 4.2 shows, the graph of family size can be very strongly skewed. It would be better not to attempt to convert hearths into people if it were not for the fact that one has other sources of population data than hearths – poll taxes, muster rolls, communicants – and one needs, for purposes of comparison, to convert them all to a single unit. In using a multiplier of five persons to the hearth one is risking an error of perhaps as much as 15 per cent. One can expect no higher level of accuracy in statistics derived from medieval sources.

One may, lastly, question the accuracy of the hearth rolls on which historians have leaned so heavily. It is agreed that they omit much. They contain no reference to the land-owning classes and the Church. There was presumably at least one priest in every parish, and his household would in all probability have included a servant. There is likely also to have been a monastic grange, a castle or a manor house; there may have been a chantry chapel with a priest living in an adjoining priest's house, a leper-house – in the Rouen *pouillé* these were specifically mentioned – or a monastic foundation. Then there were the poor, those from whom no tax payment could be expected and who were therefore not worth the trouble of counting. Sometimes the hearths of the poor were specifically mentioned, as in the Brabant hearth lists. More often there is silence on this matter, and one does not know whether or not they were included in the formal lists and then excused when it came to collecting the tax.

When one turns from rural areas to the towns the problems increase: the numbers of priests and of members of the religious orders grew greatly. The poor were more numerous and on the question whether transients were included or excluded one usually has no knowledge at all. It is likely that the addition of not more than 3 per cent in rural areas and 5 per cent in urban would take care of the excluded categories, but, in the absence of documentary record, there is no means of estimating the fluctuating numbers of the poor.

## DEMOGRAPHIC HISTORY

The demographic history of Europe during the Middle Ages divides readily into three periods: the early Middle Ages, when population was either declining or stable; the period of population growth, from the tenth or eleventh century until the end of the thirteenth, and the last two centuries of the Middle Ages, when population at first declined, and then fluctuated, before beginning an upward trend late in the fifteenth century.

## The early Middle Ages

It is generally assumed that population began to decline during the later centuries of the Roman Empire. For this there is little hard evidence, and its reality has in fact been questioned.[28] It would be surprising if a period of invasion and war did not result in some diminution of the total population. Town population, as is clear from the literary sources, did in fact decline to the point at which, in parts of north-western Europe, urban life ceased to exist.

The period from A.D. 543 to 950, wrote Russell 'marks the lowest ebb of population in Europe since the early Roman Empire'.[29] Hay may well be right, but the evidence to support such a claim is not forthcoming. Skeletal evidence from cemeteries suggests that the expectation of life was short and that infant mortality was high. Mortality from the outbreak of the bubonic plauge under Justinian, and from successive occurrences during the next two centuries was probably very great, but there is no evidence that its demographic effects were as serious as those of the better known and more widespread plague of the fourteenth century.[30] It is not until the ninth century that we at last have firm data on population in the polyptyque of Irminon (see p. 49).

If some of the fiscs surveyed in that document can be equated with later parishes, their densities must have approached twenty-five to the square kilometre. Ferdinand Lot, who first used these data to estimate the population of France,[31] concluded that the estates of Saint-Germain were as densely peopled as rural France in his own age, and the total population would have been about 15 million. This figure is, however, excessive. Lot had made the elementary mistake of assuming that the rest of France was capable of supporting as many people to the square kilometre as the fertile communes of the Paris Basin. Over much of the country the density could only have been a small fraction of that estimated for this region.

Attempts have been made to estimate the population from the numbers of inhabited places that have been recorded. There is no reason to suppose that the names of all villages and hamlets got into the scanty records, nor that their average size is in any way determinable. A familiar study of medieval population estimates the population of Europe, excluding 'Slavia' (whatever that means), as 23·2 million in 800 and 28·7 two centuries later. For neither of these totals, nor for the regional figures on which they are based, is there a shred of acceptable evidence.

## The period of population growth

It is impossible to say when the population of Europe began to expand after its stagnation or contraction during the early Middle Ages. Russell dates the period of growth, with a precision which is unsupported by the sources, from 950 until 1348. It would be highly improbable that an upsurge occurred over large areas of Europe at the same time. More likely the population fluctuated greatly during the early Middle Ages, as it also did in the late fourteenth and fifteenth centuries, as periods of recovery were interrupted by famine, pestilence or war. One can only say that at some time between the eighth and eleventh centuries, in one area of Europe after another, the periods of growth became more prolonged and the demographic crises less serious. The evidence for this vital revolution of the Middle Ages is, by and large, indirect: other events and trends can only be understood in the light of a very considerable increase in population.

The clearest evidence comes from England. Between the compilation of Domesday Book (1085) and the preparation of the poll tax lists (1377) there was, however one interprets these texts, an increase of population of approximately threefold. Now and again one finds evidence, particularly from the thirteenth century, which shows how the number of tenants on a particular manor, or group of manors, increased. In the Taunton manor of the Bishop of Winchester every male above the age of twelve was called upon to pay a penny each year to the court on the occasion of the view of frankpledge. The amounts thus collected were recorded, and, for the period from 1209 until early in the fourteenth century, they show a very sharp rise. The payments increased from 612 pennies in 1209 to 1448 in 1311, an annual rate of increase of 0·85 per cent.[32]

The increase of population on the continent of Europe may have been at a slower rate than in England. Some of the fiscs of Saint-Germain, as well as of the manors of the abbeys Saint-Rémi, Lobbes and Montierender showed so high a population in the ninth and tenth centuries that no great increase could have been possible. It is probable, however, that in the frontier areas of eastern Europe the population may have grown at a faster rate. Russell has estimated that the population of Europe, including the Slav lands but with the exception of Russia, increased between 1000 and 1340 from 30·4 million to 61·9. This is nothing more than intelligent guesswork. The population *may* have increased twofold, it certainly showed a very considerable growth.

Two important questions are raised by the subject of Europe's population increase; when did the rate of increase begin to slacken and eventually end, and, secondly, was there, near the end of this period of growth, a condition of acute overpopulation? The sources which might have provided an answer to both these questions are very far from unambiguous. While we have many estimates of the numbers of hearths and of parishioners and communicants, there are very few indeed which constitute a sequence of estimates for any one place or district. The head tax on the manor of Taunton is quite exceptional in having left a record over a long period of time, but even here the record becomes valueless in the fourteenth century because the payments became stereotyped. Take, for example, the graph shown in Fig. 4.3. It shows

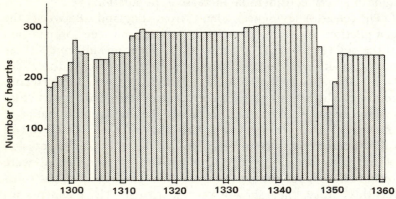

Fig. 4.3  Number of hearths in seven parishes near Montmélian, Savoy; based on Pierre Duparc, 'Evolution démographique de quelques paroisses de Savoie depuis la fin du XIII$^e$ siècle', *Bull. Phil. Hist.*, 1962, pp. 247–74.

the estimated number of hearths in seven parishes near Montmélian in Savoy from 1296 until 1364. There was a steady increase from the beginning of the period covered until 1315, a bad year throughout western Europe. The number of hearths seems then to have been frozen and to have remained so for eighteen years, after which growth at a slower rate was continued until the outbreak of the Black Death. Recovery from the plague was rapid but in 1360 the number of hearths remained 20 per cent below that of 1347.

It is very doubtful indeed whether this graph reflects accurately the trends in *total* population. There is likely to have been a fall after the crisis years of 1315–17; perhaps the *average* size of hearths fell; perhaps the lord demanded during the years 1316 to 1333 the same income as he had previously enjoyed, and the number of hearths became for this period a purely notional quantity. In any event, the number of hearths ceased to be an accurate measure of population.

Other evidence suggests strongly, even if it does not prove, that population was continuing to increase, at least in some areas, during the first two decades of the fourteenth century. Two seigneuries in Bas Languedoc, for which comparable data exists from different periods, show an increase during these years.

**Table 4.1 Population density per square kilometre**

| Seigneurie | Density 1295 | Density 1304–6 | Density 1321–2 |
|---|---|---|---|
| Vézenobres | 33·9 | — | 36·6 |
| Nogaret | — | 26·1 | 32.2 |

A comparison of estimates based on the *pouillés* of the diocese of Rouen for the mid-thirteenth century and those derived from the French hearth list of 1328 also suggests an increase in the density of population in the *bailliages* of Caux and Rouen from 65 to 72·4 per square kilometre.[33] These figures at least make it improbable that the downward turn occurred much before the Black Death.

The early years of the fourteenth century saw a number of famine crises. None spanned the continent, but all influenced extensive areas. The years 1302 to 1305 were famine years in Languedoc. In the whole of north-western Europe 1315, 1316 and 1317 were years of adverse weather and severe famine, followed by pestilence, though the Montmélian figures might be taken to suggest that this particular crisis was barely felt in the Alps of Savoy. This sequence of what Creighton termed 'famine-pestilences' must have made a large dent in the total population, and one that would have been perpetuated for many generations if the mortality happened to be particularly severe amongst the young. Perhaps it was in the first two or three decades of the fourteenth century that the vital revolution of the Middle Ages came at last to an end.

The second question, which was postulated earlier, asks whether a Malthusian condition had arisen by the end of the thirteenth century, with population pressing so hard on resources that famine and pestilence were the inevitable consequences. It is widely, though not universally, accepted that this was the case. The argument commonly accepted runs thus: during the period of medieval growth there was abundant land and a growing population. But the frontier of settlement came in time to be used up, and there developed in the villages a pool of underemployed and perhaps also unmarried peasants. Holdings were divided and subdivided, and standards of living, already very low, sank yet more because the volume of food production per head became too small to provide an adequate diet. This in turn exposed the population both to the ravages of famine and also to epidemic disease. These factors applied the Malthusian check; birth rates were lowered, mortality increased and the population began to decline.

This argument is too mechanistic. It represents the curve of population as gradually approaching that of food production, with catastrophe at the moment when the former crossed the latter. It implies a finite amount of land which was being fully used at the time when the crisis broke. It suggests, furthermore, that improvements in the technology and the productivity of agriculture were beyond the wit of medieval man. Neither, of course, was true. Much good land went uncultivated or undercultivated. The productivity of the soil varied enormously and these variations were not altogether a function of its quality. The problem was rather that in medieval Europe, as in modern India, there was a reluctance to innovate. The medieval village community did nothing to encourage innovation, and there can be little doubt that medieval man failed in fact even to make the most of the limited technology which he had at his command (see p. 281). Overpopulation was not a condition which the observant and the well informed could see gradually approaching. There were good harvest years and there were bad. After a good harvest people could live adequately, if not well; then the crops might fail and the Malthusian conditions were revealed.

Figure 4.4 represents the amount of cropland necessary to support one person. It varies, of course, with the yield ratio of the crops and with the field system used. If a fourfold return was normal on the seed sown, one person required about 1·5 hectares (3·6 acres), assuming that the land was under fallow every third

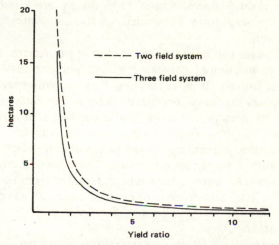

Fig. 4.4 The area required for the food supply of one person with increasing yield-ratios; after Slicher van Bath, in *A.A.G.Bij.*, No. 9.

year. Titow has estimated[34] that on the Bishop of Winchester's manor of Taunton each person had on average 3·3 acres in 1248, but only 2·5 in 1311. One tends to assume that the poorer tenants performed wage labour and were thus enabled to purchase grain in the open market. It is difficult to know how otherwise they could have survived; it is no less difficult to discover where there were holdings large enough to require their services.

The hearth lists allow one to make a very rough computation of the total extent of all land, inclusive of woodland, grazing and waste, that was on average available to the peasant. In the *bailliages* of Caen and Rouen, in Normandy, the estimated population was over seventy to the square kilometre, or 1·43 hectares per person. This included the area of the demesne, where it existed, which was cultivated by the peasant who did not enjoy its usufruct. This is, of course, total land, not merely cropland, but in this part of Normandy there was little woodland or waste, and the density was inflated by the inclusion of the city of Rouen. In some exclusively rural areas in the Rouergue, a region very far from noted for the excellence of its soil, densities rose to more than forty to the square kilometre, while in the plain of Languedoc, where the hot, dry summers placed severe limitations on crop-growing, densities of over thirty per square kilometre were recorded in several places. About 33 to the square kilometre were found in the Sergeantry of Porcien, on the moderately good soils of Champagne.

These figures can only be regarded as approximate. Even so, if the average household consisted of five persons this was over-population indeed. It is surprising that no widespread famine crisis appears to have occurred before the early fourteenth century. The reason may have lain in the fact that different districts, even neighbouring parishes, showed varying degrees of overpopulation, depending on the physical and social conditions of the locality. One cannot generalise. There were districts where the situation was acute; others where, to judge from the silence of the records, little catastrophic or even unusual can have occurred.

*The later Middle Ages*
By all odds the Black Death was the most widespread and the most devastating epidemic ever to strike Europe. In some respects it constituted a watershed between the central period of the Middle Ages and the later medieval period. Where the population had not taken a downward turn before its onset it most certainly did so in the course of the spread of the epidemic across the continent. The Black Death, or bubonic plague, was brought to Europe from Asia. It had been endemic in China, and was carried from there in the 1340s across Central Asia to the Crimea by the Tatars. At Caffa, in 1347, the Genoese traders became infected and the disease was taken to Italy, along with their spices, aboard a Genoese galley. It appeared wherever the galley touched shore: Sicily and Calabria and the port cities of Marseilles and Genoa were all infected by the end of 1347 or early 1348. By the end of 1348 it had spread

across much of western Europe, and in the following year reached most of the British Isles and Germany, and began to be felt in Scandinavia (Fig. 4.5). By the end of 1351 the disease died away

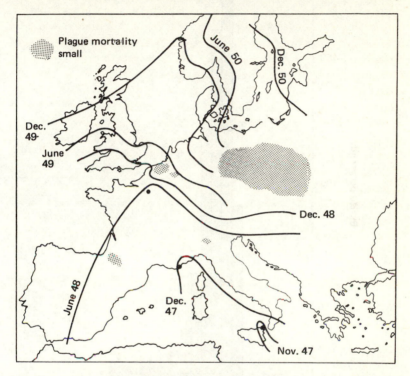

Fig. 4.5    The spread of the Black Death; after E. Carpentier, 'Autour de la Peste Noire', *Ann. E.S.C.*, xvii (1962).

on the northern fringes of Europe. Few areas were spared: a small area in Flanders, another in the western Pyrenees, together with central Poland seem alone to have escaped. Elsewhere the mortality was catastrophic. Whole communities, such as monasteries, were wiped out. The mortality seems in general to have been greater in towns than in rural areas, and many urban dwellers, like the characters in Boccaccio's *Decameron*, found refuge from it in the countryside.

The bacillus of the bubonic plague normally lives within the bloodstream of a rodent; in medieval Europe, the black rat. From here it is distributed to human beings by the flea. It is not

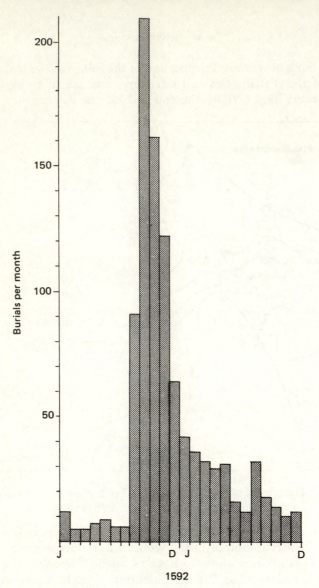

Fig. 4.6 Plague mortality: an English case from the late sixteenth century – mortality in Exeter, 1591–92; based on tables in Ransom Pickard, *The Population and Epidemics of Exeter*, Exeter, published privately, 1947.

particularly infectious and physical contact with an infected person does not necessarily lead to its contraction. There is, however, a variant of the disease, known as the pneumonic plague, which infects the lungs and is spread by coughing and in the spittle. It was particularly lethal and commonly occurred in the course of the Black Death.

It is impossible to say what fraction of the population of Europe succumbed to the plague in its several forms. Contemporary estimates were in all probability greatly exaggerated, and attempts to juggle with the few statistics available lead to no acceptable conclusions. One can only say that in some areas the mortality was very heavy, perhaps a half or more of the total population, and that others escaped with little or no mortality that can be directly attributed to it. As with overpopulation and also with the earlier non-plague epidemics and famines, one cannot generalise for the continent as a whole. Each region, each locality had its own, individual pattern of population development and of incidence of epidemic and plague.

The parish of Givry, in Burgundy, is exceptional in having kept a record of burials in the church and churchyard through part of the fourteenth century, and even more unusual in having preserved it.[35] The parish register shows how suddenly the plague hit the village in August 1348; how short was its duration, and how devastating while it lasted. Before the onset of the plague, recorded deaths had averaged almost forty a year, suggesting a population of at least 1000. During the plague year 1348 the total number of deaths rose to 649, of which 630 occurred during the months of July to November. This would suggest that the population of the parish was reduced to about a third of its previous size.

Estimates of the number of taxable hearths have survived for a number of towns. Amongst them is Millau,[36] a town of the Central Massif of France (Fig. 4.7). They suggest that the population had been declining for almost forty years before the onslaught of the plague, and that it was then reduced by more than a third. Hearth lists for certain Italian towns show an even sharper decline in the number of hearths. At both Volterra and San Gimignano, the number was reduced by the plague to less than half and subsequently fell to about a quarter of the pre-plague total.[37] At Albi, a town in the south of France which appears to have suffered severely, the number of hearths fell from 2669 in 1343 to an estimated 1200 in 1357.[38] The population may have fallen proportionately more, because one must assume that the average size of the household also decreased. From his study of the 'estimes', or city taxes at Toulouse, Philippe Wolff estimated the population of the city to have been:[39]

| 1335 | 30,000 |
| 1385 | 26,000 |
| 1398 | 20,400 |
| 1405 | 19,000 |

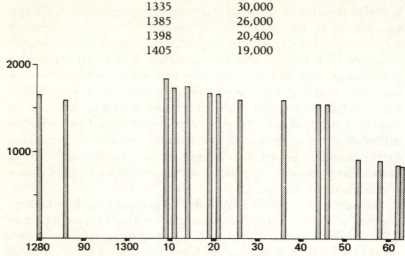

Fig. 4.7   Number of hearths at Millau; based on table in Philippe Wolff, 'Trois études de démographie médiévale en France méridionale', in *Studi in Onore di Amando Sapori*, Milan, 1957, i, 493–503.

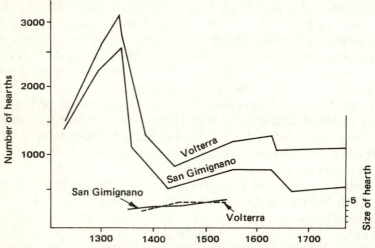

Fig. 4.8   Hearths and hearth size at Volterra and San Gimignano; after Enrico Fiumi, 'La populazione del territorio volterrano sangimignanese ed il problema demografico dell'età communale', *Studi in Onore di*

A feature of this table, as of several earlier tables and graphs, is that the decline in population appears to have continued long after the initial outbreak of the epidemic in 1347–51 was over. Its devastating effects were reinforced by later, though in general more sporadic outbreaks. There was a widespread occurrence in 1363–6 and others, more localised, in 1374, 1383, 1389 and at subsequent dates. An important reason for the continued decline of population even when the great pestilence was only a memory, lies in the probably heavy child mortality. The parents of the next generation were very much fewer. The ghost of the Black Death hung over Europe during the later Middle Ages, and was not exorcised until the late fifteenth century.

Figure 4.9 is an attempt to represent by means of a series of population pyramids the *possible* structure of the population during the century following the Black Death. It is theoretical, and based on a series of assumptions which cannot be positively established.

The century and a half following the great pestilence was characterised by fluctuations in which it is difficult to discern any regular pattern. An increase in population in one area appears to have accompanied decline in another. The period was one of almost continuous war, when the destruction of life and property reached a level not known for many centuries. The evidence for Burgundy is overwhelming. The *cerches des feux* records for village after village that the houses had been burned and the crops destroyed. The number of taxable hearths declined and reached its lowest level between 1420 and 1440. Figure 4.10 shows the general trend in parts of Burgundy and the Low Countries. Other factors contributed to the fluctuation in the population totals during the period following the Black Death. People were more mobile; crop failures were more frequent, and the plague kept returning in a sporadic fashion to many parts of Europe. Lastly, if it can be assumed that the plague was particularly fatal to the young, each outbreak must have led to several generations of diminished birthrate until its effects had been eradicated.

*Amintore Fanfani*, Milan, 1962, 249–90, and Christine Klapisch, 'Fiscalité et démographie en Toscane (1427–1430)', *Ann. E.S.C.*, xxiv (1969), 1313–37.

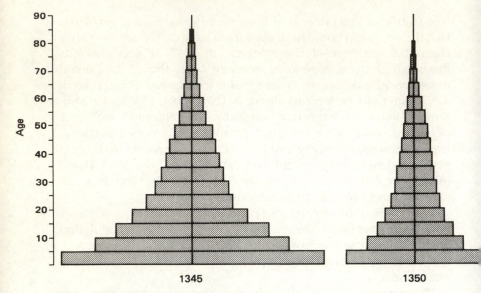

Fig. 4.9  Pyramids showing the structure of the population of Western Europe before and after the Black Death.

If, in western Europe, the downward trend initiated at or even before the time of the Black Death was continued until the middle years of the fifteenth century, this pattern does not appear in central and eastern Europe. The scanty evidence suggests that in Hungary the population may have very nearly doubled between 1300 and the early sixteenth century. In Poland, not the best documented but certainly the most fully studied country of central and eastern Europe, the population is estimated[40] to have grown from some 2 million in the mid-thirteenth century to 7·5 million in the sixteenth, an annual rate of growth of about 0·35 per cent.

For this more favourable situation in central and eastern Europe there were two important reasons. In the first place the great plague was experienced only lightly, if at all. The second reason was that the frontier of settlement was not effectively exhausted, as it had been in the west. There was always more land awaiting settlers, and a Malthusian situation, with its consequent checks on population growth, did not appear until modern times.

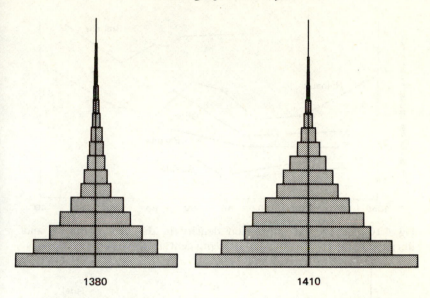

1380                        1410

This relative abundance of land throughout the Middle Ages also helps to explain the different character assumed by feudalism in eastern Europe (see p. 474). Eastern Europe, furthermore, was not seriously disturbed by wars until the Turkish invasions of the late fourteenth and fifteenth centuries, and Poland not until the wars of the mid-seventeenth century. The graph, Fig. 4.11, based upon the work of Irena Gieysztorowa, suggests that the growth of population in Poland was virtually uninterrupted from the eleventh century until the seventeenth.

Very little is known of the history of population in Scandinavia before the sixteenth century. Central and southern Sweden, and perhaps other areas exposed to a strong Germanic influence are thought to have had a decline in their total population in the fifteenth century.[41] Elsewhere the very sparse population was probably unaffected by the epidemics which swept so much of Europe, and may have increased slowly within the limits of its primitive and self-sufficing economy.

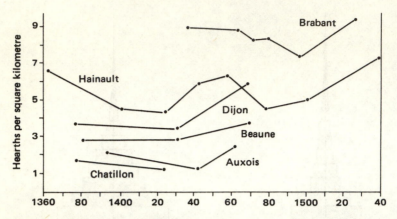

Fig. 4.10 Changes in population density in the Low Countries and Burgundy in the fourteenth and fifteenth centuries; based on hearth lists.

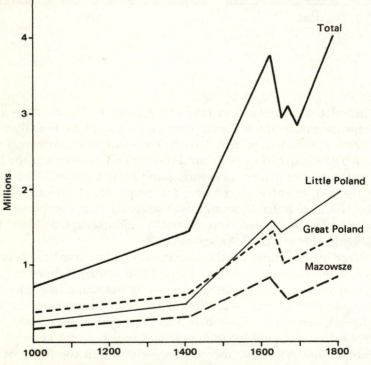

Fig. 4.11 Growth of population in Poland; after I. Gieysztorowa, in *Kwart. Hist. Mat. Kult. Mat.*, xi (1963), 523–62.

POPULATION ESTIMATES

The preceding pages have shown that only rarely and for a very few places is it possible to suggest, even within a wide margin of error, the probable population during the Middle Ages. To derive totals for Europe or even for its constituent countries is all too often to argue from inadequate evidence towards untenable conclusions. Each such estimate must be treated as one man's guess. The greater abundance of hearth lists and similar documents for the later Middle Ages do perhaps diminish the risk in suggesting the size of populations. At least they allow one to set limits between which the true population is likely to lie. As one moves into modern times these limits come closer together and the margin of error diminishes.

Perhaps the best approach to an estimate of the population of Europe in the fifteenth century – the sources are quite inadequate before this date – is by way of estimated densities. It is usually an easy matter to compute the areas of the administrative units for which the totals of hearths or parishioners are available, and the number of hearths can be calculated per unit area.

Despite the not inconsiderable sources of error one derives an approximate idea of the density of population in certain parts of fifteenth century Europe. There were great variations between the Ardennes and the Jura, each with only three or four to the square kilometre, and the densely populated Low Countries. Similar data, capable of being represented in the same way, are available for parts of southern France and Germany. Is it possible to extrapolate from these data, to supply as it were, the missing pieces, and so to construct a population map for a large part of Europe? There are two guides in making such an extension to the map: the density and size of towns, which in its broad outline are known, and the nature of the terrain which was a major factor in rural landuse. Nevertheless, such a map must be presented only with great diffidence. One can expect that as more and more local historical studies are published, any map such as that which appears in Fig. 4.12 can be gradually refined and its accuracy tested.

Total numbers can be suggested, however, only with the greatest caution. For France, on the basis of the hearth list of 1328 Lot has put the population of that part of the country which was subject directly to the king at about 13·5 million, and has estimated that of the whole of France within its 1794 boundaries

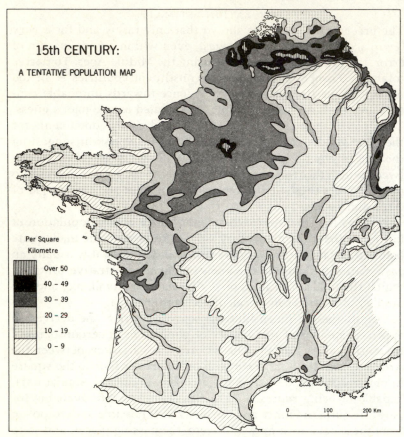

15th CENTURY:

A TENTATIVE POPULATION MAP

Per Square
Kilometre

Over 50
40 – 49
30 – 39
20 – 29
10 – 19
0 – 9

0    100    200 Km

Fig. 4.12  A hypothetical map of population density in Western
Europe during the fifteenth century.

at 17·6 million. The evidence for western Switzerland consists
largely in the lists for the Canton of Zurich and the Diocese of
Lausanne, supplemented by data for Basel and Geneva (see p.
126). Ammann, after a careful examination of the statistical data,
has given it as his opinion that the population of western (Rom-
ance) Switzerland in the first half of the fifteenth century was
some 140,000 to 145,000. Bickel has used these figures to estimate
the population of the whole of Switzerland, within its present
boundaries, at 600 to 650,000.[42]

In Germany the data for towns is relatively abundant, but there
is little evidence for the rural population. For the mid-sixteenth

century Blaschke estimated a population of about 553,000 in Ducal Saxony, or twenty-two to the square kilometre.[43] It must have been considerably less in the fifteenth century.

A hearth list for Mecklenburg,[44] dating from about 1495 shows a thinly peopled and largely rural region, with an average density of no more than eight or ten to the square kilometre. German estimates of the population of the whole of Germany have ranged as high as 15 million. This, in view of the very low densities which have been established in eastern Germany, seems excessive. Ten to twelve million *might* be more acceptable estimates.

Of Poland and eastern Europe generally one can only say that in the later Middle Ages the population density was very low, but increasing steadily. Irena Gieysztorowa has suggested that in the three historic provinces of Poland there were:

| 1340 | 1,250,000 | 8·6 per square km. |
| 1580 | 3,100,000 | 21·3 per square km. |

On the basis of the *porta*, or hearth tax of 1494–5, Kovaçsics has estimated[45] a population of some 3·6 million in the historic Hungarian lands, which included both Slovakia and Transylvania.

Little is known of the population of the Balkans. There was a fringe of commercial cities, all of them much decayed in the fifteenth century, around the coast. Even Constantinople, for much of the medieval period the largest city by far in Europe, probably had no more than 100,000 after the Turkish conquest in 1453, and was not a great deal larger before. A hearth tax levied by Suleiman between 1520 and 1535,[46] gives some measure of population of the European provinces of the Turkish Empire, after they had begun to recover from the Ottoman conquest: 1,061,799 hearths, or somewhat over 5 million people living between the Danube and the southern headlands of Greece. The population was almost certainly smaller in the mid-fifteenth century.

Italy is in some respects the best documented country in Europe, yet the evaluation of its population presents very considerable difficulties. Hearth counts are more numerous than anywhere else, but they relate almost wholly to the cities. Rural population had been dense before the Black Death, but the late medieval decline was catastrophic. Nearly two-thirds of Pistoia's rural communes, for example, disappeared.[47] On the basis of lists of hearths and 'mouths' Beloch suggested an Italian population of about nine millions in the sixteenth century. It would have been less during the fifteenth, perhaps between seven and eight.[48]

In Spain the data for an estimate of the size of the late medieval population is almost wholly lacking except for Catalonia. Apart from the valuable bills of mortality for Barcelona, recorded in view of the severity of the plague epidemics, there are few sources that can be used before the sixteenth century. The population was sparse almost everywhere. There were clusters of denser population near the coast, in Catalonia, Valencia, Andalusia and near Lisbon. The least sparsely populated area of the interior was the plateau of Old Castile. During the fifteenth century Portugal may have had about a million inhabitants; Catalonia, about 400,000, and Castile perhaps 4 million. Moorish Spain, at this time a small area in the south, could not have had more than a quarter of a million.

For Scandinavia there is no direct evidence. It was of the order of 2 million in the mid-seventeenth century, and a great deal less in the later Middle Ages.

These figures for the population of late medieval and Renaissance Europe are offered with great diffidence. For a few small areas one can be fairly confident that the margin of error does not greatly exceed that which is inherent in the assumption that the

**Table 4.2 An estimate of the population of Europe in the mid-fifteenth century**

| Country | Est. pop. |
|---|---|
| Low Countries | 1·2–1·500,000 |
| France | 17–18,000,000 |
| Germany, including Netherlands, Austria and Bohemia | 10–12,000,000 |
| Switzerland | 600–650,000 |
| Poland | 1,500–3,000,000 |
| Hungary (Historic lands) | 3–4,000,000 |
| Balkan Peninsula | 4–6,000,000 |
| Italy | 7–9,000,000 |
| Spain and Portugal | 5–7,000,000 |
| Scandinavia | 1–2,000,000 |
| Total | 49–67,000,000 |

average 'hearth' consisted of five persons. For others, the omission of the towns or of the poor, coupled with the rounded nature of the statistics, diminishes their level of reliability. The densities shown in Fig. 4.12 and the figures in Table 4.2 are raw estimates, to be tested and refined as more data becomes available.

# 5

# Agriculture and rural life

In medieval Europe the broad shoulders of the peasant were made to support the whole superstructure of the political and feudal hierarchy; the towns, their merchants and their craftsmen, and – perhaps the heaviest burden of all – the Church. He paid taxes on his hearth and his head, and his crops were tithed for the support of his local church. He may have been called upon for labour services on the demesne, and he paid rent in money or in kind and perhaps both. The burden was a heavy one and, as a general rule, far exceeded what we might regard as the economic rent for his land. It did not spring from a freely negotiated contract; it arose from the harsh necessities of the peasant, from his need for protection and from his inability to resist increased demands in a time of increasing population and growing shortage of land.

The peasantry, it has been said, made up some 90 per cent of the population of Europe in the earlier Middle Ages. This proportion fell during later centuries, with the emergence of towns and the absorption of increased numbers in trade and crafts. It is doubtful, however, whether it fell much below 80 per cent except in a few highly urbanised areas, such as northern Italy and the Low Countries. Statistics are scanty, and, even when hearth tax lists can be made to yield acceptable totals for the rural population, figures are often missing for the towns. Totals are, however, available for a few restricted areas during the later Middle Ages.

Brabant was a highly urbanised province, and in Brussels contained one of the largest towns of its age. A hearth list, compiled in 1437, suggests that a third of the population was urban,[1] but Brabant did include, besides Brussels, the cities of Louvain and

164

Antwerp, and the urban total was further inflated by the agricultural component of the town population.

The lists, compiled at about the same time, for the Duchy of Burgundy show a very different relationship of urban and rural population. Towns were fewer than in Brabant, and the largest of them, Dijon, Beaune and Nuits, were very much smaller than those of the Low Countries. Here, with a very much lower overall density of population, the urban population made up no more than fifteen to twenty per cent of the total.[2]

Lastly, the hearth list of the Duchy of Mecklenburg prepared in 1495,[3] shows us a highly rural population. In the area subject to the tax, urban population made up less than 5 per cent of the total, and part of this must have been fully employed in the fields which surrounded the few, small towns.

Though parts of Italy, Tuscany in particular, may have had a lower proportion of farm population even than Brabant, the latter may, together with Mecklenburg, be taken as representing the extremes. Perhaps Burgundy, with from 80 to 85 per cent of its population rural, represents the average for western, central and southern Europe during the later Middle Ages. Any smaller proportion, in all probability, could not have supported the non-rural population under the conditions of medieval agriculture.

## SETTLEMENT

The population of western, central and southern Europe may have increased from about 30 million in the ninth century, to more than 60 million in the early fourteenth. This would have necessitated the approximate doubling of total food production. There is little evidence for any greatly increased intensity of cultivation, and the increase was, by and large, obtained by extending the area under cultivation.

### The internal frontier

The process of breaking in new land for cultivation was interrupted during the period of the Germanic invasions. It had certainly been resumed by the time of Charlemagne, and the polyptyque of Saint-Germain records that Irminon had himself caused land to be cleared for cultivation. This does not necessarily reflect an increasing population pressure; it could be that wornout fields were exchanged for new. Of the significance of developments in the following centuries, however, there can be no doubt. Land abandoned during the invasions of the ninth and tenth centuries was reoccupied, and men began to colonise areas newly taken in from the waste. The process continued until the early years of the fourteenth century, after which it ceased. The period of medieval colonisation was over; the greatest achievement of medieval man was completed, and locally there was recession and contraction, not unlike that which characterised the closing years of the Roman Empire in the West.

The extension of medieval settlement and agriculture assumed three distinct forms, each of which was reflected in its distinctive structures of villages and fields. The first and simplest method took the form of the enlargement of existing clusters of cottages and the adding of field to field. There can be little doubt that villages increased in size by the partition of hut sites, and the building of two dwellings where there had previously been one, just as the *manse* was itself divided into halves, quarters and even smaller fractions. This process is implicit in the ground plan of many villages and in the system of fields which surrounded them, but it is extraordinarily difficult to document it during the period of medieval growth.

One can argue that there was an effective limit to the size to which a village community could grow. This limit was set by the area required for its support. A farm family could not live on a cultivated area of much less than ten hectares. Add to this the garden plots around the cottages; the meadow, woodland, and inevitable areas of wasteland, and one requires for a community of fifty 'hearths' a total area of not less than about ten square kilometres. This area would have varied greatly with the quality of the soil and the technical level of farming. It would have been appreciably larger in areas of poor soil and in those in which pastoral farming was relatively important. The question is at what point a community became too large; its fields too extended and fragmented, and the diseconomies of its continued growth too great. In well settled areas, such as the central plain of Belgium, settlements were, as a general rule, closely spaced from the first, and the scope for expansion was even less than in most other areas.

Hearth lists (see p. 124) for various parts of western Europe give evidence of rural communities of considerably greater size than the hypothetical fifty households or 250 inhabitants. This is often because these statistics relate, not to discrete settlements of closely spaced huts, but rather to unit areas, such as parishes, within which there may have been two or more separate communities.

A second form of medieval colonisation was the departure of groups from the parent community and the formation of new settlements on land which had not previously been cultivated – at least not in the recent past. When in the early fifteenth century Paul de Limbourg came to illustrate the rural labours of each

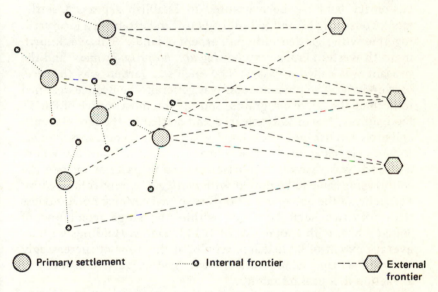

| | | |
|---|---|---|
| ⬡ Primary settlement | ·····o Internal frontier | ----⬡ External frontier |

Fig. 5.1   A model of German eastward colonisation and settlement.

month of the year, he chose for his portrayal of February a distant view of a village under the snow, with, in the foreground, an isolated farm. The latter consisted of a hut, cut away to show its interior, a dovecote, and sheds for storage and for the protection of farm animals, the whole surrounded by a fence cutting it off from the fields. The essential feature of this scene is the isolated farm, a colony established from the village, but within the latter's particular frontier of settlement. This must have represented the most frequent way in which communities grew and multiplied.

Abbot Suger of Saint-Denis described, in the account which he wrote of his administration of the monastery's lands, how

> at Vaucresson we have laid out a township, constructed a church and house, and caused land which was uncultivated to be brought under the plough. . . . There are already there about 60 tenants [*hospites*] and many more would choose to come if there were anyone to provide for them [*si sit qui provideat*]. The place before . . . had more than two (square?) miles of barren land, and was of no profit at all to our church.[4]

Latouche has quoted a grant of land in Maine of 1086: 'as is customary land has been granted to establish a peasant settlement, consisting of land to build a house and establish a farmyard, together with a garden and a half arpent of land'.[5] This was known in north-western France as a *bordagium*, *hospitia*, or *meix*, and the peasant was called a *hospes*. The enclosed garden was the *olca*, *osca* or *ouche*. The phenomenon was general. The Beauce destined to become the 'mère des grains' and the foremost source of Paris's food supply, began to be cleared and settled in the late eleventh and early twelfth centuries. Land was granted to peasants *in plano et bosco*, in clearances already made and also in forest whose clearance was thereby authorised. In many parts of Europe the countryside came to be dotted with *bordagia*. A rent roll, cited by Latouche, of the abbey of La Couture, near Le Mans, noted no less than fifty-two such bordages within the single commune of Joué-l'Abbé, with a total area of 1013 hectares. Holdings with an average extent of 20 hectares would, at this time of increasingly crowded village communities, have had a very considerable attraction to a peasant family.

In all parts of France, the Rhineland and western Germany the process went on. Europe's internal frontier was expanded at the expense of forest, marsh and moor. 'It was the waste land,' wrote Archibald Lewis,[6] 'which Europe's peasants settled and largely put into cultivation between the years 1000 and 1200. . . . A vast new area of virgin soil capable of sustaining a growing population was put to the plough or made available for pasturing increased flocks of sheep and cattle.' This change brought about a fundamental alteration in tenurial arrangements. The scattered settlements of only one or two peasant households could not easily be called upon to perform labour services. Instead they usually paid a money rent. The records of the Brabant abbey of Saint-Trond, for example, early in the twelfth century, showed three farm-steads, 'which pay 18 denarii, where formerly no use was made of the land'.[7]

This extension of settlement and agriculture brought about, not only a radical alteration in the pattern of human settlement on the land, but also a change in methods of cultivation and even in the crops grown and the animals reared. Early man was a shrewd judge of the quality of the land which he broke up for cultivation, but he had of necessity to compromise between the soils which were inherently fertile and those which could be most easily cultivated with the tools which he possessed. The best from his point of view were the light soils, made of loess or *limon*. This was a dustlike deposit, intrinsically fertile, naturally dry and well drained, and easily turned even with a clumsy wooden plough. These soils lay in a discontinuous belt across northern Europe from Normandy in the west, through the Low Countries, Saxony, Silesia and southern Poland. Many of the large, bipartite villas of the Carolingian period had been established on them and there is in all probability a causal connection between soil quality and the spread of large estates. There was in these areas a more dense rural population than elsewhere, easier to supervise and control and subjected more readily to the rigours of a bipartite manorial economy. The rewards of manorial farming in such areas were much greater than elsewhere.

Bordering this region of good soil, or enclosed like islands within it, lay areas of poor or more difficult soil. These might be sandy soils, easily ploughed but unrewarding, or they might, at the opposite extreme, be heavy clays, intrinsically fertile but difficult to clear of their cover of oak wood, expensive to drain and almost impossible to plough without a large team. Other types of physical environment which proved less tempting to the early medieval peasant were the marshes of the coastal regions (see p. 170), the damp floodplains of the river valleys, and uplands such as the Ardennes, Auvergne and Harz, with their shallow, acid soils, their longer periods of snow cover, and their heavier rainfall.

One can take the map of early medieval Europe and analyse it on a macro-scale with reference to its suitability for the medieval farmer. There was a movement throughout central and western Europe from good to less good soils, as the former came gradually to be fully settled and developed, and younger sons were obliged to migrate and try their luck elsewhere. The same phenomenon can be examined on a micro-scale. Within any small area there were variations in soil. The earliest settlements were on or close to those which seemed the easiest to use. In any river valley these were likely to be the terraces which the river had formed in earlier phases of its history. Below them was damp meadowland; higher up the valley slopes there may have been forest or rough grazing. In such a setting the progress of settlement was both up and down the valley side from the initial settlement on the light terrace soils.

Countless papers have examined the spread of medieval settlement and agriculture on this micro-scale. In some instances this dispersal can be traced from the grants of land and the receipt of rents from it; more often place-names provide a guide to the medieval landscape. Words indicative of cutting trees and tearing out their roots, of burning the vegetation and breaking up the land are legion in all the languages of western and central Europe.[8] In most cases these relate to clearance during the period from the tenth to the fourteenth centuries.

The reclamation of marshland is a special case of land reclamation during the Middle Ages, differing from that of the waste in that it called for the efforts of a large body of people and required some kind of overall direction or supervision. It took place at many points, both on the coast and inland. The foremost medieval example of the reclamation of marshland occurred in Flanders. The marshes were used for grazing in summer – Saint-Pierre of Ghent in the ninth century had a marsh which was unique in that it could be grazed even in winter – and also for cutting rushes and fodder. Small patches of land could even be cultivated, usually with oats which would grow and ripen in late spring and summer. In the eleventh century areas of marshland began to be enclosed by dykes, drained and brought under cultivation. *Wateringues*, or drainage canals, were cut and the dykes carefully maintained. The peasants were charged with the latter responsibility and were held responsible for any losses through flooding by river or sea. At the beginning of the eleventh century Lambert of Ardres described West Flanders as 'waste and desolate'. A century later, the Count was making grants of land 'which . . . has been recovered from the marsh', as well as that which 'has grown through the surge of the tide'.[9] By 1180 a church was consecrated to serve an area which had previously been 'watery and unin-habitable' (*in loco aquoso et inhabitabili*).

Areas of marshland bordering the English Channel and Bay of Biscay were first reclaimed. The greatest progress, however, was in Italy. While some areas in central and southern Italy, notably the Campagna (see p. 206), reverted to their earlier condition of a sparsely inhabited wilderness, great progress was made in northern Italy. Here the process was stimulated by the demand for a larger food production and the need to control the floods on the Po and its tributaries. Dykes were built for miles along the river banks; the marshes and damp woodland of the flood plains were reclaimed, and immense areas brought under cultivation. Mantua became the focus of a vast reclamation system. In a Mediterranean climate land drainage cannot be divorced from irrigation. Irrigation canals were constructed, especially around Milan, for the cultivation of summer crops on the drier terrace lands which bordered the plain.[10] Land reclamation was active in the eleventh and twelfth centuries, and culminated in the thirteenth. Thereafter only the more intractable lands remained unused for agriculture. Population growth had been checked and breadcrops were being imported on an increasing scale from more distant lands. In the late thirteenth and fourteenth centuries the great work of land clearance and reclamation came to an end in Italy as it did elsewhere in Europe, and, locally at least, marginal lands were lost to arable farming.

In this internal colonisation of western and central Europe monasteries played an important role. The earlier foundations were primarily Benedictine. The monks did not consciously and deliberately seek wild and barren sites. They had to use the lands they were given, and these appear to have been, as often as not, lands which had formerly been occupied and cultivated, even if settlement had been temporarily abandoned. The older founda-tions, nevertheless, were also given large areas of uncultivated forest and waste, and in these, as occasion offered, they established colonies of peasants. It was the later wave of monastic founda-tions, including those of the Cistercian and Praemonstratensian orders, which made the greatest impact on the waste. These later orders sought deliberately the uncleared and uncultivated areas, perhaps because this was all that they were likely to get. They made a virtue of their necessities, preached the gospel of work, and made immense clearings in the forest and waste.

The role of the Cistercians was the most spectacular. Their earliest houses were in the forests of Burgundy, but they founded their daughter monasteries across Europe from the moors of Yorkshire to the wastes of Little Poland. Everywhere they built their austere churches, laid out their farms and established their granges. Cultivation was carried on as a general rule, not by peasants who lived with their families in their own huts, but by lay brethren, or *conversi* who were unmarried, lived at the granges and were subject to the discipline of their order. The result was a highly efficient, streamlined form of estate management, which proved to be very effective as long as the supply of *conversi* continued.

The total impact of the monastic orders in clearing and settling the land is very difficult to assess. Until the coming of the Cistercian and similar orders their role was to direct, to supervise, perhaps to infuse some degree of order into the processes of land clearance and settlement. They did not participate directly in it. The lands of the abbey of Lobbes, in the Sambre valley near Maubeuge, have been carefully studied.[11] They had been mostly acquired by gift from Merovingian magnates, and many of the monastic *villae* occupied sites previously used by the Romans. The initial clearing of the land had been carried out centuries earlier, and, though the monks may have encouraged peasants to settle on their lands, the latter were probably *vestiti* – 'clothed', or furnished with manpower, when the monks received them. Gregory of Tours described how Chrodin 'would lay out . . . estates, planting vineyards, building houses, and putting land under cultivation'. These he would give to the church, 'with the labourers and tilled lands, together with plate, hangings, utensils, servants and slaves'.[12] Irminon is credited with initiating land clearance in the Paris region, but according to his polyptyque, the area involved was very small. In marginal areas, such as the Eifel and Ardennes, in which lay most of the lands of Prüm, Stavelot and Cornelimünster, settlements were unquestionably established under monastic supervision, but it is highly probable that the lands would also have been cleared and brought under cultivation if they had remained in lay hands. In one respect only were the monasteries able to reclaim and settle lands in a way in which most laymen could not. Well endowed monasteries had an income which permitted them to invest large sums in the process. The piecemeal erosion of the forest and heath called for no great capital outlay; the reclamation of marshland, on the contrary, necessitated not only a considerable expenditure, but also the employment of a large body of workers. In the reclamation of the coastal marshes, especially those of the Low Countries, the monasteries played a prominent role.[13]

Of the importance of the later wave of monasticism there can be no doubt. The monks received some cleared and settled lands by gift, but were mostly endowed with forest and waste whose value was contingent on their development of it. The Norbertine houses of Tongerloo, Averbode and Postel, in the Campine to the east of Antwerp, for example, inherited some cleared and cultivated lands which had previously been in the possession of the Benedictines, but they also received large areas of the infertile heathland which still makes up much of this region; these they were able to bring under some form of profitable land use by their own labours.[14] Throughout western and central Europe the Cistercian lay brethren worked in the fields, filling the monastic granges, and contributing to the fortunes of the merchants who handled their wool.

One must not exaggerate the contribution even of the Cistercians to the processes of land-clearing, settlement and cultivation. In all there were only about 700 Cistercian houses and the largest of them could have had little more than 100 to 200 lay brothers even at the peak of their prosperity;[15] most would have had only a fraction of this number. They were employed in working the Cistercian estates, not in continuously clearing land and broadening their limits. It is clearly impossible to arrive at a measure of the land brought into use by the monks; much of it was grazing land of only marginal value. Seen against the total achievement of western man in clearing and reclaiming land and bringing it under cultivation, the *direct* achievement of the monks was important, but not large.

The internal frontier of Europe continued to expand until late in the thirteenth century. In some areas new settlements continued to be made into the fourteenth, but the movement had lost its impetus long before 1300. The reasons were complex. Beyond a certain point it was not practicable to clear forest; woodland was as important to the rural economy as meadowland. Continued encroachment on the dry heathland, like the Lüneburg Heath, the Campine and the English Breckland, was soon found to yield diminishing returns. Above all population was growing less rapidly in the late thirteenth century, and in most parts of Europe it ceased to expand early in the fourteenth (see p. 155).

## The external frontier

Europe's external frontier of settlement lay in Scandinavia, in east-central and south-eastern Europe and in Spain. It was a series of thinly peopled areas into which settlers migrated from the more developed and more densely populated areas of Europe. This movement towards the periphery of Europe can be dated with greater precision than the settlement of the internal frontier which has already been discussed, but of the numbers involved and of the mechanics of the settlement process very little is known.

The Scandinavian frontier of settlement can be dismissed quite briefly because the numbers involved were small and the lasting importance of the settlements slight. The movement was, essentially, from the hard environment of the fjords of Norway and of the plains of Sweden to the yet harsher environment of the high plateaux and the northern forests. Migration from the over-populated areas of Scandinavia did not readily take this route; most people moved to the British Isles and to the shores of north-west Europe and the Baltic Sea, where population was more dense but opportunity was greater. The Icelandic *Landnámabok*,[16] however, gives us a picture of settlers laying out their fields and establishing villages in one of the most forbidding environments of any of those to which European peoples went.

This is corroborated from the Sagas, with their picture of small enclosures fenced from the waste, where hay was made; of the extensive upland pastures, where the cattle and sheep were grazed for as long a period of the year as the climate permitted. In Scandinavia itself the early settlements lay close to the coast, on the lower and more sheltered land. Here also were small, enclosed fields, where oats, rye and, above all, hay were grown. Animals were, however, grazed on the high plateaux – the fjeld – and in the forests during the summer months, when the cultivated lands in the lowlands were bearing crops of hay and grain. In autumn they were brought back to their lowland quarters for the winter, but sometimes were overtaken by early snows. Egil's Saga tells how Skellagrim, finding his 'livestock . . . much increased', took to driving them up to the high fells in summer. Here he found that his 'beasts became better and fatter . . . (and) that his sheep throve in winters in the mountain dales, even though they could not be driven down.' He therefore 'let make a farmstead up by the fell and had a dwelling there: let there tend his sheep.'[17] And so settlement was advanced from the valleys to the high fells.

No doubt a similar process took place in central and northern Sweden and even in Finland. Amongst the settlers of this northern frontier there were colonies of miners and workers in metal. It was the peasants who dredged up the bog ore from the shallow lakes and smelted it with charcoal on simple hearths. By the mid-thirteenth century, if not earlier, the iron was being exported to north-western Europe.[18] The penetration of the wilderness of northern Sweden was, in all probability, as much for its wealth of metals as for the scanty resources of the soil.

The Spanish peninsula was also a frontier of settlement from the twelfth to the thirteenth centuries. At first 'Franks' occupied the cities, founded new ones and colonised the mountainous belt of northern Spain. In the cities and the small plains along the Mediterranean coast the Christian settlers remained a small minority in a Muslim world until well into the sixteenth century. On the plateau of central Spain, however, there were broad areas requiring settlers when the reconquest had been completed, and here, as in eastern Europe, rural communities were established of immigrants.

The frontier *par excellence* of medieval Europe lay in the east. It was here that the movement of settlers took place on the largest scale; that the most profound changes were made in the landscape and the economy, and the long-term consequences of the migration were of the greatest significance. The general movement of migration in Europe had been westwards during the invasion period. It is not clear when this trend was replaced by one of migration towards the east; probably Charlemagne's conquest of Saxony (772–785) and the development of trade with the Slavs marked the beginning of the eastward movement. The latter did not, however, gain much momentum before the eleventh century and, as a migration of peoples in search of new homes, it probably did not outlast the thirteenth.

Few aspects of medieval history and certainly none in the sphere of the history of settlement, arouse stronger and more emotional feelings than the eastward movement of the Germans.

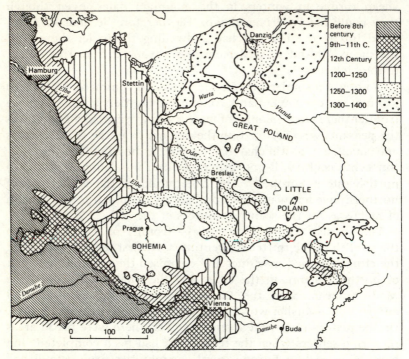

Fig. 5.2  The eastward spread of German settlement.

To some it was a great civilising mission, an eastward march on a broad front into the lands of the Slavs; 'an irrepressible conflict in which race supremacy, religion, language, trade, customs and land to live in were the issues . . . a gigantic series of missionary campaigns and colonising conquests protracted through centuries.'[19] In other words, something like the American occupation and settlement of the West. To others, especially the Slav historians, it was a diffusion of western technology and trade rather than the physical replacement of Slavs by Germans. The term which is unfortunately all too often used for the process – *Drang nach Osten* – implies a coordinated and violent movement, so dear to the Teutonic mentality, in which Germans seized and occupied the eastern lands. A German historian thus described the movement (the thinking is throughout in terms of military strategy):

> They moved forward on a broad but irregular front. The southern wing was far ahead, and had reached. . . . Transylvania and the foot of the Tatra in the second half of the twelfth century. The northern front, down to 1200, lay about the line – western Bohemia, the Lusatias, the Middle Mark of Brandenburg, central Mecklenburg.[20]

A second source of misunderstanding has been the confusion between human settlement and the imposition of military and political control. The latter ran far ahead of settlement, and Bismarck in the later nineteenth century found himself trying to make good Germans out of Poles whose ancestors had been conquered many centuries earlier by the armies of Brandenburg. The imposition of German political authority may have been accompanied by the settlement of colonies of Germans. On the other hand there are instances of the establishment of Germans, in Transylvania for example, in areas which never came under the control of a German state – at least before the Second World War.

The eastward movement consisted in part of the uncoordinated migration of countless small groups. Early in the twelfth century, Count Adolf of Holstein began to resettle his lands after the Slavic wars.

> As the land was without inhabitants, he sent messengers into all parts, namely, to Flanders and Holland, to Utrecht, Westphalia and Frisia, proclaiming that whosoever were in straits for lack of fields should come with their families and receive a very good land. . . . An innumerable multitude of different people rose up at his call and they came with their families and their goods into the land of Wagria.[21]

It is often said that German migrants came to the east in search of more abundant land, a less burdensome tenurial system, and greater personal liberty. Some came of their own volition; others because they were sent by their lords to the wide, empty spaces of eastern Germany. The latter had fallen under the control of ecclesiastical or lay lords, but without settlers the lands were valueless. Like the Archbishop of Bremen before them, they arranged for colonists to be brought from the west. *Locatores*

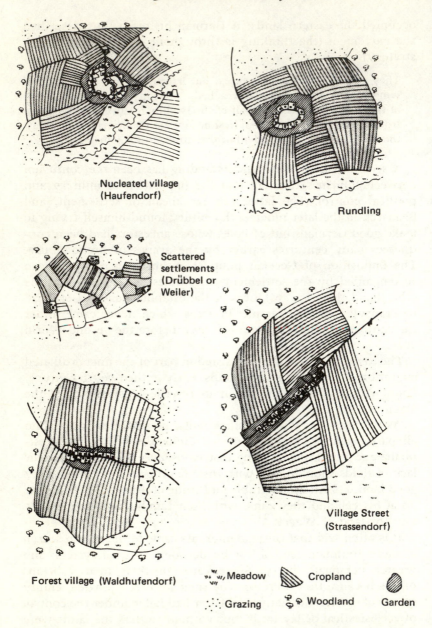

Nucleated village
(Haufendorf)

Rundling

Scattered
settlements
(Drübbel or
Weiler)

Village Street
(Strassendorf)

Forest village (Waldhufendorf)

Meadow    Cropland

Grazing    Woodland    Garden

Fig. 5.3   Plans of village types in Central Europe during the late Middle Ages.

served as middlemen, negotiating for a group of families, organising their transport, and establishing them in their new home.[22]

No doubt some peasants did well in their new lands, and attempted to rise in the social scale. The thirteenth-century epic of Meier Helmbrecht satirises the aspiring peasant of the Danube valley – it is in fact located in Upper Austria – who tries to enter the ranks of the lesser nobility. Such social climbing may not have been uncommon in the eastern frontier; it was less common in the crowded lands of western Europe.

Once settled in their new homes, the Germans found themselves amongst Slavs. They may have formed their own separate and distinct communities; more likely they constituted, along with the Slavs, a village under German law. The ratio of German immigrants to local Slavs is something which we shall never know. It is nevertheless true that a large part of Upper Silesia, in which a majority of the villagers lived in the fourteenth century under *deutsches Recht*, was Polish-speaking in the eighteenth.[23]

It is difficult to estimate the scale of German eastern colonisation. The documentation of this vast enterprise is scanty indeed. It has been claimed that some 1200 villages were established in Silesia before 1350 and no less than 1400 in the Prussian lands of the Church and of the German Knights.[24] Such estimates are based largely on the evidence of place-names. The villages whose names have been recorded are likely to have contained large numbers of Slav peasants, and many of them were undoubtedly not primary settlements established by colonists from the west, but secondary settlements resulting from migration within Silesia and Prussia. The number of colonists who came from west of the Elbe may well have been a great deal less than the 150,000 suggested by Aubin for these two provinces.

In eastern Europe, as in western, few new settlements were established in the early fourteenth century, and the movement, for practical purposes, ceased with the Black Death. Only in areas little affected by the Plague, such as parts of eastern Poland and Ruthenia did new settlements continue to be made. The later Middle Ages were, in most of Europe, a period of contraction. The colonising activity of western man reached its peak in the twelfth and thirteenth centuries, but of its precise chronology we know little. It would be natural to suppose that internal colonisation developed before the large-scale migration to the external frontier. The well known pollen diagram of Overbeck[25] shows an increase in the amount of pollen of the bread grains and also of the plantain, a weed of the cornfield, and a diminution in that of beech and hornbeam, from the Roman period until the twelfth century. Thereafter the grain pollens diminished until about 1400, when the volume again increased to a maximum in the mid-sixteenth. This data was obtained from a peat moor high on the plateau of the Rhöngebirge, to the east of Frankfurt-on-Main. It suggests that in this far from fertile and productive region population, and hence the area of cultivated land, increased until the twelfth century, and that it then declined, only to increase again in the fifteenth and much of the sixteenth century. The decline of cultivation at a time when land clearance and settlement were still expanding in many other parts of Europe suggests that marginal areas of the *internal* frontier were abandoned as the external frontier opened up.

*Village settlement*
The forms adopted by rural settlement in all parts of Europe were not only influenced in some measure by the physical conditions of the terrain, but also – and to a more important degree – by the level of the economy and the social structure of the settlers themselves. A century ago Meitzen argued[26] that the morphology of a settlement was to be linked with the ethnic origins of the settlers; that the compact and clustered village was related to Germanic settlement; that a pattern of scattered farms was Celtic, and the ring-fence village Slavic. Meitzen played an important role in emphasising the variety of settlements that emerged during the Middle Ages, even if he was wrong in his analysis of their origins. The study of villages and settlement types, however, cannot be dissociated from that of fields. The latter derive, no less than houses and farms, from social and economic conditions, and in the following pages, field systems will be examined along with the human settlements which they enclose.

The earliest settlements, at least in Europe north of the Alps, were probably small hut clusters around which a shifting agriculture was practised. Small and probably irregular fields were cleared, brought under cultivation and then abandoned to the waste. This system of *Feldgraswirtschaft* can be inferred from Tacitus. It was probably practised by the Slavs when the Germans intruded amongst them,[27] and, under the name of infield-outfield farming, it survived in parts of Great Britain into modern times. It is to be presumed that this small settlement of only a few households grew in size; that the land was tilled more frequently, and that a field *system* replaced the irregular cultivation of earlier times. Physical conditions would in many instances set limits to this process of growth; on the other hand, the small hamlet might expand into a large compact village. The latter could happen only where the soil was naturally fertile, because only in such areas could a large rural community be supported by the produce of its surrounding fields.

The large village developed institutions and structures which differed greatly from those of a small hamlet. In the latter co-operative ploughing may never have taken place; there might never have been enough draught animals for the heavy plough, and the peasants might have been obliged to rely on some lighter instrument. In the larger village, on the other hand, there was greater scope for the mutuality of the rural community and at the same time for those restrictions on individual freedom imposed by the tyranny of custom. By the time of the invasions of the ninth and tenth centuries most village communities in western and central Europe had passed or were passing under some form of seigneurial control. Whereas the isolated settlement or the hamlet might be difficult to supervise, the village was more easily managed and, given its greater size and productivity, more worth the trouble of close supervision and control.

The small hamlet, if left to its own internal processes of development and growth, might have moved towards a system of organising its fields and of sharing its ploughing beasts, its meadow and its woodland such as we find in the bipartite manor. When a lord had a share in the lands of the community and could demand the services of its members, the process was greatly hastened. A *system* was imposed; the occasional became the regular. The demesne was cultivated by the labours of the peasants, and the mutuality of the lord and his tenants, crystallised in the customs and practices of the manorial court, came into being.

To the question when did this village community take shape there can be no simple answer. There are instances of village communities which derived from *villae* of the later Roman Empire, their peasants being descended from the late Roman colonate and slaves. There are also cases of the deliberate creation of bipartite manors, in which social relations and field systems were made to conform as closely as was practicable to the current concept of how a village community should operate. When Abbot Suger established the village of Vaucresson (see p. 168), settling there sixty families, he was in all probability doing just this. And when, as he claimed, he increased the revenues which the monastery obtained from certain manors what he probably did was to streamline their administration, and organise the peasant obligations so that they contributed in the highest degree possible to the profitability of the demesne.[28] The extreme case of the creation of the model village is to be found in the organisation of the Cistercian granges.[29]

The area of Europe where the large clustered village, surrounded by its open fields, was the normal way of settling and using the land, was in fact severely restricted. It covered much of northern France and western Germany, but even here there were large areas where hamlets and scattered settlements were to be found. Wherever the terrain was more hilly or the soils less fertile – in the hills of Perche, in the Ardennes, on the clays of Champagne Humide, in the Vosges and the scattered hill-masses of Germany – large, nucleated villages became less frequent and the prevailing settlement form was the hamlet or the isolated farmstead. There was a difference also in the landscape, implicit in the medieval phrase *in plano et in bosco*, between the countryside of the open fields and nucleated villages on the one hand, and that of small settlements and enclosed fields on the other. Wace caught the social consequences when he wrote:[30]

> Li paisan et li villain,
> Cil des bocages et cil des plains

The villein, descendant of slave and colonus, was unfree as against his lord, constrained to work on his demesne, regimented in most aspects of his daily life, and subject to the *Feldzwang* of the village economy. The peasant, by contrast, was in effect free. Even if he was not a freeholder he could nevertheless adapt his farming to his own needs provided only that he paid his rent to his lord.

The movement of people into Europe's external frontier imposed new and different conditions on their settlements. Fresh patterns of villages and fields emerged in response to changed social and economic needs. It was, in the first place, a relatively disciplined and orderly process of settlement. Communities, together with their tools, beasts and equipment, were taken to the new site and 'located'. They probably occupied virgin sites. If there had previously been a Slav settlement, it was absorbed into the new village and its fields largely or wholly obliterated in the process. The most common form assumed by the new settlements was that of the street village. Peasant houses were aligned along both sides of a road or track. Their frontages on to the road were approximately equal, and their cropland, commonly made up of a small number of very large open fields, reached out to the boundaries of the settlement. Sometimes the two lines of cottages diverged, enclosing an oval or spindle-shaped green – the *Angerdorf* of the Germans, or *owalnica* of the Poles. The whole was tidier and more orderly than the clustered village of western Europe. It is unlikely that there was a demesne, at least in the first century or two of the village's existence, and the peasants in all probability paid a rent in cash or in kind. Although the street village was subject to some of the constraints – routine of ploughing, sowing and reaping, of fallowing and of common grazing after harvest – of the open-field village of the West, there was, nevertheless, a greater degree of personal freedom than in the latter. Serfdom appears to have been rare and if the peasantry had to be liberated in the eighteenth and nineteenth centuries, this was only because their status had been downgraded with the formation of the great estates of eastern Europe in early modern times (see p. 474).

Many variants of the street village appeared in the landscape of eastern Europe. The most common was the forest village, or *Waldhufendorf*, consisting, like the street village, of a double line of houses, but lacking the open fields of the latter. Instead, each house was backed by its own enclosed land, which formed a narrow strip, perhaps 50 to 100 metres in breadth, extending for a kilometre or more to the farthest limits of cultivated land. The forest village was common, as indeed it remains today, in the hill country of northern Bohemia and southern Poland. It snaked its way into the foothills of the mountains, often following a valley for miles, its narrow strips of cultivation reaching up the hills on each side. The marshland village, or *Marschhufendorf*, was similar except that the cottages lay along the sinuous dyke constructed to protect newly reclaimed farmland. Individual holdings, made up mainly of meadowland, extended back from the line of cottages across the flat and newly drained land.

A village type, associated in particular with the areas east of the Elbe river which were occupied and settled by the Germans in the twelfth and thirteenth centuries, was the *Rundling* or ring-fence village. The cottages were arranged very approximately in a circle, so that their fenced garden-plots formed a ring within which the farm animals could be corralled. Meitzen regarded it as a specifically Slavic form of settlement. This it certainly was not; it was one which was particularly well suited to the disturbed conditions of the frontier. The street and forest village, as well as the *Rundling*, are shown in Figure 5.3.

The typically west European forms – the clustered village and the hamlet – are not found in significant numbers east of the Elbe. Instead the street and forest villages predominate, with a sprinkling of ring-fence villages in the Elbe valley itself.

*Late medieval contraction*

The medieval economy took a downward turn with the decline in population during the fourteenth century. This resulted inevitably in a contraction in the cultivated area and, locally at least, the abandonment of settlements. The pressure of population in the thirteenth century had made necessary the settlement and cultivation of large areas of marginal land. Some, as is suggested by the pollen analysis from the Rhöngebirge, had been abandoned much earlier. One would expect, with the contraction of the total population by as much as a quarter, that there would have been a widespread reduction of cultivation and the abandonment of much of the poorer quality land. There are two ways in which settlement and cultivation can contract.[31] Individual settlements may become a little smaller; some cottages may fall to ruin and the remoter fields may be abandoned. Alternatively there may be the total abandonment of some settlements and the concentration of their inhabitants at a smaller number of more favoured sites.

Undoubtedly both processes occurred. There is evidence of abandoned fields around large settlements in the estate maps and cadasters of early modern times. At the same time, in some areas of central Europe, the number of settlements which were wholly abandoned and never again reoccupied is so great that the phenomenon can be explained only in terms of the concentration of population at fewer places.

The abandonment of settlements, what the Germans call *Wüstungen*, is not easy to document. It is generally assumed that they were deserted as a result of the plagues and resulting high mortality of the second half of the fourteenth century. What one looks for, then, is evidence for the existence of a named settlement before the mid-fourteenth century and its disappearance from the records at some date thereafter. There are many examples of this. It is, however, more difficult to discover the size, both before and after the Plague, of the villages which survived. Most of the hearth lists relate to the century and a half following the Black Death. Nevertheless there is enough evidence to suggest very strongly that, although population decline was general, the *Wüstungen* were a local phenomenon.

Abel's well-known and much quoted study of the lost settlements of Germany[32] shows that in northern Thuringia two-thirds of the named places disappeared during the later Middle Ages, and that the wastage was only a little less in Anhalt and around the eastern Harz mountains. At the same time it was at the rate of a fifth or less in south-western Germany and only a third in the Rhenish Palatinate. These figures cannot be reconciled with what we know about the decline of population, unless we assume that only very small settlements disappeared and that there was a concentration of population in the larger.

In France, it is often said, there was little abandonment of settlements in the later Middle Ages. This view is supported by a study of the so-called polyptyque of Eudes Rigaud, which lists the parishes of the Rouen diocese with the estimated number of parishioners. The diocese lay mainly north of the river Seine in an area of fertile soil, long characterised by large, clustered villages. The names listed by Eudes Rigaud can be identified on either the eighteenth century maps of Cassini or on modern topographical sheets, and it cannot be doubted that here there was no loss amongst the villages which gave their names to the parishes of the diocese. They may have contracted – almost certainly they did – but they did not disappear, and the only losses that could have taken place were of isolated farmsteads and clearings. The lands which the Count of Champagne held in the district of Porcien were surveyed in the early thirteenth century.[33] Here also all the names of settlements can be identified and located on the modern map, thus suggesting again that none of the larger rural settlements was abandoned.

If there was a significant loss of settlements in Burgundy, Brabant, Hainault, Luxembourg and in the diocese of Lausanne, it must have taken place before the earliest surviving hearth lists were compiled early in the fifteenth century (see p. 124). Slicher van Bath has given it as his judgment that lost villages were comparatively rare in the Netherlands, but admits that there was some contraction in the number of isolated farmsteads in the notably infertile area of Twente in the eastern Netherlands.[34] In Italy also there was a widespread abandonment of fields and of the smaller and more remote settlements, reflecting in all probability a concentration of population in larger and more favourably situated villages.[35]

The conclusion appears to be irresistible that in fertile and productive areas, characterised by nucleated villages, there was a contraction of settlement size, but that in relatively few instances was a settlement wholly abandoned. On the other hand, there was unquestionably wholesale abandonment of settlements in some parts of England and in Central Europe, but it seems probable that the lost settlements were in the main small in size and situated in areas of marginal productivity. The abandonment of such sites seems to have been accompanied by some degree of concentration of settlement in the larger villages. Nor was the abandonment of marginal settlements a feature only of the period of declining population. If the dating of pollen evidence is correct (see p. 180) such sites were abandoned during the period of most vigorous population growth, since this also saw the opening up of the eastern frontier.

Discussion has so far been predicated on the assumption that the abandonment of settlements and of cropland was a consequence of the decline of population during the later Middle Ages. No doubt this was the principal cause, but it was by no means the only one. There is evidence for the abandonment of settlements as early as the twelfth century as peasants migrated first to peripheral areas near their homes and then to better but more distant land. Other reasons for the abandonment of settlements were the creation of 'forests' for purposes of hunting, of granges for the management of Cistercian estates, and of sheep runs when the price of wool was rising. But of all the secondary reasons for the loss of villages the foremost was war.

Medieval man, at least the humbler class of medieval man, was primarily a bread-eater. He ate peas and beans, which were his principal source of protein, but meat and dairy produce formed no significant part of his diet. His croplands were, therefore, the most important part of his possessions, and were very often the only parts of his farm holding which he did not share with others. Estimates of the area needed to support a peasant household were always expressed in units of cropland, even though part of it might at any time be under fallow. Only in mountainous areas and in Scandinavia did the products of animal husbandry contribute significantly to human diet.

Yet the rural community could not have lived on its cropland alone. Its woodland was no less necessary. Without trees it could could not build and roof its cottages; without the fallen limbs of trees it had no fuel either to heat them in winter or to cook the bread crops which were otherwise indigestible. The woodland, or at least part of it, yielded pannage for pigs, which in turn provided most of the animal protein consumed by medieval man. Meadow was no less essential, though in a different way. It provided hay, and the commonest measure of meadowland was the number of loads of hay which it might be expected to yield. Without hay the ploughing beasts and the riding horses could not be kept through the winter. Meadowland was usually the scarcest category of land and the most valuable per hectare. Its area could not be increased without great difficulty because it was to be found only on the damp, alluvial soils along the valleys. Pasture, or rough grazing land, was present in most rural communities, but was usually less important. It provided grazing for sheep and cattle and from its flowering bushes the bees gathered the honey which was the only source of sweetening.

Few communities were without a mill, since the bread grains had to be ground before they could be used for human food. The water-powered mill had been rare in classical antiquity, perhaps because the general availability of slave labour had made the use of mechanical power unnecessary. The water mill, at first operated by a small, undershot wheel, became increasingly common in the early Middle Ages, and the hand quern gradually disappeared from the cottage. In its place came the distaff and spindle and sometimes also a tall, narrow loom. Wool obtained from the local sheep together with flax and hemp grown in the garden plots of the peasants, provided most of the cloth needed. The chief drink was a light beer, preferably brewed from malted barley, but also in emergency from oats or any other grain that might be available. Hops were used for flavouring the beer only occasionally. Usually there was a *camba*, or brewhouse, where the peasants were required to bring their malt for brewing, just as they took their grain to the lord's mill to be ground.

Such was the self-sufficing village community. The area which it controlled was limited. The nucleated village of northern France could command, on an average, about 2000 hectares. Within this the community had to maintain a balance between the several kinds of land use. Any increase in the area of cropland might lead to a shortage of building timber and of fuel. Some land had, furthermore, to be spared from crop-farming for the support of the animals, without which the cropland could not be ploughed.

The previous pages have traced in broad outline the expansion of settlement and agriculture in the high Middle Ages and their contraction during the later centuries. At the peak of its medieval expansion, at the end of the thirteenth and early in the fourteenth centuries, the density of rural population was probably as great as at any time in Europe's history, and in some areas it probably could not have been increased without significant changes in agricultural technology.[36]

Factors in the later medieval contraction of agriculture, it has been argued, were a deterioration of the climate and an exhaustion, or at least impoverishment, of the soil. Indeed, one theory of the late medieval decline has been predicated upon these assumptions. For neither is there any compelling evidence. In the first place a soil may be eroded and destroyed, but it is not easily exhausted, or deprived of nutrients to the point where it can no longer support a crop. If a tract of land were continuously cultivated with the same crop and without the addition of manure, its yield would decline over a period of many years to a lower level, but this level would in all probability be maintained. Medieval man did not sow his fields intensively and he secured only a very low yield ratio (see p. 198). Furthermore he both rotated his crops and used a system of fallow, and when he practised an infield-outfield system, the land may have been left for many years without any sown crops. Lastly, he was aware of the value of both marl and manure, and in fact used the small supply that was available.

The evidence which we have does not suggest that yield ratios declined in the later Middle Ages[37]; indeed, everything points to the contrary. It can, of course, be argued that, since the cultivated area contracted and marginal land was abandoned, one would expect yield ratios on average to rise. Further, it could be said that the rise in average yields from the better soils might disguise some degree of soil deterioration on some of the less good. This is entirely possible, but the extent of the improvement in yield ratios during the fourteenth and fifteenth centuries surely rules out soil deterioration as a general phenomenon. On a local scale, however, there was some degree of soil loss. Reclaimed marshlands were extensively inundated in the fifteenth century. There is some evidence that damp valley-lands in many areas, but especially in central Europe, became incultivable. Doubtless there was then, as there is today, some blowing of dry soils left under bare fallow, and washing of soils on steep hillsides which should never have been brought under cultivation. But these were small-scale and local phenomena. There is no evidence for a widespread and progressive deterioration of the soil.

The related question of climatic change during the later Middle Ages can be dismissed less easily. There is abundant evidence during the fourteenth and fifteenth centuries for wet summers which did not allow the crops to ripen, and severe winters which froze them in the ground; for late spring frosts and disastrous floods. There is a strong probability that these add up to a cyclical change in climate during the later years of the thirteenth century, and for this there is some evidence in pollen analyses and in tree-rings. In all probability the change took the form of increased storminess, higher rainfall and cooler and more cloudy summers. It is impossible to say whether and to what extent harvests were affected. Yield ratios showed some improvement during the later Middle Ages, but, as has been seen, some marginal land, which would have included damp valley floors and wet lowlands, had passed out of cultivation. The

189

resulting improvement might have more than offset a deterioration due to cooler and wetter climatic conditions.

## The crops

The fields which surrounded every medieval settlement were for the greater part under cereal or bread crops. These provided most of the food supply and consumed the greater part of the peasants' labour. The farmer's year was organised round the autumn and spring ploughing and the sowing and reaping of the bread crops. The great barns of the monasteries were built to store grain, and it was the abundance or scarcity of bread crops which spelled wellbeing or famine for the peasant.

In most parts of Europe, irrespective of the field system actually in use, a three-course rotation was generally practised, consisting of an autumn sown crop, a spring sown crop, and fallow, before the land was again prepared for the next autumn sowing. Variations in this routine were imposed by the quality of the land, by the vagaries of the weather and by the necessities of man. Spring sown crop had sometimes to follow spring sown crop, as when winter frost or flooding destroyed the autumn sown grain before it could germinate and grow.[38]

The preferred grains were wheat and rye. These were not the plump, refined grains known to the modern farmer, but smaller and less hardy varieties which by an unconscious process of selection, had been developed from the wild grains of antiquity. Rye had emerged in central Europe only within the historical period, and oats had been disseminated in all probability as a weed of the wheat field. Wheat and rye could usually be threshed free of their husks or glumes; they milled easily, and yielded a flour which could be baked into a bread. Medieval varieties of wheat and rye were relatively slow-growing. Throughout Europe they had to be sown in autumn, and they matured between June and August. They did not grow well on poor and acid soil, and they succumbed readily to the rigours of a hard winter. There were, however, variants which were in some degree adjusted to their physical environments. Among them were dinkel, a hardy variety of wheat, much grown in northern Switzerland and Swabia, and spelt, a similar variant of wheat, which was common in the Low Countries and the lower Rhineland.

The most important spring sown crops were oats and barley,

sometimes mixed under the name of meteil or maslin. They were usually sown in March and were often described as tremois, or three-month crops. They cropped better than wheat or even rye, on areas of poor soil, and there can be little doubt that they were grown to the exclusion of the latter in some areas. The Prüm polyptyque, much of which related to areas of poor and infertile soil, recorded that at Aldenselen in the Netherlands there was a tract of land which took oats 'whenever it was sown'. At Vilancia, on the Eifel, there were seven fields where only oats were sown. Oats were rarely sown in southern Europe, where the long, dry summer made it difficult for a 'three-month' crop to grow and mature before growth was halted by the heat and drought.

Oats were one of the most widely cultivated crops in northern Europe because they could be grown on almost any soil. They had the great disadvantages, however, of being difficult to thresh and mill and of yielding a flour which would not 'rise' when baked. Oats were fed to the horses, malted for brewing when barley was in short supply, and occasionally used as human food for the deserving poor. The records of St Pantaleon of Cologne show, in words reminiscent of Dr Johnson's strictures on the diet of the Scots, that the monastery received large quantities of oats which were used to feed the horses of the lord abbot and any travellers who might arrive.

It was the object of monastic and doubtless also of lay landholders to impose a regular cropping routine because, within the limits set by weather, this would be likely to yield a steady supply of food. No doubt also this was resisted by the peasantry, and the compulsion of the medieval cropping system seems often to have been honoured in the breach. No doubt the lord could generally dictate the cropping on his own demesne, and there is abundant evidence of a regular three-field practice on fields of approximately equal size, but exceptions had to be made for the peasants. Guillaume de Ryckel, the thirteenth century abbot of Saint-Trond, near Liège, was obliged to make an agreement with a group of peasants whereby

all . . . who till the said land, for the first six years [of their tenancy] may sow whatever pleases them and in whatever quantity they wish. In the six years following, however, they will observe and follow the communal sowing practice, so that in the first year they will sow wheat or rye, in the second year, barley or oats or any other grain which it is customary to sow in spring, and in the third year they will sow nothing on this same land.[39]

A regular three-field system might be expected to yield approximately equal quantities of autumn and spring sown grains. Very rarely indeed is this equation satisfied by the cropping figures that are available. At the grange at Veulerent, belonging to the abbey of Chaalis the cropland was divided into three parts (*in tres aristas*), the areas and agricultural use of which were:[40]

| | | |
|---|---|---|
| I. | 365½ arpents | wheat |
| II. | 323 arpents 9 perches | fallow |
| III. | 333 arpents 10 perches | mixed grain |

But this streamlined operation belonged to the Cistercians, and was worked by its own *conversi*. More often we find the cropping pattern distorted by the greater demand for the panifiable grains – wheat and rye; by conditions of soil and weather which might make spring sown crops more desirable; by the wilfulness of the peasants, or the exactions of their lords. Rents were often paid in the form of the autumn-sown grains. According to Guillaume de Ryckel's notebook,[41] the abbey of Saint-Trond required annually:

| | |
|---|---|
| wheat | 227 modii |
| rye | 291 modii |
| spelt | 40 modii |

while from its demesne lands it obtained:

| *Autumn sown* | | *Spring sown* | |
|---|---|---|---|
| wheat | 400 modii | barley | 15 modii |
| rye | 410 modii | oats | 40 modii |
| spelt | 170 modii | | |

The demands of the monastery and the supply from the lands which it could control were thus tipped heavily in favour of panifiable, autumn sown grains. Tithe payments might be taken to reflect more accurately the actual cropping system of the peasants, and these show a preponderance of the non-panifiable grains, barley and oats. Very rarely do we find clear evidence for the general and widespread use of a three-field system, in which autumn and spring sown crops and fallow succeed one another. Everywhere we find evidence that the market or the lord demanded a surplus of wheat or rye, while soil and climate were perhaps more conducive to oats and barley. A remedy, where conditions of soil and climate made it possible, was to revert to a two-field system, such as continued to be practised in much of the Mediterranean region, with alternating wheat–barley and fallow. In the highly urbanised middle Rhineland, where there was a heavy demand for bread grains, we actually find the three-course system, which yielded a considerable amount of unwanted oats and barley, being given up in favour of a two-field system which yielded a smaller total volume of grain, but rather more of the desirable wheat and rye.[42]

A close examination of Guillaume de Ryckel's notebook shows not only a lack of harmony between autumn and winter grains but also the clearly marked local characteristics of the cropping pattern. There were manors which appear to have grown only rye and oats; those which produced mainly rye and spelt (was the latter spring sown?), or spelt and oats, or oats and barley, or oats alone. One needs to study these cropping patterns against the background of soil, of water-level in the fields and of other physical conditions over which the peasant had little or no control. One asks did these variations spring from the institutional structure of the community, from the unchanging custom of the village and from the nature of conventional rents; and was it difficult, or even impossible for a peasant to acquire the seed necessary to change his methods of cultivation?

The pattern of cereal-growing showed strongly marked regional characteristics. There were areas dominated by a single crop or by a couple of crops in joint production. What we need is a map of Europe showing quantitatively the contribution of each cereal to the total production.

Most distinctive is the Mediterranean region, with its two-field system and its dominance of autumn sown wheat and barley. There is, however, some evidence that attempts were made in southern France, and perhaps elsewhere, to introduce a three-field system with a spring sown crop. The Paris basin and northern France is the only part of Europe where one can say without qualification that a three-field system was widely practised and that there was an approximate equality in the production of the two categories of grain. Wheat was perhaps the more important autumn-sown grain, while oats predominated amongst those sown in spring. Even so, there were many areas within this region where the cropping practice was highly irregular. West of the Paris basin, in the *bocage* region of north-western France, with its predominance of hamlets and scattered *bordagia*, there was probably no established system. Rye and oats were most commonly grown and on the poorest soils a crop of oats was perhaps taken at irregular intervals. It seems probable that a three-field system prevailed on the good soils of Hainault, Brabant and Liège, though it was in the latter province that the erratic cropping of Saint-Trond was encountered. On the good soils of the Lower Rhineland, of Saxony and of Bohemia there seems also to have been a system of approximately equal autumn and spring sown crops. But elsewhere one cannot speak with certainty of the existence of any particular system.

*The cultivation of the soil*

During the Middle Ages the heavy plough came to be used throughout most of western and central Europe. It was a cumbersome instrument, fitted with wheels which controlled the depth to which the share cut into the soil; a coulter, which made a vertical cut through the soil, and a mouldboard, which undercut the sward and turned it over. Thus the plough not only buried the weeds, but also brought up to the surface a lower soil level in which percolating water tended to concentrate the plant nutrients. This type of plough was illustrated in countless medieval manuscripts (Fig. 5.4), and when the Sieur de Joinville was in Egypt during the crusade of Louis IX, he expressed his astonishment that the fellahin ploughed 'with a wheel-less plough'.[43] If only he had looked more closely in western Europe, he would have found that the mouldboard plough was not always supported on wheels.

The ploughman in Aelfric's dialogue told of his work:

> I work very hard; I go out at daybreak, drive the oxen to the field and yoke them to the plough. Never is winter weather so severe that I dare to remain at home; for I fear my master. But when the oxen are yoked

to the plough and the *share* and *coulter* fastened on, every day I must plough a full acre or more.[44]

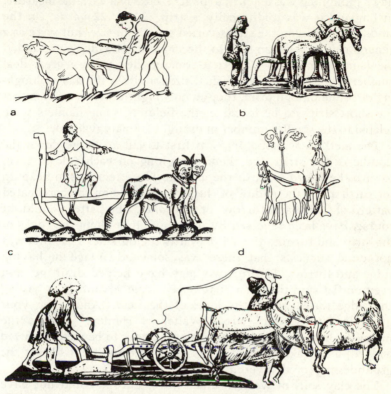

Fig. 5.4   Types of ploughs: (*a*) and (*b*) light classical plough;
(*c*) early medieval light plough in north-western Europe;
(*d*) light plough in Moravia, eleventh century;
(*e*) heavy plough in Bohemia, fourteenth century.

It was the heavy plough, the *carruca* of the records, which bit into the heavy clay soils of northern Europe and the forest lands of the east. It was commonly drawn by several pairs of oxen, though developments in harness design, especially the introduction of the padded collar, allowed horses to be used more extensively. Walter of Henley recommended the addition of a couple of horses to the ox-team, thus combining the greater speed of the former with the strength of the latter.

The heavy plough was difficult to turn, and was usually made to cut a long furrow, a 'furlong' indeed, before being turned. A day's ploughing was a 'journal' or acre, clearly a variable measure. In England it was traditionally a strip 220 by 22 yards. On the lands of Saint-Rémi the strips varied greatly in size, but were as a general rule larger than this. In the small fields which surrounded the hamlets in north-western Germany they were a great deal smaller. There was no established size for either the day's plough-ing or of the plough team, though one might perhaps assume that the short strips to be found in the fields of some hamlets were related to the smaller number of draught animals available.

The method of ploughing was first to cut a furrow down the middle of the strip, and then, ploughing on each side in turn, to turn the sward towards the middle. The effect was to heap up the earth along the middle of the strip, producing the corrugated pattern of 'ridge-and-furrow' or *Hochaker*. The pattern could, of course, have been reversed by ploughing first along the edges of the strip and turning the soil towards the outside. That this was not done suggests that there was some advantage in having ridge-and-furrow. The furrows may have helped drainage, and even on flat land there may have been some advantage in having the ridge raised above the level of the field. 'And when your groundes are sowen,' wrote Walter of Henley,[45] 'cause the marryshe [marshy] landes and waterie landes to be well forrowed [ridged] and make the water forrowes [free running] so that the grounde may be delyvered from the water.'

The clay soils of western and central Europe could not have been broken up and cultivated without the heavy plough. It may be questioned whether this plough was equally useful and wide-spread on the light soils. In the three-field area of the Paris basin and northern France it was probably in universal use, or Joinville would have been aware of the light plough. But it would be very surprising if some lighter instrument was not known and used in the *bocage* regions of the west, where even the breastplough and caschrom remained in use into modern times. Nor did the heavy plough altogether replace the light in the frontier areas of eastern Europe.

The traditional Slavic plough was a simple wooden instru-ment.[46] Two types were in use; one was hooked (Fig. 5.4) and tore through the soil; the other had a horizontal base com-monly fitted with a metal tip. It slid through the soil, undercutting

196

the weeds and plant growth, and was clearly an improvement on the hooked plough. These ploughs are known from the Baltic coast to Greece. A thirteenth-century fresco at Znojmo (Moravia) shows King Přemysl of Bohemia with a simple hooked plough pulled by two oxen (Fig. 5.4d). This may, of course be a piece of deliberate archaism, but at least the simplest of ploughs was still familiar on the border of the Ostmark at this date. There can be little doubt that the heavy wheeled plough with mouldboard was introduced from the West, and there is at least the presumption that it was the Germans who brought it. It is noteworthy that the simpler *araire* type of plough survived into modern times most widely in those areas of eastern and south-eastern Europe where the Germans did not settle.

It is commonly assumed that the character of the plough dictated the shape and arrangement of the fields. Strips could unquestionably be tilled with a light plough and conversely small square fields with the heavy, but such methods would entail a greater expenditure of effort and in the long run would not have been economic. One must suppose that when fields were first laid out they were adjusted to the technical demands of the tools used, whatever changes may subsequently have taken place in both.

Ploughing duties were the heaviest obligations owed by the peasant, and there can be no doubt that the land was well and truly ploughed. Figure 5.5 shows the frequency of ploughing

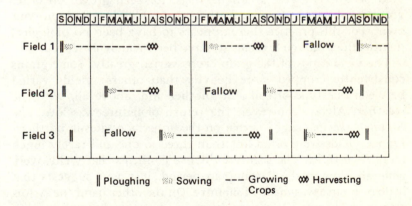

Fig. 5.5 Ploughing, sowing and harvesting routine in a three-field system.

197

in a regular three-field system. The fields were ploughed before sowing. Walter of Henley recommended that the furrows be 'little and well laid together, that the seed may fall evenly'. Seed was sown broadcast and a harrow was then drawn over the field to spread the earth over it.

The grain was harvested with the sickle. Unless the straw was needed for thatching, the ears were cut off high above the ground and the stubble was ploughed in. Walter of Henley recommended that as much as possible of the straw should be returned to the soil in this way. Later in the Middle Ages the sickle began, at least locally, to be replaced by the scythe, which cut close to the ground. In this way large quantities of straw became available and were spread in the cowsheds and stables, ultimately making their way back to the fields as manure.

Tithe was usually taken before the sheaves were removed from the field. The grain was then threshed and a portion set aside for the next year's crop. In northern Europe threshing was carried out in a barn with a jointed flail, and was often work for the dark days of autumn and winter. Only in the warm dry Mediterranean autumn were the tasks of flailing and winnowing normally carried on out of doors. It was the custom of some great landowners to sow seed taken from another field or a different manor. Charlemagne had enjoined this practice in the *Capitulare de Villis* (see p. 61), and Walter of Henley's advice was to 'change your seed every year at Michaelmas, for seed grown on other ground will bring more profit than that which is grown on your own'. For this practice there appears to have been no biological justification, though it seems to have been widely observed.

The yield ratios of the grain crops varied greatly. Some grains consistently cropped more heavily than others; yields varied between one type of soil and another and, above all, with the weather. Always, however, the return of nature was low. The *Brevium exempla* suggests that on the imperial estates in northern France yields were often less than three to one and rarely much more than three. The scanty evidence confirms that yields were generally low in the Carolingian period, just as it suggests that little or no use was made of manure. On the other hand the Artois estates of Thierry d'Hireçon in the early fourteenth century were, more often than not, yielding an eightfold return of wheat and in one year a return of more than elevenfold.[47] But he kept a large number of animals and appears from his surviving accounts to have made good use of their manure. Barley usually yielded the highest returns, followed by rye and wheat, with oats usually showing the lowest yield ratios. It is difficult, however, to make such comparisons because, unless we are dealing with a regular three-field system, there is at least a suspicion that the bread grains *par excellence* were grown on the best soil and the ill-regarded oats banished to the poorest.

Few rural communities were without a mill. Gone were the times when bread grains were ground by the housewife or a slave in a handworked quern. The waterwheel came in during the early Middle Ages and quickly spread. Domesday Book lists more than 5000 mills in over 3000 separate communities in late eleventh century England.[48] The reason is easy to see. The erection of a watermill was a profitable investment for the lord, provided that he could compel his tenants to use it. With increasing seigneurial control over the manor this was usually not difficult, and rent rolls and similar documents show a large and growing income as the lord took his cut of all the grain that was sent to the manorial mill, or leased it at farm.

Part of the grain was malted. Barley was preferred for this purpose, but oats were used more often. When, in the early twelfth century, Flanders was faced with famine, the Count ordered that not even oats should be used for brewing, but that instead they should be made into bread, so that the poor might at least maintain life on bread and water.[49] Much of the malt (*bracia*), which was so often recorded amongst the peasants' dues, must have been made from oats.

Some indication has already been given of the vast quantities of grain which some of the richer monasteries received annually from their own demesnes as well as in the form of rent and tithe. It greatly exceeded their normal requirements, and the surplus was sold into the markets. Without it towns would not have grown or specialised rural crafts have developed. We must visualise a great many petty dealers going from village to village, buying up the peasants' surplus and doubtless making loans on the security of the next crop, while merchants operating on a larger scale bought up the stores which accumulated in monastic tithe barns and shipped them by cart and boat to distant markets. Thierry d'Hireçon was able to sell his own not inconsiderable surplus in the towns of Flanders, and on one occasion he shipped two boat loads from the small river port of Aire to Ghent.

Around every cottage in the village community was an enclosed garden. The cottager, indeed, had no other land than this small plot. Here he grew a few vegetables and a fruit tree or two; here he might keep a dairy cow or a goat, and dig into the ground whatever manure became available. The garden was the principal source of the *companagium*, the accompaniment of the monotonous and unbalanced diet of grain. Beans and peas were essential in a diet which otherwise consisted mainly of starch. They form, nevertheless, one of the darkest corners of medieval agriculture, in part because the produce of the gardens was not usually subject to tithe, and rarely contributed to the peasant's obligations to his lord. Vegetables were grown, domesticated variants of the wild varieties which still grew in the surrounding fields and woodlands: the onion, cabbage, and turnip.[50] The number of such plants increased greatly in the fifteenth century as varieties introduced from the Arab world were domesticated and diffused.

The gardens of the rich had long been made to produce a great many exotic vegetables and herbs. Charlemagne had prescribed a list of impracticable length for the imperial manors (see p. 61), but by the fifteenth century a not dissimilar variety might have been found in the châteaux gardens in much of western Europe. But the garden of the peasant probably produced little more than peas and beans, cabbage and turnips. It is probable that peas and beans were also grown as field crops in rotation with grains, and were often included with the *bladum minutum*, the 'lesser grains'.

By the later Middle Ages the cultivation of vegetables had become a specialised occupation around many of the larger towns. Fresh vegetables as well as the less perishable roots were sold in the town markets. The 'market gardens' were most often to be found on the humid, alluvial soil, often inundated in winter, which lay along the valleys. It was here in the marshes, the *marais*, that the *maraîchers*, or market gardeners, grew their vegetables for the nearby town market. The *hortillonages* which lie along the Somme valley, below Amiens, are one of many survivals of this medieval practice. Food crops were obliged to share the soil with industrial plants, which played a small but important role in the medieval economy. Foremost amongst the latter were hemp and flax. They grew best in a humid climate and in a damp, well fertilised soil. They were crops of northern rather than of southern Europe, but in the former were probably grown in most rural communities, usually in small, enclosed gardens. Hemp was grown for making rope and twine, which were no less widely used in the Middle Ages than today. Flax was cultivated essentially for the manufacture of linen. Both plants required a great deal of labour in planting, pulling, soaking or retting, and in scutching, or breaking up the stiff fibres into workable thread. But it was work which demanded little skill and which could easily be carried on in or around the peasant cottages. The ninth and tenth century polyptyques show that there was a heavy production of vegetable fibres and that bundles of flax were prominent among the dues owed by the peasants to their lords. Some areas, whether owing to their natural advantages for the cultivation of flax and hemp or to careful management by their lords, acquired a considerable reputation and importance for the production of these crops. Brittany thus came to be noted for its rope and coarse canvas, and the Low Countries and western and southern Germany for their flax and linen (see p. 314).

## Viticulture

Foremost amongst the specialised crops of the Middle Ages was the fruit of the vine. The consumption of good wine, like the wearing of expensive cloth, was a mark of rank and a form of conspicuous consumption. The Church required wine for the performance of its liturgy, though there is no evidence that the quality of the wine was in this case of significance. The cultivation of the grape vine had spread during the classical period over much of the Roman Empire. Only in Britain and northern and north-western Gaul was the vine wholly absent. Dion has argued[51] that certain areas lying near the frontier of viticulture and favoured with good means of transport, became the sources of wine for the more distant regions of the Empire. Such an area was the Rhône valley. Here vine-growing was intensively developed and survived the Germanic invasions. The polyptyques of the ninth century show that the cultivation of the vine was widespread in areas where it is today unimportant or not even known.[52] The slowness and difficulty of medieval transport led some lords, as far north as Artois and Flanders, Mecklenburg and Brandenburg, to produce their own wine, a practice which was gradually abandoned as trade developed and better wines became available from more southerly vineyards.

Almost every manor in the wine-producing areas of Europe had its small vineyard. In some areas, particularly those which combined the advantages of a favourable climate and easy transport, commercial viticulture was developed almost to the exclusion of other agricultural activities. In the Rhône and Saône valleys, along the headwaters of the Seine and its tributaries, in the Moselle and Rhine valleys, in the Bordelais and the Tyrol and along the Austrian margin of the Hungarian Plain, vineyards covered much of the cultivated land. Around the larger towns of central and southern France, of southern Germany and of Italy there were vineyards, often owned and worked in very small parcels by the citizens themselves. Fra Salimbene in the mid-thirteenth century noted that around Auxerre, in the Yonne valley, 'people sow nothing, reap nothing and gather nothing into their barns. They only need to send their wine to Paris on the nearby river. . . . The sale of wine in this city brings them in a good profit which pays entirely for their food and clothing.'[53]

The cultivation of the vine was a demanding occupation. The planting and tending of the vinestocks consumed a great deal of time, and they represented a heavy investment which yielded returns only slowly. Few peasants were able to maintain vineyards on their own account. At most they might hope to develop a small vineyard on a share-cropping basis. A common form of tenure was to lease a small tract of land to a peasant on condition that he planted and tended the vines until they were grown. At the expiry of the lease, when the vineyard was coming into production, it was divided between the lord and the tenant, who thus acquired a small but valuable freehold. Most of the great vineyards of the Middle Ages, whose wine was sought after by merchants and eagerly bought by the rich, were managed directly by their lords, whether secular or ecclesiastical, with the help, as a general rule, of hired labour.

The olive continued to be cultivated in southern Europe, but it is doubtful whether it was anywhere as important as it had been under the Roman Empire. There is no evidence for an important trade in olive oil, though there was an export from Apulia and Sicily.[54] The reasons are not far to seek. No crop was as vulnerable to war as the olive. The trees did not usually mature in less than twenty years and, once destroyed, they were not likely to be replanted in those uncertain times. Nevertheless, many monasteries in southern France owned olive groves, and trees – even single olive trees – are recorded amongst the possessions of individual peasants.

*Animal Farming*

For most people the rearing of animals was only a marginal activity. The peasant needed an ox which, yoked with those of his neighbours, pulled his plough. He might have a cow, and a pig or two in the forest, but most farm animals belonged to his lord. The chief restraint on animal rearing was the shortage of winter fodder. A little vetch was grown, but there was, as a general rule, nothing except hay on which to feed the animals through the winter. Ploughing oxen had a prior claim on the food supply, and oats were, of course, fed to the horses and occasionally the cattle. Some animals were turned loose in the woodland, and those which survived the winter were rounded up in the spring. For the pigs there was a wholesale slaughter every autumn, and salted pork was the only meat that many people ever tasted.

A consequence of the small number of animals kept on most manors was the very small supply of manure. Medieval man was very slow to learn that an increase in the number of farm animals would be likely to result in better crop yields. When, towards the end of the Middle Ages, yield ratios began to improve, this is probably to be attributed, at least in part, to the increased availability and use of farmyard manure.

If the peasant owned few farm animals, his lord commonly possessed a considerable number. He might on any sizeable manor have enough oxen for two or more teams. He would have a number of cows, kept more for breeding purposes than for the milk, butter and cheese which they could yield, and he might produce cattle for sale to the butchers of the nearby town. He always kept a stable of horses. He and his retinue travelled on horseback; the horse was an instrument of war, as well as a mark of prestige, literally raising the knight above the level of the mass of the peasantry. The principal food of the horse, apart from grass and hay, was oats, and the widespread cultivation of the low-yielding oats is not unrelated to its importance in feeding horses.

The pig was the only animal which was kept exclusively for its ability to supply food. Pigs were found everywhere except in southern Europe. They were scavengers, but their chief source of food was in the woodlands which yielded acorns and beechmast. High forest was measured by its ability to support pigs; 'woodland for so many pigs' was a common item in manorial inventories, and the common medieval illustrations of the labours of the months frequently represented one of the tasks of November as knocking down the fruits of the beech and oak for the benefit of the herd of ravenous pigs seen rooting below.

Since prehistoric times there had been a tendency for the number of sheep to be inversely proportionate to that of pigs. The latter fed in the forests; the former on the grassy downland from which trees had largely been cleared. The Neolithic expansion of cultivation at the expense of the forest appears to have been accompanied by a diminution in the number of pigs and an increase in that of other animals. Sheep were valued chiefly for their wool. The fleece varied greatly in quality from one part of Europe to another. The value attached to English, Spanish or North African wool not only led to an important trade, but inevitably brought about an increased concentration of sheep-breeding. Sheep capable of producing a good quality fleece were bought and transported from one country to another. The merino sheep of North Africa was introduced into Spain, and, crossbred with local strains, led to an improvement in the quality of Spanish wool.

The records give a false impression of the number of farm animals because they relate, as a general rule, only to the demesne. While peasant obligations were listed, peasant assets were not. Thus we may have good evidence for large flocks and herds on the demesne, while the peasants' relative lack of animals went undocumented. The four large Carolingian manors in the north of France were unusually well stocked, and the record, contained in the *Brevium exempla*, gives a very detailed list of the animals. Grouped according to the four broad categories, the totals are:

|         | Annappes | Vitry | Cysoing | Somain | Total |
|---------|---------|-------|---------|--------|-------|
| Horses  | 72      | 101   | 53      | 62     | 288   |
| Cattle  | 127     | 53    | 30      | 42     | 252   |

| | | | | |
|---|---|---|---|---|
| Pigs | 365 | 250 | 160 | 250 | 1025 |
| Sheep | 470 | 220 | 358 | 450 | 1498 |

On these Artois manors sheep already in the ninth century showed a marked predominance over pigs, reflecting perhaps a growing demand for wool in what was to become the cloth-producing region of the Low Countries. Thierry d'Hireçon's account books, kept in the same area five centuries later, suggest that by then the predominance of sheep was much more strongly marked. The total numbers of farm animals, as well as the ratio of one kind to another, changed during the Middle Ages.[55] There is reason to believe that on good cropland, such as parts of the Paris Basin, there was a decline in animal husbandry, as crop farming expanded into the forest and waste. Elsewhere, in northern France and England for example, the expanding market for wool led to an increase in the size of the flocks. In Germany, however, especially eastern, where the forests remained extensive pigs were numerous and important. The number of ploughing oxen must have increased with the extension of arable, but dairy cows remained few except in restricted areas, which included the reclaimed marshlands of the Low Countries and of the north German coast. The accounts of the Count of Flanders for the year 1187 record extensive pasture land, and the *vaccaria*, or dairy farms, produced a considerable income in cheese.[56]

In the Alps also dairy cattle were important in the Middle Ages as they had been during the Roman period. Fortunately the economy of many of the Alpine valleys of Austria is revealed in the *Urbäre*, or extents, of the possessions of a number of Austrian monasteries.[57] Self-sufficing village communities had been established along the valleys, where they had been able to produce hardy cereals, such as rye and oats, and also fodder. Cattle-rearing and dairy farming were important in the earliest records. The pressure of population drove these mountain communities to broaden their use of resources and to extend their agriculture to the higher levels within the mountains where crops could not be grown, but grass was abundant during the summer months. Mountain settlements, usually clusters of small and roughly built huts, known as *swaigae* or *Schwaighofe*, were established on the higher slopes. They were inhabited in summer, and in some of them shepherds and cowherds may have lived throughout the year (compare the Norwegian example, p. 174). At the *swaiga* the cattle were milked and cheese was made. The rents of countless Alpine settlements were discharged in cheese, and throughout the Alpine region cheese was the principal product and export.[58]

Many of the animals in Alpine settlements migrated seasonally between the valley settlements, where some cropfarming was practised, and the higher pastures which could be grazed only in summer. This practice of transhumance made possible the maximum use of such marginal land. It was adopted not only throughout the Alpine range but also in the Pyrenees and Apennines. A Provençal record [59] shows that over 20,000 sheep came down from the Alps to the winter grazing grounds near Saint-Maximin, east of Aix, and a few years later a flock of over 1400 set out for the mountains from the Hospitallers' lands at Manosque, in the Durance valley. Provence and Languedoc appear in winter to have been a huge sheep-run. Tolls were levied on migrating sheep, and the flocks were usually allowed to pause and graze the lands which lay along their route, provided that they could be counted on to contribute as much in the form of manure than they removed as feed.

Similar seasonal movements of stock are recorded in many other parts of Europe. The economy of the Pyrenees was closely similar to that of the Alps.[60] In the Apennines also there was a seasonal movement between the summer and the winter grazing lands. The mountains of the Abruzzi and Basilicata served, as they had done in classical times, as the meeting place for the shepherds and their flocks from the Campagna, the plains of Apulia and all others of the coastal lowlands which border the Italian peninsula. Taxes were levied, just as in Roman times, on the transhumant sheep. The monastery of Camaldoli, in the northern Apennines, leased its mountain pastures to the owners of the huge flocks which in winter grazed the Tuscan Maremma.[61] In the Roman Campagna, in turn exploited by the Popes and ravaged by their enemies, agriculture decayed until, in the words of J. W. Thompson, it became 'a sodden wilderness into which shepherds with their flocks already [fourteenth century] were descending as they do today from the Abruzzi'.[62]

The most extensive and highly organised of such transhumant movements, however, was that which developed in Spain. In the course of the Middle Ages a vast transhumant movement developed between the northern grazing lands where the sheep passed the summer, and those of New Castile, the Guadalquivir valley and the coastal lowlands. Its course was dictated by the climatic conditions and the availability of grazing. The seasonal migration of sheep was here of great antiquity. It probably antedated the Roman conquest; it was recognised in the Visigothic Law, which guaranteed to the shepherds the right to use their migration tracks, but it grew to an immense size and international importance only after the reconquest of the Meseta from the Muslims. The depopulation and destruction which resulted from the wars not only made large areas available for pasture but also removed obstacles to the migrations themselves. At the same time sheep-rearing was one of the few ways in which the dry, empty plains of Spain could be used.

The shepherds had been accustomed to meet at local *mestas* to sort out stray animals and to discuss their common problems of safeguarding their grazing lands and migration routes, or *cañadas* from encroachment by agriculturists. In 1273 King Alfonso X, known as the Wise, of Castile granted a charter to all the shepherds of his realm, thus founding the national Mesta, which continued to grow in importance until the sixteenth century.[63] About 1520 the number of sheep subject to the Mesta reached three million. The breed of sheep was greatly improved by the introduction in the thirteenth century of the merino from North Africa. The quality of the fleece was raised and Spain became, with the decline in England's export, the chief commercial source of wool. The wool trade led to a great increase in the size of the flocks and lay at the basis of the political power of the Mesta. Until the nineteenth century the twice yearly migration of the sheep and the maintenance of their grazing grounds along the *cañadas* continued to be an obstacle to the spread of crop farming.

## Demesne farming

Throughout much of western and central Europe the demesne, where it had not derived from the villa system of the later Roman Empire, was forged from countless parcels of land acquired by purchase or by gift. The process of building the demesne and of organising peasants' obligations and services continued into the thirteenth and even the fourteenth centuries in some parts of Europe. In others the process of establishing the demesne had long since come to an end, and in some it was moving into reverse, and the demesnes were being leased or fragmented. Demesne farming with the labour provided by villein tenants was far from universal. It would probably be true to say that it was usual in the region of three-field agriculture and nucleated villages of northern France and that it extended north-eastwards across Hainault and Brabant towards the Rhine. Even here there were many settlements in which the lord had no demesne and received from his tenants a rent in cash or in kind.[64] West of the open-field region of northern France, the bipartite manor, in which the peasants provided the labour to cultivate the lord's demesne, was rarer, but by no means unknown. In Germany, also, it was usual only in a few areas, chiefly those which had been well settled under the Carolingians. Elsewhere it was uncommon, and on the newly colonised lands of the east it was rare. In Italy, as in northern France, the demesne, *mansus indominicatus*, was frequently met with, but was by no means general.

The twelfth century was a period of change in the tenurial relations of lord and peasant. The role of money in the economy was increasing at this time, and a market in land was beginning to appear. Donations continued to be made to monasteries and other religious institutions, but they were fewer than in earlier centuries. The following table shows how the generosity of laymen in the County of Namur declined in the later Middle Ages:[65]

| | Number of gifts to the Abbey of | | |
| | Floreffe | Geronsart | Waulsort |
| --- | --- | --- | --- |
| 1100–1200 | 87 | 9 | 17 |
| 1200–1250 | 53 | 29 | 20 |
| 1250–1300 | 38 | 27 | 5 |
| 1300–1350 | 11 | 2 | 3 |
| 1350–1431 | 5 | 10 | 8 |

Those lords who would at an earlier age have given lands to religious houses, now sold them for cash. Even the institutions of the Church were short of money. It was a period of ambitious building enterprises. Suger's rebuilding of the abbey of Saint-Denis and his difficulty in raising the money for it, or the continuing financial problems of Peter the Venerable at Cluny, must have been paralleled in hundreds of other institutions as well as in lay households. At the same time the costly luxuries of pilgrimage and crusade, the building of castles and manor houses, and the urge towards conspicuous consumption, all combined to increase the financial needs of lay lords. Both categories of landholders tended to sell off small or marginal units of their estates, and at the same time to consolidate and to operate with greater efficiency the lands which they retained. Such a process is well illustrated on the lands of Saint-Bavon at Ghent.[66] The manors had here been created at a relatively late date – mostly in the eleventh century, by the consolidation of smallholdings, supplemented by reclamation from the waste. Peasant obligations do not appear to have been fully organised before, in the thirteenth century, the monastery began to rid itself of its demesne by leasing it at a money rent.

The needs of the manorial lords went farther. The stereotyped services of their tenants could rarely be made to generate the cash which they needed. It seemed more rewarding to lease some part of the demesne, either as a unit or broken up into *mansi*, and, since the ploughing and other services of the peasants would no longer be needed, to commute these for a money payment. The trend is far from clear, and it is probable that the commutation of peasant services came first, and was followed by a period when the demesnes were worked with hired labour, before it was itself leased. The history of demesne farming in continental Europe remains obscure. There were lords who tried to make their lands more remunerative by exacting to the full the services and payments to which they were entitled and by depressing the status and adding to the burdens of the peasantry. In this they drew some support from current studies in Roman Law with its emphatic recognition of the status of slave. There was a certain tendency amongst the lawyers to equate the half-free villein – a status barely recognised in Roman Law – with the slave whose position was all too well known to the lawyers. A not dissimilar movement of enserfment was to take place several centuries later in eastern Europe (see p. 474).

In general, however, the trend in much of western and central Europe was towards raising the status of the peasant, the elimination of serfdom, and the placing of tenurial arrangements on a cash basis. The progress of this movement is not easy to document in detail, but in rentals and censiers one finds progressively more and more of the peasant obligations assessed and presumably discharged in terms of money. At the Bavarian abbey of Baumburg[67] most obligations in the twelfth century were discharged in kind, while by the mid-thirteenth most of the land was held at a money rent. Early in the fourteenth century even the Cistercian grange at Veulerent, whose tidy management has already been commented upon, was leased at a money rent. The sequence of polyptyques and censiers of the Alsatian monastery of Marmoutier also suggests the gradual abandonment of demesne farming and the spread of a cash nexus between the abbey and its tenants.[68]

In its extreme form, the surrender of labour services and dues in kind took the shape of the grant of franchise. The rural community became free; it was no longer liable for payments of chevage (head-tax) and heriot; for burdensome and unpredictable services, and for other quasi-servile obligations. The desire of the peasants for a free status was compulsive, but freedom was often purchased at a high price. The lord never gave up all his rights; he continued to exact a heavy rent, the profits of the manorial courts, which were essentially the fines imposed on the peasantry, were considerable, and he demanded a payment whenever a piece of land changed hands. And for the franchise itself the payment was sometimes enormous, far exceeding the monetary assets of the community and forcing the peasants to bear a heavy burden of debt for many years.[69]

As a general rule the lord continued to own the mill and leased it to the miller. His *ban* included a monopoly of corn-milling, and he was able to charge whatever the traffic would bear for grinding the peasants' grain. At the same time, in his political role as the local representative of legitimate power, he began to levy taxes. In England the king managed to keep this function in his own hands, and taxes on person or on property were paid into the Exchequer. In much of continental Europe, however, this *taille* or tallage went to the lord. It was arbitrary and oppressive; it came in general to be attached to land, and in some instances became the lord's major source of income.

The peasant thus appears to have replaced one tyranny by another, to have achieved the status of a free man, but to have retained many of his quasi-servile obligations. Although the movement towards money payments and a higher personal status was general throughout Europe, there were some areas where it did not occur. These were as a general rule in remote areas, away from the main stream of medieval life, and here in some instances serfdom and labour services lasted until the eighteenth century.

The commutation of peasant services for a money rent did bring about one gratuitous benefit for the cultivator. The period was marked by rising prices and the falling real value of money. The purchasing power of the rents paid was thus reduced, and represented a diminishing fraction of the income of the peasant household. The lord, of course, attempted to remedy the situation by exacting, in the form of *taille* and as mill-tolls and other payments, what he had lost in rent. He did not everywhere succeed, and there were peasants whose material condition was marginally improved by the commutation of services and the purchase of their freedom from servile obligations.

The spread of cultivation and settlement, especially in the twelfth and thirteenth centuries, was also accompanied by the upgrading of the status of the peasant. The fringe of small and commonly isolated settlements which spread round the older and larger villages was inhabited in general by free, rent-paying peasants. They were too remote from the demesne to be called upon to assist in its cultivation; their tenement was too small for a rent in kind to be worth the trouble of carting to the barn. 'As a general rule,' wrote Verriest[70] of the County of Hainault, 'the lands brought under cultivation in the thirteenth century were let at a rent, either in money or kind.' On the eastern frontier of settlement, similar conditions prevailed. Rents, however, were sometimes paid in kind, perhaps because insufficient money was in circulation.

Furthermore, since much of the grain contributed as rent payment was destined for sale, it was more convenient and possibly more profitable for the lord to sell it himself. Fourteenth-century records[71] show large quantities of grain, chiefly rye, shipped down the Elbe to Hamburg from the newly settled lands to the east of the river. The retention of payments in kind, instead of commuting them for cash, marked the beginning of the depression of the peasantry of eastern Europe. Their reduction to serfdom followed as a reaction to market conditions in the west in the fifteenth and sixteenth centuries.

The joint process of leasing the demesne and commuting peasant services began earlier and was probably carried farther in Italy than in most other parts of Europe. Estates, in particular those of the Church, had formerly been very extensive, as the surveys of the possessions of St Giulia of Brescia and Bobbio show. They appear, furthermore, to have consisted largely of bipartite manors, doubtless deriving in many cases from late Roman *villae*. In the tenth century the monasteries began to divide their demesnes, alienating parcels of land to reward some and to win the goodwill of others. Gerbert of Aurillac, as Pope Sylvester II, in fact, complained of the unnecessary liberality of Bobbio. Some such alienations were nominally for a term of years and in return for a rent payment. All too often, however, the lands were lost for good, and rent or services proved to be difficult or impossible to exact. On the lands of San Martino of Lucca there was no trace of a demesne by the late eleventh century; all had been dissipated. The same was happening on lay estates. There were retainers to be rewarded; ready cash was needed and, above all, the landed class tended to move to the towns where it preferred to live, rentier-fashion, on the revenues of its rural estates. Demesne farming may have survived in remote parts of Italy, but over the country as a whole agriculture had passed by the thirteenth century into the hands of free peasants. Fra Salimbene described how during the wars of the Guelphs and the Ghibellines of the thirteenth century the citizens of many north Italian towns provided armed guards for the peasants as they worked in the fields nearby. The peasants may not have dwelled in the towns, but it was probably the citizens who owned the fields.

In Spain the situation resembled that in central and eastern Europe, and for the same reason. Within the security of the northern mountains, one tended to find large estates, bipartite manors and a servile peasantry. To the south, on the plains of Old Castile and later of New, the land was being resettled as the Moors withdrew southwards. As in central Europe, *locatores* arranged for the transport and settlement of groups of peasants, who, like their central European counterparts, enjoyed a greater degree of personal freedom than those who remained in the north. In Spain also, especially in New Castile, large areas were left thinly peopled and without any recognised seigneurs. In these circumstances, the leaders of the northern forces, exercising their right of *aprisio*, carved out large estates for themselves. This was the origin of the *latifundia* of Spain. The free peasants who were established on them came in time to be depressed, just as were those on the similar great estates in the east. Most often the peasants bought protection at the price of accepting some degree of subservience to a seigneur.[72]

In the earlier Middle Ages there was in most parts of Europe a clear idea of how much land the peasant household needed. It was the *mansus* or *hoba*, a variable area of cropland, but on average from ten to fifteen hectares. There may have been a time when every household had just this, but already in the ninth century the polyptyques show that many *mansi* had been divided. During the following three centuries *mansi* came to be divided and subdivided until a quarter-*mansus* was thought to be, if not sufficient, then at least as much as a peasant family could expect. By the late thirteenth and early fourteenth century the pattern of peasant holdings presented a picture of utmost confusion, with many of the peasant holdings reduced to a few *journaux* or ploughlands. A survey of the manor of Longueil, in Normandy, of the early fourteenth century, showed an extreme subdivision of holdings, in which the smallest had been reduced to only a half-verge – about an eighth of an acre.[73] Dubled has shown[74] a similar extreme division of holdings in Alsace, and Genicot in the County of Namur.[75] In three villages in the latter, at the end of the thirteenth century, most peasant holdings were of less than six hectares and many were of under two. At the manor of Beuvrequem, no less than 43 per cent of the peasants had each under two hectares.

The most extreme form of fragmentation and division of peasant holdings was probably to be found around the towns. In some measure this was a consequence of the more specialised and intensive cultivation adopted in order to supply the urban market; to some extent also it reflected the part-time agricultural pursuits of many of the citizens, and their tendency to invest in the purchase of small parcels of land. The extremes of subdivision were probably to be found in Flanders and around Paris. At one village in the former more than two-thirds of its households each had no more than a single arpent (about an acre) of vineyard or cropland, and a further sixth had only two. The *Veil Rentier*,[76] a polyptyque of about 1275 of the lands of Jehan de Pamele-

Audenarde, mostly lying between the Scheldt and the Dendre, shows an extreme subdivision of farm holdings. Many were reduced to two or three bonniers (3 to 4 acres), and none appear to have been capable of supporting a family. At a village in the Paris region, cropland measuring 155 arpents (about 150 acres) was fragmented into no less than 271 separate parcels.[77]

The division and subdivision of farm holdings was undoubtedly most intense in areas which had been longest settled. It was not as serious – if, indeed, it was serious at all – in the eastern frontier of settlement, and in such western areas of sparse population and poor soil, such as the Auvergne, it seems never to have been carried to the extremes found, for example, near Paris. This division of land, in some measure, brought about its own remedy. Some peasants, driven from the land by the smallness of their holdings and their consequent inability in a bad year to extract even a bare livelihood from them, sold out to wealthier and more successful neighbours. A market developed in land, and gradually larger, and perhaps more compact holdings were created in a piecemeal fashion. Herlihy has demonstrated[78] that in southern France and Italy this movement towards the reconsolidation of holdings made great progress from the eleventh century, while the dispossessed moved away and made their clearances elsewhere.

No doubt increasing population was the principal factor in the division of farm holdings, just as the demand for land sent up the payments – entry fines and the like – payable by the peasants when they took over a tenement. But, if a whole *mansus* or *hoba* had been considered necessary in the early Middle Ages to support a peasant family, it is inconceivable that, without any other change, a small fraction of a manse could have sufficed in the thirteenth century. No doubt, the peasants were able to supplement their diminishing holding with their rights in the meadow, common and woodland, though these were also, presumably, subject to the same process of division and subdivision. There must have been an increase in the productivity of arable farming, perhaps, as Duby suggests,[79] as a result of a shorter period of fallow; perhaps through the introduction of more efficient tools and equipment, including the wheeled mouldboard plough, and more efficient types of harness; perhaps even by the more careful selection of seed. The yield ratios appear, from the scanty evidence available, to have increased during the period. Marginal changes in the productivity of farming must have helped to compensate for the diminishing size of the average holding; but not completely. Everything points to the progressive impoverishment of the peasantry. The emergence of a small class of wealthy farmers, able to buy up parcels of land and lease the demesne, like the kulaks in modern Russia, was made possible only by the depression of the rest.

*Land-values and grain prices*
Unfortunately there are too few records to allow one to trace in detail the changes in the price of land. The local land market became increasingly vigorous but demand was continually forcing up the level of prices. Herlihy has shown[80] that in Tuscany land values continued to rise until the third quarter of the thirteenth century, after which they began to drop in sympathy with falling grain prices. The latter was probably a response to the development of a long-distance grain trade and the import of wheat from less urbanised areas of Italy as much as to the reduced population. Elsewhere, where there were no cheap imports to deflate the price of local grain, the price levels probably kept up, and with them, in all probability, the value of land.

It is not until the later fourteenth century that price series became available. They all show extreme year to year fluctuations, depending on the quality of the harvest and the resulting abundance or scarcity of grain (Fig. 5.6). At the same time, there were sharp variations in price within quite small areas, reflecting the local incidence of drought, frost or excessive rainfall. Transport was so undeveloped that we do not have a grain market covering a large area, except perhaps in such regions as Tuscany or Flanders, where there were large imports and a developed system of internal communications. Instead, there was a series of local markets within each of which prices were regulated by local conditions. They were not, however, a simple function of the supply and demand of foodstuffs. There were other and more complicating factors. The peasant may himself have been in debt to a money lender; he may have mortgaged his crop for a loan with which, perhaps, to redeem some of his servile obligations or to discharge one of his traditional, social duties. He may even have sold his crop 'forward' before it had even matured, he himself gambling

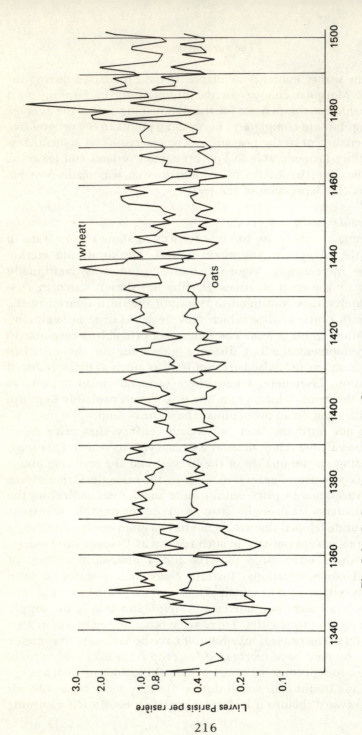

Fig. 5.6 Grain prices at Douai, after Monique Mestayer, 'Les prix du blé et de l'avoine de 1329 à 1793', *Ann. E.S.C.*, xlv (1963), 157–76.

on a low and the merchant on a high market price after harvest.

A second factor lay in the circumstances of cropping. In most areas two or more grain crops were in joint production. If the panifiable grain, wheat or rye, was the primary object of husbandry, then one can regard the oats as a byproduct, the output of which in good years might even be in excess of local needs. The result was in general, to keep the price of oats fairly low. When one considers that the labour of growing oats was as great as that of cultivating wheat or rye, and that the yield ratio was appreciably lower, oats appear to have been an uneconomic crop, grown, apart from their consumption by animals and their use in brewing, because the system demanded a spring sown crop.

Artois and West Flanders were an important source of breadcrops for the towns of the Low Countries. Douai, on the river Scarpe, was a collecting centre for cereals which were taken by boat downriver to Ghent and other towns, and it is likely that Thierry d'Hireçon's wheat moved by this route to the market. A run of wheat and oats prices exists for Douai – from 1329, with only slight interruptions, until the French Revolution.[81] Prices were fairly low at the beginning of this period, but rose in the early 1340s. Prices moved higher in the last third of the century, but if any long-term change can be discerned through the violent short-term fluctuations of the fifteenth century, it is in a downward direction until about 1460. Thereafter the trend was clearly upwards, and continued so until the mid-seventeenth century (Fig. 5.6). At other markets in northern France and the Low Countries, particularly at Valenciennes, there was a fall in prices in the last quarter of the fourteenth century, and a rise in the first third of the fifteenth. It is difficult to relate these changes to fluctuations in demand, resulting from changes in population. It is more likely that they reflect political and economic conditions, the interruption of supplies from France or the import of grain to the Flemish towns from overseas.[82]

## THE LATER MIDDLE AGES

The effect of the Black Death was to reduce the supply of rural labour, and to hasten the fragmentation or leasing of the demesne. The landlords tended first to commute labour services for a money payment and then to give up the direct cultivation of the demesne. This had been happening before the Black Death; it was intensified by the shortage of farm labour in the later fourteenth and the fifteenth centuries. There was, on the part of the seigneurs, an undoubted desire to retain possession of some part of their land under their own direct control. There was a certain prestige in growing or producing their own food supply, and this was especially true of wine. Demesne vineyards were often retained in the lord's hands long after the demesne itself had been leased. On the other hand, labour to work the demesne was scarce and expensive. Labour services had been widely commuted before the Black Death; domestic slaves had long since disappeared from most of Europe, and the seigneurs had, as a general rule, learned to work their lands with hired labour. The cost of the latter now rose so high that the profits of direct farming, especially if any significant part of the produce was sold in the open market, were neutralised.

The seigneurs had long been accustomed to granting, leasing or selling small and outlying parcels of land. They would thus have rid themselves, usually for a money rent, of demesnes which had ceased to be worth the trouble of working. The process continued. Demesnes, where they were retained, were reduced in size until they could be managed with the available resources. There seems to have been a certain reluctance on the part of seigneurs, both lay and ecclesiastic, to fragment the demesne. Such a step was likely to be irreversible; on the other hand, if the demesne were leased to a 'farmer' for a term of years there was always a possibility that it could again be worked directly by its lord if he wished. Data are at present too scanty to permit one to assess the relative importance of the several ways of disposing of the demesne. It seems, however, that leasing the demesne to a farmer, who worked himself together with his family and hired supplementary labour, was perhaps the commonest method, especially on the lands of the Church.

It would be surprising if suitable lessees could always be found. They had to be skilled and successful farmers, and they needed considerable capital to work a large demesne farm. They were probably found amongst the ranks of the richer peasants, who thus gravitated toward the status of the English yeoman of a later age. In continental Europe a successful 'farmer' could approximate the ranks of the lowest aristocracy. Scarcity of 'farmers' may have been a factor in the development and spread of the practice of *métayage*, or share-cropping.

This practice consisted in leasing a parcel of land for a term of years, or of lives, in return for a fraction of the crop. This was rarely less than a third and sometimes as much as two-thirds. In return, the lord provided part or even all of the capital needed to operate the tenancy: seed corn, tools, equipment, and draught animals. The peasant thus had a kind of insurance against bad years, since his rent payment fell with a diminished yield, and he was able to overcome his lack of working capital. The lord, on the other hand, got his lands worked, usually on conditions favourable to himself; he could continue to oversee their management, and could, at the expiry of any lease, take them back, if he wished, into his own hands.

Leases in métayage were known and used in the twelfth century, but did not become widespread until the late thirteenth and fourteenth. Even so, they were not much used except in Italy and southern France. Métayage was relatively common around towns, and was probably not unconnected with the acquisition by burgesses of rural plots which they wanted to have cultivated without too much effort on their own part. In parts of Italy and France, it is claimed, up to three-quarters of the farmland was held by contracts of métayage, a system which continued, with no fundamental change, into the nineteenth century.

These trends in tenurial relations were not common to the whole of Europe. There were many remote areas which lagged in their economic and social development behind the rest of the continent. Here the demesne continued to be worked directly, and labour dues to be demanded of the peasants. Such areas were parts of the Massif Central of France, of Brittany, and of the hilly areas of Germany. This conservatism arose in large measure from the relative isolation of these areas, their remoteness from urban markets and the feeble extent to which a money economy had penetrated them. In general they were areas which had been urbanised to only a slight degree.

This is not altogether true of eastern Europe. This broad belt of territory, stretching from the Baltic Sea southwards and eastwards towards the Danube basin and the Russian steppe, was not without towns, some of which became large and important commercial centres. The region was not merely conservative in its economic and tenurial organisation; it was reactionary. Its trend of development in the later Middle Ages was towards the great estate, a servile peasantry, and the exaction of labour obligations. A market economy had never developed here as it had in western Europe, and there was a smaller volume of circulating money. On the other hand, the peasants' obligations to their lords were less onerous than in the west, and the urge to escape them or to commute them for a money payment was less compelling. In these circumstances the seigneurs were able to maintain their rights, and even to extend and enlarge them.

Their inducement was in very large measure economic. The demand for bread crops was beginning to increase in western Europe during the later Middle Ages. Population was again increasing, and it was easier for the towns of north-western Europe to satisfy their needs by means of imports than by expanding internal cultivation. Hence a market slowly developed for the bread cereals of eastern Europe, chiefly rye and wheat, shipped down the Baltic rivers to the ports at their mouths and thence by sea to the west. It was the profits to be obtained from the grain trade which, more than anything else, led the seigneurs along the eastern borderlands of Europe to increase both the obligations of their peasants and the amount of grain available to sell to the merchants of Hamburg, Lübeck, Stettin, and Danzig.

In the rest of Europe demesne farming was less secure than ever before. The lords were faced not only with low grain prices, possibly made yet lower by competition from eastern Europe, but also with the shortage and high price of farm labour. How they must have wished that they could put back the clock and restore the corvée once owed by the peasants. Some may, indeed, have tried to do so, and here and there a few may even have succeeded. Yet the prestige that went with the ownership of an estate and the direct management of a 'home' farm had never been so high. Not since the classical period were so many treatises on agriculture and the management of estates written and published for the guidance of the landed gentry.

The fifteenth century has sometimes been regarded as the golden age of the European peasant. Food prices – and thus the cost of living – were sagging, and the real value of money rents had been depreciated by the earlier inflation. But the number of those who could profit from these conditions was probably small. There had never been a time when peasant holdings had been approximately equal; indeed, the polyptyques showed a great inequality in both status and possessions as early as the ninth century. By the later Middle Ages the difference between the well-to-do peasant and the poorest had greatly increased. The rich peasant was able to hire labour, the higher cost of which was offset by his diminished rent payments. The poorest, with little or no land to cultivate, were obliged to sell their services. While there was a market for farm labour, it is not improbable that this market was only locally important and that it originated in the needs of demesne farming and of the more wealthy peasants. If in any rural community these were not present, there was likely to be little demand for the services of the cottagers. In any event, the circumstances of the farming year were such that the labour needs were considerable at the time of the autumn and spring ploughing and at harvest time, and slight at other periods of the year. The day labourer, whose wage at the best of times was at little more than a subsistence level, was thus likely to be un-employed for a significant part of the year.

One may fairly ask why there should have been landless peasants at a time when the population had been reduced by pestilence and the area of cultivated land had, as a whole, been contracting. The answer probably lies in the fact that it was marginal land and marginal settlements which were in general abandoned. Large villages on good soil were probably little, if at all, reduced in size. The cottager could not go to the abandoned lands on the frontier of settlement not only because these lands were poor in quality and difficult to cultivate, but also because, being a cottager, he did not have the tools and equipment to cultivate them. Such conditions favoured a métayage tenancy, which was, in fact widely adopted in Italy and much of France. But conditions of métayage were often onerous in the extreme, and at their easiest never made a wealthy man out of the peasant.

In the more fluid social conditions of the later Middle Ages, when the population was fluctuating and mobile and the relations of lord and peasant were changing, there was abundant oppor-tunity for the clever and the unscrupulous. Speculation in com-modities and in land was rife. Estates were broken up, but new estates were pieced together. Well-to-do peasants became mer-chants, bought more land, and aspired to the ranks of the gentry. The poorer, the less clever, or the less fortunate were, by contrast, obliged to mortgage or sell their lands, and sank both socially and economically in the scale of peasant society. It was an age of opportunity, as indeed are all periods of relatively rapid social change, but not all persons were in a position to benefit from it and few, in all probability, reaped any great rewards.

# 6

# The development of the medieval town

There have been three periods in the history of Europe when the founding of towns was a major preoccupation of European man. The town, as an institution, originated outside Europe, and the earliest European urban revolution was anticipated by at least two thousand years in the Middle East, in the Indian subcontinent and in China. The idea of living in towns took root in the Greek world of the seventh or eighth century B.C. By the fifth century urban living had become the norm, and Greek culture was unthinkable outside the framework of the πολις (*polis*). To Aristotle civilised man was essentially a creature suited to living in the *polis*.

The Greek *polis*, or something closely akin to it, was diffused through much of the Mediterranean basin by the Greeks themselves, by the Etruscans, the extent of whose debt to the Greeks is far from clear, and by the Romans. The Greeks carried their own idea of the city to the Middle East and even to central Asia. The civilisation of Rome, no less than that of Greece, was conceived within an urban framework, and urban institutions were established on the farthest frontiers of the Empire.

The fourth and later centuries of our era were marked by the decay of urban life and by the contraction in size and even the abandonment of towns. A second period of urban growth, with which this chapter is primarily concerned, began in the tenth century and culminated in the thirteenth. There followed a second period of stagnation in urban life. Most towns ceased to grow in the fifteenth century; some declined in size, and very few new towns were founded except on Europe's eastern frontier.

223

Even the sixteenth century saw no general revival of urban growth. Rather, a small number of cities grew rapidly: Antwerp, Cadiz, Lisbon, Paris, Madrid and Amsterdam, but most were little larger than they had been a century earlier. The seventeenth and eighteenth centuries were also years of stagnation in urban life or, at best, of only very slow growth. It was not until the nineteenth century that the third urban revolution produced the pattern of cities and towns we know today.

There was, of course, a degree of continuity between each of these three phases of urban expansion and growth. Though the majority of Greek *poleis* had disappeared well before the end of the classical period, most of those of the Roman Empire in the West survived, though greatly reduced in size. It was thus on classical foundations that the medieval network of towns was built. Similarly, the latter provided the framework within which, by a process of selective growth, the industrial and commercial cities of nineteenth and twentieth century Europe emerged.

Comparison between these three phases of urban development must not, however, be pressed too far, for urbanism meant different things at different times. The Greek *polis* was not the same kind of an institution as the medieval town; it was not even identical with the Roman *civitas*, and all differed fundamentally from the modern industrial city. It is impossible to formulate, except in the most general terms, a definition of town or city which is applicable to all three phases of urban development.

The dichotomy between town and country, between urban and rural pursuits, which prevails today, was absent from the classical town, and was not a regular feature of the medieval. Juridically the *polis* and the *civitas* were part and parcel of their surrounding territory. The medieval town, by contrast, was separate in law and in institutions from its countryside, just as it was physically cut off by its walls. Two features, however, towns of all ages had in common. In the first place they were compactly or densely built; in other words, they were highly nucleated, and secondly, non-agricultural pursuits were relatively important in them. They contained craftsmen, traders and merchants, but one cannot exclude agriculture from amongst their occupations. Indeed, most of the Greek *poleis* were predominantly agricultural, and in all except the largest medieval towns, rural pursuits continued to be important and in some instances dominant.

The distinction between town and village has always been difficult to draw. In function they might be closely similar; in status they were poles apart. The central place or town of the Roman *civitas* was the provincial symbol of Rome, a seat of local government and of the imperial cult, and the residence of local rentiers and 'gentry'. Stripped of these functions it reverted to a semirural community like any provincial *vicus*.

With the revival of urban living from the tenth century onwards, towns developed new functions, but these were not necessarily those which had characterised the towns of the classical world. The Roman *civitas*-capital was to only a small degree a centre of crafts and manufactures. In some medieval towns, by contrast, this role was generally important and sometimes preponderant. The Roman towns lay, in many instances, at the focus of routes, but the Roman road system was not thronged by merchants carting goods from one town to another, nor were urban markets as a general rule engaged in a large scale in long-distance trade. The medieval town, by contrast, was essentially a market centre, and the larger the town the more far-reaching was its nexus of commercial relations.

### THE URBAN REVOLUTION

But what distinguished the medieval town from contemporary villages and also from both the capitals of the *civitates* of the Romans and the *poleis* of the Greeks was the special status enjoyed by its citizens. At a time when rural population was bound to the soil, subjected to servile obligations, made to perform day-works and boon-works, and to pay heriot and merchet at death, the citizen of the town was free, or at least relatively so. He could move about as he wished; he could change his occupation; he could have his son educated and allow him to take orders in the Church without first obtaining leave of a lord.

Towns had a communal organisation – as also did many villages– but they were freer than rural communities to organise their own affairs. They could levy taxes on persons and commodities. They had a court and administered justice in some limited respects. But there were degrees of freedom between medieval towns, and these were spelled out in the charters by which the towns were incorporated and granted their privileges. In many instances the charters were given to towns which already existed in embryo;

sometimes they constituted a confirmation and legal recognition of privilieges which already existed by a kind of prescriptive right. In other cases the grant of a charter antedated the growth of the town and was intended to encourage citizens to come and settle. The priority in time of the grant of a charter and the creation of an urban settlement is not an easy one to decide.

The lords or seigneurs who granted the charters of incorporation to new towns rarely surrendered all rights over their inhabitants. Burgage rents, market dues and the profits of courts continued to flow into the lord's coffers, and privileges were usually granted to a town in the hope that it would grow and the revenue to be gained from it would continue to increase. The burgesses rarely obtained more than a restricted and conditional freedom to practise trade and the crafts and to act in a corporate capacity. Many are the instances of the suppression of urban privileges, and of the renewal of a charter only at a high price.

As towns grew in size and wealth the burgesses of many of them were emboldened to demand greater freedom, amounting in some instances to an almost complete autonomy. In this way the communal movement of the eleventh, twelfth and thirteenth centuries was born. The earliest towns to experience this revolutionary movement were episcopal, because in the eleventh century the larger and more prosperous among them were the seats of bishops. From the tenth century the bishops and, for that matter, the abbots of urban monasteries, had encouraged the growth of their towns, but had attempted to impose their own control upon them. The two policies were in mutual conflict, and prosperity bred revolt among the burgesses of the towns.

The communal movement appeared first in Italy, and it was there that it achieved its greatest successes. The tradition of urban organisation was older here than in other parts of Europe, and, indeed, derived from the *civitates* of the Roman Empire. Long-distance trade revived earlier here, and there was already in the tenth century a sizeable body of merchants eager to increase their control over markets and routes. Lastly, rural feudalism was never as strongly developed in Italy as it was to the north of the Alps. Indeed, as will be noted later, the tendency was for the rural and landowning aristocracy to live in the towns and to provide from their ranks not only the merchants but also the patricians into whose hands the destinies of the towns passed.

The idea of the town as an autonomous community of merchants, traders and craftsmen spread northwards from the Mediterranean. In north-western Europe, however, it faced more vigorous opposition, from both ecclesiastical and lay lords. In 1070 the citizens of Le Mans threw off the control of their bishop and declared themselves a commune. Their example was followed in the cities of the Rhineland, particularly in Worms and Cologne. Conflict continued for some two centuries with victory by and large resting with the cities. Their cause was greatly helped by the support given to it by the German emperors who found in the cities a powerful ally against the Church. All the larger German towns became 'imperial cities', dependent only on the emperor, and as imperial power diminished the autonomy of the cities approximated more closely to political sovereignty.

The communal movement had little success in France and none at all in England, despite the efforts in this direction of the city of London. In both countries the crown succeeded in curbing the pretensions of the cities without, as a general rule, alienating them. Indeed, it found in the commercial classes of the towns a convenient ally against the pretensions of the feudal nobility, and in England it drew them into the system of parliamentary representation in the course of the thirteenth century. Only in Italy, Germany and, to a more limited extent, the Low Countries did the cities achieve a sufficient degree of freedom and independence to allow them to pursue their own policies. In Switzerland (part of the German Empire) some of them entered the Swiss Confederation as individual cantons. Indeed, Zug, Zurich and Bern were the earliest accessions to the original Forest Cantons. In Germany itself they formed leagues to assist one another against the princes who still had claims on their obedience. In north Germany, no less than about a hundred cities and towns belonged at one time or another to the Hanseatic League,[1] which itself acted as an independent and sovereign body (see p. 378).

In northern and central Italy the sovereignty and independence of the city were carried to their extreme. The towns annexed the surrounding territory and eliminated what remained of rural feudalism, until they bordered on one another, and the whole country became a mosaic of city states. The absorption of the surrounding rural areas became a necessity as the city grew to be more and more independent. In England and France the king's law guaranteed to every community the right to purchase foodstuffs as well as the raw materials for its crafts in the surrounding villages and rural areas. As the city became more nearly sovereign and independent, so it displaced or destroyed the one authority which might have guaranteed its access to the rural sources of food and materials. Thus the city became a city–state, using the *contado* which it controlled to supply at least part of its physical needs.

Urban control of rural territory was carried to its extreme in Italy, but it was not unknown elsewhere. It was an accepted principle in much of Europe that any town might exercise its authority over a narrow tract of surrounding territory. In Germany, at least, this was established by convention as the *Bannmeile*, the mile-wide strip which encircled the walls of the town. In a few instances German cities came close to Italian in their subjugation of rural territory. The limits of Basel, Zug and Schaffhausen, and of Hamburg and Bremen have been perpetuated in cantonal and *Land* boundaries. The extreme case in Germany of the Middle Ages was Nuremberg, where the city fathers exercised jurisdiction over 66 square kilometres of territory, within which they both acquired land and produced a significant part of the city's requirements in food.[2]

The medieval town, at least in continental Europe, was walled, and without its defences it was no town. In England only about a hundred out of a total of several hundred incorporated towns were ever walled.[3] A few others – Cambridge, for example – were protected by a ditch, and doubtless there were some, like Bridgwater in Somerset, whose outermost houses were interconnected to present a continuous wall, broken only where roads crossed it from within the town to the surrounding countryside. But on the continent even the humblest *Zwergstadt* was protected by walls of some kind. These range from massively built curtain walls with drum towers at intervals, like those which survive at Goslar and Nuremberg, to fences constructed of wood, with large wooden entrance towers, together with the further protection of a ditch. Such towns are represented in the seventeenth-century topographical writings of the Merians.[4]

In England town walls were symbolic and decorative. Those of Coventry were maintained in some kind of repair, because, it was said, they allowed people to move dry-foot from one part of the city to another along the rampart walk. In continental Europe their intent was more serious. At Cologne control of the walls, and thus of the defence and security of the city, was fiercely disputed between the archbishop and the citizens – a struggle in which the citizens ultimately triumphed. A town's walls were symbolic of the separation of the town from the countryside. The small number of gates by which it could be entered were often decorated with a coat-of-arms, symbol of the town's corporate identity, and with other iconographic detail intended to impress the visitor with its might and majesty. One is continually amazed at the size and elaboration of the walls, towers and gates even of very small towns. Mainbernheim, in Bavaria, for example, retains today a circuit of walls of about 1000 metres in length, with two gates and several towers. The area enclosed by them is only 8 hectares.[5] Its population could never have been much more than 500 and the little town was in the Middle Ages, as it remains today, predominantly agricultural. One is left wondering how a small and mainly rural community could have been able to afford the luxury of so ambitious a building operation as these walls and towers represent.

The immense number of urban sieges that have been recorded in both Germany and Italy show that the walls had a grimmer purpose than mere ostentation. They are a reflection of that dichotomy which existed between urban society and the feudal order, and they served to protect the hard-won liberties of the former from the claims and infringements of the latter. The cost, nevertheless, of their construction and maintenance must have been a severe burden on the finances of every town that built them and kept them in good fighting order (see p. 272).

The public buildings of the medieval town, no less than its walls, gave emphasis to its corporate existence, and the prominence which these received at the hands of the planner and builder was, in a rough kind of way, a measure of the strength and autonomy of the town. Public buildings, other than ecclesiastical, were relatively humble in England and in much of France. They were built on a vastly more lavish scale in Italy, but it was in northern France, the Low Countries and the great commercial cities of Germany and east-central Europe that their scale and elaboration overshadowed that of the city churches. The Old Hall at Bruges, the Cloth Hall at Ypres, the *Ratusz* at Wrocław (Breslau) and gild halls at countless European cities were the

Fig. 6.1    Seal of the city of Ypres.

outward expression of the wealth, pride and independence of their burgesses. It is no accident that the secular monuments of the medieval cities were conceived on the largest scale in just those areas where the communal movement was most vigorous.

The relation between the growth and spread of the city during the Middle Ages and the economic fortunes of the continent is a close one. The towns were the focal points in the nexus of trading relations and also the chief – but by no means the only – centres of manufacture. The growth in the volume both of specialised production and of trade was necessarily accompanied by the expansion of the centres in which they were carried on. The town was the product of regional and inter-regional trade. The existence of specialised urban crafts was predicated on that of an extensive market and of the availability of a mechanism for distributing their products. The town was not only a centre of manufacture; it was also a centre of consumption, and as the wealth of merchants and entrepreneurs increased, so also did the volume and range of its transactions.

The growth, stagnation and renewed growth of the towns reflects the curve of medieval economic history. It is extra-ordinarily difficult to measure the increase in number and in size of the medieval towns. The data on their population are scanty, and town size can at best be inferred from the numbers of hearths or of fighting men or by walled area (see p. 251). Nor are the data on the foundation of towns particularly helpful. Most grew from a pre-urban nucleus (see p. 238), and at some stage in this development the community was granted a charter and endowed with urban privileges. It was made a town by a particular act on the part of its suzerain, and for this we often know the precise date. We do not always know when traders and craftsmen first gathered there.

The eastward progression of the town from western Germany into east-central Europe, so often mapped and described, does not portray the diffusion across the continent of a particular form of economic activity, but rather the spread of the act of incorporating communities which, in very many instances had existed previously, by the grant of a charter of privileges. Nor was the possession of a charter any guarantee that economic growth would continue. In all too many instances the incorporation of a small community was a desperate and ultimately vain attempt to stimulate growth and expansion.

Nevertheless the graph of town foundation, in the legal sense of that term, is a measure, however approximate, of economic growth (Fig. 3.1). In England the granting of charters on a lavish scale was a feature of the period which on other grounds is known to have been one of vigorous expansion. The evidence of German towns is even clearer, because here, except in the Rhineland, there was no heritage of urban settlements from the Roman Empire. An increasing number of new towns was founded until the closing decades of the thirteenth century. The first half of the fourteenth witnessed a falling-off in their number, and this decline became yet more marked in the later fourteenth century and throughout the fifteenth.

Few towns were founded after the beginning of the fourteenth century, at least in western and central Europe, and existing towns showed little evidence of growth. The previous century had been one in which the more important commercial centres had grown rapidly. This growth was reflected in the built-up, or at least in the walled area of the town. All the larger cities of the continent could show successive lines of walls, as suburbs were included within the walled area. Cologne, Ghent, Bruges, Basel, Paris, indeed almost all the larger trading cities of western and central Europe and many of those of northern Italy underwent

231

this process. In few instances, however, do we find any major extension of the walled area after 1300, and there is no important case later than the Black Death. One of the last important examples is the building, described by Giovanni Villani, of the walls of Florence between 1284 and 1333. The enlarged city area was never, until modern times, more than partially built up; the growth of population had already been halted when the walls were being built, though it is doubtful whether the patricians who controlled the city could have been aware of the fact.

Clearly, then, cities ceased in all parts of Europe except eastern, to grow both in size and in number towards the end of the thirteenth century and early in the fourteenth. Thereafter their fortunes fluctuated. Both the pattern of trade and the structure of demand were changing. Some cities, prominent amongst them the traditional clothing centres of Flanders, stagnated or decayed. Others adapted more readily to the changing economic conditions, amongst them Lyons, Geneva, Brussels, and continued to prosper, though their rate of growth was very much slower than it had been in the thirteenth century.

## The Mediterranean: region of urban continuity

Edith Ennen[6] has emphasised the contrast in urban history between Italy and southern France; north-western Europe, and the areas of Europe which lay outside the boundaries of the Roman Empire (p. 71).

In the Mediterranean region towns declined in importance during the centuries which followed the collapse of the Western Empire, but they continued to be inhabited. Rentiers disappeared from their villas; merchants became fewer in their markets, and some towns became little more than refuges for the rural population of surrounding areas. But there was no general, prolonged or widespread interruption of urban life in Italy, and in Spain also most of the larger cities continued to be inhabited. The Lombards perpetuated, by the Edict of Rothari (643), a system of urban territories which closely resembled that of the Roman *civitates*.[7] The population of Rome itself fell to a mere fraction of its size under the Empire. The more southerly parts of the city were abandoned; religious institutions invaded the area once dignified by palaces and temples, and the citizens were concentrated in the area of flat land which had once been the *Campus Martius*.

But the evidence for the continuity of urban and commercial life is overwhelming. Ravenna remained a port and trading centre, in close contact with Constantinople, and it was not until the sixth century that its basilicas, with their Byzantine inspired mosaics were built. But the harbour of Ravenna was poor and, furthermore was silting rapidly. In the course of the seventh and eighth centuries its commercial activity began gradually to pass to settlements which lay around the Gulf of Venice, foremost amongst them Venice itself. Within the Lombard plain the cities of the later Roman Empire continued to be the seats of bishops and the scene of an active trade. Pavia in particular became a centre from which goods, imported from the Byzantine Empire through Ravenna or Venice, were distributed by way of the Alpine routes to north-western Europe.

The size and commercial activity of the north Italian cities may have fallen well below even their late Roman level. Trade was, apart from the salt from the Venetian lagoons, restricted to luxury goods, but there can be no doubt that most Italian cities, unlike those of north-western Europe, continued to carry on specifically urban activities. The course of trade was strongly influenced by political considerations. Seaborne trade was mainly with the Byzantine Empire and only to a small degree with Spain and North Africa. The Byzantine Empire continued to exercise at least a nominal control over southern Italy and also over a few coastal enclaves farther to the north, including Venice itself. These territories offered considerable advantages for trade with the Levant, and it was their coastal settlements which became the earliest trading communities of medieval Italy.

Earliest to achieve commercial predominance was Amalfi. Its trade developed in the ninth century and culminated in the eleventh before, in 1077, it fell to the Normans under Robert Guiscard. The city occupied a cleft in the rugged south coast of the Sorrento peninsula. It had no Roman antecedents; its citizens could never have practised agriculture. It was, like the later port-city of Dubrovnik (Ragusa) given over entirely to trade. Amongst contemporary cities its only rivals in the trade between West and East were its neighbours, Salerno, Naples, and Gaeta; Bari in Apulia, and ultimately Venice. Why, one may ask, did so unpropitious a site with so indifferent a harbour give rise to the greatest commercial city of the tenth and eleventh centuries? The

233

answer probably lies in the fact that here, on the west coast of Italy, merchants could at once enjoy the protection of Byzantine rule and proximity to the cities and commercial routes of northern Italy (see p. 104).

Venice was heir to the trade of Amalfi. Like the latter, it lay within the jurisdiction of the Byzantine Empire, but so remote from its centralised administration that it could enjoy the advantages without any of the liabilities of imperial rule. Its Roman predecessor had been Aquileia, on the mainland to the north-east, destroyed first by the Huns and finally by the Lombards in 568. The islands of the Venetian lagoon provided security for refugees from the mainland; the shallow waters which surrounded them yielded salt, which became one of their earliest articles of trade. By the mid-tenth century a prosperous trading community had grown up, and was to continue to grow and spread over the islands during the succeeding four centuries. Venice differed, however, in an important respect from other cities of early medieval Italy. Byzantine authority gradually lapsed, leaving Venice endowed with an effective sovereignty not only over its own lagoon, but also over the Byzantine enclave on the mainland. Venice was, in fact, born a city state.

Other cities of early medieval Italy were of Roman origin; their relative size and commercial importance had changed. Pisa near the mouth of the river Arno, in Tuscany, had been held back by the Lombards who controlled its hinterland. But in the tenth century it developed as a trading city in close contact with Amalfi to the south and with Provence and Lombardy to the north. Siena, Lucca, Pistoia, Prato, and Florence were the more important of the cities of Tuscany, and amongst them Florence, a comparatively unimportant town under the Roman Empire, had established its primacy by the thirteenth century and was in fact to conquer most of the Tuscan region by the early fifteenth.

Genoa had, perhaps, decayed more than most Roman towns during the early Middle Ages, and its revival came relatively late with the development of trade in the western basin of the Mediterranean Sea. In the Lombard Plain, most of the cities of the later Roman Empire had served as centres of crafts and trade, but a process of selective growth greatly changed their relative prominence. Pavia, linked by the navigable river Po with the ports of the Adriatic Sea, first emerged as a centre of trade. It was then

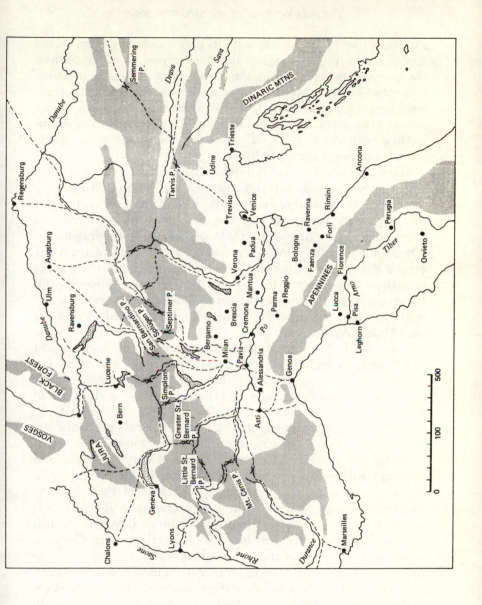

Fig. 6.2    Italy and Italian towns during the later Middle Ages.

235

supplanted by Milan which, with its easy access to the most used Alpine routes (p. 359), became the chief emporium of the plain in the later Middle Ages. Along the central river axis of the plain lay Piacenza, Cremona, Mantua and Ferrara; near the Alpine foothills were Como, Bergamo, Brescia and Verona, and close to the Apennines on the south, Parma and Bologna. All were centres of manufacture, with cloth, in all its immense variety, and metal goods foremost amongst their products.

In the later Middle Ages Italy was characterised by its considerable number of large cities; Venice, Genoa, Milan and Florence were, with the probable exceptions of Paris and Constantinople, the biggest in Europe before the emergence of Antwerp and Amsterdam. This phenomenon was largely due to the fragmentation of much of Italy into city states. Within each of them the central city tended to increase its predominance by restricting the growth of rivals within its *contado*. In few cases, however, did Italian cities continue to grow after the mid-fourteenth century and many of those of the second rank actually declined during the later Middle Ages.

Spain, with the exception of the province of Baetica, had never been as highly urbanised as Italy. In the course of the Germanic and of the subsequent Moorish invasions, many towns disappeared, but in the larger and more important of them urban functions probably survived. Toledo became the seat of the Visigothic kings. Saragossa, Barcelona and Valencia probably saw little interruption of their urban life. The Moors themselves occupied and developed the coastal towns of southern Spain, and Seville, Cordoba and Granada experienced, in the early Middle Ages, one of the most distinguished periods of their history. The coastal towns shared in the commercial revival which was common to the whole western Mediterranean from the twelfth century. Barcelona grew to be a major port-city, but Christian Spain nevertheless remained very much less urbanised than the rest of western Europe. Towns were fewer and very much smaller, and the trend towards urban self-government was less marked. Moorish Spain, however, shared the common Mediterranean trend towards the creation of large towns. Seville, Cordoba and Granada grew earlier and faster than the towns of Christian Spain. Vicens Vives claims[8] that Cordoba had a population of a quarter of a million in the tenth century. Even if this figure is somewhat exaggerated, it was nevertheless the largest city in Europe at this time, with the possible exception of Constantinople.

In the Balkan peninsula urban life decayed and over large areas disappeared during the early Middle Ages. It had never been a vigorous growth, and many of the small towns of the region had been brought into being by the requirements of the military and were sustained by the need to supply the Roman frontier garrisons (see p. 81). They had been overrun and probably destroyed by the Gothic and Slav invaders of the peninsula. Only around the coast did any semblance of urban life continue. The towns of Greece, notably Thessaloniki, Thebes and Corinth survived the invasions, though continuously threatened by them. Athens was reduced to a small community living beneath the steep face of the Acropolis. Along the Adriatic coast, Roman towns were abandoned, some never to be reoccupied, and refugees crowded on to small islands, like Ragusa, or behind ready made defences, like Diocletians's palace on the water's edge at Split (Spalato).

In the course of Justinian's attempts to pacify or reconquer the mountainous interior of the Balkans a large number of towns was founded or restored and fortified. Procopius has left us the names of no less than 215 of them in Epirus, Macedonia and Thrace. The Balkan peninsula was thus, like the north-western fringes of the Empire, an area where urban life disappeared and had to be recreated, slowly and painfully, in very much later centuries.

To this there was one highly important exception. The capital city of the Byzantine Empire saw no interruption and but little contraction in its urban functions since the time when it was refounded by the emperor Constantine early in the fourth century. At a time when cities in the west were becoming smaller its area was enlarged. The defensive walls of Constantine were replaced by the enlarged defences of Theodosius, thus making it the largest city in area after Rome itself. The city may in the sixth century have had a population of half a million. It was, and remained for almost two centuries, the administrative centre of a vast empire. It was, as indeed it had to be with so large a population, the biggest trading centre in Europe, and probably also its largest centre of manufactures.

Constantinople owed its immunity from conquest and the continuity of its urban life in part at least to its site. It lay on a steepsided peninsula, protected on all sides except the west by the waters of the Sea of Marmara and the Bosporus. Its food supply was largely brought in by ship from the Black Sea coast and the Aegean, and a large part of its trade was seaborne. The Levant, furthermore, was by far the richer part of the Roman Empire and, if the Balkans were poorly developed and overrun by invaders at a relatively early date, Syria, Egypt and parts of Anatolia were amongst the richest areas of the civilised world. The Eastern Empire was, lastly, far better administered than the Western. Its central institutions of government never broke down, except when they were seized by the Crusaders or the Turks. Trade and taxes continued to flow into Constantinople until the time when, in 1453, it was beleaguered and ultimately conquered by the Ottoman Turks.

### Urban revival in north-western Europe

In northern Spain, most of France and the Rhineland urban life was interrupted, though in most instances the cities themselves seem never to have been wholly abandoned. It was noted in chapter 2 that the institutions of the Church provided a thread of continuity, and when, in the course of the eleventh century, the cities of northern France again appear in the records, they seem to have been under the firm and authoritarian control of their bishops.

Such cities as Tours, Reims, and Lyons were, under the Merovingians, centres of trade and manufacture, on however small a scale. There is no evidence that they declined in importance in the eighth and ninth centuries; they surely did not cease to be inhabited, except perhaps temporarily and locally under the impact of the Viking raids. Rather, they existed as 'pre-urban nuclei', to use Ganshof's expression, ready to grow again into cities in the tenth and eleventh centuries. The topography of the early medieval city throws some light on its history during the period of its early medieval growth. Many are binary cities; they have two distinct nuclei; the one Roman in origin; the other early medieval; the one administrative and ecclesiastical, the other commercial.

The city of Arras is not only typical of the cities of France but has the further advantage of having been elucidated topographically by Lestocquoy.[9] The Roman *civitas* capital of the Atrebates,

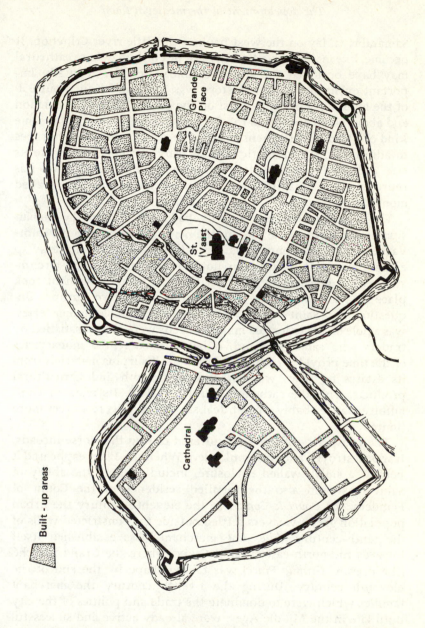

Grande
Place

St.
Vaast

Cathedral

Built - up areas

Fig. 6.3   Arras as a binary town; based on plan of Arras in 1435, in
J. Lestocquoy, *Les Dynasties Bourgeoises d'Arras*, Mém. Comm. Dépt.
Pas-de-Calais.

Samarabriva, lay on the west bank of the little river Crinchon. It became, like many such cities, the seat of a bishop, whose cathedral may have occupied the site of a Roman temple. A vitally important event in the city's history was the foundation about 650 of the monastery of Saint-Vaast on the other side of the Crinchon and about 600 metres from the Roman city. By 800 there was some kind of a trading settlement close to the abbey, with two churches in addition to the monastic church. Any attempt to estimate its size can be little more than guesswork, but Lestocquoy has represented its inhabited area as entirely surrounding the walled monastic precinct.

The focus of economic activity had shifted from the Roman site, now known as the *Cité*, to the new settlement around Saint-Vaast, known by contrast as the *Ville* (Fig. 6). It is not easy to explain this shift. That it was not due primarily to local circumstances is suggested by the fact that a similar movement took place in a dozen or more similar cities of western Europe. Unquestionably Saint-Vaast, like many comparable monasteries, was a pole of attraction. Its material needs were in part satisfied by traders who came here and, if better documented monasteries of the time provide any model, it had itself surplus materials from its estates for sale: woollen and linen cloth and agricultural products. This the cathedral could not rival. Its resident community was probably a great deal smaller, and its resources more limited.

The prosperity of the *Ville* suffered during the Norse inroads. It was destroyed and the monks fled. When the *Ville* reappeared it became a small, walled enclosure, including both the abbey of Saint-Vaast and also the fortified residence of the Count of Flanders, the *Court-le-Comte*. In the eleventh century the urban population grew; weavers settled outside the constricted walls of the tenth-century *Ville*. The merchant class established itself towards the north-east of Saint-Croix, where the Grand Marché (the present *Grande Place*) was taking shape by the end of the eleventh century. During the twelfth century the merchant families which were to dominate the trade and politics of the city until late in the Middle Ages, were already active and successful in the city's trade.[10]

It was the *Ville* of Arras which grew and prospered. Markets were not to be found in the *Cité*, and only a few wealthy merchants made their residence there. Even after the area within the enlarged walls of the *Ville* had been filled up, the citizens were slow in overflowing into the *Cité*, and when they did so they encountered difficulties with the cathedral authorities. In consequence, Arras during the last century of the Middle Ages continued to demonstrate in its topography the twin nuclei from which it had sprung. The *Ville* was densely settled, its merchants were rich (see p. 349), and the majority of its citizens were engaged in craft industries, of which the textile branch, was the most important. By contrast the *Cité* consisted, within its walls, of only three streets, between which lay the cathedral. The rest was made up of gardens and open spaces (Fig. 6.3).

The development of Arras has been traced because its history was typical of that of many cities in north-western Europe. One can list a dozen or twenty which grew round the twin poles of cathedral and monastery. Indeed, almost every medieval episcopal city of France shows this dichotomy, commercial and craft activities always tending to gravitate towards a monastic nucleus. Here the fair was most likely to be held, like that of St Remigius, the wine fair at the monastery of Saint-Rémi at Reims, and the Lendit Fair at the abbey of Saint-Denis, near Paris. The 'city', by contrast, retained its episcopal calm, invaded, as a general rule, to only a small degree by craftsmen and the business activities of merchants.

The *ville*, or *bourg*, lay in some instances very close to the *cité*, so that an extension of the walls of the latter could eventually be built to enclose it. In other cases, the *cité* and *ville* formed separate and distinct walled enclosures, as at Dijon and Périgueux, where a space of some 300 metres separated them. Sometimes the *ville* was established on the far side of the river, as at Verdun and Metz. It is noteworthy that two Roman towns of northern Gaul, Bavai and Cassel, never became the seats of bishops, and neither attracted any significant monastic foundation. Both remained small towns of only local importance. Without the institutions of the Church, the gap between the *civitas* and the medieval city could not readily be bridged.

*New towns of the twelfth century*
Not all towns in western Europe derived from Roman settlements; many, indeed most, grew up each around a primary nucleus

provided by a monastery or a castle. Many Benedictine monasteries of the seventh and eighth centuries were founded, not in the suburbs of former Roman *civitas* capitals but in the depth of the countryside. A small agricultural community grew up around each of them; in some instances, these acquired certain urban functions, and, in a few, gave rise to towns of not inconsiderable size and importance. Among these were Saint-Omer, Saint-Riquier, Corbie, Saint-Trond, Fulda and, at a later date, Cluny.

Far more numerous were the towns which grew up within the shadow and under the protection of a castle. Indeed, this is almost the classic form of the medieval town in western and central Europe.[11] It is useless to argue whether the town grew from a village, and its citizens from the local peasantry. Neither castle nor monastery was, as a general rule, built far from a rural community. Both required labour for the constructon and maintenance of their fabrics, and a steady food supply for those who lived in them.

The development of the monastic or castle town must have followed some such course as this. Permission was first given for a market to be held in the village, and this is likely to have been accompanied or followed by the grant of restricted privileges. The community thus became in legal terms a town, though its urban functions may have consisted of little more than a weekly market. The grant of a charter was essentially an attempt on the part of the lord to profit from market dues, burgage rents and the profits of courts which were likely to arise in a town. Incorporation came, not infrequently, before the development of strictly urban functions, and in many instances the latter never really materialised. The result was the *Agrarstadt*, the small community with urban status and some of the trappings of towns, such as defences and gates; it had the right to hold a market but it lacked specialised crafts and a community of merchants and traders.

The grants of privileges with which these embryonic towns were endowed, came in time to be stereotyped. Those granted to certain towns provided convenient models for other sets of urban rules. Doubtless the wouldbe citizens claimed to have a grant of the same 'laws' as those of neighbouring towns, and their lords knew too little about urban institutions to be able to modify them. Thus the Laws of Breteuil, granted in the first instance to the obscure Norman town of that name, were generalised in Normandy and parts of western England.[12] Similarly, newly incorporated towns in central Europe tended to receive the 'laws' of Magdeburg, of Lübeck, or of the Bohemian town of Iglau (Jihlava). The 'laws' of Louvain were adopted elsewhere in Brabant, and in Luxembourg a number of towns adopted the *droit de Beaumont*, which was itself a town in little more than name.

The Counts of Flanders had founded a number of palaces or castles in the County by the late tenth or early eleventh century. Each was the centre of a castellany, from which it derived supplies and soldiers and for which it provided some kind of refuge. The Counts during this and succeeding centuries showed a quite unusual administrative skill. They kept a firm grip on their castellans and appear to have made the development of commercial settlements beside their castles a deliberate object of policy.[13] They were assisted by the contemporary growth of population and expansion of trade. In the course of the tenth century, after the Viking raids had ceased, small urban communities began to form beside most of the residences of the counts, and during the eleventh century their growth became rapid. A network of towns grew almost from nothing. By the end of the century Ypres, Lille, Tournai, Valenciennes and Douai had emerged as commercial towns in West Flanders, together with a number of less distinguished places: Messines, Aire, Thourout, Audenarde. By 1100 or, at latest, a few years later, a sequence of fairs had been established at several of them.

East Flanders developed later than west, but Bruges and Ghent were already prominent as trading centres by the end of the eleventh century. The nucleus of each was a castle of the Count of Flanders, on which first a local and then a long-distance trade were concentrated. A fourteenth-century chronicler somewhat imaginatively reconstructed the birth of the city of Bruges:

> In order to satisfy the needs of the castle folk, there began to throng before his gate near the castle bridge traders and merchants selling costly goods, then inn-keepers to feed and house those doing business with the prince . . . ; they built houses and set up inns where those who could not be put up at the castle were accommodated. . . . The houses increased to such an extent that there soon grew up a large town which in the common speech of the lower classes is still called 'Bridge', for Bruges means 'bridge' in their patois.[14]

The Flemish cities began as centres of trade, as communities

243

of merchants. But it cannot be emphasised too strongly that the community which grew up beside the Count's castle also contained peasants and craftsmen and was, at least in its earliest years, more agricultural than it was commercial. It has already been suggested that part at least of the merchandise handled derived from the surplus production, especially cloth, of the monasteries. Craft industries, however, came to dominate in all except Bruges, which remained a predominantly commercial city. The thirteenth century saw the peak of prosperity of the Flemish cloth manufacture. Thereafter it was weakened by external competition and internal discords (see p. 459).

Towns developed later, perhaps by a century, in Brabant and Hainault, but here too most grew up round castles or monasteries. Brussels, which was to become by far the largest, developed around a ducal castle built beside the river Senne. Tongeren (Tongres) was of Roman origin, but ceased to grow after its bishops had in the eighth century abandoned it. Its place was taken by the riverside settlement of Liège which grew around its episcopal nucleus to be one of the largest cities of the Low Countries. Louvain and Malines were also later developments, stimulated by the growing industrial production and trade of Brabant in the twelfth and thirteenth centuries.

The successful towns of the medieval Low Countries had one thing in common. They lay on navigable rivers; their commerce could be moved by boat, and many of them were, at least in the earlier Middle Ages, accessible to seaborne shipping. This elementary fact brings out a fundamental distinction between the Roman and the medieval city in this region; the one oriented towards Gaul, from which its garrisons and its supplies had once derived; the other towards the sea and the sea routes to England and northern and western Europe; the one dependent on its roads, the other on its rivers.

*Urban development in central Europe*
Urban life, as it was understood in the ancient world, ended at the frontiers of the Roman Empire. Indeed, many of the urban settlements along the Rhine and Danube were far from having the status and significance of *civitates* capitals. Most were legionary forts, alongside some of which *cannabae*, settlements of petty traders and of others who provided for the wants of the garrisons,

had grown up. A few, such as *Regnum* (Regensburg), survived as inhabited places. Others, like the legionary fortress of *Vindonissa* near Basel, and *Carnuntum* (Petronell) on the Danube below Vienna, were destroyed during the Germanic invasions and never reoccupied. The survival rate amongst the Rhineland towns was rather greater than in those along the Danube. Strasbourg, Speyer, Worms, Mainz and Cologne survived as inhabited places, and at some time in the seventh or eighth century each became the seat of a bishop. By the later years of the tenth century or, at latest, early in the eleventh each had attracted a small pre-urban community which grew into a town of several thousands during the twelfth century.

Regensburg, though never the capital of a Roman *civitas*, nevertheless became the seat of a petty Bavarian duke. The monastery of St Emmeran was founded outside its walls to the west, and in the tenth century the bishopric was established and a cathedral built within the walled enclosure of the Romans. In other words, the history of Regensburg, in its broad outlines, repeated that of Arras and Reims, Tours and Toulouse, though at a later date by several centuries. Similar lines of development can be demonstrated at other frontier settlements, notably in the Rhineland towns of Bonn and Xanten, where the Frankish settlement grew up outside the fortifications of the Roman town.

The urban history of the lands lying beyond the Rhine and Danube is one of extraordinary complexity. There was no tradition of urbanism. Towns grew up at first where there was a need for the services which they could provide. They developed round nuclei, fixed points which offered protection or an advantageous site to the traders who frequented them. In the absence of Roman towns, the nuclei could have been gathering places of itinerant merchants, villages, the strongholds of Germanic or Slavic tribes, monastic settlements, the palaces of the early emperors or the castles of their vassals. Many towns incorporated several such nuclei, closely spaced, but, at least in origin, independent of one another.

Traders tended at a very early date to form small communities. We do not know how they chose their sites. Perhaps, by some kind of mutual consent, they agreed that a particular place was a convenient one at which they might forgather at agreed times. A commonly used term for such a gathering of traders was *wik*.

The cluster outside the walls of a monastery or in the *suburbium* of a Roman *civitas* was a *wik*. There were also *wiks* which had emerged in isolation. Hedeby, at the head of a narrow arm of the Baltic Sea near the base of the Danish peninsula, was such a settlement. It lay on a convenient route from the Baltic to the North Sea. It owed nothing to any previous settlement; everything to its logistic value within the framework of north European trade in the early Middle Ages. It was small in area, surrounded by a defensive bank and palisade, within which were the huts of the traders. How they organised and administered their settlement we do not know, but we can be sure that their rights were not dependent on any formal grant of privileges. If the town had survived – it was in fact destroyed in the mid-eleventh century and the site abandoned – it would have claimed that its rights were prescriptive.

It is difficult to estimate the number of such self-sustaining *wiks*. Quentovic on the north coast of France may have been one, though its site is not precisely known.[15] Duurstede on the lower Rhine and perhaps Hamburg belong to this group, as also do Sigtuna, Birka and other trading centres established around the Baltic Sea by the Norse. Clearly, however, the number of independent *wiks* was small, and perhaps they were occupied only during the sailing and trading season. Most appear in the end to have been either abandoned or destroyed; they did not, by themselves, give rise to permanent medieval towns. This, of course, only serves to reinforce the view that patronage and protection were necessary for a medieval commercial community to survive and prosper.

Some towns may have grown from villages. The distinction between village and town was always blurred. Many a village became a market centre, and the needs of a weekly market could easily have led to the emergence of a handful of craftsmen. It was not unusual for villages to act in a corporate capacity, and in time to claim the prescriptive rights of a town, which might then be confirmed by charter.

Castle and monastery served in central, as in western Europe, as the points around which a town might develop. East of the Rhine, however, amongst the most important nuclei, at least of the earlier towns, were the tribal fortresses known to the Germans as burgwalls and to the Slavs as *grody* or *hrady*. They were small earthworks which served as places of refuge in time of invasion and war. Helmold's Slavic Chronicle describes how, even after the wars against the Wagrians of Holstein and Mecklenburg had ended, the local peasantry felt insecure because their fortress, or *burh*, had not been rebuilt. In Nordalbingia (Holstein) people 'came out of the strongholds in which they were keeping themselves shut up for fear of the wars. And they returned, each one to his own village'.[16] No less than ninety such *Burgwalle* have been counted in Brandenburg alone. Their number in East Germany is so great that no village could have been too far from one. Most were quite small, covering only a few hectares. They commonly occupied low-lying sites, naturally protected by river or marsh, and were usually enclosed by ditch, bank and palisade, with a single well guarded entrance.

A number of large defensive works of this kinds was associated with the ninth century state of Great Moravia. Its focal points were *hrady*, many of them larger and more strongly built than the German burgwalls. They contained masonry buildings, and the foundations of a number of apsidal churches and rotundas have been excavated. Archaeological finds include goods which can only have been acquired by long-distance trade and they show that iron-workings and other crafts were carried on. The largest of them, such as Mikulčice and Staré Město, may have had a permanent population of several hundreds. It cannot be doubted that many of these *hrady* contained at this time a small population engaged in manufacturing and trade, and in terms of urban development they were probably not behind contemporary towns in Carolingian Europe.[17] They were the seats of power of the local Slav princes who probably inhabited some strong point within their extensive area. They must also have served as refuges for the local peasantry. Yet most of them did not outlast the Great Moravian Empire which had provided the conditions for their growth. The state was destroyed by the invading Magyars, and most of these incipient towns were abandoned, never to be reoccupied.

In the tenth century the Jewish trader and traveller, Ibrahim Ibn Ja'kub, crossed Bohemia on his way to Kraków in southern Poland. He passed by way of Prague, and described the town which lay on the summit of the steep hill to the west of the Vltava. It was built of stone and contained both the residence of the local prince and also a large masonry church – evidently the church of St George which still survives within the Hradčany. There was a community of craftsmen and traders, similar doubtless to that which had existed a century earlier at Staré Město and elsewhere in Moravia.[18]

Such a burg, whether or not it was the seat of a local prince and a centre of craft industries, lies at the core of many, perhaps of most of the earlier towns of central Europe. The burg attracted a community of traders and craftsmen, who dwelled outside its walls and ditches, but close enough to enjoy its protection. They formed a small, unplanned town, which may itself in time have come to have its own defensive walls. In some instances the development of the town went no further, but in others a new town was grafted on to the old. This was, as a general rule, associated with the arrival of settlers from the west and with the grant of extended privileges. The new town was usually planned, with a large market place and streets intersecting at right angles.[19]

This sequence of events is well illustrated at Kraków, where the Slavic town grew up below the *gród*, here known as the Wawel. This was the town *zu polnische Recht*, whose privileges derived from local custom. Then, in 1257, the planned town was established *zu germanische Recht*, with its straight streets, its large market place and its cloth hall. It is likely that the Germans who created it could be persuaded to come only by the grant of a formal charter of privileges – German law, as it was termed; the Polish custom was too indefinite and uncertain to attract them. Poznań, Breslau (Wrocław), Prague and many other towns of central Europe show in the layout of their streets and squares an evolution closely similar to that of Kraków.

In Germany itself the course of evolution of some of the older towns was a great deal more complex even than that of Prague or Breslau. There are instances of four or even more separate nuclei. The burg occupied a local strong point; below it lay the *Altstadt*, formed by the earliest colony of traders and craftsmen; nearby a community gathered around a monastic foundation, and finally a *Neustadt*, with a planned lay-out, was established. To these might even have been added a cathedral precinct. Such were the cells of which Hildesheim, Brunswick, Brandenburg and Magdeburg were composed. Most of these elements are discernible also in Münster, Osnabrück, Hamburg and Stettin (Szczecin), and

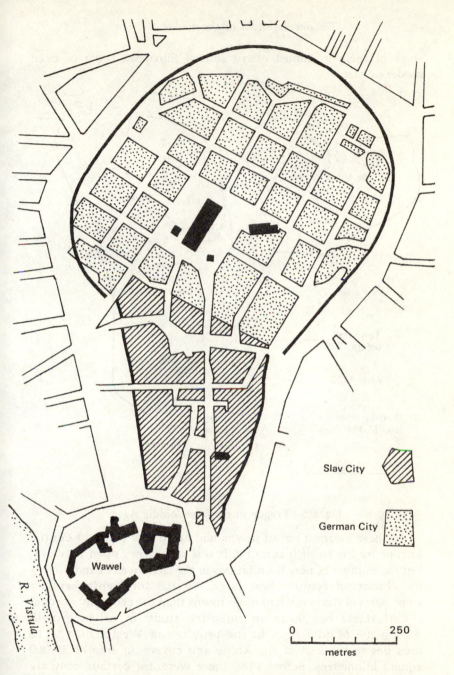

Fig. 6.4 Kraków in the later Middle Ages.

some of them in almost every central European town of even moderate size.

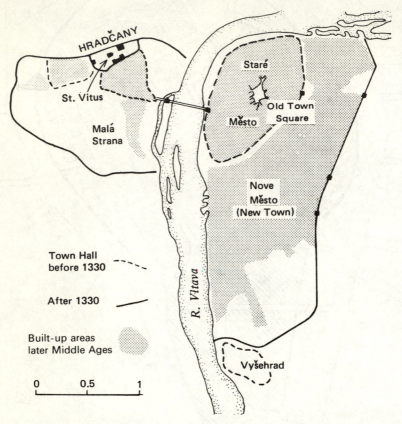

Fig. 6.5   Prague in the later Middle Ages.

By these means a net of towns had come into being in Central Europe by the twelfth century. It was still a very open network, but the number of new foundations in the later twelfth and during the thirteenth century was large. By the fourteenth century some parts of Germany had more towns than the economy needed.

Carl Haase has made an intensive study of urban growth during the Middle Ages in the province of Westphalia.[20] The area lies to the east of the Rhine and covers an area of 38,000 square kilometres. Before 1180 there were, for certain, only six towns, together with another half-dozen whose status and function at this date are far from clear. In the period from 1180 until 1350 no less than 132 towns appeared within this area, so that by the mid-fourteenth century the urban density was such that each served, on average, an area of about 300 square kilometres. The dates of foundation of the towns of Westphalia, in so far as they can be established, were:

| | |
|---|---|
| Before 1180 | 6 |
| 1180–1240 | 36 |
| 1240–1290 | 39 |
| 1290–1350 | 57 |
| Total | 138 |

There is no means of determining the size of these towns during the later Middle Ages beyond the topographical evidence afforded by the enclosed area of the towns themselves. This line of reasoning must be used only with the greatest caution; urban population is not a simple function of urban area. Nevertheless, the areas of the medieval towns of Westphalia suggest that only those founded in the first and second of the four periods ever attained a size that can be considered large by medieval standards. Most of those founded in the last period remained very small. Their founders appear to have misread the economic indicators, and to have continued to establish towns and to endow them with privileges long after an economic recession had cut back drastically on the opportunities for urban growth.

Elsewhere in central Europe towns began to proliferate. In the Main valley of Franconia as many as forty-two were founded.[21] No less than twelve owed their origin to the enterprise of the bishops of Würzburg between 1232 and 1354, and nine other territorial princes also participated in the undertaking, establishing between them as many as thirty towns.[22] Swabia was, more than any other region of Germany, a land of small towns, founded under princely auspices in the thirteenth and later centuries. Württemberg alone had 148. In Luxembourg there were 361 places which had received grants of privileges,[23] the great majority of which can only have been villages.

Many historians, notably in Germany, have described an eastward diffusion of the town and of urban institutions, and have related it to the contemporary movement of rural population into the less densely populated areas of east-central Europe. The reality of this movement cannot be disputed. The desire of the lords to create towns and to profit from them, communicated itself eastwards. Stoob and Weczerka have mapped the resulting diffusion of the town in their rather tendentious *Atlas Ostmitteleuropas.*[24] It must, however, be emphasised that what these maps show is the eastward spread, not of urban functions, but of legal institutions. In many instances the two went together. A new urban settlement was laid out on a site which had probably been chosen with considerable care. A call went out for settlers, together with a promise of privileges, which would normally include freedom from arbitrary and onerous obligations, the right to have a market, to own urban property, to organise and administer their own affairs, and to have a court to settle their own disputes.

The new town was created at a particular moment in time; it did not grow slowly through the years, as most earlier towns had done. In consequence it had to be planned. Streets were laid out, and frontages divided into lots, in readiness for the future citizens to come and occupy them. The streets of older towns may have derived from meandering cattle paths; they curved in order to avoid or to link up properties. In the newly planned towns there were, as a general rule, no such restrictions. Streets were straight, and were made to intersect at right angles – or at least very nearly so. Since the market was to be a feature of the new town, an open space, also rectangular in plan, was left near its centre.

Such towns spread through central Germany and into the Slav lands beyond. Can we be sure that each was the first town in the medieval sense to appear in its locality? Take for example the small town of Parchim, in Mecklenburg-Schwerin, some 100 kilometres to the east of Hamburg. It consisted of three parts.[25] The first was a Burg, probably deriving from an earlier refuge. Adjacent to it lay a small, unplanned town, and to the west of this, the new town, with a regular street plan. It is, in fact, a Kraków in miniature. The *Neustadt* is first noted in 1249, so that the older town must have been appreciably earlier than this. Parchim would appear from the records to have been a new town founded in the mid-thirteenth century. This is the date when German law was introduced at Parchim; but urban functions are likely to have been first carried on here very considerably earlier.

## The new towns of the later Middle Ages
The planned towns which spread across Germany and eastern

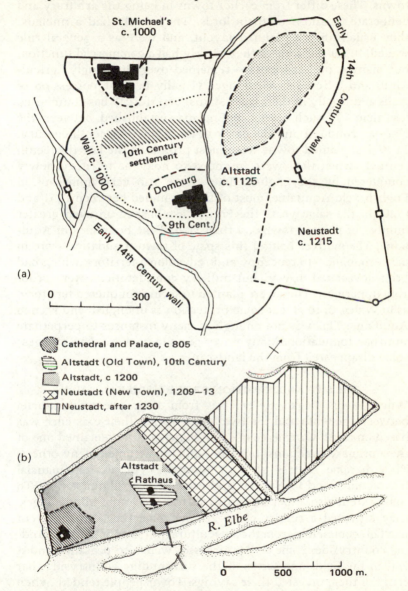

(a)

St. Michael's
c. 1000

Early 14th Century wall

Wall c. 1000

10th Century
settlement

Domburg

Altstadt
c. 1125

9th Cent.

Neustadt
c. 1215

Early 14th Century wall

0      300

(b)

⬧ Cathedral and Palace, c 805
⬨ Altstadt (Old Town), 10th Century
▦ Altstadt, c 1200
⧆ Neustadt (New Town), 1209–13
▥ Neustadt, after 1230

Altstadt
Rathaus

R. Elbe

0     500     1000 m.

Fig. 6.6   Late medieval German towns: (a) Hildesheim and (b) Magdeburg

253

Europe in the thirteenth and fourteenth centuries are only a special case in a broad class of medieval towns, the so-called new towns. These differ from earlier towns in being the arbitrary and deliberate creations of their lords. They rarely had a nucleus; they usually had a planned layout, and were as a general rule walled. In some instances they clearly had a commercial function, but many – perhaps most – remained overwhelmingly agricultural, and differed from villages visually in their possession of walls and legally in their freer status. Beresford[26] has counted no less than 172 such towns in England, established between the Norman conquest and the early years of the fourteenth century. In Wales, planted towns were most prolific in the late thirteenth century, when they were intended to hold the territory newly conquered by the English. They were also very numerous in English-held Aquitaine, most of them founded between 1251 and 1320. In the same years the French established an even greater number of planted towns on their side of the boundary in Aquitaine. The motives behind this spate of town foundation were in part economic – to reoccupy and redevelop a territory which had been devastated in war, but military considerations were probably uppermost. They were planted to secure conquered territory, as in Wales, or to give it some protection as in English and French Aquitaine. This was not enough in many instances to perpetuate an urban foundation. Many never grew to be more than villages; some disappeared from the landscape.

### THE SIZE AND FUNCTION OF THE MEDIEVAL TOWN

When towns began to emerge from their pre-urban nuclei between the tenth and the twelfth centuries, their existence was based on trade. Commerce in some shape or form remained one of their primary functions, but they quickly assumed many others. They became centres of craft industries, places for financial transactions, and for secular and ecclesiastical administation. To some extent also, especially towards the end of the Middle Ages, they attracted a rentier class. At the same time, no town cut itself off completely from the agricultural pursuits of the surrounding countryside. Some of its burgesses were also peasants, and it was in the fields and farms of the surrounding countryside that many of them invested their savings. Townspeople tended, when they engaged in agricultural pursuits, to practise a very intensive cultivation on small parcels of land. In southern Europe they were heavily engaged in viticulture. At Amiens they practised market gardening along the Somme valley.

The variety of functions performed by any town was closely related to its size. The agricultural component always formed a much higher percentage of the total urban activity of small towns than of large. In small towns, on the other hand, manufacturing occupied only a small proportion of its total population, and satisfied primarily the needs of the local area. Specialised production was always relatively more important in the larger towns, and aimed to supply a very much wider market. The more extensive market, in turn, necessitated a community of merchants, and the whole complex of craftsmen and merchants called into being a large tertiary employment, builders, butchers, bakers, servants, and others, whose function it was to satisfy the material needs of the specialised workers. One is constantly surprised at the large numbers of the latter which appear in tax assessments, muster rolls and other lists of the citizens of medieval towns. At Toulouse, for example, there were 177 butchers in 1322.[27] The total population cannot have exceeded 30,000, so that there was one butcher for every 175 persons. When one considers the conditions of poverty in which the majority lived, there appears to have been more than adequate provision for the supply of meat

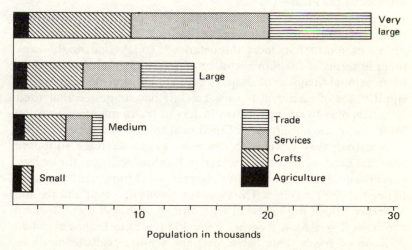

Fig. 6.7   A schematic representation of the functions of medieval towns.

255

to the more affluent citizens. Bonvesin della Riva claimed that there were more than 440 butchers in Milan, which suggests an even higher ratio of butchers to total population. He added that there were 300 bakeries subject to city tax, since they baked for sale to the citizens, as well as more than a hundred 'which serve monks or religious'. At Florence, according to Giovanni Villani, there were 146 bakeries – a very much lower density.

It is extremely difficult to compile a list of medieval towns. Of course the large towns, and also those of medium size were familiar to contemporaries, and are well known today. It is the vast number of small and dwarf towns that it is almost impossible to enumerate. In England the lists of towns which sent rep-representatives to the meetings of Parliament differed from one occasion to another. Similarly in France there was no consistency in the lists of those summoned to the fourteenth century assemblies of towns.[28] Le Goff has commented[29] that in the Middle Ages there was no accepted definition of a town nor any kind of list of the places that might qualify. The kings and their officials just did not know which were the towns of the kingdom. In 1316, 227 towns were summoned to send representatives to the assemblies of the kings of France, and altogether 570 were represented at one time or another.

## The size of the medieval town

How many amongst this great number of cities and towns had truly urban functions and were recognised by contemporaries as places of more than local importance? Today one might rank them in terms of the number of branch banks, of chain stores, or of the annual turnover of shops. There are no such measures of the significance of medieval towns. Le Goff has suggested that their attractiveness to the mendicant orders of friars might serve as an indicator of the importance of medieval towns. Almost all friaries were urban; they were established as a response to the supposed spiritual needs of the towns, and their location reflected the orders' perception of which towns were largest, most important and most in need of their services. Thirty-seven towns in 'royal' France and a further fifteen in the rest of the country each had three or more convents (Fig. 6.8). Altogether, only 155 towns in France ever had a house of friars. This list is perhaps a more realistic guide to the towns of economic significance than the much longer lists of those which were summoned to send representatives to the king's assemblies.

In Germany the situation was incomparably more confused. The number of towns was greatly increased by the feudal division of the territory and the presence of many territorial enclaves and exclaves of the German states.[30] There were some three

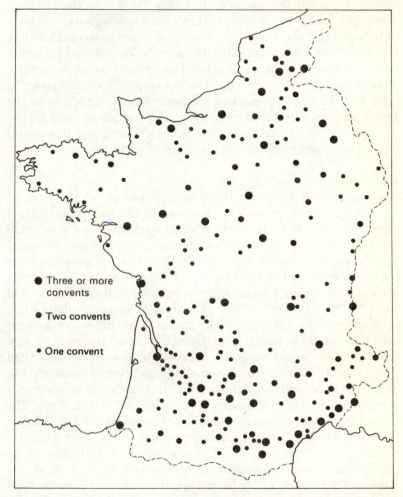

● Three or more
   convents

● Two convents

• One convent

Fig. 6.8   The distribution of urban friaries in France; based on J. Le Goff, 'Ordres mendiants et urbanisation dans la France médiévale', *Ann. E.S.C.*, xxv (1970), 924–46.

thousand places with urban pretensions. Bechtel has estimated[31] that out of this total, large and medium sized towns made up less than fifty; that 150 were small towns, and the rest, about 2800, were very small or dwarf towns, of which the vast majority contained little more than some seventy households each.

Elsewhere in Europe the preponderance of small towns may have been much less marked, but they were nonetheless very numerous. In Europe's most highly urbanised regions, northern Italy and the Low Countries, towns of small and intermediate size were few compared with the number in Germany; urban functions tended to be concentrated in a relatively small number of large and very large towns. The development of city states in Italy and the strongly marked tendency in that direction in the Low Countries had the effect of subjecting extensive rural areas – the *contadi* – to the authority of the central city, and this would clearly have inhibited the proliferation of small towns.

*Giant cities*

It is convenient to group the towns of Europe at the peak of their demographic growth – let us say in the half century from about 1275 to 1325 – into size groups. First there is a very small group of what we might term *giant cities*, those whose estimated population was in excess of 50,000. Very few fell into this category, and most lay in Italy. Florence, if we may accept the estimate made by Giovanni Villani, shortly before the Black Death, had some 90,000 'mouths'. Milan, according to Bonvesin della Riva, who wrote about 1288, had no less than 12,500 houses each opening on to one of the streets, and added that many sheltered several families. This would suggest a total population of not less than about 75,000. Venice probably had a population of some 90,000, and Genoa was only a little smaller. It is difficult to form any estimate of the size of Spanish cities during the Middle Ages. The largest of the Moorish cities, Seville, Cordoba and Granada, almost certainly fell into the giant category, but the only other Mediterranean city of this size was Constantinople.[32] Estimates of its population at the time of Justinian vary from half a million to a million. These figures may be exaggerated; in any event the total declined during the following centuries and fell catastrophically after the seizure of the city by the crusaders in 1204. It may, at the time of its siege by the Turks in 1453 have fallen to 80,000. It remained a 'giant' city, though no longer the foremost in size in the whole of Europe.

North of the Alps there were fewer cities of 'giant' size. Paris unquestionably belonged to this category, but considerable doubt surrounds the estimates that have been made of its total population.[33] The well-known hearth list of 1328 (see p. 125) credits the city together with its suburbs, with no less than 61,098 hearths together with a further 2351 at Saint-Denis. Other estimates, derived from the area of the city, from the scanty evidence for its food consumption, and from the numbers of craftsmen and traders, suggest a total of less than 100,000. The only other 'giant' towns of northern Europe lay in the Low Countries. In the fourteenth century Ghent must have turned 50,000, and Bruges probably ran it close. Brussels developed somewhat later, with the economic growth of Brabant, but must have reached a similar total in the fifteenth century.

*Very large cities*
These had an estimated population of more than some 25,000. They were more numerous than the 'giants' but one can, nevertheless, point to no more than fifteen or twenty, a large proportion of which were to be found in Italy. Among these were the major cities of the Lombard plain: Padua, Bologna and perhaps Verona and Pavia. The list would have included the Tuscan city of Lucca and also Rome, Naples and perhaps Palermo. The chief 'industry' at Rome was, of course, the Church, but one cannot point to any dominant economic activity in Naples and Palermo that could have justified so large a population. They served, as indeed they have since continued to do, as refuges for the surplus population of a crowded countryside. All the larger medieval cities had a high proportion of poor and underemployed, none more conspicuously than those of southern Italy and Sicily.

Spain had at least two very large cities, Barcelona and Valencia, both important ports and commercial centres. At the same time Lisbon, a relatively small and unimportant port in the fourteenth century, grew rapidly in the fifteenth with the expansion of the African trade. By the end of the Middle Ages it was unquestionably a 'very large' city.

There were few very large cities north of the Pyrenees and Alps. Bruges unquestionably belonged to this category, and may even have exceeded it. Brussels reached this size in the fifteenth century, but was appreciably smaller when Bruges and Ghent were at the peak of their prosperity. In France, Toulouse and Bordeaux certainly; Rouen probably, and possibly Lyons were very large cities. In Germany, Cologne fell into this category, and Lübeck, the most important of the Hanseatic towns, probably reached this size in the fifteenth century. Nuremberg approached it very close and Prague almost certainly had a population of between 30 and 40,000 before the outbreak of the Hussite wars.

### Large cities
The category of large cities is made up of those with populations of between 10 and 25,000. They were far more numerous than the cities belonging to the categories already discussed. Most of the cities of the Plain of Lombardy were of this size: Cremona, Mantua, Modena, Parma, Pavia, Rimini, Forli and perhaps also Faenza, Ravenna and Cesena; and, in peninsular Italy, Orvieto, Perugia, Siena, Pistoia, Pisa. Doubt surrounds the cities of southern Italy. They were probably larger than their international and commercial significance might have suggested because of their tendency to absorb rural population that had been squeezed off the land. Among the large cities of southern Italy and Sicily were certainly Bari, Messina and Palermo, and possibly also Syracuse and Enna. The situation in Spain is no clearer. Saragosa fell within this size range, but most towns of Christian Spain remained small until the fifteenth century. Valladolid had 6750 *vecinos* or hearths in 1530,[34] and may have had somewhat in excess of 10,000 inhabitants in the previous century. The same may also have been true of Salamanca, Segovia and Burgos.

Large towns were relatively more numerous in north-western Europe. The majority of the significant clothing and industrial towns of the Low Countries were of this category: Abbeville and Amiens, Arras and Douai, Ypres and Lille, Valenciennes and Mons, Louvain and Liège, Bois-le-Duc and the rising port of Antwerp. Many, perhaps most, of the episcopal cities of France, such as Beauvais, Chartres, Troyes, Metz, Dijon, Lyons also fell within this size range. Avignon belonged to this category until it was lifted into the range of 'very large' cities by the arrival in 1309 of the papal court and its retinue.[35] One is constantly surprised at the large size of many little known and relatively unimportant French towns, especially of those in southern France. This is, of course, part of the general tendency met with in southern Europe for many of the people who would, if they had been in northern Europe, have lived in rural areas, to move to the towns. Millau, situated amid the barren Causses, had in 1309, 1835 hearths and little short of 10,000 people. Castres and Albi almost certainly exceeded 10,000 before the Black Death.[36]

Most of the well-known commercial cities of medieval Germany also belonged to this category: the Rhineland cities of Frankfurt, Mainz, Speyer, Worms, Strasbourg and Basel; the northern ports of Bremen and Hamburg and the inland cities of Münster, Osnabrück and Magdeburg; the Baltic ports of Rostock and perhaps also of Wismar and Stralsund and, farther afield, of Königsberg, Riga and Reval; in south Germany, Augsburg, Ulm and Zurich, and, in eastern Germany and Poland, Erfurt, Wrocław (Breslau) and Kraków.

## Medium-sized and small towns

Medium-sized towns are taken to be those with from 2,000 to 10,000 inhabitants. Their number was immense, and was exceeded only by that of small and dwarf towns. Some twenty are shown in the area of the Low Countries and northern France represented in Fig. 7.1. In France this category must have included most towns of more than local importance, just as in England it embraced the majority of county towns.

The function of the medieval town was closely related to its size. The *small* and *dwarf* towns, with a population of less than 2000, did little if anything more than serve local needs. Let Rheinfelden in Switzerland and Espalion in Guyenne serve as examples. Rheinfelden was a small walled town, lying on the Rhine about 15 kilometres above Basel. It grew up under the protection of a castle belonging to the Zähringen dukes, who had granted it a charter. Its walls, built in the thirteenth century, enclosed an area of about ten hectares. In the fourteenth century there were about 220 households in the town, representing a population of around a thousand. Crafts were well represented. There were about ten metal-workers; some twenty to thirty tanners and leather workers and a similar number of weavers, as well as builders, carpenters and a few others. Perhaps half to two-thirds of the households were headed by craftsmen. Most of the others, one assumes, were engaged more or less directly in agriculture, and they sent grain to the half-dozen mills in the town. In addition, it is likely that most of the craftsmen also played some part in local agriculture. They may have shared in the vineyards which surrounded the town, kept a few animals, or cultivated small parcels of cropland.[37]

The approximate market area of Rheinfelden is known because a list of places which sold wheat in the town has survived. It was a rounded area extending some 15 kilometres along the Rhine, a similar distance into the Jura to the south and a very much shorter distance northwards into the foothills of the Black Forest. No doubt this area of about 300 square kilometres overlapped the service area of neighbouring towns, but within much of this area Rheinfelden served as the only practicable outlet for agricultural surpluses and as the chief source of manufactured articles and consumers' goods. Articles of distant origin were available in the town. Good Alsatian wine could be bought as well as the local *Landwein*; salt came from Salzburg and Lorraine; timber was rafted down·the river; fish, salted and dried, was brought from the lower Rhine, as well as spices, sugar, rice, dyestuffs, cotton and luxury fabrics. The amounts were doubtless very small indeed, but there was nevertheless a demand amongst the richer citizens of the small town for such goods. Such imports into the local region had to be paid for. There is no evidence that Rheinfelden earned any significant amount of currency from its services to travellers and river shipping. Its trade must therefore have been balanced by the movement of agricultural goods and perhaps of the products of local crafts into the regional market.

Espalion, by contrast, lay close to the uplands of the Auvergne, and had no close neighbours. It was walled, except along the side which bordered the river Lot. Within this area there were only three main streets and about 175 houses. It was, perhaps, a little smaller than Rheinfelden. Our knowledge of the town is derived in the main from two tax rolls of the early fifteenth century,[38] which tell us more about its social structure than its economic activities. The houses were mostly very humble, and there is little evidence that crafts were practised on more than a very small scale. Agriculture was proportionately more important, and most citizens appear to have held some land outside the walls. Indeed, well over a third of the value of the citizens' real estate was in the fields and vineyards surrounding the town. The tax rolls unfortunately tell us nothing of those whose assessment was nil on account of their poverty. In 1403, 144 citizens were assessed, seventy at less than 6 deniers, and six at more than 31. The range of wealth was evidently not particularly great.

By contrast with Rheinfelden, crafts were relatively unimportant. There was a mill, but only two weavers were mentioned. Tanning was carried on along the river. There was a market and a fair, at which it is probable that the pastoral products of the mountains were exchanged for grain from the lowlands to the west. But Espalion seems not to have had the long-distance relations of Rheinfelden. Even its population, to judge from their toponymic surnames, came mainly from the surrounding countryside. It is likely that more small towns of western and central Europe resembled Espalion than Rheinfelden in their economic structures. Yet it was the latter which supported regional trade, supplied goods to the towns of intermediate size and in turn provided a market for the products of the latter.

The towns of intermediate size partook in some respects of the characteristics of the small towns. Their agricultural component was important and their local markets served the needs of their immediate localities. But they also manufactured goods which were sold over a very much broader area and, in turn, they constituted a regional far more than a local market. The occupational structure of the intermediate towns was at one and the same time broader and more specialised. There were almost as many separate crafts in a town like Frankfurt-on-Main – admittedly one lying at the uppermost of the rather arbitrary limits of this class of towns – as there were craftsmen in one like Rheinfelden. In the latter the industrial structure must have resembled that which Aristotle found in a small Greek *polis* and described in his *Cyropaedia* (quoted on p. 31). In the former there were enough practitioners of each of the more important crafts, for some form of corporate or gild organisation to have been possible.

The non-agricultural functions of towns of intermediate size can be grouped, first, into those, the basic occupations, which served the needs of the region as a whole and indeed reached far beyond its limits and brought money into the town, and the service or non-basic functions. The latter included the retailers and servants, whose contribution to the 'export' industries of the town was indirect. The number of those who followed these occu-pations might be expected to vary very roughly with the size of the town. They would, however, include the notaries and scriven-ers, whose services were essential in any town that carried on any volume of long-distance trade. These constituted only a handful in most towns of intermediate size, but in those, such as Florence, Augsburg, Nuremberg and Frankfurt, in which trade and monetary transactions were important, they would have formed a large community (see p. 267).

Since goods made in the town were sold over a relatively large area, transport costs were a more significant factor, than was the case with small towns. In consequence there was a greater emphasis on quality. It is true that intermediate and large towns produced some poor quality fabrics, mostly for local consump-tion, but they also wove quality cloth, capable of bearing the high costs of transport to distant markets. Almost all the intermediate and large towns of northern France and the Low Countries made a type of cloth which they each regarded as their speciality and for which they could normally expect to find a continuing demand in distant markets. The account books of the Bonis brothers of Montauban (see p. 351), in the south of France, kept during the years 1339 to 1345, show how widely these northern towns were known and respected for the quality of their products. The cloth industry provides the best examples of this emphasis on quality production in the larger producing centres. It was of course carried to its extreme in the production of heavy broadcloth in the cities of Flanders; in that of the artistically finished and decorated cloths of Florence, and in the silk produc-tion of Lucca, Bologna and Milan.

A not dissimilar situation can be detected in tanning and leather-working, with the production of the coarser qualities in most towns and that of a superior type in only a few, of which Fribourg and Basel, in Switzerland, were important examples. Little Rheinfelden had a handful of metal-workers, who doubtless shoed the horses and produced the simple ironware required by an agricultural society. But a more refined metal industry – the production of weapons and armour – was to be found mainly in a few of the larger towns, of which Milan, Toledo and Liège were the most prominent.

Dinant, a town of intermediate size – its population probably did not exceed 6000 – had a few tanyards, but its basic industry was the production of metal goods, especially pots and pans, metal tools, and farm equipment – what came to be called *dinanderie*.[39] The agricultural component of the town's occupational structure was small – the surrounding area offered little scope for farming. A relatively large – how big one cannot say – proportion of the labour force was engaged in the basic metal industries. Much of the town's food supply was brought from a considerable distance, and was, of course, paid for by the export of the town's basic products. Dinant must have been one of the most highly specialised of medieval towns, until its destruction in 1466 by the armies of Charles the Bold. Cities such as Ypres and Abbeville showed a not dissimilar concentration on the textile industries, and perhaps also Lucca on silk, and Ulm, Memmingen and Ravensburg on fustians and barchents (see p. 314). In others, the industrial specialisation was less narrow, but all except the small towns must have provided goods or services for an extensive area; they could not otherwise have maintained themselves.

Activities related to the Church and to monasteries and other ecclesiastical institutions were unquestionably an economic stimulus in many cities and towns. The numbers of regular and other clergy varied greatly. In small towns, which often constituted a single parish or even only a part of a parish, the clerical component of the population was negligible. In large towns there were very many parish churches – Norwich, a town of not much more than 13,000, had about forty parishes, but this density was exceptional. Many had monasteries, the houses of the mendicant orders, hospitals and other endowed institutions, and some were furthermore the seats of bishops and their cathedral chapters. It is easy to exaggerate the numbers directly involved in such institutions. The cathedral priory of Canterbury probably never had much more than seventy monks, with perhaps as many servants, and this was a large monastery. Food supply for monasteries and similar institutions was in the main brought in from their rural manors, at least until these were leased, but there must have been a marginal demand for goods in the town markets. It is likely that the religious institutions were dependent on the town more for services than for goods. Servants, carters and, above all, masons, glaziers, metal-workers and others concerned with the building and maintenance of the churches and conventual buildings must have made up a considerable number. One can only guess at the volume of ecclesiastical expenditure on building, on food and entertainment, and on the employees of the church. The arrival of the papal court at Avignon in 1309 brought with it over 4000 *curialistes*. The population of the town may perhaps have been increased overall by 10,000, and probably more if we include the somewhat transitory workers engaged in the very considerable building programme. The impact of the institutions of the Church on the economy of medium-sized and large towns of medieval Europe has yet to be studied.

There was a limit to the size to which towns could grow when their functions were primarily manufacturing. Very few ever grew to a size much in excess of 20,000. Towns of larger size normally had an important commercial function. Some, like Ghent and Bruges, served as collecting and forwarding centres for a cloth producing region. Venice, Genoa, Pisa and Barcelona were ports through which Middle Eastern, North African and Spanish goods were imported and the products of Europe exported. Milan and, to a lesser extent, Verona, Bergamo and other north Italian cities, were entrepots in the trade between northern and southern Europe; Florence became a major commercial centre in the thirteenth century and played a vital role, despite its lack of direct contact with ports and shipping, in the Mediterranean cloth trade. Nuremberg, Augsburg, Cologne and, on a smaller scale, Frankfurt-on-Main, Basel and Strasbourg, were also centres of long-distance trade.

Toulouse, with a population which may have reached 30,000 before the Black Death and certainly exceeded 20,000 at the end of the century, was one of the largest cities in southern France, and was exceeded only by Bordeaux. It was thus a 'very large' city. One can in very general terms assess the relative importance of its several functions. Its citizens practised agriculture and cultivated the vineyards which lay close to the city; a significant part of its food supply was thus produced locally. The clerical population is said to have made up five per cent of the total. Manufacturing was relatively unimportant for a city of this size; it satisfied mainly local and regional demand, but supplied some cloth, leather and metal goods for long-distance trade. Its basic function lay, rather, in commerce. It was a gathering place for the wines of southern Aquitaine and Languedoc, and it despatched them, in general by the Garonne, to Bordeaux for shipment. It was the major centre in Europe for the dyestuff known as *pastel*. It imported salt fish, English and Flemish cloth and Cornish tin; salt was brought from the lagoons along the coast of Languedoc, and animals from both the Pyrenees and the Massif Central. It was well served by water routes as well as by a nexus of land routes. The merchants of Toulouse were a large and rich community. Their wealth allowed them to keep numerous servants and retainers; they made heavy demands on local retail businesses, and their own commercial transactions must have necessitated large numbers of notaries and scriveners, and of men who packed, loaded and transported their merchandise. In all the larger towns there was a very large number of such persons who made up the infrastructure of commerce. In Genoa, for example, there were no less than 200 notaries in the mid-thirteenth century, while in Pisa there were nearly 300, and in Milan more than 500.

The population of Toulouse, as of most large cities of southern Europe, was inflated by the influx of rural landowners, who lived within the city walls, segregated within the *turres*, or urban castles. 'It is not of small importance,' wrote Giovanni Botero when considering the reasons for the size and greatness of cities,

> that the gentlemen in Italy do dwell in cities, and in France in their castles. . . . For the Italian divideth his expense and endeavours part in the city, part in the country, but the greater part he bestows in the city. But the Frenchman employs all that he may wholly in the country, regarding the city little or nothing at all.[40]

The towers of the urban nobility were as much a feature of Toulouse, which in this respect belonged to the Mediterranean, as they were of Bologna and Siena, and their households must have contributed greatly to the urban demand for goods and services.

## Urban migration

It is generally and probably rightly assumed that the reproduction rate was very much higher in rural than in urban areas. There were, however, exceptions. Wolff[41] has demonstrated from his study of wills that at Rodez, in the Rouergue, there were in the early fifteenth century on average 3·77 children living at the time of death of each testator. This was exceptional; the corresponding figure at Toulouse was 2·43. All cities and towns were populated by immigration from rural areas, and most were maintained only by continued migration. This may help to explain the very great fluctuations in urban population for which there is evidence in the late Middle Ages.

There is no direct evidence for the areas which supplied cities with their population, but a fraction of the immigrants – how large one cannot know – continued to be known by the name of their native village. A number of studies has been made of the personal names of burgesses of French cities, notably for Amiens, Provins, Toulouse and Bordeaux. These suggest that only a very small fraction covered distances of a hundred or more kilometres, and that most travelled no more than a day's journey to reach the city. They knew what lay ahead of them when they set out on an already familiar road to the town, and they could keep in touch with their native village. This is very far from supporting the view that a significant fraction of the urban population had actually absconded from seigneurial control, and journeyed to a distant city without the knowledge and consent of their lords. It is true, in the well known German phrase, that *Stadt Luft macht frei*, but the number of those who secreted themselves in a town for a year and a day, and thus achieved this freedom must always have been small.

A recent study[42] of the small towns of the Forez, in the Central Massif of France, emphasises the shortness of the journey made by most migrants to the towns. The earliest immigrants to Mont-

**Table 6.1 Migrants to Montbrison, as percentage of total migrants in each period (after Etienne Fournial)**

| Source of migrant (km) | Date of migration | | |
|---|---|---|---|
| | *Before* 1260 | 1260–1300 | 1300–49 |
| Less than 10 | 40 | 33 | 13 |
| 10–20 | 38 | 26 | 22 |
| 20–30 | 10 | 20 | 22 |
| 30–40 | 3 | 4 | 10 |
| 40–50 | | 5 | 6 |
| 50–60 | 9 | 3 | 7 |
| Over 60 | | 9 | 20 |

brison came from the nearby villages, more than three-quarters from less than 20 kilometres. Subsequent migrants came from farther afield, and after 1300, a third travelled distances of more than 40 kilometres. As the town grew it became a centre of attraction for an ever-broadening area.

## Urban food supply

A community in which the pursuit of agriculture was the principal or only occupation was necessarily small. It is unlikely that any villagers could have regularly made a journey to their most distant fields of more than two or three kilometres, though communal woodland and waste were often more remote. This would have prescribed a maximum area which they were able to cultivate and thus have set a limit to the size of the village. A cultivated area of 10 to 15 square kilometres – the area within a radius of about two kilometres of a village – would appear to have been the maximum that could be conveniently ploughed and reaped. When allowance is made for woodland, meadow, common grazing and waste land, a community of some 150 households would appear to have been about the maximum size of farming settlements in regions of moderate to good farmland.

The same argument applies to towns. There are examples, notably in the Hungarian Plain, of huge agricultural towns, whose 'citizens' tilled vast areas and made, at least occasionally, very long journeys to the fields. But these were unusual, and were justified by the quite exceptional circumstances of the Plain of Hungary. In any event, the peasants usually established temporary huts, or *tanyak*, in their more remote fields, and these ultimately developed into permanent dwellings. No city or town can have cultivated directly and regularly lands lying much beyond three or four kilometres from its walls. But the urban lands appear to have been relatively valuable and to have been cultivated perhaps more intensively than those of villages. Many citizens, even in north-western Europe, had urban vineyards, from which they satisfied part at least of the demand for cheap wine.

A very small town might have been expected to satisfy most, if not all, its agricultural needs from its own fields and by the labours of its own citizens. But this 'domestic' production of food would not have increased in volume with growth in the size of the town. Towns of intermediate size would have been heavily dependent on food brought in from the villages of the region and sold in the urban markets. Large towns might well have exhausted the potentialities of their local regions, and 'very large' and 'giant' cities were undoubtedly dependent for the supply of basic food-stuffs, especially the breadgrains on long-distance trade.

The relationship between urban growth and the agricultural productivity of the surrounding region is close, and questions of food supply must have limited the expansion of many cities. Botero, whose sixteenth-century treatise on cities has already been cited, noted 'the fruitfulness of the country' as one of the fundamental reasons for the growth of a city, and was clearly mystified when he found fertile provinces 'that have never a good city in them; as, for example, Piedmont'.

The military conquest and political control of the *contado* by some Italian cities was motivated in part by the desire to have undivided control over its resources. The *contado* formed, to-gether with its central city, an economic unit, and self-sufficiency in most of the requisites of daily life was the ideal of the Italian city state. Padua – not one of the larger Italian cities – appears to have achieved this ideal.[43] Pisa attempted similarly to live off the produce of the Pisan plain and of the nearby Maremma marshes. But the land was inherently less productive than the Po plain, and, despite a fairly ruthless policy of exploitation by the citizens, supplementary grain had to be imported from Sicily.[44] In his eulogy of the wealth and prosperity of Milan, Bonvesin della Riva described how 'in our territories . . . all kinds of cereals are produced . . . in such an amazing quantity that . . . they not only make good the deficiency of foodstuffs in the city of Como but also are transported and distributed to feed peoples beyond the Alps'. But the Lombardy Plain, especially as it was exploited in the thirteenth and later centuries, was one of the most fertile and productive areas of Europe. This was a precondition of the urban growth of northern Italy.

The port cities of Venice and Genoa had a less ready access to the food surplus of a fertile hinterland. Genoa, like Pisa, drew bread crops from Sicily and even from Spain and North Africa. Venice obtained grain from the whole Adriatic region. Romagna and the Marches regularly supplied Venice and, somewhat less regularly, Rome itself.[45] There was also a considerable movement of grain from Apulia and Sicily to the cities of northern Italy. The

Dalmatian coast was too rugged to yield any significant surplus, but the plain of Albania appears to have enjoyed a degree of prosperity as a major source of the Venetian bread supply.

The urban food supply presented no less a problem in northern France and the Low Countries. Medieval land reclamation in Flanders must have been related as much to the demand for food in the Flemish cities as the growth of the rural population. During the Middle Ages, however, the major source of supply of bread crops was the fertile but comparatively lightly urbanised regions of Artois and Picardy. Grain was carted to the limit of navigation on the Lys, Scarpe and Scheldt, where small river-ports had grown up, and was carried down-river to the cities. A complicated system of waterways and staple rights developed with the upstream cities and markets having the advantage over those lower down. The Flemish cities, unlike the Italian, never fully established their political control over their surrounding territories; they never became city-states.[46] They had a limited authority to control the rural cloth industry (see p. 308), but they could not compel the rural area to satisfy their needs for bread grains and other food-stuffs. It was not until Baltic rye began in the fifteenth century to supplement the grain of northern France that the food supply of the Flemish cities was secure.

The cities of Brabant, including Brussels, the largest of them, appear to have derived their food supply from the fertile plains of southern Brabant, so much more productive than the alternating polders and sands of Flanders. Food supply was relatively easy in the Rhineland cities. Cologne drew upon the plain of Westphalia and relied heavily on the Rhine itself for the movement of food-stuffs.[47] Other Rhineland cities – which were, in any event, very much smaller – could be supplied from the plains of Baden and Alsace, the Rheingau and Wetterau. Here too the river had the effect of greatly extending the area from which supplies could be drawn and the *Marktschiff*, or market-boat, was a well established institutions at such towns as Frankfurt and Mainz.[48]

Paris was, at least from the eleventh or twelfth century, the largest city in the Christian west, and its food supply was propor-tionately important. Its situation, near the convergence of several navigable rivers, gave it a great advantage, and much of its food supply, not to mention its requirements in salt, building timber and fuel, were brought to the city by boat. The principal quays for unloading the produce lay on the right bank of the Seine; very little was unloaded on the left bank. A report on Paris' food supply of the late seventeenth century[49] showed that grain was received from areas as distant as Picardy, but the chief source was unquestionably the plains of Beauce. The chief grain market in Paris was, in fact, known as *le Marché de Beauce*. There was, however, some production in the vicinity of the city, and Etienne Boileau's transcription of its gild regulations (see p. 293) recorded that a burgess might sell his grain in the city without payment of toll.

Some wine was produced in the close vicinity of Paris, but it enjoyed no high reputation. Most abundant in the city's markets was burgundy, brought down river to the city, through Gascon and even Rhenish wines were sometimes brought up from the coastal ports. Animals were in the seventeenth century driven overland from as far afield as Brittany. In the Middle Ages the city cast its net less widely, but Normandy was certainly an important source of fatstock.

### URBAN FINANCES

In most of Europe cities and towns were taxed for the support of their ruler; they usually made some kind of payment to the territorial lord to whom they owed their liberties, and their citizens taxed themselves in order to defray the expenses of municipal government. The right to make levies of this last kind was usually explicit or implicit in their charters. The expenses of urban government were often very high; they were also very variable. Building and maintaining the walls and gates were commonly the most costly item in a town's budget. At Namur at one period their cost consumed two-thirds of the city's income; at Dijon they were a very heavy burden, and when Brussels rebuilt its walls late in the fourteenth century it also faced the expense of the compulsory purchase and demolition of houses which stood in their path. The expenditure of cities included, in very many instances, extraordinary taxes levied by the king. Salaries and pensions, feasting and pageantry, the upkeep of wells and fountains, and some rudimentary attempts to keep the city both clean and secure all entered into its accounts.

The sources of municipal income normally consisted both of direct impositions on its citizens and of indirect taxes on the goods which they consumed.[50] The latter tended to predominate. In the Tuscan cities they commonly made up 80 to 85 per cent of income; at Basel 85, and at Bruges 93 per cent. At Perigueux, on the other hand, a *taille*, levied on all heads of household, was the chief municipal tax. Indirect taxes were levied primarily on foodstuffs. Wine has always attracted a heavy rate of duty, and there seem to have been few medieval towns which did not make wine consumption contribute heavily to their income. In many cities there was a toll, *gabella*, on all foodstuffs brought in for sale. Most cities owned corporate property: mills, halls and buildings in which goods were offered for sale, the grazing in the ditch which encircled its walls, even municipal brick and lime kilns and quarries. All could be made to yield a revenue.

Urban budgets have been little studied, but the few examples which are available suggest that the volume of receipts was large and that it increased sharply in the thirteenth century. That of Pisa rose from under 2400 livres in 1230 to about 40,000 livres in 1288.[51] At Dijon, which almost alone has been the subject of a full and careful study,[52] the total income of the town consisted of a fairly steady revenue from municipal property, tolls and the profits of jurisdiction. On this was superimposed in most years a variable direct levy, usually for a specific purpose such as repairing the town's walls or discharging its obligations to the Duke of Burgundy, which sometimes amounted to many times the regular income.

Municipal taxation appears in general to have been regressive in so far as a very large part of the taxation was in many, perhaps most, cases a flat levy on goods of everyday consumption and use. Direct taxes were usually made proportionate to the assessed wealth of the taxpayer, though the property of the wealthy was undervalued. The Church appears, as a general rule, to have contributed little to the tax income of the towns. At Dijon, the several monastic and other ecclesiastical institutions made a substantial contribution to the costs of its fortifications, but to nothing else. Cities with large religious institutions must, like American cities blessed with universities, have found them a considerable fiscal liability.

Most of the larger cities covered extraordinary expenditures by means of forced loans from its wealthier citizens;[53] many Italian cities in this way built up an enormous indebtedness, which was converted into a consolidated debt paying a fixed rate of interest.

Service on the debt became a major lien on the city's income from direct taxes. There can be no doubt that urban expenditure and indebtedness increased several times during the last two centuries of the Middle Ages, and that this was due primarily to the increased frequency and the high social cost of war.

## THE URBAN SCENE

Little except the ground plan remains of most medieval towns. Except in the case of a few of the later – and by definition smaller – towns, there was no discernible plan in their layout. The streets were rarely straight. They linked together the irregular spaces which served as markets. Except in the 'new' towns these were in their layout reminiscent of the village green, from which, in fact, many had derived. The central *place* was often dominated by a parish church or, in the case of the episcopal cities, by a cathedral. The English practice of hiding the cathedral behind a battlemented wall, in the security of its close, was very rarely followed in continental Europe, in part because European cathedrals, outside southern Italy, were not monastic. Parish churches were numerous in all except the smallest towns, and the panoramic city views, which became increasingly popular in the sixteenth century, always made much of their steeples and towers. There were also civic buildings, which served as centres of city administration, as headquarters of its gilds and as meeting places for its merchants.

The city was constrained by its walls, which in the faster growing urban centres, brought about a denser occupation of the urban area than might otherwise have been the case. Genoa, one of the most closely built of European cities, is said to have had over 150 houses to the hectare in some part of its urban area.[54] On the other hand, many towns had not, at the end of the period of medieval growth, filled out the area within their walls. Many of the sixteenth-century city views of Braun and Hogenberg, of Deventer and of Sebastian Münster show gardens and even cultivated fields within the walls.

Whether or not the walled area had been fully built up, there were usually suburbs, straggling rows of houses or clusters of cottages, which lay on the far side of the town ditch. They were roughly built, and always liable to immediate destruction if the city were attacked. Most towns appear to have tried to keep a clear field of fire around their walls. An inquisition held at Calais

early in the fifteenth century shows how at least one highly
vulnerable town failed in this.

> Outside the gates of Calais houses and buildings are erected . . . by
> which . . . great damage is liable to come . . . for under cover of the
> same enemies could be lodged. . . . Hitherto there was an ordinance
> kept whereby no man . . . could build houses there, which was
> continued until the land outside the said gates was granted by the
> king's letters patent to certain persons who have erected the said
> houses . . . contrary to the common good.[55]

Suburbs were sometimes of great extent; Bonvesin della
Riva reported that the number of houses beyond the moat of the
city of Milan 'would be enough to constitute a city'. Those suburbs
which developed in the twelfth and thirteenth centuries were
likely to have been enclosed by an extension of the walls by the
fourteenth, but few additions to town walls were made after the
mid-fourteenth century, and suburbs went unprotected. There
seems generally to have been a degree of uncertainty regarding
the size of suburbs. No doubt the number of suburban inhabitants
fluctuated more than that of the area within the walls. Suburban
living may have had financial advantages, in so far as goods commonly paid toll as they passed through the city's gates, but it was
precarious and lacking in the kind of protection which walls gave
to those who lived within them.

Very little of the housing of the medieval town has survived,
and this has in every instance been the masonry-built homes of
the patricians rather than the humbler dwellings of artisans.
More have survived in Italy, because there a far greater use was
made of stone than in northern Europe, where wood was cheap
and abundant. A few medieval houses remain in Nuremberg and
Troyes, and careful search reveals fragments of medieval housing
in many other north European cities. Most were of two, occasionally of three storeys. They were built in rows along the streets,
each backed by a small courtyard.[56] Shops and workshops often
occupied the ground floor levels, just as in the Roman *tabernae*.
In Paris, houses of three storeys became common from the mid-
thirteenth century, and Heers has shown that in Genoa, admittedly
a highly congested city, houses sometimes ran to seven storeys.
Few houses in the larger towns retained gardens until the end of

the Middle Ages. The garden plots, which had once lain behind the streets of houses in the larger cities, were in time divided up, and built upon.[57] Small, crowded and insanitary courtyards thus developed, which must in many respects have resembled those ugly and malodorous courts described by Friedrich Engels in nineteenth century Manchester.

Most of the city houses seem to have been single-family dwellings, but the tall houses of Genoa must, in effect, have been tenements, and Bonvesin della Riva, while counting the number of families, nevertheless added that there were 'very many houses in which many families live together'. At Valladolid, in the sixteenth century almost all town houses were occupied each by a single family,[58] and this must have been the general rule in all except the few cities where space was at a great premium.

Much of the housing was built of wood and roofed with thatch. Away from the town centre, where most of the patricians lived, the houses were of one or at most two storeys. Their walls were commonly built of timber framing, infilled with wickerwork and clay. They were insubstantial; their structure decayed readily, especially in the damp climate of northern Europe. They were infested by rats, and, above all, they burned easily. Fire was a perennial danger to all medieval towns, and there is little evidence that much was ever done to combat it beyond requiring, in a few instances, that houses be built of masonry and roofed with tile or slate. Toulouse, within the period 1343–1451, suffered no less than five disastrous fires. The *Bourgeois of Mons*, at the beginning of the sixteenth century described the fire which destroyed Valenciennes in 1522.[59] Every medieval town must at some time have been devastated by fire.

No doubt much of the urban property, especially in smaller towns, was owned by the families which occupied them. Some form of burgage tenure, in which a small, almost nominal conventional rent was paid, was widespread. But in many cities there was speculation in urban property. The rich burgesses of Arras, described by Lestocquoy,[60] owned urban property, and the unscrupulous Jehan de Franche, in the late thirteenth century, made a fortune by acquiring and manipulating urban real estate.[61] We are left in no doubt that the medieval real-estate operator, who bought up property and rented it to artisans and labourers, had nothing to learn from his modern counterpart.

In every medieval city, except the smallest, a social distinction was to be drawn between the various quarters, and in large cities this distinction was particularly strongly marked. The differential in wealth and income between the richest citizens and the broad mass of the labouring poor was enormous. The valuations of property for tax purposes, made at Basel in 1446, show a range from under 30 gulden to over 20,000 (Table 6.2).[62] About half of those assessed fell into the lowest category, and below these were the unknown masses who were too poor to have been assessed at all.

The well-to-do and patrician classes usually lived close to the market place, the business centre of the town. The sixteenth-century houses of the Grande Place at Brussels are the successors

**Table 6.2  Taxable wealth in Basel, 1446**

| Gulden | Persons | Percentage |
|---|---|---|
| Less than 100 | 1926 | 67·8 |
| 100–   500 | 622 | 21·3 |
| 500–  1000 | 128 | 4·7 |
| 1000–  1500 | 46 | 1·7 |
| 1500–  2000 | 22 | 0·9 |
| 2000–  2500 | 25 | 0·9 |
| 2500–  3000 | 9 |  |
| 3000–  3500 | 12 |  |
| 3500–  4000 | 3 |  |
| 4000–  4500 | 12 | 2·6 |
| 4500–  5000 | 3 |  |
| 5000–10,000 | 23 |  |
| 10,000–20,000 | 9 |  |
| Over 20,000 | 1 |  |
|  | 2841 | 100·0 |

Those assessed were presumably heads of households. There is no evidence for the number of those too poor to have been assessed. Based on Gustav Schönberg, *Finanzverhältnisse der Stadt Basel im XIV. und XV. Jahrhundert*, Tübingen, 1879.

to the less elaborate houses of the medieval merchants. In Paris, where the number of affluent citizens was probably greater than in most other cities, they tended to live on the right bank in the quarters of Sainte-Oppotune, Saint-Jacques la Boucherie and

Saint-Denis.[63] The south-eastern parts of the city were the poorest. This may have derived from the earlier tendency for the exploited workers to live outside the walls; the patricians and masters, inside, protected from the workers' revolts which were not uncommon in the twelfth and thirteenth centuries. At Basel, the linen-weavers continued to be concentrated in the *Vorstadt*, even after this had been enclosed by the city walls. Within the working class areas there was a tendency for certain crafts to group themselves. In Paris the tanners were concentrated along the right bank above the Ile de la Cité, and the mercers and clothiers were to be found in those quarters where the richer citizens, who were their customers, lived. Money-lenders and jewellers were mostly to be found in the same area.

No less conspicuous was the tendency for certain ethnic and cultural groups to live as small, closed societies. The 'nations' at the medieval universities formed such groups. The Syrians had done so in the earliest medieval towns, the Italians in Constantinople, and above all, the Jews did so in the later Middle Ages.[64] The origin of the ghetto is to be found more in Jewish exclusiveness than in Christian intolerance, extreme as the latter unquestionably was. In the eleventh century a question addressed by a Jewish community to its Talmudic scholars was: 'one of the home owners in an alley, exclusively inhabited by Jews, wanted to sell or lease his courtyard to a non-Jew. May the other inhabitants of that alley legally restrain him from settling a non-Jew in their midst?'[65] It appears that Jews often desired to maintain the Jewishness of the sectors of the city in which they lived.

The streets of the medieval town were unpaved, unlighted and ill-kept. At Valladolid in the sixteenth century waste was merely tossed into the street, or thrown into the river which had to be cleaned out periodically to allow its water to flow freely. Farm animals were kept in the small courts and yards behind city houses and dung-heaps accumulated before their doors. In 1481 the authorities in Frankfurt forbade the rearing of pigs within the *Altstadt*, because they fouled the streets in a manner unworthy of a great city. It is generally assumed that the streets were very narrow, and a few such alleys have survived. Some streets, however, were wide, and most urban fairs, including those of Champagne, were in fact held in the streets of the towns, where rows of wooden stalls were erected for the purpose.

# 7

# Medieval manufacturing

Medieval society was predominantly agricultural. If it were possible to calculate its gross national product, farming would be seen as its largest sector by far. Yet manufacturing was important, and its contribution to medieval society was an essential one. Throughout the Middle Ages cloth was woven and clothing made; leather was tanned and fabricated into footwear, protective clothing and saddlery; minerals were extracted from the earth and smelted, and metals were refined. Weapons and armour were continually in demand; metal tools and utensils were used around the home and on the land. Stone was quarried and buildings erected; glass and pottery were made. Doubtless many of these activities were carried on by people whose primary occupation was in agriculture; by non-specialists who engaged in them when the land demanded something less than their full attention, or they were cottage industries designed to supplement a farm income or to strengthen the self-sufficient rural family.

Yet in the thousand years which separated the end of the ancient world from the beginning of modern times two important changes occurred in the scale and organisation of manufacturing in Europe. The volume of manufactures increased very many times during the period, and the manufacturing processes passed increasingly into the hands of specialists for whom their craft was their only means of livelihood. These developments were necessarily accompanied, both as cause and as consequence, by the development of trade in the goods produced. This also tended in many branches of productive activity to pass into the hands of specialists. The cobbler still made a pair of shoes for a particular customer, as indeed he still does in many parts of Europe, but the weaver produced more and more for a distant market. The merchant thus intervened between the producer of the cloth and its purchaser, as he also did between the wool-grower and each of the subsequent stages in the spinning of the thread and production of the finished cloth.

The growing role of specialisation in manufacturing brought with it an increasing volume of production. The volume of goods increased from, perhaps, the tenth or eleventh century until the fourteenth. It then suffered a setback, and again mounted in the fifteenth and sixteenth centuries. The curve of expansion, contraction and renewed expansion was doubtless far from even, but there are no runs of figures, except for a few localised industries and for short periods of time. Any evaluation of the overall rate of change, and of its variations between one area and another is entirely qualitative, derived from estimates of population and of the nature of demand. It is by no means certain, however, that the production of goods increased faster than the population which consumed them. In the later fourteenth and early fifteenth centuries population declined, and with it the volume of demand. Production was cut back, but it is probable that, in many branches of manufacturing, output was higher in relation to population than it had been before the Black Death.

It is difficult, however, to make comparisons. Not only is an adequate statistical base wholly lacking, but there was also a shift in the pattern of demand, so that one is in fact comparing different commodities. The cloth industry was the largest and most pervasive branch of manufacturing during the Middle Ages. In the thirteenth century cloth production and the cloth trade were dominated by the quality woollens marketed by the Flemish cities; by the fifteenth century such fabrics had lost their primacy. A cheaper, lighter cloth, made in different places and by different methods, had displaced it. The 'new draperies' were made in vastly greater quantities, but their costs of production were less, and they did not wear as well as the traditional Flemish cloth. They were worn, however, by a far greater number of people, and must be taken to represent a real improvement in living standards. There were other changes. Pewter tended amongst the bourgeois classes to replace ware on the table, and glass came to be more widely used in windows.

Medieval manufacturing was remarkably unprogressive, both in the techniques of production and also in its organisational structure. In very few respects did medieval industry show any technical advance on that of classical times, and knowledge of some industrial processes was even lost during the early Middle Ages and not regained until modern times. Advances were made in the later Middle Ages in the design and construction of ships and in the art of navigation, but one can point to few comparable developments in the field of industrial production. Foremost amongst those that were made were improvements in the use of water as a source of power, the invention of the windmill and, above all, the introduction in the fifteenth century of the blast furnace.

Units of industrial production remained very small throughout the medieval period. There was nothing even faintly resembling the factory before the sixteenth century, and the largest single industrial operation was almost certainly the Arsenal at Venice. But this was owned and operated by the Venetian Republic, and its purpose was to build and fit out its ships for military and commercial purposes. It is worth noting that the earliest large 'factory' in England was the comparable dockyard at Chatham, built early in the eighteenth century. Mines, particularly towards the end of the Middle Ages, sometimes employed a large labour force by medieval standards. But in all other respects the unit of industrial production remained the small workshop.

To some degree this predominance throughout the period of very small units of production was due to the lack of investment capital (see p. 299). Above all, however, it sprang from popular attitudes to manufacturing, and was reinforced by the organisations of craftsmen, known as gilds. The medieval ideal, or at least our modern concept of that ideal, envisaged a master producing cloth, leather goods or metal wares, or even loaves of bread or joints of meat, with the help of a journeyman and an apprentice. Quality would have been supervised by the gild. The master was prevented from engrossing his raw materials, even if he had the opportunity. He worked under the public eye, and he was expected to charge the 'just price' for his product, and to live modestly as became his station. Reality fell short of the ideal. Quality was not always the foremost consideration of the craftsman, and the precise regulations drawn up by gilds and public authorities, together with their frequent repetition, suggest that enforcement was not always easy. Most medieval craftsmen lived close to the margin of subsistence, and their capital assets, as shown by their wills – and only the more well-to-do left wills – were often pathetically small.

This chapter will trace the growth and spread of manufacturing during the medieval centuries; it will examine the institutional framework within which it was carried on, and will assess, in so far as sources make it possible, the contribution of manufacturing to the total production of medieval Europe.

MANUFACTURING: RURAL AND URBAN

The history of manufacturing during this period is readily divisible into three phases. Precise time limits cannot be given for them, because they were stages in an evolutionary process which proceeded at different rates in different parts of the continent. In general, central Europe lagged behind western and southern, and eastern and northern behind central.

The first phase was that of the restricted production of manufactured goods under conditions which approached those of local self-sufficiency, the 'economy of no markets' of Pirenne. There were, of course, markets, and there is no reason to suppose that trade, even long-distance trade, ever ceased, but the goods traded were of relatively high value, and the market in the coarse, simple goods of everyday use was probably very small. The household or the village community produced its own cloth and such rough tools, weapons and consumers' goods as it needed. Long before the end of Roman rule in the West there was a tendency (see p. 30) for large estates to have their own workshops and weaving sheds, satisfying from their own raw materials and by the labour of their own slaves most of their material wants.

Long-distance trade was hampered and restricted in many ways. Low value goods could not justify the labour, time and risk involved in transporting them far. Local regions had always been self-sufficing in the simpler and cheaper goods, but these had under the Roman Empire been in large measure produced by specialists and sold in local shops and markets. The near self-sufficiency of the local region now gave place to a similar autonomy within the limits of the community or of the estate or fisc. The tendency was strong for each feudally controlled territory to become almost as self-sufficing in manufactured goods as it was in foodstuffs, with the exception only of the exotic and luxury goods which the estate lacked the means to produce.

We can only occasionally get a glimpse of this feudal organisation of manufacturing. There was the Anglo-Saxon earl who took with him when he travelled his own blacksmith and iron-worker, whose obligation it was to make and repair his master's weapons and armour. There were the monastic estates, surveyed in the polyptyques of the ninth and later centuries, which produced cloth, salt, timber for building, and even iron from their own land and by the labour of their own dependants and serfs.

Manufactured goods formed part of the dues owed by the peasants to their lords. A monastery, such as Prüm or Lobbes, in the ninth and tenth centuries received an immense amount of cloth, woven from flax or wool, as well as hundreds of bundles of raw flax. Some monasteries even ran workshops – *gynaecea* – in which women, presumably of servile status, prepared and span fibre and wove cloth. Such an institution as a monastery, together with the communities of peasants by which it was sustained, was clearly self-sufficing in all except a few esoteric items, and may have had a marketable surplus in some of the articles, such as cloth, which it produced.

The Benedictine houses of the ninth and tenth centuries in Western Europe, or the manors which they controlled, thus served as centres of industrial production. In east-central Europe, Cistercian houses were performing the same role in the twelfth century, at a time when, in western and southern Europe, manufacturing was becoming a specialised occupation and passing into the hands of urban craftsmen.

At some time between the tenth and the twelfth centuries manufacturing processes gradually shifted from monasteries and rural areas to the new but expanding urban centres. At the same time they tended to pass from the non-specialised hands of the peasantry to those of the specialised craftsmen. These two events were clearly related. Specialist craftsmen worked for a wider market than non-specialised. In very many instances it was necessary for a merchant or trader to interpose between the artificer and the consumer, and the former found that he could operate effectively only when he had access to the market or a trader had access to him. A series of commercial institutions and arrangements developed: periodic fairs and regular markets, always in or close to towns, were established, and these in turn declined in importance as their role was taken over by the continuous operation of urban trading centres.

The tenth and eleventh centuries witnessed a growth in population and probably also an increase in per capita demand for goods. This was most conspicuous in the ambitious building programmes which were undertaken at this time. The wealth that accrued from the more widespread and intensive cultivation of the soil was in part channelled towards increasing the demand for consumers' goods. Since much of this new wealth inevitably found its way into the hands of the feudal classes, it was used to finance the consumption of quality or luxury goods. This in turn contributed to the importance of the specialised urban craftsman.

For three or more centuries manufacturing was predominantly, though by no means exclusively, an urban pursuit. There were of course exceptions. Certain crafts were of necessity pursued mainly in rural areas. Mining and quarrying were from their very nature, primarily rural, though many towns had their own quarries from which they extracted materials for their building programmes. A few – Tournai is a notable example – even produced a well-known ornamental stone which was distributed and sold over a wide area. The smelting of metals was also a rural pursuit. The preparation of foodstuffs, in so far, at least, as it was the work of specialised crafts, was almost exclusively urban, and the very large numbers of butchers and bakers has already been noted (see p. 256).

Towards the end of the Middle Ages there was a gradual movement of craft industries from the towns to the countryside. This trend continued through the sixteenth and seventeenth centuries, and provides a partial explanation of the failure of most towns to grow significantly after the fourteenth century. By the eighteenth century a large proportion of the craft industries was carried on in a rural setting, and the Industrial Revolution, when it came, was at first a rural, not an urban phenomenon.

There were several reasons for this dispersal of manufacturing during the later Middle Ages. Foremost amongst them was the increasing use of simple machines powered by water. The undershot water wheel came into general use. Mills were built in immense numbers. Not only did they grind corn; they were also made to full cloth, crush pigments, and power the bellows of iron refineries, and, late in the fifteenth century, of the newly developed blast-furnaces.

More important, however, was the rigidity of the urban crafts in the face of a changing pattern of demand. The gild structure had been important in maintaining quality at a time when market demand was strongly oriented towards luxury goods. During the later Middle Ages the pattern of demand was becoming more broadbased, and the consumption of goods of medium quality, especially cloth, was greater. By and large, the traditional centres of manufacture failed to accommodate themselves to the new market, and production, especially of cloth and metal goods, but also to some extent of leather, shifted gradually from town to country.

A further reason for the drift of manufacturing to the countryside was that labour was cheaper in the latter. No one supposes that the urban journeyman was overpaid, but there were charges upon urban craftsmen that were not known in rural areas. The rural craftsman was furthermore very often a part-time farmer. His craft was a supplement to his agricultural activities, though there were doubtless many cases where the reverse would have been true. The rural craft thus tended to be a marginal occupation, less highly rewarded than the urban craft which provided a full-time employment. Poverty and overcrowding in the rural areas served only to increase the need for the supplementary income that a craft could bring to a rural household. Rural industry, furthermore, was less regimented and controlled than urban. The resistance of the urban gilds to innovation and change was possibly the most important factor in the rise of rural industries.

The balance shifted in favour of the villages. The woollen and linen industry of Normandy and Brittany in the late Middle Ages and early modern times, was almost exclusively rural. The manufacture of fustian and barchent in South Germany and of linen in Switzerland was similarly a domestic industry, carried on in the cottages of the peasantry. But the clearest case of the migration of craft industries from the town to the country, apart from the example provided by England, is to be found in the Low Countries (see p. 459).

The new pattern of industry called for a new type of industrial organisation. The rural craftsman did not have as easy an access to the market as his urban counterpart, and he probably lacked the capital to purchase a stock of whatever raw materials he used and to hold it, perhaps for many months, until he could sell his product. The merchant capitalist, a class which did not exist during the early medieval phase of rural industry, provided the answer. He made raw wool available for the spinner, and spun thread for the weaver, while he himself often controlled the more capital-intensive finishing processes. Furthermore, he provided the link between the rural craftsman and the market, visiting the former at regular intervals to deposit raw materials and to collect the output of the previous period of work.[1]

Such was the domestic, or 'putting-out' system (*Verlags-system*), the earliest manifestation of anything resembling modern capitalism. The craftsman worked for the merchant; the latter provided the materials and paid a kind of piece-rate for the work. The system lent itself more readily to abuses than the urban gild system, and gave the craftsman no protection against the merchant. Rural craftsmen could not easily combine; they became in fact the servants of the merchant capitalist, without whose supply of materials they could not employ themselves, and without whose command of the market they could not dispose of their product.

One last factor in the development of rural industry was the growth of population. The period of urban expansion had been one of increasing population, when the surplus of rural areas, or some part of it had migrated to find employment in the towns. In the fifteenth century population in much of Europe was recovering from its earlier setbacks. This time country folk did not migrate to the towns; urban occupations were brought to them. Changing conditions of land tenure now made it possible for a peasant to lease a fraction of a family tenement, sufficient to give him a part-time employment on the land, while the rest of his time was given to weaving or iron-working. In some parts of England, it has been argued, the custom of partible inheritance, that is, of division between heirs, encouraged the formation of small holdings, which had, if they were to provide a living, to be supplemented by part-time crafts. The same may have happened in continental Europe.

### THE ORGANISATION OF MEDIEVAL MANUFACTURING

Manufacturing never wholly deserted the towns. Indeed there

must have been many branches which never really experienced the competition of rural craftsmen. It was primarily the textile industries, and only secondly those which fabricated iron and leather goods, which were thus dispersed through the countryside. Most others, including the finishing processes in the textile industries, remained within the walls of towns until the end of the Middle Ages.

Within the towns the craftsmen were organised into confraternities or gilds. Medieval society was dominated by such societies. Their purposes varied. Many were charitable, educational or eleemosynary; most had a religious purpose. All served in some way to provide, in the anonymous society of the town, that mutuality and interdependence which were a feature of the rural community. Foremost amongst these corporations were the craft gilds in the narrower sense of the term. These were organisations of men who practised the same craft. They grew up in the larger towns in the twelfth and thirteenth centuries, but their origin is far from clear. We may be sure, however, that they owed nothing to the *collegia* of the later Roman Empire, just as they in their turn were in so sense the origin of trades unions. It was inevitable that groups of men, following the same calling, living close to one another, standing together in the same church, buying in the same market, at the mercy of the same merchants and traders, should combine for their mutual protection and help. Such combinations were commonly in part religious, for nowhere is it possible to draw a clear distinction between the secular and economic functions of gilds on the one hand, and the spiritual and eleemosynary on the other. Indeed, the gild regulations, which the masters formulated and enforced, derived in part from contemporary religious teaching on man and society, price and profit.

## The Gild Merchant

There was a strong element of revolt against the established order in the formation of craft gilds. No two towns had the same, or even closely similar histories, and generalisation is unwise, but there can be no doubt that in many the craft gilds represented to a considerable degree the poorer and less privileged craftsmen, who combined to resist the pretensions of the long-established patrician class.

The Gild Merchant was the primary organisation of urban

traders. Licence for them to unite and organise was granted by the lord who endowed the town with its privileges. They formed a corporation within the body of citizens or burgesses. In 1127 the Count of Flanders granted a charter to the citizens of Saint-Omer; they became free of certain burdensome obligations, and had easier recourse to law in settling disputes. Amongst their number were 'those who have their gild and belong to it'. These citizens the Count made 'free of toll at the port of Dixmude and at the port of Gravelines, and throughout all the land of Flanders'.[2] Such privileges would in all probability have been of no value to most of the citizens, but to the élite of traders, who made up the Gild Merchant, they were invaluable, opening up to them commercial opportunities in the nearby ports and throughout Flanders.

The traders of the twelfth and thirteenth centuries not only dealt in whatever goods were in demand; they also supervised the work of craftsmen, providing them with raw materials and marketing the fruits of their labours. The merchants became rich; they acquired urban property, which they rented to craftsmen, perhaps to those already heavily dependent on them. They made loans at interest, and from being well-to-do they became rich. As traders they were comparatively unspecialised at first. In the larger towns, however, many of them tended to focus their activities on a narrow range of goods. They dealt in wool, cloth, or spices, though ever watchful for any business opportunity which they might turn to their advantage.

Specialisation brought division within the merchants' gild. Groups were formed of merchants dealing in wool or cloth, in skins and furs, in wine, spices or other related commodities. In this way the more prestigious gilds, like the 'greater misteries' of London, came into being. They were gilds of traders rather than of craftsmen; they did their business in the *gild*-hall or cloth-hall, rather than in humble workshops along the side streets of the town, and they employed craftsmen, commonly on a piecework basis. These were the greater gilds. In Florence there were seven of them, out of a total number of gilds which ultimately rose to over seventy. In London, where there had never been a Gild Merchant, there came to be twelve such gilds, though the gulf between the greater and the lesser companies was here neither so clearcut not so absolute as in many other cities.[3] The earliest London gilds to separate from the mass of traders and craftsmen were the mercers, tailors and drapers, who all dealt in some way in cloth; the grocers, who imported spices, the fishmongers, vintners, goldsmiths and salters.

In Paris there had been a general association of merchants, the *marchands de l'eau*, those, that is, who brought goods to the city by water. It was not until the thirteenth century that more specialised trading gilds and artisans gilds began to form.

The merchants who were grouped into a small number of traders' gilds seem rarely to have restricted themselves to a narrow range of commodities. They commonly spread across the whole field of trade, making profit where they could. They regularly invested in urban real estate, and sometimes also in rural. They were not infrequently the landlords of the craftsmen to whom they supplied both fixed and working capital, always at a generous rate of interest. In London, 'of fifty-three bakers inspected in 1303, only seven owned their own bakehouses; most were held under lease from wholesalers, who, together with the fishmongers held a commanding interest in half the twenty-eight mills near the city'.[4] The same situation prevailed in the larger cities of continental Europe. Jehan Boinebroke of Douai and the Crespin and Lanstiers of Arras yielded nothing to the grocers and haberdashers of London in the variety of their business enterprises and their ability to make profit from them.

The merchants employed craftsmen in a variety of ways. Most often, it would appear, they advanced operating capital in the form of raw wool, spun thread, hides, metals and dyestuffs, and took back the processed goods, paying a commission for the work done. In a manufacturing process involving a series of distinct activities, the merchant would in all probability put out the materials to several craftsmen in turn, making as many payments for fabrication or processing. In other instances the merchant owned the fixed capital, as in the case of the bakers noted above. It was clearly in the interests of the merchant to prevent the development of combinations amongst the craftsmen and to keep their costs as low as possible. When in the end they failed to hold the craftsmen in this subordinate position, they took their business to the rural areas, where combination amongst the part-time weavers and other craftsmen was more difficult and correspondingly less likely. In doing so they succeeded in some instances in destroying the urban crafts.

The merchant class, lastly, often held a monopoly of political power in the towns. They provided the town government, and formed and élite which, whether or not it was in a formal position of power, controlled the town's destinies. They were the patricians, the *pluis sufficeauntz*, the *potentiores*. Wealth meant power in the Middles Ages no less than today.

It was only in the larger towns of medieval Europe that the merchant class came into its own; only here was to be found the range of opportunity in trade, manufacturing and manipulating real estate which they required. 'The simpler the town's economic life', in the words of Professor Thrupp,

> the more it approximated to a mere market town serving a small district, the more the independent artisan and shopkeeper predominated. In proportion as the town took part in inter-regional trade and especially as it developed industries that were dependent on distant markets for their supply or outlet the merchant came into ascendency and tended to control the government structure.[5]

### The Artisans' Gilds

Merchants' gilds crystallised from the gild merchant or from the general community of traders. They were the most prestigious of the confraternities; their members were the most wealthy and politically important citizens, and the less well-to-do were excluded from them by high entrance fees and obligatory feasts and liveries. Gross has presented a model[6] which represents the craft gilds as emerging similarly from the Gild Merchant which had previously monopolised commercial activity within the borough. The gilds emerged in so many ways that generalisation is difficult and dangerous. Gross's model is oversimplified. It assumes the coalescence of free and independent craftsmen for the maintenance of standards of workmanship and the preservation of their interests. The craftsmen may have been free and independent in the small market towns, where they were probably too few in most instances to be able to organise specialised crafts. In the larger towns, where they would have been much more numerous, the majority were probably far from independent.

Most urban crafts called for a considerable fixed capital, and, in some instances, a large working capital. The weaver's loom and the tools of the cobbler or carpenter were of no high value, but others, the tanners, bakers, metal-workers, for example, needed more extensive working quarters and larger equipment. Most industrial processes were slow, and material that was being processed represented a not inconsiderable investment for a prolonged period. In the case of goldsmiths, pewterers, silk-weavers, and the embroiderers of certain luxury fabrics, the stock of materials must have represented a very large outlay. In the small towns this problem of capital outlay on materials either did not arise or was of minor importance. The crafts were more simple; they produced for a local rather than a distant market, and there were few raw materials that were not of local origin.

The craftsmen were, as a general rule, short of capital. If they had been even moderately well-to-do they would have been employers of craftsmen. In view of the large amount of urban property in the hands of the Church and of merchant capitalists, few can have owned their own houses and shops. These they rented or leased from, in many instances, the same men who provided their raw materials and marketed part at least of their product. In the larger cities and especially in those branches of industry which made or processed goods for distant markets, the artisan was in the grip of the merchant capitalist fully as much as any nineteenth century mill-hand was at the mercy of the factory owner.

It was in such circumstances that many of the craft gilds were formed. They did not evolve slowly from merchants' gilds; rather, they were the result of successful revolt against the economic and political power of the merchant capitalists. The fact is that the medieval craftsman was extremely poor, living always on the edge of starvation. The weaver could ill afford to wear the cloth which he wove on commission for the merchant clothier. The complaint of the worker comes through to us in the verses of Chrestien de Troyes:

> Toujours tisserons draps de soie,
> Jamais n'en serons mieux vêtues,
> Toujours serons pauvres et rues,
> Et toujours aurons faim et soif. . . .
> Nous avons du pain à grand' peine,
> Peu le matin et le soir moins. . .
> Mais notre travail enrichit
> Celui pour qui nous travaillons.[7]

It was in 'a London . . . imbued with the revolutionary spirit'[8] that the lesser mysteries, made up of ordinary craftsmen, began to form in the later thirteenth century. For over a century new crafts were struggling into being, and fighting for a voice in the government of the city and in the control of their own destinies. By 1376 there were in London some fifty mysteries; in 1422 the Brewers' Gild compiled a list of 111 other gilds. Throughout western and central Europe there was conflict between the organised merchants and the crafts. In general, the crafts gained a pyrrhic victory, organising themselves and participating in town government, but all too often losing the economic fruits of victory, as manufacturing moved from town to country.

The town of Huy, lying within the bishopric of Liège, had at the beginning of the fourteenth century a probable population of no more than 6,000. Nevertheless, its communal strife bears a certain resemblance to that of London. In 1299 the members of the crafts revolted and seized the reins of government from the merchants and patricians. A new bishop came to the rescue of the latter, and the privileges of the craftsmen were suppressed. Within a few years, however, the craftsmen again asserted themselves, but, it would appear, more judiciously. They never again controlled the town's government, but they participated in it – a compromise which was followed in some other towns of the Low Countries.[9]

At Florence, the *popolo grasso*, the well-fed and well-to-do who controlled the seven *Arti Maggiori* and thus the destinies of the city, battened on the 'little people', the *popolo minuto*, the mass of semi- and unskilled workmen. The latter had on many occasions attempted to organise, to influence the patricians, to increase their wages and improve their conditions of work. In 1324, the 'fat people' legislated that

> every league or society of persons is forbidden if not sanctioned by the public authorities; wherefore we decree that any member of any *Arte*, and especially workmen of the *Arte della Lana*, under which many different persons of different conditions exercise trades, cannot assemble in any place, for any motive, nor make laws and ordinances under any title of brotherhood for any motive or pretence of religion, of funerals or of oblations, without permission of the *Consoli*.[10]

292

Later in the century (1378–81) the discontents of the 'little people' came to a head in the bloody riots of the *Ciompi*.[11] The solution adopted was to detach from the rebels the members of the more skilled trades by allowing them to incorporate themselves as gilds, and to suppress rigorously all attempts on the part of the others to organise.[12]

The gilds never formed a system. They were congeries of people, held together by self-interest, on which public authority sometimes imposed certain obligations. Amongst the large towns no two ever had an identical or even similar gild organisation. Towns of intermediate size often had a small number of gilds, whose economic functions must have been a great deal broader than their names would suggest. The gilds which one finds in any town were in part a response to such industrial specialisation as the town may have adopted; in part, also, to the play of urban politics; to the degree of success of the patrician class in resisting the pretensions of the artisans, and to the political skill and organising capacity of the latter. We have already seen how different was the outcome of the struggle within the city between *majores* and *minores* in the Low Countries, in Italy and in London.

In 1258, or soon afterwards, Etienne Boileau, *prévôt* or chief magistrate of Paris, undertook, on the orders of Louis IX, a review of the regulations of the city's gilds.[13] Each was called upon to send representatives to the Châtelet, there to present its rules and customs, which were then written down for future reference in controlling disputes between them. Boileau's register contains the regulations of a hundred crafts. Some are long and detailed; others are made up of only a few short paragraphs. In some cases the number of journeymen and apprentices was regulated; in others, the master was free to take on what labour he could. Occasionally the age was specified at which an apprentice could be engaged. It was usual for the regulations to specify the quality of the raw materials which might be used; to prohibit working by candlelight and on Sundays and certain feast days of the Church. Sometimes it was prescribed where the product might be sold. A few crafts had rules which might have been dictated by the police. Locksmiths, for example, were prohibited from making copies of the keys that might be presented to them; they had also to have the actual lock in their possession. Presumably the object was to prevent keys from passing into the hands of unauthorised persons. The old-clothes dealer, or *fripier*, was forbidden to purchase garments stained with blood. Some of the food industries – the *talemeliers*, or bakers, for example – were so closely controlled that many of the regulations must have been imposed on the gild by the city authorities.

Boileau's enrolment of the gild regulations is silent upon the size of each gild. Lists survive of the numbers of artisans in Paris for the years 1292 and 1300.[14] That for the latter year appears to be the more complete. In all 5844 artisans – masters, presumably – are accounted for, and the number of crafts recorded in the two lists reaches the extraordinary total of 448. It is admitted that a number of gilds escaped Boileau's enquiry, but clearly not enough to raise their total to this level. Several of the more esoteric crafts were pursued by only one or two masters, such as that of copper-founding, of metal-polishing, or of making buckles. Such crafts-men may have been subsumed under the name of a craft similar to their own, or, more likely, they belonged to no gild at all. It is, however, worth noting that the *Blasoniers* – men who made leather shields and blazoned them with the heraldic devices of their owners – inscribed their rules in Boileau's book, but the artisan lists of both 1292 and 1300 recorded only two members of the craft.

Some crafts, on the other hand, were very large. The weavers of woollen cloth numbered 360, and there were further groups of silk and linen weavers. There were 338 skinners and an extra-ordinarily large total of 251 goldsmiths. There were 129 mercers, 160 tailors, and 163 old clothes dealers; 131 bakers and 70 butchers; 122 masons and 108 carpenters. Not all these crafts are represented in Boileau's list. The ordinances of the silk-weavers were inscribed, but there are no regulations that clearly apply to the large number of cloth-weavers. One must conclude that the gild structure of Paris was fluid; that some gilds were very much broader in scope than their names might be taken to suggest, and that there was a considerable, perhaps a large mass of labour, much of it only semiskilled, which was not organised into craft gilds at all.

Cologne was the largest city in the Rhineland during the later Middle Ages, and its craft organisation was relatively complex. By the end of the fourteenth century there were thirty-six gilds.[15] Several new gilds was established in the fifteenth century, but at the same time four of the older crafts – the blanket makers (*Bettdeckenweber*), fustian-weavers (*Tirtiweber*), purse-makers and glove-makers – disappeared. By the end of the fifteenth century there were forty-four or forty-five gilds. A few lists survive of gild-members, mainly of the late fourteenth and the fifteenth centuries. These are an uncertain guide to the size of the crafts, but they may perhaps be taken to indicate their relative importance. The woollen cloth industry in all its branches was the largest by far, but the goldsmiths in 1395 listed no less than 122 masters.

Frankfurt-on-Main was a great deal smaller than either Cologne or Paris, and it is doubtful whether its medieval population ever greatly exceeded 10,000. In 1355 it had fourteen gilds.[16] By 1387 they had increased to twenty, and in the course of the fifteenth century reached 28, but by the early sixteenth century five of these had disappeared. In 1387 there were 1544 separate business undertakings, divided between the twenty gilds, most of which must have embraced more than one craft (see Table 7.1).

**Table 7.1**

|  | Undertakings | Percentage |
|---|---|---|
| Primary production (gardening, viti- | | |
| culture, fishing, etc.) | 107 | 6·1 |
| Secondary production | | |
| Textile manufacture | 334 | 21·7 |
| Clothing | 272 | 17·7 |
| Food industries | 179 | 11·7 |
| Building and construction | 141 | 9·3 |
| Metalworking | 123 | 8·0 |
| Wood-working | 118 | 7·7 |
| Leather working | 66 | 4·4 |
| Fuel and lighting | 13 | 0·9 |
| Tertiary occupations | | |
| Innkeeping, trade, transport | 156 | 10·1 |
| Personal service, and others | 35 | 2·2 |
|  | 1544 | 100·0 |

(Based on Karl Bücher, *Die Bevölkerung von Frankfurt am Main*, Tübingen, 1886, pp. 141–6.)

A feature of the occupational structure of Frankfurt is the absence, or at least the extreme rarity of luxury crafts. Not a single goldsmith appears. There were very few pursuits that could not have been found in a small town, serving the needs of its local region. It seems likely that an extreme proliferation of crafts, including those of a luxury nature, was to be found only in the few very large and large cities. Liège, a city similar in size to Frankfurt, had thirty-two gilds, whereas Mulhouse, a small town deeply involved in agriculture, had only six: the tailors, butchers, bakers, 'vignerons' (*Räbleuth*), smiths, and gardeners and agricultural workers.[17] Düren, a town of not dissimilar size in the lower Rhineland, had seven gilds: smiths, weavers, brewers, bakers, tailors, shoemakers and woodworkers.[18] Each was broad in scope, but they nevertheless, were basically those which catered for the needs of a small and partly agricultural town.

Much has been written of the functions of the gilds. They have been idealised as the essential institutional structure of a stable urban society, as the guarantee of quality in workmanship and of a fair price to the consumer, and as an avenue by which the humblest artisan could rise to the highest ranks in urban society. More recently gilds have been dismissed as the inefficient instruments of sectional interests, as a brake on technical progress and a hindrance to efficient business organisation. It is indicative of the current view of their relative unimportance that certain recent books on European economic history have barely recognised their existence. That they did not perform the civilising role which their nineteenth-century eulogists have ascribed to them is clear; yet they were not unimportant instruments in the formulation and implementation of local economic policy. They reflected the balance of political and social interests in a town, and in their ossified, late medieval and early modern forms they became a bastion of vested interests and an obstacle to economic progress. In much of Europe their influence was undermined in the eighteenth century, and in very few areas did they survive the French Revolution as instruments of economic policy. Where they have continued to exist, it has generally been as the colourful and convivial administrators of charitable endowments.

Yet a careful reading of any set of gild regulations shows a concern both for the physical conditions under which the craft was carried on and for the welfare of the consuming public.

Indeed, the latter is so conspicuous in most that the whole gild structure appears to have been consumer oriented. Nevertheless, the gilds were born of conflict; stripped of all their religious and social trappings, they are seen as attempts on the part of the poorer craftsmen to protect their interests by means of combinations. This they had in common with the later trades unions.

Gild regulations were, in a sense, the product of compromise between the artisans, aiming to safeguard their own livelihood, and urban society as represented by the patricians. The artisans might form gilds, but in order to gain recognition, they incorporated into their rules many clauses whose purpose was to protect the consumer. Medieval subterfuge was remarkably unsubtle, like the mixing of poor quality materials with good, and the re-use of old materials. In some instances a scale of fines was promulgated for these petty breaches of gild ordinances. The quality of the workmanship was supposedly guaranteed by the requirement that the 'master' be adequately trained in his 'mystery' and that he work only during the hours of daylight. Time after time the gilds pronounced against work by candlelight. The number of apprentices which a master might have was usually limited to two or three at most, and in some instances the lowest age at which they might be bound apprentice was specified. The purpose was clearly to prevent the master from packing his workshop with cheap but inadequately trained workmen. The institution of apprenticeship, during which the young artisan learned his mystery, was also designed to secure properly trained 'masters'.

*Economic role of the gilds*

It has been held against the gilds that they were monopolistic, that they resisted technical progress, and, like some trade unions today, were hostile to innovation. Indeed, it has been claimed that any substantial technical and industrial progress had to await the effective suppression of gild activity in the late eighteenth and nineteenth centuries. This is to exaggerate the importance of their role.

The artisans' gild, it is true, held by the terms of its own charter of recognition a local monopoly of its particular craft. But the consequences of this monopolistic position were modified by the fact that the local authorities which incorporated the gilds could also modify the conditions under which they operated.

Membership of the gild was open to all who could satisfy its minimum requirement that the 'master' should be competent within his craft. Most gilds, it is true, limited the number of apprentices that a master might have, and thus prevented a rapid expansion of a craft. On the other hand, there is no reason to suppose that the activity of many crafts would have been expanded without this restriction. Population was not growing rapidly during the period of greatest gild activity, and it is doubtful whether overall demand for manufactured goods was increasing. In any event, it was not the artisan who studied the economic indicators and judged the market possibilities. The merchant capitalists did this, and all the evidence suggests that if the latter desired an increased production they had the means to secure it. The urban artisan in the later Middle Ages was in a weak economic position, and unlikely to combine to restrict production or to force up prices. Although there is abundant evidence of friction and even of open hostility between merchants, masters and artisans, there is very little to suggest that monopolistic and restrictive powers were used for economic ends. Lastly, any restrictive movement by the urban crafts could, in effect, be broken by an appeal to the rural workers. Combination, monopoly and restriction could be effective only in those industries which satisfied a mass demand. In the class of luxury manufactures the elasticity of demand was such that these methods could have had little effect.

The gilds in the second place, are accused of resisting innovation. The Middle Ages, it has already been noted, were not an inventive period, and very few mechanical inventions or developments were made. The most significant, such as the blast-furnace, the waterwheel and the spinning wheel were not seriously obstructed or their diffusion hindered by any form of gild action. The water-wheel was increasingly used during the later Middle Ages, and such opposition as there was to powered mills seems to have been directed more against their capitalist owners than against the mills themselves. Indeed, there are instances of communal construction and operation of grinding and fulling mills.[19]

Medieval manufacturing rose above a domestic scale in very few instances. Except in mining and metallurgy, its fixed capital remained small, and the institution of the factory did not make its appearance. Gild regulations, as a general rule, kept the number of journeymen and apprentices low, but it is doubtful whether this was the main reason for the absence of large industrial under-takings. The reason is more likely to have been inadequate capital than lack of initiative. The Republic of Venice established at its *Arsenal* a factory with a quite remarkable division of labour for the purpose of fitting out its ships.[20] There were also ship-yards at Genoa, but such large undertakings were in general financed from public funds.

A factory system implies the use of mechanical power on a large scale. In the later Middle Ages growing use was being made of water-power, and waterwheels of increasing size and sophistication were being constructed. Flour mills were sometimes operated by several wheels, but these seem generally to have been mounted on moored boats from which the wheels dipped into the stream. A power source capable of activating even a small factory had not been developed by the end of the Middle Ages. In fact, large and highly complex pieces of water-powered machinery did not come until the seventeenth and above all the eighteenth centuries, and it is likely that they were pioneered in the closing years of the Middle Ages in the metalliferous mines.

Factories, then, offered no advantage in the use of mechanical power. Nor, in all probability, would they have given any cost advantage over the domestic worker. Jack of Newbury and other 'factory' clothiers of the sixteenth century set up large numbers of looms under one roof, but they were hand-looms, and there was no effective power-loom until the end of the eighteenth century. There might have been some advantage in the closer supervision of work which this system made possible, but costs of production may well have been lower under the putting-out system. The Malmesbury 'factory' lasted for only a short while, and we find no comparable development in continental Europe before the innovations of Colbert. The merchant capitalists were quite capable of introducing a rudimentary form of factory system. They did not do so, and we can only assume that there was too little profit in it. Merchant capitalism gave rise to industrial capitalism only on an insignificant scale.

BRANCHES OF MEDIEVAL MANUFACTURING

The medieval crafts can be conveniently divided into those which produced consumer goods and prepared foodstuffs for the market, mainly in an urban environment; those which carried on the extraction, smelting and refining of metals, and the broad group of building and construction industries. To these should be added the service occupations – notaries, innkeepers, servants and the like.

The medieval crafts were carried on at more than one level. Some processed materials of local origin to produce coarse and simple goods to satisfy local needs. Others employed more refined methods on raw materials of superior quality to make luxury goods which could bear the cost of transport across the continent. In no craft was this more true than in the manufacture of textiles.

Textiles were the medieval manufacture *par excellence*. Weavers constituted the largest group of craftsmen in the few towns for which we have data. Raw materials of the textile industries, together with finished cloth, made up a very large fraction, perhaps as much as two-thirds, of the total volume of trade by both land and water. Cloth was woven from wool, cotton, silk, flax and hemp. The processes, from the initial spinning of the thread to the finishing of the cloth, were highly specialised, and, in the towns engaged the attentions of different gilds. Immense numbers of people were engaged in the textile industries, and family names, at least in the English-speaking world, are more redolent of the cloth-working crafts than we sometimes realise. The reason for this predominance of the cloth industry, quite apart from the universal need for clothing, lies in the fact that dress was a badge of rank and one of the few forms of conspicuous consumption available to medieval man.

### The Woollen Industry

The woollen industry was throughout the Middle Ages the most important branch of the textile industry. It had been an important craft in the later centuries of the Roman Empire. Cloth was woven, fulled and dyed on many of the late Roman villas that are known to us. Long-distance trade in cloth must have been reduced to negligible significance during the early Middle Ages, but the production of cloth for family and local use continued through these dark centuries. In the Carolingian period cloth was being woven, as in the later years of the Roman Empire, by the women in *gynaecea*, or small workshops. These had by now, however, become appendages of monasteries rather than of villas, and there is evidence that the cloth, especially that woven in northern

France and the Low Countries, was beginning to enter into long-distance trade (see p. 76).

During the following centuries the manufacture and trade in cloth became increasingly important, both at the local level and for distant and specialised markets. Sheep were reared in all parts of Europe, and no place was without a local source of wool. The quality of the wool, however, varied very greatly. Pegolotti's treatise of the first half of the fourteenth century lists an immense number of wools of different quality, and in England the average price of the wool produced in Shropshire and Lincolnshire was almost three times that of wool from Cornwall. Many factors influenced the value of the wool, including the breed of sheep and the conditions under which they were grazed. The wool shorn from a living sheep was worth a good deal more than the fleece of one which had died or been slaughtered. Furthermore, some parts of the individual fleece were more highly esteemed than others, and were used in the weaving of superior qualities of cloth.

The manufacture of woollen cloth was made up of more separate processes, carried on by different people in different places, than any other medieval industry.[21] The wool itself was sorted into qualities; at Saint-Omer four grades were recognised, and this seems to have been the general practice. It was then cleansed of the foreign matter that clings to the fleece; washed to get rid of the grease, and beaten to open up its texture and improve its felting properties. These processes were commonly carried on in the villages and on the farms. The wool was then combed into long bundles preparatory to spinning; some was also carded, but this process, which bruised and split the fibres, was not always approved, and in any case was not used for threads which were to form the warp. Until the later Middle Ages spinning was done with distaff and spindle, and was, of course, regarded as women's work. The spinning-wheel appeared in the thirteenth century, but its use was resisted – possibly the only known instance of medieval resistance to innovation. The spinning wheel, it was held, yielded a weaker and less even thread than the distaff and spindle, and was never used for the warp thread. The spun thread was then doubled to produce the requisite thickness and strength.

The thread to be used as weft was then wound on to the shuttle, and the warp was fastened to the warp-beam of the loom. Even this was a specialised occupation in some weaving areas. The Greeks and Romans had used a small vertical loom, shown on Greek painted vases and Roman bas-reliefs. The warp hung vertically within the frame, and was not wound round a warp-beam. The largest cloth that could be woven was thus no bigger than the frame itself.[22] This primitive loom survived into the Middle Ages. It was well suited to the confined space of the peasant's cottage, but the growing demand for cloth led to the adoption of a more sophisticated instrument. At least from the thirteenth century a horizontal loom was used for all except the coarsest cloth. It was supported by four uprights. At the far end was the warp-beam, a cylinder, around which the warp, sometimes as long as 50 metres, was wound. In front of the weaver was another roller, with the warp ends attached, on to which the cloth was wound as it was woven. Pedals fixed beneath were used to operate the shed mechanism, and the weaver, sitting on a bench in front of the loom, passed the shuttle to and fro, from side to side, through the shed as it opened and closed.

On this simple frame a variety of fabrics could be woven, according to the tightness of the weave, the thickness of the thread, its degree of smoothness or coarseness, and the quality of the wool from which it had been spun. The width of the cloth was determined by the number of warp threads attached to the beam, but it could not in any case, exceed that of the frame. The warp threads were usually counted in hundreds, and thus ranged from $10^c$ to $16^c$.

After the cloth had been woven it was again washed to eliminate the grease and dirt which it had inevitably picked up in the course of spinning and weaving. Fuller's earth was commonly used at this stage. The cloth was then stamped by the bare feet of the fuller or beaten with the paddles of the water-powered fulling-mill to thicken and felt the cloth. There are many classical bas-reliefs and medieval paintings which show this laborious process. It was the earliest process in the whole field of textile manufacture to be mechanised. The fulling mill appeared in England in the late twelfth century, and even earlier in the Low Countries[23] and northern France.

Fulling was followed by a further rinsing of the cloth. A nap was then raised on the cloth by 'teasing' it with the sharp spines of

302

the heads of the teasel plant, and was then shorn to produce an even finish. In the course of all these processes the cloth had probably shrunk. A final stage, before dyeing, was to pull it into shape again by attaching it to hooks (tenterhooks) and stretching it over a frame.

There were many ways of accomplishing each of these finishing processes, and the method used helped to determine the type and quality of the cloth. Sometimes one of the stages was repeated or extended. The raising of the nap, the shearing and the stretching could each be performed at different times and in different ways. Each weaving centre had its own particular method of doing things. Valenciennes finished its cloth somewhat differently from Arras or Ypres or Saint-Omer, and in this lay the chief reasons for the small differences between one cloth and another, which were so important to the medieval purchaser. Some cloths were sold before the finishing processes had been completed; they were *mi-parues*, to be finished elsewhere and in accordance with other people's tastes.

Medieval man loved bright colours, and these he could enjoy most easily in the clothes which he wore. Dyeing was thus a highly important operation, and was usually handled by specialist dyers. Although mineral dyes were used in stained and painted glass and also in pigments for painting, only vegetable dyes were used in finishing cloth. Their production was a basic occupation of several areas, and trade in dyestuffs provided a living for countless middlemen.

The *Capitulare de Villis* of Charlemagne enjoined the cultivation of woad (*gauda*), cochineal red and madder (*garantia*), but woad remained the most used of medieval dyestuffs. It was prepared from the leaves of a herbaceous plant, grown especially in the Toulouse area of southern France, around Lille, and in Saxony and Thuringia. It was prepared by grinding the leaves in a mill and allowing the resulting paste to ferment. It was then dried and was ready for use. Dissolved in water, it produced, according to the strength of the solution and the number of times the cloth was dipped, every shade from black to pale blue, and with the addition of madder, it yielded a purple.

Madder, the principal source of the red dye, was obtained from the roots of the madder plant, which was widely grown in the southern Low Countries, in Germany and in southern France.

The kermes insect, in fact a minute species of parasitical louse, which forms small galls on certain trees, was also used. Occasionally one finds peasants burdened with the obligation to collect these *vermiculi*, or 'little worms'. When crushed the galls yielded a scarlet dye; indeed, the word 'scarlet', together with its French and German cognates, derives from the word 'kermes' (*Arabic*: Dûd il Quîrmis; *Iranian:* kerema). It was the kermes dye which was adopted in 1467 by Pope Paul II as the colour of the robes of the cardinals of the Roman curia. It was always an expensive dye, and for that reason much sought after by the rich and powerful. Venice became a centre for the trade in kermes – by and large a Mediterranean dyestuff – and the cloth dyed with it was often termed Venetian scarlet. A yellow dye was obtained from the weld plant and also from saffron. Many other vegetable dyes were also used, especially in the production of coarse cloth for local use.

Fully as important as the quality of the dyestuff was the mordant used both to cleanse the fabric and to provide a film on the fibres with which the dyestuff bonded. Several chemical substances were used for this, but by far the most important was alum, a name given to a complex sulphate of potassium and aluminium.[24] Though it occurs in southern Italy and Spain, the chief sources of dyer's alum in medieval Europe was near Phocaea, on the Aegean coast of Anatolia. The island fell under the control of the Genoese, who grew rich on the alum trade (see p. 470). The earliest Genoese galley to reach north-western Europe, about 1280, was laden, it is said, not with the silks and spices of the Orient, but – in some ways a more desirable cargo – with common alum. Phocaea was overrun by the Turks in the fifteenth century and ceased to be important as a source of alum. In 1462, however, the large deposits of Tolfa were discovered. Henceforward the Tolfa mines not only supplied most of the mordant used in Europe, but contributed greatly to the wealth of the papacy.

The dyeing process could take place at almost any stage in the sequence of cloth-making processes. The spun thread, the woven cloth, and even the cleaned wool could be put into the dyer's vat. Raw wool absorbed the dye more readily, but dyed wool was less easy to manipulate than undyed. Plain colours seem, in general, to have been dyed after weaving, but mixed cloths, in which the warp and weft were of different colours, had clearly to be woven from wool which had already been dyed. The wool or the cloth was first impregnated with a solution of alum, and then dipped, repeatedly in many instances, into the vat of dye. Medieval drawings sometimes represent the cloth as being boiled over a fire; in some instances a winching device is shown to lift the heavy piece of wet cloth from the vat.

When dried and folded the cloth was ready for the market. The size of each type of cloth was standardised, and craftsmen were commonly punished for selling pieces which did not conform with their local standards. Cloths were generally fairly small; narrow, because they had been woven on a narrow loom, and short, because many medieval weavers never really developed the technique of attaching a long warp to the warp-beam.

There was thus an almost infinite range in the variety of fabrics available to those able to afford them. One has, for example, only to read through the account books of the Bonis brothers,[25] merchants in the small Languedoc town of Montauban; their clients demanded cloth of every colour, quality and price. The Bonis dealt in the local 'rosets', 'greys' and rough serges at eight shillings the *canne* (about 1·84 m), in the brown and white cloth of Rouergue, the chequered patterns from Rodez, and in the more elegant fabrics from Ypres, Brussels and Malines. The Beauvais and Montvilliers cloth, far from the most expensive, sold at 38 shillings the *canne*. Pegolotti[26] listed the sizes of countless different types of cloth, and added the prices commonly paid for the wool of no less than 195 English and Scottish monasteries and of eleven separate wool-growing regions.

The coarse cloths made by the peasantry for their own use were no less varied, though they acquired no distinctive names and may never have been sold outside the communities which produced them. They had not passed through all the processes to which the quality cloths were subjected, and they were dyed, if indeed they were dyed at all, with the vegetable dyes that were available locally. Most of the cloth woven and worn was of this latter kind, because most of the population was rural and poor. Nevertheless, the well-to-do peasant could hope at some time in his life to be able to buy a piece of cloth of better than average quality, though the price differential between the quality cloth and the common was immense.

## The cloth-making regions

The quality cloth which entered into long-distance trade and was retailed by merchants like the Bonis brothers, was made in a restricted number of places, foremost amongst them the Low Countries, together with nearby areas of northern France, and northern Italy. In addition there was a number of towns outside these regions in which the cloth industry was well developed. In most the refined cloth industry of the later Middle Ages emerged slowly from the earlier peasant manufacture of coarse fabrics; in a few – Ath, in Brabant, for example[27] – the industry was deliberately established by the local prince who offered special privileges to cloth-workers.

## The Flanders cloth industry

In Flanders the cloth industry grew from a monastic and peasant craft. Sometime in the tenth or eleventh century it became established in the towns. By the late eleventh century it was a well organised industry, and its cloth sold in the Flanders fairs. A few years later it began to appear at the fairs of Champagne and to be purchased by the merchants of Italy. This cloth was made in the three Flanders cities of Bruges, Ghent and Ypres, as well as in Arras, Saint-Omer, Douai and a few other towns. It was a heavy cloth, tightly woven from strong, thick thread which had been spun from quality wool, and well fulled. It was passed through a complex series of processes, and was in consequence a very expensive fabric. The market for it was small, but within this market it had few rivals. Much of it came in the twelfth century to be shipped by way of the fairs of Champagne to Italy where some of it was further processed and finished before being exported by Italian merchants.

The production of quality cloth spread from the cities of Flanders southwards and eastwards to Hainault and Brabant, and south-westwards through west Flanders to Artois and Picardy. Brussels and Malines developed as centres for the production of quality cloth in the course of the thirteenth century. Valenciennes, Douai, Lille, Arras and Saint-Omer were no less important. It is not easy to explain why this small region of north-western Europe became the leading centre of the most important manufacturing industry of medieval Europe. Its decline in the later Middle Ages is much more readily explicable. Much has been made of the fact that wool was produced locally; that the monastery of Saint-Bertin at Saint-Omer, for example, owned extensive sheep runs; that a high quality wool was available from England, and was being imported as early as the twelfth century; that woad was grown; fuller's earth was found locally, and the manufacturing centres lay close to shipping routes. None of these factors helps to explain *why* the production of a quality cloth became a specialised occupation. A cloth-making tradition may have been inherited from the Romans; the monasteries were unquestionably centres of cloth production, and it is possible that by the ninth century some system had been developed to market it. The *pallia fresonica*, mentioned by Ermoldus Niger and the Monk of St Gall, was almost certainly woven in the southern

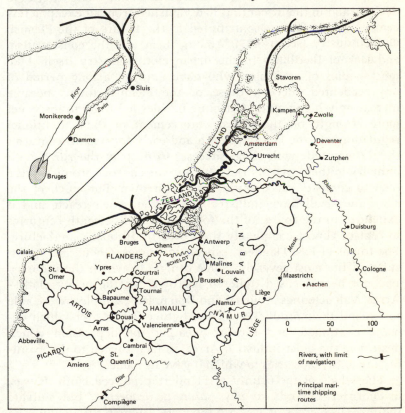

Fig. 7.1   Textile manufacturing centres of the Low Countries; inset, Bruges and its links with the sea.

Low Countries.[28] But when did the rural craft move to the towns; when was the superior English wool first used; when did cloth begin to be shipped regularly to southern France and Italy? Above all, perhaps, what was the role of the Count of Flanders in providing the conditions in which urban cloth-workers could pursue their crafts and merchants buy and transport the cloth. It might be claimed, though the evidence is scanty, that the good government of the counts was an important factor in the growth both of the towns and of their manufactures, and that these essential developments had begun well before the middle years of the eleventh century.

The Flanders cloth industry reached its peak of prosperity in the thirteenth century. In the fourteenth, its importance began to decline, and in the fifteenth it had vanished from all except a few centres. Many factors contributed to the failure of the Flemish cloth industry (see p. 457). Among them was the conservatism and lack of flexibility in the urban cloth industry itself. Like most bodies of craftsmen who have enjoyed a long period of unprecedented success, those of the Flemish towns became increasingly hidebound. A decline in sales led them to insist yet more strongly on the fullest enforcement of their traditional regulations. In the late thirteenth and early fourteenth centuries they attempted, with some success, to destroy the rural cloth industry in their own districts, because its cheaper products were seen to compete successfully with their own. But much of the rural and small town industry was beyond their reach, and it expanded in the course of the fourteenth and fifteenth centuries to replace almost completely their own traditional manufacture. The towns of East Flanders, especially Bruges, Ghent and Ypres, suffered the most severely. Some others, in which the industry had not been focused quite so narrowly on the heavy cloth – Arras, Valenciennes, Tournai and Douai, for example – were able to expand their production of the lighter fabrics, for which demand continued, and thus to weather the depression which destroyed the older industry. Arras, in fact, turned to the manufacture of the tapestries to which it gave its name.

The whole of the county of Flanders produced cloth. It was, in Coornaert's words, *un pays saturé de draperie*,[29] but, outside the few large cities, it was a lighter cloth which was made. The weave was looser; it used a poorer quality wool than the *grande draperie*, much of it from the sheep of Artois, and some from Spain. The finishing processes were simplified and abbreviated, and a serviceable but cheaper cloth was produced. It was for such a fabric that the market was expanding during the later Middle Ages, with the growth of the urban middle class and the formation of a rural élite amongst the peasantry. The words which Clapham used of the Yorkshire woollen industry in the nineteenth century are no less applicable to rural cloth-working in fourteenth and fifteenth-century Flanders. It was, he said, 'the ordinary case of a pushing, hardworking locality with certain slight advantages, attacking the lower grades of an expanding market'.[30]

These lighter fabrics were the 'new draperies'. They had long been made by the rural population. Now the scale of production was increased; better wool was used for some of them, and the merchants who had previously handled the quality cloth, now began to put out their wool to the rural weavers. The cloth was cheaper, in part because the manufacturing processes had been simplified; in part also because labour was less costly. Rural weavers were not organised into gilds; the merchant clothier could watch the quality of their work, and in this populous and poverty-stricken countryside he could exploit the labour of the peasantry. The traditional cloth industry had priced itself out of the market as effectively as the East Anglian worsted or the West Country serge industry did during the Industrial Revolution.

New manufacturing centres emerged. Some had been clothing towns of minor importance, overtaken and eclipsed by the *villes drapantes* in the thirteenth century. Now they again became weaving centres. They lay in a ring around Ypres, showing how ineffective had been the opposition of the latter to the rural and small town industry: Poperinghe, Cassel, Bailleul, Dixmude and, above all, Hondschoote. They lay along the Lys valley: Courtrai, Werwicq and Comines. Hondschoote, thanks to the researches of Coornaert, has become one of the best known of the centres of the 'new draperies'. It lies today just within the borders of France. In the Middle Ages it was relatively remote from the larger towns and happily immune to their civil strife. Its development was held back by the wars of the fourteenth century, and it was not until the last quarter of the century that its industry began to develop. Nevertheless, Pegolotti, writing in all probability before the mid-fourteenth century, gave a short paragraph of his manual to the white 'says' of *Dondiscatto in Fiandra*. Every village produced says, but Hondeschoote became the undisputed focus of the new draperies in West Flanders. Their manufacture, however, spread into some of the centres of the older draperies, as well as into Artois and Normandy.

## The Italian cloth industry

The Italian cloth industry stood in marked contrast to that of Flanders and the Low Countries. A direct continuity with the cloth manufacture of the later Roman Empire is possible. Many parts of Italy were well suited to sheep-rearing, and there must have been an abundant production of wool. Much, however, was of poor quality, and medieval Italy seems always to have been dependent on imports for the supply of wool of better quality. This goes far towards explaining why Italy, despite its cultural inheritance from the Roman Empire, became dependent upon a distant region in northern Europe for the supply of quality cloth. From the late eleventh century Lombard merchants were importing cloth from the Low Countries.

The Italians were well aware of the needs of their Middle Eastern markets, and were quite capable of finishing cloth imported from north-western Europe to satisfy the requirements of their customers. They took the Flemish cloth; some of it they again fulled, raising the nap, shearing and dyeing it. The cloth-finishing industry was established in Genoa, but spread to other towns. It was in Florence, however, that it was most developed, and there the merchants who controlled the industry formed the most prestigious of the gilds, the *Arte di Calimala*, so named from the small street in which it was concentrated. The cloth-finishing industry reached its peak in the late thirteenth century. Villani estimated that some 10,000 pieces of Flemish cloth were imported yearly about 1330, and a single merchant, Neri di Buonaccorsi, is said to have finished no less than 1100 pieces.[31] The *Arte di Calimala* had its agents in Paris, at the Champagne fairs, and at many places along the routes which lead from Flanders to the Mediterranean. But in the fourteenth century the industry was of diminishing importance, and in this it reflected the fortunes of the Flemish crafts with which it was so intimately connected. In 1458 the import of cloth into Florence was forbidden. The domestic cloth industry had come of age, and the *Arte di Calimala* disappeared.

About 1300 the *Arte della Lana*, the gild of Florentine clothiers, produced ten times as many pieces of cloth as were finished by the *Arte di Calimala*. Everywhere in northern Italy the domestic weaving industry was expanding and the quality of its cloth steadily improving. The production of a superior cloth was helped by the increasing use of a better quality wool. Italians appear to have begun to use English wool early in the thirteenth century. Pegolotti represented it as being shipped from England to Gascony, and then transported overland to the Mediterranean coast for final shipment to Tuscany. In 1307 the first direct shipment of English wool was made by sea to Genoa. At the same time increasing use was being made of wool from North Africa and Spain. The merino sheep was introduced from Africa into the Iberian Peninsula, possibly by Italian merchants, eager to purchase its better quality fleece.

The largest centre of woollen cloth production, after Florence, was probably Verona. Craftsmen from Verona were attracted to Bologna and Mantua, but they could always be tempted away by other towns. The extraordinary mobility of Italian labour is one of its characteristic features. The wide demand for skilled weavers did much to raise both the status of labour and also its remuneration. The Bolognese industry was, in Professor Mazzaoui's words, 'an artificial creation of the mercantile dominated commune'.[32] The local merchants had previously imported Flemish cloth, and had dyed and prepared it for the market. 'The successful launching of a home industry based upon imported labour and techniques presupposed a political authority favorable to commercial and industrial interests, a substantial capital investment and a commercial organization capable of meeting the needs of an industry which required not only imported raw materials but also foreign outlets for its products.'[32] The Italian cloth industry, in short, was organised on a capitalist basis and was controlled by cloth merchants. Their powers of organisation were probably greater than those of the Flemish clothiers, and their business sophistication incomparably higher.

Most towns of northern Italy developed a textile industry, though that of Venice did not become important until the Middle Ages were over and the fortunes of the Republic in decline. South of Tuscany and Umbria the production of cloth for the market ceased to be important. Indeed, Orvieto was probably the most southerly weaving centre of significance. Rome imported cloth from northern Italy, and Naples was a leading market for the products of Florence.

Almost nothing is known of the volume of cloth production or of the number of people it employed. Villani's estimate of 30,000 cloth-workers in Florence is clearly a gross exaggeration. Only for England is there a run of trustworthy statistics. Exports rose from less than a thousand pieces after the Black Death to about 46,000 at the end of the century. After dropping to less than 30,000 during the first two decades of the fifteenth century, the volume rose again to about 50,000 by the mid-century. Miller has estimated[33] that the English cloth industry must have employed, about 1400, 'only the equivalent of about 15,000 fully employed persons' – perhaps a half of one per cent of the total population. Professor Mazzaoui has found the names of only about 150 craftsmen who migrated to Bologna, and has estimated that in the total population of over 30,000, the number of textile workers can have been only some five or six hundred. The numbers of the Flemish weavers who fled to England under Edward III has been put at 'une bonne centaine' in London and rather less over the rest of the country.[34] These figures suggest how small in absolute terms was the medieval cloth industry. At Paris, a not unimportant centre of the textile industries, only about 600 textile artisans – 360 of them weavers – paid the *taille* in 1300. This total would in all probability have excluded apprentices and perhaps some journeymen, but it did include drapers and wool-dealers. The total labour force engaged in the textile industry may not have exceeded a thousand.

The Low Countries and Northern Italy were the two largest and most important concentrations of the clothing industry during the later Middle Ages. They were, however, neither given over exclusively to woollen textiles, nor did they supply more than a fraction of the long-distance trade in cloth. Leaving aside the peasant product, which never sold beyond its local area, there were hundreds of towns which produced cloth of respectable quality and sold it in distant markets. The Bonis brothers handled far more cloth from Rodez than from Flanders or Florence. Pegolotti thought the cloths of Chalon-sur-Saône, Troyes, Paris, Montivilliers, Caen, Amiens, Provins, Lagny, Cambrai each worth a paragraph in his manual. There are numerous other examples.

## Italian cotton and fustian weaving

One thinks of the European cotton industry as a development of modern times, when ships could bring cargoes of raw cotton from southern Asia. In fact, cotton was known to the Romans, though it does not appear to have been grown north of the Mediterranean Sea. The actual cultivation of the plant was introduced into southern Spain by the Arabs, and their agricultural and geographical writings contained directions for planting and harvesting it. In the twelfth century, and probably earlier, it was being grown in Sicity, and the port of Genoa was importing *bombacium di Sicilia* in the twelfth century and despatching it to the towns of Lombardy.

In the twelfth and thirteenth centuries the wearing of cotton spread through the towns of Tuscany and northern Italy. There was a demand for a light fabric in the hot Italian summers, and both flax and cotton were used. There is some evidence for the widespread cultivation of flax in Lombardy, though linen may never have been as important as in South Germany. It was, however, cotton, or rather a mixture of cotton and wool, which was used increasingly for the summer clothing of the Italians. The weaving of pure cottons does not seem to have been common, except perhaps in Southern Italy and Sicily, where some cotton was grown. A reason probably lay in the poor quality of the cotton itself. South Italian and, in fact, most western Mediterranean cotton was of short staple and yielded a weak thread, generally held to be unsuitable for the warp. It was imported by Genoa and distributed to the towns of its hinterland, whose fustians were generally held to be inferior to those woven from Middle Eastern cotton. The latter was imported mainly by Venice from Syria, Egypt, and even Armenia, and was distributed to the towns of the eastern part of the Lombardy Plain, especially Verona, Padua and Bologna, and subsequently to the fustian weavers of southern Germany. The gild regulations of Ulm, the leading German centre of cotton-weaving, required that the raw material should have been brought across the Alps from Venice, a guarantee, perhaps, that it was of good Syrian or Cypriot quality. The same regulations insisted that the warp, which took most of the strain in the weaving process, should be of flax, and the best South German flax at that, while the weaker cotton might be used only in the weft. The question thus arises whether the Italians ever produced a pure cotton, rather than a mixed fabric or fustian. Pegolotti referred on several occasions to trade in 'cottons', but it seems probable that most Italian cottons, like the South German barchents, were in fact mixed fabrics, or fustians, though the manufacture of pure cottons cannot be excluded.[35] The spinning and weaving of cotton form one of the least understood of all branches of medieval industry, and it is possible that further research will show that pure cottons, as well as fustians, were far more important than has been supposed by historians obsessed with the predominance of the woollens.

The Italian fustian industry reached its peak in the thirteenth and early fourteenth century. Its weavers had been amongst the humblest of Italian cloth-workers, and doubtless had played a role in the social disturbances of the Italian cities. The industry was controlled by the merchants who imported the cotton and sold the cloth. In the course of the fourteenth century the fustian weavers succeeded in organising and in taking over the control of the industry. The inevitable result was a loss of markets. Only at Cremona did fustian weaving retain its importance in the later Middle Ages, and here the merchant capitalists remained in firm control of industry.

Italian fustians had at first been sold over the whole Mediterranean basin and also in much of central and western Europe. They moved northwards across the Alpine passes to Germany. Now, with the decline of the Italian industry, the German merchants were encouraged to produce a fustian themselves.

### German linen and barchent manufacture
A mid-eleventh century poem represents the sheep and the flax plant as disputing which of the two performed the greater service to man.[36] The flax plant had, indeed, a strong case. There is abundant evidence for the spinning and weaving of flax as early as the Neolithic period and its use may in fact, have been older than that of wool.[37] The flax plant had spread from the Mediterranean, but even in prehistoric times it seems to have been used most intensively in the Alpine region and Germany. Flax offered great advantages as a textile fibre. The peasant, too poor to raise sheep, could nevertheless cultivate a small patch of flax. The preparation of the thread was laborious but far from difficult, and it made small demands on fixed capital. The spinning of flax was

simpler than that of wool, and the thread could be woven on a small loom. Furthermore the cloth needed to be bleached, but did not otherwise call for complex finishing processes. The classical civilisations had made a great use of flax both for clothing and for sail-cloth. Plutarch praised it as providing 'the wearer with a smooth and always clean attire'. It did not 'burden him with its weight, is fitting for all seasons, and is avoided by troublesome vermin'. Its cleanliness, or rather the ease with which it could be laundered, has always been an important recommendation. On the other hand it was less warm in winter, and needed to be supplemented at this season with woollen cloth.

It is unlikely that the cultivation of flax and the weaving of linen ever died out in central Europe between the Bronze Age and the Middle Ages. Payments in flax were prescribed in some of the early German codes, and in the ninth century polyptyques dues in flax and linen were no less common than those payable in woollen cloth. One gets the impression that monasteries such as those of Prüm, Corvey and Lobbes made as great a contribution to the manufacture of linen as they did to that of woollen cloth.

The flax plant grows well in the moist climate and under the cloudy skies of central and north-western Europe. It was 'pulled' before the seeds had ripened. The stalks were then cleaned and 'retted'. Packed in boxes, they were allowed to soak in water. The soft tissues were broken down by bacterial action, and the fibres separated and softened. This malodorous process was carried on beside the streams and rivers; even today one detects its presence amid the farms and fields of Belgium. The flax was 'broken' either by beating it or by pulling it between the jaws of a 'brake', which crushed the woody tissues of the stalks. It was then 'scutched' or hackled to remove unwanted matter and to reduce the flax to fine, smooth threads. It was then ready for spinning, which was, given the length of the fibres, a somewhat simpler process than that of wool.

Flax weaving seems to have been almost crowded out from the Low Countries and northern France by the rural draperies. It seems also to have been reduced to insignificance in Italy, but in Switzerland and South Germany it came into its own, and from here it spread to North Germany and eastwards into the Slav lands. Until the thirteenth century flax-weaving remained a peasant industry, and linen rarely came on to the market. Then the growing interest in light textiles, combined with the increasing urban demand for cloth, led merchants to market linen in the Rhineland towns and at the Champagne fairs. Demand increased, especially after the technique had been developed of combining the flax with either cotton or wool. The barchents or fustians of South Germany were made with a flax warp and a cotton weft. In the lower Rhineland, especially at Cologne, wool was sometimes used instead of cotton.

During the fourteenth century the market for these cheap, light and serviceable fabrics expanded greatly, and a veritable industrial region emerged in northern Switzerland, Swabia and Bavaria.[38] The Swiss industry was concentrated in Constance and St Gall, but was spread in fact, from Schaffhausen on the Rhine to Lindau at the head of Lake Constance. The South German manufacture lay mainly within a rectangle bounded by Ulm, Augsburg, Kempten and Ravensburg. The Swiss concentrated on pure linens; the South German craftsmen on barchents woven from a mixture of flax and cotton. The linen and barchent industry followed a similar historical pattern to that of the woollen cloth manufacture. A more refined branch parted company with the coarse peasant manufacture, and moved to the towns. Ulm, where cotton first appeared about 1320, became the most important centre of the industry.[39] At the same time merchant capitalists took control of the manufacture, imported cotton from Venice, bought up the prepared flax from the villages and commissioned urban weavers to produce cloth for them. They finished the cloth, if it had not already been bleached and dyed, and then marketed it. The linens and barchents from Switzerland and south Germany were distributed over as wide an area as Flemish cloth had been. The largest market was probably that of Italy. Immense quantities were transported over the Alpine passes, and much was shipped from Venice to the Middle Eastern countries which supplied the raw cotton, and from Genoa to the ports of North Africa. South German barchents made their way down the Rhine to the Low Countries and across central Europe to the fairs of Leipzig and beyond.

Foremost amongst the merchants who, in the later Middle Ages, managed the linen and barchent industry of South Germany was the company of Ravensburg. This association of merchants was formed in the fifteenth century.[40] Its headquarters were in the small Swabian town of Ravensburg, and much of its business consisted in the collection and shipment of linen, fustian and barchent. It even sent bales of South German cloth as far afield as Spain.

The chief areas for flax-growing and linen-weaving in North Germany lay around the towns of Münster, Bielefeld and Herford. The industry here passed through the same stages as that of South Germany. A more refined cloth production emerged in the thirteenth century and moved to the towns. Here specialised weavers produced enough cloth for the local merchants to sell in Cologne and Osnabrück, whence it was sent to Scandinavia and the Baltic, and from the early sixteenth century, to the New World.

Hemp was grown no less widely than flax. It is a similar, but more hardy plant, and is prepared in much the same way. It yields, however, a coarse thread and, if woven, a rough fabric. Hempen cloth was worn during the Middle Ages, but it was considered a mark of extreme poverty. Hemp was chiefly used in making rope and coarse fabrics for packing wool, cloth and other goods. Its preparation and fabrication seem, except in a few rare cases, to have been rural pursuits. Venice, which showed a marked capacity for industrial organisation, established a rope factory in 1303 for the purpose of outfitting its ships. Venice relied at first on hemp grown and processed at Bologna, regarded as the best suited for ships' rigging, as, indeed, it remained into the eighteenth century. But Bologna used its monopolistic position to the full, and forced the Venetians to develop, though with some difficulty, the cultivation of a high quality hemp near Padua. Other areas of Europe, notably Britanny, the Central Massif of France and parts of Germany, produced hemp, but nowhere, except in Venice, did it give rise to a significant urban industry.

## The silk industry

Silk was the luxury fabric par excellence. Unlike other textiles, its manufacture did not graduate from the ranks of the peasant crafts. It was carried on in a few well-known urban centres, in each of which it had been deliberately established by the ruling classes. The Romans had been familiar with silk, which they imported from Asia, but they never learned the secrets of its manufacture. The cultivation of the silk-worm, according to Procopius, was introduced into the Byzantine Empire under

Justinian. The industry was expanded, but remained an imperial monopoly.[41] The weaving and dyeing of silks were strictly controlled, and their export prohibited. Silk, in Lopez's words, was 'not just another commodity, but a symbol of authority'. It was woven by small and highly privileged gilds, which supplied the emperor, his court and his friends. Only silk of second quality was ever exposed for sale.

Silk cloth was produced on a more abundant scale in the Arab world, both from locally grown material and also from raw silk imported from eastern Asia. As far as most of Europe was concerned, the specialists in silk-weaving were not the handful of Byzantine craftsmen, however refined their products may have been, but the Arabs. It was from the latter that the silk-weaving of southern Spain and Sicily derived. Silk-growing had been introduced into Sicily before the time of Roger II, but it was probably he who encouraged a trade in silk cloth. From Sicily the craft spread to northern Italy, and thence across the Alps to France. By the late twelfth century it was established in Lucca and Florence. It was developed soon afterwards in Genoa and Venice, and in the late thirteenth century at Milan. Sericulture spread less quickly, and was dependent on the slow growth of the mulberry. The industry in northern Italy was at first dependent on raw silk imported in part from southern Italy and Spain, but mainly from the Middle East and the Caucasus region.

Until the civil disturbances of the mid-fourteenth century, Lucca dominated the silk market. There were, according to Mrs Edler de Roover, at one time about 240 silk weavers, a measure of the small scale of this, the greatest luxury industry of its age. It was entirely in the hands of male craftsmen, thus emphasising the lack of roots in the rural crafts of the region, and was controlled, like other quality textile industries, by merchant capitalists. In the later fourteenth century many of the craftsmen fled to other Italian towns, and some even settled beyond the Alps. Bologna and Venice were the foremost heirs to the technical supremacy of Lucca. Several towns in southern France, including Avignon, where the papal court must have constituted a large market, established the industry. Eventually, however, it was Lyons which developed the most important silk manufacture in France, but, despite the encouragement given by Charles VII and Louis XI, it remained small until the end of the Middle Ages.

Silk-weaving was also introduced into Paris, Cologne and other towns in north-western Europe, but it was dependent on imported raw materials and never became either large or prosperous. The modern silk industry of Krefeld, in West Germany, was developed by the von der Leyen family in the early eighteenth century, and owed nothing to the medieval craft of silk-weaving.

Not unrelated to the production of silk fabrics was the embroidery and decoration of these and other luxury fabrics with gold, silver and silk thread. Examples of such fabrics have survived from the later years of the Roman Empire, and such works of art continued to be produced, especially for church use, during the centuries which followed. Cloth of gold and other highly decorated fabrics were made in very few centres. At Paris there was a gild which specialised in beating out the gold and silver thread for embroidery, and there were also workshops for these rich fabrics at Cologne, Florence, Venice and Lucca.

*Tanning and the leather industries*
This group of industries, second in importance only to the making of textiles, developed, like the latter, as rural occupations, and invaded the towns only in the later Middle Ages. The process of tanning skins and hides and their conversion into articles of clothing and of everyday use consists essentially in removing the epidermis and hair, as well as particles of flesh, and in so treating the hide that it will not putrify or decay. A number of chemicals was used for this purpose: alum, manure and various organic substances. Most important, however, was tannin, derived primarily from the bark and galls of the oak tree. The process gives off an offensive smell, consumes large quantities of water, and produces a highly polluted effluent. Urban tanneries were usually situated by the river bank, as far as possible from human habitation and water supply. In Moorish Cordoba they were relegated to the down-stream side of the city.

There were almost as many ways of preparing leather as there were of finishing cloth. Sometimes hides were thinned by shaving away their surfaces to produce a fine and flexible leather; oil was used to make it soft and supple, and dyestuffs were used to produce coloured leather. In southern Spain, a soft Cordovan leather was made, and the craft, practised by the cordwainers, spread through much of Europe. A number of crafts – tanners, curriers, cordwainers – used particular processes in making leather. Tanning was a very slow process, and a large amount of capital was tied up in the hides as they lay soaking in solutions of tannin. In consequence, the tanner, like the weaver, was often obliged to work for a merchant entrepreneur who provided his raw materials and marketed his product.

### The metal industries

Metals were essential to medieval civilisation, but they were used in small amounts and were relatively valuable. Most widely used was iron, indispensible for tools, weapons and armour. But lead was much used in roofing and in making water-ducts, and, alloyed with tin, in pewter. Copper was used for bronze, and the precious metals, gold and silver, were in demand for currency as well as for making vessels for ecclesiastical and lay use and for decoration. Metals were never produced in sufficient quantities, owing in part to the technical difficulties of mining and smelting, but also to their highly localised occurrence. There was furthermore, a drain of certain metals, especially lead, tin and the precious metals, from Europe to the Middle East.

*Iron-working.* This was the most widespread of all the metal industries. Iron ores were found very extensively, though often of a quality which would be rejected today, and wood, the universal fuel, was generally abundant. The iron-working industries consisted, on the one hand, of the mining, smelting and refining of the metal, and, on the other, of the fabrication of tools, weapons and small pieces of hardware. The former was of necessity a rural pursuit; the latter usually an urban occupation, carried on in full view of the consumers. The one was practised by miners and smelters working independently of one another, though often under some form of feudal or communal control; the other under the strict control of the swordsmiths', the blacksmiths' or the helmet-makers' gild.

Iron was the least tractable of the metals known and used during the Middle Ages. It smelted at a high temperature, was difficult to rid of its impurities, and was almost impossible to produce in large, homogeneous masses. Furthermore, the ore occurred in a great many varieties, no two of which required precisely the same treatment. Smelters learned empirically how to handle the ores which they used, and thus built up a body of technical knowledge which they jealously guarded.

The mining and smelting of iron ore are poorly documented, in part because these crafts were carried on chiefly in remote areas; in part also because their labour force was unorganised and kept few if any records. The ore itself was obtained from shallow pits, or, as bog-ore, was dredged from the floors of shallow lakes. It was smelted with charcoal, at first in small furnaces built of stones and clay and often set in a hillside so that the wind supplied a natural draught. The ore was reduced to an impure, pasty mass, which had to be further refined before it could be used. This primitive furnace came in time to be replaced by a hearth in which bellows, operated by a waterwheel, supplied the draught. This permitted a closer control over the process, and it became possible, by working the 'bloom' of iron with metal rods and by exposing all parts of it to the oxidising effects of a blast of air, to produce a mass of relatively pure iron. This was the 'direct' method, by which a lump of usable iron was produced directly and in one process from the ore.

The hearth in its many local forms began to replace the primitive furnace which had done service since prehistoric times. With its more powerful blast – yet another consequence of the medieval rediscovery of water-power – larger masses of more homogeneous metal could be made. The bloom of iron could then be reheated and forged into helmets, breastplates and other pieces of armour; it could be drawn into wire, which in turn could be made into nails; it could be fabricated by the smith into locks, bolts, hinges and that wide range of hardware which building practice was beginning to require; it could, lastly, be case-hardened and made to yield a kind of steel, which in turn could be used to sharpen chisels and saws. Medieval man had a wide knowledge of the technical processes involved, but it was all acquired empirically, treasured in secrecy, and passed on only to trusted members of the family or company. It was, in fact a kind of magic. This is how Theophilus, in the fourteenth century, recommended that a steel file be made from a rough bar of soft iron:

> Burn the horn of an ox in the fire, and scrape it, and mix with it a third part salt, and grind it strongly. Then put the file in the fire, and when it glows sprinkle this preparation over it everywhere, and, some hot coals being applied, you will blow quickly upon the whole,

yet so that the tempering may not fall off . . . [then] extinguish it in water.[42]

In more scientific terms, the metal was made to absorb sufficient carbon at its surface to bring this within the chemical and physical range of steel.

The use of the hearth greatly increased the volume of iron available, and much improved its quality. Further improvements ushered in the most revolutionary change of all, the introduction of the blast furnace. Neither the date nor the place of this epoch-making discovery is known, though it probably occurred during the middle years of the fifteenth century in eastern France or the Rhineland. The blast-furnace developed from the hearth. The sides of the latter were built higher. It ceased to be possible to manipulate the bloom, but the increased size of the furnace and the use of a more powerful blast led to higher temperatures and a more complete fusion of the metal. Instead of a pasty bloom of soft iron, a pool of liquid metal formed on the floor of the hearth. At first the sides of the latter were dismantled to allow the metal to be recovered. This was the stage known to the Germans as the *Stückofen*. It was, however, soon discovered that a vent, built into the lower wall of the furnace and plugged with clay when it was in blast, could be used for tapping a stream of liquid metal.

Many years must have passed before man learned to control and to use this new instrument which he had, perhaps unconsciously, created. The blast furnace was by far the most important in its long-term consequences of the few technical innovations made by medieval man. In the first place it increased manyfold the amount of metal that could be produced, but it was an iron which differed chemically from the soft iron from the bloomery. In its condition of complete fusion within the furnace it had absorbed carbon – up to as much as 5 per cent of its own weight. This gave it great fluidity, but, when cold, it also imparted to it great hardness and brittleness. It was in fact cast-iron. It could take the shape of a mould; cannon and firebacks could be cast from it, but it would not make cutting tools. A sword cast from it would be shivered at the first blow, and armour of cast-iron would have been heavy and fragile. Vast quantities of cast-iron began to be made for use in both peace and war, but for the uses to which iron had tradition-ally been put, the metal drawn from the blast furnace had to be further refined. The masses – pigs, as they were called – of cast iron were converted to soft, malleable iron, or even directly into steel, on a hearth. The jet of air from the bellows was played on the hot metal so that it oxidised and removed much or all of the carbon which it contained. The resulting iron, shaped into convenient pieces, was the bar-iron of commerce, the raw material of the iron-using industries during the later Middle Ages. This combination of blast-furnace and refining hearth constituted the *indirect* method of producing iron, the one which, with profound technical changes, remains in use today.

The primitive wind-furnace had disappeared from western Europe by the end of the thirteenth century, replaced by the bloomery, with its water-powered bellows. The latter spread eastwards across Europe. In the early thirteenth century it began to be adopted in the iron-workings of Styria and Carinthia. From here it spread into Hungary, and in the early years of the fourteenth was to be found in the mountains of Slovakia, in Silesia and in southern Poland. At about the same time the use of the hearth spread into Sweden. In this diffusion of more sophisticated techniques of iron-making, German technicians played a vital role. It was they who carried the new methods with them in their migrations, and who became the first proponents of the hearth and its water-powered bellows in central, eastern and northern Europe.

Some two hundred years or more later the blast-furnace, the next significant technological development in the field of ferrous metallurgy, began to spread through Europe in a similar fashion. It reached England by 1500, and at the same time spread through the rest of Germany. It was in use in the western Alps at the beginning of the sixteenth century; it reached the eastern Alps somewhat later, and Bohemia, Moravia and Slovakia by the end of the sixteenth century or early in the seventeenth. The revolution effected by the blast furnace was even more profound than that which resulted from the introduction of the bloomery, but its political, social and economic consequences belong to modern European history rather than to medieval.

It is impossible to estimate the number of hearths and furnaces erected and worked during the Middle Ages, nor can we tell, except in a few instances, how much metal they produced in a year. The earliest wind-furnaces were small and shortlived. Enormous numbers have been excavated in, for example, the Siegen district of West Germany and the Holy Cross Mountains of Poland, and, to judge from the small amounts of slag found nearby, each can have been operated for only a very short time. They represented, however, a small investment, and could be readily abandoned and rebuilt elsewhere. They were, as they were sometimes called, *forgiae errantes*, established wherever there was ore and the fuel to smelt it with. They were built near very small ore bodies, such as in later centuries would have passed unnoticed.

The adoption of the bloomery, and still more of the blast-furnace, represented a large fixed capital. It could not be moved, and would not readily be abandoned as long as there were ore and fuel in the vicinity. It required a more abundant supply of ore and charcoal than earlier smelting devices, and was, as a general rule, built only near ore-bodies of proven size and within a short distance of forests which could satisfy its ravenous appetite for fuel. The result was inevitably a concentration of iron-smelting in a small number of areas which could satisfy its needs. The primitive manorial smelting hearth disappeared, and the trend – maintained until the present – towards fewer and larger units of production was initiated.

It was not until the eighteenth century that hearths and furnaces were worked throughout the year. Many things interrupted their work. Charcoal-burning was a seasonal occupation, and the transport of ore and fuel could be held up by the condition of the roads. The blast was dependent on water-power, and this in turn on the level of water in the streams. A dry season often led to the closure of works. Harvest, too, often took precedence over tending the furnace. Styria, probably one of the more productive of the iron smelting regions, is estimated to have produced about 2,000 tons of metal a year at the beginning of the fourteenth century. A single bloomery, on the basis of English evidence, produced less than three tons of iron in a year in the fourteenth century and not much more in the fifteenth.[43] The earliest blast furnaces had a daily output of a ton or more of metal. No doubt there was every temptation to make the maximum use of this fixed capital, but the plant must have been idle much of the time. Sprandel[44] has estimated that the total European output of iron about 1400 was no more than 25 to 30,000 tons, and that it rose only to 40,000 by 1500.

Comparatively little is known of the social and economic conditions under which iron was produced during the Middle Ages. The polyptyques contain few references to iron amongst their lists of peasant obligations. Saint-Germain received 100-pound blooms from certain of its tenants in Normandy, and Fulda and Lörsch also received dues in iron from some villages. It appears that these were collective obligations, presupposing some form of communal iron-working. Such undertakings were probably widespread during the early Middle Ages, and since they were based on village custom they resulted in few written records. How to absorb such autonomous societies into a system of feudal obligations and dependence was a crucial problem in the Middle Ages. The lord claimed the land on which the rural communities had long been accustomed to dig for ores. In 1047 the Emperor Henry III granted to all the inhabitants of the Val di Scalve, in the Alps to the north of Milan, the right to work iron and to sell it within a prescribed area, subject only to the payment to the emperor of a thousand pounds of iron annually.[45] This appears to have been the pattern generally followed. The lord granted, or rather, confirmed a traditional practice, sometimes on condition that the ore was not sold outside the area, receiving in return a payment, usually proportionate to the amount of metal worked. The Count of Champagne confirmed such rights to communities of iron-workers in the Forêt d'Othe; the Count of Foix, to those of Vicdessos, in Ariège; the Count of Savoy, to those of Allevard, high in the Alps, above Grenoble. There is also evidence for collective or communal ironworks at several places in Italy and Germany.

In 1289, the rights and privileges, commonly known as the 'customs', of the ironworkers in the hills of Normandy were codified, and on several later occasions they were confirmed by the king of France.[46] The miners were organised; they elected representatives, who exercised certain judicial functions and protected their interests against the landed nobility. Metal workers thus tended to constitute an immunity within the feudal system of tenurial relations. The tin miners of south-western England probably constituted the extreme example of a privileged craft group, but throughout Europe there were mining communities, both in the ferrous and the non-ferrous metals, who enjoyed privileges which were denied to other groups.

In the twelfth and thirteenth centuries the monastic orders, especially the Cistercians and Carthusians, undertook the task of working iron. They did so on land which had been given them, and the work was accomplished by lay-brethern, or *conversi*. The abbey of Clairvaux, in Burgundy, owned perhaps a dozen iron-works, each probably consisting of a single bloomery, and was the largest iron producer in the region in the later Middle Ages.[47] Everywhere the Cistercians showed themselves active in iron-working, and in eastern Europe, particularly in Poland, their pioneering work was of great long-term importance. The Carthusian order entered the metallurgical field rather later than the Cistercians. It was not until the end of the twelfth century that they began to exploit the mineral and forest resources of the vast Alpine regions which they had acquired. In some cases the monks worked the bloomeries themselves; in others, they leased them, but always iron-working provided one of the surest and most important sources of income. As investment in fixed capital became larger, it was found desirable to use it for as long a period of the year as possible. Metal-working gradually ceased to be a part-time occupation of the farming community, and became the full-time pursuit for professional iron-workers. At the same time, the growing volume of production necessitated wider markets, until, by the end of the Middle Ages, there was a trading network which spanned the continent. In these circumstances, the merchant capitalist who dealt in bar iron, first invested in ironworks, and then leased and operated them. Thus the Count of Savoy, in the late thirteenth century, granted to Lucchese and Florentine merchants the right to open up mines and to establish ironworks in his territories. Genoese and Tuscan merchants were active in the mines of Elba in the fourteenth century; Milanese in the Alps of Bergamo, and merchants from many towns, in the industry of Normandy, Champagne and the Alps.[48]

*The non-ferrous metals.* Only five metals, other than iron, were regularly used. Two of them were the precious metals, gold and silver; the others were lead, tin and copper. Zinc, in the form of calamine, was used, though medieval man never succeeded in reducing it to its metallic form. The non-ferrous metals differed from iron in their much more restricted distribution, in the greater technical difficulties in mining their ores, and the greater ease of smelting them. Except gold, which is found in its 'native' state, the non-ferrous metals occur most often as sulphides, in veins or lodes. This meant, of course, that many deposits could be pursued downwards from the surface and that their richness often increased with their distance from the surface.

The ores of iron – at least those that were worked during the Middle Ages – were found at a very shallow depth, and it was impossible to exploit them without seriously disturbing the surface of the ground. The owner of the land was held to own also the ores of iron which might lie beneath it; it never occurred to people to separate the one from the other. With minerals which were usually mined from a greater depth such a separation of ownership became possible, and even desirable. Land might be leased or sold, reserving rights to the non-ferrous minerals. This was, in itself, an important legal advance. It allowed mineral resources to be acquired by parties with the technical knowledge and financial resources to exploit them. It provided the legal framework within which the Fuggers, Welsers, and other mining capitalists of the sixteenth century were able to work.

An extension of this view, that surface and mineral rights were separable, was the doctrine of regalian rights, the idea that the king or prince himself held an exclusive right to some or all minerals that might be extracted from the subsoil. The doctrine was of classical origin, and gradually gained acceptance in medieval Europe with the revived interest in Roman law. It was asserted by the Emperor Frederick I in 1158, and was subsequently adopted in most of Europe. Within the German Empire the regalian right devolved as a general rule on the princes who exercised effective power. Sometimes it was asserted only with regard to the precious metals. It was never made to apply to the so-called 'earths', even when these, as was the case with calamine, were in fact metalliferous ores. If the king 'owned' certain minerals lying beneath the surface, it was clearly to his advantage that they should be mined, smelted and sold. As a general rule, medieval rulers did not engage directly in mining and smelting; the Rammelsberg mine, near Goslar, is an apparent exception, because it lay on an imperial estate. Instead, princes commonly welcomed all who were able and willing to extract the minerals, and exacted from them a royalty in proportion to the amount of metal obtained. Furthermore, the prince's right to the regalian minerals beneath the soil usually took precedence over the landowner's right to the usufruct of the surface. The two were clearly incompatible, and the disputes which arose contributed to the assertion by the mining communities of their separate status.

The history of tin-mining in Devon and Cornwall provides a clear and well documented case study in the law and practice of medieval mining. Here the tinners were authorised to turn over the surface in their search for tin ore. Such mining, as repeated complaints made clear, was highly destructive of the soil. Furthermore, the miners needed to channel water to their workings, and this often necessitated interference with surface rights over a large area. Yet the tin royalty was an important source of royal revenue, and it was in the king's interest that the tin be mined. The royal charter of 1201 and subsequent confirmations gave to the tinners the right, without prior consent, to 'bound' or establish small concessions, on wasteland, on payment of a royalty to the king and a small toll to the landowner. They could also construct ducts to carry water to their workings. The only condition was that the mine be worked continuously; any interruption, and the concession lapsed, and another might 'bound' in the same area.

No system could have made for greater conflict between the miners and the owners and cultivators of the soil. A court, with jurisdiction over all matters relating to mining, existed outside the system of common-law courts. The tinners thus constituted a small but autonomous body, with its own peculiar laws and customs and its own means of judging cases and enforcing its decisions.

The tinners constituted an extreme case, but it was one which bore close similarities to the organisation of many mining communities in continental Europe. The miners of the Harz Mountains, of the Ore Mountains of Saxony and Bohemia, of Kutná Hora and Přibram, and, above all, of the Carpathian Mountains in northern Hungary, all had similar privileges. These were remote and mountainous areas, in which the miners settled in considerable numbers. They created small mining towns: Freiberg in Saxony, Kutná Hora, and the Slovakian towns of Kremnica and Baňská Bystrica, which combined the autonomy of incorporated towns with the juridical independence of mining communities. The privileges of the central European miners were embodied in the 'Laws' of Jihlava (Iglau), a small mining town in southern Bohemia. These were first codified in 1249, but, with local modifications, were adopted over much of east-central and south-eastern Europe. The central European miners were mainly German, and the opening up of metalliferous mines in the Slav lands was a facet of German eastward colonisation.

Western Germany was the most important source of the non-ferrous metals during the earlier Middle Ages. The chief mines were in the Harz Mountains. The Rammelsberg mine was opened in the tenth century and quickly became a major source of silver. The fortunes of the Saxon dynasty, and also of the town of Goslar, one of the most frequented of imperial residences, were founded on it. Along with many other mines in the Harz, the Rammelsberg continued to be productive until, in the fourteenth century, problems of drainage became too great, and production fell off. It was not until the fifteenth century that the technical problems were overcome, and the Harz again became a major source of silver.

Bohemia was also highly mineralised. The Krušny Hory, or Ore Mountains, became in the last century of the Middle Ages one of the most productive mining areas of Europe. It was here that the earliest school of mines, the *Bergakademie* of Freiberg, was later founded. Here too George Agricola practised as a doctor and acquired that knowledge of mining practice which he used in writing his *De Re Metallica*.[49] Silver was here the mainstay of mining. In central Bohemia, at Příbram and Kutná Hora, mining was controlled by the Bohemian crown, which pre-empted the metal for the royal mint. Mining had begun in the twelfth century, if not earlier. It was greatly expanded during the later Middle Ages, and at the same time the mining passed from the small men, who did little more than scratch the surface, to capitalists, able to open, equip and operate large mines, with dozens, perhaps hundreds of workers. Amongst these merchant capitalists of the late fifteenth century was Jan Thurzo, who made one fortune from the mines near Kutná Hora and another from those of Slovakia. A painting of the last quarter of the fifteenth century, contained in the Kutná Hora *gradual*,[50] illustrates life at the mining centre. An immense number of scantily clad but hooded miners climb through crevices in the rocks, lighted by small lamps. They are shown cleaving the rock with wedges; pulling shallow baskets of ore through the workings, and hauling it by ropes to the surface. At the surface, a horse-operated *whim* hoists the ore to the ground level, where it is washed and the larger lumps broken up. It is an intimate and revealing picture of a large silver mine at the end of the Middle Ages, clearly a well organised and highly capitalised undertaking.

The Slovak silver mines were opened up by Germans in the thirteenth century, but waited for their fullest expansion for the coming of the merchant capitalists,[51] like the Fuggers, Thurzos, Paumgartners and Welsers.

The smelting of the complex silver-copper ores was made possible by the discovery by Lazarus Ercker of the cupellation process, in the mid-fifteenth century. The Slovak ores were smelted within the mountains where there was no shortage of fuel. The Fuggers and Thurzos also owned the furnaces, and marketed the metal in the Baltic towns, in Nuremberg and in Venice and the North Italian cities. The mines of Upper Hungary, as the Slovak area was commonly called, reached their peak during the first third of the sixteenth century. In the ten years 1495 to 1504, 190,000 Centner (about 10,000 tons) of copper were sold, almost three-quarters of it on Fugger account. Silver production from the Fugger mines near Baňská Bystrica was in 1510–13 worth 51,847 marks. The Fuggers and Thurzos paid highly to the king of Hungary for their privileges, but they made enormous profits from them. The price revolution of the sixteenth century probably owed as much, at least in its early stages, to the silver which flowed from the mines of Bohemia and Slovakia as it did to the bullion from the New World. In 1526 King Lewis of Hungary drove a hard bargain with the mining magnates, and the Thurzos withdrew from the enterprise, leaving the Fuggers alone. A year later Lewis was dead, drowned as he fled from the battlefield of Mohacs. The Turks controlled the Plain of Hungary and the routes leading from the south to the mines of Slovakia. Mining dwindled, and the Fuggers eventually withdrew to their very considerable undertakings in the Austrian Alps.

German miners also made their way into Transylvania and the Balkan Peninsula, and in the thirteenth century began to open up the varied resources of Bosnia and Serbia. Gold, silver and lead were mined, especially near Novo Brdo, which became the most active mining centre in the Balkans. This was a wild and insecure region. The miners lived in small but strongly fortified towns, and the metals moved in convoys through the mountains to the coast. Dubrovnik and Split became the most important commercial outlets, from which the metals were shipped to Italy.

Southern Spain had been a major source of metals under the Roman Empire. The mines, primarily in the Sierra Morena, and the more southerly parts of the Meseta, were revived by the Arab conquerors. Mining flourished during the earlier Middle Ages, but little seems to have been exported to the rest of Europe. The mineral resources of Sweden began to be opened up in the later Middle Ages. Some silver was obtained, but mining came to be dominated by copper. From the first there was a strong German influence in Swedish mining, and the Falun copper mines are said to have been opened up by men from the Rammelsberg.

We know where the metalliferous ores were obtained during the Middle Ages, but not, in general, the quantities produced. The precious metals were mined in only small amounts. It has been estimated that Kutná Hora at the height of its prosperity yielded only about 200 cwt of silver a year. With the sole exception of the tin production of south-western England, there are no statistical series of metal output. There are fragmentary data on the volume of metal produced by the Fuggers and Thurzos, and we have the figures collated by Soetbeer for the precious metals during the later Middle Ages.[52] For earlier centuries almost nothing is known.

Craftsmen in the non-ferrous metals were not to be found in every town. They worked with expensive raw materials, and served a wealthy and influential clientèle. Some were mobile, moving from one building site to another. Most were to be found only in the larger towns. In London there was a gild of pewterers, who alloyed lead with tin to make the table-ware and drinking pots of the rich; there were bronze-founders, who cast bells and statuary; brass-workers, who, little though they knew it, added zinc to copper to produce brass, and those who decorated baser metals with inlays of copper. In the largest cities, the workers in fine metals, the goldsmiths and silversmiths, were to be counted in their hundreds. Florence had a bell-founders' gild, and Balthazar Behem's illustrations of the trades of Kraków includes that of the *Erzgiesser* whose craft included the casting of church bells.[53] Florence also had a gild which combined the forging of helmets with working in brass. There was even one town in medieval

Europe, Dinant, which was given over almost wholly to the fabrication of metal goods (see page 265).[54]

*Coal mining.* Coal, which has since become one of the most valuable of the riches of the earth's crust, was little used during the Middle Ages. For this there was good reason. In much of Europe the forests were still extensive enough to yield charcoal, and coal, without being first converted to coke, was a difficult and unpleasant fuel in the cottage and was unsuited to the smelting of metals. It was only in those densely populated areas in which the forests had been reduced to a few copses, that coal was used. It was burned in England and the Low Countries, but its use continued until the eighteenth century to arouse considerable hostility. In the early sixteenth century the Greek traveller, Nicander Nucius, visited Liège. 'In this city,' he wrote, 'and all the neighbouring country, they are accustomed to burn a certain black substance, stony and shining, and producing hot embers without smoke . . . These stones they dig out of the deepest recesses of the earth, finding veins from which they extract them.'[55] It was, indeed, in the vicinity of Liège that the earliest regular mining of coal developed. The Cistercian house of Val Saint-Lambert, as early as 1228, reserved rights in coal when it leased land (see p. 327),[56] and the earliest agreement to mine coal on the monastery's lands was reached in 1278. Thereafter many mines were opened up, and coal came to be regularly used for such purposes as the burning of bricks, tiles and lime, which was inordinately extravagant of fuel. In the late thirteenth century coal began to be mined also in the Ruhr valley of West Germany, and was carried by boat to the Rhineland towns. Elsewhere in Europe the peasants may have scratched at the rocks and extracted small quantities, but coal was, by and large, of negligible importance before the seventeenth century.

Wood, charcoal and, in a few areas, peat, were the only forms of fuel in general use. No community could exist without some woodland in which the peasants had rights to 'estovers', and in the larger forest areas the charcoal burners were active. These cut down the whole tree and carbonised it in slow fires. They could only do this with the consent of the lords of the soil, and there was considerable reluctance on the part of the latter to allowing the extent of forest to be greatly reduced. On the other hand, the larger mining and smelting centres were extravagant of fuel. Kutná Hora, which must have ranked as one of the largest smelting centres in Europe, was served by societies or gilds of charcoal-burners, who held a monopoly of the supply of fuel, and acted together both to secure rights to cut trees and to profit from the needs of the smelters.

*Salt working.* Common salt has been the mineral in most wide-spread demand at all stages of human history, and was one of the earliest commodities to enter into trade. It lay at the root of the prosperity of many towns, including Venice, and the frequency with which one finds the word 'salt' as a place-name element is evidence of its importance. In the Middle Ages salt was obtained in two ways. The simpler was to evaporate sea-water in shallow lagoons along the coast. The other was to evaporate over fires the brine that rose in salt-springs.

Salt-pans lined the European coast, from the Aegean Sea to the Bay of Biscay. North of the Loire mouth, the cloudy skies and cool summers restricted evaporation. Nevertheless, there were salt-pans on the coast of Normandy, and Domesday recorded many on the English coast. The flat coasts around the tideless Mediterranean Sea were the most suited for the evaporation of brine. Salt was made in Macedonia and Thrace for the supply of Constantinople; along the coast of Epirus and Albania, in the lagoons of Venice, around the shores of Apulia, in Tuscany and Provence, on the coast of Andalusia, and above all along the shores of the Bay of Biscay. The Bay which gave its name to 'Bay salt,' the variety in the greatest demand in north-western Europe, was in fact the *Baie de Bourgneuf*, an opening off the more familiar Bay of Biscay. The greatest demand for salt came from the populous areas of north-western Europe and from those northern regions where the fisheries were important. The most abundant production was on those coasts which lay nearest to the market and at the same time had the right physical and climatic conditions. These were without question the flat shores of the Bay of Biscay and of Languedoc and Provence. They had suitable means of transport to northern Europe, either by coastwise shipping or up the valley of the Rhône. Saltpans had been worked in these areas since early in the Middle Ages. They were owned in many instances by monastic landowners who leased them to individuals or small groups of men who made the salt.

There are many salt-springs where the brine was evaporated in large pans over fires. The abbey of Prüm had such a salt-work at the end of the ninth century (see p. 77). In the later Middle Ages salt springs were used near Paderborn and at Lüneburg, and in the Danube valley of Upper Austria. These inland saltworks in general supplied areas not easily accessible to salt brought inland from the coast.

The volume of salt produced must have been very large, though few statistics exist. English ports are estimated to have imported some 16,000 quarters a year in the late fourteenth century.[57] The consumption in the Low Countries and the Baltic, where much was used in curing fish, must have been considerably larger.

## The building industries

Building construction was one of the major industries of the Middle Ages. The great buildings, both ecclesiastical and lay, are too often taken for granted or dismissed as the products of religious euphoria. They were designed and erected by professionals, able to turn their hand as easily to Gothic tracery as to castle walls. The sheer volume of building construction undertaken from early in the eleventh century, when Europe began to put on 'its white robe of churches', to the end of the fifteenth is staggering, the more so when one thinks of the relatively small size and general poverty of the population. One asks how could it have been paid for, and to what extent was economic growth inhibited by so huge an investment in what was, economically speaking, an unproductive expenditure.

There is no means of knowing how many were engaged at any one time in the building industries. They can, however, be divided into the urban workers, many of whom belonged to gilds and whose numbers can thus in a few instances be estimated, and those who moved from one large building to another, like the architects who designed them. At Paris in 1300, 383 craftsmen of the building industries paid *taille*. Of these 122 were masons; 108 were carpenters, and 31 *couvreurs* who put the roofs on houses. This list does not even exhaust the skilled craftsmen in the building trades; it certainly omits the doubtless very much larger numbers of semiskilled and unskilled: the hod-carriers, quarrymen and those who mixed mortar and dragged materials to the building site. In general few masons and workers in stone lived in the towns. Coventry had only seven out of 603 craftsmen in 1450. There were only twenty at Norwich, and scarcely more at Oxford. This is because medieval town building, outside the Mediterranean region, was predominantly in wood. Town house construction offered little work for the mason, though there was a tendency in the fifteenth century, if not earlier, to replace the thatched roof with slate or tile and to build large fire-places and chimneys of masonry.[58]

The more ambitious buildings, however, whether large churches or civic architecture, were of stone, and the use of wood was restricted to the roofs and floors. The masons who worked on them were highly skilled, relatively well paid, and very mobile. They moved from one building site to another, thus assisting in the diffusion of architectural styles. Urban masons and carpenters were commonly grouped into gilds. Peripatetic craftsmen could have no such organisation, but at any major building site, where work continued perhaps for decades, they had their 'lodges'. Their purpose was to give some permanence to the shifting body of craftsmen, to canalise their efforts to help one another, to represent their interests as against the persons and institutions whom they served, and doubtless to collect information on where the next job was to be found. Inevitably the travelling masons maintained links between the lodges, so that an informal association developed between them.

The supply of building materials was often of critical importance, whether construction was in wood or stone. It was not easy to acquire the large beams required for roofing. Abbot Suger relates how, after being told that the large timbers required for the new abbey of Saint-Denis were unobtainable, he went into the woods and searched for them himself – successfully as the event proved. Time after time we find grants by the lord of the soil of permission to cut timber or to quarry stone for the construction of a church or a monastery. Building materials were customarily transported very great distances, especially if water-transport was available. Paris obtained building stone from the nearby limestone plateau of Brie, but timber was floated down the rivers from Burgundy. Southern England obtained some of its ashlar masonry from Normandy, and Venice from the Dalmatian coast. Certain ornamental stones – the black marble of Tournai or the reddish tufa from Andernach – can be recognised over large areas of north-western Europe. The cost of gathering the materials to the building site was a not inconsiderable fraction of total expenses.

In certain parts of Europe, where there was no building stone and the cost of transporting it from distant quarries excessive, builders turned to the use of bricks. The art of burning bricks and tiles was rediscovered in the Middle Ages. It was most developed in the North German Plain, where suitable clays were abundant and the forests could satisfy the huge demand of the brick-kilns for fuel. In the fifteenth century north German towns, from Lüneburg, through Lübeck and Danzig, to Riga, developed an austere form of brick-gothic architecture. In the following century the Dutch evolved a style of domestic architecture particularly well suited to the use of brick. It was only very slowly that brick replaced wood. Its use was encouraged by the disastrous fires from which every medieval town suffered at one time or another; its wider use was restricted by the high cost of the bricks themselves. Little is known of such ancillary crafts as lime-burning, which must have been carried on near most towns and on every major construction site. At Florence there was a minor gild which embraced brick and lime-burners, as well as those who made coarse earthenware pots. It is probable, however, that the lime-burners, like the masons, drifted from building site to building site.

MANUFACTURING IN THE MEDIEVAL ECONOMY

It is very difficult to evaluate the significance of manufacturing in the medieval economy. That it was, in terms both of the volume of employment and the value of the product, inferior to agriculture cannot be denied. It is no less apparent that, at least until the early fourteenth century, it accounted for an increasing proportion of an expanding gross product. Urban population, however, grew from one or two per cent in the eleventh century to perhaps 12 to 15 per cent at the beginning of the fourteenth. It included an agricultural component, as well as a merchant and entrepreneurial class. In no town did the crafts occupy more than a minority of the working population, and there was only a handful of specialised craftsmen in most of the smaller towns.

On the other hand many crafts, especially in the later Middle

Ages, were also practised in rural areas, and some – the smelting of metals, for example – exclusively so. It is quite impossible, except in a few instances, to estimate the numbers employed wholly, part-time or seasonally in rural industries. No doubt the numbers fluctuated greatly, with a tendency to increase in the fifteenth century. It is entirely possible that rural employment in mining and the crafts was at least as large as urban in the later Middle Ages. This would suggest that in the developed areas of Europe, from northern Spain to central Germany and from central Italy to the Baltic, between five and ten per cent of the population was engaged in mining, metallurgy and the crafts. The service industries – the innkeepers and servants, porters and *Weinknechte*, retailers and notaries – would have made up a significantly smaller proportion of the urban population and would have been very few in the rural areas.

# 8

# The trade of the
# Middle Ages

The Europe of the ninth century had, in the well-worn judgment of
Pirenne, 'an economy of no markets'. This opinion is not, however,
supported by the evidence. There was a good deal of trade, and in
very few parts of Europe were local communities entirely without
commercial contacts with other peoples and other regions. 'The
whole theory of the closed household economy and the "autarchy"
of the great estate of the Middle Ages', wrote Dopsch,[1] 'is clearly
based on a very shaky foundation', and in this he is surely right.
Yet one must be careful not to exaggerate. The volume of trade was
small compared with that of the later Middle Ages. Though a
certain amount of coarse cloth entered into trade as well as a perhaps considerable amount of salt, the movement was in the main
one of luxury articles, and, again with the exception of salt, the
vast majority of the people never acquired any goods that had not
been produced in their immediate vicinity. Trade, furthermore,
was sporadic. A *system* of trade, made up of interlocking and inter-
dependent components and functioning regularly or continuously, had not yet made its appearance.

### EARLY MEDIEVAL TRADE

Yet the later medieval trading system can in the ninth and tenth
centuries be discerned in embryo. There were markets as well as
fairs, which met less frequently. There were merchants who
apparently gave themselves wholly to trade, and were beginning
to frequent certain centres and to establish recognised routes
between them. Inevitably the passage, however irregular and
infrequent, of such traders led to the emergence of ferries across

338

the rivers, overnight accommodation, markets, even toll stations. At the same time the idea came to be accepted that in certain places the presence of traders was to be expected, and they in turn formed associations to protect both themselves and their merchandise. This led then to an intensification of trade along certain routes. Markets and fairs came to be held regularly; traders could expect to meet one another on these occasions, and so a commercial system gradually took shape. At the same time financial instruments were devised. The promissory note and then the bill of exchange came to be used to settle debts; banks remitted large sums of money from one end of Europe to the other; double-entry book-keeping permitted merchants to keep their accounts with ever-increasing precision. By the fourteenth century a commercial system of quite exceptional elaboration and complexity had been evolved. Indeed, no fundamental advances in business organisation and management were made between the fifteenth century and the end of the eighteenth.

But in the tenth century this system lay far in the future. The trade of the Carolingian Empire had been disrupted and in some areas destroyed by the invasions of the ninth and early tenth centuries. The Carolingian port of Quentovic disappeared so completely that there is today some doubt regarding its precise location. In many parts of Europe villages were destroyed, the movement of traders interrupted, and human energies diverted from capital accumulation and production for trade to the tasks of defence and reconstruction. Yet the interruption of trade was not universal. Throughout the period of the invasions markets continued to be held; merchants transported their wares and consumers compared the prices of luxury goods in different markets. About 900, when the inroads of the Norse, the Magyars and the Muslims were at their most severe, Gerbert of Aurillac was offered eastern silks and spices by Venetian merchants in the market of Pavia, and declined them because he had already purchased a supply – and, apparently, at a more favourable price – in Rome.[2]

The pattern of trade which had begun to emerge at the beginning of the ninth century was distorted, but not destroyed by the invasions of the tenth. Traffic flowed after the period of the invasions along much of the same routes as it had done before. It consisted in the main of the movement of goods from the Byzantine Empire and the Middle East to the Italian ports, and thence by road and river to north-western Europe.

There was, in general, a preference for water-borne transport, either by river or along the coasts of Europe. The system of Roman roads was of little importance. Their purpose had been military, and they were designed for marching armies rather than the carts and wagons of merchants. In all too many cases their paving had been robbed, and the bridges, without which no road system can be effective, were neglected and often ruinous. 'The lack of decent roads,' wrote Lopez, 'was one of the principal reasons for the rapid disintegration of' the Carolingian state.[3] The restricted trade of the early Middle Ages could hardly be held to justify their restoration and maintenance, even if this were financially and administratively practicable. From the fifth to the tenth centuries the relative importance of the rivers increased, a trend which continued until, in the later Middle Ages, traffic began to move back from the rivers to the roads. From the time of Charlemagne the polyptyques and cartularies are strewn with reference to river transport, to the services of boatmen, and to exemptions from river tolls.[4] The vineyards which supplied the monasteries were located, more often than not, close to navigable rivers, and monastic wine must have been a frequent cargo on the Moselle and Rhine. Salt production was also to a large extent in the hands of the monks, and salt made its journey to the market very largely by water. From the lagoons of Commachio and Venice it moved up the Po, and from the salt-pans of the Bay of Biscay coast up the Loire to the heart of France and by short road journeys to the Paris rivers.

The commercial axis which linked north-western Europe with the Byzantine Empire ran southwards from the Low Countries to the Mediterranean and continued by sea from Italy to the ports of the Aegean and the Levant. It was a highly vulnerable route. It was exposed at several points to Berber pirates in the Mediterranean, and to avoid these it was necessary to cross mountainous regions which presented difficulties of a different kind. The river Meuse provided the most northerly segment of the route.[5]

The river route even tempted the bishops of Tongeren to abandon their city on the plateau of central Belgium and to move to Liège. Other towns on the Meuse – Maastricht, Huy, Dinant – were amongst the earliest to develop in the Low Countries. On

Early medieval trade

one of the branches of its delta lay Duurstede, one of the chief
ports of Carolingian Austrasia, and before the end of the tenth
century there was a fair at Visé, near Liège, at which traders
gathered from much of western Europe.

## The Mediterranean
From the Meuse valley the route ran overland to the Saône river
and thus to the Rhône. The ports of Languedoc and Provence,
which lay close to the mouth of the Rhône, had by the Carolingian
period lost much of their earlier prosperity. In the late eighth
century an emissary from the Pope to the Carolingian court went
by sea to Marseilles rather than brave the Lombards who controlled the Alpine passes. In the middle years of the ninth century all
the important ports of Languedoc and Provence: Narbonne, Arles,
Marseilles, were raided by the Muslims, who also established a
piratical base near Saint-Tropez (see p. 72). Commerce diminished
in the ports of southern France as it was forced to cross the Alps to
northern Italy rather than follow the Mediterranean coast. But
trade continued through the Italian ports to the Aegean, Asia
Minor, Syria and Egypt. This commerce had formerly been largely
in the hands of Syrians, Jews and the subjects of the Byzantine
Empire themselves. Much of it had once passed through Ravenna,
but the port had now silted, and its role had passed to the traders
who lived around the Venetian lagoons. These were in the tenth
and eleventh centuries extending their control along the shores of
the Adriatic Sea, tapping the commerce of Dalmatia, exporting
iron from Carinthia and Friuli and slaves from the Slav lands, and
reaching out towards the routes to Constantinople and the Levant.
As intermediaries in this east–west trade they nevertheless had
formidable rivals. Foremost amongst these were the towns of
southern Italy: Gaeta, Amalfi and Bari.

Amalfi dominated this early trade between the eastern and the
western Mediterranean. It developed a complex triangular trade
which spanned much of the Mediterranean Sea.[6] Its merchants
exported the products of southern Italy – wheat, timber, cloth,
wines and fruits – not to Constantinople, which could be supplied
more cheaply from nearer sources, but to North Africa. In the
ports of the latter, from Tunis to Alexandria, they were exchanged
for olive oil, wax and gold from the Sudan. These were the goods
which the Byzantines were prepared to accept in return for their

silks and ceremonial robes, their spices, jewellery and works of art.

The Arab writer, Ibn Kordadbeh, described Amalfi as 'the most prosperous town in Lombardy (Italy), the most noble, the most illustrious . . . the most affluent and opulent'.[7] The linen cloth which its merchants exported, was the product of Naples, where 'I have seen pieces the like of which I found in no other country, and there is no craftsman in any other workshop in the world who is able to manufacture it'. The Song of Guiscard, who conquered the town in 1077 praised its power and opulence.[8] After the Norman conquest the commercial importance of Amalfi in the Middle Eastern trade declined. Its pre-eminence had clearly depended upon its quasi-autonomous position within the Byzantine Empire. As subjects of the Norman kingdom of Sicily the Amalfitans found their trade subordinated to the political policies of their rulers. They were no longer able to buy up the grain surplus of southern Italy and sell it to the Muslims in North Africa. For the rest of the Middle Ages Amalfi remained a prosperous little port serving the needs of the local trade of its Neapolitan and Salernian hinterland.

With Amalfi were associated Gaeta, to the north of Naples, and Bari in Apulia. The latter suffered the same fate as Amalfi. Occupied by the Normans, it was made to serve the needs of the Norman state. Gaeta became a port of only local significance, and primacy in the trade of the west coast of Italy passed to Pisa, and then to Genoa.

The eastern termini of this trade were the ports of Egypt and the Levant, especially Alexandria, Jaffa, Antioch, and, above all, Constantinople. The Muslim lands of North Africa and the Middle East enjoyed a period of prosperity in the tenth century, and the Arab conquest of Crete and Cyprus, and occasional raids on the coast of the mainland, did little to interrupt the flow of trade. Byzantine sea-power had weakened, but still maintained a firm grip on the Aegean Sea and on much of the Black Sea coast. The life of St Gregory the Decapolite[9] presents a picture of the Aegean in the ninth century, its ports full of shipping and trade disturbed only occasionally by the threat of a raid by Muslim pirates. The sea-borne trade of the Aegean and Black Seas was intended essentially for Constantinople, as that of the Mediterranean had been for Rome. Its population – perhaps 800,000 – was fed with grain brought by ship from the Black Sea coast and Asia Minor, wine from the Aegean and olive oil from as far afield as North Africa.

In addition to the local trade in foodstuffs was the long-distance commerce in luxury goods with Russia, Central Asia and the Middle East. Spices, raw silk, cotton, gemstones and ivory were brought from India by way either of the Persian Gulf or of Iran and Turkestan. Skins, furs and amber came down the Russian rivers to the Black Sea coast, from which they were shipped to Constantinople. The Russian trade was an important one. It was, wrote Constantine Porphyrogenitus,[10] in the hands of the Russians, who built boats in the northern forests during winter, and brought them to Kiev when the ice melted. Here they formed a fleet which sailed down the Dnepr, portaging around the rapids, until they reached the shore of the Black Sea. Here the ships were equipped with sails, and followed the coast westward until they reached Constantinople, where 'their voyage, fraught with such travail and terror, such difficulty and danger, is at an end'.

The eastern trade of the Byzantines was an unbalanced one. Though their artistic products were in demand in the West, they held little attraction in Asia. The spices, raw silk, ivory had to be paid for, in part, by the export of bullion. Gold was in perpetual demand, and much of the precious metals which western merchants shipped to Constantinople either from North Africa or from coin hoards in Europe ultimately made its way to Iran, India and beyond.

The so-called *Book of the Eparch*,[11] compiled about 900, attempted to codify the regulations which governed the merchants and craftsmen of Constantinople. It makes clear how much the city was dependent upon imported raw materials and how closely the merchants who imported them were controlled. The most important European port of the Empire, after Constantinople, was Thessaloniki. It supplied some grain, as well as animals, to the capital, but the conquest of most of the Balkan peninsula by the Slavs had cut off much of its hinterland.

### The Viking North

The trading links with the Levant accounted for only a part of Europe's trade. A very different though no less important route linked the Carolingian heartland with the Baltic Sea, with Scandinavia and with Russia. The tumult and confusion of the Viking raids tends to disguise the trading relations which were established in the same areas and at the same time. The first traders into these areas during the Middle Ages appear to have been the Frisians. In the seventh and eighth centuries their small ships had sailed within the protecting line of the Frisian Islands to the Danish peninsula, and from here both northwards to Norway and, after portaging their wares across the base of the Danish peninsula, eastwards to the island of Gotland and the Uppland region of central Sweden. Their exports probably included Frankish pottery and glass, which have been found in large quantities in Scandinavian burials, together with cloth and salt. Their return cargoes included furs and skins, the staple products of the northern forests, as well as amber, wax and salted and dried fish.

In the course of the ninth century the Scandinavian peoples themselves took over most of the trade of the Baltic, and restricted the sphere of Frisian activity largely to the shores of the North Sea.[12] The focus of this northern trade came to be Hedeby (Haithabu), lying at the head of the Schlei fjord, near the later town of Schleswig (see p. 86). On the coast of Pomerania, Wollin grew up as a trading settlement, and somewhere near the mouth of the Vistula lay Truso, to which King Alfred's informant, Wulfstan, had sailed late in the ninth century.[13] On the southern shore of Lake Mälaren, near the site of the modern Stockholm, lay Birka, perhaps the most important of these trading places of the Baltic region. Not only did it carry on trade with Hedeby and the west, but also with the coast of Finland, the eastern Baltic, and Staraya Ladoga in Russia. Birka was, about the year 1000, replaced by Sigtuna, near Uppsala, and the destruction of Sigtuna in 1187 prepared the way for the rise of Stockholm and Visby as the chief trading towns of Scandinavia. Othere of Halogaland, another of Alfred's informants, described a trading place in southern Norway.[14] This has been identified with Kaupang, a farm close to the western shore of Oslo fjord in southern Norway. The site has been excavated, but the finds suggest barter rather than trade. The settlement was very small and unfortified and may have been occupied for only the summer season.[15] Other traders' settlements were probably similar; easily destroyed and occupied only intermittently, they could readily disappear from the landscape leaving no trace.

The Viking dominaton of the Baltic Sea was followed by their penetration of Russia. Bases were established along much of the coastline, and from these the Vikings penetrated the valleys which guided them into the hinterland. In this way they made forays into the Oder and Vistula valleys, but their most important expeditions took them up the Dvina, Volkhov and Neva rivers. From these slow-flowing and navigable waterways, portages led them through the forests to the head-waters of the Volga, Don, Dnepr and Dnestr, and thus to the Caspian or Black Seas.

The most important of these Viking routes was that which followed the Volga river to its mouth in the Caspian Sea. It was by this route that Persian and Middle Eastern goods reached the Baltic, and Itil, lying on the Volga river near the head of its delta, was in the ninth and tenth centuries a market where Norse, Tartars, Persians and Armenians were brought together. The earlier coin hoards found in Scandinavia are of Arab and Persian coins. These are often taken as a measure of the volume of trade. It is doubtful, however, whether Scandinavian exports to the Middle East would have been so much in excess of imports that the trade balance would require to be adjusted by the import of gold, unless the trade in slaves reached very large proportions. It is more likely that the Vikings drew no distinction between trade, piracy and raiding, turning from one to the other as occasion offered. The Persians, so eager to acquire gold from the Byzantines, are unlikely to have been ready to release it to the Vikings. The hoards are more likely to represent the profits of successful raids.

Greater importance in the long run attached to the routes which followed the courses of the Black Sea rivers. As in western Europe, Viking raids in this direction led to permanent settlement and to the foundation of trading towns in which the Vikings themselves must have formed a local aristocracy among the Slav and Tatar masses. An association of such towns, not altogether correctly described as the first Russian State, came into being in the later years of the ninth century. Their merchants transmitted the northern products to the Black Sea coast, whence they were taken to Constantinople (see p. 88). This commerce developed somewhat later than that which linked the Baltic Sea with the Caspian and the Middle East. Hoards of Byzantine *nomisma* do not appear in Scandinavia until the middle years of the ninth century. In the course of the late tenth and early eleventh centuries, both of these routes were cut by renewed invasion from the Steppe, and communication across the so-called isthmus of Europe was ended for several centuries.

Sea-routes did not provide the only ways by which trade was carried on between western Europe and Russia. Charlemagne's ordinances had provided for an overland trade between his empire and eastern Europe (see p. 77), and, though the volume of commerce which passed his frontier stations may have been small in the early ninth century, it increased greatly in the tenth and began to assume the proportions of a regular and predictable movement. Mainz became the chief point of departure. From here merchants, many of them Jewish, travelled up the Main, and by way of Bamberg, one of Charlemagne's 'ports of entry', reached Prague (see p. 247). The route continued through the Moravian Gate to Kraków and thence across the plains of southern Poland to Przemyśl, where there was a large Jewish community, and on to Kiev. Regensburg was a western terminus of secondary importance at first, because the disturbed conditions in the Hungarian Plain made travel difficult. Eventually, however, a route was developed across the Carpathian Mountains from Przemyśl to the future site of Budapest and thence by river to South Germany.

This west to east land route was supplemented by others which linked it with the Baltic route from north-western Europe to Russia. One of these followed the Polish rivers. In the tenth century central Poland, especially the towns of Gniezno and Poznań, became, as archaeological finds have demonstrated, the focus of long-distance trade.

The volume of commerce which moved along these routes was doubtless small. The route through Prague and Przemyśl made no use of water-borne transport and was dependent on pack animals and carts. This we know from the story of the company of Jewish traders from Regensburg which was held up because they had lost a wheel. Doubtless the goods which made their way to Przemyśl by way of the Hungarian Plain used the Danube for part of the way. The supplementary routes which linked Kraków and Przemyśl with the Baltic coast unquestionably made great use of the Polish rivers.

Such was the pattern of trade which emerged in Europe during the years immediately following the cataclysms of the late ninth and early tenth centuries. To some extent its development accompanied the Viking, Magyar and Arab raids and was shaped by them. There can be no doubt that Viking raids and Norse trade were closely interconnected, the former supplying part of the materials required in the more peaceful pursuit of the latter.

## THE MERCHANTS

Little is known of the merchants who carried their wares across Europe, and even less of the source of their trading capital. Within the Mediterranean basin Syrians and Jews had long been prominent in trade. In the second half of the ninth century Ibn Kordadbeh seems to have implied that much of the trade was in the hands of Jews, who

> travel from the East to the West and from the West to the East by land as well as by sea. . . . They embark in the land of the Franks on the Western Sea, and they sail toward al-Farama [Pelusium, in Egypt]. There they load their merchandise on the backs of camels and proceed by land to al-Qulzum [on the Gulf of Suez]. . . . Some of them sail for Constantinople in order to sell their merchandise to the Romans. Others proceed to the residence of the king of the Franks to dispose of their articles.[16]

It has been suggested that, as the Italians gradually took over the commerce of Italian ports, the Jewish traders were obliged to turn their attention to more northerly and less developed routes. The scanty sources certainly suggest that the number of Jews increased along the overland routes from the Rhine and Danube to Przemyśl and Kiev. They nevertheless remained active in the Mediterranean ports. When, about 1170, Benjamin of Tudela travelled from his Spanish homeland to Constantinople, he noted the number and size of the Jewish communities along his route.[17] He found more than forty communities, some of which, he claimed, counted their numbers in hundreds.

The growing activity of Jewish merchants along the overland route is shown by the travel narrative of Ibrahim Ibn Ja'kub, written about 965. There were Jewish communities in many of the Rhineland towns, as well as in those which lay along the routes to Przemyśl Jewish traders were not, however, to be found in significant numbers in the northern ports and along the North Sea and Baltic routes. Trade was dominated by the Nordic peoples, who had ousted the Frisians from the Baltic and were active also in north-western Europe. It was northern peoples also, who sailed the Russian rivers and brought their forest products to the markets of the Crimea and Constantinople, or to the fair of Itil on the Volga.

Trading journeys were long and slow; the merchant required capital to purchase his wares and to support himself on the long voyage from Italy to Syria, or the journey from Mainz to Kiev. The latter could not have taken much less than a hundred days. He had, in some way, to cover himself against losses along the route, and, even if he sold at the end of it at a substantial profit, he could not, in the rudimentary commercial system of the tenth and eleventh centuries, anticipate, this profit and live on it before it had been earned. The trader, on however small a scale, had to be a man of some limited means. It is evident, however, that quite small resources were adequate to start with.

King Alfred included in his translation of the History of Orosius the narrations of the two Norse traders already mentioned. Ohthere went to northern Norway in search of skins, hides and whalebone, but he was also a farmer in the intervals between his trading voyages. He sold his merchandise in the market at Sciringesheal, whence it was probably sent to Hedeby at the base of the Danish peninsula. Wulfstan made Hedeby his base, and from there he sailed eastwards along the Baltic coast to Truso, near the mouth of the Vistula. Both men had their own ships, but they worked alone, except for the crews which manned their ships. They bought the products of the forest and the sea, probably by barter, and they seem each to have made a single trip during the sailing season. The scale of their operations was clearly very small.

The story, recorded in the life of St Godric of Finchale,[18] shows how at least one eleventh-century merchant rose to affluence and eventually sainthood. He became a petty merchant, travelling from fair to fair and market to market. He travelled over much of north-western Europe; he learned the nature of local demand, and was able to buy goods cheaply in one place and sell them at high profit in another. His travels appear to have followed no regular pattern; he went wherever profit was to be made. He appears to have worked alone, and to have handled only a small quantity of merchandise at a time. Nevertheless, Godric prospered and amassed a considerable fortune, enough, indeed, to endow the priory of Finchale in County Durham.

This story, which may well in its general outline be typical of the rise of many merchants, leaves many questions unanswered. Did he as a general rule use coin or did he engage mainly in a barter trade? Where did he keep, or invest his profits until they amounted to a substantial endowment? Did he purchase real estate? Was he merely a footloose wanderer, or did he have a permanent base which he could call home, and to which he returned periodically?

It was the growth of towns and the appearance of regular fairs which gave some regularity to the movements of traders. The towns became their bases and their excursions from them gradually came to assume a regular pattern. With an urban base it became easier for a merchant to accumulate capital. Many of the later medieval merchants who have become well known to us, owned extensive urban property. The Lanstier family at Arras owned many houses in the town as early as 1110, but it is far from clear whether these derived from the profits earned from trade or rather represented the source of their trading capital. The family subsequently became prominent both in trade and in banking and money-lending. Arras was remarkable for the number of its rich, patrician families.[19] Most were described as merchants. They certainly engaged in trade, but they also lent money at high rates of interest and speculated in housing and land. In the late thirteenth century, there were no less than eighty-eight families with fortunes of over 3000 livres. The Huquedieu family possessed a fortune of 40 to 50,000 livres, and the Crespins had perhaps a quarter of a million.

It is doubtful whether the profit margin in dealing in cloth, wine and other commodities in general demand was particularly large, though big profits were sometimes made on luxury goods. There was strong competition between merchants; trading risks were great and the rewards of those who were successful, not exceptional. Large fortunes are more likely to have been built up by speculating in land and by money-lending. More likely the successful merchant used these means to increase the small fortune which he had earned by legitimate trade.

Most of the wealthy merchants of the thirteenth and fourteenth centuries of whom we have knowledge were active in many fields besides trade. Jehan Boinebroke (see p. 289) of Douai must have resembled the Lanstiers and Crespins of Arras in the breadth of his interests, from the putting out of wool to domestic weavers to rack-renting local property and lending money at exorbitant rates of interest. All that we know of them suggests that this race of merchant capitalists was as ruthless and grasping, as masterful and arrogant, as any nineteenth century factory owner.

This does not explain how they got their start, where they obtained the first few livres which put them in business, and the social stratum from which they derived. Lestocquoy found that at Arras most of the patrician families derived from the petty functionaries of the Count of Flanders and of the abbey of Saint-Vaast, rather than from footloose wanderers like Godric. Their founders would have been well placed both to learn the conditions of supply and demand and to acquire an initial capital. Most were probably small landowners, but it is unlikely at least in northern Europe, that landowners used profits from their estates in commercial enterprises on any considerable scale before the late Middle Ages.

In southern Europe, especially in northern and central Italy, conditions were different. Here the rural landowner tended, if not to abandon the countryside for the city, at least to have an urban residence, and to spend much of his time in the city. The profits of his rural possessions were in large part remitted to the town, either in cash or in kind, and there he became familiar with commercial pursuits and rubbed shoulders with traders. The landed urban patriciate invested in trade, and younger sons participated in it. The division between the feudal classes and the bourgeoisie was blurred. Princes were also traders, and the most elegant and distinguished of all Italian princely houses, the Medici of Florence, owed much of its wealth to commerce and banking. The precocious commercial development of Italy was greatly aided by – if, indeed, it did not owe its existence to – the supply of capital made available through the participation of the landed classes.

The number of merchants greatly increased in the course of the twelfth and thirteenth centuries. The Cossets, Lanstiers and Huquedieus carried on their business on a continental scale. In the lesser towns merchants operated on a smaller scale, tailoring their business to suit the demands and potentialities of the region which they served. Such were the Bonis brothers of Montauban, whose account books for the years 1339–45 have survived.[20]

Their activities were fully as diverse as those of Jehan Boinebroke. They dealt in cloth, spices, candles, jewellery; they would purchase on commission articles suitable for baptismal and wedding gifts; they lent money at interest; they even had horses for rent, and they served as bankers and as rent and tithe collectors. They had no agents in the towns of the Low Countries and Italy, not even in Toulouse and Bordeaux, which were the largest cities of their region, but they must have made a very comfortable living in Montauban and the small towns of Rouergue and Quercy. Occasionally they travelled to Paris, Lyons, or even to Italy, to purchase goods, but usually they remained within the region of their home town of Montauban. Their book-keeping methods were unsophisticated, and if the accounts are difficult to understand, this is probably because the Bonis probably carried much of their business in their heads.

Francesco di Marco Datini of Prato, in Tuscany, was also a merchant on a small scale, at least by the standards of fourteenth-century Italy. After an apprenticeship in Avignon, at a time when the Papacy had brought a rich and varied commerce to the city, he returned to Tuscany and settled in Florence, where he conducted his business from a shop in Por S. Maria. He bought and sold in many of the commercial centres of France and the western Mediterranean. Most of his business was conducted by means of *compagnie*, in which Francesco Datini was associated with one or more merchants, who each subscribed to the undertaking. Datini always remained the dominant partner, and placed one of his associates as factor (*fattor*) in the *fondacho*, or trading-base in the city with which the company was doing business. Several such companies might be operative at the same time; none knew better than Datini how to spread his risks.

Francesco Datini made a fortune, much of which he invested in the purchase of houses in his native Prato and farms in Tuscany. He owed his success primarily to his command of detail, his dedication to business, and his capacity for long periods of intensely hard work. His fortune came, 'not so much by a series of brilliant *coups*, as by an infinitely patient accumulation of small profits – an avoidance of dangers, quite as much as a seizure of opportunities'.[21]

Andrea Barbarigo of Venice provides an interesting parallel to Datini. He came of a noble Venetian family which had long been engaged in trade, but had lost heavily when an important venture was shipwrecked on the Dalmatian coast. It fell to Andrea to rebuild the family fortunes. This he did by buying cotton in the Levant, olive oil in Valencia, cloth in England and the Low Countries; importing them to Venice, and selling them at a profit.[22] He formed shortlived partnerships, as did Datini, but remained all the while in Venice, employing *commissi*, on a commission basis, as his representatives in foreign ports. Like Datini, he dealt in a very wide range of commodities, never allowing his assets to be tied up in any one venture except for short periods of time. These two men, shrewd, immensely energetic and at times ruthless and grasping, were typical of Italian, and perhaps also of European, merchants of their age.

The trader during the earlier Middle Ages seems in general to have acted alone, to have moved only in such company as he met on the road, and to have enjoyed little protection from either his prince or his fellow merchants. Not so those who did business in the later Middle Ages. The richer among them travelled relatively little; instead, they maintained factors in distant cities, with whom they maintained a regular service by courier. They formed partnerships, often for a single voyage or expedition, and shared in the profits. Sometimes, these partnerships were with a merchant in a distant city, each undertaking to buy and sell on behalf of the other. The Kress family of Nuremberg, for example, established such a relationship with the Amadi of Venice in the late fourteenth century.[23] The Kresses were heavily engaged in distributing in South Germany the raw cotton imported by the Venetians, and in forwarding wool from England to the Italian centres of cloth manufacture.

The practice grew because it was well suited to the needs of the small merchant whose business was insufficient to justify a factor in each of several ports. The correspondence between the Bombergen of Antwerp and the Grimani of Venice[24] throws much light on the practice. Each worked for the other on a commission basis. The rates appear to have been low, commonly 3 per cent and sometimes as low as 2. Some merchants entered upon commission trading on a large scale; the Van der Molen of Antwerp, for example, accepted commissions on behalf of principals in many Italian towns.[25] In this way a merchant could engage in long-distance trade on a small scale without himself facing either the hardships of travel or the need for a large capital outlay.

The merchant in the later Middle Ages, from the thirteenth century onwards, lived under the protection of his town. Reciprocal guarantees were often given between towns. The Italian city-states were particularly active in supporting their merchants, on whose success many of them were heavily dependent. The merchants of Venice, it has been said, formed a large regulated company, within which each pursued his own ends, under the paternal supervision of the Venetian state. Genoa, Milan and many other city-states also made the protection of their merchants an object of policy.

In foreign places the merchants from a particular town, or even a group of towns, tended to live together for mutual protection and consolation. In some instances this was really necessary, as in the Hanseatic merchant's *kontors* in Novgorod or Bergen, or even in their Steelyard in London. The German merchants – in the main from South Germany – lived in Venice in their *Fondaco dei Tedeschi*, close to the Rialto bridge. This communal living became even more necessary for western merchants living in the Byzantine Empire and the Levant. They had their 'forts' at Modon, and in the Crimean, Syrian and Egyptian ports. In Constantinople itself the western merchants lived always in enclosed and fortified 'factories'. They were, in fact, similar to the forts established by the British on the coast of India in the seventeenth century.

The growing complexity of trade meant that the future merchant had much to learn. A kind of apprenticeship was instituted. Those merchants' sons who were destined to follow in their fathers' footsteps often learned the business as factors in foreign cities. Many merchants also took outsiders into their service for the purpose of teaching them the difficult business of commerce.

Handbooks were compiled for the guidance of fledgling merchants. Of these the *Pratica della Mercatura* of Pegolotti is by far the best known. A merchant needed to know the relationship of the currencies which he was likely to handle; the many sizes and qualities of the goods in which he dealt, and the places where they might be obtained most cheaply. All this he would learn most readily as a member of a small community of factors and merchants living together in a foreign city.[26]

### FAIRS AND MARKETS

During the Carolingian period and the centuries immediately following commerce amounted only to an irregular and intermittent trickle of commodities. It was insufficient to justify permanent trading centres, open to receive merchants and to do business at all times. How one merchant could arrange to meet with others was a problem solved only by the establishment of fairs. A fair was a periodic and regular meeting of traders, commonly for a period of days or even weeks and usually held not more than twice in a year. Here one merchant could count on meeting others, be sure of finding the commodities he needed, and usually of selling those which he carried with him. Fairs played an important role in giving pattern and regularity to his wanderings. On the other hand goods, such as cloth, metal ware and foodstuffs, were produced for the market in only small quantities. The regional fair served to gather them together under conditions that would be most likely to lead to their sale and distribution.

Fairs are commonly associated with markets. Indeed, the medieval charters which established them commonly linked them together as a grant of a weekly market and a twice or thrice yearly fair. There were, however, important differences between them. The fair assembled only infrequently; it may have lasted several weeks; it may have been frequented by local people, but its essential business was in commodities of distant origin and between merchants from remote places. Inevitably the goods were relatively valuable; otherwise they could not have supported the costs of transport. By contrast the market served the needs of its local area. It was held frequently – usually once a week – as befitted an outlet for cheap and perishable goods. The area which a market could serve was thus defined by Bracton: a man could travel 20 miles in a day. He would normally spend a third of the day at the market, which would leave two-thirds for travel time. Therefore his journey could not be more than $6\frac{2}{3}$ m. This rule of thumb was commonly used in England to determine whether a newly established market would be to the detriment of those already in existence. In this way a theoretical maximum density was established. In reality this was rarely achieved.

Though different in function, markets and fairs were in some measure integrated into a system. The merchants who sold their goods at the fairs had in some instances acquired them by visiting in turn a series of weekly markets. Conversely, the villagers were likely to acquire what few exotic goods they were ever likely to possess at their local market, perhaps after selling their corn or an animal successfully. These items would be likely to have been brought to the local market by traders who had acquired them at the regional fair. Fairs became in the later Middle Ages particularly important as outlets for the products of domestic industries in rural areas (see p. 358). These goods, such as the South German fustians and barchents, more often than not reached the fairs by way of the markets.

Market and fair were similar in requiring the protection of the law. Permission to hold them was formally given, or at least was conceived to have been granted, by the lord on whose land they were held. European fairs began to develop after the confusion and destruction of the Norse and Viking raids. Many grew up in the close proximity of monasteries. The Lendit fair, one of the most important in western Europe, had been established even earlier at the abbey of Saint-Denis, near Paris. The Visé fair, held on the bank of the Meuse near Liège, was mentioned in 983, and may have been held well before this date. It carried on an important business in metals for which the Ardennes to the south were noted. It probably also transmitted copper from the newly opened mines in the Harz.[27] The number of fairs greatly increased in the closing years of the eleventh century and first part of the twelfth. A tendency showed itself for fairs to be held in sequence at each of a group of towns. The first such cycle of fairs to develop was that held in the Flanders towns of Lille, Messines, Ypres, Thourout and Bruges. Some had come into being well before 1100; the cycle was completed some twenty-five years later. The sequence of fairs lasted throughout most of the season when merchants were normally able to travel and conduct their business. The Flanders fairs declined in importance with the rise of the Flemish cities as business centres in continuous operation. They retained, however, some significance as animal fairs throughout the Middle Ages.

The cycle of Champagne fairs forms the most noteworthy and commercially the most important in medieval Europe. It came to be a cycle of six fairs, two each in Troyes and Provins and one each in Lagny and Bar-sur-Aube, and each lasted at least six weeks. The year opened with the fair of Lagny, on the Marne near

Paris (Fig. 8.1). This was followed by that of Bar-sur-Aube in mid-Lent and the first Provins fair in the week of the feast of the Ascension. The first Troyes fair followed after the feast of St John the Baptist; the second Provins, on September 14, and the cycle ended with the second Troyes fair on the second of November. The dates of the second and third fairs of the sequence varied

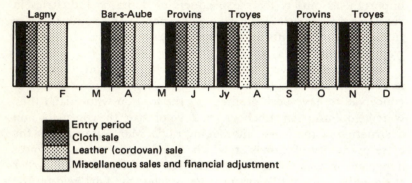

Fig. 8.1   The sequence of Champagne fairs.

with the date of Easter, but as a general rule there was an interval of at most a week or two between fairs. The winter fairs of Lagny and Bar-sur-Aube appear to have been the least significant, and the importance of Troyes and Provins was overwhelming.[28]

The fairs developed during the first half of the twelfth century as regional fairs, at which the sale of horses was important. It is not clearly known how they grew from markets of only regional importance into international fairs of European significance. Unquestionably the growing trade between the Low Countries and Italy called for a meeting place of their respective merchants somewhere in eastern France, but the Italians do not appear to have come to the fairs before the late twelfth century. A route much used at an earlier date between north and south had followed the lines of the Meuse, Saône and Rhône. A more direct route between the Rhône valley and the cities of West Flanders ran from the Saône, across the upland of Langres to the head-waters of the Paris rivers, and thence northwards towards Lille and Arras. The fair towns lay on, or close to this route.[29] Furthermore the region had been unified during the eleventh century under the Counts of Champagne, whose firm but enlightened rule bore a certain similarity to that of the Counts of Flanders.

At a time when government had difficulty in enforcing its will, it is not surprising that any ruler who could ensure the safety and welfare of merchants and travellers, attracted them to his territory.

The system of Champagne fairs had probably not evolved fully before the last quarter of the twelfth century. It lasted through the thirteenth, but its importance was declining by 1300. The fairs retained some local importance until the mid-fourteenth century, but were finally extinguished by the Hundred Years' War. Each was strictly organised. The first week was occupied with setting up stalls along the streets of the town; this was followed by a ten-day cloth sale; an eleven-day period when the soft cordovan leather was offered for sale, and nineteen days when various other goods were handled. The fair concluded with a few days devoted to the settling of accounts. [30]

Merchandise travelled slowly, often conveyed by professional carters, or *vectuarii*. The merchants set out for the fairs after they had actually opened, but couriers travelled ahead at a much greater speed, with news of the varieties and amounts of merchandise that were on the road. Much of the goods was then sold unseen, and credit instruments were exchanged between merchants. No coin passed at this stage. At the end of the fair, books were balanced, and any debit or credit balance was settled by a notarial bill (see p. 415). In this way merchants were under no obligation to travel with large sums of money. The fairs were well on their way to becoming an occasion, not for the display of merchandise, but for the settling of accounts, a trend which was carried farther still in the fifteenth century fairs of Lyons, Antwerp and Bergen-op-Zoom.

The decline of the Champagne fairs in the fourteenth century has been attributed to the breakdown of law and order, the absorption of the County of Champagne into the royal domain of France and the end of the rule of the paternal Counts of Champagne; the outbreak of the Hundred Years' War, and the use of the sea route from Italy to the Low Countries. All these factors were doubtless important, but the underlying fact was that the fairs were no longer essential to the overland trade of western Europe. Financial transactions could be completed as easily and doubtless more comfortably in the counting houses of Florence or Bruges than at the fairs. Goods were becoming standardised (see p. 305) and it was becoming less necessary to examine them before purchase.

Above all, the merchants – or at least the wealthier amongst them – did business with many places in which they maintained agents. Couriers moved between them with orders and commercial information, and the goods were moved by professional carters who often arranged amongst themselves to travel in convoy.

The international fairs of western Europe were thus of declining importance in the later Middle Ages, but they never disappeared. Many became little more than markets of regional importance, at which farm stock was sold. Some handled goods which became available only seasonally, such as the wine fairs of Bozen or Compiègne, or the herring fair of Scania, in southern Sweden.

In central and eastern Europe fairs were of increasing importance in the fourteenth and fifteenth centuries. This is because fairs are an indication of a pioneer, rather than of a mature economy. A group of fairs became established in the upper Rhineland and south Germany. It is sometimes said that they replaced the Champagne fairs. This, however, they did not do; they handled different commodities and satisfied different needs. Economic conditions in South Germany, Switzerland and Austria in the fourteenth century resembled in certain respects those in western Europe a century earlier, with the creation of new branches of the textile industries and the development of distant markets.

The Frankfurt-on-Main fairs were in existence in the early thirteenth century, but did not achieve international importance until the fourteenth. Their rise, and also that of the fairs of Friedberg, Nördlingen, Zurzach and Geneva were clearly related to the eastward shift in commercial routes (see p. 373) which were

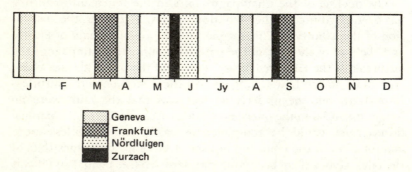

Fig. 8.2 The sequence of South German fairs.

beginning to use the passes of the central and even the eastern Alps. The opening of the St Gotthard pass about 1230 was of crucial importance. The Nördlingen fairs were as closely related to the south German cloth industry as those of Champagne had been to that of the Low Countries. The Zurzach fairs grew up on the bank of the Rhine about 50 kilometres above Basel. It served a smaller area than the Nördlingen and Frankfurt fairs. Cloth from northern Switzerland, Alsace and south-west Germany predominated, but Alpine products – skins, hides and cheese – were also important.

Geneva was well placed to command the more westerly Alpine passes, especially the much used Great and Little St Bernard passes, as well as the Mont Cenis and St Gotthard (see Fig. 6.2). Its fairs began, like those of Frankfurt, in the thirteenth century, but did not acquire any international importance until the fourteenth. They became important for the sale of Swiss cloth and of metals and metal goods, especially the armour and weaponry of Milan. They also inherited an important function which the Champagne fairs had formerly served: they became meeting places of merchants for the settlement of their trading accounts. The Geneva fairs achieved their greatest importance in the middle years of the fifteenth century, and then steadily declined in importance (see p. 361). The fate of the South German and Swiss fairs was similar to that of the Champagne fairs: business became permanent and regular and moved gradually to the shops and commercial houses of the towns.

The fate of late medieval fairs is well illustrated by the fortunes of that of Nuremberg. The right to hold a fair was granted by the emperor in 1423–24 and confirmed in 1431. Nuremberg was at this time the largest commercial town in south Germany, yet its fair failed to attract merchants and was abandoned. This apparent paradox can be simply explained. Nuremberg did not need a fair; all the business normally transacted at a fair could be handled within the walls of the city *and at any time*. In the same period, however, fairs were far from declining in east-central Europe. The Leipzig fair was gaining importance in the fifteenth century, and in Poland fairs were active at Poznań and Gniezno. But this was a pioneer region in which few large towns had developed.

. Another area in which fairs developed during the later Middle Ages, only to fail, as their functions were merged with those of the

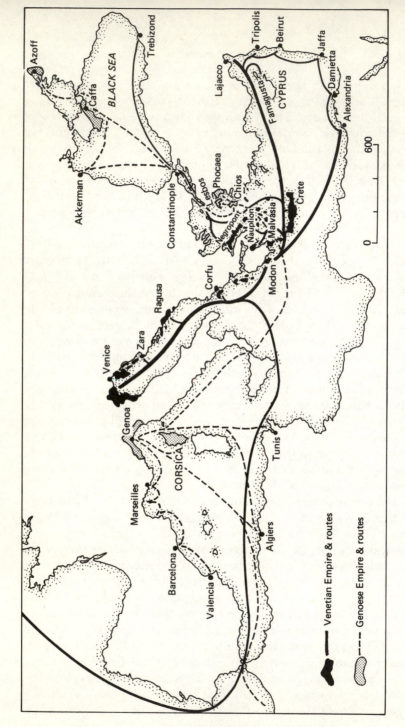

Fig. 8.3  Venetian and Genoese commercial empires.

BLACK SEA

Azoff
Caffa
Trebizond
Tripolis
Beirut
Jaffa
Lajacco
Famagusta
CYPRUS
Damietta
Alexandria
Akkerman
Constantinople
Lesbos
Phocaea
Chios
Negropont
Nauplion
Malvasia
Crete
Modon
Corfu
Ragusa
Zara
Venice
Genoa
Tunis
CORSICA
Marseilles
Algiers
Barcelona
Valencia

600

0

Venetian Empire & routes

Genoese Empire & routes

360

cities, was the northern Low Countries and lower Rhineland. The oldest fairs in this region were at Deventer and Utrecht, on waterways which at this time were much used between the Rhine and the North Sea. The fairs at Antwerp and Bergen-op-Zoom were developed in the fourteenth century and took over some of the functions of those of Deventer and Utrecht. Both Antwerp and Bergen were easily accessible by sea and served for the import of English wool and cloth. They were convenient outlets for the relatively undeveloped northern Low Countries, and as such achieved a high level of prosperity in the later years of the fifteenth century. In 1479–88, the Bergen fairs were very greatly extended, and the Antwerp fairs came gradually to be held almost continuously; in other words, they ceased to be fairs.[31] The Antwerp fairs were never formally discontinued; in the sixteenth century their activities merged with those of the largest city in north-western Europe. Bergen, on the other hand, declined in importance as a fair town. It became less accessible to seaborne shipping and in the sixteenth century succumbed to the competition of nearby Antwerp.

In the fifteenth and early sixteenth centuries, at a time when the business of the fairs was steadily passing to the towns, the fairs themselves became pawns in the game of national politics. In 1463 the Lyons fairs were established as part of the policy of Louis XI, and the French were forbidden to visit the Geneva fairs. The Lyons fairs enjoyed a period of prosperity, based largely on the financial business which was transacted here rather than at Geneva (see p. 359).

Markets underwent no such cycle of rise and decline. Few grants of market rights were made, except in Eastern Europe, after the fourteenth century, but by this date a network of markets, adequate for local needs, had been established. It was not until the nineteenth century that they showed signs of decline and decay. They were occasions when the peasants could expect to meet one another, and the itinerent trader could be certain of finding customers.[32]

### THE PATTERN OF TRADE

In the commercial and economic expansion which marked the period from the eleventh to the fourteenth centuries it was Italy – especially northern Italy – which set the pace. A greater volume of trade, however it is measured, passed through the hands of the Italian merchants than was handled in any other region of comparable size in Europe. All important innovations in commerce and accounting were made in Italy, and the Italian merchants or their agents were to be found at every fair and in every city of significance in western and central Europe. At first the primacy of the Italians in Europe's trade was undisputed. Inevitably, however, other foci of trade emerged, encouraged by the example of the Italians and assisted by their pioneering developments. The gap between the Italians and less developed communities was narrowed until by the end of the Middle Ages or at latest the first century of modern times, the Italians were overtaken by the peoples of north-western Europe in the fields in which they had once been pre-eminent.

The first area to rival the commercial and industrial preeminence of Italy was the Low Countries. Their manufacturing and commerce began to be raised above the level of merely local importance in the late eleventh century. By the thirteenth they were of international significance. Centres of trade multiplied in northern France and the lower Rhineland. A change in the geographical pattern of routes brought commerce on an increasing scale across Switzerland and South Germany, and there too active centres of trade emerged. The commerce of the Low Countries and Rhineland was extended eastwards and north-eastwards, absorbing what was left of the Viking trading activity, until a trading system of immense complexity spanned the European continent from Spain to the borders of Russia.

## Italy

An important change occurred in the second half of the eleventh century in the pattern of Italian trade. Amalfi and the ports of southern Italy succumbed to the growing pressure of the Normans and the increasing weakness of their protectors, the Byzantine emperors, and their role passed to Venice, Pisa and Genoa. Venice had already emerged as the leading commercial city of the Adriatic. It had inherited the role of Ravenna; it enjoyed better links with its hinterland than the latter by way of the river Po, and lay closer to the Alpine passes and the vast but undeveloped market of central Europe. At the same time the great length of the Adriatic Sea gave it a degree of immunity from Normans and

Saracens who had been the undoing of Amalfi. Nevertheless, the rise of Venice cannot be wholly explained by these circumstances. Its internal stability, the orderly system of government created and maintained over a period of centuries by its patrician families; the continuity and sheer persistence of its policy, all combined to impress the imagination with its power, just as it delighted the eye by its grace and beauty. 'They little thought', wrote Ruskin, 'who first drove the stakes into the sand, and strewed the ocean reeds for their rest, that their children were to be the princes of that ocean [the Adriatic], and their palaces its pride.'

Before the end of the eleventh century the Venetians were extending their authority along the shores of the Adriatic and intensifying their trade in Constantinople. The volume of their commerce was, doubtless, still small, and in 1084 they suffered a military defeat at the hands of Robert Guiscard and the Normans, though their quasi-independence was not threatened. It was the Crusades which gave the greatest impetus to the expansion of Venetian trade. Not that they participated directly, except in the Fourth Crusade (1204), in those bloody and brutal forays – that was not the Venetian way of doing things; they lent their ships and offered the services of merchants who were second to none in their knowledge of the eastern Mediterranean, and they were rewarded generously. They extended their commercial privileges in Constantinople, and acquired trading concessions in every significant port of the Levant. The Venetian fleet was not the largest to carry crusaders from Italy to the east – that was the Pisan – but its rewards were amongst the most lavish. In the Fourth Crusade of 1204 the Venetians were able to divert the whole expedition from its primary purpose, the re-capture of Jerusalem, to the conquest of Constantinople and the acquisition for themselves of trading bases throughout the Aegean.

Thus an overseas empire was built up, consisting of a large number of strategically placed bases. Except on the mainland of Italy, Venice occupied no extensive territory and the Venezia was acquired late and primarily as a source of food and basic commodities. The Venetian empire resembled the Asiatic empire of Great Britain in the seventeenth and early years of the eighteenth century. Most of its possessions were small in area, merely *comptoirs* to which goods were brought for sale. Most were self-

sufficing in foodstuffs and, apart from a little wheat and cotton and a considerable volume of wine – foremost the 'malmsey' from Monemvasia in the Morea, they produced little for the export trade. The most important bases lay along the eastern shore of the Adriatic, around the shores of Greece, where Coron, Modon and Monemvasia were the most important, and in the Aegean (Fig. 8.3).[33] The Venetians had a commercial establishment on the southern shore of the Golden Horn as well as another on the coast of Syria. Their fortunes in the eastern Mediterranean were closely linked with those of the Crusades, but even after the destruction of the Latin Kingdom and the expulsion of the crusaders, the Venetians continued throughout the later Middle Ages to maintain small communities of merchants.

The Venetian state opened as a vast regulated company – another point of similarity with British enterprise in the seventeenth century. It established the legal and institutional framework within which the merchants acted, and provided the military and diplomatic protection which they needed. The merchants themselves acted individually or in small partnerships. They chartered ships and maintained, often jointly, agents who lived in the overseas ports, within the shelter of walls built by the Venetian state and guarded by the soldiers of the Republic.

The overseas empire of Venice would have been meaningless without access to its European hinterland. The latter provided the exports of Venice and consumed most of its imports. There was a gradual change in the direction of Venice's inland trade. This had been at first largely channelled by the river Po in a westward direction. Venice supplied the fairs of Pavia, and thus, by way of the more westerly Alpine passes, the Rhône valley and France. This outlet for Venetian trade appears to have dwindled as trade revived in the western Mediterranean and Venetian contacts with Germany were intensified. German merchants were in Italy in the twelfth century, and by 1228 at the very latest they had their *Fondaco* in the city.[34] The Germans brought metals from the eastern Alps, especially iron and copper, and cloth, in particular

Fig. 8.4 Types of ships in use in the Middle Ages.
*Long ships:* (a) Venetian galley; (b) Viking ship.
*Round ships:* (c) Mediterranean, *c.* 1100; (d) Mediterranean, early 16th century; (e) North-west European (Jacques Coeur's ship), *c.* 1450.

the lightweight fustians and linens, in greatest demand in the warmer regions of the eastern Mediterranean. They took away wine from Greece and Crete; raw cotton, which was in increasing demand in Germany in the later Middle Ages (see p. 316), as well as the more valuable and less bulky products of the East.

Pisa and Genoa developed a comparable trading system from their bases on the western shore of Italy. They had a later start than Venice, and Pisa, the earlier of the two to develop, lived long under the shadow of Amalfi. In the eleventh century Pisa, lying on the Arno river only 10 kilometres from its mouth, became the port for Tuscany, and built up a trade with Corsica and Sardinia so successfully that the Pisan contingent was the largest in the fleet that was brought together to carry the crusaders to the Levant in 1097. The twelfth century was the age of Pisa. In 1135 it attacked Amalfi and gave a *coup de grace* to the Amalfitans' pretensions in Mediterranean trade. For several decades the Pisans were the only significant rivals of the Venetians. Then they succumbed, as the Amalfitans had done before them. At this time Lucca was the most developed city of Tuscany, but the region fell far short in its commercial potential to the hinterland of Venice. Pisa's routes into northern Italy were the rough tracks across the Apennines and its coastwise route to the Rhône delta and France could be cut by Genoa. The early cooperation between Pisa and Genoa gave way to hostility as the two competed for markets. Intermittent war between the two cities occupied much of the twelfth century. Weakened by this struggle, the Pisans succumbed to the Florentines in the following century.

Genoa occupied a site only a degree more propitious than that of Amalfi. At the time when the latter was at the height of its prosperity, Genoa was nothing more than a fishing village on a narrow shelf of land between the Apennines and the sea. It has no immediate hinterland with which to trade, as did Pisa, but it had other advantages. The Apennines are here narrow and more easily crossed than at other points, and beyond lay the Lombardy Plain and the passes which led to Germany.

The overseas trade of Genoa was at first confined to the western Mediterranean. At the time when the Normans were overwhelming southern Italy, the Genoese, in alliance with the Pisans, were chasing the Saracens from the islands and raiding the North African coast. This gave place in the twelfth century to trade with the Berbers of Africa and the Muslims of Spain – a trade from which the Genoese appear to have benefited far more than the Pisans. From Tripoli westwards to Morocco the trade of North Africa fell largely into their hands. They displaced the Syrians and Jews who had previously controlled this trade, and exchanged Italian fustian and linen for raw cotton, dyestuffs, spices, alum, skins, and hides from the Atlas region and even gold dust brought across the Sahara Desert from Senegal. A major consideration in Genoese trade was the fact that the territory of Genoa could produce very little food. Unlike Venice and Pisa, Genoa was obliged to import most of its requirements by sea. Wine and salt came from Spain, wheat from Sicily and, in the fourteenth century, from the Black Sea region; meat and cheese from southern Italy and the Mediterranean islands.

The Genoese followed the Venetians into the eastern Mediterranean, but their trade was of little significance before 1100. They profited from the Crusades, but tended, in general, to trade with areas where the Venetians had not established themselves. Their base in Constantinople – it lay in Pera, to the north of the Golden Horn – was relatively small; they established no permanent bases in either Greece or Syria, but became very important in the commerce of Cyprus, western Asia Minor and the Black Sea coast (Fig. 8.3). Their chief base in the eastern Mediterranean was the island of Chios, and the chief commodity of their trade the alum which began about 1275 to be produced in quantity from the mines of Phocaea, on the mainland nearby. They did not establish bases on the Black Sea coast until the second half of the thirteenth century, and then, within the span of some fifteen years they cast a ring of trading stations along its coastline.[35] Soldaia and Caffa, in the Crimea, were amongst the earliest, but their possessions came to include Tana, at the mouth of the Don, Trebizond and Moncastro (the future Cetatea Alba) on the estuary of the Dnestr. Silks and spices were brought across Central Asia to the eastern shore of the Black Sea, to be shipped thence to Pera and Genoa, but grain was the most important commodity handled by the Genoese. It was grown around the periphery of the Black Sea; the Genoese shipped it to supply Constantinople as well as to satisfy their needs in Genoa itself. The Genoese were probably responsible for a very large fraction of the total Mediterranean grain trade.[36] It was a feature of Genoese trade in the Mediterranean basin that silks and spices played only a minor role. Cargoes were made up of bulky goods of low value: wheat, alum, salt, cotton and wool.

## The Western Mediterranean

The trade of Genoa was closely bound up with that of the ports of the south of France and of Catalonia and Spain. With the retreat of the Arabs from these regions their commerce began to revive. Barcelona grew to be the most important port, but Marseilles, Narbonne and the ports of the Rhône delta all carried on a considerable volume of trade. Much of it was coastwise, the transport of grain and wool, wine and oil from the little ports to the larger emporia. The pattern of trade changed not only with changes in demand but also with the choking of ports and the shallowing of waterways. Arles and Saint-Gilles, Montpellier and Béziers, all of them used during the earlier Middle Ages, came in time to be abandoned as ports. Louis IX, about 1250, founded the port of Aigues Mortes on one of the branches of the Rhône delta as a place of embarkation for his Crusade. Within a couple of centuries it too had silted and could no longer be reached by any except the smallest ships. Only Marseilles and Barcelona were wholly unaffected by these natural changes.

The ports of Languedoc and Provence had as their hinterland the whole valley of the Rhône, which canalised their trade with the interior. This traffic was vital for the port of Genoa. Genoese merchants either shipped their goods along the Ligurian coast to one of the ports of southern France and thence moved them inland by road or river or they used one of the several land routes to the Rhône valley. The trade of the Champagne fairs had come this way. The decline of the fairs led to a certain diminution in the volume of commerce that moved to and from the Mediterranean coast, but the establishment of the Papal court at Avignon (1305) did much to restore the balance. The papacy returned to Rome, but the foundation of the Lyons fairs continued to bring merchants, especially the Genoese, to the Rhône valley.

A large part – perhaps the largest part – of the European commerce of Venice and Genoa was not with Germany and France, but with the cities of the Plain of Lombardy. These were reached from Genoa by way of the Giovi Pass, almost too gentle and easy a route to deserve the name. From Venice many were accessible by the Po, navigable at least as far as Piacenza. Many towns of the Plain served primarily as banking centres and as staging points on the routes from the ports to the Alpine crossings. Such were Asti, Cremona, Piacenza and Mantua. When, in 1220, the Mantuans threatened to control the shipping on the Po, the citizens of Cremona and Reggio nell' Emilia combined to cut a canal some 60 kilometres in length to circumvent Mantuan territory. All the larger towns of the Plain were linked by navigable waterway with the Po, and each had its fleet of river boats and its small port. Many developed textile and metal industries (see pp. 310–14 and 325), importing some of their raw materials and shipping out their finished goods through Mediterranean ports of northern Italy.

Milan grew to be the largest manufacturing and commercial city of Lombardy. Bonvesin della Riva, writing about 1288, described the city's four fairs and several markets. 'It is amazing', he wrote, 'to see almost innumerable merchants with their variety of wares and buyers flocking to all these fairs . . . practically anything that man may need is brought daily not only into special places but even into the open squares.'[37] The commercial pre-eminence of Milan was certainly due in part to its navigable connection with the Po and its command of a number of trans-Alpine routes. Of these the Simplon pass came into general use in the middle years of the thirteenth century and the St Gotthard pass – the easiest route across the central Alps – was opened up a few years earlier.

Florence had no such advantages. Indeed, its rise to become the fourth of the giant cities of Italy is not easy to explain. When Pisa was a flourishing port, the chief city of Tuscany was Lucca, which as early as the eleventh century had a cloth manufacture and export. Yet sometime in the twelfth or early thirteenth century Lucca was overtaken by its rival. Florence lay on the Arno, a navigable river only in winter, but it could rarely count on using the port of Pisa at its mouth. Until, in 1406, Pisa was conquered by the Florentines, its citizens were more often than not hostile to their Tuscan neighbour. Florence used the port of Ancona, but this necessitated transporting merchandise across the Apennines. Most often, however, they used the ships of the Genoese, moving their goods to and from the port through the hills of northern Tuscany and Liguria.[38] Florence, as befitted a city with such tenuous links with the outside, developed labour intensive industries, thus reducing to a minimum its dependence upon trade in bulky goods (see p. 310). It imported Flemish cloth and English and Spanish wool, together with such foodstuffs and metals as were necessary to supplement the output of Tuscany itself.

In 1406 Florence conquered her neighbour and rival, Pisa. Access to the sea, however, gave her no immediate commercial advantage, for the Arno had silted and Pisa was no longer accessible to seagoing ships. The Pisans had themselves used Porto Pisano, to the south of the Arno mouth, but this was small and shallow, and the Florentines were obliged to develop the harbour of Leghorn (Livorno), an insalubrious spot on the malarial Tuscan coast.

Despite its lack of a port before the later fifteenth century, Florence had in fact built up a small fleet which made its home in the ports of friendly allies.[39] Galleys were built and owned by the Florentine state, but were leased to merchants who used them in the Levant trade. Florentine galleys continued to operate until the later years of the century, but were supplemented by a large number of smaller, privately owned vessels.

Ships in use in Mediterranean trade, at least during the later Middle Ages, were of two kinds, the galley and the smaller round ship, or nef (*navis*) (Fig. 8.4). The former was propelled by oars, but had supplementary sail. Its advantage was its speed under conditions when a sailing ship would have been becalmed. It was thus a safer ship to use on seas that were infested with pirates. On the other hand, much of its space was occupied by the oarsmen, whose physical needs furthermore called for frequent stops to take on food and water. The galley could therefore carry relatively little cargo, and was, as a general rule, used for such valuable commodities as silk and spices. It was expensive to operate, and only the larger trading cities were able to maintain a fleet of galleys, which were thus, by and large, restricted to Venice, Genoa and Florence.[40]

The largest fleet of galleys in the later Middle Ages belonged to Venice, the city which engaged most heavily in the trade in esoteric products of the East. Genoa had galleys in the late thirteenth, but then abandoned them in favour of the nef, better suited to the bulk commodities of low value in which the Genoese dealt. In the fifteenth century the Florentines began to operate

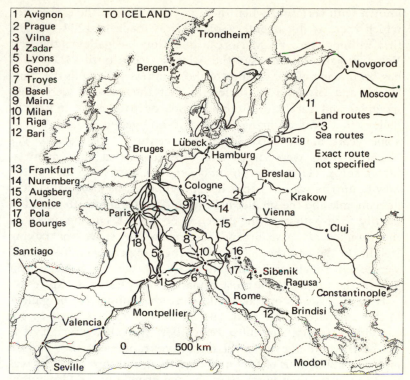

| | |
|---|---|
| 1 | Avignon |
| 2 | Prague |
| 3 | Vilna |
| 4 | Zadar |
| 5 | Lyons |
| 6 | Genoa |
| 7 | Troyes |
| 8 | Basel |
| 9 | Mainz |
| 10 | Milan |
| 11 | Riga |
| 12 | Bari |
| 13 | Frankfurt |
| 14 | Nuremberg |
| 15 | Augsberg |
| 16 | Venice |
| 17 | Pola |
| 18 | Bourges |

TO ICELAND
Trondheim
Bergen
Novgorod
Moscow
Land routes
Sea routes
Exact route not specified
Lübeck
Bruges
Hamburg
Danzig
Breslau
Cologne
Krakow
Paris
Vienna
Cluj
Santiago
Sibenik
Ragusa
Constantinople
Rome
Brindisi
Montpellier
Valencia
Seville
Modon

0      500 km

Fig. 8.5   The Itinerary of Bruges.

galleys for their Levant trade in valuable cloth and spices. Fleets of as many as fourteen 'great' galleys left the Tuscan ports in summer, each powered by as many as 150 oarsmen and with a total crew of over 200. The cargo however did not generally exceed 250 tons.

The nef was the general purpose ship of the Mediterranean. It came in every size. It was broader in the beam, of deeper draught and generally slower than the galley. Its crew was much smaller, though it commonly included a few crossbowmen, but its cargo capacity was large in relation to its size. The nef was used for the bulky cargoes of low value: wheat, salt, wool, alum, timber, which in fact dominated the commerce of the Mediterranean Sea.

It was, however, the galley which first made the ocean voyage from the Mediterranean ports to north-western Europe. It is not

371

known with certainty when these voyages began; the earliest for which there is documentary record was made in 1277–78. The first sailings were by Marjorcan and Genoese galleys; the first Venetian galley did not sail the Atlantic Ocean until 1312. Much has been made of the sailings of the Flanders galleys in the fourteenth and fifteenth centuries. In fact the sailings were both irregular and barely profitable. Genoa despatched at most four galleys in a year. In many years only one galley set sail, and in some years in the early fourteenth century, none at all. The Venetian fleets were larger, and often consisted of as many as fifteen ships. The basic problem of sending ships from Italy to the Low Countries was, as Lopez has shown, that the large galley was uneconomic and the smaller nef unsafe. The Genoese attempted to modify their galleys in the direction of the nef, cutting down on the number of oarsmen and increasing the space for paying freight. In the end they abandoned these expensive expeditions. Venice alone maintained its galley sailings, because it had a firm grip on the supply of the most valuable of pay-cargoes – spices.

How significant, one may ask, were the sailings of the galleys in the commercial pattern of late medieval Europe? Their cargo-carrying capacity, one must remember, was always small. It is doubtful whether, even in the most favourable year, they carried more than 3000 tons of freight. Three thousand tons of spices was probably more than north-west Europe needed or could pay for; a similar weight of wool or cloth, salt or alum was of little significance. Some galleys, especially the Genoese, did in fact carry considerable quantities of such coarse and heavy commodities – which is a major reason for their financial failure. But it is very doubtful whether this movement detracted significantly from the volume of overland trade between Italy and north-western Europe.

From the eleventh century overland trade between Italy and north-western Europe was by way of the Rhône valley and either Champagne or Lorraine. This commercial axis was displaced eastwards in the thirteenth century and later, and the flow of commodities between the two focal regions in European trade began to cross the Alps and follow the Rhine valley. The decline of the more westerly routes was, however, more relative than absolute. Chalon, in the Saône valley, inherited some of the functions of the Champagne fairs; Lyons developed as a commercial and financial centre, and the towns of the Meuse valley remained important throughout the Middle Ages.[41]

There was, then, within the bundle of routes by which northern Italy and north-western Europe were linked, a change of emphasis in the period from the eleventh to the fifteenth centuries, an eastward shift in their centre of gravity.

The Rhine became the most important routeway of the later Middle Ages. It was, even in its unimproved condition, an easily navigated river, and was in fact well used all the way from the Falls of Schaffhausen, north of Zurich, to the sea. Furthermore the passes of the central Alps, particularly the St Gotthard route, first mentioned in an itinerary in 1236, converged on the valley of the upper Rhine (Fig. 6.2). The Venetians, however, tended to use the passes of the eastern Alps, of which the Brenner was the easiest to negotiate. These led to Augsburg, Regensburg, Nuremberg and Prague. In the volume of goods handled they probably fell short of the Rhineland routes, but their importance was increasing in the later Middle Ages, with the economic development of central Europe.[42]

Discussion of the major routes necessarily distracts attention from the many minor roads which were used on occasion and the vast number of tracks which linked one town with another without ever being integrated into a road system of continental scale. In the later Middle Ages, no less than in the earlier, the road was wherever the traveller went (see p. 386), and there was no limit to his willingness to try new ways for the sake of speed, convenience and safety. In recent years a number of local studies, especially in France, has demonstrated how dense the network of tracks actually was, and how obscure local paths could occasionally be integrated into a long distance route, achieve a brief period of fame or notoriety, and then again be abandoned to the local peasants and their cattle.

## The Low Countries

In the archives of Brussels is a road book, compiled about 1380 and commonly known as the Itinerary of Bruges.[43] It is the longest and most compendious of medieval itineraries to have survived, and it gives the names of the stations and their distances apart along a large number of routes radiating from Bruges. It was put together from many sources; it contains both pilgrim routes, such as those to Compostella, Rome and Jerusalem, and also the

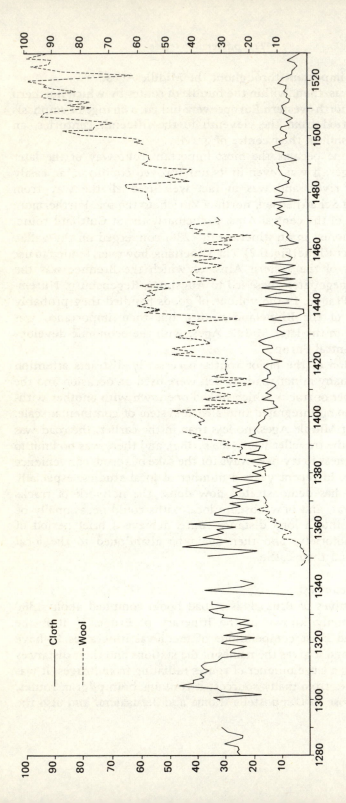

Fig. 8.6 The export of English wool and cloth: based on E. M. Carus-Wilson and O. Coleman, *England's Export Trade, 1275–1547*, Oxford, 1963

routes regularly used by traders. Many routes and some Alpine passes, known to have been in use at this time, are omitted, but the itinerary (Fig. 8.5) nevertheless gives a picture of Flanders as the focus and route centre of north-western Europe.

> For the little land of Flanders is
> But a staple to other lands ywis

The more westerly trans-continental routes, those in regular use in the eleventh and twelfth centuries, impinged on the cities of West Flanders and Artois: Saint-Omer, Arras and Douai. The commercial focus of the Low Countries then shifted towards the east, and first Bruges and Ghent, and then Antwerp became the most important centres. An important reason, apart from the favour and protection given to these cities by the Counts of Flanders, was the growing importance of maritime trade. Bruges had grown up around one of the castles of the Count. During the first half of the twelfth century, a waterway, the Zwin, was opened up from the coast entirely as a consequence of floods and storm-surges. It has often been said that the river Zwin created the port of Bruges and that with its silting in the later Middle Ages, Bruges lost its pre-eminence as a commercial centre. This is to distort the record; Bruges was never a port for seagoing ships. At best they were able to reach Damme, about 5 km. below the city. It was Damme, not Bruges, which silted in the thirteenth century, and was replaced by Sluys, near the mouth of the river (Fig. 7.1). The *Libel of English Policie* described how merchandise

> Is unto Flanders shipped full craftily,
> Unto Bruges as to her staple fayre:
> The Haven of Scluse hir haven for her repayre
> Which is cleped Swyn tho shippes giding:
> Where many vessels and fayre are abiding.

The Flanders galleys from the Mediterranean were accustomed to unload at Sluys, and from Damme or Sluys goods were brought up-river to Bruges.

The manufactures of Flanders from the twelfth century on-wards required large quantities of imported wool. They also produced large quantities of cloth for sale. Bruges became the central market for this business. It was more a commercial than a manufacturing town. It gathered the cloth from the surrounding towns and villages and prepared it for export. It lay in the midst of the richest and most highly urbanised area of Europe outside northern Italy, and it handled the necessities as well as the luxuries of the rich bourgeoisie of the southern Low Countries. It was a place where the Italian merchants maintained their *fattori*, placed their orders and watched the movement of prices and the changes in supply and demand in north-west Europe.

Bruges attained the peak of its prosperity in the first half of the fourteenth century. Its fortunes then began to decline. The import of English wool fell off, and was in any case made to flow through other ports than Bruges. Cloth production tended to move away from East Flanders to Brabant and the Lower Rhineland, and the eastward shift of emphasis within the European system of routes was to the disadvantage of Bruges. Flanders was disturbed by war in the late thirteenth century and the first quarter of the fourteenth, and its cities were torn by civil strife. All combined to lessen the commercial importance of Bruges.

The principal and ultimately successful rival of Bruges was Antwerp. The latter lay on the east bank of the Scheldt, a river far more easily navigated than the Zwin and linked by waterways both with Brabant and the Rhine. It was not particularly well placed to profit from the local trade of Flanders or that with the Champagne fairs, but when commerce developed with the Baltic, the Rhineland and Germany, Antwerp found itself endowed with advantages that were denied to Bruges. Antwerp lay in northern Brabant. During the thirteenth century, when the development of Flanders was at full flood, Brabant was still a relatively backward and underdeveloped region. In the late thirteenth century the textile manufactures, specifically the production of lighter fabrics, were diffused through Brabant, and Brussels and Louvain in the south, Antwerp in the north began to rival the older clothing cities of Flanders. The disturbances which troubled the Flemish towns could only contribute to the prosperity of Brabant, and the Flemings watched with dismay the growing fortunes of Antwerp, on the opposite bank of the Scheldt to themselves. In 1356 they captured Antwerp in an attempt to supress this rival. Its port stagnated for half a century, until in 1406 it was reintegrated into Brabant. From that moment Antwerp never looked back, until its prosperity was destroyed in the course of the wars of the late sixteenth century.

Comparison between Bruges and Antwerp is inevitable, and it is easy to visualise Antwerp as the commercial heir of Bruges. Yet their roles were far from identical. They reached respectively the peak of their prosperity perhaps two centuries apart, and during this period the needs and opportunities of European commerce had greatly changed. They responded to different needs. Bruges was not primarily an international port; it was not an entrepot at which were gathered and exchanged the products of western and central Europe. Its imports consisted mainly of the goods – wool, dyestuffs, wine, metals, salt – required by its Flemish hinterland, and its exports were dominated by the products, especially cloth, of this same region.[44]

That Antwerp became an international market was due in the first place to the economic growth of Europe's pioneer regions, the Scandinavian north and the Slavic east. Antwerp, after it had been rejoined to the Duchy of Brabant (1406), became the most important centre in which the salt and wine of the south, the cloth of the Low Countries, the metals of Germany, and the rye, salted fish and timber of the North could be assembled and exchanged. In the heyday of Bruges's prosperity the need for such an emporium was only beginning to be felt; by the fifteenth century the volume of international trade which impinged upon north-western Europe became overwhelming. The need for an international port in this general region was urgent, and after the destruction of Antwerp (1576) the palm passed to Amsterdam, and the role of intermediaries in the commerce of western Europe was assumed by the Dutch.

From the ports of the Low Countries routes fanned out, westwards to Brittany and England, north-eastwards to Scandinavia, eastwards to the coast of Germany and the Baltic. From all these directions goods converged on Bruges, Antwerp and the many smaller ports of the region, just as they did from the whole Mediterranean basin to the ports of Venice and Genoa. In these northern seas, as in the Mediterranean, there was a lively coastal trade.[45] Small vessels brought Gascon wine, salt from the 'Bay' and coarse Breton fabrics and sailcloth. In return they carried metals, wool, timber for shipbuilding, rye and fish.

The trade with England is better documented and better known than that with the Atlantic coasts of Europe. Wool was the most important of the goods which the Low Countries derived from England. The customs accounts record the amount of wool shipped from English ports for much of the period after 1279. In exceptional years it exceeded 40,000 sacks, but the amount diminished steadily during the later years of the fourteenth century, and in the fifteenth only rarely exceeded 10,000 sacks. Much of this wool was used in the Low Countries; most was imported through the ports of this region (Fig. 8.6). It became the practice of the English kings, in order to control the trade in wool and to make sure that custom had been paid, to direct it through a single European port, the staple. The location of the staple was changed several times according to the vicissitudes of English relations with the Low Countries. It was moved between Dordrecht, Antwerp, Saint-Omer and Bruges, and was finally established in Calais.

Until the mid-fourteenth century the exports of England – and indeed, of the whole of the British Isles – had been primarily foodstuffs and raw materials, and trade in these commodities was mainly in the hands of foreign merchants, chiefly Flemings and Italians. Pegolotti's treatise contains a great deal of information to guide his fellow countrymen in purchasing wool. After about 1350 the decline in wool exports was compensated by an increase in the volume of cloth shipped. The trend continued throughout the remaining years of the Middle Ages, until, by the early sixteenth century the roles of wool and cloth in the English export trade had been almost exactly reversed (Fig. 8.6). Much of the English cloth was imported through the ports of the Low Countries, but this time it was English merchants, the Merchant Adventurers, who took the lead. Despite the complaint in the *Libel of English Policie* that foreigners

> . . . bare hence our best chaffare:
> Cloth, woll, and tinne. . . .

it is clear that much of the trade to the ports of north-western Europe was in the hands of English merchants and carried in English 'bottoms'.

## The Hanseatic League

A similar trend was also apparent in these years in the trade between north-western Europe on the one hand and north Germany, Scandinavia and the Baltic region on the other. These also had been pioneer regions to which the western traders, Frisians and Flemings, had come to sell their manufactured products and to buy what goods the northern forests had to offer. From the twelfth century this began to change. The Frisians ceased gradually to be active in this field, and during the twelfth century they seem to have disappeared from the commercial scene. The Vikings, who had long dominated the Baltic Sea, were less active, and the dominant commercial role passed to the Germans. There has been a tendency to underrate the importance of the Vikings as traders, and to assume that Scandinavia and the Baltic region were backward and undeveloped at the time when the Germans began to build their cities and to develop their trade. In fact, the German achievement in northern Europe was founded upon that of the Scandinavian people. The heroic age of the North had long been over in the twelfth century, but its tumult and migration had left a legacy of peaceful commerce. 'There is much evidence', wrote Christensen,[46] "that the Scandinavians followed the old trade routes well into the thirteenth century . . . up to the year 1200 Scandinavian trade with the Baltic regions is much more strongly authenticated than Lübeck and German trade.'[47] The German merchants at first did business in the Baltic 'as companions of the Scandinavians and later as their heirs'.

The centres of Viking trade: Hedeby, Birka, Jumna and others, had disappeared by the twelfth century, destroyed in most cases by the Vikings themselves in the course of their raids. But they had in every instance been replaced by another in the same general area. Schleswig replaced Hedeby and appears to have been no less busy and prosperous. The focal point of pre-Hanseatic commerce was the island of Gotland. It was the 'peasant sailors' of Gotland, to use the term coined by Dollinger,[48] who in the intervals of their farming, spread over the Baltic Sea and did business with the Russians at Novgorod.

The growth of the Hanse is intimately bound up with the eastward spread of German settlers in the twelfth and thirteenth centuries. The city of Lübeck was founded in 1158 by the Count of Holstein. A site was chosen on the navigable river Trave, only 20 kilometres from the Baltic Sea. In its location the city was heir to Hedeby, but, instead of being a south-western outpost of the Vikings, it was the vanguard of the advancing Germans. Early in the thirteenth century, the Wendish cities of Rostock, Wismar, Stralsund and Stettin, were established. All were built on or near the coast, accessible to seaborne shipping. From their foundation their primary purpose was to resume and to continue the traditional trade of the Baltic region, but this time to bring it under the control of the Germans and to link it with the rising commercial centres of north-western Europe.

This early Germanic trade in the Baltic was carried on very largely with the Russian lands to the east, where Scandinavians from Gotland had kept open the commercial routes established three centuries earlier. The Germans, following in the footsteps of the Gotlanders, established a trading base, the Peterhof, in Novgorod. Here they bought the furs and wax, brought in from the northern forests, as well as goods of higher value brought overland from Central Asia and the Middle East. The island of Gotland was strategically situated for this trade, and the Gotlanders, from their port of Visby, had long played a prominent role. Here the German merchants from the Wendish towns established a base beside that of the native Gotlanders.

The community of German Merchants frequenting Gotland (*universi mercatores imperii Romani Gotlandiam frequentantes*) was the nucleus from which the Hanse later evolved. It was natural that the German merchants trading with a distant and foreign land like Russia, should seek to organise for their mutual protection. Yet the Gotland community had no clear constitution. It was recognised by the German emperor, Lothair III, but it operated under Swedish sovereignty. Nevertheless, the German community of Visby changed in the course of the thirteenth century from a floating population of merchants to a settled, urban community.

At the same time the German merchants extended their activities westward. They established a *kontor*, similar in most respects to their *Fondaco* in Venice, in Bruges and another in London. The latter, known as the Steelyard, or *Stalhof* (place of sale), remained active until it was suppressed by Elizabeth I in 1598. The merchants of Lübeck and of the Wendish towns were allied with those of Hamburg and of the Rhineland towns like Cologne and Dortmund. The lead in these commercial activities, as also in the negotiations with foreign powers, was taken by the loosely organised community of merchants, based in Visby. Its activities were, however, closely watched by the cities, primarily Lübeck, from which most of these merchants had originally come.

Leagues of towns were far from unknown in the Germany of the thirteenth century. There was an urban league in Swabia; another shortlived league emerged in the lower Rhineland, and in 1264 the Wendish towns came together to form a league, though an attempt to include all which had been established according to the 'laws' of Lübeck failed. The reasons for the formation of a league of commercial cities in the western Baltic were clear. On the one hand they were jealous of the power and privileges of the Gotland community; on the other, the latter association was inadequate to suppress piracy and to protect the interests of the merchants. Furthermore, the towns were themselves under pressure from the princes of northern Germany, anxious to restore their authority over them.

The Germans gained entry to the lands lying to the east of the Baltic by way of Novgorod, but access to the city by way of the Neva river, Lake Ladoga and the Volkhov river was circuitous and difficult. More southerly rivers, the Dvina and Niemen, offered an easier route into the Russian hinterland, but were blocked by the warlike tribes of Livonia and Lithuania. Not until the early thirteenth century did German settlers make progress in this area. In 1202 the order of the Brethren of the Sword was founded by the archbishop of Bremen who claimed spiritual jurisdiction over the east Baltic region. The order, which included merchants amongst its members, combined the conversion of the heathen with the pursuit of trade in a manner that would have done justice to nineteenth century British enterprise in Africa. In 1201 Riga was founded, quickly followed by Reval on the Estonian coast, and Dorpat, Narva and other towns of the interior.

But the area between Livonia and the Polish lands still remained in the hands of the Prussians and Lithuanians. In 1226 the order, which came subsequently to be known as that of the Teutonic or German Knights, was invited to come to the area by the Polish prince, Konrad of Mazowsze. It had found little scope for its particular kind of proselytizing in Transylvania, where it had been established, and eagerly accepted. In the middle years of the thirteenth century the knights conquered Prussia and threatened Poland. They absorbed the Brethren of the Sword and gave a more violent and incisive character to the German penetration of the Baltic region. In the wake of the military conquest came the foundation of German towns and an expansion of German trade.

It was this market which the Hanse was organised to exploit. Almost a century passed between the organisation of the league of Wendish cities and the formation of the larger and more powerful Hanseatic League. In 1356 a meeting was convened of the towns of the Hanse. The reason was the precarious position of the German merchants in the Low Countries, and the events of the following years showed convincingly that the combined economic and military power of the towns could achieve significant victories. Diplomatic triumph over Flanders and military victory over Denmark followed. At the same time German merchants blockaded Novgorod and forced the Russians to terminate their practice of molesting the trade of the Hanse.

The Hanseatic League was the peak of its power and prosperity at the end of the fourteenth century, but despite its power and importance it is extraordinarily difficult to define. Before the formation, in 1356, of the Hanse of the towns, membership was defined by the right to use the *Kontors* of the German merchants at Novgorod and at Bruges, London and Bergen. It is far from clear how membership was determined thereafter, though a series of lists[48] shows the number of members fluctuating between seventy and eighty. The league was dominated by Lübeck and a dozen or so large towns (Fig. 8.7), but most of its members were small places of only a thousand or so inhabitants. The league had a diet, the *Hansetag*, which met irregularly, usually on the initiative of Lübeck, and formulated its ordinances or *Recesse*.

The focal points in the commerce of the Hanse were its four Kontors, each of them, except that at Bruges, an enclosure housing the merchants and their wares and capable of defence. In addition, the Hanse had some kind of control over trading settlements at Pskov and Kovno in Russia, and in Norway. The traffic consisted essentially of the movement of bulky goods of low value from the east Baltic region to the west and the return movement of lightweight goods of greater value. It retained this character throughout the medieval period, though there were changes in the relative value of the different commodities.

The goods were in general carried from ports such as Danzig, Königsberg, Riga and Reval to Lübeck and other Wendish ports. Some were transhipped and taken on by way of the Sound to the west. The rest was carried overland to Hamburg for reshipment. Return cargoes, much of it from Bruges and London, followed

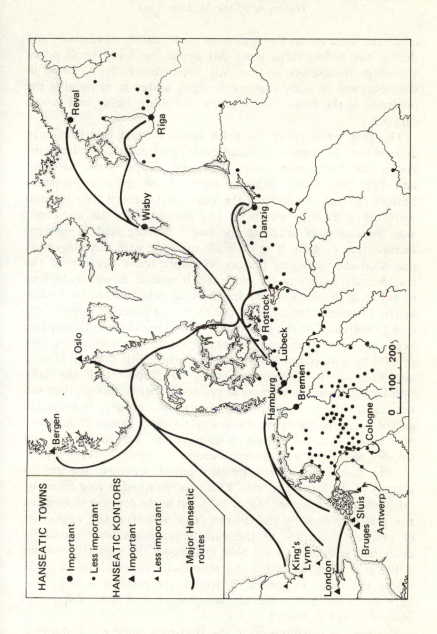

Fig. 8.7 The Hanseatic League in the fifteenth century.

383

much the same route. Voyages were made mainly in summer, and during the winter ships were tied up in the many small ports. The ships themselves were mostly cogs, stoutly built, broad in the beam and of fairly shallow draught, suited to navigating the estuaries of the Baltic rivers and to handling bulky and heavy cargoes.

The chief products of the Baltic lands were at first furs, wax and timber. To these was added grain, particularly rye from the Polish and Lithuanian lands; iron and copper from Sweden, and fish. The Baltic fisheries were of no great importance, though herring shoaled off the coast of southern Sweden and were taken in large numbers. The autumn fish fair at Skanör was the source of much of the salted herring sold in western Europe (see p. 402). It is difficult to trace with any degree of precision the changing pattern of Baltic trade because of the fragmentary nature of the evidence. It would, however, be true to say that the fur exports and herring sales tended to decline in the fifteenth century, and the export of Swedish copper and iron to increase. At the same time refined metals, chiefly copper, began to move from the mountains of northern Hungary (see p. 476) by way of the Polish rivers, to the Baltic ports of Danzig and Königsberg. The most notable development of the later Middle Ages was the increase in grain shipments, though they did not reach their peak until the seventeenth century. Norway lay on the fringe of the Hanseatic realm. Its chief export commodity was salted cod, which was bought at the Bergen Kontor and shipped to the ports of western Europe.

Only one basic raw material figured amongst the return cargoes of the Hansards: salt. This was obtained at first from the salt springs of Lüneburg (see p. 398), but in the fourteenth century this was displaced by the cheaper 'Bay' salt from the west coast of France. The trade of the east Baltic ports was summarily described as *in unde ut mit solte und roggen* (in with salt and out with rye).[49] But the eastward traffic included also English cloth, spices and wine. In general, however, the eastbound cargo was very much less bulky than the westbound, and many ships were obliged to sail in ballast.

Commercial organisation in the Hanseatic sphere is commonly thought of as relatively unsophisticated, even undeveloped. This was indeed the case in the twelfth century, and perhaps even for the whole period before the creation of the Hanse of the towns. The merchants were unlettered and travelled with their goods. In the fourteenth century this ceased. After a period of youthful travel, when they familiarised themselves with all aspects of their business, they tended to remain in their home towns, only occasionally visiting one of the Kontors. They rented space in ships and either employed men to accompany their cargoes or used agents at foreign ports to buy and sell for them. Their business was less diversified than that of Italian merchants; there were fewer opportunities for making large speculative profits and little opportunity to profit from money-lending and banking. There were many well-to-do merchants in Lübeck and Hamburg, but their fortunes bore no comparison with those of the merchants of Flanders or of Italy.

Merchant ventures during the heyday of Hanseatic prosperity were most often partnerships of two or more merchants, who contributed their capital and shared the risk of a venture between them. The richer merchants participated, exactly as Datini had done in Florence, in several separate partnerships at the same time. They do not, however, appear to have engaged in a voluminous correspondence, as Datini did, and in very few instances is it possible to see these Hanseatic merchants as men. The few merchants' records that have survived are untidy and unsystematic. They did not even begin to use double-entry book-keeping until the sixteenth century. They took over the bill of exchange from the Italians in Bruges, but made little use of it. Instruments of credit, in fact, remained undeveloped and much of their trade was on a cash basis. In the Russian lands and in Scandinavia it was often a simple barter. One cannot but surmise how much more developed Hanseatic trade might have been if the Hansards had evolved a more sophisticated financial and credit system.

All the evidence suggests that the fortunes of the Hanseatic League declined during the fifteenth century, though as an effective political and economic force it lasted into the second half of the seventeenth century. The volume of grain, of metals and ores, and of English cloth handled by the Hansards actually increased, but they lost their near monopoly of Baltic trade. They had never been able to interdict the Baltic Sea to the Dutch and Germans from non-Hanseatic cities. In the fifteenth century the activities of these peoples increased, though there is no means of knowing what proportion of the total Baltic trade fell into their hands. They were assisted by the lack of unity within the Hanse. The more easterly members were eager primarily to market the grain, wax, timber and other commodities delivered to them from their Russian and Lithuanian hinterlands. They did not greatly care in whose 'bottoms' these goods reached the west, and felt no compulsion to reserve this business for their rivals of Lübeck or Hamburg.

The Hanseatic towns had always been obliged to fight against the pretensions of the territorial princes. In the fourteenth century they had defeated the King of Denmark militarily, but in the fifteenth and later centuries the power and pretensions of rulers – the kings of Sweden, Denmark, Poland and England, the Tsar of Russia and the princes of north Germany – was increasing. They did not scruple to deal with traders other than members of the Hanseatic League. The number of towns represented at the *Hansetage*, the only evidence there is for membership, decreased, and trade gradually slipped from the hands of the Hansards.

### ROAD AND RIVER TRANSPORT

The general trend from the tenth or eleventh century until the end of the Middle Ages was towards an increasing volume of trade and an intensification of the network of routes which it followed. Roads, rivers and canals, and the sea were all used, but their relative importance changed during the period. The cost of transport was always high. Valuable commodities – the silks and spices of the East – could bear this cost; bulky goods of low value – alum, grain and building materials – could not, and one sees throughout the later Middle Ages repeated attempts to create some cheap means of bulk transport.

Medieval man, at least in western and southern Europe, inherited from the Roman Empire, a system of well built roads. Their purpose was, however, military rather than commercial. They ran where the legions might expect to go; they were too narrow for the carts and wagons of traders, and their paved surface required careful maintenance. This they never received despite injunctions in the Germanic codes that the roads should be kept in good repair. Medieval people developed roads to suit their needs. These, more often than not, consisted in local pathways and animal tracks integrated into a system. There was a multiplicity of such trackways. Between any two towns of importance there might be a multiplicity of roads, none of them adequately maintained and differing from one another only in their degrees of obstruction and interruption.

If it were ever possible to calculate in ton/miles the volume of freight that was moved in medieval Europe, we should probably find that the greater part was transported by road. Human porterage was used. Much was carried on the backs of pack animals, and many of the bridges were too narrow for anything larger to have passed. Some was transported in two-wheeled carts and four-wheeled wagons. Many medieval drawings show vehicles very similar indeed to those used by the peasants today in parts of eastern Europe. All kinds of goods travelled by road, but wherever possible waterways were used to move bulky goods. Foodstuffs like grain and wine were moved on the backs of horses and mules – one dreads to think what it might have done to the quality of the vintage – as well as wool, alum and salt. Even building stone was sometimes transported immense distances by land from the quarry to the building site. The city of Troyes, for example, obtained stone from Tonnerre, 50 kilometres to the south and from Saint-Dizier, 70 kilometres to the north-east. It took two days to drag the stone over this distance, usually on carts which carried on average about 2300 kilogrammes of cut stone, though on occasion the load was as large as 3900 kilogrammes – a very heavy load for the clumsy vehicles and rough unsurfaced roads.[50]

Travel was slow and the risks great. Few people ever travelled alone. Usually they formed groups for mutual protection, and this further reduced their speed which had to be adjusted to that of their slowest members. Freight was most often conveyed by professional wagoners who were thoroughly familiar with the routes they followed. The choice of route was influenced by the state of the roads, the amount of toll charged, and the danger from robbers. No less important was the availability of overnight accommodation. The many surviving itineraries, listing in many instances places of very inconsiderable importance, were in fact lists of places where the traveller might expect to be able to stay overnight. On no routes was the provision of overnight accommodation more important than on those which crossed the Alps.

Indeed, the mountains could not be crossed without it, and the opening of a new route often consisted in the building of a hospice somewhere near its summit. Most famous of such hospices was that founded in Carolingian times at the summit of the Great St Bernard Pass, but there were others on all the well used Alpine routes.[51]

In the later Middle Ages the merchant very rarely travelled with the goods he owned; they were entrusted to regular carters. It thus became all the more necessary for him to get his instructions to his agents quickly, to receive their replies, and to appraise conditions in the markets with which he did business. For this he relied upon couriers who travelled much more quickly than the carters. It was noted above that the business of the Champagne fairs relied heavily on information brought in this way. There developed a regular courier service between the major trading centres. Most of the great trading companies of Italy employed their own couriers, but the smaller men made use of professional couriers who might travel with a large bag of missives from many merchants. The mail service was far from safe. Datini would sometimes send more than one copy of an important letter by different routes. They were also liable to be opened and read en route. 'There are many,' wrote Datini 'who strive to seize letters that pass through their hands', and letters containing confidential information, he added, should be entrusted only to known and tried friends.

The speed of travel varied greatly. A courier on horseback could cover up to 100 kilometres in a day, but if he travelled on foot he could not expect to do more than 30 to 40. Laden carts and wagons travelled even more slowly. The spacing of stations along the medieval itineraries, such as that of Bruges, give some indication of the length of a day's journey for a slow moving caravan of wagons and pedestrians. It ranged from 18 to 30 kilometres. All roads had toll stations, established by the local lord, who demanded payment for the privilege of travelling within his jurisdiction, or by the king or prince who levied a custom on goods entering or leaving his realm. But the multiplicity of roads often made it easy to evade a toll station. Only where the roads were forced to converge to cross a bridge or to pass a defile in the Jura or on the approaches to the Alps was it possible to levy toll on the greater part of the traffic. In some areas boundaries were well provided with toll stations. It was, for example, very difficult for merchandise to evade the customs levied by the king of France as it passed from Flanders into Artois. The most used crossing point was Bapaume and a great deal is known of the tolls exacted here. Another well documented toll station was the Col de Jougne,[52] where the road from the passes of the Central Alps and the upper Rhône valley to Champagne and Flanders crossed the Jura. The records show how large were the quantities of bulky goods of low value – wool, leather, salt – which made this difficult journey.

At no time were rivers of greater importance for the transport of freight than during the Middle Ages. The 'fluvialisation', to use Lopez's term,[53] of land transport increased during the early Middle Ages, as Roman roads and bridges fell into disrepair. Every river that was capable of bearing a boat, however small, was used. Swift streams which were not easily navigated were used in one direction only. Merchandise, or even timber alone, was rafted down them from the hills to the plains. Europe's rivers were, in general, well suited for navigation. Except in the southern areas of Mediterranean climate, their flow was fairly even throughout the year. They seldom ran dry, and, except in central Europe, navigation was rarely hindered by ice. In most of Spain, Italy – south of the Lombardy Plain, and the Balkan peninsula, however, rivers were of little value. Most were short; they dried out or were reduced to a mere trickle during the long dry summer. A very great use was made during the earlier Middle Ages of such broad rivers with their steady flow as the Po, the Rhine, and the Seine and its tributaries. One gets the impression that during the Carolingian period the movement of goods was very largely by water.

Rivers provided natural highways across Europe, but it should not be supposed that they presented no difficulties for the medieval traveller and merchant. Rivers, like the Roman roads, did not always lie in the directions in which travellers wished to go; the movement from one river basin to another had necessarily to be made overland, and such portages were all too often costly, dangerous and difficult. River boats were either towed or propelled by the wind. Towing necessitated the provision of towpaths, and these were even more difficult to maintain than the roads, always liable to crumble under heavy rain, and to be washed away by floods. The record of transport on the Rhine is filled with complaints of the disappearance of the towing path. The use of sail also presented difficulties, though most boats, to judge from Renaissance engravings and woodcuts, relied heavily on the wind. They were often becalmed, and found it difficult to tack in the narrow confines of a twisting river.

River transport was safer than that by road. It was a great deal less easy to rob a ship than a caravan, but the river boat could less easily escape the attentions of a toll collector nor could it evade the staple rights claimed by many cities along the river's course. Manmade restrictions on the use of rivers increased as the Middle Ages progressed. Most burdensome were tolls. All rivers had toll stations, established by the local princes. Those on the Rhine are the best known, largely because their physical remains in the shape of castles and towers can be seen today. At most there were some thirty toll stations, the majority between Mainz and Cologne, where shipping can be most easily controlled, and it is claimed that their impositions almost doubled the cost of goods which moved by this route. On the river Seine toll was paid no less than eighteen times in the 130 kilometres between La Roche-Guyon, near Mantes, and Paris.[54] In 1273 the *Parlement* forbade the establishment of new tolls, and during the fourteenth century several were suppressed. Nevertheless, both here and on other rivers the boatmen and the merchants fought a losing battle against the feudal right to establish toll stations and exact what the traffic would bear. In some cases, when the boat carried a homogeneous cargo of a commodity of low value, the toll consisted of a fraction of the freight. The salt boats, sailing up the Seine to Paris, are said to have paid about one-twenty-seventh of their cargo in tolls. This increased to one-twentieth in the sixteenth century. Many of the toll stations were owned by monasteries: Saint-Denis of Paris received the profits of no less than five of those located on the Seine. On the other hand, it was common for the cargoes destined for religious institutions to gain exemption from the tolls. Even on as unimportant a river as the Weser there were tolls, and the only rivers that were not burdened in this way were those that carried so little traffic that tolls were not worth the trouble of collecting.

The staple rights of many European towns were an affliction of a somewhat different character. They consisted in the privilege of forcing all passing ships to stop, unload, and offer their goods for sale, and to reload and proceed on their way only if there was no demand for them. Conditions varied from one town to another. Some goods were exempt and for others there might be little demand. In some towns it was required that goods remain exposed for as much as two weeks.[55] The staple right (*Stapelrecht*) was rigorously enforced in the Rhineland towns which possessed it: Cologne, Mainz, Strasbourg and Basel. Paris and Rouen possessed staple rights on the Seine; Münden and Bremen on the Weser; and Frankfurt, on the Oder. On the Scheldt and its tributaries upstream towns sometimes cut off the supply of grain to those, like Ghent, Bruges, and Ypres, which lay nearer their mouths. In extreme cases, the exercise of the *Stapelrecht* brought river traffic to a standstill. Frankfurt-on-Oder, for example, placed a virtual embargo on trade, preventing all goods from the south from passing the city towards the Baltic.[56] The effect was not only to inhibit economic growth in the upper Oder valley, but also to cut the port of Stettin off from part of its natural hinterland.

Closely connected with the *Stapelrecht* was the *Umschlagsrecht*. This meant, not only that ships should be unloaded at certain points along a river, but that their cargoes, if allowed to continue, should be reloaded into *different* ships. In origin this burden on trade was based on the assumption that ships of varying draught and size were required on the several segments of the river's course. The desirability of using different ships became institutionalised. It ceased to be a convenience, and became a burden. The *Umschlagsrecht* was particularly prominent on the Rhine, where it was coupled with the *Stapelrecht*.

It was difficult to evade such burdens and restrictions on river trade. Cremona and Reggio together cut a canal to evade the exactions of Mantua, but this was a rare occurrence, technically and financially beyond the scope of most of the medieval towns which suffered from this kind of legalised extortion by their neighbours. The effect of tolls was generally to stifle river traffic and to force the movement of goods back to the roads.[57] In the later Middle Ages rivers were of declining importance. In early modern times they were, in general, very little used, and it was not until the restrictions had been removed in the course of the French Revolution and the Napoleonic wars that river transport again became important in Europe.

During the early Middle Ages all kinds of goods moved by

boat. The poem of Ermoldus Niger refers to the Frisian cloth which was carried up the Rhine to its market in Switzerland; imports from the East were carried up the river Po from Venice. But in time such goods deserted the rivers and were carried by road, and in the later Middle Ages, the rivers were used chiefly for bulk cargoes. This change springs, in part, from the heavy tolls imposed on the river traffic, and the losses sustained in the leaky holds of the ships; in part also from the improvements made in the roads. They were integrated into a system; bridges were built and accommodation provided, and, if the cost of land transport was high, it was in general valuable freights that used it. What then was carried by river boat in the fourteenth and fifteenth centuries? On many rivers salt represented the largest cargo. On the Loire in 1355–56 out of 1397 barges, no less than 989, or 70 per cent, were loaded wholly with salt.[58] Most was produced on the coast and could be carried inland conveniently and cheaply by river. Grain and wine were also prominent amongst the freight of river craft. Paris and the cities of the Low Countries and northern Italy imported large amounts of grain in this way. Much of it came by barge. In the later Middle Ages, when the rye of Eastern Europe began to furnish the needs of western cities, transport by river began to assume an overwhelming importance. It was taken by roughly constructed boats down the Oder, Vistula, Niemen and other rivers to the sea. The grain was loaded on to sea-going ships, and the crude boats were then broken up and their timbers sold for building or fuel.

Maritime trade assumed an ever increasing role in the commerce of Europe. This was in part due to the fact that the seas became safer for peaceful shipping in the later Middle Ages than they had been in the earlier. In part, also, it reflected the overall increase in the volume of trade and, in particular, of that in bulky commodities for which transport by sea was very well suited. This was accompanied by a growth in the size of ships and an increasing specialisation in their design.

On the northern seas the commonest vessel was the round ship, broad in the beam, with a large cargo capacity, and propelled by sail. The *cog* was usually single-masted and of up to 250 tons. Some ships were larger, and carried as many as three masts. The prevailing Mediterranean ship, the *nef*, was basically similar. Most carried square sails, but in the later Middle Ages, the caravel, a lightly built round ship with a lateen sail, appeared. It could sail closer to the wind than the square-rigged ship, and was well adapted to sailing into and out of the many small ports of the Mediterranean littoral.

In sharp contrast were the long ships. The Viking vessels had been long ships, but the type disappeared from northern waters. It was, however, perpetuated in the Mediterranean as the galley. It had both sails and oars. It was fast, could be moved even in a dead calm, and was thus safer where piracy was rife. On the other hand, its cargo capacity was small, and it tended to be used mainly for transporting goods of small bulk and high value.

Most sea-going ships were small – of less than 100 tons. They plied between the many little ports, with a shallow depth of water and scanty protection against storms. In the Mediterranean, roads running parallel with the coast were almost abandoned in favour of coastal shipping. From southern Spain to the headlands of Greece the coastal waters were busy with the movement of little ships in the summer season. The same was true of north-western Europe, where there was a succession of busy little ports all the way from the 'Bay' where salt was loaded, to the base of the Danish peninsula. Much of this traffic was in the hands of the Bretons, the Normans and the Dutch. They were unspecialised, willing to carry whatever cargo was available, and if none offered, prepared to turn pirate on occasion. Much of the cross-channel trade between the French and English ports was in these small craft.[59] Farther to the east, there were dozens of little ports around the Zuider Zee and on the islands of the Rhine delta, whose ships sailed the inshore waterways of the Netherlands and north-west Germany.

### THE COMMODITIES OF MEDIEVAL TRADE

Professor Lopez has advised us not to allow 'the glitter and glamour of trade in luxuries . . . to overshadow the heavy trade in cheap bulky goods'.[60] It was the latter which filled the holds of most ships and river boats and even provided a large part of the freight that travelled by road. It is, unhappily, quite impossible to assess the relative values and volumes of the luxury goods and of the basic commodities which entered into European trade. Occasionally is there a hint in customs accounts, bills of lading or the correspondence of merchants of their respective amounts, and in general the luxury goods are found to come a very poor second.

## The spice trade

This, it has been seen (p. 363), was essentially the movement of goods from certain emporia in the Levant to the Italian ports and their distribution, generally overland, to much of western and central Europe. The spice trade was dominated by pepper, but ginger, cinnamon, nutmeg were also imported. The Venetians handled a large part of the spice trade. In the first half of the fifteenth century they had only some twenty merchant galleys, and Lane[61] has estimated that they could not, on the basis of a single voyage to the Levant each summer, have carried between them more than 4500 tons of freight, only part of which was made up of spices. If we add the spice imports of Genoa, Pisa, Florence and Barcelona, we still have a very small trade, even though unit values were high.

Spices were not the only goods of Asiatic origin which were brought to Europe in the galleys of the Venetians. There was also a quantity of dyestuffs: Brazil-wood and indigo which yielded colours unobtainable with the dyes in common use in the west (see p. 303). There were sugar, ivory and gemstones; small quantities of steel from India, but relayed through Damascus which gave it the name it commonly bore. Amounts of each of these commodities were small and the trade probably erratic.

## The grain trade

There was no long distance trade in grain during the early Middle Ages, except for the supply of Constantinople and perhaps Rome. By the end of the Middle Ages the bread crops were moved over great distances and in large quantities. The principal reason was, of course, the urbanisation of Europe. A mechanism was created for shipping grain over long distances to satisfy urban needs; it could then be used to remedy those local shortages which arose through crop-failure and which in earlier times had led to starvation and death.

The most severe shortages, as might be expected, were experienced in Italy and the Low-Countries. The surplus areas of Italy were, as they had been in classical times, Sicily and Apulia, the coastal plains of both the east and west of the Italian peninsula, and the Plain of Lombardy. Every city constituted a deficit area, and the larger cities imposed demands which even their *contadi* were quite incapable of meeting. Venice, Genoa and Florence imported grain by sea; Milan and the northern cities relied heavily on the productive capacity of the Lombardy Plain.

The Italian production of grain had to be supplemented by imports from other regions of the Mediterranean. Venice drew upon the resources of the thinly peopled plain of Albania and even on North Africa. Grain was carried by coastal shipping from Languedoc to Genoa and Pisa. Wheat was the dominant grain crop, and made up most of the grain trade. Barley did not enter largely into trade, and rye, the mainstay of the northern grain trade, was virtually unknown in the Mediterranan basin.

The Flanders cities were in a no less precarious position than those of northern Italy. The plain itself was not a grain growing region; its sandy soils were too infertile, and its clays too damp. The chief source of import during most of the Middle Ages was Artois and Picardy, a region of light and fertile soil where, if Thierry d'Hireçon was in any way typical of its landowners (see pp. 198–9), farming was practised efficiently and yields were high. Grain – here wheat, spelt and rye – was carted to the limits of navigation on the Scheldt tributaries, at Valenciennes, Douai and Aire. From here it was taken down-river by barge.[62] There was fierce competition between the Flemish cities for access to the grain of Artois and control of the waterways, and many were the towns which exercised a kind of *Stapelrecht*, allowing to pass only the grain for which they could see no pressing need.

Brabant and Hainault supplemented the grain supply of Artois, but their own urban growth in the later Middle Ages reduced their importance in this regard. Picardy had a surplus, much of which was sent down the Somme and along the coast to Flanders.[63] Holland and the Netherlands, though not highly urbanised like Flanders or even Brabant, were nevertheless deficit areas. As in Flanders, the soils were unsuited to crop-farming. Grain was imported by coasting ships from northern France and also brought by river craft from the lower Rhineland. The latter region, basically Guelders, Jülich and Cleves, also supplied the city of Cologne. The cities of the middle Rhineland were largely supplied from the plains of Alsace and Baden.

In the later Middle Ages north-western Europe was ceasing to satisfy its needs in bread crops from its traditional markets and began to turn to more distant sources. Baltic grain began to reach western Europe in the thirteenth century, and the supply subsequently increased in volume and became more regular. Rye dominated. At the end of the fifteenth century, when figures first became available, 97 per cent of the grain shipment from Danzig was made up of rye. The grain came at first from Mecklenburg and Pomerania. Then the cultivation of grain for export was developed on a large scale in Poland and Lithuania. The grain was shipped by way of the Polish and Russian rivers, and Danzig acquired – and held until the nineteenth century – a dominating role in Europe's grain supply. Some of the Baltic grain went to Norway, which periodically suffered severe shortages, but most was consumed in the highly urbanised areas of north-western Europe. Not until the late sixteenth century did Baltic grain reach the Mediterranean market on a considerable scale.

## The wine trade

From the eleventh century attempts to cultivate the grape vine and to make wine in climatically marginal areas were gradually abandoned (see p. 201), and northern Europe began to rely on imports from more favoured regions. The Mediterranean lands, with the exception of those under Muslim control, continued to produce the wine they needed, but to export little. They lay too far from the importing regions of northern Europe. Nevertheless, the Crusaders returned with a taste for some southern wines, notably that produced in southern Greece. This sweet and heavy wine was brought to western Europe by the Venetians, and, under the name of Malmsey, was marketed as far away as England. The Turkish conquest ended the trade in Malmsey, and its place was taken by the not dissimilar wines of Madeira and Portugal.

With this not very important exception, the trade in wine was carried on with areas which combined the advantages of a warm and sunny climate with means of easy transport to the north European markets. Very broadly there were four such areas during the later Middle Ages. The first lay from the Aunis and Saintonge southwards into Guyenne and Gascony. To a small degree its wines were exported northwards overland to Normandy, Brittany and the Paris region, but most were exported by sea. Vineyards lined the Garonne river, which each autumn carried the barrels down to Bordeaux for export to Great Britain and the Low Countries. Before the Hundred Years' War, it has been claimed, 50,000 barrels a year were exported. The vineyards were severely damaged in the course of the fighting, and exports after the war never regained their previous level.

The second area of intensive viticulture was Burgundy. It lay close to the climatic limit of the vine, but lacked Gascony's great advantage, a ready access to the sea. Even river transport did not greatly favour it. The chief areas of viticulture within Burgundy lay along the foot of the Côte d'Or, to the north and south of Beaune, where the great vintages continue to be produced today. The market for Burgundian wines lay to the north, and the barrels were carted across the Langres Plateau to reach the navigable tributaries of the Seine. Here, at Auxerre, Chablis and Saint-Dizier the wine was put on the river boats which carried it to the markets of Paris and Rouen. Some of the Burgundian wines continued their journey by sea to England; they were taken up the Oise to the wine fairs at Compiègne and thence by river and short portages to the Low Countries. Cheaper wines could be had from Champagne and the Paris region. Paris itself was surrounded by vineyards but those who could afford them drank burgundies, brought down river, and clarets from Bordeaux, shipped upstream from the port of Rouen.

The establishment of the Papacy at Avignon created a vastly inflated demand for many commodities, amongst them quality wines. The most favoured were the burgundies from Beaune and Saint-Pourçain. The former was taken down the Saône and Rhône to Avignon, but the much prized Saint-Pourçain was taken by wagon the 175 kilometres through the mountains of Charolais to the Saône at Chalon. The wine suffered; its price was high, and the Papal court, doubtless with great reluctance, gave up drinking Saint-Pourçain.[64]

A third area which produced wine for export was the Rhineland, from Alsace northwards to Bonn. It was the northern part of this region, however, which produced then, as it does today, the greater part of the export wine. There were local wine markets at Speyer, Mainz, Frankfurt and Strasbourg, but these were over-shadowed in importance by Cologne, which as a wine market was probably rivalled only by Paris. Cologne dealt in wines from as far away as Switzerland and Austria. Clarets from Aquitaine were brought by sea and river and burgundies by a variety of routes, but its chief business was with the Rhine and Moselle wines. These were distributed over the Low Countries and were despatched by ship to Great Britain and the Baltic.

The Alps placed an insuperable barrier to the transport of Italian wines to northern Europe. Only at the Brenner Pass was it practicable to send them across the mountains. The wines of Tyrol were sold at the wine fair at Bozen and distributed over much of South Germany, even selling as far away as Cologne.

*The salt trade*

The greater part of the salt which entered into long-distance trade came from the coastal salt-pans. Within the Mediterranean there was a movement of salt towards the larger consuming centres, particularly in northern Italy. It filled the holds or formed part-cargoes in the nefs. The Spanish coast, the Balearic Islands and Languedoc sent salt in small coasting vessels to Genoa, Barcelona, Pisa and other ports. Venice derived salt from lagoons on the Dalmatian and Albanian coasts, and Constantinople from the coasts of Macedonia and Thrace. But the largest movement of salt was from the 'Bay', which shipped large amounts in late summer to northern Europe.

The maritime salt trade developed steadily from the twelfth century. The market for Bay salt was extended from the Channel ports to the Low Countries, and then, with the development of Hanseatic trade, salt began to form the largest eastbound cargo of the Hansards. Away from the coasts of western and northern Europe sea salt met the competition of salt derived from springs or quarried from the rock, as at Wieliczka in southern Poland. In the Netherlands salt was derived by burning the peat and dissolving it from the ashes that were formed. Gradually, however, imported sea salt cut into the market for all other forms, until only areas remote from the sea, like Bohemia and Austria, were secure from its competition.

*The wool trade*

The trade in wool was made necessary both by the variations in the quality of wool and by the concentration of the weaving industry in a few areas. Three were pre-eminent for the quality of their wool: England, Spain and North Africa. It was English wool which was most in demand during the period of expansion in the thirteenth and early fourteenth centuries. The broadcloth manufacture of the Low Countries was based on English wool, though the local wool from Artois may have been important in the earlier phases of its growth. English wool was in the thirteenth century in demand in Italy and made the costly journey overland from the Channel ports to the Plain of Lombardy. At first it was sent across France, but the French prohibition of the export of wool forced it to take a more easterly route to Basel and so across the central passes of the Alps to Italy. English wool was being carried on the backs of pack animals across the St Gotthard Pass before 1300.

The export of English wool began to decline about the middle of the fourteenth century, and continental Europe was obliged to turn to other sources. The new draperies could use wool of medium quality and this in turn encouraged the use of many local wools. But it was Spanish wool which, by and large, entered the European market to replace the English. The Mesta was formed in the late thirteenth century (see p. 207), and the export of wool both to Italy and to northern Europe grew in volume. It probably reached its peak in the early fifteenth century, when immense quantities were sent from the wool fairs at Medina del Campo, near Valladolid, to the northern ports of Spain for shipment to north-west Europe.

## The cloth trade

Cloth was by far the most important of all manufactured goods in medieval trade. No other commodity was available in such a rich variety of quality, texture, colour and size. In no other field were there such changes in fashion and in the structure of demand. We thus find developing a pattern of trade so complex that with the limited sources available it defies analysis. Reference has already been made (p. 351) to the books of the Bonis of Montauban and the Datini of Prato. They dealt in the cloth of obscure and distant places, presumably because a customer wanted it, as well as in the great fabrics of Flanders or Florence which, like the great vintages, were known and in demand almost everywhere. Dollinger has shown how,[65] in the mutual trade of two towns – neither of them of the first rank – Fribourg in Switzerland and Strasbourg in Alsace, they exchanged cloth of indifferent quality with one another. The shopping list of a well-to-do lady of Quercy, in south-western France,[66] recorded the purchase of fourteen pieces of cloth in the very small town of Villeneuve. They came from: Saint-Quentin, Lille, Sens, Provins, Beauvais, Cambrai, Ypres, Avignon and Louviers (Normandy). In addition there was a 'say' from Germany. The only cloth of local origin was another say from Cahors. She had all Europe from which to make her choice, and she used this freedom to the full.

In the confused pattern of the medieval cloth trade one can, nevertheless, discern certain movements which transcended this fluctuating and local scale. They represented on the one hand, a large-scale production in certain specialised centres; on the other, a continuing demand for a cloth of established quality. Foremost amongst such producing and exporting centres were the Low Countries, with a predominance first of the broadcloths of Flanders and, towards the end of the Middle Ages, of the new draperies of Brabant and the rural areas of Flanders. The movement of the Flanders cloth was, in the main, to Italy, by way of the Champagne fairs as long as they were active and, after their collapse, by way of the Rhineland and the passes of the Central Alps. In the later Middle Ages English cloth to some extent replaced that of Flanders in the Italian market.

A feature of trade in the later Middle Ages is the broadening basis of demand, the increasing demand for goods of medium quality. This is shown in the growing popularity not only of the new draperies but also of the mixed fabrics and fustians. The latter were produced in South Germany and Switzerland, and were marketed by the merchants of the Ravensburg Company of Ravensburg, near Lake Constance. Its chief market was in Italy, but the South German cloth was diffused far more widely than the Flemish cloth had been. It was marketed in the Rhineland towns; it was sold in the Baltic by the Hansards, and in Eastern Europe by the merchants of Nuremberg and Prague.

*Trade in metals*
Metals and metal goods share the obscurity and anonymity which mark medieval mining and smelting. Almost nothing is known of the volume of metals entering into commerce, and very little of the geographical pattern of this trade. The metals which were significant during the Middle Ages were, first and foremost, iron

and steel, followed by lead, tin, copper and calamine which was used in brass founding.

One must assume that much of the iron was used where it was produced in the fabrication of domestic hardware. There were, however, certain areas in which iron production greatly exceeded local demand and which were thus able to supply the metal to much of western Europe. Foremost among them was the Basque region of northern Spain.

One assumes that Sweden was, at least during the later Middle Ages, second in importance. The earliest recorded exports, of the mid-thirteenth century, came from Gotland, but central Sweden was unquestionably the most important Scandinavian source of iron. Iron was exported, chiefly from Stockholm, by the merchants of the Hanse. The volume of export could not, it is claimed,[67] have exceeded 300 to 500 tons yearly in 1368–9, but may have risen to 900 tons a year at the end of the century. Exports continued to increase through the fifteenth century and that from Stockholm alone reached about 3000 tons by the middle years of the sixteenth century. Much of the iron was shipped to Lübeck, whence it was distributed to western Europe.

The non-ferrous metals – copper, tin and lead – did not, unlike iron, occur widely, and trade in them was important. The chief source of tin was Cornwall, which held almost a monopoly in western Europe. It was shipped, mainly from London, to the Low Countries, and, alloyed with lead to form pewter, it found its way across Europe and by sea to the Middle East. Copper was less highly localised. The mines in the Harz Mountains of Germany were an important source, but in the later Middle Ages the vast reserves of the eastern Alps and of the mountains of Slovakia were opened up, in part at least by the activities of the Fuggers. Hungarian copper followed the route of Hungarian iron to the markets of western Europe, and as the Middle Ages were closing Antwerp developed as the foremost copper market of the continent. Amongst the leading consumers of copper was Dinant, on the Meuse, which, before its destruction in 1466, seems to have received most of its metal from the Harz mountains and the market of Goslar. As early as the twelfth century merchants from Dinant were buying copper in Cologne, and in the thirteenth copper dealers – *si vero de Goslaria vel undecumque* – were paying a special toll in the city.[68]

The previous pages have merely summarised our knowledge of the principal categories of medieval trade. There was, in fact, no limit to the variety of goods which made their way along medieval roads or were carried in small boats along the rivers. One might add to these already discussed butter, cheese and salted fish, the skins and furs used to trim the clothing of the rich, the hides from which coarse leather was made and the finer skins, which, tanned with greater care, yielded cordovan for making gloves and ladies' shoes. Some of these goods, even those of low value, sometimes travelled great distances. Hides from Fribourg (Switzerland) were sold in Strasbourg, and the Cologne records show that a wagon-load of hides from Münster, destined for the city, was thrown during a storm from the bridge over the river Lippe and lost. Herring, cured at small towns on the Dutch coast, were carried up the Rhine and, doubtless, many another river for sale in urban markets, and about 1400 a couple of merchants of Kampen, a small port town near the shore of the Zuider Zee, were accused of 'falsely' offering for sale in Cologne the herring which they had themselves salted and cured in Scania in southern Sweden. Nothing shows better the immense range of medieval commerce in the latter Middle Ages than the commercial records of Cologne or the books of such merchant families as the Bonis and the Datini.

# 9

# The commercial revolution

A commercial revolution, in the words of the late Raymond de Roover, is 'a complete or drastic change in the methods of doing business or in the organization of business enterprise'. Such a revolution, he claims, occurred at the end of the thirteenth and early in the fourteenth century. It was characterised by a change in the activities of merchants, who ceased gradually to travel with their wares and, instead, entrusted them to 'common carriers', and sent their orders and made payment by couriers. It was marked by the development of new forms of partnership; by the appearance of the bill of exchange, which eliminated the necessity to transport large amounts of specie, together with the mechanism for clearing or discounting them, and by the increasing use of credit, which the bill of exchange made possible. Lastly, more sophisticated methods of book-keeping made their appearance.

All these developments in the practice of commerce appeared first in Italy, though some were indebted to Middle Eastern example. They spread during the last two centuries of the Middle Ages over much of Western Europe. They were adopted in Germany, but had little influence on the trade of the Baltic region and almost none on that of eastern Europe. Beyond serving as bankers to English kings, the Italians made little contribution to economic organisation in Great Britain,[1] and the commercial revolution was not experienced here until the sixteenth century.

Before the commercial revolution the merchant travelled as a general rule with his wares. The volume of his goods was limited by the means of transport at his disposal, and the speed of his

403

turnover by the slowness of his rate of travel. He carried little currency, in part because it was unsafe to do so, but partly also because the amount in circulation was inadequate for the needs of commerce. Much of his trading was done at fairs, where he could buy goods on the security of goods still in his possession, and wait until the conclusion of the fair before clearing his obligations with other merchants. It was, in fact, a highly refined form of barter. At the conclusion of the accounting period which brought a fair to a close only small sums of money actually changed hands.

Such had been the practice at the fairs and in the cities which lay along the commercial axis from Italy to north-western Europe. To the east and to the north trade often had a yet more 'natural' character. It was barter in which the concept of money rarely entered. Heckscher[2] has described how, in sixteenth-century Sweden, the value of herring was sometimes expressed in terms of grain or iron, commodities for which the fish was often exchanged. A debt to the city of Lübeck was discharged in butter, and taxes were often paid in kind.

On the other hand one must not emphasise unduly, as Werner Sombart has done, the small scale of medieval business and trade. One can readily admit that the total tonnage of goods imported from the Levant by all the Italian cities in a year would not today fill the hold of a single small freighter and that the size of the total European market for exotic wares was, compared with that of modern times, minute. Sombart described the merchant as 'girding himself with a sword,' and, in order 'to get his few pack safely to their destination,' as 'for weeks and months performing the tasks of carriage driver and innkeeper.'[3] This was true of the blessed Godric of Finchale, who nevertheless succeeded in amassing a considerable fortune; it was no longer true of the age of the Bardi, the Peruzzi, and the Acciaiuoli. Their business was conducted on the largest scale known hitherto. They lent money to kings; they maintained factors in most of the leading commercial cities of Europe, and their orders and commercial paper were carried between them at the speed of a horse.

### CREDIT AND USURY

At the root of the commercial revolution was the institution of credit. One of the most severe obstacles to the development of trade in the ancient world had been the failure of the classical civilisations to evolve any adequate instruments of credit. If they had done so, the strictures of the Church Fathers on the practice of usury might have been less severe, for in the long run Christian moral values always adjust themselves to economic necessity. For much of the Middle Ages, however, the Church formally condemned the taking of interest on a loan, however that loan might be disguised, and it required great ingenuity upon the part of the canon lawyers to reconcile the most elementary and necessary commercial practices with the teachings of the Church. A rigid doctrine on usury was formulated by Gratian in the early twelfth century. It was based on biblical precept, reinforced by the writings of the Fathers and the canons of the early Church. It defined usury as 'the receiving of more than the sum lent, not only of money but of anything in kind. . . . Any excess demanded, though it be a small gift, is usury.'[4] Usury was condemned, though medieval thinkers never faced up to the double standard enjoined in the text of Deuteronomy: 'thou shalt not lend upon usury to thy brother . . . Unto a stranger though mayest lend upon usury.' That this biblical passage was much in the minds of Renaissance people is shown in Shakespeare's *Merchant of Venice*:

> If thou wilt lend this money, lend it not
> As to thy friends, – for when did friendship take
> A breed for barren metal of his friend? –
> But lend it rather to thine enemy:
> Who if he break, thou mayst with better face
> Exact the penalty.

The earning of a profit, however, was acceptable, provided it represented the just return for services performed or even a reward for risk taking.

The first objection to the Christian doctrine on usury came from the civil law. The Codex of Justinian had accepted the payment of interest on a debt as a useful practice. The canonists conveniently overcame this by asserting the superiority of canon law to civil law in case of conflict. To this they added the specious arguments that money is sterile and cannot be made to breed, and that to charge interest is to demand payment for time which is common to all. Early Christian doctrine was basically hostile to the merchant and to the practice of trade. 'Trade', enunciated one of the early canons, 'can scarcely, if ever, be pleasing to God.' Usury seems to have been regarded as a theological offence rather than as a crime against society. It was taken for granted that the Jews could charge interest on their loans, and the Lateran Council of 1215 was merely concerned that they should not exact *immoderatas usuras*. The Christian who offended by accepting or paying interest subjected himself only to spiritual penalties and his offence was rarely, if ever, amenable to the civil courts.

Various methods were adopted of making a loan and receiving interest. An article might be sold and then brought back at the end of a specified period (*venditio* and *emptio ad tempus*), the difference between the two prices constituting the interest on a loan, which was the real object of the transaction. Such a practice was condemned by the canon lawyers unless there was a genuine uncertainty regarding the future price of the article at the time of the original contract. In other words, the contract was legitimised if an element of risk entered into it. Again, a loan might be made on the security of something, a horse, for example, which could be made to yield a profit. Such a loan was held to be usurious. On the other hand, if the creditor could show that he suffered loss as a result of lending money – *damnum emergens* – he was entitled to some compensation; or he might withdraw money from some lucrative employment (*lucrum cessans*) in order to help a friend. In this case he might also exact *interesse* on his loan. Arguments became so subtle that only a canonist could have had the patience or the interest to follow them. Certainly the line separating legitimate from sinful financial operations became so blurred that there can have been few instances in which laymen felt that their souls were imperilled by their business transactions.

The canon lawyers became increasingly broad in their interpretations of the canons as the commercial need for credit grew. In practice a distinction came to be drawn between business loans and what one might term distress loans. In the case of the former the borrower commonly expected to use the money he had borrowed for profit; it was therefore only reasonable that he should be required to pay for the privilege of using someone else's money for his own gain. A distress loan, however, was commonly made to someone who had sustained loss through accident or misfortune. Such a one was to be pitied and helped; not forced deeper into debt by the obligation to pay high rates of

interest. It was the pawnbroker who was most likely to be called
upon to make distress loans, and it was his activities which were
denounced most frequently.[5] Indeed in some cities a *mons
pietatis* was established, a fund for the help of the needy, which
demanded in interest only enough to cover the cost of administration.

Apart from the loans made by Italian banking houses to kings
and princes, the largest sums which entered into credit transactions were specified in bills of exchange. Money received in one
place was repaid at a later date, in a distant place, and in a different currency. Clearly this was a credit transaction, but it
embraced an element of risk in so far as it was impossible to
predict with certainty the rates of exchange at the place where a
bill would be discounted. In de Roover's words, the 'speculative
profits on exchange served as a cloak to cover interest charges'.[6]
The canonists did not even wince, and the most usurious monetary transactions of the later Middle Ages, those on which the
fortunes of the Medici and many other banks were founded, was,
theologically speaking, above reproach.

It has become an article of faith of the Weber-Tawney school,
which links the rise of modern capitalism with the Reformation,
that the medieval injunctions against usury restricted economic
growth and hindered the activities of the entrepreneurs. This
judgment is at the least overstated. One may readily admit that
the injunctions of the Church led to the adoption of subterfuges
which consumed time and were probably wasteful. They caused
banking operations pure and simple to be disguised as exchange
contracts. In the end the overwhelming need for credit led the
theologians to excel themselves in finding ways to circumvent
the obstacles which they had themselves erected, until their
sophisticated casuistry brought discredit upon the whole
apparatus of scholastic economics.

The largest loans, it has already been noted, were made to
kings, princes and public bodies. The Italian cities frequently
resorted to forced loans, and in many cases the municipal debts
became consolidated and paid interest at a fixed rate. The canonists in general admitted that those who were compelled to lend
their money to the city were entitled to interest upon it. When
city bonds were sold as if they were annuities or rent charges,
objections were sometimes made on theological grounds, but there

is no evidence that the practice was significantly inhibited thereby.

Kings sometimes borrowed heavily from companies such as the Florentine houses of Bardi and Peruzzi, often on the security of revenue to be derived from specific taxes. All too often the royal debtors defaulted, and the failure of Edward III to honour his debts led to the collapse of the Florentine banking houses to which he was indebted. The Medici in the following century faced the same problem. Too much of their capital was immobilised in long-term loans, many of them to the king of England, which was the precarious condition of doing business in foreign countries. Perhaps the risk inherent in any loan to a ruling prince exempted it from the injunctions against usury.

The canon lawyers condemned no less strongly – and here they were joined by the great body of consumers – other forms of gain, amongst them the formation of price rings and the engrossing or monopolising of certain commodities, especially foodstuffs. The margin between engrossing the grain supply of a community and the legitimate speculation in wheat was a fine one, which the canonists never defined satisfactorily. They contented themselves with a blanket condemnation of all forms of monopoly.

The labourer was entitled to a 'just wage' just as commodities should be sold at a 'just price'. The scholastic economists, however, never distinguished clearly between cost and price. It was held by a few that the price at which an article was offered for sale in the market should be the sum of the costs of the material of which it was made and of the labour which had been expended in making and marketing it. Such a theory was too divorced from reality to be taken seriously. Aquinas considered that price depended upon usefulness, utility or human wants. Price was determined by the market. In the words of his contemporary, Accursius, *res tantum valet quantum vendi potest*. According to San Bernardino the correct price was that which was established as a result of the haggling of the market.[7] The theologians gave little thought to the question of price regulation. They admitted that in times of scarcity, it was desirable or even necessary, and accepted the idea that it should be related to the cost of producing the commodity in question.

It seems also to have been assumed that labour was a commodity, whose value was also to be established by market conditions. The 'just wage', like the 'just price', was to be fixed by competition and free bargaining. Here we again see the medieval condemnation of monopoly. San Bernardino claimed that the skilled worker commanded a higher wage than the unskilled because his skills gave him a scarcity value, and it was admitted that the unskilled masses might be compelled to accept something less than a living wage. In general, combinations amongst workers to raise wages or to improve conditions of work were condemned as interference with the free play of market forces. The canonists would probably have condemned both regulatory governmental practice, such as the Statute of Labourers, enacted shortly after the Black Death (1351), and also such proletarian movements as that of the Ciompi, of which the Florentine moralists might well have had bitter memories. It is with good reason that de Roover has found in the sermons of the fifteenth-century Florentine, Sant' Antonio, a remarkable anticipation of the ideas of Adam Smith.

## MEDIEVAL BANKING

Many, perhaps most, of the loans made in medieval society were from one individual to another, often on the security of some item of personal property. Banking developed when deposits made with a banker were used both to make loans to third parties and, by book transfers, to effect payments from one individual to another. Medieval banking developed almost certainly from the activities of money-changers. The latter provided a necessary service in view of the various currencies in circulation and the debased condition of much of the coinage. Nothing would have been simpler than for a money-changer to accept coins of one currency against the future payment of those of another, or to have made an advance under similar conditions. In the course of the twelfth century deposits were increasingly made with the money-changers, who used the deposits to make loans. This primitive form of banking was fraught with grave dangers. A run on the money-changer might find him without the liquid assets to meet the demands of his creditors. Such bankruptcies were sometimes severely punished.

By the end of the twelfth century the Templars were serving, in effect, as bankers to the kings of France and England, and were lending money which they were in process of transferring from the Papal tax collectors to Rome. In the early years of the thirteenth century Italians were making loans to German and other ecclesiastics visiting Rome, repayable sometimes at the fairs of Champagne. Clearly some form of international clearance had been devised. The money-changers, in fact, played a very valuable role at the fairs, making book entries of deposits and loans, transferring credits in their books from one merchant to another, and rendering a final accounting at the conclusion of the fairs.

Banking in the twelfth and thirteenth centuries was a relatively simple operation, calling for little capital and few records. The banker sat and did business at a bench or counter (Italian: *banca*). His ledger, in which all transactions were entered, was the only legally valid record of his transactions. These had necessarily to be done verbally, and in person. A well-known sixteenth-century painting by Marinus of Romenwael shows the banker seated at his table, his journal opened in front of him, while a client whispers instructions for the transfer of money or payment of a debt into his ear. The banker had thus to be accessible. In Florence he set up his table on the Rialto. He travelled from fair to fair, carrying relatively little money, but expecting to receive payment of sums owing to him, often on the security of goods brought to the fairs for sale.

The use of written instructions to a banker developed slowly, and the negotiable cheque had barely made its appearance at the end of the Middle Ages. Bankers had necessarily to be in close touch with one another, so that they could adjust their claims against one another. This was simple in those Italian cities which became noted for their banking services, Piacenza, Lucca or Florence. Elsewhere, however, it was the fairs which acted as periodic meeting places for bankers. They provided periodic clearing-houses, at which bankers could adjust their interregional claims. The fairs became, in fact, the scenes of a very large part of Europe's long-distance commercial transactions, and at certain periods they were the most important single centres of commercial and financial activity. Usher has described how the system operated:

In the great fairs, credit was organised in the simplest possible manner. A buyer was required to make a transfer of credit on the books of a fair banker to be completed at the close of the fair. . . . The

410

entry on the banker's book was a special kind of time obligation. It was a guarantee by the banker, but it was not a loan. The buyer was presumed to have credits on his account at that moment or to have goods for sale which would enable him to put the banker in funds before payment could be demanded.[8]

Each of the Champagne fairs had concluded (see p. 356) with a period of several days when accounts were balanced and settlements made. After the decline of the fairs early in the fourteenth century their financial functions were transferred to Chalon-sur-Saône, and then to Geneva, whose long-established fairs, reconfirmed in 1420, served the same role, though in rather less organised fashion, as the earlier Champagne fairs. About 1462, thanks in large measure to the manipulations of Louis XI of France, its commercial functions both as mart and as clearing-house, passed to the fairs of Lyons. At the central European fairs also bankers kept a record of transactions and settled accounts at intervals. At the great wool fairs of Medina del Campo, in Castile, all transactions were cleared by the bankers, who compared balances every second day throughout the period of the fair, 'so that many payments were liquidated or reduced to a form that would make it possible for the individual merchant to apply all his credits to the payment of all his debts'.[9] At the peak of their prosperity the Medina del Campo fairs, it is said, had the services of fourteen or fifteen bankers.

In the fourteenth century the bill of exchange evolved as the chief means of making a banking transaction at a distance. It was not a cheque because it was not a negotiable document. It was a request to a banker to make a disbursement (see below, p. 415), and its growing use in the the later Middle Ages added immeasurably to the volume of banking transactions.

The early bankers were small men who set up their counters and did business, moving from one site to another according to the commercial 'season'. But financial transactions were never divorced from trade. Merchants needed to remit funds, to grant credit and make loans. The large family 'companies' which emerged in the north Italian cities in the thirteenth century combined all these functions with the purchase and sale of wool and cloth. The bigger they became, the more they tended to emphasise their financial operations. The tendency, from the late thirteenth century for the merchants to sit at home in their counting houses and to emply *fattori* in the cities with which they did business, allowed them to increase enormously the scale of their business and to become immensely wealthy.

Italian merchant-bankers and their agents appeared in London as early as 1224. By the mid-thirteenth century their numbers and their commercial and financial methods shocked the English chronicler, Matthew Paris, who denounced their usurious practices. Their numbers increased as more and more of the Italian merchant-banking houses established factors in the cities of north-western Europe. The earliest of these international banking houses were based in Piacenza, Lucca and Siena, but towards the end of the thirteenth century the focus of banking activity shifted to Florence. A large number of banks was established. Most appear to have been family partnerships, though some admitted outsiders to membership. The largest – the Bardi, Peruzzi and Acciaiuoli – were centralised companies, in each of which all operations were controlled from the central counting house in Florence. They were also companies with unlimited liability, and when in 1341 Edward III of England defaulted on his debts he brought about the bankruptcy of the Peruzzi (1343) and of the Bardi (1346).[10] The profits of these large banking companies were not large, perhaps 10 to 12 per cent, far too little to bear the loss of about £180,000 on their transactions in London.

No banks of comparable size emerged after the collapse of these Florentine enterprises. The Datini undertakings (see p. 351) were a series of shortlived partnerships between members of the Datini family, or between a Datini and one or more outsiders. These were separate and autonomous undertakings, and the failure of any one of them had no direct effect on any of the others. The Medici bank, the most famous financial institution of the late Middle Ages, was also a group of partnerships, in each of which a member of the Medici family figured as a principal. The bank received deposits which were safe from confiscation for political reasons. The Despencers had, in the concluding years of the reign of Edward II, stowed away immense sums with the Bardi and Peruzzi, in much the same way that modern adventurers have secreted their gains in Switzerland. The deposits with the Medici bank in the less certain times of the fifteenth century were even larger, and gave the Medici partnership greater security in their financial manipulations. The Medici were also used to transmit funds derived from papal taxation to Rome, an obligation which caused them no little trouble and inconvenience because of the unbalanced nature of late medieval trade between Italy and north-western Europe.

The business of the Medici bank was assisted at one time or another by its control of no less than ten branches. In addition to the public bank at Florence, known as the *Tavola*, the company controlled branches at Rome, Pisa and Venice. A subsidiary at Naples proved to be unprofitable and was closed – a comment on the economic decline of southern Italy. On the other hand, a branch was established at Milan, mainly to provide services for the court and government of the Sforza. Outside Italy the chief regional branch of the bank was at Bruges, for which the London office served as a kind of satellite. An office in Avignon declined in importance after the Popes had abandoned the city, and was closed. Another in Marseilles was shortlived. The only other branches were at the fair town of Geneva, which remained an important centre of banking activity until about 1465, when the activities of the Medici bank were transferred to Lyons (see p. 438).

The Medici bank had fewer branches or factors than the great banks of the fourteenth century. Its activities were more circumscribed, and it took fewer risks. Nevertheless the scale of its activities and the extent of its profits contracted sharply in the last third of the fifteenth century. Very many of its smaller rivals became bankrupt during this period. For this there were several reasons. Foremost amongst them was the unbalanced nature of late medieval trade. Italian exports to north-western Europe were insufficiently requited by the movement of cloth and English wool, and the flow of central European silver into the international trading system was inadequate to restore a balance in visible trade. In consequence the Medici and other banks were accumulating assets in the books of their Bruges subsidiary, which they were quite unable to remit to Florence or to use commercially in other directions. Events might have been quite different if the Italian commercial bankers had been able to establish trading relations with the German Hanse. The failure of the Mediterranean and Baltic spheres of commercial activity to establish a productive association with one another may have been the most significant factor in the economic decline of both.

A second factor in the decline of the Medici and of other Italian banks was the war in the Levant. The Florentines were deeply committed financially to Venetian trade with the eastern Mediterranean. The volume of this trade was in any event declining during the later fifteenth century. It was interrupted by the Turkish war of 1463–79, which was followed by the siege of Rhodes and a Muslim attack on southern Italy. The Medici bank lost heavily in the military defeat of Venice. Add to these two factors the unprofitability of much of the Medici investment. Political circumstances compelled them to lend heavily to governments and to subsidise the civil strife within Italy which was at the same time stifling the trade which supported it. It was, however, none of these which finally brought the activities of this, the greatest of the late medieval banking enterprises, to a close. In 1494 the French armies of Charles VIII entered Italy. Late in the year they occupied Florence. The Medici fled; their bank ceased to function, and a crippling fine was imposed on the city.

The glamour which surrounds the international banks, such as that of the Medici, tends to distract attention from the hundreds of small enterprises which continued throughout both the later Middle Ages and also modern times to provide for local needs. It might even be the case that in hard times their services became even more necessary. Pawnbroking, carried on in some areas under licence from the local authorities, was generally condemned by the Church and widely used by the laity. Money-changers continued to combine the exchanging of currency with dealing in jewellery and the making of small, short-term loans. Such activities are poorly documented, but there is no reason to assume that they shared in any way in the fortunes of the great banks.

At almost exactly the time when the commercial empire of the Medici was extinguished, that of the Fuggers was greatly extended by their involvement in the copper and silver mines of Slovakia (see p. 476). The family had been weavers and cloth merchants in Augsburg. Late in the fifteenth century they diversified their holdings, perhaps as an insurance against the decline of the Italian and Levantine cloth trade. They chose to invest in the non-ferrous metal industries at a time when these were expanding. Their usual procedure was to lend on the security of the mine itself. They thus received the Schwaz silver mine in Tyrol when the previous operators defaulted on their debt. By the end of the century the Fuggers had established a virtual monopoly of the central European copper market. 'About 1525,' wrote Ehrenberg,[11] 'the Fuggers were, beyond dispute, the most influential financiers of their time', and their speculations and investments were spread from Spain to Poland, from Antwerp to Naples. The mantle of Lorenzo di Medici of Florence had fallen upon Jacob Fugger of Augsburg. The change was symbolic in several ways. It marked the end of the Italian style of international banking; it represented a shift away from the production of consumers' goods and towards investment in capital goods. Above all it denoted a movement of the locus of economic activity away from Italy and the Mediterranean and towards central and northern Europe.

## THE BILL OF EXCHANGE

The activity and the profits of the Italian banking and commercial houses were founded upon the use of the bill of exchange. This simple, almost laconic, but highly flexible instrument allowed vast sums of money to be moved from one account to another, from one part of Europe to another in as short a time as it took for a courier to make the journey between them. The earliest surviving bills of exchange were drawn in the first half of the fourteenth century. They were, however, preceded by more formal financial instruments, the notarial acts. This was a document drawn up by a notary recording the fact that *A* had received a loan in, let us say, Genoa, in the local currency, and promised to repay at, say, the fair at Provins, a given sum in livres tournois to the lender or his agent.

The circumstances of such a loan, which must have been made many thousands of times in the Italian cities in the course of the fourteenth and early fifteenth centuries, are easy to understand. *A* wishes to take a consignment of merchandise for sale at the Champagne fairs. He borrows a sum of money to allow him to purchase the goods, and undertakes, after he has disposed of them successfully, to repay the loan, but in the different currency which he will have received for them. This notarial act was formally recorded in the books of the notary, and this served as legal proof that the loan had been paid. One must assume that the agent for the creditor, who received repayment at Provins, looked for someone who would borrow a similar sum for the purchase of, let us say, Flemish cloth, which could be transmitted to Genoa and sold, thus allowing the original creditor to be repaid.

The system was simple. The notarial act covered both a loan and an exchange. Interest had, of course, to be paid on the loan, and thus was subsumed in the sum which had to be paid to the creditor's account at Provins. The uncertainty of the exchange was sufficient to introduce a small element of uncertainty into the transaction, and this proved adequate to circumvent the rules of the Church. This kind of exchange contract was devised in the interests of long-distance trade. It came to be used, however, as a means of disguising a direct loan as an exchange transaction and thus evading the canonical rules. Such was known as a 'dry exchange' contract. It provided for repayment in a different currency and at a different place, but incorporated an option by which the borrower might elect to repay the loan at the place at which he had negotiated it originally.

The following is a somewhat abbreviated dry exchange contract, drawn up at Genoa in 1188:[12] 'We, Girardo de Valle and Tommaso de Valle, acknowledge that we have received from you, Beltrame Bertaldo, banker, a number of (deniers) Genoese for which (we promise to pay) £4 Provisine (i.e. currency of Provins) to you or your accredited messenger at the next May fair of Provins.' So far it is a normal contract by which a merchant obtained credit to carry on his business. The notary adds, however, 'And if we do not do this, we promise to pay you on our next return from the same fair for every 12 (deniers) Provisine 16 (deniers) Genoese until you are fully paid.' The sum originally lent is not specified, so that it is impossible to calculate the rate of interest. The option to repay at Provins was not to be taken seriously, and the journey to Champagne was probably fictitious. This was, in reality, a simple loan to be repaid, along with a probably high rate of interest, at the place at which it was originally contracted.

Each exchange contract, whether or not it genuinely related to long-distance trade, required the services of a notary, who wrote out the conditions clearly and unambiguously. This was probably necessary at a time when most traders could neither read nor write. But in the fourteenth century the growing volume of business and the greater sophistication of merchants themselves suggested a somewhat simpler method of conducting their financial business. The result was the bill of exchange. The validity of the notarial instrument had been guaranteed by the name of the notary who had drawn it, and by those of its witnesses. The bill of exchange, on the other hand, was a holograph. It was written in a handwriting that was readily identifiable by the person to whom it was sent. Cases are known of the rejection of a bill because the drawee did not recognise the style of calligraphy. The following is a typical bill of exchange:

> To: Francesco di Marco and Luca del Sera in Barcelona (1) In the name of God, the 12th of February 1399 Pay at usance by this first of exchange, to Giovanni Asopardo (2) £306 13s. 4d. Barcelonisi, which are for 400 florins received here from Bartolemo Garzoni (3), at 15s. 4d. per florin. Pay and charge to our account there and reply. God keep you Francesco and Andrea (di Bonanno), (4), greetings from Genoa.

(and in a different hand)

> Accepted March 13. Set down in Red Book B, f.97.[13]

In this, as in most bills of exchange, there were four parties: Bartolomeo Garzoni (3) has bought a bill for 400 Genoese florins from Francesco and Andrea di Bonanno (4), who declare that they have received the money. The bill is then sent by Garzoni to Francesco di Marco and Luca del Sera (1), bankers in Barcelona, in whose books the di Bonanno brothers have an account; di Marco and del Sera accept the bill, since there is sufficient money in the di Bonanno account. They pay the amount specified in Barcelona currency to Giovanni Asopardo (2); mark the bill as accepted, with the date, and make the appropriate transfers in their ledger. The whole transaction can be represented in simple, diagrammatic form (Fig. 9.1). Garzoni has purchased currency of Barcelona. This may, of course, have been used to discharge a commercial obligation; Asopardo *may* have shipped merchandise to him previously. On the other hand, he may have sought to acquire money in Barcelona at a time when it was cheap, relative to other currencies. It is not without significance that the whole transaction took place in February and March. According to a fifteenth century merchants' manual, *El libro di mercatantie et usanze de' paesi*,[14] 'In Barcelona it (i.e. the local currency) is dear from June continuously up to August – in June on account of the wool and in July on account of the grain and rice harvested in Valencia. And it is dear throughout October also, because of the saffron.'

417

**Figure 9.1 A typical bill of exchange transaction**

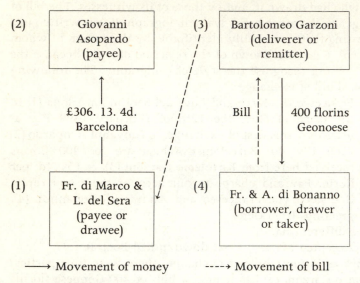

⟶ Movement of money     ----⟶ Movement of bill

It is probable, though this is pure conjecture, that the Barcelona currency was, in this instance, held until the summer following in the account of Giovanni Asopardo, and was then used to purchase grain which was shipped to Italy. Alternatively the sum held in Garzoni's account in Barcelona may have been used just to remit money to Genoa at a time when the exchange rates had tipped in favour of the Spanish and against the Italian currency. In this way the exchange operation was completed; the original deliverer (3) received back his money as a credit or in the form of merchandise.

Large profits were to be made on such transactions. Bankers were aware of the fluctuations in the exchange. When a shipment of spices left Venice for the Low Countries they well knew that Venetian ducats would be in great demand in Bruges a month hence. The regular and rapid courier service between financial centres allowed the Italian merchant to make ducats available at the right time to secure the maximum advantage from the exchange. The idea that a bill of exchange was only a means of payment in a commercial transaction is, wrote de Roover, *tout simplement, de la haute fantaisie.*[15] Of the thousands of bills of exchange which survive in the Datini archives, the majority

418

probably relate to such speculative exchanges. It was the speculative character of such contracts which kept them clear of ecclesiastical condemnation.

The bill of exchange quoted above called upon the drawee to 'pay at usance' the given sum in the currency of Barcelona. A period of time necessarily elapsed between the drawing of a bill and the time when it was presented for payment. In this particular case it was a little over four weeks. Usance was the term given to the period of time which by common consent should elapse between the drawing and the paying of a bill. It varied according to the distance that the bill had to be transmitted, and for every banking centre there was an agreed schedule of usance for every other. A table of usance from Florence is:[16]

| Town | days | Town | days |
|------|------|------|------|
| Avignon | 30 | Barcelona | 60 |
| Bologna | 6 | Bruges | 60 |
| Geneva | next fair | Genoa | 8 |
| London | 90 | Naples | 10 |
| Palermo | 30 | Pisa | 3 |
| Rome | 10 | Valencia | 60 |
| Venice | 5 | | |

Nothing shows more clearly than this table, and others which might have been compiled for every city in the list, the high level of international organisation of medieval finance and the regularity with which financial transactions were conducted. The bill of exchange was a simple and flexible instrument; it lent itself to many modifications and a variety of uses during the later Middle Ages. A network of financial interdependence of extraordinary complexity was built up. In the last resort the movement of commodities or of bullion was necessary to redress a financial balance, but any commercial transaction was likely to be hedged by complicated financial manoeuvres. Andrea Barbarigo of Venice, in order to purchase cotton in Damascus or wool in Spain, found it necessary to make drafts on London and Bruges. Europe was never again to know such financial unity until recent years.

One financial instrument was not significantly used during the Middle Ages: the negotiable cheque. A bill of exchange was not a negotiable document. It was drawn by one party and accepted (or not) by another. That was all; it could not, suitably endorsed, be passed on from one person to another for the satisfaction of their debts, as if it were a form of paper money, until it at last came home to the bank on which it was drawn. The cheque would have solved a number of the problems of the merchant-banker, though it would not altogether have served the speculative ends to which the bill of exchange was put.

In the previous chapter a short sketch was presented of the medieval merchant. Most, it was seen, rose from humble beginnings. Few families remained in commerce for more than two or three generations, and the most successful of them tended to invest their savings in land, which offered them a quieter life and a more secure income. The fortunes of some, such as Jacques Cœur, collapsed as suddenly as they had grown. Merchants, or at least the more fortunate of them, began to accumulate wealth, when they abandoned the road themselves and controlled trade from their counting houses in the commercial cities. Long-distance trade had always been fraught with grave dangers, and none more so than sea-borne trade. The merchant rarely, if ever, entrusted all his wealth to a single voyage. He quickly learned to spread his risks, and developed a number of contractual forms which answered his needs.

One of the earliest of such contracts between the sedentary merchant on the one hand and the trader who ventured with his cargo to distant parts was the sea-loan. It derived from a classical maritime contract. The merchant lent money or merchandise to a ship's master, who repaid them only if the voyage was successful. Conditions were apt to vary greatly, but the not inconsiderable risk assumed by the stay-at-home partner in the transaction was in general held to justify the interest he received. Later, however, the sea-loan was pronounced usurious, until it became the custom to provide in the contract for the return of the principal, together with a share of the profit, in a different currency. In this *cambium maritimum*, as in the bill of exchange, interest or profit was disguised in the rate of exchange.

From the sea-loan evolved the more usual *commenda* or *societas maris*. The investor contributed a fraction of the capital in an overseas venture, while a partner assumed responsibility for the voyage and for disposing of the cargo. At the end of the voyage the profit was divided in pre-arranged proportions, commonly three-quarters for the sedentary and one-quarter for the travelling partner. The *commenda* bears the marks of a straightforward investment by a capitalist in a maritime venture over which he had no control. In fact, the contract evolved into very many distinct forms. The travelling partner, often called the *tractator* in the contract, might make agreements with more than one *stans*, or sleeping partner. The latter might, in fact, play a very active role in the venture, short, however, of going on the voyage. Canon law tended to regard the *commenda* as a partnership, in which risk was borne equally by all involved in the transaction. There were doubtless many cases in which it was in fact little better than usury.

The *commenda* contract had been devised to meet the needs of sea-borne trade. Institutional forms were also developed for trade by land. The latter differed from maritime trade, at least as far as the Italian city republics were concerned, in its smaller element of risk and in the fact that it did not call for capital investment in a ship. The result was the *compagnia*, a form of partnership in which two or more advanced the capital and shared the profit, though none of them, in all probability, accompanied the merchandise. This was the general form assumed by the partnerships in which the Datini (see p. 351) and many other familiar medieval merchants carried on their business.

The high degree of risk in medieval travel and trade called for some form of insurance. Risks were greatest by sea, but there is no evidence that the travelling merchant ever took steps, other than travelling in convoy, to protect his goods. The sedentary trader who entered into a sea-loan or a partnership probably did nothing more than spread his risks over as many ventures as possible. Genuine insurance, as Mrs Edler de Roover has shown, 'was a product of the commercial revolution which occurred . . . from 1275 to 1325 or thereabouts'.[17]

The earliest sea-loans had incorporated no element of insurance, in so far as the sedentary partner received back his investment only if the cargo reached its destination. Towards the end of the thirteenth century instances became more frequent in the notarial records of the precise division of the risk between the parties to the venture. It was not until the mid-fourteenth century, so the surviving records show, that attempts were made to spread the risk beyond the partners. In 1350 a premium of 18 per cent was paid on a cargo of wheat shipped from Sicily to Tunis. Thereafter the number of known cases increases rapidly. The Datini instructed their agents not to ship any merchandise without insurance. It does not appear that the insurance was for the whole consignment, nor did a single underwriter cover the whole risk. It was usual, before a ship sailed, to invite several underwriters to cover a fraction of its cargo. Even so, it was not always easy to secure sufficient insurance on some ventures. War and marine risks were usually covered, but damage to the goods through neglect and arrest by foreign authorities seem not to have been.

The premium was likely to vary with the season of sailing and the type of ship. Cargoes carried by galleys, perhaps naturally, paid a lower premium than those shipped in the slower nefs and cogs. War and piratical action would send up the premium. A table of premia paid by the Florentine merchant, Barnardo Cambri, has been published by Mrs de Roover. They range from one per cent on a short Italian coasting voyage to fourteen per cent for winter voyages with cargoes of wine from La Rochelle to the Low Countries. It is evident that insurance rates were high, higher, it would appear than the actual risks merited. The medieval underwriters lacked a statistical basis for the assessment of risks, and thus tended to panic and raise their rates sharply when they received news of maritime danger. Some merchants did not insure their cargoes. The practice did not become general in England until the late sixteenth century, and even in Venice some merchants are said not to have insured cargoes shipped on galleys.

Goods travelling by land were occasionally insured in the fifteenth century, but the practice appears to have been rare. Known cases related in general to goods which were transported partly by sea, partly by land, and a single premium was quoted for the whole journey.

## MEDIEVAL BOOK-KEEPING

The sophisticated financial manipulations of the Italian merchants and bankers in the fourteenth and fifteenth centuries called for a no less developed method of keeping their accounts. Such early account books as have survived show a confusing medley of entries relating to purchases and sales, with occasional notes of an entirely private nature. Such methods of book-keeping were quite inadequate for the needs of the Italian merchant-banker who dealt in bills of exchange as well as in merchandise from all parts of Europe. In the course of the thirteenth century he learned to keep his credit and debit entries separate from one another, either on different pages or in different ledgers. By the early fourteenth century a form of double-entry book-keeping was in use in Genoa, and had probably been evolved even earlier in Tuscany. It came to be used by the factors and representatives of the Italian banking houses in the chief financial centres of western Europe, but apart from this was not widely accepted outside Italy.

The following passage is quoted from an account book of the first half of the fourteenth century, kept by a merchant of Carcassonne:

> Senher Ber of St Esteve, nobleman, lord of Lastours, owes 4s. which we lent him. To be paid . . . on October 3.
>
> Mosenher the mayor judge of Carcassonne owes 18s for 3 palms of medley French, which was for the lining of the cape which Maestro Crestia Rocafort took. Paid 18s.
>
> Riquart, wife of the late En Adam of Rovenay, of the city of Carcassonne, owes 10s for 2 palms of vermilion and for $1\frac{1}{2}$ palms of white, which was for hose with edging for her, which she took on Wednesday, October 4th. Also she owes 1d. Also, she owes 1d. Also, she owes 1d. Also, she owes 1d. Remains (to be paid) 10s 4d. Also, she owes 1d. Paid 3s 11d medal. Paid 6s 5d medal.
>
> Senher Uc Garie, £11 for 4 canas of cameli (cloth). Paid £11.
>
> Senher Peyre Fabre of Pomas owes 4d. which we lent to James Rog of Villefranche de Conflent. Also, he owes 15 *gold dobles* because of what we lent him on Sunday, October 8. Paid in full.[18]

It is a far cry from such confusion to the careful double-entry accounting of the following excerpt from the Venetian archives.[19] Here each transaction appears twice as a credit and as a debit entry. Each client of a banker or merchant would have a separate page or pages, so that it could be seen at a glance how business relations with him stood.

How important, it has been asked, was the introduction and spread of double-entry book-keeping? Sombart and many other historians of the rise of modern capitalist institutions have treated it as a corner-stone of capitalism, permitting the analysis of each business transaction and the more careful and profitable planning of future actions. It depersonalised business, it was held, and

+ Jesus Mcccc° xxij j

Mr. John Mantegan )f Spilimbergo *Dr.* on 17th March for 12 parcels of *mosto vallieri* of Como and for 11 webs of cloth at 16½ ducats the web – amount net, as entered in the book kept for Mr. D. and Mr. James, page 71, in this book page 97£xvii    i    ii —

+ Jesus Mcccc° xxij j

Mr. John per contra *Cr.* on the 15th December, per Mr. Andrew di Priuli, on account of monies received, as entered in the book kept for Mr. D. and Mr. James at page 71, in this book page 72 £xvii — — — and at same date, for moneys deposited by his factor, as appears as above at page 71, in this book page 103 £—    i    ii —

Mr. Rasmo de Viena of Neustadt *Dr.* on 11th May for 11 parcels of pepper, weight 86 pounds . . . ounces net at 93½ ducats per c a n t a r r o (?). Amount net, as entered in the book kept for Mr. D. and Mr. James page 71, in this book page 92 £xviiii xviij vi 12

Mr. Rasmo *Cr.* per contra on the 12th May per Mr. Nicholas Cocco and Mr. Anthony Miorati for pepper, as entered as above page 71, in this book page 85 £xviiii xviij vi 12

isolated the pursuit of profit as the principal, indeed, the only object of the trader. On the other hand, there is no clear evidence that the medieval merchant regularly or periodically cast up his accounts and struck a balance. The use of double-entry book-keeping could bring order to a merchant's records. It is very doubtful whether merchants 'required anything more from their ledgers and journals than a clear and ready record of transactions for easy reference, and descriptive details of their cash, merchandise, and other assets bought and sold.'[20] Double-entry bookkeeping was a convenience but its introduction in the fourteenth century clearly had no revolutionary consequences.

## THE MERCHANTS' LAW

The conduct of merchants was governed by a body of customary law known as the *lex mercatoria*. It was not completely consistent in all parts of western and southern Europe. It grew up in response to local conditions, but in the course of time certain general principles came to prevail. Though sometimes reaffirmed by statute law, the basis of the merchants' law was custom, the way things were normally done in Visby or Oléron or Barcelona. Everywhere, however, it provided for summary procedures and prompt justice; the trader had no time to wait upon the pleasure of the royal courts. The interpretation of the merchants' law, lastly, was founded on equity. Its courts were not bound by the legal and institutional subtlety of the courts of the land; they gave their judgments on the basis of what seemed equitable and right.

From as early as the ninth century merchants began to acquire exclusive jurisdiction over the disputes which arose between them. This was confirmed by various royal enactments, above all, in charters authorising the creation of merchant gilds. This was especially the case in Italy, where some gilds even claimed the right to hear in the gild courts cases between merchants and non-merchants, provided they related to commercial matters. It was at the fairs and markets, however, that courts held under the merchants' law acquired the greatest importance. This was in part due to the fact that speedy decisions were essential, but partly because many cases inevitably related to disputes between merchants of more than one nation. It was important that the travelling merchant should be subject to a law whose broad principles he knew and understood. The court of 'pie-powder', or *pied poudré*, acquired a reputation for its speedy and equitable justice.

The Law Merchant was concerned primarily with sales and contracts between merchants and with the right of merchants to travel and do business without fear of illicit restrictions or of having their goods sequestrated for the debts of others. The decline of the fairs as commodity markets detracted greatly from the significance of the merchants' courts, but business was, in effect, only transferred to those of the urban merchant gilds. These, especially in the Italian cities, were faced with a considerable body of cases touching mainly the interpretation and breach of com-

425

mercial contracts of all kinds. It is not difficult to see in this body of custom the origins of international law.

Trade was burdened throughout the Middle Ages by a serious shortage of currency. There had long been a drain of specie towards the East (see p. 116). This was partially remedied as the precious metals were brought out of hoards and minted, and new metal came on to the market from the mines. But there was a strict limit to the former, and medieval mining was not, until the later years of the fifteenth century, notably successful. Specie continued in the fourteenth century to be drained eastwards. The Tartars, to whom the Italians were turning increasingly for their supply of spices and oriental products, used only a silver currency. So, too, did the Egyptians, who constituted the alternative source of such wares.

At the same time demand increased for small currency. Armies had to be paid and supplies procured, and for these purposes the silver penny and the smaller pieces of 'black money', minted mainly from copper with only a trace of silver, were in demand. There were periods in the mid-fourteenth century – such was the scarcity of silver – when the royal moneyers in France could mint no new money at all. Even without the financial stringencies of governments, which led them to reduce the silver content of their coinage, there would have been a progressive debasement owing to the shortage of metal.[21] The depreciation of the silver currency, noted in chapter 3, continued in the later Middle Ages. The number of grammes of silver to the pound-tale (i.e. 240 pennies) fell in France, between 1250 and 1500, from 80 to 22; in Genoa, from 70 to 13, and in Milan from 70 to 9. At Venice and Florence the drop was from 20 to 6 and 35 to 6 respectively.

The debasement of the coinage was, in most countries, carefully controlled. This, in turn, necessitated a strict licensing and supervision of the moneyers who struck the coins. They were told exactly how many coins were to be struck from a given weight of metal.[22] The older and intrinsically more valuable coins were recalled and melted, except, of course, for the doubtless considerable number which were driven out of circulation, surreptitiously melted down, and the metal exported, perhaps to the Levant.

Depreciation brought with it a need for units of higher value.[23]
Quite early in the thirteenth century, a groat or *grosso* had been
minted at Venice. It was of finer metal than the denarius as well as
larger, and was equated with 24 of the latter. Other Italian cities
followed with their variously named *grossi*. Most were worth
twelve denarii, and were thus related, if only in name, to the
shilling. Later in the thirteenth century a *gros* was minted in
France, and later in most states of western Europe. In the Empire it
was known as the *groschen*. In England a groat, worth four silver
pennies, was issued regularly from 1351. Even the *grossi* were
progressively debased over much of Europe by reducing the
fineness of the silver. The denarii, or pennies, and their fractional
units, the halfpenny and farthing, were, in the meanwhile,
reduced to 'black money', billon or vellon, which consisted
largely of copper or other base metal, with only a few percentage
points of silver. Such small change was important in an economy
which centred increasingly in the market, and it was always in
short supply. On the other hand these small coins cost as much to
strike as the larger and more reputable currency, while the
rewards to the moneyers were very much smaller. Unquestionably far less was minted than the economy needed, and this helps
to explain the retention in some parts of Europe of a system of
small-scale barter throughout the Middle Ages.

The need of commerce for large denominations was met
finally by the minting of gold coins. A debased hyperperon
continued to be used in the Byzantine Empire, and Muslim gold
dinars continued to circulate, but in the West the minting of gold
coins had been interrupted since the eighth century. In 1252 both
Genoa and Florence returned to a gold currency with respectively
the *genovino* and the *florin*, and were followed by Venice with its
gold ducat. The French produced a variety of gold coins from the
late thirteenth century, until in 1385 they began to mint the *écu*,
known also as the crown, which continued until the seventeenth
century to be the élite French coinage. Gold coinages were also
minted in the fifteenth century by Dukes of Burgundy and by
some of the princes of the Rhineland. Even the gold coinage of the
later Middle Ages went the way of the silver, and was gradually
debased, though in England the rate of devaluation was a great
deal less than in most other countries. Only the élite coinages of
Florence and Venice, the florin and the ducat, maintained their

427

gold content and provided a model for other and newer currencies.

A disconcerting feature of the currency systems of the later Middle Ages was the failure of the several units within any one system to maintain a steady relationship to one another. The silver denarii, for example, fluctuated in value against the gold currency, with a general tendency, however, to depreciate. This is, of course, the perennial problem with a bimetal system of currency. It is, perhaps, more remarkable that the silver coinages within a single system should not maintain a constant relationship with one another. The denarius, or 'little' penny, tended in general to depreciate as against the *grosso*. The relationship of currencies to one another was a constant preoccupation of the merchant. So also was their integration into the system of money of account which he used in his bookkeeping (see p. 119). He was helped by the tendency to fit a new coinage into the existing system. In much of southern and western Europe the *grosso* was conceived as the equivalent of twelve pennies, and thus as a sou or a shilling in the money of account. Where this was not the case, as in Venice, two systems of account came into use and lasted until the 'little' penny ceased to be current.

Most of the coins struck by the medieval moneyers circulated in

Fig. 9.2   Some typical late ancient and medieval coins:

(a) A bronze *nummia* of Justinian of 538–9. The reverse shows the date of the minting.
(b) A silver dirhem of Umaiyad Spain, 772.
(c) A gold dinar of Harun-al-Rashid of the Abbasid Caliphate, 801.
(d) A silver penny (*denarius*) of Charlemagne; his name appears on the obverse and the name of the mint (*Mogontia*, Mainz) on the reverse.
(e) A silver penny of Philip II of France, 1180–1223. Note the broad similarity to the Carolingian penny.
(f) A French écu (crown) of Charles VI of France, 1380–1422: gold.
(g) A gold *solidus* of Constantine the Great, 324–337.
(h) A gold Florentine florin of 1252; note the lily emblem of Florence.
(j) A gold Venetian ducat of 1284. On the obverse the Doge is shown kneeling before St. Mark; the reverse shows a figure of Christ, with the words around the edge: *sit tibi christe datus quem tu regis iste ducatus*. The last word of this inscription is the origin of the word ducat.
The obverse is shown to the left, and the reverse to the right. All coins are reproduced true size.

their local areas. Even some of the gold coins had no wide circulation. It would have been impossible to use the silver pennies,
which were for a long period the only effective coins, in long-
distance trade. Their weight alone would have made it impractical,
though small numbers would, of course, have circulated outside
the areas in which they were minted. A few gold hyperperons and
dinars were current in western and southern Europe before the
thirteenth century. Then, from the late thirteenth century, the
highly regarded gold currency of the Italian republics acquired
and retained a European reputation. It is interesting that the Low
Countries, the other leading commercial centre, never attempted
to produce a currency which would rival the Italian. In this, as in
almost every other aspect of economic development, the Italians
were the pioneers. Indeed, in some of these fields of activity they
found few imitators before the sixteenth century.

### THE ROLE OF GOVERNMENT

Governments cannot be said to have had an economic policy
before the later Middle Ages. In a feudal society, king or prince,
like any petty feudal lord, was expected to live of his own, to
derive all that he needed for the support of himself and his
retinue, for the conduct of his political affairs, and the waging of
his wars from the lands which he held and the feudal obligations
which were owed to him. Any attempt to broaden the basis of his
income was likely to be strenuously resisted. The first important
step was to separate off the treasury or exchequer from the household, to draw a distinction between the income and expenditure
of government and that of the royal 'family'. In the territories
which were administratively the most advanced – Flanders,
Normandy, England – this step had been taken by the early
twelfth century. France did not achieve this stage of development
for perhaps another century.

By the thirteenth century the traditional sources of governmental income – the royal domain, the profits of justice, and
feudal obligations – were shrinking in value at a time when the
obligations of government were beginning to increase. This
necessitated in every political unit, from the kingdom of France
to the city republics of Italy, a growing resort to taxation – of
property, of persons, of trade – for the support of government.
Any form of taxation is discriminatory, in so far as it cannot be

made to apply equally and fairly to all people. Almost from the start governments used their powers to tax for the purpose of aiding one sector relative to another. A crudely conceived economic policy dictated that the foreigner should be made to pay more dearly for his wool or that the king's subjects should be penalised financially for consuming an imported commodity, such as wine. Salt was taxed almost everywhere, partly because it was in universal demand, partly because its movement could be controlled.

At the same time the economic sphere of governmental action was broadened in another direction. Economic growth required that exceptions be made in the nexus of personal relations and obligations which is known as feudalism. The growth of towns, the commercial activity of markets, and the movement of traders lay, in a sense, outside the feudal order. They had to be authorised and then protected. Government – specifically the king or the terri- torial lord – granted permission for a town to be established with its own rules, an enclave, as it were, in a feudally dominated land. It extended its protection to merchants; it even attempted to control prices.

For several centuries such governmental actions were unco- ordinated and even ill-considered. They impinged on economic life, but hardly amounted to an economic policy. Indeed many of them were conceived within a feudal framework. They consisted in the delegating of regulatory powers from a government which could not or would not exercise them, to a smaller authority on a local scale which was expected to do so. The town was authorised by its charter to hold a court and, within prescribed limits and in return, usually, for a certain payment, to conduct its own affairs. The gilds were similarly charged with the supervision of their own members and the regulation of their trade and crafts. There were rulers for whom the creation of towns and stimulation of markets was an objective carefully conceived and consciously pursued, amounting to an economic policy. To many, however, the grant of a charter was a reward for services or a return for a financial payment.

In the later Middle Ages governments came to assume a more positive attitude towards economic policy. This reflected the growing power and the centralising tendencies which fore- shadowed the nation-state of modern times. The mounting scale of warfare, the growing complexity of political relations, the increase in population, all combined to place new obligations on government.

Foremost amongst the factors which led to this change in the obligations of governments was the increase in the scale of war. Armies in the eleventh and twelfth centuries, and even in much of the thirteenth in some parts of Europe, remained small and non-professional. Campaigns were short; weapons and armour, unsophisticated, and the scale of fortification relatively modest. This began to change in the course of the thirteenth century. Many of the territorial states engaged in campaigns of territorial conquest; warfare no longer consisted mainly of short, seasonal campaigns, and the soldiers became professionals, more elaborately armed and equipped and paid a wage. The building of the royal castle of Dover cost the exchequer some £16,000 during the late twelfth and the thirteenth centuries, in addition to the expenses of its garrison.[24] Such a scale of expenditure was beyond the scope of government without the imposition of special taxes.

In both England and France a general system of taxation was instituted in the late thirteenth century. It consisted of a levy or subsidy, based upon property, supplemented by poll taxes and customs duties on the export and import of specified goods. The system, developed in England under Edward I, underwent little change before the end of the Middle Ages. The French system of taxation, less clearly conceived and logically implemented, collapsed, and it was not until the closing years of the fourteenth century that direct taxes and taxes on sales were regularly levied. At about the same time, the kings of both Castile and Aragon began to impose heavy indirect taxes on the sale of commodities and on the production of certain goods, such as cloth. In Castile a major source of income was the tax on sheep, and one of the functions of the Mesta (see p. 207) was to systematise and broaden the basis of this levy.[25] The German emperors, on the other hand, failed to obtain from the Empire as a whole a tax income that could supplement the financial resources of their own dynastic estates. They did succeed in imposing a small direct levy on the imperial cities, but in emergencies had generally to rely on loans from German and occasionally Italian merchant houses. The political weakness of the later emperors is to be related to their failure to establish a regular system of taxation. The more powerful of the territorial princes of the German Empire were, in several instances, better placed financially than the emperor himself. It was their possessions in Austria which provided the larger part of the Habsburg's income. Nevertheless, the finances of the German states were as a general rule poorly managed, and the demands made upon them in the fiercely competitive atmosphere of late medieval Germany were heavy. There were few princes who were not heavily indebted most of their time to merchant bankers.

It was in Italy that the burden of public expenditure reached its highest level in relation to the size of the population. The manpower and resources of most of the city republics were relatively small; warfare was frequent, and preparation for war a continuing obligation. Extraordinary expenses, such as the cost of a campaign or the burden of rebuilding the city walls, were commonly met by the levy of forced loans on those citizens able to bear them. Money was set aside in times of peace to amortise these vast and growing obligations. Nevertheless, the debt of the city of Florence grew from about 300,000 florins early in the fourteenth century, to 3 million by 1400. Even the service of this debt was at times beyond the capacity of the city governments. 'Such an assumption of fiscal liability on the part of the government', wrote Becker,[26] 'was awesome,' and the search for revenue 'led to integration of Florentine territory, the rise of empire and a strenuous programme of mercantilism'. It became the practice to consolidate the city's debts, to pay a fixed rate of interest, and to allow shares in it to be bought and sold. Day to day expenses of government in Florence, together with debt service, were largely covered by the gabelles – taxes on sales, on commodities entering the city, and even on service.[27]

The Venetian debt was even larger. It began in the midthirteenth century, with a forced loan. Shortly afterwards this was consolidated as the *Monte Vecchio*, paying five per cent to the creditors.[28] Despite the establishment of a sinking fund to buy back the city bonds, the debt steadily increased:

| | |
|---|---|
| 1255 | 15,000 *lire a grossi* |
| 1299 | 1,500,000 |
| 1353 | 3,100,000 |
| 1395 | 10,000,000 |
| 1438 | 16,000,000 |
| 1482 | 21,500,000 (= about 8,260,000 ducats) |

Borrowing also served as a means of financing governments outside Italy. All rulers borrowed on occasion, and from the later years of the thirteenth century onwards such loans became normal. Many were short-term, and it was not until the end of the Middle Ages that the territorial states began to establish funded debts as the Italian city republics had already done. Often loans were secured on the proceeds of a particular tax; sometimes jewels or sacred relics were pledged. But always there was so considerable an element of risk in lending to princes – the losses of the Bardi and Peruzzi in their dealings with Edward III are a case in point – that it is surprising that bankers were prepared to continue the practice. The fact is, as we have already seen, that they had little alternative. Loans to the crown were, for example, the price paid by the Medici bank for shipping wool at Southampton instead of through the staple port of Calais. In many other ways the privileges of the Italians were dependent upon their willingness to accede to the demands of the English and other rulers.

During the thirteenth century the French kings relied on the Templars for loans and, in fact, kept their treasury in the Paris Temple. In 1312 Philip the Fair secured the dissolution of the Order of the Temple and himself appropriated much of their possessions in France. This was a convenient way of extinguishing his debt to them. It was not uncommon for the Jews to be treated in much the same way. Neither Philip the Fair nor most of his successors were good payers, and in the end they found it difficult to secure loans. During the closing decades of the Hundred Years' War, the needs of the French crown were overwhelming. Charles VII employed the merchant, Jacques Cœur of Bourges, to raise loans for the king's service. This he did with great success, and thus played an important role in the final reconquest of Normandy from the English. But Jacques Cœur, like many who had made their financial services available to the French kings, outlived his usefulness. He was arrested on charges which were almost certainly spurious; his possessions were confiscated, and the king's debts to him extinguished.

The rich burgesses of the cities of the Low Countries were an important source of loans. The ambitious schemes of the Dukes of Burgundy were in part financed by loans from Italian bankers, amongst whom the Medici bank was a prominent lender. Here, as in Italy, political power was less a function of population and resources than of the ability to secure credits and raise armies of mercenaries.

*A Policy of Plenty*

It has long been debated whether that body of ideas which is known as mercantilism aimed rather towards abundance of goods or towards political power; whether their object was to secure the wellbeing of the population or the security of the state. During the later Middle Ages, when these ideas took shape, both objects were pursued, though intermittently and without careful consideration of their implications.

Governments were faced, at least until the fourteenth century, with a rising population and an increasing demand for food and land. It is very doubtful whether those in authority ever had any perception of the problem in its historical perspective. They were faintly aware of its urgency at a particular moment. Locally and half-heartedly they encouraged the reclamation of the waste and the extension of cropland. The Counts of Flanders promoted the dyking and draining of fields and the creation of polders. At various times during the Middle Ages the Italian city republics saw to it that more land was brought under the plough. But, in so far as kings and princes encouraged the clearing and cultivation of land, it was in their capacity as landholders. Their objective was to increase the revenue from their own domain rather than the food supply of their kingdom. The clearing of the forest and the reclamation of the waste were, by and large, left to the local lords and seigneurs.

In time of emergency the government might take action, though not always wisely. Famine and flood stirred the authorities into action. Count Charles the Good of Flanders, early in the twelfth century, forbade the use of oats for malting and brewing in a period of famine so that the supply of grain for bread-making might be increased. Such acts can be paralleled in many parts of Europe, but very rarely is there any suggestion of a *policy* which would prevent such catastrophes, or at least reduce the gravity of their consequences.

Any catastrophe in a predominantly agricultural society was followed by a rise in food prices. Although medieval society, with the consent of the canonists, allowed prices to be determined by the haggling of the market, there were times when, for the public good, it was necessary to override the market mechanism. Such a time was the period of grave shortages which accompanied the bad crop seasons of 1315–17, or that which followed immediately on the Black Death. Prices (see p. 442) rose alarmingly and the poor ceased to be able to buy bread. It was held to be the task of government to insure a certain minimum standard for all, and the authorities intervened with attempts to control prices. It is notoriously difficult in any society to regulate prices. The impersonal market forces were little understood in the Middle Ages and, in the long run, such efforts achieved little success.

Authority, both ecclesiastical and lay, also set its face sternly against monopoly. The engrosser, the forestaller and the regrater,[29] the threefold embodiment of commercial malfeasance, were roundly condemned by both the spiritual and the lay arm, and humiliating punishments were reserved by the secular courts for those found guilty of these offences. At the same time, however, it was the institutional framework of medieval society which did much to encourage monopoly. In its anxiety to preserve standards of craftsmanship, public authority entrusted regulatory and supervisory powers to the gilds, which it endowed with monopolistic powers. In the later Middle Ages, powerful gilds became guilty of price-fixing and of condoning poor workmanship by their members. The problem of monopoly was, despite the urgings of the moralists, one which medieval society never successfully faced.

It was in the sphere of food supply that governments showed their greatest concern for welfare. As long as society was largely rural and towns remained very small, there was no acute problem except when crops failed or were destroyed. The growth of larger cities in the thirteenth century raised more serious problems. They could not be supplied, even with the basic bread grains necessary for their food supply, from their immediate area, and long-distance trade was necessary. From the thirteenth century onwards rulers showed a great concern for the supply of their larger cities – in particular, their capitals. The reasons were obvious; quite apart from any humanitarian instincts which might have been present, they were deeply concerned for the preservation of law and order. They knew all too well that a hungry and unruly mob made up of the urban proletariat constituted a very serious threat to their own authority.

Nowhere was the problem of urban food supply more difficult than in the cities of the Low Countries and the city republics of Italy. The former were obliged to rely upon supplies from Artois, Picardy and the lower Rhineland, areas beyond the control of both themselves and their territorial princes. In Italy, the persistent warfare between the city-states was aimed, in part at least, to increase the territory from which they could derive an exclusive food supply. Even in France, wrote Miller, 'there are times when the economic policy of the government . . . has the appearance of being little more than a local policy of provision for Paris'.[30]

## A policy of power

It is generally agreed that the pursuit of power was central to mercantilist thought.[31] In the late Middle Ages most other aspects of economic policy were subordinated to this end. The heavy borrowing and even heavier taxation which characterised most governments were in the main directed to the maintenance of armies and the pursuit of war. These, in turn, had as their principal objective the enlargement of territory and the increase of political power.

Control of trade has always been an important aspect of mercantilist policy. The purpose of trade, it came to be held in later centuries, was the increase in the sum total of wealth. A positive balance on visible trade was held to be desirable, and the consequent accumulation of bullion a mark of wealth and power. Medieval governments never acted as if they accepted the full implications of this view. One nevertheless finds strong expressions of the government's alarm when it seemed convenient to merchants to export bullion to correct a persistently adverse balance. The drain of bullion was heavily to the Middle East, but unfortunately we do not know the extent to which this was corrected by the production of new metal from the mines of central Europe. The movement of bullion within Europe was not, it would appear, on a significant scale, partly because the points outside which it was profitable to export or import specie were far more widely separated than is the case today. It is worth noting that the Medici bank had no means, in the absence of suitable commodity trade, of remitting to Florence the very considerable balances which it accumulated at its branch at Bruges.

Governments made great use of embargoes on trade and of the forced canalisation of trade through specific channels. The prohibition of the export of weapons and of the instruments of war can be traced back to Roman imperial policy. During the Middle Ages, the prohibition against trading with the enemy was very difficult to enforce owing to the multiplicity of routes over which trade could move. England was better placed than most states to control its foreign trade, because the number of ports through which it could pass was limited. It is presumably for this reason that England made greater and more successful use of export and import duties than any other country of medieval Europe. English kings persistently used the export of wool – one of the most valuable raw materials to be had anywhere in medieval Europe – in the advancement of political policy. In the first place the foreign exchange received for wool was used to pay the armies fighting on French soil during the Hundred Years' War. Then, through its power to withhold supplies, the English government was in a position, which it used to the full, to influence policy in the Low Countries. From the end of the thirteenth century, the wool was exported to Europe through a 'staple' port – Bruges, Dordrecht or Antwerp and, after 1363, Calais. The privilege of obtaining wool through any other channel, as the Medici bank was accustomed to do through Southampton, was rarely granted and always in return for some persuasive consideration.

It was easier, however, to control trade by restricting access to fairs and markets. It was not uncommon for a prince to exclude the merchants of a rival or hostile power. Such prohibitions were usually shortlived, but could nevertheless give rise to a lasting change in the direction of trade. An interesting case is the replacement of the Geneva fairs by those of Lyons. In 1462, when the Geneva fairs were at the peak of their prosperity, Louis XI forbade French merchants to visit them and at the same time granted privileges and concessions to Lyons. The Lyons fairs developed remarkably rapidly, and the Geneva fairs declined steadily in importance and ceased to be held during the following century. This, however, was not the end of the affair. The emperor Charles V established a fair at Besançon, in Franche Compté, in an attempt, unsuccessful, as it proved, to undermine the trade and business of Lyons. There are other instances of the foundation of a fair or market for the express purpose of detracting from one already in existence.

The fostering of manufactures was a feature of mercantile policy. The deliberate encouragement of new industries rarely entered into the economic policies of medieval governments. The migration of Flemish weavers to England under Edward III and the dispersion of the Lucchese silk weavers might be cited. There are instances in northern Italy of competition between cities to attract textile artisans and to build up an export industry in cloth. In the Low Countries also the prince occasionally gave his powerful support to a new industry. The development of the manufacture of light woollen cloth at Ath, early in the fourteenth century, was due to the personal efforts of William of Avesnes, Count of Hainault.[32] But such cases are rare. Though medieval rulers occasionally fostered the industrial crafts, any consistent policy of industrial development was totally beyond their powers either to conceive or to implement.

It is easy to exaggerate the role of government policy in the economic history of the Middle Ages because in a few instances, some of which have been cited, it was effective. All rulers did their utmost to maximise their income from the royal domain, because it was a major source of revenue. Outside this, however, their action was hesitant and vacillating, lacking both in a clearly conceived objective and a knowledge of economic conditions. Only in the field of taxation did they in general achieve any success. They felt their way gropingly towards a system of taxation that yielded the revenue they needed with a minimum of outlay and inconvenience. When they had arrived at a system which appeared to work smoothly they made little further change. Nonetheless, taxation was heavy. Henry of Eastry, the prior of Canterbury who did much to improve the estates of Christ Church, was called upon to disburse a third of the house's income in royal and papal taxation. In this instance taxation almost certainly cut into the capital which would otherwise have been available for investment and development. The slowing down of the rate of economic growth during the later Middle Ages, Miller noted, 'was probably partly due to fiscal causes'.[33]

# 10

# The late Middle Ages

The Black Death appeared on the coast of the Crimea in 1347, and in the following winter was carried in the ships of the Genoese merchants to Constantinople and on to Italy. By the spring of 1348. the plague had reached the ports of the western Mediterranean, and in the heat of the following summer it spread through much of western Europe. The cold of winter hindered its progess, since the bacilli did not readily multiply in the cooler temperatures. In 1349 the plague reached the north of Europe, and in 1350 it died away in Scandinavia and on the borders of Russia. The Black Death was over, but the plague had come to Europe to stay for a long while. Its last serious outbreak in the West was at Marseilles in 1720. But no subsequent outbreak was as virulent or as widespread as that of the mid-fourteenth century, when only parts of eastern and northern Europe, and, strangely enough, of the Low Countries appear to have escaped it. It is doubtful, however, whether any part of Europe was wholly immune to the later epidemics, and many places were repeatedly ravaged by them.

It is very difficult to estimate the mortality caused by the Black Death. It may, locally at least, have destroyed half the population, and over western Europe as a whole it probably accounted for at least a quarter. Its sudden impact, and the drastic reduction which resulted in both producing and consuming power led to fundamental changes in the economy. Indeed, in the whole course of European history there has been in all probability no such abrupt reversal of the course of economic development. The Black Death was a divide in the history of medieval Europe. It marked, in a widely accepted view, an end to the period of medieval growth. Construction work on cathedrals and monasteries ended, and those which had not been completed remained unfinished into modern times. The thirteenth had been, in an overworked phrase, 'the greatest of centuries', when a kind of euphoria diffused through Europe. The century and a half which followed the Black Death marked, by contrast, the 'waning of the Middle Ages', when pessimism and economic depression replaced the brightness and the sense of achievement of earlier centuries.

Many writers have combined to spread a blanket of gloom over the last century and a half of the Middle Ages.[1] They have emphasised the feeling of despondency which marks much of its literature, the violent tenor of its life, the decay of traditional institutions, and the almost continuous warfare. They have interpreted it as a period of depression in which small local and sectional economic gains were more than outweighed by the general recession.

This now familiar historical judgment may be exaggerated or even unfounded. Pessimism, it is true, does pervade the literature of the period. There was a preoccupation with death. The shortness and misery of life were a constant theme of ballads and romances. Sepulchral monuments began to assume the forms of skeletons and of other emblems of human frailty.[2] To what extent, one may ask, was this a literary and artistic convention? In large measure it undoubtedly was, and the ease with which it could yield to a confident humanism shows how shallow was its basis. Yet the ever-present danger of the plague and the certainty that wherever it struck, mortality would be high and no respecter of rank or age, cannot have been without its influence on literature and art and perhaps also on men's attitude to business and investment. The threat of plague must have hung over the later Middle Ages as that of nuclear war has done over our own recent past. It cannot be said that the last twenty-five years have been marked by any great exuberance and buoyancy of spirit. Nor, on the other hand, can it be said that visions of a nuclear holocaust have deterred men from experimenting, inventing, and increasing the total productivity of the earth several times.

THE ECONOMIC CONSEQUENCES OF THE BLACK DEATH

The Black Death, like any major cataclysm, caused an immediate dislocation of life. Fields went unploughed and crops were not harvested. The miller died and there was no one to grind the corn. There were immediate shortages, accompanied inevitably by panic buying by those who had the money to do so. Prices rose, and there was much hardship and suffering. But these were short-term consequences of the plague. Within three or four years they had passed, and Europe was left with the long-term results of the epidemic. These were aggravated by later and more localised outbreaks, and these continued to be experienced for the remainder of the medieval period.

Before the plague Europe had been overpopulated, even though the peak of population growth had probably been experienced up to half a century earlier. Of the three factors of production – land, labour and capital – the first had long been relatively scarce, and the second overabundant. Capital played only a small role. The peasant had his ploughs, draught oxen and other equipment; the craftsman possessed the tools of his trade and in some instances a sizeable store of raw materials. But in general only a small stock was needed, and this could have been expanded without putting any great pressure on the other factors of production.

The essential condition was the relationship of man to land. During the earlier period of high population the area of land under cultivation had been pushed to an extreme. Land of indifferent or even of poor quality had been brought under cultivation, and the marginal productivity of land was low. So also, of course, was that of the marginal unit of labour, which was used to till unproductive soil for a scant return. A consequence of this was that land values, as expressed in rents and entry fines, ruled high, and wages, reflecting the low marginal utility of labour, were relatively low. The 'greatest of centuries', the age of Aquinas and Frederick II, was no paradise for the peasant who must have made up four-fifths of the population of Europe.

The revolutionary effect of the Black Death was to reverse the relative abundance of land and labour. The reduction of the labour force by 25 per cent – to take a conservative estimate – made it a relatively scarce commodity. At manorial courts the peasants, instead of bidding against one another for land, found themselves able to impose their own terms, and to demand higher wages, the commutation of services, and lower rents. Of course, such demands did not go unresisted. Attempts were made to put the clock back, to re-impose servile obligations which did not need to be paid for in coin, to control wages by statute, and to restrict the rise in prices. These measures provoked a bitter peasant reaction in many parts of Europe. The Peasants' Revolt in England (1381) was only one example, albeit the most familiar, of a movement which was widespread in western Europe. Nonetheless, the labour force had improved its material position by becoming scarcer and thus more valuable.

At the same time total demand was reduced, in proportion, very approximately, to the reduction of population. Less bread crops were needed, and thus a smaller area of land had to be cultivated. The village community could abandon its least productive land and concentrate its efforts on soils of better quality. Some settlements – generally those which had come into being late when the better land had already been colonised – were abandoned, and such of their inhabitants as had survived must have merged with neighbouring communities (see p. 185). Throughout north-western Europe, from the English Midlands and the Paris Basin eastwards to central Germany and Poland, there is evidence for lost villages.

The cultivated area of Europe is made up of patches of soil of high quality, surrounded by areas of intermediate and poor. Soil quality was dependent not only on the intrinsic properties of the soil itself, but also upon such conditions as slope, drainage, liability to flooding, and ease of ploughing. As the cultivated area contracted, so the community withdrew to the better soil. Fig. 10.1 represents successive stages in the history of a typical settlement. Under pre-plague conditions the community culti-cultivated the area a'-a'' on the abscissa. This is made up of all the land indicated as of high quality as well as that of intermediate quality. After the plague the area under cultivation was reduced to that represented by b'-b'', and this, it will be seen, is made up entirely of land of high quality. If inputs of labour and capital remained constant per unit area – a not unreasonable assumption – then the output per unit area would be likely to increase, because the other factors were now concentrated on land of superior quality. The peasant's labour was thus rewarded by a higher

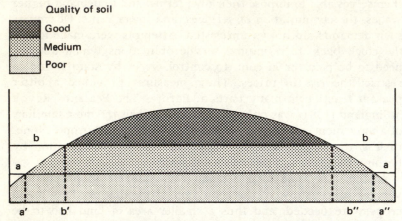

Quality of soil
Good
Medium
Poor

Fig. 10.1   Model showing the late medieval reduction of cropland.

crop-yield, which he was free to use as he pleased: to consume as food or to sell in the market. Thus far, it would appear, the welfare of the peasant can, as a general rule, only have been improved by the reduction in population and the consequent changes in the factors of production.

A feature of the agricultural situation in much of Europe had been the small average size of peasant holdings, which had been divided and subdivided as population increased. The reduction in the number of peasant proprietors allowed, in some measure, small and fragmented holdings to be recombined. To some extent, this resulted from inheritance; to some extent also from grant or lease of land in the manorial court, at which rents and entry fines were reduced in order to attract tenants. There was yet another factor leading to the concentration of parcels of land in fewer hands. Many peasants inherited small sums of money and small amounts of personal goods through the premature death of parents and relatives, and used them to acquire parcels of land or to round out their holdings. The peasant, whose holding was too small to support him and his family, had previously sought wage labour on the lands of more adequately endowed peasants or on the demesne. Now the inducement to find work outside his own holding was less pressing. Many peasants could employ themselves profitably on their own land for a greater proportion of their time, and thus denied to their lord those services which he had never needed more urgently. And so we again find that the peasant appears to have been the beneficiary of the changes in land-ownership which resulted from the decrease in population.

The misfortunes of demesne farming were complementary to the successes of the peasantry. Over much of Europe the demesne had already been leased in part. The remainder was dependent upon a reduced labour supply. Those estates which were still owed ploughing duties and other servile obligations were fortunate in that they were not forced to pay inflated wage rates for their labour. Servile labour was, however, increasingly restless, and knowledge of the good fortune of other peasants merely increased the expectations of the less fortunate, and led them into the peasant risings which were a feature of the later fourteenth century.

Demesne farming was faced with increased labour costs, even when an adequate labour supply could be obtained. Landlords tended either to turn to other forms of land use which demanded less labour than the cultivation of bread crops, or to more diversified crops which might be expected to bring in greater monetary rewards. There was, locally at least, an increase in viticulture, which, in spite of its heavy demands on labour, yielded higher returns than cereal-farming. The production of industrial crops: flax, hemp and vegetable dyes, was also increased. But the most important alternative form of land use was grazing. The grassing down of arable to make sheep-runs was most common – or at least best documented – in England, but was a feature of much of western Europe.

It was not only the scarcity and high cost of labour which induced the lord to turn to sheep. The trend of prices led him in the same direction. Before the Black Death, when peasant holdings had been small and population pressed severely against the local food resources, there had been little surplus grain for the market. Towns had been hard put to it to secure an adequate supply. Italian citites had conquered their *contadi* in part at least to ensure for themselves whatever grain surplus there was, and even so the larger of them had become dependent on the wheatfields of Apulia and Sicily. We have already seen (p. 395) how precarious was the grain supply of Flemish cities, and Paris and other large towns experienced acute problems of food supply. In such circumstances grain prices ruled high, and the lord who marketed only a small quantity could often secure a very good price for it.

The Black Death and the altered balance of the rural economy changed this. The size of the average crop did not contract with the area of the cultivated land. The larger peasant holdings were more likely to have a surplus for the market, and the leasing of the demesne merely increased the number of peasants who were adding their quota. More grain was coming on to the market than at any time previously.

At the same time urban demand was contracting. Towns suffered no less acutely than rural areas from the Great Plague. There was thus a reduced demand in the face of increased production, and prices fell sharply in the later years of the fourteenth century. The difficulty in marketing his grain surplus, and the reduced income from what he did manage to sell, began to influence the economic status of the peasant. He may have benefited from smaller rents and entry fines; he certainly found his monetary income declining. Was he, in the final analysis, better off than his ancestors before the Great Plague? Any answer to this question can be based only on a subjective evaluation of the factors. In terms of the purchase of consumers' goods in the market, he probably had not improved his position (see p. 447), but if we think in terms of his subsistence economy, his ability to feed himself and his family from his own resources, he was probably better off than his forebears had ever been. He had, on balance, a larger holding; its average soil quality was better; he could produce a greater volume of food, and was able to substitute in some degree protein for the predominantly starch diet which had previously sufficed. There is, in fact, abundant evidence that the diet of very many people improved in the fifteenth century. The coarse grains, oats and barley, disappeared from the human diet in many parts of Europe. In the plain of the middle Rhineland cultivators reverted from a three-field to a two-field system because the latter yielded (see p. 446) a greater quantity of panifiable grains and less of the coarse. Miskimin has shown that there was a marked increase in the consumption of beer, as more coarse grains, especially barley, became available for malting. Gilles le Bouvier, writing in the fifteenth century, pointed repeatedly to the large production of animal foods, and the Flemings, he wrote, were 'grans mengeurs de chers (chair), de poisson, de lait et de beures'.[3] Such appears to have been the situation in much of Europe. The human diet was improved, and it is difficult not to see in this a factor in the renewed population increase which became apparent in the later fifteenth century.

Thus in rural areas a fall in population was accompanied by a less than commensurate reduction in grain production. More grain became available for the urban markets and at a lower price than previously. One might expect the urban population to have profited from this situation. It is doubtful whether, in the long run, it actually did so. The urban consumers paid for their grain purchases by the sale of the products of crafts – cloth, metal goods, leather goods – and of goods such as spices, salt and salted fish, which they retailed. The price elasticity of the goods which the towns had to sell was a very great deal less than that of the food products of the rural areas. Nothing had happened to increase the marginal productivity of urban labour. The reduced population of the towns *may* have increased the ratio of capital to labour, but in most urban crafts this could have had little or no significance. It was of no advantage to the craftsman to have more tools than he could use. Nor was the productivity of mining and smelting increased, or the prices of imported spices reduced. The price of urban products did not fall like that of agricultural goods, and the rural population found itself unable to purchase as much as it had formerly done. This was, of course, a simple instance of the price 'scissors' – the fall in the price of farm products without a comparable reduction in that of manufactured goods – not unlike that which affected the whole world in the 1930s. Its consequence was a reduction in the volume of goods exchanged.

Such, in very general terms, was the course of economic development in western, central and, in some measure, in southern Europe during the period following the Black Death. Its chronology is less clear. The European market consisted in fact of an immense number of local markets, some overlapping; many operating in relative isolation. Each was linked by a tenuous chain with regional and larger markets. In consequence, impulses were diffused slowly through this system. Local reactions to the prevailing European trends might come quickly or slowly. In some areas the distortion of the pre-Black Death economic balance might have been slight; in others, profound.

The great pestilence had affected most of Europe. It was followed in the 1360s by severe and widespread outbreaks, and by further recurrences throughout the later fourteenth and the fifteenth centuries, less widespread and disastrous but sufficient to distort yet again an economy which was slowly adjusting itself to the changed conditions of production and demand. Superimposed upon this sequence of natural cataclysms was the manmade scourge of war. It can scarcely be doubted that wars were more frequent and more damaging in the later Middle Ages than in the earlier, and it can be argued that the whole quality of life became more violent. The result was to create local scarcities, to destroy the accumulated capital of generations, and to throw upon the roads or drive into the towns large numbers of poverty-stricken people for whom war had destroyed their very means of livelihood. Violence bred violence; warfare led to banditry, and, in an unending spiral, destroyed the substance of life.

To the scourges of pestilence and war some would add the consequences of climatic change. There is some evidence that the frequency of crop failures was greater during the later Middle Ages than it had been previously. Storm surges occurred along the coasts, inundating large areas, and the water-table rose in many valleys, making them unfit for crop cultivation. Surveys made in the fifteenth and early sixteenth centuries of lands near Lille and Douai, in west Flanders, bear evidence of extensive flooding and of marshes spreading over low-lying land.[4] The disruption of life and the loss of agricultural land were serious in the Low Countries, and there is similar evidence in other parts of northern Europe. It is improbable, however, that climatic change had any significant influence on the late medieval economy except in a few marginal areas which were especially vulnerable.

### MANUFACTURING PRODUCTION

Both the production of manufactured goods and the demand for them declined sharply after the Black Death. The shortage of skilled craftsmen was so acute that in some cities gild regulations were waived, and masters were encouraged to take on more apprentices than they had hitherto been permitted. The rural market failed to develop significantly because, as has been seen, the purchasing power of the peasants remained small. Within the towns, the contraction in the demand for manufactured goods was less marked. The urban population benefited from low grain prices, and thus was able to spend more on consumers' goods. At the same time there was an increase in spending, as wealth came to be concentrated in fewer hands, and was spent with a reckless abandon. Matteo Villani, shortly after the plague had subsided, described the increased consumption which resulted:

> The common people by reason of the abundance and superfluity that they found would no longer work at their accustomed trades; they wanted the dearest and most delicate foods . . . while children and common women clad themselves in all the fair and costly garments of the illustrious who had died.[5]

A taste for extravagant dress and elaborate furnishings continued long after the windfalls induced by the Black Death had been consumed. There were evidently many rich burgesses in most of the larger towns able to gratify their tastes and to build costly and artistic town houses. Indeed, the range of wealth between the richest citizens and the poorest appears to have increased. The luxury crafts flourished; the demand for colourful and costly cloths continued high, and the production of pewter ware for the table and of articles of copper and bronze achieved heights never yet known. At the same time the number of paupers increased, and in the Duchy of Brabant in 1437 'poor' households made up no less than 23 per cent of the total.

It is extraordinarily difficult to produce statistics which can demonstrate the trends in the production of manufactured goods. It is claimed on the one hand, that there was an overall decline in industrial production, that the known instances of increased output, as in the English cloth manufacture, were more than offset by the decline in other areas of production. It is said, on the other, that the structure of demand was changing, that public taste was turning from the traditional fabrics to the cheaper and lighter, which were being produced in increasing volume. The Florentine cloth production, which, according to Giovanni Villani, had amounted to some 70,000 pieces yearly a decade before the Black Death, had fallen to 30,000 in 1373, and to 19,000 in 1382.[6] The Flemish cloth industry was in decline long before the Black Death, and by the end of the fourteenth century the traditional manufacture was of negligible importance. One can point to peculiar and local reasons for these changes: the interruptions in the supply of English wool, the collapse of the Champagne fairs, the embargo on the movement of Flemish goods across France. But were there other factors common to the whole of Europe, such as a general contraction of demand? To this there is no easy answer.

The English cloth trade is the best documented of all branches of medieval manufacturing. The volume of cloth export was negligible at the time of the Black Death. Thereafter it rose steadily until the end of the century (Fig. 8.6), sank in the early fifteenth, and rose again to a new peak in the 1440s. A further decline in the third quarter of the fifteenth century was followed by a sharp rise in its concluding decades. It must, however, be remembered that we are dealing with very small amounts. At its peak the export consisted of little more than 60,000 pieces of cloth, a great deal less than the total production of Ypres at the height of its prosperity.

The cloth production of Ypres reached a peak of about 90,000 pieces of cloth at the beginning of the fourteenth century. It had sunk to less than half this total before the Black Death, but rose sharply again in the twenty years following the plague, thus illustrating the abnormal demand of these years, but was finally extinguished by the end of the century.[7] Cloth production at Louvain and Courtrai declined during the first half of the fifteenth century; revived in the 'seventies and 'eighties, and then underwent a very sharp reverse in the closing years of the century and early in the sixteenth.

But what of the contemporary expansion of production in the rural areas of Flanders and in the cities of Brabant? It was in 1328 that the town of Ath began to develop a cloth industry.[8] In other towns of Brabant a growing cloth industry paralleled the decline of the traditional centres of Flanders. The output of says at Hondschoote, in West Flanders, rose steadily through the fifteenth century, and that of linen at Courtrai was expanding for much of the period (Fig. 10.2). The evidence from tolls levied on merchandise in transit does nothing to support the idea that the volume of the cloth trade declined. The amounts collected varied greatly, but the trend was generally upwards until the 1480s.[9]

The situation was not dissimilar in northern Italy. The decline of the Florentine cloth industry is well documented, but there is some evidence for an increased production in the rural areas of less costly fabrics. In northern Italy, where the cloth industry

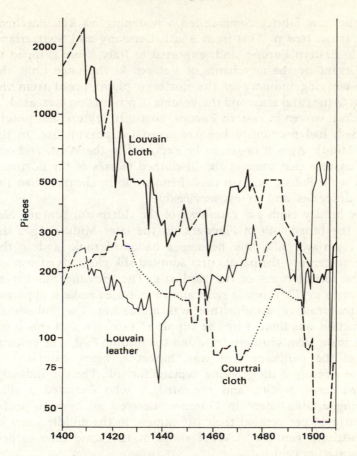

Fig. 10.2 Production of cloth at Louvain and Courtrai and of leather at Louvain, 1400–1500; after R. Van Uytven, 'La Flandre et le Brabant terres de promission sous les ducs de Bourgogne,' *Rev. Nord.*, xliii (1961), 281–317.

had hitherto been of minor importance, the quality of the local wool was improved and, together with imported Spanish wool, gave rise to an expanded cloth manufacture. New types of cloth were developed, and these found a market not only in Italy and the Balkans, but also on the opposite shores of the Mediterranean Sea.

In South Germany also the cloth industry was expanding in the later Middle Ages.[10] The use of mixed fibres became common, and the new fabrics commanded a widening market. Barchent and fustian (see p. 314) from South Germany and Switzerland sold in Eastern Europe, and, exported to Italy, were shipped to the Levant by the merchants of Venice. At the same time, the linen-weaving industry of the northern plain spread from the towns to the rural areas and the volume of production increased.[11] The cloth woven in eastern Europe, coarse in texture and poorly finished, had previously been reserved for peasant use. In the later Middle Ages it began to be exported to the West, and one must assume that some of the ill-clothed masses of the northern cities wore Polish, Silesian or Bohemian cloth, cheaper than the 'new draperies' and no less serviceable.

The luxury cloth *par excellence* of the thirteenth century had been the broadcloth of Flanders. In the later Middle Ages the élite cloth was silk. Silk became a badge of rank, and in the fifteenth century the papal curia adopted silk cloth, dyed scarlet, for the formal robes of the cardinals. The growing number of references to silk robes in wills and inventories make it apparent that the scale of manufacture was increasing. The volume of production was limited by the supply of raw silk, and this came in the main from southern Italy and the Middle East. The cultivation of the mulberry tree was, however, being extended in Italy as a result of the growing demand for silk. The silk industry yielded large profits, and the Medici, who operated a silk-weaving establishment in Florence, derived an average profit of nearly 16 per cent on their investment in the middle years of the fifteenth century.[12] Wool shops at the same time earned barely six per cent.

The decline of the traditional industries is well documented. There were vested interests which complained and protested; the mechanism for recording and taxing the output was well established. But new branches of manufacture crept on to the scene unnoticed – deliberately so, for to advertise their presence was to invite hostility and repression. There are no statistics to show how rapidly the new crafts expanded their production. The statistics are all on the side of those who see in the later Middle Ages a long and deep depression.

There is evidence also for the expansion of the metal-producing industries during the concluding century of the Middle Ages. It is extraordinarily difficult to discover for any period before the nineteenth century the volume and value of minerals extracted and smelted. The increasing number of references to bar iron exported from Sweden, northern Spain, or the hills of central Germany must surely indicate an expanding volume of production and consumption. The blast furnace, furthermore, was developed from the hearth at some time in the fifteenth century. Technological innovation does not normally characterise a declining or even a stagnant industry.

An expanding production of bar iron implies a commensurate increase in the iron-using industries. Military hardware was growing in volume and complexity. Cannon were in use from the second quarter of the fourteenth century, and a fifteenth-century suit of armour consumed a great deal more metal than one of the twelfth or thirteenth, and called for an incomparably greater amount of skilled labour. Milan alone is said to have had more than a hundred workshops producing body-armour, and there must surely have been a not dissimilar activity in Paris, Liège, Cologne and many others amongst the larger cities. There was also an increasing demand for bar iron in the production of hardware for hearth and home: firedogs and spits, locks and hinges, grills for windows and coulters for ploughs. The blacksmith was present at every building site and every major construction called for large quantities of bar iron.

The growth in the metals industries extended also to the more important of the non-ferrous metals. The production of tin, of which Cornwall held a near monopoly, increased steadily in the later fourteenth century, and reached its medieval peak about 1400.[13] Output then sank until the 1460s, after which it again increased. There is no statistical basis for a study of the other non-ferrous metals. Production of most of them seems to have declined in the second half of the fifteenth century. Demand certainly contracted somewhat, but it is also highly probable that technical difficulties arising from the increasing depth of mines and the growing problem of pumping water from them strongly influenced production. It is not without significance that the price of lead increased steadily in the market of Kraków – not far from the mining regions of Bohemia and Hungary – throughout the fifteenth century, at a time when the prices of most other commodities were tending to fall.[14] To this generalisation silver was a conspicuous exception; output increased sharply from the mid-fifteenth century, and reached its maximum some seventy years later.

Building activity is a sensitive economic indicator. Major building projects presuppose an income to pay for them and, in some instances, an expectation of the profit which they will yield. The commencement of a major building project was, in the later Middle Ages, a very rough indicator of the buoyancy of the economy. No major ecclesiastical buildings were commenced from the time of the Black Death until the early sixteenth century, when St Peter's, Rome, was begun, though some were completed or modified. At the parochial level the cessation of church building was very much less marked. Parish churches were enlarged and rebuilt throughout Europe. Large brick-Gothic churches were erected in the Baltic region, and stately limestone churches in the limestone belt of England. From one end of Europe to the other, city churches were rebuilt and enlarged. Only in areas which, on other grounds, we know to have been depressed, do we find as a general rule, any conspicuous absence of new building at the parochial level.

The building activity of the later Middle Ages differed from that of the thirteenth and earlier centuries. The latter had been oriented towards the ecclesiastical hierarchy and the monastic orders, but the later building was mostly commissioned for the laity which paid for it. One has only to contrast the overextended naves – the area where the congregation stood or knelt – of a church, such as those of Lavenham or Chipping Campden, with the older and smaller choirs on which little money had been spent. Art and architecture were passing from the Church into the control of the well-to-do laity. Merchants and the burgesses of the large cities undertook elaborate constructions. They rebuilt churches in their own names and added chapels in which they and their descendants might lie in appropriate splendour. The secularisation of architecture was even more apparent in the building of town halls and merchants' halls, as well as of town houses of rich burgesses. Jacques Cœur's splendid house at Bourges and cloth-halls from Ypres to Kraków remain as evidence of this.

It is difficult, indeed impossible, to compare the investment in art and achitecture in the period following the Black Death with that in the century which preceded. It was different in nature, but it should not be assumed that it was necessarily smaller in volume or that it consumed a lesser proportion of man's productive activity.

In summary, one may say that the drastic reduction of the population as a result of the Great Plague and of later epidemics led to a contraction in total production throughout southern, western and central Europe. At the same time the abandonment of

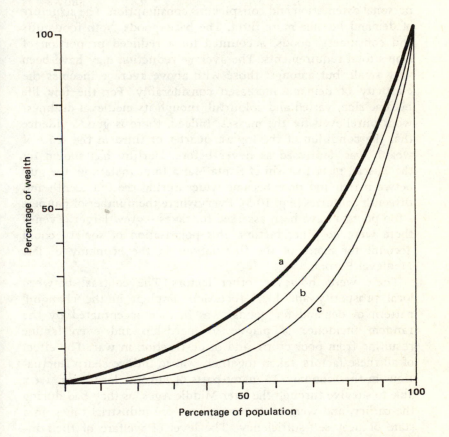

Fig. 10.3 Lorenz curve, showing the growing concentration of wealth at Santa Maria Impruneta, near Florence; after D. Herlihy, 'Santa Maria Impruneta: A rural commune in the late Middle Ages', in *Florentine Studies*, ed Nicolai Rubinstein, London, Faber, 1968, 242–76. (*a*) wealth in 1307; (*b*) in 1330; (*c*) in 1427.

455

marginal units of production, especially in agriculture, led, in all probability to an increase in the productivity of labour. Real incomes were on average increased, but society probably became even less egalitarian than it had been before the outbreak of the pestilence. Death and inheritence led to a concentration of wealth, and put increased purchasing power in the hands of the few. Amongst the psychological consequences of the plague was an orgy of spending, and the later Middle Ages became an age of personal ostentation and conspicuous consumption. The structure of demand became more fluid. The basic goods, both foodstuffs and consumers' goods, accounted for a reduced proportion of man's total requirements. The average reduction may have been very small, but amongst those with above average incomes the elasticity of demand increased considerably. For the few life became rich, varied and colourful, though its medieval drabness went unrelieved for the masses. Indeed, there is good evidence that the condition of the lowest quarter or third in the scale of wealth was depressed as never before. Herlihy has shown for the Tuscan *pieve* (parish) of Santa Maria Impruneta how the gulf between rich and poor became wider during the fourteenth and fifteenth centuries (Fig. 10.3). Everywhere the number of paupers – too poor to have been assessed for taxes – grew larger. Even if there were no other factors, this polarisation of society could account for many of the fluctuations in the economy of late Medieval Europe.

There were, however, other factors. The contrast between local prosperity and local recession, implicit in the changing pattern of demand for goods, was further accentuated by the random incidence of plague; of hardship and even famine resulting from poor crops, and of destruction in war. The effect of all these factors, taken together, was to induce sharp fluctuations in the economy. In many parts of Europe, local areas were able to survive through the later Middle Ages, as they had during the earlier, and were to do throughout pre-industrial times, in a state of near self-sufficiency. The level of welfare of their inhabitants varied, in the main, with fluctuations in the yield of crops. Elsewhere, there were conditions of local depression, as basic industries declined or the ravages of war destroyed capital assets and decimated the population. On the other hand, new manufactures in new areas – the northern Low Countries,

South Germany, the Plain of Lombardy – reflected new demands and brought about a rising level of prosperity.

In the following pages an attempt will be made to trace the economic fortunes during the later Middle Ages of three areas of critical importance: the Low Countries, northern Italy and eastern Europe. Lack both of space and of adequate documentation prevents the similar discussion of other areas.

### THE LOW COUNTRIES

The decline of Flanders and of neighbouring areas of northern France and the Low Countries is the best documented and most often cited instance of economic crisis during the later Middle Ages. A well-known series demonstrates the decay and virtual extinction of the cloth export of Ypres.[15] The port of Bruges, it is said, gradually silted until ships could no longer reach the city. Flemish broadcloth ceased to be exported for finishing in Italy, and the business of the Champagne fairs, on which the trade of Flanders had formerly been heavily dependent, had long been in decline when the Hundred Years' War brought it to a standstill.

This is all, of course, incontrovertible. The mistake is to exaggerate both the scale of manufacturing in Flanders and the commercial role of its cities before the fourteenth century, and, at the same time, to fail to recognise that in some measure the decline of the traditional crafts was compensated by the rise of new branches of manufacture. Flanders had, in the course of the twelfth and thirteenth centuries, developed only one important export industry, that of luxury cloth. A region which rests its prosperity on so narrow an industrial base is taking a grave risk. Flanders never really diversified its economy, and its great cities remained markets of regional rather than of continental importance. Bruges may have been the 'Venice of the North', but in the scale and variety of its economy it fell very far short of the Adriatic city.

The Zwin and Reye were silting and becoming unnavigable in the later Middle Ages, but the galleys and nefs continued to dock at Sluys, as they had always done and were to continue to do long after Bruges had ceased to be an important centre of cloth manufacture. The *Libel of English Policie* described how merchandise:

Is into Flanders shipped full craftily,
Unto Bruges as to her staple fayre:
The Haven of Scluse hir Haven for her repayre
Which is cleped Swyn tho shippes giding:
Where many vessels and fayre are abiding.

The decline of the Flanders cities and the loss of their markets is to be linked, not with silting along the Flemish coast or the extinction of the Champagne fairs, but rather with changes in the pattern of demand in other parts of Europe. Unquestionably

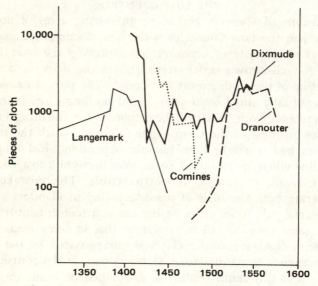

Fig. 10.4 Cloth production in the Ypres region, 1350–1600; after Rolf Sprandel, 'Die Stückzahlen der Tuchproduction in Dixmude, Comines, Langemark, Dranouter, Eecke and Lo', *Viertel. Soz. Wirtsch.*, liv (1967), 336–3.

the wars of the fourteenth and fifteenth centuries interfered with the transport of merchandise and led to a contraction of demand, while the size of the consuming public was smaller after the epidemics of the fourteenth century, but, above all, the cloth industry now catered for a different class.

It would be wrong to assume that after the fourteenth century the cloth industry disappeared from Flanders and the southern Low Countries, and that quality cloth ceased entirely to be made. Cloth continued to make its way to Italy, though in greatly diminished quantities. The manufacture of a coarse but durable cloth, in wider and more plebeian demand than broadcloth, was expanded, but it found its market amongst the better-off peasants and the burgesses of the northern cities. The former pattern of trade was destroyed. The galleys of the Italian cities continued in the fifteenth century to bring their cargoes of alum, silk, spices and wines to the havens of the Zwin and to the rising port of Antwerp, but there was no local cargo waiting for them. They sailed across to Southampton and loaded a cargo of English wool. The flow of southern merchandise to Flanders became contingent on a return cargo of English wool, and as the latter ceased gradually to be available, so the galleys abandoned their voyages to north-western Europe. The industry of Flanders had been based upon the supply of English wool. Its failure brought the commercial prosperity of Bruges finally to an end. The city came to be dominated by 'brokers, inn-keepers, *drapiers*, and commission agents'[16] until even these deserted Bruges for Antwerp.

One cannot say to what degree the decline in the manufacture of quality cloth was compensated over the Low Countries as a whole by the increase in the production of linen and by the rise of the 'new draperies'. The latter was, by and large, a rural manufacture, carried on in the villages and the small and generally unincorporated towns. The important Hondschoote industry received its charter from the Count in 1374. At this time also the 'new draperies' of Comines and Dixmude cut into the market for the cloth of nearby Ypres. There is evidence for an increasing production of coarse cloth during the fifteenth century, though there were sharp fluctuations throughout the period.

The manufacture of linen increased in importance during the later Middle Ages. Larger areas were planted with flax than formerly, and there was also an import from the Baltic region. Spinning of flax and weaving of linen spread through the rural areas, especially in North Brabant and neighbouring Zeeland. Linen was worn to an increasing extent by a small segment of the population, a mark of improved living standards. There is evidence also for an increase in the tanning of leather and the preparation of skins. This in turn suggests that there was a contraction of arable farming, perhaps under the influence of falling grain prices. Carpet manufacture was also expanded during the fifteenth century, to some extent replacing the textile industry

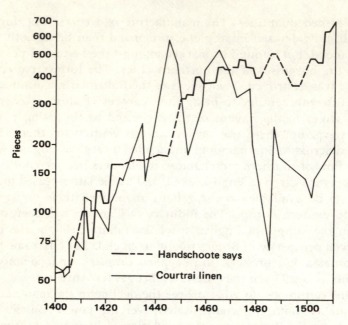

Fig. 10.5   Production of says at Hondschoote and of linen at Courtrai; after R. Van Uytven, 'La Flandre et le Brabant terres de promission sous les ducs de Bourgogne,' *Rev. Nord.*, xliii (1961), 281–317.

in such cities as Ghent. Arras was able to develop the weaving of tapestries to which it gave its name.[17]

North Brabant developed in the second half of the fourteenth century into an important area for the manufacture of the coarser textiles. Lier in 1367 greatly increased the size of its cloth-hall, and at Turnhout a new cloth-hall was built in 1373. At the same time the cloth fairs at the small port-city of Antwerp were growing in importance. In 1357, the town, with its surrounding territory, was annexed to Flanders, and its economic growth inhibited until in 1406 it was re-united with Brabant. Thereafter its expansion was unrestricted until it was ravaged by the Spaniards in 1576. Antwerp served the commercial needs of North Brabant. For a short period in the fourteenth century it had been the staple through which English wool was distributed over the Low Countries. It continued to import wool to satisfy the needs of

Malines, Louvain, Brussels and other cities in its hinterland. It had closer links with the Rhineland than the Flemish cities ever had, and it stood to profit as the north–south trade of western Europe shifted slowly from the routes which followed the Rhône valley and converged on the fairs of Champagne, eastwards towards the German cities and the Alpine passes. German merchants frequented Antwerp, and the Italian banking houses which maintained their factors at Bruges, nevertheless kept themselves fully informed of what went on in the city by the Scheldt.

The growth of Antwerp in the later Middle Ages reflected the increasing importance of the commerce of northern Europe. Bruges in its heyday had been linked primarily with southern Europe. Antwerp's commercial ties were rather with Great Britain, the Rhineland and North Germany. English cloth became one of the most important commodities traded at the fairs of Bergen-op-Zoom and Antwerp. English, German and Italian merchants settled here; the Venetian galleys began to visit the Scheldt, and at the close of the fifteenth century the Portuguese established here an emporium for the spices which they had brought from India. In the course of the fifteenth century Antwerp became the most important international market in north-western Europe. In 1478 the Medici closed their bank in Bruges, thus marking symbolically the end of the city's commercial hegemony. A generation later work began on the Bourse of Antwerp, which then began to dominate the finance and trade of northern Europe.

One must not assume too readily that there was a decline in productivity, at least in productivity per head. There were unquestionably extreme fluctuations, as one clothing centre after another expanded its production in response to market opportunities, only to reduce it again within a few years. Perhaps, on balance, there may have been a downward trend in the later years of the fifteenth century owing to the Burgundian wars and the commercial manipulations of the Dukes of Burgundy.

The southern Low Countries do not seem to have suffered severely from the Plague epidemics of the mid-fourteenth century, and population does not appear to have contracted as sharply as it did in Italy and many parts of western Europe. Registers of fees and land-holding, compiled for Hainault in the late fifteenth and early sixteenth centuries, show an extreme fragmentation of the land. 'Many small-holders,' wrote Koenigsberger,[18] 'can hardly have lived on the income from their holdings at all unless they, or some members of their families, supplemented it by working as craftsmen or as spinners and weavers in the growing rural textile industries.' It was, indeed, in such circumstances that much of the cloth of the Low Countries was made during the fifteenth century. Any contraction in sales would have been disastrous for the rural population, and there were many occasions on which war and the destruction of villages and of farm-stock must have brought all business to a standstill. In some areas of Hainault almost half the rural houses were destroyed in the course of fighting in the late fifteenth century.

A somewhat similar series of surveys was made for lands in West Flanders between 1449 and 1549.[19] They present a comparable picture of crops destroyed by the weather, of farmland inundated and rendered useless, and, above all, of recurring destruction at the hands of the marauding armies of Burgundy and France. A comparison of the successive inquiries into land-holding and the use made of land reveals at best a condition of stagnation; at worst, the utter destruction of resources. During the last decade of the century conditions appear to have changed. The unbridled warfare and destruction of the previous century and a half ceased, or was, at least, greatly reduced in scale. Henceforward wars were, by and large, fought between national monarchies rather than contending local princes. Campaigns were more controlled, and widespread destruction of people and resources, with one or two conspicuous exceptions, became less common. Population began to increase during the early decades of the sixteenth century, if not before. The cloth manufacture revived, and a period of renewed economic growth ushered in the modern period.

## ITALY IN THE LATER MIDDLE AGES

The prosperity of the Low Countries had been narrowly based. At its foundation lay the cloth industry, and the decline of the latter struck at the prosperity of the whole region. Northern Italy, by contrast, derived its prosperity during the earlier centuries of the Middle Ages from the transit traffic which it handled between Europe and the Mediterranean and Middle Eastern regions. Its largest cities were commercial rather than industrial as far as their basic function was concerned.

There were, of course, manufacturing industries, as there had to be to satisfy the needs of the local people, but Italy was slow in developing a basic export industry. The textile industry was inhibited by the lack of a local wool of sufficient fineness. It was this fact, more than any other, which led to the import of Flemish broadcloth. The most illustrious branch of the Italian clothing industry in the late thirteenth and early fourteenth centuries consisted essentially in the finishing and embroidering of imported cloth.

This, however, was changing. Florence developed as a cloth-making centre in its own right (see p. 311), and early in the fourteenth century the luxury cloth industry employed only a small fraction of the city's cloth workers. It is indicative also of the relative newness of the clothing industry that a great many of the weavers were in fact Germans. At the same time the textile industry was growing in many of the North Italian towns. Only in the great port cities did it remain of relatively minor importance. Bologna, which had formerly engaged, like Florence, in the finishing of cloth imported from north-western Europe, developed in the thirteenth century a cloth-weaving industry of its own. The quality of the local wool was improved, and at the same time a good quality wool, known as *garbo*, became available from Spain. In the fifteenth century English wool provided a return cargo for the Italian galleys which sailed to the Low Countries, though its volume must always have remained small. Flax-spinning and linen-weaving were expanded, and cotton from Sicily and the Middle East were imported and used increasingly in weaving mixed fabrics.

The manufacturing industries of Italy were in full growth when the Black Death struck early in 1348. Mortality was very heavy. Urban population, it has been claimed, was reduced to about half of its level before the spread of the epidemic. Output of cloth and of other manufactured goods fell off sharply, and some branches of production had not recovered by the end of the Middle Ages. Much has been written of the change which came over Italian art during the *trecento*. The joy and naturalness of the age of Dante and Giotto gave place to a more sombre atmosphere, to 'a darker realm of fearful, strenuous yet often uncertain piety, brightened only by mystical transports and visions of supernatural splendour'.[20] The emotional impact of the Great Plague and of subsequent epidemics was profound. It appears, on the evidence of painting and of some literature, to have induced a deeper religious feeling. It may have led to a reluctance to invest in long-term enterprises, though for this the evidence is very uncertain; it certainly contributed in the minds of some to a more hedonistic attitude to life. Never, perhaps, was consumption more ostentatious, or the pursuit of pleasure more open than amongst some of the more well-to-do Italians of the age of the Renaissance.

High mortality led to the concentration of wealth in fewer hands. Some found themselves suddenly rich, and bought town houses and rural estates. Others had neither the luck nor the wit for self-aggrandisement, and their poverty became more abject. The extremes of wealth were exaggerated. Both rich and poor moved to the towns, the former to enjoy their luxury and security, the latter to seek work or to live on the urban charities. There arose an intense mobility, both social and geographic. The cities were filled with 'new' men, intent, like most such, to further their economic interests. It is not altogether surprising that the Florentine *catasto* of 1427 showed that less than half the men aged from twenty-eight to thirty-two were married, and that the percentage rose only to 65·5 for those of thirty-three to thirty-seven.[21] They had other pursuits to follow, and the low urban birth rate which resulted contributed yet more to the rural influx into the cities. In the Pistoian countryside more than three-quarters of the men of twenty-eight to thirty-two were married, and almost 90 per cent of those from thirty-three to thirty-seven. Only in this way could the supply of manpower to the cities be maintained.

This mobility had profound economic consequences. It checked the growth of rural industries, and drew craftsmen to the towns. It influenced the structure of demand, increasing the consumption of luxury goods and the demand for the services of builders, decorators and artists. It encouraged the successful members of the bourgeoisie to invest in rural estates, which they commonly leased on a share-cropping or *mezzadria* basis to the local peasantry.

Before the population declined in the middle years of the fourteenth century the food supply of the larger cities had posed a serious problem. Most had obtained grain from the plains of peninsular Italy – the Romagna and Apulia – from Sicily and even from North Africa and the Black Sea. All except the largest could now satisfy their needs from their local regions, or *contadi*. The grain export of Apulia and Sicily declined to negligible proportions, and with it went what prosperity there had been in the Italian *Mezzogiorno*. Attempts to develop crafts, chiefly in Campania, met with little success, and the South became, and indeed remained, until the present century, a depressed region, contributing little to the economy of northern Italy and deriving little from it.

*Florence*
In the course of the thirteenth century Florence attracted the banking activities of central Italy and became the most important financial centre in the western world. It is difficult to explain how Florence came to play the role of Europe's banker. It lay 80 kilometres from the sea, and until the early fifteenth century had neither port nor commercial fleet of its own. It had no conspicuous advantages, and it differed from its rivals, in all probability, chiefly in the character, skill and initiative of some of its leading citizens. In the early fourteenth century, its leading banking houses, the Bardi, Peruzzi and Acciaiuoli, did business throughout western and southern Europe. The *Pratica della Mercatura* of Francesco Balduccio Pegolotti, an employee of the Bardi, may perhaps be taken as in some way reflecting the company's broad business interests. If this was so, they are seen to penetrate every country and to impinge on every branch of European trade. All was centred in Florence. According to Giovanni Villani, there were no less than eighty banks, large and small, in Florence about 1340. Some were overextended, and several of the largest failed during the difficult years about the middle of the fourteenth century. The banking business continued, however, to focus in Florence, though none of the later banks, not even that of the Medici, ever rivalled the size of the Bardi or the Peruzzi. Not until the last quarter of the fifteenth century was there a conspicuous decline in the importance of the Florentine banking. By 1494, when the Medici bank finally closed its doors, only half a dozen banks remained in the city. Italy's pre-eminence in the world of banking and finance ended, and the lead passed to Antwerp, and then to Amsterdam and London.

One cannot use the fortunes of the Italian banks as a barometer of economic conditions in Italy, because their downfall reflected crises in other parts of Europe rather than in Italy itself. A major factor in the final crisis of the Medici bank was the large assets which it held frozen in the Low Countries or in the hands of princely debtors. There was, however, a general decline in the fifteenth century in the international transfer of funds and the discounting of bills, which had constituted a major part of the business of the Medici and of other Florentine banks. This was part of that general process whereby the economic focus of the continent slowly shifted from Italy and the Mediterranean to the lands which surrounded the North Sea.

Florence, a leading manufacturing centre and, in the later Middle Ages, by far the most important city in banking and finance, had played no direct role in Mediterranean commerce before the fifteenth century. Indeed, until 1406, when Pisa was conquered, Florence had no direct access to the sea, and her trade was conducted with the help of 'hired ships and a borrowed port'.[22] It was another fifteen years before the Florentines acquired Porto Pisano and Leghorn (Livorno), and were able to operate a fleet of galleys of their own.

The Florentine fleet operated from 1422 until 1480. The galleys were built and owned by the Republic, but were leased to merchants for specific voyages, They normally sailed to the eastern Mediterranean, where they loaded spices; to the coasts of Spain and Barbary, and to Flanders and England. At the peak of its prosperity the Florentine merchant fleet consisted of some thirty galleys as well as a number of smaller craft. The galleys were capable of carrying from 100 to 250 tons of merchandise, and the volume of freight which they could together transport in the course of a year was relatively small. Their cargoes were very varied. The chief exports were cloth and the alum from the papal mines at Tolfa. Imports included cotton, hides and skins, spices and foodstuffs. The galleys were expensive to operate and were unprofitable unless they could be restricted to high value cargoes. The galley fleet, in fact, made a loss, and the state eventually ceased to maintain it. This does not mean that smaller ships, more like the capacious cog of northern seas, did not continue to sail under the control of private merchants. Nevertheless, the failure of the Florentine galley fleet serves to emphasise the fact that the era of the traditional Mediterranean commerce, on which the prosperity of Italy had been based, was drawing to a close. It was difficult for a new competitor to break into the long-distance trade, dominated by Venice and Genoa, especially when the volume of the trade was itself in decline.

## Venice

Despite the tendency to couple together the names of Venice and Genoa, one must not exaggerate their similarities in the later Middle Ages. Both were, of course, city-republics of small territorial extent and limited agricultural resources. Both had certain manufactures, notably shipbuilding and the preparation of ships' supplies, but in neither was there a basic export industry. Both were dedicated to international trade, and their profit margins came from the exchange of the products of Europe for those of North Africa, the Middle East and the Black Sea region. Here, however, their close similarities ended. The areas which they exploited overlapped, but each handled its own distinctive types of cargo and employed appropriately designed ships. Even business methods and commercial organisation differed between the two cities.

Both Venice and Genoa carried on their trade under the shadow of the Turks. The later years of the thirteenth and the early decades of the fourteenth century had been an era of relative peace in the Levant and around the shores of the Black Sea and even in Central Asia. 'Nowhere,' wrote Ibn Battuta of Asia Minor in 1333, 'will you find men so eager to welcome travellers, so prompt to serve food and to satisfy the wants of others.'[23] Traders and missionaries were able to cross Asia from the Black Sea to China, and silks and spices made the journey from the Orient by sea to the ports of the Persian Gulf and Red Sea, and were taken on by caravan to the Mediterranean. In the middle years of the fourteenth century this began to change. The Ottoman Turks became more aggressive and fanatical, and they organised a disciplined and effective fighting force, the Janissaries. In 1350 they overran the province of Nicaea, the last foothold of the Byzantine Empire in Asia Minor. Only a few years later they landed in Thrace, spread into the Balkan peninsula and, in 1389, overwhelmed the Serb state at Kosovo.

There followed a lull in the campaign of Turkish conquest for the greater part of a century. Then the Ottoman armies advanced again. Parts of Asia Minor, such as Karamania and Trebizond, which had not previously been annexed to the Ottoman Empire, were conquered. Within the Balkan Peninsula, the Peloponnese, Epirus, Albania, Bosnia and Wallachia fell to the Turks, and one by one the islands of the Aegean and eastern Mediterranean were taken. Rhodes held out until 1522; Naxos until 1516, and Cyprus till 1571. A few Italian bases on the coast of Greece were retained into the sixteenth century, and Dubrovnik (Ragusa), thanks to Venetian sea-power, never succumbed to the Turks. The Ottoman Turks did not occupy Syria until 1516, and Egypt not until the following year, but Italian commercial supremacy in the Levant was effectively ended by the Venetian-Turkish war of 1463–79.

The Venetian share in the diminishing trade of the Levant was dominated by the traffic in spices, of which pepper was by far the most important. These were obtained mainly from Alexandria and the ports of Syria. The trade was thus not seriously threatened by the Turks until early in the sixteenth century. Spices formed a valuable cargo, and were in the later Middle Ages carried by the swift galleys from the Levantine ports to Venice, while slower vessels, with a greater cargo capacity, were left to transport the less valuable wares which made up much of Venetian trade. These consisted of grain from North Africa and southern Italy, of wine from Greece and Crete, of cotton from Egypt, together with skins and hides, timber for building ships and houses, and salt. These were paid for primarily by the export of cloth, especially barchents and fustians from south Germany. The latter became increasingly important in the fifteenth century. The German merchants had their *Fondaco* beside the Grand Canal, in which they lived, stored their wares and did their business. In 1505 this immense building was reconstructed; surely the Germans foresaw no significant interruption of their trade with Venice or of Venetian exports to the Levant.

The Venetian commercial empire was supported by a large number of bases which, like the later 'factories' of the British in India, were fortified and ruled as parts of the Republic (see p. 363). It was with the southern Balkans and the Aegean region that Venice conducted the bulk of its trade, other than that in spices. At Constantinople the Venetians had only a 'comptoir' on the southern shore of the Golden Horn, and in the Black Sea their only trading post was at Tana. The whole of this area became peripheral to their interests, and they tended to abandon it to the Genoese, especially after the war of 1350–55.

Venetian commerce appears to have held up fairly well during the later Middle Ages, and the chain of bases was even extended early in the fifteenth century. Although the Negropont was lost in the war of 1463, Venice nevertheless succeeded in extending its authority in the Peloponnese, and later occupied Cyprus and islands close to the Greek coast. The Venetians had no hesitation in doing business with the Turks during the long periods of peace which separated the Turkish wars, and for this they were roundly condemned by the Pope. The Turkish conquests led to an increase in piracy and thus in the dangers of doing business in the Levant. Nevertheless, Venetian trade in Greece and the Aegean was not seriously threatened until the closing years of the fifteenth century, and the débacle did not come until the sixteenth.

The spice trade was little affected by events in the Aegean. It continued to be the most profitable branch of Venetian commerce. That well documented merchant, Andrea Barbarigo, dealt mainly in cotton and spices from Syria and Egypt (see p. 351). It has often been held that when, in 1498, the Portuguese reached India, the supply of spices to the Levantine ports was abruptly cut off. Nothing could be farther from the truth. For a brief period the supply was interrupted, and Portuguese competition forced up the price. But in the long run the Portuguese pepper, brought by sea around the Cape of Good Hope, proved to be no cheaper, and the Venetian spice trade continued far into the sixteenth century. The economy of the Republic was undermined rather by the eventual loss of its Greek and Aegean trade. It was malmsey wine and olive oil, rather than pepper and cinnamon, which dried up on the Venetian market.

Another and very different factor in the changing economy of the Venetian Republic during the later Middle Ages lay in the attitude of the merchants towards risk-taking. Early in the fifteenth century the Republic had begun to extend its narrow territory on the Italian mainland, and by the end of the century Venetian rule extended from Bergamo to Udine. This new empire on the *terrafirma* proved to be very profitable, and provided for the state a larger and more secure income than its overseas possessions had done. The profits from successful trading ventures came increasingly to be invested in landed estates rather than in snips and new commercial undertakings. The patrician families of Venice by no means abandoned the trade on which their fortunes had been based, but times were uncertain, and who can blame them for hedging against bad times which the more far-sighted amongst them must have seen approaching.

*Genoa*

Throughout the later Middle Ages the Genoese state was the commercial rival of the Venetian. Territorially it consisted of a narrow strip of land between the Ligurian Apennines and the Mediterranean Sea, and its local resources were even more slender than those of Venice. Its earliest trade had been with southern Italy, North Africa and Spain, and this traffic, in which it had few significant rivals, it retained throughout the Middle Ages. It was Genoa's attempts to break into the Levantine trade, especially that of Constantinople and the Aegean, that led to the wars with Venice in the thirteenth and fourteenth centuries.

After 1204 the Venetians had been dominant in Constantinople, but the restored Palaeologi, in 1261, granted exceptional privileges to the Genoese. The latter gained control of the fortress of Galata, across the Golden Horn from the city, and of the suburb of Pera. The virtual control of the straits, which they thus acquired, allowed them to monopolise the trade of the Black Sea. Silks and spices reached their bases at Caffa, in the Crimea, Azof, and Trebizond by the overland route from China. Some were sent north-westwards from Moncastro (Cetatea Alba) by the route which followed the Dnestr valley towards Poland and the Baltic. The Genoese managed to hold the mouth of the Dnestr until the Ottoman conquest in 1484. Much of their merchandise was gathered at Pera and shipped thence to Italy. In the Aegean Sea the Genoese held only the island of Chios, but this they transformed into one of the most important trading centres of the later Middle Ages. Here were collected the alum of Phocaea, raw cotton from Asia Minor, grain, skins and hides, in addition to the more valuable silks and spices.

The Genoese traded also with Cyprus, but their bases in Syria had been lost in the course of their conflicts with the Venetians. Their commerce was mainly in bulky goods of low value. For this reason they abandoned the construction of galleys, and concentrated on the 'nef', which had a very much larger hold. It was the nef which carried Phocaean alum, Turkish cotton and Italian grain to their home port. The larger part of Genoese trade was within the western basin of the Mediterranean Sea, with the ports of Spain, southern France and North Africa. From the late thirteenth century Genoese galleys sailed for north-western Europe, laden mainly with alum, for which wool generally provided a return cargo. Genoa's overland links with central and northern Europe were inferior to those of Venice. While the latter came in the fifteenth century to control the approaches to the Alpine passes, Genoa remained dependent on the goodwill of the dukes of Milan or were obliged to send their merchandise northwards by way of the Rhône valley.

While Venice provided a model of good administration and internal harmony, the city government of Genoa was factious and turbulent. Its divisions weakened the Republic politically and led at the end of the fifteenth century to the acceptance of French suzerainty. In the meanwhile Genoa had fared very badly – more through lack of judgment than of resources – in its last war with Venice, the so-called War of Chioggia (1378–81). Its power in the eastern Mediterranean was gravely undermined. In the mid-fifteenth century the Turks overran Phocaea, and Genoa lost control of the source of the alum which had played so important a role in its commerce. Shortly afterwards, the papal alum from Tolfa completely dominated the European market.

The fifteenth century was a period at best of stagnation in the Genoese economy, and, after about 1460, of decline, as Levantine bases were taken by the Turks and the Genoese lost their monopoly of a lucrative trading commodity. Despite the weakness of its competitive position during the later Middle Ages, Genoa used comparatively advanced commercial techniques. It is paradoxical that the accounting and financial methods of the Genoese were considerably in advance of those of their successful rivals, the Venetians.

## North Italian Plain

In the last century of the Middle Ages, the economy of Venice and of Florence was stagnating, and that of Genoa and of southern Italy was in decline. The slight evidence points to a modest revival in the north. The cloth industry was pursued in the towns; there was an active market in land, and the urban middle class was investing heavily in rural property. The bourgeoisie, indeed, poured money into its newly acquired lands, draining and dyking them, extending dairy-farming and improving agriculture. No comparable investment seems to have been made in urban crafts. Population was again increasing slowly, but it was the rural rather than the urban population which grew.

In Piedmont, which had during earlier centuries been very much less developed than Lombardy, there was also some growth in the size of towns, in the volume of trade and in total population. Transport facilities were improved, and in many small ways the increased prosperity of Lombardy communicated itself westwards to Piedmont.

Italy thus presents, like the Low Countries during the same period, a picture of general stagnation, with some areas in which productivity had declined sharply and others in which a modest prosperity showed itself. It was one which might be expected to appear in a society in which the structure of demand was changing and external circumstances both restricted markets and cut off the supply of some materials.

### EASTERN EUROPE

The vast area lying to the east of the Elbe had been the pioneer fringe of medieval Europe, into which settlers were advancing as late as the early years of the fourteenth century. It had clearly been an area of economic growth, as land was cleared, agriculture extended, and towns established. This growth did not cease with the end of the great migration; instead, as if by the momentum which it had built up, it continued until the end of the Middle Ages. Certain factors in this continued economic growth are apparent. The epidemics of the fourteenth century were very much less disastrous in eastern than in western and southern Europe. The population was not significantly reduced, though its overall density remained fairly low. There was a highly favourable ratio of land to people, as there had been in western Europe during the earlier Middle Ages.

The population of the three western provinces of Poland – Great and Little Poland and Mazowsze – is estimated to have risen from less than 700,000 about 1000 to 1·25 million in 1340, and 3.1 million in the sixteenth century. In the more realistic terms of density to the square kilometre, the population rose in this period from 4·8 to 8·6 in the fourteenth century and to 21·3 in the sixteenth. Poland cannot be said to have been overpopulated anywhere or at any time in the Middle Ages. Evidence is lacking for the Czech lands of Bohemia and Moravia, but the fragmentary sources for Hungary suggests that there also a sparse population was growing steadily during the concluding centuries of the Middle Ages.

The growth of an internal market is reflected in the continued foundations of towns, at least until early in the fifteenth century. The most intense activity, it is true, had been in the closing decades of the thirteenth century, but throughout the fourteenth and the first half of the fifteenth centuries, a period when virtually no towns were established in western and southern Europe, the foundation of new towns continued, and indeed, was checked only during the difficult years of the later fifteenth century.[24] This activity, it is true, was more intense towards the eastern border of the region than in western Poland or in Bohemia, where an adequate net of urban centres had already perhaps been established by the end of the thirteenth century.

The spread of small towns across the whole of eastern Europe implies both a rural market for the products of urban crafts and also a demand for the agricultural products of the area. There is evidence for the expansion of textile and metal industries during the later Middle Ages in Bohemia and Poland, for the increasing use of iron in agricultural implements, and for a growing demand for consumers' goods. Petty rural traders, Jewish, Armenian and Greek, made their appearance, and long-distance trade developed with the west. Even the coarse cloth of Poland and Bohemia commanded a market amongst the poor in central Europe, and Bohemian merchants were to be met in the *Fondaco dei Tedeschi* in Venice. Landowners and well-to-do members of bourgeoisie in eastern Europe created a demand for the more refined cloth produced in the Low Countries and Germany, for wines and for other consumers' goods from the West. Many of these goods were distributed over eastern Europe by the merchants of Cologne, Aachen and Nuremberg from the fairs of Frankfort on Main.[25]

The most used routes were those which ran from Saxony to Poznań and through Silesia to Wrocław and Kraków; across

Bohemia by way of Cheb and Prague, and from Austria through Brno in Moravia to Poland, and eastwards into Hungary. Trade brought prosperity to cities such as Wrocław, Prague, Brno, Olomouc, and, above all, Kraków, upon which many of the routes converged. Large numbers of animals, especially cattle, reared in less populous parts of Europe, like Galicia and the Hungarian Plain, were driven westwards along these routes to supply the cities of central Europe. Even the spices and silks of the East were sometimes brought from the Black Sea coast by way of the market centre of L'vov (Lwów) to Kraków and Prague.

Superimposed on the general development of production and trade throughout most of eastern Europe were two developments of particular significance for Europe as a whole: the increase of commercial grain production and the opening up of mines in Austria, Bohemia and Hungary. A market developed in north-western Europe, and later in southern, for East European and Baltic grain. It was mainly produced on estates in central Poland, and was transported overland to shipping points on the Vistula and its tributaries. Małowist considers that shipments of rye to the West had begun before the Thirteen Years' War (1454–66) with the German Knights; it developed steadily in the later fifteenth and early sixteenth centuries. The profit of the landlords in a time of falling agricultural prices, was dependent upon reducing production and transport costs to a minimum, and this they achieved, in part, by the re-creation of great estates, which they cultivated directly; in part, by the re-establishment of serfdom. They resumed possession of peasants' holdings and depressed the status of the half-free peasantry. 'By the end of the fifteenth century,' wrote Blum, 'from the Elbe to the Volga, most of the peasantry were well on their way to becoming serfs.'[26] By the end of the sixteenth the process of enserfment was virtually complete. This development was made possible by the growing political power of the nobility and by the extension of their seigneurial jurisdiction.

Seigneurial power was no less hostile to towns than to a free peasantry. Whereas the latter would have sold their surplus in an urban market, the noble landowners bypassed the towns, selling directly to merchants, who exported their grain, skins, hides and lumber. The peasantry, depressed by ever more severe labour obligations, ceased to provide a market for urban crafts. At the same time the nobility used their political power to control the prices of urban products, and in doing so destroyed the feeble urban industries. All except the largest and most strategically located towns decayed and were reduced functionally, if not legally, to the status of villages.

Thus, in eastern Europe, the collapse of grain prices led, in contrast to the course of events in the West, to the re-establishment of great estates and to the reassertion of seigneurial control over the peasantry. This contrast arose in some measure from the fact that the weakness of monarchy in eastern Europe left too great a power in the possession of the nobility, while in the west the general land trend was towards reducing the power of the latter. Another factor is likely to have been the different trends in population. In the west, the plague epidemics of the fourteenth century had so reduced the population that there was real scarcity of labour. In eastern Europe there were instances of the abandonment of villages and cropland, but the loss of population was overall on a very much smaller scale than in the west. Blaschke has calculated that in Saxony there was a loss of only 8·7 per cent of the rural population, and that a considerable proportion of these in fact migrated to the towns.[27] The sixteenth-century population is said to have been about a fifth larger than before the Black Death. Estimates already quoted for Poland suggest that the rate of increase in the later Middle Ages must have been steeper than in Saxony, and losses through the plague much less. Labour was in consequence a cheaper commodity in eastern than in western, and the landowners were thus able to impose harsher conditions.

The second development which so greatly influenced eastern Europe during the later Middle Ages was the growth of the mining and smelting industries. In the second half of the fifteenth century, adit-drainage, the introduction of new and more efficient pumps, and the adoption of new methods of underground mining contributed to a revival in Bohemia and to a vigorous development in Slovakia.

In the mid-fifteenth century merchants from the south German cities began to invest in mining enterprises in the Alps, probably because trade with Italy and the Levant was less remunerative than it had previously been. Among them was Jakob Fugger the second. His family had been cloth merchants of Augsburg, and he had himself done business in the German *Fondaco* at Venice. Late in the fifteenth century he gained possession of a mine in the Tyrol (see p. 329). He then extended his activities to Carinthia, Bohemia and the mountains of Upper Hungary. The Fuggers, in association with the Thurzos, carried on mining in Slovakia for half a century before the Turkish invasion brought it to a close. Their partnership was one of the largest, if not the largest capitalist undertaking in Europe up to this time – and without any benefit of the Protestant ethic.

Silver from Tyrol, Bohemia and Slovakia contributed to the price inflation in Europe well before that from the New World began to flood the European market. Copper from Hungary travelled westwards and northwards across Europe to supply the brass and bronze industries of Germany and the Low Countries. The peak of Slovak copper mining was reached in the second decade of the sixteenth century. Much of it was sent by a combination of land, river and sea transport to Antwerp, which became for a period in the sixteenth century the chief copper market in Europe. In 1546 the Fuggers began to relinquish their mining interests.[28] New World silver was beginning to undermine the profitability of mining in central and eastern Europe. The Fugger interests were taken over by other German financial houses, the Paumgartner and the Manlich, but mining declined during the sixteenth century and was finally terminated in the course of the wars of the seventeenth.

The shortlived mining output of Bohemia and Slovakia led to the building of a few attractive towns amid the mountains, but contributed little to the prosperity of these regions. Labour was exploited and profits went to the western entrepreneurs. There is nothing to show that peasant purchasing power was stimulated to more than a very modest degree by mining development. Eastern Europe, in short, experienced a short-lived period of prosperity. This was then overtaken by a spreading depression which was marked by the decay of towns and the reduction of the peasantry to serfdom. Even the mining developments of the later Middle Ages did little to redeem this picture of gloom which lasted until recent times.

### WAGES AND PRICES

The prices at which commodities sell in the market is the most sensitive barometer of economic conditions available to us. Labour is a commodity, no less than grain or wool, and its price also reflects its abundance relative to demand. Medieval economic opinion, as a general rule, regarded the just price and the just wage as those which were arrived at as a result of open competition in the market. Attempts to fix the level of either were strongly opposed, and only in an emergency was government intervention and control either attempted or tolerated. It was difficult under medieval conditions to control wages and prices. Attempts to do so were, as a general rule, made only in time of crisis induced by harvest failure or epidemic disease. Such a situation was usually shortlived, so that conditions in any event would have tended to return to normal within a relatively short period of time. Nevertheless, it does not appear that such regulatory efforts achieved any considerable measure of success.

The price of land fluctuated no less than that of commodities. Indeed, since the chief commodities traded in were the products of the soil, the two tended to move in harmony with one another. Contractual and institutional factors, however, made it very difficult for levels of rent to move quickly in response to changes in demand. It was, however, possible to vary the entrance fine, paid when a new tenant took up the tenement. Changes in the level of fines are a measure of the relative scarcity and abundance of land, but they are likely to be so delayed that their value as a measure of economic conditions is slight.

Most useful are runs of prices of the basic foodstuffs: wheat, rye and oats, as well as of other agricultural products, such as malt, livestock and wool. These, especially the bread grains, were in inelastic demand, so that price fluctuations can be regarded, by and large, as a measure of the adequacy of supply. Demand for luxury goods and for many manufactured goods, on the other hand, was relatively elastic. They could be dispensed with. If their price rose sharply sales diminished, and price levels were restored fairly quickly.

Examination of any price series for the basic foodstuffs shows very wide fluctuations. In any series the price levels are likely to reflect a number of factors, of which the most important are:

1. an annual cycle of price change. Prices of agricultural products tend to be low after harvest. The farmer, hard pressed for storage space or in urgent need of cash, placed a proportion –

perhaps a high proportion of his disposable surplus on the market. Prices then tended to rise during the year, and reached their highest levels shortly before the next harvest.

2. Superimposed on this annual cycle are less regular fluctuations induced by the abundance or failure of the harvest. The latter always led to sudden and extreme increases in grain prices, which, however, were relatively shortlived. To some extent, import of grain from distant areas, unaffected by the shortage, remedied the situation, though the medieval market was not a flexible one, and such corrections could not be counted on. The inevitability of good harvests following bad, coupled with the equally inevitable loss of life during a famine crisis, restored the situation.

3. A final group of factors in the level of prices and wages was the size of the stock of money, its quality, and the rapidity with which it circulated. Currency was always in short supply in medieval Europe, and there were prolonged periods when royal mints could not operate owing to their shortage of silver (see p. 115). On the other hand the reminting of old coins and the creation of a debased currency on a large scale within a short period of time could flood the market with poor currency and lead to a sharp rise in prices. Miskimin[29] has demonstrated that a very abrupt increase in French grain prices in 1360, which has all the outward characteristics of a crisis due to crop failure, was in fact, due to the quite unusual activity in the royal mints of France. The very sharp price rise of wheat in Ghent in the 1480s and 1490s was due primarily to the debasement of the Flemish groat which took place in these years. Farmer has demonstrated[30] a similar relationship between price changes and the recoinage of the currency in England.

The movement of prices has been linked with the amount of currency, its speed of circulation and the volume of transactions in the so-called Fisher formula:

$$P = \frac{M.V}{T}$$

where $P$ represents the price; $M$, the quality of money; $V$, the velocity of its circulation, and $T$, the volume of transactions. Any increase in the amount of money in circulation, or in the speed with which it passed from hand to hand would thus contribute to a price increase. An increase in the volume of business, without any commensurate increase in that of circulating money, would bring about a fall in prices. In so far as monetary considerations were a factor in the late medieval decline in prices, they must have assumed the form of a physical decline in the supply of money and in the speed with which it circulated. If this was the case, it was corrected late in the fifteenth century by the increased minting of silver. The issue of debased coins would have had the effect of raising prices, since the intrinsic value of each unit of the currency became smaller. It remains probable, despite the monetary arguments of Kosminsky and others, that the basic reason for the long-term decline in prices was the result of reduced demand, which was itself the consequence of the fall in population. Until the middle years of the fourteenth century prices tended to rise. The high mortality during the Black Death and subsequent outbreaks of the plague led to a reduction in demand and to stable or even slightly falling prices, even though the dislocations caused by the emergency itself may have brought about large temporary increases.

Materials for the study of prices are so much more abundant for

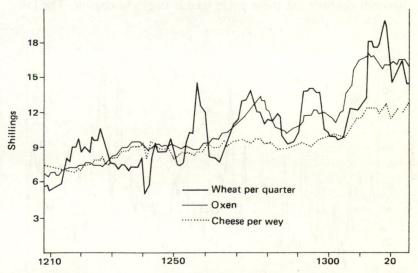

Fig. 10.6  Prices of wheat, oxen and cheese in England before the Black Death; after M. M. Postan, *The Medieval Economy and Society*, London, Weidenfeld and Nicolson, 1972, p. 242.

England than for continental Europe that it is convenient to illustrate price trends before the Black Death from English sources. Figure 10.6 shows the increases in the price of wheat and cheese during the thirteenth and early fourteenth centuries. Fluctuations were greatest, as might have been expected, in the commodity for which there was the smaller elasticity of demand. The severe harvest crises of 1315–17 are reflected in the highest grain prices recorded during the period. The price of cheese, on the other hand, showed only minor fluctuations. It is of interest that the prices of both cheese and oxen rose during the period 1230–53, when grain prices were particularly low. One can, perhaps, assume that the low price of grain allowed more money to be used in purchasing meat and cheese, thus raising the prices of the latter.

This phenomenon became very conspicuous after the Black Death, when, for almost a century and a half the prices of bread grains were either stable or even falling. At the same time wages were somewhat inflated owing to the scarcity of labour, and demand for meat and other animal products, as well as of durable consumers' goods, was much increased. Not until late in the fifteenth century did these price trends begin to change. The fall

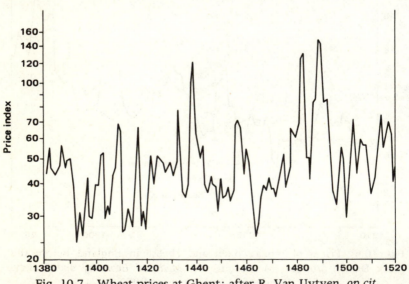

Fig. 10.7 Wheat prices at Ghent; after R. Van Uytven, *op.cit.*

in grain prices ended, and from about 1465–75 began to rise in most parts of Europe. The simplest explanation is, of course, that a rising population led to an increase in demand for, and thus to a rise in the price of, the basic bread grains, and that this left a smaller purchasing power for other goods.

Price series are fewer and less adequate in continental Europe than in England. There is no body of material comparable with the enormous compilation of Thorold Rogers. D'Avenal's tables for France are both less adequate and less reliable, and for few other places are there runs of prices at all. The graphs in Figs. 10.7 and 10.8 show very broadly the trend in grain prices at Ghent, and Kraków. The smoothness of the latter hides the very considerable fluctuations resulting from the ravages of weather and war.

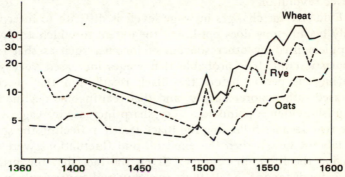

Fig. 10.8   Grain prices at Kraków; after J. Pelc, *Ceny w Krakowie w Latach 1369–1600*. Badania Ch. Dziejów Spolecznych i Gospodarczych, Nr 14, Lwów, 1935. part 2, 151.

The upward turn, apparent in the graphs during the later years of the fifteenth century, passed into the price revolution of the sixteenth. The latter has, as is well known, been attributed to the influx of New World silver. This, however, did not become a significant factor until the second quarter of the century. It was preceded by an increased output from the mines of central Europe. But variations in the supply of money cannot be made to bear all the blame for the price rise. Different categories of goods were affected in varying degrees, agricultural products showing a steeper rate of increase than other goods. Without any other influences, increasing population would have led to an increase in the price of foodstuffs. In fact, many local factors influenced prices. Cipolla has shown[31] that in Italy the increase in building activity in the mid-sixteenth century led to a price rise because a larger volume of money was being disbursed in wages without a commensurate increase in the amount of disposable goods. Money, furthermore, may have circulated faster; indeed, it probably did, since shops, open for business on all except the holidays of the Church, largely replaced the periodic markets and fairs. None of these factors, however, can wholly explain the sharp but uneven rise in prices which began in the late fifteenth century, was intensified in the middle years of the sixteenth and flattened off early in the seventeenth. One cannot escape the fact that the volume of circulating money greatly increased, and that this was the most important cause of the 'price revolution'.

Evidence for changes in wage levels is difficult to interpret, if only because one does not know the extent to which a wage was supplemented by other sources of income, such as that from a domestic craft. It is probable that wages increased very slowly during the period before the Black Death, but that prices increased rather more sharply, and that real income declined. The English evidence points to a very sharp increase in wages within the two decades following the Black Death, reflecting the scarcity of labour. Levels then flattened off and fluctuations were slight during the fifteenth century. Given the fact that the prices of basic foods tended to fall, there was thus and appreciable increase in real incomes. Figure 10.9 shows the *real* income of a craftsman from the late thirteenth century; there was a steady rise from the late fourteenth century until about 1500, after which there was a catastrophic fall.[32] Not all the English peasantry, however, was able to benefit from a fixed monetary income, and it is likely that only a small proportion was able to derive much profit from the contrary movement of wages and prices.

In continental Europe a smaller proportion of the rural labour was actually in receipt of a fixed money wage than in England. In France, vineyards were commonly worked with hired labourers, whose wages tended to be low and stable.[33] The same might be said of craftsmen's wages in the towns. In France wage rates remained depressed throughout the later Middle Ages. In Germany, on the other hand, the trend was similar to that in England,

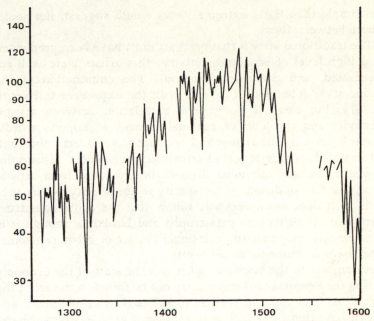

Fig. 10.9   Real income of a building craftsman expressed in the folume of consumables, in southern England, after E. H. Phelps Brown and Sheila V. Hopkins, 'Seven Centuries of the Prices of Consumables, compared with Builders' Wage-rates', *Economica*, xxiii (1956), 296–314.

with wage rates tending to rise until the later years of the fifteenth century, and then to decline.

### A DEPRESSION OF THE RENAISSANCE?

One of the most vigorous historical controversies of recent years has concerned the level of economic activity in the period from the Black Death until about 1500. The earlier view appears to have been that the high level of creativity displayed by Renaissance painters, sculptors and architects must have been sustained by a comparatively high level of economic activity; in short, that large profits were necessary for the support of great art. This has now given place to the contrasted view, supported by what few statistics are available, that the concluding century and a half of the Middle Ages were marked by diminishing production, lowered standards of living and widespread distress. The controversy remains unresolved, though it is likely that the truth, a great deal less simple than these extreme views would suggest, lies some-where between them.

The traditional view is that great art must have been predicated on a high level of economic activity; that artists were well re-munerated, and patronage generous. The culmination of the Gothic style coincided, it is true, with the expansive thirteenth century, but there is no general correlation between artistic creativity and the level of national income. In Lopez's words, 'there is no heap of riches and no depth of poverty that will automatically insure or forbid artistic achievement'.[34] This point is well made, and one must dismiss the argument from artistic creativity for conditions of prosperity in the society which sup-ports it. It does not necessarily follow that the contrary is true, that great art thrives on catastrophe and hardship, though it is undoubtedly true that the emotional impact of crisis can some-times have an immense creative effect.

An answer to the question, what was the state of the economy during the Renaissance? can clearly not be found in the art of the period. At best this can give us some insight into its mood, and this, it has often been said, was not one of great exuberance and vitality. Renaissance man lived under the joint shadow of pesti-lence and war. The devastation wrought by each has been emphasised repeatedly in this book. It would be surprising if men's attitudes were not influenced by it. 'At the close of the Middle Ages', wrote Huizinga, 'a sombre melancholy weighs on people's souls. Whether we read a chronicle, a poem, a sermon, a legal document even, the same impression of immense sadness is produced by them all.'[35] One can, however, no more argue for depressed economic conditions from the gloom and despondency of the preacher than one can for a bursting economy from the paintings of Giotto and of the Siena school.

Depressed economic conditions imply a contraction of total production, and thus of trade and consumption. Population was reduced drastically during the fourteenth century, so that de-mand fell sharply. The consequences for agriculture and manu-facturing have already been noted (pp. 444–48). What matters however is not whether total production fell sharply during the century following the Black Death – there is no question but that it did – but whether this fall was greater or less than that of the population. In other words, we need to know what changes took place in the gross product per head.

This coefficient, calculable with difficulty for modern times, cannot possibly be determined for the later Middle Ages. Indeed, it is the very sparsity of statistics which allows the controversy regarding the economy of the Renaissance to go unresolved for so long. The advocates of gloom and despondency rely upon a few statistical series, the evidence of prices, and the fact that the number of those too poor to be assessed for taxes appears to have increased. But in all these changes the contraction of the population was a highly significant factor. The question resolves itself into this: was the contraction in production and in the volume of services performed greater than can be explained in terms of a reduced population? The answer is that we do not know.

The inequality of development – or of recession – in different regions of Europe has been emphasised earlier in this chapter, and is, in general, not in dispute. The proponents of the depression of the Renaissance admit that, for example, the English cloth manufacture and export increased during the period; that the cloth manufacture of Brabant was expanded, that it spread north-wards into what is today the Netherlands, and that in many parts of Europe there were signs of local prosperity. They only claim that 'the rapid progress of a few younger countries may be in-sufficient to make up for the slow decline of the old economic giants'.[36] The article from which this quotation was taken evoked a spirited reply from Cipolla. He claimed that the economy of the fifteenth century was 'still flexible and dynamic'; that 'a reshaping of the international division of labour' was taking place, and that all we can say is that 'in some areas woollen production was declining while in others it was growing, and . . . it is not unreasonable to believe that the two facts were inti-mately related'[37].

Others have shared this view. 'A story of success', according to Waley, 'can be set beside almost every story of decline, and there is inadequate information to measure the two against each other.'[38] An extreme view was expressed by Bridbury, with reference, it must be added, to England. The later Middle Ages, he claimed,[39] were 'a period of tremendous advance not only constitutionally, but also in social and economic affairs'. The Russian economic historian, Kosminsky, found the economy of the fifteenth century expanding, as a result of the decline in the importance of feudal rents and their replacement by a money economy. What happened in the Low Countries, so often cited as evidence of economic decline, was, he claimed, 'a displacement of production into another economic region'.[40]

Both views of the economy of the Renaissance are based on a very restricted body of evidence. It is impossible to choose between them because, statistically speaking, there is no basis from which to view the behaviour of the European economy as a whole. The period of growth had unquestionably ended some time in the early fourteenth century. One can agree with Cipolla that profound changes were taking place in the international division of labour, and one can perhaps add that nowhere, except perhaps in the English cloth industry and, late in the fifteenth century, in the Central European mining industries, was there any spectacular expansion. Indeed, in an age so clouded by pestilence and war as the later Middle Ages one would not expect to find any significant or widespread evidence of economic growth. The scale of capital investment was small enough during the earlier period of expansion; it was almost certainly a great deal less during the closing century and a half of the Middle Ages, when taxation absorbed a staggeringly high proportion of current income. The high financial and social costs of warfare constituted a very restrictive factor, especially in France, which probably suffered more disastrously than most other parts of Europe. The sheer destruction of capital assets appears to have been, at least locally, as in Burgundy[41] and Gascony,[42] on a far greater scale than society could repair. Inevitably there was economic depression in such regions, and this, through reduced demand for goods from outside the region, communicated itself to other areas. Regions, such as parts of Gascony, which were devastated during the Hundred Years' War, had been, only shortly before that war began, not unimportant markets for cloth from northern France. There must have been a cessation, not merely a slackening, of economic growth in many other parts of Europe, which were seriously disturbed by war. Yet 'there was never a breakdown in the fabric of commercial interdependence . . . local specialisation could make new advances'.[43]

The depression of the Renaissance was not only a local or regional phenomenon. It also affected some segments of every society. We have seen that in some areas the peasant who was fortunate enough to hold his farm by copyhold, at a low fixed rent, could in all probability live more comfortably than his ancestors had been able to do. A small number of people was able to lay acre to acre and thus to build up a sizeable farm. In doing so, however, they inevitably deprived many a small peasant of his inheritance. The tendency, in very general terms, was for the middle to fall out of medieval society, for the rich to become richer, and the impoverished to become more numerous. This, as the Marxist historians have repeatedly emphasised, is a feature of capitalist society, which in these years began to replace the structured society of feudalism.

# Abbreviations

| | |
|---|---|
| A.A.A.G. | *Annals of the Association of American Geographers* (Washington) |
| A.A.G.Bij. | *Afdeling Agrarische Geschiedenis Bijdragen* (Wageningen, Netherlands) |
| Acad. Inscr. C.R. | *Comptes Rendus, Académie des Inscriptions et Belles Lettres* (Paris) |
| Actes Coll. Int. Dém. Hist. | *Actes du Colloque International de Démographie Historique* (Liège, 1964) |
| Agric. Hist. Rev. | *Agricultural History Review* (Reading) |
| Am. Hist. Rev. | *The American Historical Review* (Washington, D.C.) |
| Ann. Dém. Hist. | *Annales de Démographie Historique* (Paris) |
| Ann. E.S.C. | *Annales: Economies – Sociétés – Civilisations* (Paris) |
| Ann. Géog. | *Annales de Géographie* (Paris) |
| Ann. Hist. Econ. Soc. | *Annales d'Histoire Economique et Sociale* (Paris) |
| Ann. Midi | *Annales du Midi* (Toulouse) |
| Ann. Norm. | *Annales de Normandie* (Caen) |
| Ann. Rept. Am. Hist. Soc. | *Annual Report, American Historical Society* (Washington, D.C.) |
| Bibl. Ec. Chartres | *Bibliothèque de l'Ecole des Chartes* (Paris) |
| Bibl. Ec. Franç. Ath. Rome | *Bibliothèque des Ecoles Françaises d'Athènes et de Rome* |
| Bull. Comm. Roy. Hist. | *Bulletin de la Commission Royale d'Histoire* (Brussels) |
| Bull. Phil. Hist. | *Bulletin Philologique et Historique de la Comité des Travaux Historiques et Scientifiques* (Paris) |
| Bibl. Ec. Htes. Et. | *Bibliothèque de l'Ecole des Hautes Etudes* (Paris) |
| Cah. Hist. Mond. | *Cahiers d'Histoire Mondiale* (Paris) |
| Camb. Econ. Hist. | *Cambridge Economic History of Europe* (London) |
| Cib. Rev. | *Ciba Review* (Basel) |

| | |
|---|---|
| Comm. Roy. Hist. | *Commission Royale d'Histoire de Belgique* (Brussels) |
| Comp. Stud. Soc. Hist. | *Comparative Studies in Society and History* (Chicago) |
| Conf. Int. Hist. Econ. | *Conférence Internationale d'Histoire Economique* |
| Deutsch. Akad. Wiss. | *Deutsche Akademie der Wissenschaften* (Berlin) |
| Ec. Prat. Htes Et. | *Ecole Pratique des Hautes Etudes* (Paris) |
| Econ. Hist. Rev. | *The Economic History Review* (London) |
| Et. Rur. | *Etudes Rurales* (Paris) |
| Hans. Geschichtsbl. | *Hansische Geschichtsblätter* (Leipzig) |
| Hist. | *Historica* (Prague) |
| Htes Et. Med. Mod. | *Hautes Etudes Médiévales et Modernes* (Geneva) |
| Jahrb. Nat. Stat. | *Jahrbücher für Nationalökönomie und Statistik* (Jena, Stuttgart) |
| Jahrb. Ver. Meckl. Gesch. | *Jahrbuch des Vereins für Mecklenburgische Geschichte* (Schwerin) |
| Jnl Eccl. Hist. | *Journal of Ecclesiastical History* |
| Jnl Econ. Bus Hist. | *Journal of Economic and Business History* (Cambridge, Mass.) |
| Jnl Econ. Hist. | *The Journal of Economic History* |
| Jnl Econ. Soc. Hist. Orient | *Journal of Economic and Social History of the Orient* (Leiden) |
| Jnl Interdisc. Hist. | *Journal of Interdisciplinary History* (Pittsburgh, Penn.) |
| Jnl Pol. Econ. | *Journal of Political Economy* (Chicago) |
| Jnl Rom. Stud. | *Journal of Roman Studies* (London) |
| Jnl. Soc Hist. | *Journal of Social History* (Berkeley) |
| Kwart. Hist. Kult. Mat. | *Kwartalnik Historii Kultury Materialnej* (Warsaw) |
| Med. Hum. | *Medievalia et Humanistica* (Boulder, Col.) |
| Mém. Comm. Dépt. Pas-de-Calais | *Mémoires de la Commission Départementale des des Monuments Historiques du Pas-de-Calais* (Arras) |
| Mon. Germ. Hist. | *Monumenta Germaniae Historica* |
| Moy. Age | *Le Moyen Age* (Paris) |
| Pet. Mitt. | *Petermanns Mitteilungen* (Gotha) |
| Pop. Stud. | *Population Studies* (London) |
| Rev. Belge Phil. Hist. | *Revue Belge de Philologie et d'Histoire* (Brussels) |
| Rev. Et. Anc. | *Revue des Etudes Anciennes* (Bordeaux) |
| Rev. Hist. | *Revue Historique* (Paris) |
| Rev. Hist. Econ. Soc. | *Revue d'Histoire Economique et Sociale* (Paris) |
| Rev. Hist. Sid. | *Revue d'Histoire de la Sidérurgie* (Nancy) |
| Rev. Nord | *Revue du Nord* (Paris) |
| Rev. Int. Onomast. | *Revue Internationale d'Onomastique* (Paris) |
| Spec. | *Speculum* (Boston, Mass) |

# Abbreviations

| | |
|---|---|
| Trans. Am. Phil. Soc. | *Transactions of the American Philosophical Society* (Philadelphia, Penn.) |
| Veröff. Planck Inst. Gesch. | *Veröffentlichungen des Max Planck Instituts der Geschichte* (Göttingen) |
| Viertel. Soz. Wirtsch. | *Vierteljahrschrift für Sozial- und Wirtschaftsgeschichte* (Leipzig) |
| Zeitscher. Schweiz. Gesch. | *Zeitschrift für Schweizerische Geschichte* (Zurich) |

# Notes and References

## Chapter 1. The Later Roman Empire

1. There was also a movement of gold eastwards from the Empire to India; see E. H. Warmington, *The Commerce between the Roman Empire and India*, Cambridge University Press, 1928, 272–318.
2. J. B. Bury, *History of the Later Roman Empire*, 2 vols, 1889.
3. P. A. Brunt, *Roman Manpower*, Oxford University Press, 1971, 121–30.
4. A. H. M. Jones, *The Later Roman Empire 284–602*, Oxford, Blackwell, 1964, ii, 621.
5. Ramsay MacMullen, 'Barbarian enclaves in the northern Roman Empire', *L'Antiquité Classique*, xxxii, 1963, 552–61.
6. Juvenal, *Satires*, III, 62–5. See also Seneca, *Ad Helviam*, 6.
7. Samuel Dill, *Roman Society in the Last Century of the Western Empire*, London, Macmillan, 1899, p. 276.
8. Silius Italicus, *Punica*, VII, 364–6.
9. On the relations between fields and ploughs see B. H. Slicher van Bath, *The Agrarian History of Western Europe A.D. 500–1800*, London, 1963, 54–69.
10. K. D. White, 'Wheat Farming in Roman Times', *Antiquity*, xxxvii (1963), 207–12.
11. K. D. White, 'The productivity of labour in Roman agriculture', *Antiquity*, xxxix (1965), 102–7.
12. A. J. Toynbee, *Hannibal's Legacy*, Oxford University Press, 1965, ii, 36–105.
13. In the words of Salvian, the peasants of Gaul were 'driven to flight by the tax collectors and abandon their little holdings because they cannot retain them, and seek out the estates of great men and become the tenants of the rich,' (quoted by Jones, ii, 775).
14. As quoted in Jones, ii, 801.
15. René Martin, 'Plins le Jeune et les problèmes économiques de son temps', *Rev. Et. Anc.*, lxix (1967), 62–97.
16. Petronius, *Satyricon*, iv.
17. Dill, p. 149.

18. Jones, ii, 816.

19. *ibid.*, 822.

20. The term 'town' is here used for the complex buildings. 'City' is used to translate *civitas* and implies the *territorium* together with its central place.

21. Rudi Thomsen, *The Italic Regions from Augustus to the Lombard Invasion*, Classica et Medievalia: Dissertations, Copenhagen, 1947.

22. G. E. F. Chilver, *Cisalpine Gaul*, Oxford University Press, 1941, pp. 45–50.

23. Pliny, *Natural History*, III, i, 7.

24. M. Rostovtzeff, *The Social and Economic History of the Roman Empire*, London, 1926, p. 130.

25. Joel LeGal, *Le Tibre, Fleuve de Rome dans l'Antiquité*, Paris, 1953.

26. Xenophon, *Cyropaedia*, VIII, ii, 5.

27. *Recueil Général des Bas-Reliefs, Statues et Bustes de la Gaule Romaine*, Paris (Imprimerie Nationale), 1915, vi, 437–60.

28. F. W. Walbank, *The Awful Revolution*, Liverpool University Press, 1969, pp. 47–54.

29. R. E. Mortimer Wheeler, *Rome Beyond the Imperial Frontiers*, London, Bell, 1954, pp. 63–94.

30. H. J. Eggers, *Der römische Import im freien Germanien*, Hamburgisches Museum für Völkerkunde und Vorgeschichte, 1951, esp. maps 60–62.

## Chapter 2. The early Middle Ages

1. See Charles Higounet, 'L'occupation du sol du pays entre Tarn et Garonne au Moyen Age,' *Ann. Midi*, 65 (1953), pp. 307–30, and Jacques Boussard, 'Essai sur le peuplement de la Touraine du I$^{er}$ au VIII$^e$ siècle,' *Moy. Age*, xl (1954), 261–91.

2. Franz Petri, *Germanische Volkserbe in Wallonien und Nordfrankreich*, Bonn, 1937.

3. J. M. Wallace-Hadrill, *The Long-Haired Kings*, London, Methuen, 1962, pp.8–9.

4. Gino Luzzatto, *An Economic History of Italy from the Fall of the Roman Empire to the Beginning of the Sixteenth Century*, London, Routledge, 1961, p. 18.

5. Procopius, VII, 14, 29–30.

6. Salvianus, VI, 8 and 13.

7. Sidonius Appollinaris, *Letters*, III, no. 2.

8. Sidonius Appollinaris, *Letters*, V, no. 5.

9. Salvianus, V, 5.

10. J. V. Vives, *An Economic History of Spain*, Princeton University Press, 1969, p. 84.

11. Sidonius Appollinaris, II, 2.

12. Salvianus, V, 8.

13. Gregory of Tours, VI, 32.
14. *Ausgewählte Urkunden zur Erläuterung der Verfassungsgeschichte Deutschlands im Mittelalter*, ed. Altmann and Bernheim, Berlin, 1904, p. 289, as translated in *A Source Book for Medieval Economic History*, ed. R. C. Cave and H. H. Coulson, New York, Biblo and Tanner, 1965, pp. 27–8.
15. In full *Brevium exempla ad describendas res ecclesiasticas et fiscales*; it is printed in *Mon. Germ. Hist.*, Leges, i, 250–6, and is ascribed by its editor to 810.
16. The text has twice been published with long critical introductions: *Polyptyque de l'abbé Irminon*, ed. B. Guérard, 2 vols, Paris (Imprimerie Royale), 1844; and *Polyptyque de l'Abbaye de Saint-Germain-des-Prés*, ed. A. Longnon, Paris (H. Champion), 1895.
17. See N. J. G. Pounds, 'Northwest Europe in the ninth century, its geography in the light of the polyptyques', *A.A.A.G.*, lvii (1967), 439–61.
18. *Polyptyque de l'Abbaye de Saint-Rémi de Reims*, ed. B. Guérard, Paris, Imprimerie Impériale, 1853.
19. 'Güter-Verzeichnung der Abtei Prüm von 893,' *Urkundenbuch zur Geschichte der mittelrheinischen Territorien*, ed. Heinrich Beyer, i (1860), 142–201.
20. Liber Traditionum Sancti Petri Blandiniensis, ed. Arnold Fayem, in *Cartulaire de la Ville de Gand*, 2$^e$ série, i (Ghent, 1906), pp. 10–52.
21. This short polyptyque of only four paragraphs was printed by B. Guérard in his edition of Irminon's *Polyptyque*, i, 925–6; the author's translation.
22. Robert Latouche, *The Birth of Western Economy*, London, Methuen, 1961, p. 69.
23. Auguste Longnon, *Géographie de la Gaule au VI$^e$ siècle*, Paris, Librairie Hachette, 1878, p. 16.
24. *Vita Sancti Breoci*, cap. 47, in G. H. Doble, *Saint Brioc*, Exeter, 1928.
25. K. D. White, *Agricultural Implements of the Roman World*, Cambridge University Press, 1968.
26. Gregory of Tours, III, 19; translation of O. M. Dalton.
27. Prüm polyptyque, *cap*. 46.
28. Spelt was a sub-species of the common wheat. Its chief peculiarity is that the grain does not readily separate from the husk in threshing.
29. Prüm polyptyque, *cap*. 99.
30. Saint-Pierre of Ghent, polyptyque, *cap*. 3.
31. Printed in *Mon. Germ. Hist.*, Legum Sectio, i (Hanover, 1883), 82–9, and in J. P. Migne, *Patrologia Latina*, xcvii (Paris, 1862), 349–58.
32. Gregory of Tours, III, 19.
33. Fredegar (continuation), 47.
34. 1 October; perhaps an allusion to a wine fair at Reims.
35. L. M. Hartmann, 'Die Wirtschaft des Klosters Bobbio im 9. Jahrhundert,' in *Zur Wirtschaftgeschichte Italiens im Mittelalter*, Gotha (1904) pp. 42–73; P. S. Leicht, 'L'organisation des grands domaines dans l'Italie du Nord pendant les X$^e$–XII$^e$ siècles', *Rec. Jean Bodin*, iv (1949), 165–76; Gino Luzzatto, 'Changes in Italian agrarian economy', in *Early*

*Medieval Society*, ed. Sylvia L. Thrupp, New York, Appleton-Centum, 1967, pp. 206–18; P. J. Jones, 'The agrarian development of medieval Italy', *Deuxième Conférence Internationale d'Histoire Economique*, Aix-en-Provence, 1962. ii (1965), pp. 69–86.

36. Inventarium omnium bonarum eorumque redditum monasterii sanctimonialium S. Iuliae Brixensis, in *Codex Diplomaticus Langobardiae, Historiae Patriae Monumenta*, xiii, Turin, 1873, 709–28.

37.   A. E. Verhulst, 'De Sint-Baafsabdij te Ghent en Haar Gronbezit (VII^e–XIV^e eeuw', *Verhandelingen van de Koninklijke Vlaamse Academie voor Wetenschappen, Letteren en Schone Kunsten van België, Klasse der Letteren*, Vol. xxx, 1958.

38. The Censier of St. Emmeram is printed in P. Dollinger, *L'Evolution des classes rurales en Bavière*, Paris, 1949, pp. 504–12.

39.   R. Latouche, 'Defrichement et peuplement rural dans le Maine du IX^e au XIII^e siècles', *Moy. Age*, 4^e série, iii, 1948, 77–87; and *The Birth of the Western Economy*, pp. 64–5.

40. Sidonius Appollinaris, VII, 10.

41. Gregory of Tours, II, 24.

42. *ibid*., VI, 23–4.

43. Paulus Diaconus, VI, 58.

44. Latouche, *The Birth of the Western Economy*, p. 5.

45. Isidore of Seville, *Etymologium*, XV, 2, 6.

46. Gregory of Tours, III, 19.

47. Fredegar, cap. I. The church was notable for its rich gold ornaments. See Paulus Diaconus, III, 34.

48. Paulus Diaconus, VI, I; 58.

49. It is probable that Bath (*Aquae Sulis*) was the town described in the Anglo-Saxon poem, *The Ruin*, quoted above. See J. F. Benton, *Town Origins*, D. C. Heath & Co., Boston, Mass., 1968, pp. 46–8.

50. Henri Laurent, 'Marchands du palais et marchands d'abbayes', *Rev. Hist*., vol. 183 (1938), 281–97.

51. L' Levillain, 'Essai sur les origines du Lendit', *Rev. Hist.* vol. 152 (1927), 241–76.

52. Edith Ennen, 'The different types of formation of European towns', in *Early Medieval Society*, ed. Thrupp, pp. 174–82.

53. Henri Pirenne, *Mohammed and Charlemagne*, New York, World Pub. Co., 1957, p. 143.

54. Henri Pirenne; *Medieval Cities: their origins and the revival of trade*, New York, Doubleday Anchor Books, 1956, p. 16.

55. *Ibid.*

56. Latouche, *The Birth of the Western Economy*, p. 123.

57. Sidonius Apollinaris, IV, 8.

58. *Ibid.*, VII, 2.

59. Gregory of Tours, VI, 5.

60. Notker the Stammerer, II, 14. The Norse do not appear to have reached the Mediterranean until after the death of Charlemagne.

61. Notker the Stammerer, II, 17.

62. *Ibid.*, II, 8–9.

63. Einhard, 26.
64. J. W. Thompson, *The Dissolution of the Carolingian Fisc in the Ninth Century*, University of California Pubns in *History*, vol. xxiii, Berkeley, Calif., 1935.
65. Ermoldus Niger, *Carmina*, I, lines 115–30.
66. Notker the Stammerer, I, 34.
67. Prüm polyptyque, *cap.* 46.
68. Even this has been disputed; see P. Grierson, 'Le sou d'or d'Uzès', *Moy. Age*, Sèrie 4, ix (1954), 293–309.
69. Capitulary of Pistres (864), *cap.* 12, *Mon. Germ. Hist.*, *Capitularia Regum Francorum*, ii, 315.
70. Paulus Diaconus, III, 34.
71. *Mon. Germ. Hist.*, Capitularia, i, 132.
72. *Constantine Porphyrogenitus de Administrando Imperio*, ed. Gy. Moravcsik, Budapest., 1949, 139.
73. Strabo, III, 2, 15.
74. Ernst Kissinger, 'A survey of the early Christian town of Stobi', *Dumbarton Oaks Papers*, no. 3 (1946), pp. 81–162.
75. The text is published in E. H. Freshfield, *Roman Law in the Later Roman Empire*, Cambridge University Press, 1938, pp. 3–50.
76. The Greek text is published in W. Ashburner, *Journal of Hellenic Studies*, xxx (1910), 85–108, and in translation, *ibid.*, xxxii (1912), 68–95.
77. Alfons Dopsch, *The Economic and Social Foundations of European Civilization*, London, Routledge, 1937, p. 126.
78. *The Chronicle of the Slavs,* ed. F. J. Tschan, New York, Columbia University Press, 1935, p. 123.
79. Annales Bertiniani, *Mon. Germ. Hist., Scriptores*, i, 434.
80. Ermentaire, in *Textes d'hist. médiévale*, Paris, 1951, 132–3.
81. Prüm polyptyque, caps. 49, 103.
82. *The Primary Russian Chronicle*, ed. S. F. Cross, p. 144.
83. Archibald R. Lewis, *The Northern Seas*, Princeton University Press, 1958, pp. 214–20, 226–8.
84. *Constantine Porphyrogenitus de administrando imperio*, ed. G. Moravcsik and R. J. H. Jenkins, Budapest, 1949; the quotation is from cap. 9, pp. 57–63.
85. The term, Ρως, used by the Byzantines to denote the Nordic peoples, probably derives from the Old Finnish Rõtsi, used for the Swedes; see *De Administrando Imperii*, ed. R. J. H. Jenkins, vol. ii, *Commentary*, pp. 20–3.
86. D. Sinor, 'The outlines of Hungarian prehistory', *Cah. Hist. Mond.*, iv (1957), 513–40.

## Chapter 3. The expansion of the medieval economy

1. Henri Focillon, *The Year 1000*, New York, Ungar, 1969.
2. Raoul Glaber; the translation is that of C. G. Coulton, *Life in the Middle*

2. Rauol Glaber; the translation is that of C. G. Coulton, *Life in the Middle Ages*, Cambridge University Press, 1930, vol. i.

3. *Atlas Ostliches Mitteleuropa*, Bielefeld, 1959, Blätter, 59–60.

4. Theodor Mayer, 'Das deutsche Königtum und sein Wirkungsbereich', in *Das Reich und Europa*, Leipzig, 1941, pp. 52–63.

5. Ibrāhim Ibn Ja'kub, *Monumenta Poloniae Historica*, new series, i, (Kraków, 1949), 49.

6. *Ibid.*

7. Robert Latouche, *The Birth of the Western Economy*, London, Methuen, 1961, 269. The author does not mention the fact that Burgundy was in fact raided by a band of Danes following the siege of Paris in 885; see *Abbo*, ed. Guizot, *Collection de Mémoires*, p. 52.

8. Vita Ottonis Episcopi Babanbergensis, *Monumenta Poloniae Historica*, ii, (Lwów, 1872), 32–70.

9. R. S. Lopez, 'East and West in the early Middle Ages: Economic Relations', *Relazioni del X Congresso Internazionale di Science Storiche*, iii, (Florence, 1955), 113–63.

10. *Ibid.*

11. Arnold Toynbee, *Hannibal's Legacy*, Oxford University Press, 1965, ii, 10–35; 155–89.

12. 'Conflictus Ovis et Lini', in *Zeitschrift für Deutsches Altertum*, ix (1859), 215–38.

13. *Actes des Comtes de Flandres*, 1071–1128, ed. F. Vercauteren, *Commission Royale d'Histoire*, Brussels, 1938.

14. R. H. Hilton, 'Rent and capital formation in feudal society', *Deuxième Conférence Internationale d'Histoire Economique, Aix-en-Provence*, 1962, ii (Paris, 1965), 33–68.

15. Quoted in Carlo M. Cipolla, *Money, Prices and Civilization*, New York, Gordian Press, 1967, 16.

16. R. S. Lopez, 'The dollar of the Middle Ages', *Jnl Econ. Hist.* xi (1951), 209–34.

17. Maurice Lombard, 'L'or mussulman du VII$^e$ au IX$^e$ siècle', *Ann. ESC.*, ii (1947), 143–60, see also F.-J. Himly, 'Y a-t-il emprise musulmane sur l'économie des états européens du VIII$^e$ au X$^e$ siècle?', *Schweizerische Zeitschrift für Geschichte*, v (1955), 31–81; P. Grierson, 'Carolingian Europe and the Arabs: the myth of the Mancus'. *Rev. Belge Phil. Hist.*, xxxii (1954), 1059–74.

18. R. S. Lopez, 'East and West in the early Middle Ages', *Relazioni del X Congresso Internazionale di Scienze Storiche*, iii, (Florence, 1955), 113–63.

19. D. Herlihy, 'Treasure hoards in the Italian economy, 960–1139', *Econ. Hist. Rev.*, x (1957–8), 1–14.

20. H. S. Lucas, 'The great European famine of 1315, 1316 and 1317', *Speculum*, v (1930), 343–77.

21. David Herlihy, 'Population, plague and social change in rural Pistoia, 1201–1430', *Econ. Hist. Rev..*, xviii (1965), 225–44; idem, *Medieval and Renaissance Pistoia*, Yale University Press, 1967, pp. 62–9.

22. M. Postan, 'Some economic evidence of declining population in the later Middle Ages', *Econ. Hist. Rev.*, ii (1950), 221–46.

## Chapter 4. The population of medieval Europe

1. Ferdinand Lot, 'L'état des paroisses et des feux', *Bibl. Ec. Chartres*, xc (1929), 51–107 and 256–315.
2. L.-J. Thomas, 'La population du Bas-Languedoc à la fin du XIII<sup>e</sup> siècle au commencement du XIV<sup>e</sup>', *Ann. Midi*, (1908), 469–83; Edouard Baratier, *La Démographie Provençale du XIII<sup>e</sup> au XVI<sup>e</sup> Siècle*, Paris, 1961; *Documents relatifs au Comté de Champagne et de Brie*, ed. A. Longnon, Paris, Colln. de Docts, 1891, nos, 7304–7404; H. Ammann, 'Die Bevölkerung der Westschweiz im ausgehenden Mittelalter', in *Festschrift F. E. Welti*, Aarau, 1937, 390–447; W. Bickel, *Bevölkerungsgeschichte und Bevölkerungspolitik der Schweiz seit dem Ausgang des Mittelalters*, Zurich, 1947.
3. F. Stuhr, 'Die Bevölkerung Mecklenburgs am Ausgang des Mittelalters', *Jahrb. Ver. Meck. Gesch.*, lviii (1893); *Das Landregister der Herrschaft Sorau von 1381*, ed. J. Schulte, *Brandenburgische Landbücher*, i, Berlin, 1936.
4. *Polyptychum Rotomagensis Dioecesis, Recueil des Historiens des Gaules et de la France*, xxiii (Paris, 1894), 228–329.
5. *La Visite des Eglises du Diocèse de Lausanne en 1416–1417, Mémoires et Documents publiés par la Société d'Histoire de la Suisse Romande*, 2nd series, ii (1921).
6. Ferdinand Lot, 'Conjectures démographique sur la France au LX<sup>e</sup> siècle', *Moy. Age.*, xxxii (1921), 1–27 and 107–37.
7. Karl Lamprecht, *Deutsches Wirtschaftsleben im Mittelalter*, Verlag von Alfons Dürr, Leipzig, 1886, vol. i, 163 contains a familiar instance of the use of this fallacious method.
8. Emily Coleman, 'Medieval Marriage Characteristics: A Neglected factor in the History of Medieval Serfdom', *Jnl. Interdisc. Hist.*, ii (1971), 205–19.
9. J. C. Russell, *British Medieval Population*, University of New Mexico Press, 1948, pp. 92–117.
10. Idem, 'Late ancient and medieval population', *Trans. Am. Phil. Soc.*, xlviii (1958), part 3, p. 148.
11. H. van Werveke, 'La famine de l'an 1316 en Flandre et les régions voisines', *Rev. Nord*, xli (1959), 5–14.
12. J. Garnier, *La Recherche des Feux en Bourgogne aux XIV<sup>e</sup> et XV<sup>e</sup> siècles*, Dijon, 1876.
13. Curt Weikinn, *Quellenkunde zur Witterungsgeschichte Europas von der Zeitwende bis zum Jahre 1850*, Deutsch. Akad. Wiss. Berlin, 1958, vol. i.
14. E. Leroy Ladurie, *Times of Feast, Times of Famine*, New York, Doubleday, 1971.
15. Charles Creighton, *A History of Epidemics in Britain*, vol. i, Cambridge, 1891, though now superseded in detail, is still useful. See also Philip Ziegler, *The Black Death*, London, Collins, 1969 (Penguin, 1970); and J. F. D. Shrewsbury, *A History of the Bubonic Plague in the British Isles*, London, Cambridge University Press, 1970.
16. E. Keyser, 'Die Pest in Deutschland und ihre Erforschung', *Actes*

*Coll. Int. Dem. Hist*, University of Liège, pp. 369–77.

17. Walter Kronshage, *Die Bevölkerung Göttingens, Studien zur Geschichte der Stadt Göttingen*, i, Göttingen, 1960, 28–73.

18. H. Neveux, 'La mortalité des pauvres à Cambrai (1377–1473)', *Ann. Dém. Hist.*, 1968, 73–97.

19. M.-A. Arnould, 'Mortalité et épidémies sous l'ancien régime dans la Hainaut et quelques régions limitrophes', *Actes Coll. Int. Dem. Hist.*, pp. 465–81.

20. Robert Favreau, 'Epidémies à Poitiers et dans le Centre-Ouest à la fin du Moyen Age', *Bibl. Ec. Chartres*, vol. 125 (1967), 349–98.

21. J. C. Russell, 'Demographic pattern in history', *Pop. Studies*, i (1947–8), 388–404.

22. Guillaume de Nangis, ed. Géraud, ii, 211.

23. G. Ohlin, 'Mortality, marriage and growth in pre-industrial populations', *Pop. Studies*, xiv (1960–61), 190–7.

24. H. E. Hallam, 'Some thirteenth-century censuses', *Econ. Hist. Rev.*, x (1958), 340–61.

25. Especially Lutz K. Berkner, 'The stem family and the developmental cycle of the peasant household: an eighteenth-century Austrian example', *Am. Hist. Rev.*, lxxvii (1972), 398–418.

26. For an example see F. Maillard and R.-H. Bautier, 'Un dénombrement des feux, des individus et des fortunes dans deux villages du Fenouillèdes', *Bull. Phil. Hist.*, 1965, 309–28.

27. R.-H. Bautier, 'Feux, population et structure sociale au milieu du XV^e siècle: l'exemple de Carpentras', *Ann. ESC.*, xiv (1959), 255–68.

28. Notably by Moses I. Finlay, in reviewing A. E. R. Boak, *Man-Power Shortage and the Fall of the Roman Empire in the West*, in *Jnl Rom. Studies*, xlviii (1958), 156–64.

29. J. C. Russell, *Late Ancient and Medieval Population*, p. 88.

30. P. Riché, 'Problèmes de démographie historique du haut moyen âge', *Ann. Dém. Hist.*, 1966, pp. 37–55.

31. F. Lot, 'Conjectures démographiques', *loc. cit.*

32. J. Z. Titow, 'Some evidence of the thirteenth-century population increase', *Econ. Hist. Rev.*, xiv (1961), 218–24.

33. N. J. G. Pounds, 'Overpopulation in France and the Low Countries in the later Middle Ages', *Jnl of Soc. Hist.*, iii (1970), 225–47. This paper cites the sources used and describes the method.

34. J. Z. Titow, 'Some differences between manors and their effects on the condition of the peasant in the thirteenth century', *Agric. Hist. Rev.*, x (1962), 1–13.

35. P. Gras, 'Le registre paroissial de Givry (1334–1357) et la peste noire en Bourgogne', *Bibl. Ec. Chartes*, c (1939), 295–308.

36. Philippe Wolff, 'Trois études de démographie médiévale en France méridionale', *Studi Armando Sapori*, 493–503.

37. Enrico Fiumi, 'La popolazione del territorio volterrano-sangimignanese ed il problema demographico dell' età comunale', *Studi Amintore Fanfani*, i, 249–90.

38. Geneviève Prat, 'Albi et la Peste Noire', *Ann. Midi*, lxiv (1952), 15–25.

39. P. Wolff, *Commerce et Marchands de Toulouse, vers 1350–vers 1450*, Paris, 1954, pp. 68–72.

40. Irena Gieysztorowa, 'Badania nad historią zaludnienia Polski', *Kwart. Hist. Kult. Mat.*, xi (1963), 523–62.

41. Gustaf Utterström, 'Some notes on the present state of research in Swedish demographic history prior to 1750', *Actes Coll. Int. Dém. Hist.*, 217–25.

42. H. Ammann, 'Die Bevölkerung der Westschweiz im ausgehenden Mittelalter', *Festschrift E. E. Welti*, Aarau, 1937, 390–447; Bickel, *op. cit.*, pp. 40–2.

43. Blaschke, *op. cit.*; *idem*, 'Bevölkerungsgang und Wüstungen in Sachsen während des späten Mittelalters', *Jahrb. Nat. und Stat.*, vol. 174 (1962), 414–29.

44. Friedrich Stuhr, 'Die Bevölkerung Mecklenburgs am Ausgang des Mittelalters', *Jahrb. Ver. Meckl. Gesch.*, lviii (1893), 232–78.

45. Joseph Kovacsics, 'An account of research work in historical demography in Hungary', *Coll. Int. Dém. Hist.*, pp. 249–72.

46. Omer Lufti Barkan, 'Essai sur les données statistiques des Registres de Recensement dans l'Empire Ottoman aux XV$^e$ et XVI$^e$ Siècles', *Jnl Econ. Soc. Hist Orient*, i (1958), 9–36.

47. David Herlihy, *Medieval and Renaissance Pistoia*, Yale University Press, 1967, p. 71.

48. Carlo M. Cipolla, 'Four centuries of Italian demographic development', *Population in History*, London, Edward Arnold, 1965, 570–87; idem., 'Per la storia della populazione Lombarda nel secolo XVI', *Studi Gino Luzzatto*, ii, 144–55. Beloch's summary figures are in his *Bevölkerungsgeschichte Italiens*, iii, 339–85.

## Chapter 5. Agriculture and rural life

1. N. J. G. Pounds, 'Population and settlement in the Low Countries and northern France in the later Middle Ages', *Rev. Belge Phil. Hist.*, xlix (1971), 69–402.

2. Based on J. Garnier, *La Recherche des Feux en Bourgogne aux XIV$^e$ et XV$^e$ Siècles*, Dijon, 1876.

3. Stuhr, 'Die Bevölkerung Mecklenburgs . . .', *loc. cit.*

4. Suger, *De rebus in administratione sua gestis*, cap. 10, as translated in *The European Inheritance*, ed. E. Barker, G. Clark and P. Vaucher, Oxford University Press, 1954, pp. 499–500.

5. R. Latouche, 'Défrichements et peuplement rural dans le Maine du XI$^e$ et XIII$^e$ siècle', *Moy. Age*, iii (1948), 77–87.

6. Archibald R. Lewis, 'The Closing of the Medieval Frontier, 1250–1350', *Spec.*, xxxiii (1958), 475–83.

7. *Gesta Abbatum Trudonensium*, i, 150, as quoted in Alfred Hansay, *Etude sur la formation et l'organisation économique de la domaine de l'Abbaye de Saint-Trond*, Ghent, 1899, p. 8.

8. See A. Carnoy, 'Le défrichement dans la toponymie Belge', *Rev. Int. d'Onomast.*, xiii (1961), 81–99.

9. *Actes des Comtes de Flandres*, ed. F. Vercauteren, *Comm. Roy. Hist.*, Brussels, 1938; see also G. W. Coopland, *The Abbey of St Bertin and its Neighbourhood*, pp. 900–1350, Oxford University Press, 1914,

10. Gunnar Mickwitz, 'Medieval agrarian society in its prime', *Camb. Econ. Hist. Eur.*, i (1st edn.), 323–4.

11. L. Genicot, 'Donations de villae ou défrichements: les origines du temporel de l'abbaye de Lobbes', *Miscellanea Historica in honorem Alberti de Meyer*, Louvain, 1946, i, 286–96.

12. Gregory of Tours, VI, 13.

13. Michel Mollat, 'Les hôtes de l'abbaye de Bourbourg', *Mélanges d'Histoire du Moyen Age dédiés à la mémoire de Louis Halphen*, Paris, 1951, pp. 513–21; see also the case of the reclamation of the marshes of Kent by the Benedictines of Canterbury: R. A. L. Smith, *Canterbury Cathedral Priory*, Cambridge University Press, p. 195.

14. Hugues Lamy, 'L'Abbaye de Tongerloo depuis sa fondation jusqu'en 1263', *Recueil de Travaux, Conférence d'Histoire et de Philologie*, University of Louvain, 1914.

15. Rievaulx had 600 *conversi* at the time of Abbot Ailred; this was quite exceptional.

16. A German text is published in Thule: *Altnordische Dichtung und Prosa*, vol. xxiii, Jena, 1928.

17. *Egil's Saga*, trans. and ed. E. R. Eddison, Cambridge University Press, 1930, Book 29, p. 57.

18. Eli F. Heckscher, *An Economic History of Sweden*, Harvard University Press, 1954, pp. 41–4.

19. J. W. Thompson, 'East German colonization in the Middle Ages', *Ann. Rept., Am. Hist. Ass.*, 1915, pp. 125–50.

20. Hermann Aubin, 'Medieval society in its prime: the lands east of the Elbe and German colonisation eastwards', *Camb. Econ. Hist. Europe*, i (1st edn.), 367.

21. *The Chronicle of the Slavs*, i, 57, in the translation of F. J. Tschan, New York, 1935.

22. F. Lütge, *Deutsche Sozial- und Wirtschaftsgeschichte*, Berlin, 1966, 132.

23. Walter Kuhn, *Siedlungsgeschichte Oberschlesiens*, Würzburg, 1954, pp. 31 *et seq.* and Karte 3.

24. Aubin, *op cit.*, p. 396.

25. Reproduced in Wilhelm Abel, *Die Wüstungen des ausgehenden Mittelalters*, 2nd edn, Stuttgart, 1955, p. 47, and in G. Duby, *Rural Economy and Country Life*, London, Edward Arnold, 1968, p. 392.

26. A. Meitzen, *Siedlungen und Agrarwesen der Westgermanen und Ostgermanen, der Kelten, Römer, Finnen und Slaven*, Berlin, 1895.

27. Lubor Niederle, *Manuel de l'Antiquité Slave*, ii, 205–10.

28. Suger, *op. cit.*, cap. 5.

29. See especially the grange of Veulerent; Charles Higounet, *La Grange de Veulerent*, Paris, 1964.

30. Robert Wace, *Roman de Rou*, ed. Hugo Anderson, Heilbronn, 1879, ii, part 3, lines 819–20.

31. Hans Mortensen, 'Die mittelalterliche deutsche Kulturlandschaft und ihr Verhältnis zur Gegenwart', *Viertel. Soz. Wirtsch.* xlv (1958), 17–36.

32. Abel, *op cit.*

33. *Documents relatifs au Comté de Champagne et de Brie, 1172–1361*, ed. A. Longnon, Paris, 1891, nos. 7304–7404.

34. B. H. Slicher van Bath, *The Agrarian History of Western Europe A.D. 500–1850*, London Edward Arnold, 1963, p. 160.

35. P. J. Jones; 'The agrarian development of medieval Italy', *Deuxième Conf. Int. Hist Econ., Aix-en-Provence, 1962*, Paris, 1965, ii 69–80.

36. It has been argued on theoretical grounds that the best soil could not have supported much more than 75 persons to the square kilometre under medieval conditions of technology: W. van Egmont of Indiana University in an unpublished paper.

37. Especially B. H. Slicher van Bath, 'Yield ratios', *A. A. G. Bijdragen*, x (1963).

38. It is reported in *Le Journal d'un Bourgeois de Paris sous le règne de François I$^{er}$* (*Collection de Textes*), Paris, 1910, p. 155, that in 1522–23 the severe winter frosts destroyed the autumn sown corn 'tellement qu'il convint de nouveau ressemer les dictz bledz'.

39. *Le Livre de l'Abbé Guillaume de Ryckel* (1249–1272), Ghent, 1896, 232 (author's translation).

40. Charles Higounet, 'L'assolement triennal dans la plaine de France au XIII$^e$ siècle', *Acad. Inscr. Belles-Lettres., C. R. 1956*, pt. 507–12; see also *idem, La Grange de Veulerent*, Paris, 1965.

41. *Le Livre de l'abbé Guillaume de Ryckel*, pp. 97, 356; the spelt could have been spring sown.

42. Etienne Juillard, 'L'assolement biennal dans l'agriculture septentrionale: le cas particulier de la Basse-Alsace', *Ann. Géog.*, lxi (1952), 34–45.

43. Sieur de Joinville, *Life of St Louis*, xl, 188. It should be pointed out that not all medieval ploughs fitted with coulter and mouldboard also had wheels.

44. Aelfric of Eynsham, in A. R. Benham, *English Literature from Widsuth to Chaucer*, Yale Univ. Press, 1916, 26.

45. Dorothea Oschinsky, *Walter of Henley*, Oxford University Press, 1971, Text, 322–3; Comment, 361.

46. Bertrand Gille, 'Recherches sur les instruments du labour au moyen âge', *Bibl. Ec Chartes*, vol. 120 (1963), 5–38; Lubor Niederle, *Manuel de l'Antiquité Slave* Paris, 1926, ii, 186–92.

47. J.-M. Richard, 'Thierry d' Hireçon: agriculteur artésien', *Bibl. Ec. Chartes*, liii (1892), 383–416; 571–604.

48. Margaret T. Hodgen, 'Domesday water mills', *Antiquity*, xiii (1939), 262–79.

49. Galbert of Bruges, cap. 3.

50. Roger Grand and Raymond Delatouche, *L'Agriculture au Moyen Age*

*de la fin de l'Empire Romain au XVI$^e$ siècle,* Paris, 1950, 329-55.

51. Roger Dion, *L'Histoire de la vigne et du vin en France dès origines au XIX$^e$ siècle,* Paris, 1959.

52. A. Demangeon, 'La vigne en Picardie', *Ann. Hist. Econ. Soc.,* i (1929), 430–4; I. B. Nordhoff, *Der vormälige Weinbau in Norddeutschland,* Münster, 1877.

53. The translation is that of the *University Library of Autobiography,* ii, 96.

54. Georges Yver, *Le Commerce et les Marchands dans l'Italie méridionale au XIII$^e$ et au XIV$^e$ Siècle,* Paris, 1903, pp. 104–5.

55. Wilhelm Abel, *Geschichte der deutschen Landwirtschaft,* Stuttgart, 1962, pp. 85–9

56. *Le Compte Général de 1187 connu sous le nom de Gros Brief et les institutions financières du comtè de Flandre au XII$^e$ siècle,* ed. A. Verhulst and M. Gysseling, Comm. Roy. d'Hist., Brussels, 1962.

57. Alfons Dopsch, *Die landfürstlichen Urbare Nieder- und Ober-österreichs aus dem 13. und 14. Jahrhundert,* Vienna, 1904 *et seq.*

58. See also Phillipe Dollinger, *L'Evolution des classes rurales en Bavière,* Paris, 1949, pp. 438–41; Thérèse Scalfert, *Le Haut Dauphiné au moyen âge, Paris,* 1926; Pierre Duparc, 'Une redevance féodale alpestre: l'Auciège', *Bibl. Ec. Chartes,* vol. 105 (1944), 99–122.

59. Quoted in Duby, *op. cit.,* 147.

60. P. Tucoo-Chala, 'Forêts et landes en Béarn au XIV$^e$ siècle', *Ann. Midi,* lxvii (1955), 247–59.

61. P. J. Jones, 'A Tuscan monastic estate in the later Middle Ages: Camaldoli', *Jnl Eccl. Hist.,* v (1954), 168–83.

62. J. W. Thompson, 'Serfdom in the medieval Campagna', *Wirtschaft und Kultur: Festschrift zum 70. Geburstag von Alfons Dopsch,* Leipzig, 1938, pp. 363–81.

63. Julius Klein, *The Mesta,* Harvard University Press, 1920, p. 27.

64. See G. Fournier, *Le Peuplement rural en Basse Auvergne durant le haut moyen age,* Paris, 1962, pp. 284–306.

65. L. Genicot, 'L'évolution des dons aux abbayes dans le Comté de Namur du X$^e$ au XIV$^e$ siècle', *XXX$^e$ Congrès de la Féderation Archéologique et Hist. de Belgique,* 1935, Brussels, 1936, pp. 133–48.

66. A. E. Verhulst, *De Sint-Baafsabdij te Gent en Haar Gronbezit,* Verhand van der K. Vlaamse Academie voor Wetenschappen, Letteren en Schone Kunsten van Belgie, Klasse d. Letteren, 30, 1958.

67. Dollinger, *op. cit.,* pp. 144–52, 513; *idem,* 'Les transformations du régime domanial en Bavière au XIII$^e$ siècle d'apres deux censiers de l'Abbaye de Baumburg', *Moy. Age.,* lvi (1950), 279–306.

68. Ch.-E. Perrin, *Essai sur la fortune immobilière de l'abbaye alsacienne de Marmoutier aux X$^e$ et XI$^e$ siècles,* Strasbourg, 1935, pp. 83–4.

69. Some extreme cases are cited by Duby, *op. cit.,* p. 243.

70. L. Verriest, *Le Régime seigneurial dans le Comté de Hainaut du XI$^e$ siècle à la Révolution,* Louvain, 1956, p. 73.

71. E. Engel, 'Bürgerlicher Lehnbesitz, bäuerliche Productenrente und ältmarkisch-hamburgische Handelsbeziehungen im 14. Jahrhundert',

*Hans. Geschbl.*, lxxxii (1964), 21–41.
72. Robert S. Smith, 'Medieval agrarian society in its prime: Spain', *Camb. Econ. Hist. Europe*, i (2nd edn), 1966, 432–48; J. Vicens Vives, *An Economic History of Spain*, Princeton University Press, 1969, 130–2.
73. Jean Favier, 'Le domaine de Longueil', *Ann. Norm.*, xiii (1963), 151–64.
74. H. Dubled, 'Administration et exploitation des terres de la seign-eurie rurale en Alsace au XI$^e$ et XII$^e$ siècle', *Viert. Soc. Wirt.* xlvii (1960), (1960), 433–73.
75. L. Genicot, 'L'étendue des exploitations agricoles dans le comté de Namur à la fin du XIII$^e$ siècle', *Et. Rur.*, no 5 (1962), 5–31; *idem, L'Econo-mie rurale Namuroise au Bas Moyen Age (1199–1429)*, Louvain, 1943.
76. *Le Polyptyque illustré dit 'Veil Rentier' de Messire Jehan de Pamèle-Audenarde*, ed. Léo Verriest, Brussels, 1950.
77. As cited in Guy Fourquin, *Les Campagnes de la Région Parisienne à la fin du moyen age*, Paris, 1964, 94.
78. David Herlihy, 'The Agrarian revolution in southern France and Italy', *Spec*, xxxiii (1958), 23–41.
79. Duby, *op. cit.*, 117.
80. David Herlihy, *Medieval and Renaissance Pistoia*, Yale University Press, 1967, pp. 123–34.
81. Monique Mestayer, 'Les prix du blé et de l'avoine de 1329 à 1793', *Rev. Nord,* xlv (1963), 157–76.
82. Gérard Sivery, 'L'évolution du prix du blé à Valenciennes aux XIV$^e$ et XV$^e$ siècles', *Rev. Nord,* xlvii (1965), 177–94.

## Chapter 6. The development of the medieval town

1. Walter Stein, 'Die Hansestädte', *Hans. Geschbl.*, xix (1913), 233–94; 519–60. There are several lists in the *Hansische Urkundenbücher*.
2. Fritz Schnelbögl, 'Die wirtschaftliche Bedeutung ihre Landgebietes für die Reichsstadt Nürnberg', *Beiträge zur Wirtschaftsgeschichte Nürnbergs*, i (Nuremberg, 1967) 261–317; Gerald Strauss, *Nuremberg in the Sixteenth Century*, New York, Wiley, 1966. Ulm had no territory: see Ingrid Bátori, *'Die Reichsstadt Augsburg im 18. Jahrhundert'*, *Veröff. Planck Inst. Gesch.*, xxii (1969), 14.
3. Hilary L. Turner, *Town Defences in England and Wales*, London, John Baker, 1971.
4. Brugg in Canton Aargau, Switzerland, is a case in point; see Max Banholzer, *Geschichte der Stadt Brugg im 15. und 16. Jahrhundert*, Aarau, 1961, p. 25.
5. Erich Keyser, *Deutsches Städtebuch: Bayerisches Städtebuch*, Part 1, Stuttgart, 1971, pp. 344–46.
6. Edith Ennen, 'Les différents types de formation des villes euro-péennes', *Moy. Age*, lxii (1956), 397–411.
7. A. Dopsch, *The Economic and Social Foundations of European Civili-*

*ization*, London, Routledge, 1937, p. 311.

8. J. Vicens Vives, *An Economic History of Spain*, Princeton University Press, 1969, p. 106.

9. J. Lestocquoy, *Etudes d'Histoire Urbaine: Villes et Abbayes au Moyen Age*, Mém. Comm. Dépt. Pas-de-Calais, xii, Part 2 (1966), 122–37.

10. *Idem., Les Dynasties Bourgeoises d'Arras du XI^e au XV^e Siècle, ibid.*, Part 1, 1945.

11. See H. Pirenne, *Medieval Cities*, Princeton University Press, 1927.

12. Mary Bateson, 'The Laws of Breteuil', *Eng. Hist. Review*, xv (1900), 73–8; 302–18; 496–523; 754–57; xvi (1901), 92–110, 332–45.

13. J. Dhondt, 'Développement urbain et initiative comtale en Flandre', *Rev. Nord*, xxx (1948), 133–56.

14. Chronica Sancti Bertini, Mon. Germ. Hist., SS., XXV, 768, as quoted in G. Fagniez, *Documents relatifs à l'Histoire d l'Industrie et du Commerce en France*, Collection de Textes i (1898), 54–5.

15. Jan Dhondt, 'Les problèmes de Quentovic,' *Studi in Onore di Amintore Fanfani*, Milan, 1962, i, 181–248.

16. *The Chronicle of the Slavs*, by Helmold the Priest, ed. F. J. Tschan, Columbia University Press, 1935.

17. J. Poulik, 'The latest archaeological discoveries from the period of the Great Moravian Empire', *Hist.* (Prague), i (1959), 7–70; also F. Kavka, 'Der Stand der Forschungen über den Anfang der Städte in der Tschechoslowakei,' *Kwart. Hist Kult. Mat.*, x (1962), 546–9.

18. Jarolslav Melnik, in *Hist.* (Prague), xvii (1969), 43–91.

19. Edith Ennen, *Frühgeschichte der europäischen Stadt*, Bonn, 1953; Hans Planitz, *Die Deutsche Stadt im Mittelalter*, Cologne, 1965.

20. Carl Haase, *Die Entstehung der westfälischen Städte*, Münster, 1965.

21. Adolf Welte, 'Zur Entstehung der mainfränkischen Städte', *Pet. Mitt.*, lxxxvii (1941), 233–50.

22. Robert Gradmann, 'Schwäbische Städte', *Zeitschr. der Gesellschaft für Erdkunde zu Berlin*, 1916, pp. 425–57.

23. Camille-J. Joset, *Les Villes au Pays de Luxembourg*, Recueil de Travaux d'Histoire et de Philologie, 3^e série, fasc. 5, Brussels, 1940.

24. *Atlas Ostliches Mitteleuropa*, Bielefeld, 1959, Sheets 59 and 60.

25. Karl Hoffman, 'Die Stadtgründung Mecklenburg-Schwerins in der Kolonisationszeit vom 12. bis zum 14. Jahrhundert', *Jahrb. Ver. Meckl. Gesch*, xciv (1930), 1–200.

26. M. Beresford, *New Towns of the Middle Ages*, London, Lutterworth Press, 1967, pp. 319–75.

27. Wolff, *op. cit.*

28. C. H. Taylor, 'Assemblies of French towns in 1316', *Spec.* xiv (1939), 275–99.

31. J. Le Goff, 'Ordres mendiants et urbanisation dans la France médiévale', *Ann. E.S.C.*, xxv (1970), 924–46.

30. Greater precision is now being given to this estimate by the current publication, under the direction of Erich Keyser, of the *Deutsche Städtebücher*, Stuttgart, 1954 onwards; a volume is devoted to each of the Länder.

Notes and References

31. Heinrich Bechtel, *Wirtschaftsgeschichte Deutschlands*, Munich, 1951, i, 255–7.
32. A. H. Lybyer, 'Constantinople as capital of the Ottoman Empire', *Ann. Rept. Am. Hist. Ass.*, i (1916), 373–88.
33. A recent review of the evidence is Jean Favier, 'Les contribuables Parisiens à la fin de la Guerre de Cent Ans', *Htes Et. Méd. Mod.*, xi (1970).
34. B. Bennassar, *Valladolid au Siècle d'Or*, Paris, 1967, i, 166.
35. B. Guillemain, 'La Cour Pontificale d'Avignon,' *Bibl. Ec. Franç. Ath. Rome*, vol. 201 (1962).
36. Philippe Wolff, 'Trois études de démographie médiévale en France méridionale', *Studi in Onore Armando Sapori*, 493–503; G. Prat, 'Albi et la Peste Noire,' *Ann. Midi*, lxiv (1952), 15–25.
37. H. Ammann, *Wirtschaft und Lebensraum der Mittelalterlichen Kleinstadt: i, Rheinfelden*, n.d., privately.
38. F. Bertrand, 'Espalion en 1403 d'après un registre d'estimes', *Congrès de Rodez, Société des Lettres, Sciences et Arts de l'Aveyron*, 1958, 215–41.
39. J. Gaier-Lhoest, *L'Evolution topographique de la ville de Dinant au moyen age*, Brussels, 1964. Mols, *op. cit,* ascribes an appreciably greater population to the town.
40. G. Botero, *A Treatise Concerning the Causes of the Magnificency and Greatness of Cities*, trans. Robert Petersen, 1608; see also *Rélations des Ambassadeurs Vénitiens sur les Affaires de France au XVIᵉ Siécle*, ed. M. N. Tommaseo, Collection de Documents Inédits, Paris, 1838, ii, 491.
41. P. Wolff, 'Quelques données sur la société de Rodez autour de 1420,' *Rouergue et Confins, Congrès de Rodez*, 1958, pp. 121–33.
42. Etienne Fournial, *Les Villes et l'Economie d'Echanges en Forez aux XIIIᵉ et XIVᵉ Siècles*, Paris, 1967.
43. J. K. Hyde, *Padua in the Age of Dante*, Manchester University Press, 1966, 43–5.
44. David Herlihy, *Pisa in the Early Renaissance: A Study of Urban Growth*, Yale University Press, 1958, pp. 109–26.
45. John Larner, *The Lords of the Romagna*, London, Macmillan, 1965.
46. David M. Nicholas, 'Town and countryside: social and economic tensions in fourteenth-century Flanders', *Comp. Stud. Soc. Hist.*, x (1968), 458–85.
47. Bruno Kuske, 'Handel und Handelspolitik am Niederrhein vom 13. bis 16. Jahrhundert', *Hans. Geschbl.*, xv (1909), 301–27.
48. Alexander Dietz, *Frankfurter Handelsgeschichte,* Frankfurt, 1910–25, iii, 295–9.
49. 'Marchés de Paris', App. xi, *Mémoires des Intendants sur l'Etat des Généralités*, ed. A. M. de Boislisle, Paris 1881, pp. 656–75.
50. See *Finances et Comptabilité Urbaines du XIIIᵉ au XVIᵉ Siècle*, Pro Civitate, Collection Histoire, no. 7, Brussels, 1964.
51. D. Herlihy, in *ibid.,* 385–405.
52. Françoise Humbert, *Les Finances municipales de Dijon du milieu du XIVᵉ siècle à 1477*, Pubns de l'Université de Dijon, no 23, 1961.
53. Marvin B. Becker, 'Some common features of Italian urban experience (c. 1200–1500)', *Med. Hum.*, i (1970), 175–201; Frederic C.

Lane, 'The funded debt of the Venetian Republic, 1262–1482', in *Venice and History*, Johns Hopkins University Press, 1966, pp. 87–98.

54. Jacques Heers, 'Urbanisme et structure sociale à Gênes au moyen-âge', *Studi in Onore di Amintore Fanfani*, i, 369–412.

55. *Calendar of Inquisitions Miscellaneous* (Chancery), vii, *1399–1422*, 204–7.

56. Madeleine Jurgens and Pierre Couperie, "Le logement à Paris au XVIᵉ et XVIIᵉ siècles', *Ann. ESC.*, xvii (1962), 488–500.

57. Simone Roux, 'L'habitat urbain au moyen age: le quartier de l'Université à Paris', *Ann. ESC.*, xxiv (1969), 1196–1219.

58. B. Bennassar, *Valladolid au Siècle d'Or*, Paris, 1967, pp. 148–54.

59. *Le Journal d'un Bourgeois de Mons 1505–1536*, ed. Armand Louant, Commission Royale d'Histoire, Brussels, 1969, p. 210.

60. J. Lestocquoy, *Les Dynasties Bourgeoises d'Arras du XIᵉ au XVᵉ Siècle*, Mém. Comm. Dépt. Pas-de-Calais, 5, part 1, Arras, 1945.

61. Georges Espinas, *Les Origines du Capitalisme*, 2, *Sire Jean de France, Sire Jacques le Blond*, Bibl. de la Société d' Histoire du Droit des Pays Flamands, ix (Lille, 1936), 37–91.

62. Gustav Schönberg, *Finanzverhältnisse der Stadt Basel im XIV und XV Jahrhundert*, Tübingen, 1879, p. 252.

63. Jean Favier, 'Les contribuables parisiens à la fin de la Guerre de Cent Ans', *Htes. Et. Med. Mod.*, xi (1970), 61–9.

64. Robert Montran, *Istanbul dans la seconde moitié du XVIIᵉ siècle*, Bibliothèque Archéologique et Historique de l'Institut Français d'Arch-éologie d'Istanbul, xii (1962), 49–63.
xii (1962), 49–63.

65. Irving A. Agus, *Urban Civilization in Pre-Crusade Europe*, Leiden, E. J. Brill, 1965, no. 42.

## Chapter 7. Medieval manufacturing

1. An estimate of the time taken to produce cloth is given in Federigo Melis, *Aspetti della vita economica medievale*, Siena, 1962. From spinning to finishing woollen cloth was six months to a year; on average about eight months.

2. Quoted in R. C. Cave and H. H. Coulson, *A Source Book for Medieval Economic History*, New York, Biblo and Tanner, 1965, pp. 200–2.

3. George Unwin, *The Gilds and Companies of London*, London, Allen & Unwin, 2nd edn, 1925.

4. Gwyn A. Williams, *Medieval London*, London, Athlone Press, 1970, p. 162.

5. Sylvia L. Thrupp. *The Merchant Class of Medieval London*, University of Michigan Press, 1962, p. 14.

6. Charles Gross, *The Gild Merchant*, Oxford University Press, 1890.

7. As quoted in E. Coornaert, *Les Corporations en France avant 1789*, Paris, 1941, p. 74.

8. Unwin, *op. cit.*, p. 64.

9. A. Joris, *La Ville de Huy au Moyen Age*, Bibl. de la Faculté de Philosophie et Lettres de l'Université de Liège, vol. 152 (Paris, 1959), 433–9.

10. As quoted by Niccolò Rodolico, 'The struggle for the right of association in fourteenth-century Florence', *History*, vii (1922–3), 178–90.

11. Gene A. Brucker, 'The Ciompi revolution', in *Florentine Studies*, ed. Nicolai Rubinstein, London, Faber, 1968, pp. 314–56; Raymond de Roover, 'Labour conditions in Florence around 1400: theory, policy and reality', in *ibid.*, pp. 277–313.

12. For a Marxist interpretation see M. Małowist, *Studia z dziejów rzemiosla w okresie kryzysu feudalizmu Europie w XIV i XV wieku*, Warsaw, 1954.

13. *Réglemens sur les Arts et Métiers de Paris rédigés au XIII^e siècle, et connus sous le nom du Livre d'Etienne Boileau*, ed. G.-B. Depping, Collection de Documents Inédits sur l'Histoire de France, Paris, 1837.

14. Gustave Fagniez, *Etudes sur l'Industrie et la Classe Industrielle à Paris au XIII^e et au XIV^e Siècle*, Bibl. Ec. Htes. Et., Paris, xxxiii (1877), 7–19.

15. *Die Kölner Zunfturkunden nebst anderen Kölner Gewerbeurkunden bis zum Jahre 1500*, ed. Heinrich von Loesch, Gesellschaft für Rheinische Geschichtskunde, vol. i, Bonn, 1907.

16. Karl Bücher. *Die Bevölkerung von Frankfurt am Main*, Tübingen, 1886. The crafts listed have been identified with the help of Karl Bücher, 'Die Berufe der Stadt Frankfurt am Main', *Abhandlungen der Königlich Sachsischen Gesellschaft der Wissenschaften*, iii, no. 3 (Leipzig, 1913).

17. *Circkell der Eidtgenoschaft von Andreas Ryff*, ed. E. Meininger, Basel, 1892.

18. *Quellen zur Rechts- und Wirtschaftsgeschichte der Rheinischen Städte: Julische Städte*, vol. i, *Düren*, ed. August Schoop, Gesellschaft für Rheinische Geschichtskunde, Bonn, 1920, 130–6.

19. Sylvia L. Thrupp, *Medieval industry*, in *The Fontana Economic History of Europe*, London, Collins, 1972, p. 269.

20. F. C. Lane, *Venetian Ships and Shipbuilders of the Renaissance*, Johns Hopkins University Press, 1934, pp. 130–216.

21. This account of medieval cloth manufacture is based on: G. Espinas, *La Draperie dans la Flandre française au moyen Age*, vol. ii, Paris, 1923; G. de Poerck, *La Draperie médiévale en Flandre et en Artois: technique et terminologie*, Rijksuniversiteir te Gent, 3 vols, Bruges, 1951; Walter Endrei, *L'Evolution des techniques du filage et du tissage*, Ecole Pratique des Hautes Etudes: Industrie et Artisanat, vol. iv, Paris, 1968.

22. 'The loom', *Cib. Rev.*, no. 16, Dec. 1938.

23. A fulling mill was noted at Douai in 1220, *Recueil de documents relatifs à l'histoire de l'industrie drapière de Flandre*, ed. G. Espinas and H. Pirenne, Commission Royale d'Histoire, Brussels, 1909, no. 215, pp. 16–7.

24. Charles Singer, *The Earliest Chemical Industry*, London, The Folio Society, 1948.

25. *Les Livres de Comptes des frères Bonis*, ed. E. Forestié, Archives His-

toriques de la Gascogne, no. 20, Paris, 1890.

26. Francesco Balducci Pegolotti, *La Pratica della Mercatura*. Cambridge, Mass., The Medieval Academy of America, 1936, esp. pp. 37, 79, 109

27. Léo Verriest, *La Draperie d'Ath des Origines au XVIIIᵉ Siècle*, Brussels (chez l'auteur), 1942.

28. H. Pirenne, 'Draps de frise ou draps de Flandre?', *Viert. Jahrschr. Soz. Wirtschaftsgesch.*, vii (1909), 308–15.

29. E. Coornaert, *La Draperie-Sayetterie d'Hondschoote (XIVᵉ–XVIIIᵉ siècles)*, Rennes, 1930, p. 4.

30. *Royal Commission on the Distribution of the Industrial Population, Report*, Cmd 6153, H.M.S.O., 1940, p. 32.

31. *Florentine Merchants in the Ages of the Medici*, ed. G. R. B. Richards, Cambridge, Mass., 1932, pp. 37–41.

32. Maureen F. Mazzaoui, 'The emigration of Veronese textile artisans to Bologna in the thirteenth century', *Atti e Memorie della Accademia di Agricoltura, Scienze e Lettere di Verona*, xix (1967–8).

33. Edward Miller, 'The fortunes of the English textile industry during the thirteenth century', *Econ. Hist. Rev.*, xviii (1965), 64–82.

34. E. de Sagher, 'L'immigration des tisserands Flamands et Brabançons en Angleterre sous Edouard III', *Mélanges Henri Pirenne*, Brussels, 1926, pp. 109–26.

35. On this see the pioneer papers of Maureen F. Mazzaoui, 'L'organizzione delle industrie tessili nei secoli XIII e XIV: cotonieri Veronesi', *Studi Storici Veronesi Luigi Simeoni*, xviii–xix (1968–9), 'The cotton industry of northern Italy in the late Middle Ages: 1150–1450', *Jnl. Econ. Hist.*, xxxii (1972), 262–86.

36. *Conflictus Ovis et Lini*; printed in *Zeitschrift für Deutsches Altertum*, ix (1859), 215–38; see also A. van de Vyver and Charles Verlinden, 'L'auteur et la portée du Conflictus Ovis et Lini'', *Rev. Belge Phil. Hist.*, xii (1933), 59–81.

37. J. G. D. Clark, *Prehistoric Europe*, London, Methuen, 1952, 232–4.

38. See Hektor Ammann, 'St Gallens Wirtschaftsstellung im Mittelalter', *Aus Sozial- und Wirtschaftsgeschichte: Gedächtnisschrift für Georg von Below*, Stuttgart, 1928, pp. 131–68; *ibid.*, 'Die Anfänge der Leinenindustrie des Bodenseegebietes und der Otschweiz'. *Zeitschr. Schweiz. Gesch.*, xxiii (1943), 329–70.

39. Eugen Nübling, *Ulms Baumwollweberei im Mittelalter*, Staats und Sozialwissenschaftliche Forschungen, ix Heft 5 (1890).

40. Aloys Schulte, *Geschichte der grossen Ravensburger Handelsgesellschaft, 1380–1530*, Stuttgart, 1923.

41. R. Hennig, 'Die Einführung der Seidenraupenzucht ins Byzantinerreich', *Byzantinische Zeitschrift*, xxxiii (1933), 295–312; also 'The early history of silk', *Cib. Rev.*, no. 11, July 1938, and 'Byzantine silks', *ibid.*, no. 75, August 1949, and R. S. Lopez, 'Silk industry in the Byzantine Empire', *Spec.*, xx (1945), 1–42.

42. *An Essay upon Various Arts by Theophilus*, trans. Robert Hendrie, London, 1847, p. 223.

43. H. R. Schubert, *History of the British Iron and Steel Industry*, London,

Routledge, 1957, p. 139.

44. Rolf Sprandel, 'La production du fer au Moyen Age', *Ann. E.S.C.*, xxiv (1969), 305–21).

45. *Mon. Germ. Hist.*, *Diplomatum regum et imperatorum Germaniae*, v, Berlin, 1931, no. 199, pp. 255–7.

46. Bertrand Gille, 'L'organisation de la production du fer au moyen âge', *Rev. Hist. Sid.*, ix (1968), 95–121.

47. R. Fossier, 'L'activité métallurgique d'une abbaye cistercienne: Clairvaux', *Rev. Hist. Sid.*, ii (1961), 7–13.

48. R.-H. Bautier, 'Notes sur le commerce du fer en Europe occidentale du XIIIᵉ au XVIᵉ siècle', *Rev. Hist. Sid.*, i (1960), part 4, 7–35.

49. Published at Basel in 1556, but much of it was written well before this date.

50. Reproduced in Václav Husa, *Traditional Crafts and Skills*, Prague, 1967.

51. Su Jozef Vlachovič, 'Slovak copper boom in world markets of the sixteenth and in the first quarter of the seventeenth centuries', *Studia Historica Slovaca*, i (1963), 63–95.

52. Adolf Soetbeer, *Edelmetall-Produktion und Werthverhältniss zwischen Gold und Silber seit der Entdeckung Amerikas bis zur Gegenwart*, Petermanns Mitteilungen, Erganzungsheft, no. 57, Gotha, 1879. J. U. Nef considers that Soetbeer underestimates the totals: 'Silver production in central Europe, 1450–1618', *Jnl. Pol. Econ.*, xlix (1941), 575–91.

53. *Die Alten Zunft- und Verkehrs-Ordnungen der Stadt Krakau*, ed. Bruno Bucher, Vienna, 1889.

54. H. Pirenne, 'Les marchands-batteurs de Dinant au XIVᵉ et au XVᵉ siècle', *Viertel. Soz. Wirtsch.*, ii (1904), 442–9; also A. Joris, 'Probleme der mittelalterlichen Metallindustrie im Maasgebiet', *Hans. Geschichtsbl.*, lxxxvii (1969), 58–76.

55. *The Second Book of the Travels of Nicander Nucius of Corcyra*, Camden Society, vol. xvii (1841), p. xviii.

56. Denise Van Derveeghde, *Le Domaine de Val Saint-Lambert de 1202 à 1387*, Bibl. de la Faculté de Philosophie et Lettres de l'Université de Liège, vol. 130, Paris, 1955.

57. A. R. Bridbury, *England and the Salt Trade in the Latter Middle Ages*, Oxford University Press, 1955, 170–2.

58. On urban construction see Hugues Neveux, 'Recherches sur la construction et l'entretien des maisons à Cambrai de la fin du XIVᵉ siècle au début du XVIIIᵉ', in *Le Bâtiment: enquête d'histoire économique*, Ec. Prat. Htes Et.: Industrie et Artisanat, vi (Paris, 1971), 189–312.

## Chapter 8. The trade of the Middle Ages

1. Alfons Dopsch, *The Economic and Social Foundations of European Civilization*, London, Routledge, 1937, 328.

2. F. L. Ganshof, 'Note sur un passage de la vie de Saint-Géraud d'Auril-

lac', *Mélanges offerts à M. Nicolas Iorga*, Paris, 1933, pp. 295–307.

3. R. S. Lopez, 'The evolution of land transport in the Middle Ages', *Past and Present*, no. 9 (1956), 17–29.

4. Jean Lestocquoy, 'La navigation fluviale au IX$^e$ siècle: les flotilles monastiques', *Jumièges: Congrès Scientifique du XIII$^e$ Centenaire*, Rouen, 1955, pp. 247–52.

5. F. Rousseau, 'Le destin de la vallée la la Meuse au Moyen Age', *Bulletin de l'Institut Archéologique Liégeoise*, lxiii (1939), 107–17; J. Knaepen, 'Les anciennes foires internationales de Visé', *ibid.*, lxxix (1966), 5–143.

6. Armand O. Citarella, 'Patterns in medieval trade: the commerce of Amalfi before the Crusades', *Jnl Econ. Hist.*, xxviii (1968), 531–55.

7. R. S. Lopez and I. W. Raymond, *Medieval Trade in the Mediterranean World*, Columbia University Press, 1955, p. 54.

8. Gesta Roberti Wiscardi, *Mon. Germ. Hist.*, SS., 9 pp. 239–98, lines 476–85.

9. F. Dvornik, *La Vie de Saint Grégoire la Décapolite et les Slaves macédoines au IX$^e$ siècle*, Paris, 1926.

10. *Constantine Porphyrogenitus de Administrando Imperio*, trans. R. J. H. Jenkins, Budapest, 1949, 56–63, cap. 9.

11. E. H. Freshfield, *Roman Law in the Later Roman Empire*, Cambridge University Press, 1938.

12. Herbert Jahnkuhn, 'Der Fränkisch-Friesische Handel zur Ostsee im frühen Mittelalter', *Viertel. Soz. Wirtsch.*, xl (1953), 193–243; Alexander Bugge, 'Die Nordeuropäischen Verkehrswege im frühen Mittelalter', *ibid.*, iv (1906), 227–77.

13. *A Description of Europe and the Voyages of Othere and Wulfstan*, ed. Joseph Bosworth, London, 1855.

14. Herbert Jahnkuhn, 'Die fruhmittelalterlichen Seehandelsplätze im Nord- und Ostseeraum', *Studien zu Anfängen des europäischen Städtewesens, Vörträge und Forschungen,* iv (Lindau, 1958), 451–98.

15. Charlotte Blindheim, 'The market place in Skiringssal', *Acta Archaeologica*, xxxi (1960), 83–100.

16. Quoted in R. S. Lopez and I. W. Raymond, *Medieval Trade in the Mediterranean World*, Columbia University Press, pp. 31–3.

17. *The Itinerary of Benjamin of Tudela*, ed. Marcus Nathan Adler, London, 1907.

18. *Libellus de vita et miraculis Sancti Godrici de Finchale*, ed. J. Stevenson, Surtees Society, 1845; see also Walther Vogel, 'Ein seefahrender Kaufmann um 1100', *Hans. Geschichtsbl.*, xviii (1912), 239–48.

19. Based on J. Lestocquoy, Les Dynasties Bourgeoises d'Arras du XI$^e$ au XV$^e$ Siècle, *Mémoires de la Commission Départmentale des Monuments Historiques du Pas-de-Calais*, vol. v, fasc., Arras, 1945.

20. *Les Livres de Compte des Frères Bonis*, ed. E. Forestié, Archives de la Gascogne, 20 (1890); also Claude Cugnasse, 'Activité économique et milieu humain à Montauban au XIV$^e$ siècle d'après le registre de Barthélémy Bonis', *Ann. Midi*, lxix (1957), 207–27.

21. Iris Origo, *The Merchant of Prato*, New York, Knopf, 1957, p. 95;

Federigo Melis, *Aspetti della vita economica medievale*, Siena, 1962.

22. Frederic C. Lane, *Andrea Barbarigo, Merchant of Venice 1418–1449*, Johns Hopkins University Studies in Historical and Political Science, series 62, no. 1, 1944.

23. Philippe Braunstein, 'Rélations d'Affairs entre Nurembourgeois et Vénitiens à la fin du XIV$^e$ siècle', *Mélanges d'Archéologie et d'Histoire, Ecole Française de Rome*, lxxvi (1964), 227–69.

24. Wilfrid Brulez, 'Lettres commerciales de Daniel et Antoine van Bombergen à Antonio Grimani', *Bulletin de l'Institut Historique Belge de Rome*, xxxi (1958), 169–205.

25. Florence Edler, 'The Van der Molen, Commission Merchants of Antwerp', *Medieval and Historiographical Essays in Honor of James Westfall Thompson*, Chicago, 1938, 78–145.

26. Wilfrid Brulez, *De Firma della Faille en de Internationale Handel van Vlaamse firma's in de 16e eeuw*, Verhandelingen van de Koninklijke Vlaamse Academie voor Wetenschappen, Letteren en Schone Kunsten van België, Klasse der Letteren, vol. xxxv, Brussels, 1959.

27. Knaepen, *op. cit.*

28. La Foire, *Recueil de la Sociètè Jean Bodin*, vol. v, 1953; Félix Bourquelot, *Etudes sur les Foires de Champagne, Mémoires présentés à l'Academie des Inscriptions et Belles Lettres*, Paris, 1865.

29. E. Chapin, 'Les Villes de Foire de Champagne', *Bibl. Ec. Htes. Et.*, vol. 268 (1937).

30. R. D. Face, 'Techniques of business on the trade between the fairs of Champagne and the south of Europe in the twelfth and thirteenth centuries', *Econ. Hist. Rev.*, x (1957–8), 427–38; *idem.*, 'The Vectuarii in the overland commerce between Champagne and southern Europe', *ibid.*, xii (1959–60), 239–46.

31. E. Coornaert, 'Caractères et mouvement des foires internationales au Moyen Age et au XVI$^e$ siècle', *Studi in Onore di Armando Sapori*, Milan, 1957, vol. i, 355–71; *idem.*, *Les Français et le commerce international à Anvers*, Paris, 1961.

32. The picture of the peasant market in central Poland, given in W. Reymont's novel *Chłopi* ('The Peasants') would appear to be applicable also to the medieval market in Western Wurope.

33. Freddy Thiriet, *La Romanie Vénitienne au Moyen Age*, Bibl. des Ecoles Françaises d'Athènes et de Rome, vol. 193 (1959),

34. Henry Simonsfeld, *Der Fondaco dei Tedeschi in Venedig und die deutsch-venetianischen Handelsbeziehungen*, Stuttgart, 1887; also Philippe Braunstein, *Wirtschaftliche Beziehungen zwischen Nürnberg und Italien im Spatmittelalter, Beiträge zur Wirtschaftsgeschichte Nürmbergs*, vol. i, Nuremberg, 1967.

35. G. I. Bratianu, *Recherches sur le Commerce Génois dans la Mer Noire au XIII$^e$ siècle*, Paris, 1929.

36. Jacques Heers, *Gênes au XV$^e$ Siècle*, Paris, Ecole Pratique des Hautes Etudes, 1961.

37. Quoted in Lopez and Raymond, *Medieval Trade in the Mediterranean World*, p. 69.

38. See Yves Renouard, *Les Hommes d'Affairs Italiens du Moyen Age*, Paris, 1949, pp. 130–60.

39. Michael E. Mallett, *The Florentine Galleys in the Fifteenth Century*, Oxford University Press, 1967, p. 17ff.

40. F. C. Lane, *Venetian Ships and Shipbuilders of the Renaissance*, Johns Hopkins University Press, 1944.

41. V. Chomel and J. Ebersolt, *Cinq siècles de circulation internationale vue de Jougne*, Paris, 1951; also H. Ammann, 'Der Verkehr über den Pass von Jougne nach dem Zollregister von 1462', *Mélanges offerts à M. Paul-E. Martin*, Geneva, 1961, pp. 223–37.

42. Aloys Schulte, *Geschichte der grossen Ravensburger Handelsgesellschaft, 1380–1530*, Stuttgart, 1923.

43. It was published by J. Lelewel in *Géographie du Moyen Age* with, however, many errors in the identification of the placenames, and more recently by J. Hamy, in *Le Livre de la Description des Pays*, Paris, 1898, App. IV, 161–216.

44. J. A. van Houtte, 'Bruges et Anvers, marchés nationaux ou internationaux du XIVe au XVIe siècle', *Revue du Nord*, xxxiv (1952), 89–108.

45. Michel Mollat, *Le Commerce Maritime Normand à la fin du Moyen Age*, Paris, 1952.

46. Aksel E. Christensen, 'Scandinavia and the Advance of the Hanseatics', *Scandinavian Economic History Review*, v (1957), 87–117.

47. Philippe Dollinger, *The German Hansa*, London, Macmillan, 1970.

48. These have been published in *Hansisches Urkundenbuch*, Halle, 1876 onwards.

49. Wilhelm Stieda, *Revaler Zollbücher und Quittungen des 14. Jahrhunderts*, Hansisches Geschichtsquellens, v (Halle, 1887), no. 1381, p. 52.

50. As quoted in Jean Hubert, 'Les routes du moyen age', *Les routes de France depuis les origines jusqu'à nos jours, Colloques: Cahiers de Civilisation*, Paris, 1959, pp. 25–56.

51. See Georg Schreiber, 'Mittelalterliche Alpenpässe und ihre Hospitalkultur', *Miscellanea Giovanni Galbiati*, vol. iii, Fontes Ambrosiani; vol. xxvii, Milan, 1951, 335–52.

52. Chomel and Ebersolt, *op. cit.*

53. R. S. Lopez, 'The evolution of land transport in the Middle Ages', *Past and Present*, no. 9 (1956), 17–29.

54. Gustave Guilmoto, *Etude sur les Droits de Navigation de la Seine de Paris à La Roche-Guyon du XIe au XVIIIe siècle*, Paris, 1889, pp. 3–11.

55. See Otto Gönnenwein, *Das Stapel- und Niederschlagsrecht, Quellen und Darstellungen zur Hanisischen Geschichte*, ii (1939).

56. K. F. Klöden, *Beiträge zur Geschichte des Oderhandels*, Berlin, 1845–52.

57. On the late medieval neglect of river-borne trade see M. N. Boyer, 'Roads and rivers: their use and disuse in late medieval France', *Med. Hum.*, xiii (1960), 68–80.

58. Etienne Bougoüin, 'La navigation commerciale sur la basse Loire au milieu du XIVe siècle', *Rev. Hist.*, vol. 175 (1935), 482–96.

59. Mollat, *op. cit.*; Jacques Heers, 'Rivalité ou collaboration de la

terre et de l'eau? Position général des problèmes', *Les Voies Maritimes dans le Monde: XVᵉ–XIXᵉ siècles*, Paris, 1965, pp. 13–63.

60. *Medieval Trade in the Mediterranean World*, 116.

61. F. C. Lane, 'Venetian shipping during the commercial revolution', *Am. Hist. Rev.*, xxxviii (1932–33), 219–39.

62. G. Bigwood, 'Gand et la circulation des grains en Flandre, du XIVᵉ au XVIIIᵉ siècle', *Rev. Belge Phil. Hist.*, iv (1906), 397–460.

63. Z. W. Sneller, 'Le commerce de blé des Hollandais dans le région de la Somme au XVᵉ siècle', *Bulletins de la Société des Antiquaires de Picardie*, xlii (1947–8), 140–60.

64. Yves Renouard, 'La consommation des grands vins de Bourbonnais à la cour pontificale d'Avignon', *Annales de Bourgogne*, xxiv (1952), 221–44.

65. P. Dollinger, 'Commerce et marchands strasbourgeois à Fribourg en Suisse au Moyen Age', *Beiträge zur Wirtschafts- und Stadtgeschichte*, Wiesbaden, 1965, pp. 124–43.

66. d'Alauzier, 'Achats d'étoffes d'une dame du Quercy au XIIIᵉ siècle', *Ann. Midi*, lxx (1958), 87–8; for another such list see A. Higounet-Nadal, 'Inventaire de la marchandise d'un drapier de Périgueux (1407)', *ibid.*, lxxvii (1965), 337–40.

67. R.-H. Bautier, 'Notes sur le commerce de fer en Europe occidentale du XIIIᵉ au XVIᵉ siècle', *Rev. Hist. Sid.*, iv (1963), 35–61.

68. *Quellen zur Geschichte des Kölner Handels und Verkehrs im Mittelalter*, ed. Bruno Kuske, *Publikationen der Gesellschaft für Rheinische Geschichtskunde*, xxxiii, part 1 (Bonn, 1923), nos. 5 and 8, see also A. Joris, 'Probleme der mittelalterlichen Metallindustrie im Maasgebiet', *Hans. Geschichtsbl.*, lxxxvii (1969), 58–76.

## Chapter 9. The commercial revolution

1. M. M. Postan, 'Italy and the economic development of England in the Middle Ages', *Jnl Econ. Hist.*, ii (1951), 339–46.

2. Eli F. Heckscher, 'Natural and money economy', *Jnl Econ. Bus. Hist.*, iii (1931), 1–29.

3. Werner Sombart, as quoted in *Enterprise and Secular Change*, ed. F. C. Lane and J. C. Riemersawa, Homewood, Ill., 1953, p. 26.

4. T. P. McLaughlin, 'The teaching of the canonists on usury', *Mediaeval Studies*, i (1939), 81–147; ii (1940), 1–22.

5. As by Bernardino di Siena; see Raymond de Roover, *San Bernardino of Siena and Sant' Antonio of Florence*, Cambridge, Mass., Kress Library of Business and Economics, no. 19, 1967, pp. 32–3.

6. Raymond de Roover, *The Rise and Decline of the Medici Bank 1397–1494*, New York, Norton, 1966, 11–12.

7. Raymond de Roover, 'The concept of the just price: theory and economic policy', *Jnl Econ. Hist.*, xviii (1958), 418–38.

8. Abbot P. Usher, *The Early History of Deposit Banking in Mediter-*

*ranean Europe*, Cambridge, Mass., Harvard Economic Studies, no. 75, 1943, p. 114.

9. *Ibid.*, 128.

10. Raymond de Roover, *Money, Banking and Credit in Mediaeval Bruges*, Cambridge, Mass., Mediaeval Academy of America, 1948, p. 42.

11. Richard Ehrenberg, *Capital and Finance in the Age of the Renaissance*, London, Jonathan Cape, 1928, p. 83.

12. Printed in full in Lopez and Raymond, *Medieval Trade in the Mediterranean World*, Records of Civilisation, New York, p. 166.

13. This bill of exchange is from the Datini papers, and is printed in Iris Origo, *The Merchant of Prato*, New York, Knopf, 1957, p. 150.

14. As quoted in Lopez and Raymond, *op. cit.*, 151.

15. Raymond de Roover, *L'Evolution de la Lettre de Change, XIV<sup>e</sup>–XVIII<sup>e</sup> siècles*, Ec. Prat. Htes. Et., Paris, 1953, 62.

16. As cited in R. de Roover, *The Rise and Decline of the Medici Bank 1397–1494*, New York, Norton, 1966, p. 126.

17. Florence Edler de Roover, 'Early examples of marine insurance', *Jnl Econ. Hist.*, v (1945), 172–200. See also Jacques Heers, 'Le prix de l'assurance maritime à la fin du moyen âge', *Rev. Hist. Econ. Soc.*, xxxvii (1959), 7–19.

18. C. Portal, 'Le livre-journal de Jean Saval, marchand drapier à Carcassonne', *Bull. Hist. Phil.*, 1901, pp. 440–1; the translation is that of Lopez and Raymond, *op. cit.*, pp. 362–3.

19. As quoted in Richard Brown, ed., *A History of Accounting and Accountants*, Edinburgh, T. C. & E. C. Black, 1905, 102–3. The excerpt is from the ledgers of Donado Soranzo and Brothers, 1422.

20. B. S. Yamey, 'Scientific bookkeeping and the rise of capitalism', *Econ. Hist. Rev.*, i (1949), 99–113.

21. C. M. Cipolla, 'Currency depreciation in medieval Europe', *Econ. Hist. Rev.*, xv (1963), 413–22.

22. See Robert Favreau, 'Les changeurs du royaume sous le règne de Louis XI', *Bibl. Ec. Chartres*, vol. 122 (1964), 216–51.

23. This section is deeply indebted to P. Spufford, 'Coinage and currency', *Camb. Econ. Hist.*, iii (1963), 576–602.

24. A rough computation based on H. M. Colvin, ed., *The History of the King's Works*, H.M.S.O., 1963, ii, 629–41.

25. Jaime Vicens Vives, *An Economic History of Spain*, Princeton University Press, 1968, pp. 234–7; 285–7; also Julius Klein, *The Mesta*, Cambridge, Mass., Harvard University Press, 1920.

26. Marvin B. Becker, 'Some common features of Italian urban experience (c. 1200–1500)', *Med. Hum.*, n.s., i (1970), 175–201.

27. Charles M. de la Roncière, 'Indirect taxes or "gabelles" at Florence in the fifteenth century: the evolution of tariffs and problems of collection', *Florentine Studies*, ed. N. Rubinstein, London, Faber, 1968, pp. 140–92.

28. 'The funded debt of the Venetian Republic, 1262–1482', in Frederic C. Lane, *Venice and History*, Johns Hopkins University Press, 1966, pp. 87–98.

29. The meanings of these terms was not clearly differentiated. The

*engrosser* was one who cornered the market; the *forestaller* bought up goods on their way to the market, and the *regrater* bought up goods in order to sell them again at a higher price in the same market.
30. Edward Miller, 'The economic policies of governments', *Camb. Econ. Hist. Eur.*, iii, 287.
31. Eli F. Heckscher, 'Mercantilism', *Econ. Hist. Rev.*, vii (1936–7), 44–54.
32. Léo Verriest, *La Draperie d'Ath des origines au XVIII$^e$ siècle*, Brussels, 1942, p. 15.
33. Miller, *op. cit.*, p. 306.

## Chapter 10. The late Middle Ages

1. Especially J. Huizinga, *The Waning of the Middle Ages*, London, E. Arnold & Co., 1924.
2. See T. S. R. Boase, *Death in the Middle Ages*, London, Thames & Hudson, 1972, especially ch. 4.
3. *Le Livre de la Description des Pays de Gilles le Bouvier, dit Berry*, ed. E.-T. Hamy, Recueil de Voyages et de Documents pour servir à l'Histoire de la Géographie, vol. xxii, 1908, 47.
4. Maurice Braure, 'Etude économique sur les Châtellenies de Lille, Douai et Orchies, d'après des enquêtes fiscales des XV$^e$ et XVI$^e$ siècles', *Rev. Nord*, xiv (1928), 165–200.
5. Quoted in Millard Meiss, *Painting in Florence and Siena after the Black Death*, New York, Harper & Row, 1964, 67.
6. C. M. Cipolla, 'The trends in Italian Economic History in the later Middle Ages', *Econ. Hist. Rev.*, ii (1949–50), 181–4.
7. H. van Werveke, 'De omvang van de Ieperse lakenproductie in de veertiende eeuw', *Mededelingen van de Koninklijke* Vlaamse Academie *voor Wetenschappen, Letteren en schone Kunsten van Belgie*, ix, no. 2, (1947).
8. H. Joosen, 'L'ordonnance pour les tisserands d'Ath (1328) et son modèle malinois', *Bull. Comm. Roy. Hist.*, vol. 109 (1943), 175–86.
9. R. van Uytven, 'La Flandre et le Brabant terres de promission sous les ducs de Bourgogne', *Rev. Nord*, xliii (1961), 281–317.
10. Aloys Schulte, *Geschichte der grossen Ravensburger Handelsgesellschaft*, 1380–1530, Stuttgart, 1923.
11. Gerhard Heitz, 'Landliche Leinenproduktion in Sachsen (1470–1555)', *Deutsche Akademie der Wissenschaften*, Berlin, 1961, p. 109; H.-J. Seeger, *Westfalens Handel und Gewerbe vom 9. bis 14. Jahrhundert*, Berlin, 1926, pp. 55–76.
12. Raymond de Roover, *The Rise and Decline of the Medici Bank 1397–1494*, New York, Norton, 1966, and Harry A. Miskimin, *The Economy of the Early Renaissance, 1300–1460*, New York, Prentice-Hall, 1969, 104–5.
13. A. R. Bridbury, *Economic Growth: England in the Later Middle Ages*,

London, Allen & Unwin, 1962, p. 26.

14. Juljan Pelc, *Ceny w Krakowie w latach 1369–1600*, Badania z dziejow społecznych i gospodarczych, vol. xiv (Lwów, 1935), part 2, *Tablice Statystyczne*, 63–4. This increase was not paralleled in the price of iron.

15. Rolf Sprandel, 'Die Stückzahlen der Tuchproduction in Dixmude, Comines, Langemark, Dranouten, Eecke und Lo', *Viertel. Soz. Wirtsch.*, 54 (1967), 336.

16. Raymond de Roover, *Money, Banking and Credit in Medieval Bruges*, Cambridge, Mass., Medieval Academy of America, 1948, p. 13.

17. R. van Uytven, *op. cit.*

18. H. G. Koenigsberger, 'Property and the price revolution', *Econ. Hist. Rev.*, ix (1956–57), 1–15.

19. Braure, *op. cit.*

20. Meiss, *op. cit.*, p. 61.

21. David Herlihy, 'The Tuscan town in the Quattrocento: a demographic profile', *Med. Hum.*, n.s., i (1970), 81–109.

22. M. Mallet, *The Florentine Galleys in the Fifteenth Century*, p. 10.

23. Quoted in L. S. Stavrianos, *The Balkans since 1453*, New York, Rinehart, 1958, p. 37.

24. Heinz Stoob, 'Die Ausbreitung der abendländischen Stadt im östlichen Mitteleuropa', *Zeitschrift für Ostforschung*, x (1961), 25–84; see also map in *Atlas Ostliches Mitteleuropa*, Bielefeld, 1959, pp. 59. 60.

25. F. Graus, 'Die Handelsbeziehungen Böhmens zu Deutschland und Osterreich im 14. und zu Beginn des 15. Jahrhunderts', *Hist.*, ii (1960), 77–110; F. Lutge, 'Der Handel Nürnbergs nach dem Osten im 15/16. Jahrhundert', *Beiträge zur Wirtschaftsgeschichte Nürnbergs*, i (Nuremberg, 1967), 318–76.

26. Jerome Blum, 'The rise of serfdom in eastern Europe', *Am. Hist. Rev.*, lxii (1957), 807–36.

27. Karlheinz Blaschke, *Bevölkerungsgeschichte von Sachsen bis zur industriellen Revolution*, Weimar, 1967, pp. 81–3.

28. An inventory of Fugger mining interests is given in Ludwig Scheuermann, 'Die Fugger als Montanindustrielle in Tirol und Kärnten', *Studien zur Fugger-Geschichte*, viii (1929).

29. Harry A. Miskimin, *Money, Prices and Foreign Exchange in Fourteenth Century France*, Yale Studies in Economics, xv (1963), 67–8.

30. D. L. Farmer, 'Some livestock price movements in thirteenth-century England', *Econ. Hist. Rev.*, xxii (1969).

31. C. M. Cipolla, 'La prétendue révolution des prix', *Ann. E.S.C.*, x (1955), 513–16.

32. E. H. Phelps Brown and Sheila V. Hopkins, 'Seven centuries of the prices of consumables compared with builders' wage-rates', *Economica*, new series, xxiii (1956), 296–314.

33. E. Perroy, 'Wage labour in France in the later Middle Ages', *Econ. Hist. Rev.*, viii (1955–6), 232–9.

34. Robert S. Lopez, 'Hard times and investment in culture', *The Renaissance: A Symposium*, New York, Metropolitan Museum of Art, 1953.

35. J. Huizinga, *The Waning of the Middle Ages*, 1954, edn, p. 31.
36. R. S. Lopez and H. A. Miskimin, 'The Economic Depression of the Renaissance', *Econ. Hist. Rev.*, xiv (1962), 408–26.
37. Carlo M. Cipolla, 'Economic depression of the Renaissance', *Econ. Hist. Rev.*, xvi (1963–4), 519–24.
38. Daniel Waley, *Later Medieval Europe*, London, Longmans, 1964, 108.
39. A. R. Bridbury, *Economic Growth: England in the Later Middle Ages*, London, Allen and Unwin, 1962.
40. E. A. Kosminsky, 'Peut-on considérer le XIV et le XV siècles comme l'époque de la décadence de l'économie européenne?' *Studi in Onore di Armando Sapori*, Milan, 1957, vol. 1, 537–69.
41. Joseph Garnier, *La Recherche des Feux en Bourgogne aux XIV^e et XV^e Siécles*, Dijon, 1876.
42. Robert Boutruche, *La Crise d'une société: seigneurs et paysans du Bordelais pendant la Guerre de Cent Ans*, Paris, 1947, pp. 423–9.
43. Waley, *op. cit.*, p. 113.

# Bibliography

**ABBREVIATIONS**

| | |
|---|---|
| *AAG Bijd.* | *Afdeling Agrarische Geschiedenig Bijdragen* |
| *Am.Hist.Rev.* | *American Historical Review* |
| *Ann. . . .* | *Annales de . . .* |
| *Ann.ESC* | *Annales: Economies, sociétés, civilisation* |
| *Bibl.Ecole Chartes* | *Bibliothèque de l'Ecole des Chartes* |
| *Cah. . . .* | *Cahiers . . .* |
| *Cah.Hist.Mond.* | *Cahiers d'Histoire Mondiale* |
| *Camb.Econ.Hist.* | *Cambridge Economic History* |
| *CR Acad.Inscr. et Belles-Lettres* | *Comptes Rendus, Académie des Inscriptions et Belles-Lettres* |
| *Econ.Hist.Rev.* | *Economic History Review* |
| *Ec. Prat. Htes. Ets.* | *Ecole Pratique des Hautes Etudes* |
| *Et. . . .* | *Etudes . . .* |
| *Gesch. . . .* | *Geschichte . . .* |
| *Hans.Geschsbl.* | *Hansische Geschichtsblätter* |
| *Inst.* | *Institut, Institute* |
| *Jahrb.Nat-ökon.Stat.* | *Jährbuch für Nationalökonomie und Statistik* |
| *J. . . .* | *Journal . . .* |
| *J.Econ.Hist.* | *Journal of Economic History* |
| *J.Pol.Econ.* | *Journal of Political Economy* |
| *Med.Hum.* | *Medievalia et Humanistica* |
| *Mitteil.* | *Mitteilungen . . .* |
| *Pfingstbl. hans. Geschicht.* | *Pfingstblätter des hansischen Geschichtsverein* |

# Bibliography

| | |
|---|---|
| *Rec. Soc. Jean Bodin* | *Recueils de la Société Jean Bodin* |
| *Rev.* | *Revue . . .* |
| *Rev.Belge Phil.Hist.* | *Revue Belge de Philologie et d'Histoire* |
| *Rev.Hist.* | *Revue Historique* |
| *Rev.Hist.Sid.* | *Revue d'Histoire de la Sidérurguie* |
| *SSCI Stud.Alt.Med.* | *Settimane di Studio del Centro Italiano di Studi sull'alto Medioevo* |
| *Stud. On.* | *Studi in Onore di (Armando Sapori, Amintore Fanfani, Gino Luzzatto)* |
| *Trans.Roy.Hist.Soc.* | *Transactions of the Royal Historical Society* |
| *Vschr. Sozial- und Wirtschaftsgesch.* | *Vierteljahrschrift für Sozial- und Wirtschaftsgeschichte* |
| *Zeit.* | *Zeitschrift* |
| *Zeit. Ges. Staatswiss.* | *Zeitschrift für die Gesamte Staatswissenschaft* |

## CHAPTER 1
## The later Roman Empire

AUBIN, H. 'Der Rheinhandel in römischer Zeit', *Bonner Jahrb.* cxxx (1925), 1–37.

BAILEY, K. C. *The Elder Pliny's Chapters on Chemical Subjects*, 2 vols, Arnold, 1929–32.

BELOCH, J. 'Die Bevölkerung Italiens im Altertum', *Klio: Beiträge zur alten Geschichte* iii (1903), 471–90.

BOAK, A. E. R. *Manpower Shortage and the Fall of the Roman Empire in the West*, University of Michigan Press, 1955.

BOËTHIUS, A. 'Urbanism in Italy', *Urbanism and Town-Planning, Proceedings of the Second International Congress of Classical Studies*, Copenhagen, 1958, 87–107.

BRADFORD, J. *Ancient Landscapes*, Bell, 1957.

BROGAN, O. *Roman Gaul*, Bell, 1953.

BROWN, P. 'The later Roman Empire', *Econ. Hist. Rev.*, xx (1967), 327–43.

BROWN, P. *The World of Late Antiquity*, Thames & Hudson, 1971.

BRUNT, P. A. *Roman Manpower*, Oxford University Press, 1971.

BURY, J. B. *The Invasion of Europe by the Barbarians*, Macmillan, 1928.

CHARLESWORTH, M. P. *Trade Routes and Commerce of the Roman Empire*, Cambridge University Press, 1924.

CHILVER, G. E. F. *Cisalpine Gaul*, Oxford University Press, 1941.

DAY, J. *An Economic History of Athens under Roman Domination*, Columbia University Press, 1942.

DAY, J. 'The value of Dio Chrysostom's Euboean discourse for the economic historian', *Studies in Roman Social and Economic History in honor of Allan Chester Johnson*, Princeton University Press, 1951, 209–35.

EGGERS, H. J. *Der römische Import im freien Germanien, Atlas der Urgeschichte*, Bd 1, Hamburgisches Museum für Völkerkunde und Vorgeschichte, 1951.

FRANK, T. *An Economic Survey of Ancient Rome*, 5 vols, Johns Hopkins University Press, 1933–40.

HAVERFIELD, F. *Ancient Town-Planning*, Oxford University Press, 1913.

JASNY, N. *The Wheats of Classical Antiquity*, Johns Hopkins University Studies in Historial and Political Science, Series 52, no. 3, Baltimore, 1944.

JONES, A. H. M. 'The cities of the Roman Empire', *Rec. Soc. Jean Bodin* vi (1954), 135–76.

JONES, A. H. M. *The Cities of the Eastern Roman Provinces*, Oxford University Press, 1937.

JONES, A. H. M. *The Decline of the Ancient World*, Longmans, 1966.

JONES, A. H. M. *The Greek City from Alexander to Justinian*, Oxford University Press, 1940.

JONES, A. H. M. *The Later Roman Empire, 284–602*, 3 vols, Oxford, Blackwell, 1964.

LATOUCHE, R. *The Birth of Western Economy*, Methuen, 1961.

LOANE, H. J. *Industry and Commerce of the City of Rome*, The Johns Hopkins University Studies in Historical and Political Science, Series 56, no. 2, 1938.

MEIGGS, R. *Roman Ostia*, Oxford University Press, 1960.

OLIVA, P. *Pannonia and the Onset of Crisis in the Roman Empire*, Prague, 1962.

RIVET, A. L. F. *Town and Country in Roman Britain*, Hutchinson, University Library, 1958.

ROSTOVTZEFF, M. *The Social and Economic History of the Roman Empire*, Oxford University Press, 1926.

RUSSELL, J. C. *Late Ancient and Medieval Population, Trans. of the American Philosophical Society*, new series, vol. xlviii, part 3, 1958.

STAEHELIN, F. *Die Schweiz in Römischer Zeit*, 3rd edn, Basel, 1948.

STEVENS, C. E. 'Agriculture and rural life in the later Roman Empire', in *Camb. Econ. Hist.* i, 2nd edn, 1966, 92–127.

TOYNBEE, A. J. *Hannibal's Legacy*, 2 vols, Oxford University Press, 1965.

WALBANK, F. W. *The Decline of the Roman Empire in the West*, London, Cobbett Press, 1946.

WALBANK, F. W. *The Awful Revolution*, Liverpool University Press, 1969.

WALBANK, F. W. 'Trade and industry under the later Roman Empire', *Camb. Econ. Hist.* ii, 1952, 33–85.

# Bibliography

WARMINGTON, E. H. *The Commerce between the Roman Empire and India*, Cambridge University Press, 1928.

WEST, L. C. *Roman Gaul: The objects of trade*, Oxford, Blackwell 1935.

WHEELER, SIR MORTIMER. *Rome Beyond the Imperial Frontiers*, Bell, 1954.

WHITE, K. D. *Roman Farming*, Thames & Hudson, 1970.

WISEM'AN, F. J. *Roman Spain*, Bell, 1956.

## CHAPTER 2
## The early Middle Ages

ADELSON, H. L. 'Early medieval trade routes', *Am. Hist. Rev.* lxv (1959–60), 271–87.

BRIDBURY, A. R. 'The Dark Ages', *Econ. Hist. Rev.* xxii (1969), 526–37.

DILL, S. *Roman Society in the Last Century of the Western Empire*, Cleveland, Ohio, World Publishing Co., 1958.

DOEHAERD, R. 'Méditerranée et économie occidentale pendant le haut moyen âge', *Cah. Hist. Mond.*, i (1954), 571–93.

DOPSCH, A. *Die Wirtschaftsentwicklung der Karolingerzeit*, 2nd edn, Köln, Böhlau Verlag, 1922.

DOPSCH, A. *The Economic and Social Foundations of European Civilization*, Routledge & Kegan Paul, 1937.

GRIERSON, P. 'Carolingian Europe and the Arabs: the myth of the Mancus', *Rev. Belge Phil. Hist.* xxxii (1954), 1059–74.

HERLIHY, D. 'Treasure hoards in the Italian economy, 960–1139', *Econ. Hist. Rev.* x (1957–58), 1–14.

HIMLY, F.-J. 'Y-a-t-il emprise musulmane sur l'économie des états européens du VIIIe au Xe siècle', *Schweizerische Zeit. Gesch.* v (1955), 31–81.

KLEVEREN, J. VAN. 'Die Wikingerzüge in ihrer Bedeutung für die Belebung der Geldwirtschaft im frühen Mittelalter', *Jahr. Nat-ökon Stat.* clxviii (1956), 397–415.

KOSTRZEWSKI, J. *Les Origines de la civilisation polonaise*, Paris, Presses Universitaires, 1949.

LATOUCHE, R. *The Birth of the Western Economy*, Methuen, 1961.

LESTOCQUOY, J. 'The tenth century', *Econ. Hist. Rev.* xvii (1947), 1–14.

LEWIS, A. R. *The Northern Seas*, Princeton University Press, 1958.

LEWIS, B. *The Arabs in History*, Hutchinson, University Library, 1950.

LOMBARD, M. 'L'or mussulman du VIIe au XIe siècle', *Ann. ESC* ii (1947), 143–60.

LOPEZ, R. S. 'East and West in the early Middle Ages: economic relations', *Relazioni del X Congresso Internazionale di Scienze Storiche*, vol. iii, Florence, 113–63.

LOPEZ, R. S. 'Les influences orientales et l'éveil économique de l'Occident', *Cah. Hist. Mond.* i (1953–54), 594–622.

LOPEZ, R. S. *The Tenth Century*, Holt, Rinehart & Winston, 1959.

MOSS, H. ST L. B. 'The economic consequences of the barbarian invasions', *Econ. Hist. Rev.* vii (1936–37), 209–16.

PIRENNE, H. *Medieval Cities, their origins and the revival of trade*, Trans. F. D. Halsey, Princeton University Press, 1969.

PIRENNE, H. *Muhammad and Charlemagne*, trans. B. Miall, Allen & Unwin, 1939.

ROUSSEAU, F. 'Le destin de la vallée de la Meuse au Moyen Age', *Bull. Inst. Archéologique Liégeois* lxiii (1939), 107–17.

STENBERGER, M. and KLINDT-JENSEN, O. eds, *Vallhagar: a migration period settlement on Gotland/Sweden*, Copenhagen, 1955.

TURVILLE-PETRE, G. *The Heroic Age of Scandinavia*, Hutchinson, University Library, 1951.

VERCAUTEREN, FERNAND. 'Monnaie et circulation monétaire en Belgique et dans le nord de la France du VIe au XIe siècle', *SSCI Stud. Alt. Med. evo*, Spoleto, viii (1961), 279–311.

VERLINDEN, C. 'L'état économique de l'Alsace sous Louis le Pieux d'après Ermold le Noir', *Rev. Belge Phil. Hist.*, xiii (1934), 166–76.

WALLACE-HADRILL, J. M. *The Barbarian West, 400–1000*, Hutchinson, University Library, 1952.

WALLACE-HADRILL, J. M. *The Long-Haired Kings*, Methuen, 1962.

CHAPTER 3

## The expansion of the medieval economy

### GENERAL ECONOMIC HISTORIES OF EUROPE

*The Cambridge Economic History of Europe*, Cambridge University Press.

Vol. i *The Agrarian Life of the Middle Ages*, 1st edn, ed. J. H. Clapham and Eileen Power, 1942; 2nd and much revised edn, ed. M. M. Postan, 1966.

Vol. ii *Trade and Industry in the Middle Ages*, ed. M. Postan and E. E. Rich, 1952.

Vol. iii *Economic Organization and Policies in the Middle Ages*, ed. M. M. Postan, E. E. Rich and Edward Miller, 1963.

BAUTIER, R.-H. *The Economic Development of Medieval Europe*, London, Thames & Hudson, 1971.

CAVE, R. C. and COULSON, H. H. eds. *A Source Book for Medieval Economic History*, New York, Biblo & Tannen, 1965.

CIPOLLA, M., ed. *The Fontana Economic History of Europe*, vol. i, *The Middle Ages*, Collins, 1972.

FOURQUIN, G. *Histoire Economique de l'Occident Médiéval*, Paris, Librairie Armand Colin, 1969.

# Bibliography

GENICOT, L. *Le XIIIe Siècle Européen*, Paris, Nouvelle Clio, Presses Universitaires, 1968.

HEERS, J. *L'Occident aux XIVe et XVe Siècles*, Paris, Nouvelle Clio, Presses Universitaires, 1966.

LOPEZ, R. S. *The Birth of Europe*, New York, Evans, 1966.

NORTH, DOUGLASS C. and THOMAS, R. P. *The Rise of the Western World*, Cambridge University Press, 1973.

PIRENNE, H. *Economic and Social History of Medieval Europe*, London, Routledge & Kegan Paul, 1936.

### ECONOMIC HISTORIES OF INDIVIDUAL COUNTRIES

BÄUML, F. *Medieval Civilization in Germany*, Thames & Hudson, 1969.

HECKSCHER, E. F. *An Economic History of Sweden*, Harvard University Press, 1954.

LÜTGE, F. *Deutsche Sozial- und Wirtschaftsgeschichte*, 3rd edn, Berlin, Springer Verlag, 1966.

SAKAZOV, I. *Bulgarische Wirtschaftsgeschichte*, Berlin, Grundriss der slavischen Philologie und Kulturgeschichte, 1929.

VICENS VIVES, J. *An Economic History of Spain*, Princeton Universtity Press, 1969.

### SPECIAL SUBJECTS

BAUTIER, R.-H. 'L'or et l'argent en occident de la fin du XIIIe siècle au début du XIVe siècle', *CRS Acad. Insc. et Belles-Lettres*, 1951, 169–74.

BLOCH, M. *Feudal Society*, trans. L. A. Manyon, 2nd edn, Routledge & Kegan Paul, 1962.

GANSHOF, F. L. *Feudalism*, Longmans, 1951.

HILTON, R. H. 'Rent and capital formation in feudal society', in *Deuxième Conférence Internationale d'Histoire Economique*, vol. ii, Paris, 1965, 33–68.

LIEBER, A. E. 'Eastern business practices and medieval European commerce', *Econ. Hist. Rev.* xxi (1968), 230–43.

LOPEZ, R. S. 'The dollar of the Middle Ages', *J. Economic History*, xi (1951), 209–34.

LYON, B. and VERHULST, A. *Medieval Finance: a comparison of financial institutions in northwestern Europe*, University of Ghent, Werken uitgegeven door de Faculteit van de Letteren en Wijsbegeerte, vol. cxliii, Bruges, 1967.

WHITE, L. *Medieval Technology and Technical Change*, Oxford University Press, 1962.

## CHAPTER 4
# The population of medieval Europe

AMMANN, H. 'Die Bevölkerung der Westschweiz im ausgehenden Mittelalter', *Festschrift Friedrich Emil Welti*, Aarau, Verlag, R. Sauerländer, 1937, 390–447.

ANDRÉADÈS, A. 'La population de l'Empire Byzantin', *Actes du IVe Congrès International des Etudes byzantines*, Sofia, 1935, 117–26.

BARATIER, E. *La Démographie Provençale du XIIIe au XVIe siècle*, Ec. Prat. Htes Ets, Démographies et Sociétés, vol. v, Paris, SEVPEN, 1961.

BAUTIER, R.-H. 'Feux, Population et Structure Sociale au milieu du XVe siècle: l'exemple de Carpentras', *Ann. ESC*, xiv (1959), 255–68.

BELOCH, K. J. *Bevölkerungsgeschichte Italiens*, 3 vols, Berlin, Walter de Gruyter, 1937–61.

BICKEL, W. *Bevölkerungsgeschichte und Bevölkerungspolitik der Schweiz seit dem Ausgang des Mittelalters*, Zurich, Büchergilde Gutenberg, 1947.

BIRABEN, J.-N. and LE GOFF, J. 'La peste dans le Haut Moyen Age', *Ann. ESC* xxiv (1969), 1484–1510.

BLASCHKE, K. 'Bevölkerungsgang und Wüstungen in Sachsen während des späten Mittelalters', *Jahrb. Nat-ökon Stat.* clxxiv (1962), 414–29.

BOUMANS, R. 'L'évolution démographique d'Anvers', Belgian Ministry of Foreign Affairs, *Bulletin de Statistique,* xxxiv, part 3 (1948), 1683–93.

CAZELLES, R. 'La population de Paris avant la Peste Noire', *CR Acad. Inscr. Belles-Lettres*, 1966, 539–50.

CARPENTIER, E. 'Autour de la Peste Noire: famines et epidémies dans l'histoire du XIVe siècle', *Ann. ESC*, xvii (1962), 1062–92.

CARPENTIER, E. and GLÉNISSON, J. 'La démographie française au XIVe siècle', *Ann. ESC*, xvii (1962), 109–29.

DELATOUCHE, R. 'Agriculture médiévale et population', *Et. Sociales*, n.s. no. 28, 1955, 13–23.

DESPORTES, P. 'La population de Reims au XVe siècle', *Le Moyen Age*, xxi (1966), 463–509.

DOLLINGER, P. 'Le chiffre de population de Paris au XIVe siècle: 210 000 ou 80 000 habitants?', *Rev. Historique* ccxvi (1956), 35–44.

FABER, J. A., ROESSINGH, H. K., SLICHER VAN BATH, B. H., WOUDE, A. M. VAN DER, and XANTEN, H. J. VAN, 'Population changes and economic developments in the Netherlands: a historical survey', *AAG Bijd.*, xii (1965), 47–113.

FAHLBUSCH, O. 'Die Bevölkerungszahl der Stadt Braunschweig im Anfang des xviii Jahrhunderts', *Hans. Geschbl.*, xviii (1912), 249–56.

FOSSIER, R. 'Remarques sur les mouvements de population en Champagne méridionale au XVe siècle', in *Bibl. Ecole Chartes*, cxxii (1964), 177–215.

FOSSIER, R. *La Terre et les hommes en Picardie jusqu'à la fin du XIIIe siècle*, Paris, Béatrice-Nauwelaerts, 1968.

FOURQUIN, G. 'La population de la region parisienne aux environs de 1328', *Le Moyen Age*, ser. 4, xi (1956), 63–91.

# Bibliography

FOURQUIN, G. 'Villages et hameaux du nord-ouest de la région parisienne en 1332', *Paris et Ile-de-France*, ix (1957–58), 141–56.

GÉNICOT, L. 'Sur les témoignages d'accroisement de la population en occident du XIe au XIIIe siècle', *Cah. Hist. Mond.* i (1953), 446–62.

GIEYSZTOROWA, I. 'Badania nad historia zaludnienia Polski', *Kwartalnik Historii Kultury Materialnej*, xi (1963), 523–62.

GYÖRFFY, G. 'Einwohnerzahl und Bevölkerungsdichte in Ungarn bis zum Anfang des XIV. Jahrhunderts', *Et. Historiques* (Budapest), i (1960), 163–92.

HELLEINER, K. 'Europa's Bevölkerung und Wirtschaft im späteren Mittelalter', *Mitteil. Inst. für Osterreichische Geschichtsforschung*, lxii (1954), 254–69.

HELLEINER, K. 'Population movement and agrarian depression in the later Middle Ages', *Can. J. Econ. Pol. Sci.*, xv (1949), 368–77.

HELLEINER, K. 'The population of Europe from the Black Death to the eve of the vital revolution', in *Camb. Econ. Hist.*, iv, 1–95.

HERLIHY, D. 'The population of Verona in the first century of Venetian rule', *Renaissance Venice*, J. R. Hale, Faber, 1973.

HERLIHY, D. 'The Tuscan town in the Quattrocento: A demographic profile', *Med. Hum.*, i (1970), 81–109.

HIGOUNET, C. 'Mouvements de population dans le Midi de la France du XIe au XVe siècle', *Ann. ESC* viii (1953), 1–24.

HIGOUNET, C. 'Le peuplement de Toulouse au XIIe siècle', *Ann. du Midi* liv-lv (1942–43), 489–98.

JACOBY, D. 'La population de Constantinople à l'époque byzantine: un problème de démographie urbaine', *Byzantion*, xxxi (1961), 81–109.

KEYSER, E. 'Die Bevölkerung Danzigs und ihre Herkunft im 13. und 14. Jahrhundert', *Pfingstbl. hans. Geschicht*, xiv (1924).

KEYSER, E. *Bevölkerungsgeschichte Deutschlands*, Leipzig, Verlag von S. Hirzel, 1938.

KEYSER, E. 'Die Pest in Deutschland und ihre Erforschung', *Actes du Colloque International de Démographie Historique*, University of Liège, 1965, 369–77.

KLAPISCH, C. 'Household and family in Tuscany in 1427', *Household and Family in Past Time*, ed. P. Laslett, Cambridge University Press, 1972, 267–81.

KOVACSICS, J. 'An account of research work in historical demography in Hungary', *Actes Colloque International, Liège*, 1965, 249–72.

LE ROY, LADURIE, E. *Les Paysans de Languedoc*, Ec. Prat. Htes. Ets., Paris, SEVPEN, 1966.

LE GOFF, J. and ROMANO, R. 'Paysages et peuplement rural en Europe après le XIe siècle', *XIIe Congrès International des Sciences Historiques*, Vienna, 1965.

LESTOCQUOY, J. 'Tonlieu et peuplement urbain à Arras aux XIIe et XIIIe siècles', *Ann. ESC,* x (1955), 391–5.

LESTOCQUOY, J. 'L'origine des habitants d' Arras aux XIIe et XIIIe siècles d'après les noms de famille', *Proc. Fédération Historique et Archéologique de Belgique,* 35e Congrès, Courtrai, 1953, fasc. 3, 157–62.

LESTOCQUOY, J. 'Les villes et la population urbaine', *Cah. de Civilisation Médiévale,* i (1958), 55–62.

MOLINIER, A. 'La Sénéchaussée de Rouergue en 1341', *Bibl. Ecole Chartes* xliv (1883), 452–88.

MOLS, R. Introduction à la démographie historique des villes d'Europe du XIVe au XVIIIe siècle, 3 vols, University of Louvain, 1954.

MORLET, M.-T. 'Les noms de personne à Beauvais au XIVe siècle', *Bull. Phil. Hist. du Com. Trav. Hist. Sci.,* 1955–56, Paris (1957) 295, 309.

MORLET, M.-T. 'L'origine des habitants de Provins aux XIIIe et XIVe siècles d'après les noms de personne', *ibid.* (1961) 95–114.

MÜHLEN, H. VON ZUR 'Versuch einer soziologischen Erfassung der Bevölkerung Revals im Spätmittelalter', *Hans. Geschichtsbl.* lxxv (1957), 48–69.

OTT, C. *Bevölkerungsstatistik in der Stadt und Landschaft Nürnberg in der ersten Hälfte des 15 Jahrhunderts,* Berlin, Verlag von R. Trenkel, 1907.

PENNERS, T. 'Fragen der Zuwanderung in den Hansestädten des späten Mittelalters, *Hans. Geschichtsbl.* lxxxiii (1965), 12–45.

PIRENNE, H. 'Les dénombrements de la population d'Ypres au XVe siècle', *Vschr. Sozial- und Wirtschaftsgesch.* i (1903), 1–32.

PLESNER, J. *L'Emigration de la Campagne à la Ville libre de Florence au XIIIe Siècle,* Copenhagen, Gyldendalske Boghandel-Nordisk Forlag, 1934.

PRAT, G. 'Albi et la Peste Noire', *Ann. du Midi* lxiv (1952), 15–25.

PRÜSER, F. 'Uber die Herkunft der Mittelalterlichen Bevölkerung Bremens', Festschrift zum siebzigsten Geburtstag Professor Dr Heinrich Reinckes, *Zeit. des Vereins für Hamburgische Gesch.* xli (1951), 125–54.

REISNER, W. *Die Einwohnerzahl deutscher Städte im früheren Jahrhunderten mit besonderer Berücksichtung Lübecks,* Jena, Verlag von Gustav Fischer, 1903.

RENOUARD, Y. 'Conséquences et intérêt démographique de la peste noire de 1348', reprinted in *Et. Hist. Médiévale,* Bibliothèque Générale de l'Ecole Prat. Htes. Ets., Paris, SEVPEN, 1968, 158–64.

RICHÉ, P. 'Problèmes de démographies historique du haut moyen âge', *Ann. Démographie Historique,* 1966, 37–55.

RUSSELL, J. C. *Late Ancient and Medieval Population,* Trans. Am. Phil. Soc., xlviii, part 3, 1958.

SLICHER VAN BATH, B. H. 'The economic and social conditions in the Frisian districts from 900 to 1500', *AAG Bijd.* xiii (1965), 97–133.

SMET, J. DE 'L'effectif des milices brugeoises et la population de la ville en 1340', *Rev. Belge Phil. Hist.* xii (1933), 631–6.

SMITH, R. S. 'Barcelona "Bills of Mortality" and population, 1457–1590', *J. Pol. Econ.* xliv (1936), 84–93.

STUHR, F. 'Die Bevölkerung Mecklenburgs am Ausgang des Mittelalters', *Jahrb. des Vereins für Mecklenburgische Geschichte*, lviii (1893), 232–78.

THOMAS, L.-J. 'La population du Bas Languedoc à la fin du XIIIe siècle et au commencement du XIVe', *Ann. du Midi* (1908), 469–83.

WOLFF, P. 'Trois études de démographie médiévale en France méridionale', *Stud. On. Am. Sapori*, Milan, Instituto Editoriale Cisalpino, 1957, i, 493–503.

ZIEGLER, P. *The Black Death*, Collins, 1969.

CHAPTER 5

## Agriculture and rural life

ABEL, W. *Geschichte der deutschen Landwirtschaft*, Stuttgart, Verlag Eugen Ulmer, 1962.

APPLEBAUM, S. 'The late Gallo-Roman rural pattern in the light of the Carolingian cartularies', *Latomus* xxiii (1964), 774–87.

ASHBURNER, W. 'The farmer's law', *J. Hellenic Studies*, xxxii (1912), 68–95.

BEECH, G. T. *A Rural Society in Medieval France: the Gâtine of Poitou in the eleventh century*, Johns Hopkins University Press, 1964.

BELÉNYESY, M. 'La culture permanente et l'évolution du système biennal et triennal en Hongrie médiévale', *Kwartalnik Historii Kultury Materialnej* xiii (1960), 311–26.

BELL, C. H., ed. and trans. *Peasant Life in Old German Epics*, repr. New York, Octagon Books, 1965.

BLOCH, M. *French Rural History: an essay on its basic characteristics*, Routledge & Kegan Paul, 1966.

BLUM, J. 'The rise of serfdom in eastern Europe', *Am. Hist. Rev.* lxii (1956–7), 807–36.

BOUTRUCHE, R. *La Crise d'une Société: Seigneurs et Paysans du Bordelais pendant la Guerre de Cent Ans*, Paris, 1947.

CURSCHMANN, F. *Hungersnöte im Mittelalter*, Leipzig, Verlag von B. G. Teubner, 1900.

DÉLÉAGE, A. *La Vie rurale en Bourgogne jusqu'au début du onzième siècle*, Macon, 1941.

DELISLE, L. *Etudes sur la condition de la classe agricole et l'état de l'agriculture en Normandie au Moyen Age*, Evreux, Imprimerie de A. Hérissey, 1851.

DION, R. *Histoire de la vigne et du vin en France des Origines au XIXe siècle*, privately printed, 1959.

DOLLINGER, P. *L'Evolution des classes rurales en Bavière*, Publications de la Faculté des Lettres de l'Université de Strasbourg, fasc. 112, Paris, 1949.

DOLLINGER, P. 'Les transformations du régime domanial en Bavière au XIIIe siècle d'après deux censiers de l'abbaye de Baumburg', *Le Moyen Age* lvi (1950), 279–306.

DUBLED, H. 'Administration et exploitation des terres de la seigneurie rurale en Alsace aux XIe et XIIe siècles', *Vschr. Sozial- und Wirtschaftsgesch.* xlvii (1960), 433–73.

DUBLED, H. 'Les grandes tendances de l'exploitation au sein de la seigneurie rurale en Alsace du XIIIe au XVe siècle', *Vschrift Sozial- und Wirtschaftsgesch*, xlix (1962), 41–121.

DUBY, G. 'Le grand domaine de la fin du moyen âge en France', *International Conference of Economic History*, Stockholm, Communications, Paris, 1960, 333–42.

DUBY, G. *Rural Economy and Country Life in the Medieval West*, Edward Arnold, 1968.

DUBY, G. 'Techniques et rendements agricoles dans les Alpes du Sud en 1338', *Ann. du Midi* lxx (1958), 403–13.

ENDRES, R. 'Das Kirchengut im Bistum Lucca vom 8 bis 10 Jahrhundert', *Vschr. Sozial- und Wirtschaftsgesch.* xiv (1916–18), 240–92.

FAUCHER, D. 'L'assolement triennal en France', *Et. Rurales* i (1961) 7–17.

FÉVRIER, P.-A. 'Quelques aspects de la vie agricole en Basse Provence à la fin du moyen âge', *Bull. Phil. Hist. Com. Trav. Hist. Sci.*, 1957, 299–317.

FOSSIER, R. 'Le défrichements en Picardie', *Bull. Phil. Hist. Com. Trav. Hist. Sci.*, 1963, 75–91.

FOSSIER, R. *La Terre et les hommes en Picardie jusqu'à la fin du XIIIe siècle*, Paris, Béatrice-Nauwelaerts, 1968.

FOURNIER, G. *Le Peuplement rural en Basse Auvergne durant le Haut Moyen Age*, Publications de la Faculté des Lettres et Sciences Humaines de Clermont Ferrand, 2nd ser., vol. xii, Paris, 1962.

FOURQUIN, G. *Les Campagnes de la région Parisienne à la fin du moyen age*, Publications de la Faculté des Lettres et Sciences Humaines de Paris, vol. x, Paris, 1964.

GANSHOF, F. L. 'Manorial organization in the Low Counties in the seventh, eighth and ninth centuries', *Trans. Roy. Hist. Soc.*, 4th ser., xxxi (1949), 29–59.

GENICOT, L. *La Crise agricole du bas moyen age dans le Namurois*, Université de Louvain, Recueil de Travaux d'Histoire et de Philologie, 4e sér., fasc. 44, Louvain, 1970.

GENICOT, L. 'L'étendue des exploitations agricoles dans le comté de Namur à la fin du XIIIe siècle', *Et. Rurales* v (1962), 5–31.

GILLE, B. 'Recherches sur les instruments du labour au moyen âge',

*Bibl. Ecole Chartres* cxx (1963), 5–38.

GRAND, R. and DELATOUCHE, R. *L'Agriculture au moyen age de la fin de l'Empire Romain au XVIe siècle*, Paris, E. de Boccard, 1950.

GUÉRIN, I. *La Vie Rurale en Sologne aux XIVe et XVe siècles*, Ec. Prat. Hts. Ets. 6e section, Les Hommes et la Terre, v, Paris, SEVPEN, 1960.

GYSSELING, M. and VERHULST, A. *Het Oudste Goederenregister van de Sint-Baafsabdij te Gent*, Publications of the Faculty of Letters, University of Ghent, Bruges, 1964.

HERLIHY, D. 'The Agrarian revolution in southern France and Italy 801–1150', *Speculum* xxxiii (1958), 23–41.

HIGOUNET, C. 'L'assolement triennal dans la plaine de France au XIIIe siècle', *CR Acad. Inscr. et Belles-Lettres*, 1956, 507, 12.

HIGOUNET, C. *La Grange de Vaulerent*, Ecole Pratique des Hautes Etudes, 6e section: Les Hommes et la Terre, vol. x, Paris, SEVPEN, 1965.

JONES, P. J. 'An Italian estate, 900–1200', *Econ. Hist. Rev.* vii (1954–55), 18–32.

JONES, P. J. 'A Tuscan monastic estate in the later Middle Ages: Camaldoli', *J. Ecclesiastical History* v (1954), 168–83.

JONES, P. J. 'From manor to mezzadria: a Tuscan case-study in the medieval origins of modern agrarian society', in *Florentine Studies*, ed. N. Rubinstein, Faber, 1968, 193–241.

JONES, P. J. 'The agrarian development of medieval Italy', *Deuxième Conférence Internationale d'Histoire Economique, Aix-en-Provence, 1962* ii, Paris, Mouton, 1965, ii, 69–86.

KÖTZSCHKE, R. and EBERT, W. *Gesch. der Ostdeutschen Kolonisation*, Leipzig, Bibliographisches Institut AG, 1937.

LATOUCHE, R. 'Défrichement et peuplement rural dans le Maine du IXe au XIIIe siècle', *Le Moyen Age*, liv (1948), 77–87.

LEICHT, P. S. 'L'organisation des grands domaines dans l'Italie du nord pendant les Xe–XIIe siècles', *Rec. Soc. Jean Bodin* iv (1949), 165–76.

LEMERLE, P. Esquisse pour une histoire agraire de Byzance, *Rev. Hist.*, ccxix (1958), 32–74; 254–84.

LENTACKER, F. 'Nouveaux aperçus sur l'histoire agraire flamande', *Rev. du Nord* xli (1959), 97.

LEWIS, A. R. 'The closing of the medieval frontier', *Speculum* xxxiii (1958), 475–83.

LIVET, R. *Habitat rural et structures agraires en Provence Basse*, Publications Ann. Faculté des Lettres, Aix-en-Provence, no. 32, 1962.

LOPEZ, R.S. 'The origin of the merino sheep', *The Joshua Starr Memorial Volume, Jewish Social Studies Publications*, no. 5, 161–8.

LÜTGE, F. *Geschichte der deutschen Agrarverfassung*, Stuttgart Verlag Eugen Ulmer, 1963.

LUZZATTO, G. 'Changes in Italian agrarian economy (from the fall of the Carolingians to the Beginning of the 11th century)', in *Early Medieval*

*Society*, ed. S. L. Thrupp, New York, Appleton, 1967, 206–18.

MARTIN-LORBER, O. 'L'exploitation d'unx grange cistercienne à la fin du XIVe et au début du XVe siècle', *Ann. Bourgogne* xxix (1957), 161–80.

MERTENS, J. A. and VERHULST, A. E. 'Yield-ratios in Flanders in the fourteenth century', *Econ. Hist. Rev.* xix (1966), 175–82.

MESTAYER, M. 'Les prix du blé et de l'avoine de 1329 à 1793', *Rev. du Nord* xlv (1963), 157–76.

OLSEN, M. *Farms and Fanes of Ancient Norway*, Oslo Institutet for Sammenlignende Kulturforskning, 1928.

OSTROGORSKIJ, G. 'La commune rurale byzantine', *Byzantion* xxxii (1962), 139–66

PACH, Z. S. 'The development of feudal rent in Hungary in the fifteenth century', *Econ. Hist. Rev.* xix (1966), 1–14.

PESEZ, J.-M. and LADURIE, E. LE ROY 'Les villages désertés en France: vue d'ensemble', *Ann. ESC* xx (1965), 257–90.

PIRENNE, H., ed. *Le Livre de l'Abbé Guillaume de Ryckel (1249–1272)*, Ghent, H. Engelcke, 1896.

RENOUARD, Y. 'Vignobles, vignes et vins de France au Moyen Age', *Le Moyen Age* xv (1960), 337–49.

RICHARD, J.-M. 'Thierry d'Hireçon: agriculteur artésien', *Bibl. Ecole Chartes* liii (1892), 383–416, 571–604.

RÖMER, C. *Das Kloster Berge bei Magdeburg und seine Dorfer 968–1565*, Veröffentlichungen des Max-Planck-Instituts für Geschichte xxx (1970).

ROSDOLSKY, R. 'The distribution of the agrarian product in feudalism', *J. Econ. Hist.* xi (1951), 247–65.

SCHRÖDER LEMBKE, G. 'Zur Flurform der Karolingerzeit', *Zeit. Agrargeschichte und Agrarsoziologie* ix (1961), 143–52.

SCLAFERT, T. *Le Haut Dauphiné au Moyen Age*, Paris, 1926.

SION, J. *Les Paysans de la Normandie Orientale*, Paris, 1909.

SIVÉRY, G. 'L'évolution du prix de blé à Valenciennes aux XIVe et XVe siècles', *Rev. du Nord* xlvii (1965), 177–94.

SLICHER VAN BATH, B. H. *The Agrarian History of Western Europe, A.D. 500–1850*, Edward Arnold, 1963.

SLICHER VAN BATH, B. H. 'Le climat et les recoltes en haut moyen âge', *SSCI Stud. Alt. Med.* xiii, Spoleto, 1966, 399–425.

SLICHER VAN BATH, B. H. 'De oogstopbrengsten van verschillende gewassen, voornamelijk granen, in verhouding tot het zaaizaad, ca 810–1820', *AAG Bijd.* ix (1963), 29–125.

SLICHER VAN BATH, B. H. 'The rise of intensive husbandry in the Low Countries', in *Britain and the Netherlands*, ed. J. S. Bromley and E. H. Kossmann, Chatto & Windus, 1960, 130–53.

SLICHER VAN BATH, B. H. 'Studien betreffende de agrarische geschiedenis van de Veluwe in de Middel eeuwen', *AAG Bijd* xi (1964), 13–78.

# Bibliography

VERHULST, A. E. 'L'agriculture médiévale et ses problèmes', *Studi Medievali*, 3rd ser., ii (1961), 691–704.

VERHULST, A. E. 'En basse et moyenne Belgique pendant le haut moyen âge: Differents types de structure domaniale et agraire', *Ann. ESC* xi (1956), 61–70.

VERHULST, A. E. and GYSSELING, M. *Le Compte général de 1187 connu sous le nom de 'Gros Brief' et les institutions financières du Comté de Flandre au XIIe siècle*, Brussels, Commission Royal d'Histoire, 1962.

VERHULST, A. E. 'Differénts types de structure domaniale et agraire', *Ann. ESC*, xi (1956), 61–70.

VERHULST, A. E. 'La genèse du régime domanial classique en France au haut moyen âge', *SSCI Stud. Alt. Med.* xiii, Spoleto, 1966.

VERHULST, A. E. 'Probleme de mittelalterlichen Agrarlandschaft in Flandern', *Zeit. Agrargeschichte und Agrarsoziologie*, ix (1961), 13–19.

VERHULST, A. E. *De Sint-Baafsabdij te Gent en Haar Gronbezit*, Verhandelingen van de Koninklijke Vlaamse Academie voor Wetenschappen, Letteren en Schone Kunsten van België, Klasse der Letteren xxx, 1958.

WERVEKE, H. VAN. 'La famine de l'an 1316 en Flandre et dans les régions voisines', *Rev. du Nord* xli (1959), 5–14.

CHAPTER 6
## The development of the medieval town

AMMANN, H. 'Die schweizerische Kleinstadt in der mittelalterlichen Wirtschaft', in *Festschrift Walther Merz*, Aarau, Verlag, H. R. Sauerländer, 1928, 158–215.

AMMANN, H. 'Vom Städtewesen Spaniens und Westfrankreich in Mittelalter', *Studien zu den Anfängen des Europäischen Stadtwessens, Reichenau-Vorträge* iv (1958), 105–50.

AMMANN, H. *Wirtschaft und Lebensraum der mittelalterlichen Kleinstadt:* i *Rheinfelden*, Basel, Buchdruckerei A Fricker, n.d.

BABEL, A. *Histoire Economique de Genève des Origines au début du XVIe Siècle*, 2 vols, Geneva, Alexandre Jullien Editeur, 1963.

BECK, H. G. 'Konstantinopel: zur Sozialgeschichte einer früh-mittelalterlichen Haupstadt', *Byzantinische Zeit.* lviii (1965), 11–45.

BOESCH, G. *Sempach im Mittelalter*, Zeit. Schweizerische Gesch., Beiheft no. 5, Zurich, 1948.

BONENFANT, P. 'La fondation de villes neuves en Brabant au moyen âge', *Vschr. Sozial- und Wirtschaftsgesch.* xlix (1962), 145–70.

BOTERA, G. 'A Treatise Concerning the Causes of the Magnificency and Greatness of Cities', in *Reason of State*, trans. P. J. Waley and D. P.

Waley, Yale University Press, 1956, 225–80.

BOTHE, F. 'Frankfurts Wirtschaftsleben im Mittelalter', *Zeit. Ges. Staatswiss.* xciii (1932), 193–219.

DES MAREZ, G. *Etude sur la Propriété Foncière dans les Villes du Moyen Age*, Université de Gand: Recueil de Travaux publiés par la Faculté de Philosophie et Lettres, 20, Ghent, 1898.

DHONDT, J. 'Dévelopement urbain et initiative comtale en Flandre au XIe siècle', *Rev. du Nord* xxx (1948), 133–56.

DHONDT, J. 'L'essor urbain entre Meuse et Mer du Nord à l'époque mérvingienne', *Stud. On. A. Sapori*, Milan, Instituto Editoriale Cisalpino, n.d., 55–78.

DICKINSON, R. E. *The West European City*, Routledge & Kegan Paul, 1951.

DOLLINGER-LEONARD, Y. 'De la cité romaine à la ville médiévale dans la région de la Moselle et la Haute Marne', *Studien zu den Anfängen des Europäischen Städtewesens, Reichenau-Vorträge* iv (1958), 195–226.

DUBRULLE, H. *Cambrai à la fin du moyen âge*, Lille, Impr. Lefebvre-Ducrocq, 1904.

ENNEN, E. *Frühgeschichte der Europäischen Stadt*, Bonn, Ludwig Röhrscheid Verlag, 1953.

ENNEN, E. 'The different types of formation of European towns', reprinted in *Early Medieval Society*, ed. S. L. Thrupp, Appleton-Century-Crofts, 1967.

ENNEN, E. 'Zur Typologie des Stadt-Land-Verhältnisses im Mittelalter', *Studium Generale*, xvi (1963), 445–56.

ESPINAS, G. *La Vie urbaine de Douai*, 3 vols, Paris, 1913.

FOURNIAL, E. *Les Villes et l'economie d'échange en Forez aux XIIIe et XIVe siècles*, Paris, Les Presses du Palais Royal, 1967.

GAIER-LHOEST, J. *L'évolution topographique de la ville de Dinant au moyen âge*, Brussels, Pro Civitate: Collection Histoire, 1964.

GEERING, T. *Handel und Industrie der Stadt Basel*, Basel, Verlag Felix Schneider, 1886.

GIEYSZTOR, A. 'Villes et campagnes slaves du Xe au XIIIe siècle', *Deuxième Conférence Internationale d'Histoire Economique, Aix-en-Provence, 1962*, ii, 87–105.

GRADMANN, R. *Die Städtischen Siedlungen des Königreichs Württemberg*, Stuttgart, Forschungen zur deutschen Landes- und Volkskunde, Bd xxi, Heft 2, 1926.

GYÖRFFY, G. 'Les débuts de l'évolution urbaine en Hongrie', *Cah. de Civilisation Médiévale*, xii (1969), 127–46, 253–64.

HAASE, C. *Die Entstehung der westfälischen Städte*, Veröffentlichungen des Provinzialinstituts für Westfälische Landes- und Volkskunde, Reihe i, Heft 2, Münster, 1965.

HEERS, J. 'Urbanisme et structure sociale à Gênes au moyen âge', *Stud. On. A. Fanfani*, Milan, 1962 i, 369–412.

# Bibliography

HERLIHY, D. *Medieval and Renaissance Pistoia*, Yale University Press, 1967.

HEYMANN, F. G. 'The role of the towns in the Bohemia of the later Middle Ages', *Cah. Hist. Mond.* ii (1954), 326–46.

HERLIHY, D. *Pisa in the Early Renaissance: a study of urban growth*, Yale University Press, 1958.

HOFFMANN, K. 'Die Stadtgründungen Mecklenburg-Schwerins in der Kolonisationszeit vom 12. bis zum 14. Jahrhundert', *Jahr. des Vereins für mecklenburgische Geschichte und Altertumskunde* xcii (1930), 1–200.

HYDE, J. K. *Padua in the Age of Dante*, Manchester University Press, 1966.

JORIS, A. *Huy, Ville Médiévale*, Brussels, Collection Notre Passé, 1965.

JOSET, C.-J. *Les Villes au Pays de Luxembourg*, Université de Louvain, Recueil de Travaux d'Histoire et de Philologie, 3e ser, fasc. 5, Brussels, 1940.

KEYSER, E., ed. *Deutsches Städtebucher*: volumes published for each *Land* of West Germany, Stuttgart, W. Kohlhammer Verlag. Those published so far:

*Hessisches Städtebuch*, 1957.

*Badisches Städtebuch*, 1959.

*Rheinisches Städtebuch*, 1956.

*Städtebuch Rheinland-Pfalz und Saarland*, 1964.

*Westfälisches Städtebuch*, 1954.

*Württembergisches Städtebuch*, 1962.

LATOUCHE, R. 'La commune du Mans', *Mélanges d'Histoire du Moyen Age dédiés à la Mémoire de Louis Halphen*, Paris, Presses Universitaires, 1951, 377–82.

LAVEDAN, P. *L'Histoire de l'urbanisme*, Paris, Henri Laurens, éditeur, 1959.

LE GOFF, J. 'Ordres mendiants et urbanisation dans la France médiévale', *Ann. ESC* xxv (1970), 924–46.

LESTOCQUOY, J. 'Les étapes du développement urbain d'Arras', *Rev. Belge Phil. Hist.* xxiii (1944), 163–85.

LESTOCQUOY, J. 'Le paysage urbain en Gaule du Ve au IXe siècle', *Ann. ESC* viii (1953), 159–72.

MILLER, D. A. *Imperial Constantinople*, Wiley, 1969.

MUNDY, J. H. *Liberty and Political Power in Toulouse 1050–1230*, Columbia University Press, 1954.

NICHOLAS, D. M. 'Town and countryside: social and economic tensions in fourteenth-century Flanders', *Comparative Studies in Society and History* x (1968), 458–85.

*Niederrheinische Städteatlas*, ii. *Geldrische Städte*, Kleve, Boss-Druck und Verlag, 1956.

PERROY, E. 'Les origines urbaines en Flandre d'après un ouvrage récent', *Rev. du Nord* xxix (1947), 49–63.

PÜSCHEL, A. *Das Anwachsen der deutschen Städte in der Zeit der mittelalterlichen Kolonialbewegung*, Abhandlung zur Verkehrs- und Seegeschichte vol. iv, Berlin, 1910.

*Recueils de la Société Jean Bodin*, vol. vii: *La Ville*, Brussels, 1955.

PLANITZ, H. *Die deutsche Stadt im Mittelalter*, Cologne, Böhlau-Verlag, 1965.

RÖRIG, F. *The Medieval Town*, University of California Press, 1967.

ROUX, S. 'L'habitat urbain au moyen âge: le quartier de l'université à Paris', *Ann. ESC* xxiv (1969), 1196–1219.

SCHNELBÖGL, F. 'Die wirtschaftliche Bedeutung ihre Landgebietes für die Reichstadt Nürnberg', in *Beiträge zur Wirtschaftsgeschichte Nürnbergs*, Nuremberg, 1967, i 261–317.

STOOB, H. 'Minderstädte: Formen der Stadtentstehung im Spätmittelalter', *Vschr. Sozial- und Wirtschaftsgesch.* xlvi (1959), 1–28.

STRAUSS, G. *Nuremberg in the Sixteenth Century*, Wiley, 1966.

*Studien zu den Anfängen des Europäischen Städtwesens, Reichenau-Vorträge*, iv, 1958, 297–362.

TAFRALI, O. *Thessalonique au Quatorzième Siècle*, Paris, Librairie Paul Geuthner, 1913.

WALEY, D. *Mediaeval Orvieto*, Cambridge University Press, 1952.

WELTE, A. 'Zur Entstehung der mainfränkischen Städte', *Petermanns Mitteil.* lxxxvii (1941), 233–50.

*Villes de l'Europe méditerranéenne et de l'Europe occidentale du Moyen Age au XIXe Siècle*, Annales de la Faculté des Lettres et Sciences Humaines de Nice, no. 9–10, 1969.

WINTERFELD, L. VON. 'Handel, Kapital und Patriziat in Köln bis 1400', Pfingstbl. hans. Geschichts. xvi (1925).

WOLFF, P. *Commerce et Marchands de Toulouse (vers 1350–vers 1450)*, Paris, Librairie Plon, 1954.

WOLFF, P. 'Les luttes sociales dans les villes du Midi français, XIIIe–XVe siècles', *Ann: ESC* ii (1947), 443–54.

WOLFF, P. 'Quelques données sur la société de Rodez autour de 1420', *Rouergue et Confins: Congrès de Rodez, Juin, 1958*, Société des Lettres, Sciences et Arts de l'Aveyron, Rodez, 121–33.

G. WYMANS, 'Le déclin de Tournai au XVe siècle', *Anciens Pays et Assemblées d'Etat*, xxii (1961), 111–34.

CHAPTER 7
## Medieval manufacturing

AMMANN, H. 'Deutschland und die Tuchindustrie Nordwest-Europas', *Hans. Geschichtsbl.* lxxii (1954), 1–63.

# Bibliography

AMMANN, H. 'Die Anfänge der Leinenindustrie des Bodenseegebietes under der Ostschweiz', *Zeit. Schweizerische Gesch.* xxiii (1943), 329–70.

AMMANN, H. 'Wirtschaftliche Bedeutung der Schweiz im Mittelalter', *Historische Aufsätze: Aloys Schulte zum 70 Geburtstag*, Düsseldorf, 1927, 112–32.

AMMANN, H. 'St Gallens Wirtschaftsstellung im Mittelalter', *Aus Sozial- und Wirtschaftsgeschichte: Gedächtnisschrift für Georg von Below*, Stuttgart, W. Kohlhammer Verlag, 1928, 131–68.

BAUTIER, R.-H. 'Notes sur le commerce du fer en Europe occidentale du XIIIe au XVIe siècle', *Rev. Hist. Sid.* i (1960), part 4, 7–35.

BORLANDI, F. 'Futainiers et futaines dans l'Italie du Moyen âge', *Eventail de l'histoire vivante: hommage à Lucien Febvre*, Paris, 1953, ii, 133–40.

BROUWERS, D.-D. 'Les marchands-batteurs de Dinant à la fin du XVe siècle', *Bull. Commission Royale d'Histoire* lxxviii (1909), 113–41.

COORNAERT, E. 'Draperies rurales, draperies urbaines', *Rev. Belge Phil. Hist.* xxviii (1950), 59–96.

COORNAERT, E. *Les Corporations en France*, Paris, Gallimard, 1941.

COORNAERT, E. 'Les ghildes médiévales', *Rev. Hist.* cxcix (1948), 22–55.

DAVIDSOHN, R. 'Blüte und Niedergang der Florentiner Tuchindustrie', *Zeit. Ges. Staatswiss.* lxxxv (1928), 225–55.

DEMAISON, L. 'Documents sur les draperies de Reims au moyen âge', *Bibl. Ecole Chartes* lxxxix (1928), 5–39.

ENDREI, W. *L'Evolution des Techniques du Filage et du Tissage du Moyen Age*, Paris, Ec. Prat. Htes Ets., Industrie et Salariat, 4, 1968.

ESPINAS, G. *La Draperie dans la Flandre au Moyen Age*, 2 vols, Paris, 1923.

ESPINAS, G. *Les Origines du Capitalisme: 1. Sire Jehan Boinebroke*, Bibliothèque de la Société d'Histoire du Droit des Pays Flamands, Picards et Wallons, vol vii, 1933.

FAGNIEZ, G. *Etudes sur l'Industrie et la Classe industrielle à Paris au XIIIe et au XIVe siècle*, Paris, Bibl. Ec. Prat. Htes. Et. xxxiii (1877).

GEREMEK, B. *Le Salariat dans l'Artisanat parisien aux XIIIe–XVe Siècles*, Paris, Ec. Prat. Htes Et., Industrie et Artisanat v, 1962.

GILLE, B. 'L'organisation de la production du fer au moyen âge', *Rev. Hist. Sid.* ix (1968), 95–121.

HATCHER, JOHN, *English Tin Production and Trade before 1550*, Oxford, Clarendon Press, 1973.

HEITZ, G. *Landliche Leinenproduktion in Sachsen (1470–1555)*, Berlin, Deutsche Akademie der Wissenschafter, 1961.

HILLEBRAND, W. 'Der Goslarer Metalhandel im Mittelalter', *Hans. Geschsbl.* lxxxvii (1969), 31–57.

HOHLS, H. 'Der Leinwandhandel in Norddeutschland vom Mittelalter bis zum 17 Jahrhundert', *Hans. Geschsbl.* xxxi (1926), 116–58.

IMAMUDDIN, S. M. *Some Aspects of the Socio-Economic and Cultural History of Muslim Spain*, Leiden, E. J. Brill, 1965.

# Bibliography

JIREČEK, C. J. *Die Handelsstrassen und Bergwerke von Serbien und Bosnien während des Mittelalters*, Prague, Abhandlungen der königl. böhmischen Gesellschaft der Wissenschaften, 1879.

JIREČEK, C. J. *La Civilisation Slave au Moyen Age*, Paris, Editions Bossard, 1920.

KELLENBENZ, H. 'Industries rurales en Occident de la fin du moyen âge au XVIIIe siècle', *Ann. ESC* xviii (1963), 823–82.

KELLENBENZ, H. 'Ländliches Gewerbe und bäuerliches Unternehmertum in Westeuropa vom Spätmittelalter bis ins 18 Jahrhundert', *Deuxième Conférence Internationale d'Histoire Economique, Aix-en-Provence*, Paris, Mouton, 1965, 377–427.

KOŘAN, J. and VAŇEČEK, V. 'Czech Mining and Mining Law', *Cah. Hist. Mond.* vii (1962), 27–45.

KUMLIEN, K. 'Bergbau, Bürger und Bauer im mittelalterlichen Schweden', *Vsch. Sozial- und Wirtschaftsgesch.* lii (1965), 330–46.

LAURENT, H. *Un Grand commerce d'exploitation au moyen âge: La draperie des Pays-Bas, en France et dans les pays méditeranéens*, Paris, 1935.

LINOSSIER, M.-C. 'L'artisan lyonnais de la fin du XIVe au milieu du XVe siècle', *Colloque Franco-Suisse d'Histoire Economique et Sociale*, Publications de la Faculté des Sciences Economiques et Sociales de l'Université de Genève, 1969, 9–18.

LOPEZ, R. S. 'Silk industry in the Byzantine empire', *Speculum* xx (1945), 1–42.

MALOWIST, M. 'L'évolution industrielle en Pologne du XIVe au XVIIe siècle', *Stud. On. A. Sapori*, Milan, Instituto Editoriale Cisalpino, 1957, i, 571–603.

MARQUANT, R. *La Vie Economique à Lille sous Philippe le Bon*, Bibl. Ec. Prat. Htes Ets. no. 277 (1940).

MAZZAOUI, M. F. *The Emigration of Veronese Textile Artisans to Bologna in the Thirteenth Century*, Atti e Memorie della Accademia di Agricoltura, Scienze e Lettere di Verona, no. 19 (1967–68).

MAZZAOUI, M. F. 'The cotton industry of northern Italy in the late Middle Ages', *J. Econ. Hist.* xxxii (1972), 262–86.

MOLLAT, M. *Le Commerce Maritime Normand à la Fin du Moyen Age*, Paris, Librairie Plon, 1952.

NEF, J. U. 'Industrial Europe at the time of the Reformation, *J. Political Economy* xlix (1941), 1–40, 183–224.

NÜBLING, E. *Ulms Baumwollweberie im Mittelalter*, *Schmollers Jahrb.* ix, Heft 5 (1890).

PIRENNE, H. 'Draps de Frise ou draps de Flandre', *Vschr. Sozial- und Wirtschaftsgesch.* vii (1909), 308–15.

PIRENNE, H. 'Les marchands-batteurs de Dinant au XIVe et au XVe siècle', *Vschr. Sozial- und Wirtschaftsgesch.* ii (1904), 442–9.

POERCK, G. DE. *La Draperie médiévale en Flandre et en Artois: technique et terminologie*, 3 vols, Bruges, Rijksuniversiteit te Gent, 1951.

SEEGER, H. J. *Westfalens Handel und Gewerbe vom 9. bis 14. Jahrhundert*, Berlin, Verlag von Karl Curtius, 1926.

SPRANDEL, R. 'Die Ausbreitung des deutschen Handwerks im mittelalterlichen Frankreich', *Vschr. Sozial- und Wirtschaftsgesch.* li (1964), 66–100.

SPRANDEL, R. 'Die Handwerker in den nordwestdeutschen Städten des Spätmittelalters', *Hans. Geschsbl.* lxxxvi (1968), 37–62.

SPRANDEL, R. Die oberitalienische Eisenproduktion im Mittelalter', *Vschr. Sozial- und Wirtschaftsgesch.* lii (1965), 289–339.

SPRANDEL, R. 'La production du fer au moyen âge', *Ann. ESC*, xxiv (1969), 305–21.

SPRANDEL, R. 'Zur Tuchproduction in der Gegend von Ypern', *Vschr. Sozial- und Wirtschaftsgesch.* liv (1967), 336–40.

THRUPP, S. L. 'Medieval gilds reconsidered', *J. Econ. Hist.* ii (1942), 164–73.

VÁCZY, P. 'La transformation de la technique et de l'organisation de l'industrie textile en Flandre aux XIe–XIIIe siècles', Hungarian Academy of Sciences, *Etudes Historiques* i (1960), 291–316.

VARRON, A. 'The development of Lyons as the centre of the French silk industry', *Ciba Review*, no. 6, Feb. 1938.

VERRIEST, L. *La Draperie d'Ath des origines au XVIIIe Siècle*, Brussels, privately printed, 1942.

CHAPTER 8

**The trade of the Middle Ages**

ALBERTS, W. J. 'Beiträge zur Wirtschaftsgeschichte des Rheins in Zusammenhang mit der spätmittelalterlichen Wirtschaftsentwicklung der Niederlands', *Rheinische Vierteljahrsbl.* xxvi (1961), 297–322.

AMMANN, H. 'Die Zurzacher Messen im Mittelalter', in *Taschenbuch der Historischen Gesellschaft des Kantons Aargau für das Jahr 1923*, Aarau, H. R. Sauerländer, 1–154.

AMMANN, H. 'Neue Beiträge zur Geschichte der Zurzacher Messen', in *ibid*, 1929, 1–207.

BAUTIER, R.-H. 'Le traffic fluvial sur la Seine au Pont de Meulan au milieu du XVe siècle', *Bull. Phil. Hist. Com. Trav. Hist. Sci.*, 1959, 251–96.

BAUTIER, R.-H. 'Notes sur le commerce de fer en Europe occidentale du XIIe au XVIe siècle', *Rev. Hist. Sid.* iv (1963), 35–61.

BERGIER, J.-F. *Génève et l'Economie Européenne de la Renaissance, Ec. Prat. Htes Ets*, Paris, SEVPEN, 1963.

BERGIER, J.-F. *Problèmes de l'histoire économique de la Suisse*, Bern, Franke Editions, 1968.

BIGWOOD, G. 'Gand et la circulation des grains en Flandre du XIVe au XVIIIe siécle', *Vschr. Sozial- und Wirtschaftsgesch* iv (1906), 397–460.

BOYER, M. N. 'Roads and rivers: their use and disuse in late medieval France', *Med. Hum.* xiii (1960), 68–80.

BRATIANU, G. I. *Recherches sur le commerce génois dans la Mer Noire au XIIIe siècle*, Paris, Paul Geuthner, 1929.

COORNAERT, E. 'Caractères et mouvements des foires internationales au moyen âge et au XVIe siècle', *Stud. On. A. Sapori*, Milan, Instituto Editoriale Cisalpino, 1957, i, 355–71.

COORNAERT, E. *Les Français et le commerce international à Anvers*, 2 vols, Paris, 1961.

DENHOLM-YOUNG, N. 'The merchants of Cahors', *Med. Hum.* iv (1946), 37–44.

DHONDT, J. 'Les problèmes de Quentovic', *Stud. On. Amintore Fanfani*, Milan, 1962, i, 181–248.

DIETZ, A. *Frankfurter Handelsgesch.*, Frankfurt/Main, Gebrüder Knauer, 1925.

DOEHAERD, R. *Les Relations commerciales entre Gênes, la Belgique et l'Outremont*, 3 vols, Institut Historique Belge de Rome, 1941.

DOLLINGER, P. 'Commerce et marchands strasbourgeois à Fribourg en Suisse au moyen âge', *Beiträge zur Wirtschafts- und Städtgeschichte: Festschrift Hektor Ammann*, Wiesbaden, Franz Steiner Verlag, 1965, 124–43.

DOLLINGER, P. *German Hansa*, Macmillan, 1970.

EARLE, P. 'The commercial development of Ancona, 1479–1551', *Econ. Hist. Rev.* xxii (1969), 28–44.

FACE, R. D. 'Techniques of business in the trade between the fairs of Champagne and the south of Europe in the twelfth and thirteenth centuries', *Econ. Hist. Rev.* 10 (1957–58), 427–38.

FACE, R. D. 'The Vectuarii in the overland commerce between Champagne and Southern Europe', *Econ. Hist. Rev.* xii (1959–60), 239–46.

FAGNIEZ, G., ed. *Documents relatifs à l'histoire de l'industrie et du commerce en France*, Collection de textes pour servir à l'étude et à l'enseignement de l'histoire, Paris, 1900.

FELLMANN, W. 'Die Salzproduktion im Hanseraum', *Hansische Studien Heinrich Sproemberg zum 70 Geburstag*, Berlin, Akademie Verlag, 1961.

FINOT, J. *Etude Historique sur les Relations Commerciales entre la France et la Flandre au Moyen Age*, Paris, 1894.

FORESTIÉ, E. *Les Livres de Comptes des Frères Bonis*, Archives de la Gascogne, xx, 1890.

GODARD, J. 'Contribution à l'étude de l'histoire du commerce des grains à Douai du XIVe au XVIIe siècle', *Rev. du Nord* xxvii (1944), 171–205.

GRAUS, F. 'Die Handelsbeziehungen Böhmens zu Deutschland und

Osterreich im 14 und zu Beginn des 15 Jahrhunderts', *Historica* (Prague), ii (1960), 77–110.

GRUNDZWEIG, A. 'Florence et les Pays-Bas au Moyen Age', *Bull. Inst. Hist. Belge de Rome* xxvi (1950–51), 113–28.

GUILMOTO, G. *Etude sur les droits de navigation de la Seine de Paris à la Roche-Guyon du XIe au XVIIIe siècle*, Paris, Alphonse Picard, éditeur, 1889.

HEERS, J. *Gênes au XVe siècle*, Ec. Prat. Htes Ets., 6e section: Affairs et Gens d'Affaires, xxiv, Paris, SEVPEN, 1961.

HEERS, J. 'Rivalité ou collaboration de la terre et de l'eau?', *Les Grandes Voies Maritimes dans le Monde: XVe–XIXe Siècles*, Bibl. Générale Ec. Prat. Htes Ets., Paris, SEVPEN, 1965, 13–63.

HEERS, M.-L. 'Les Génois et le commerce de l'alun à la fin du moyen âge', *Rev. Hist. Economique et Sociale* xxxii (1954), 31–53.

HEYD, W. *Histoire du Commerce du Levant au moyen âge*, Leipzig, 1885.

HOLLIHN, G. 'Die Stapel- und Gästepolitik Rigas in der Ordenszeit', *Hans. Geschichtsbl.* lx (1935), 91–207.

HOUTTE, J. A. VAN. 'The rise and decline of the market of Bruges', *Econ. Hist. Rev.* xix (1966), 29–47.

HUBERT, J. 'Les routes du moyen âge', *Les Routes de France depuis origines jusqu'à nos jours, Colloques: Cah. de Civilisation*, Paris, 1959, 25–56.

JORIS, A. 'A propos du commerce mosan aux 13e et 14e siècles', *Féderation archéologique et Historique de Belgique*, 36e Congrès, Ghent, 1955, 227–44.

KELLENBENZ, H. 'Landverkehr, Fluss- und Seeschiffahrt im Europäischen Handel', *Les Grandes voies maritimes dans le monde: XVe–XIXe siècles*, Paris, SEVPEN, 1965, 65–174.

KERLING, N. J. M. *Commercial Relations of Holland and Zeeland with England from the late 13th Century to the Close of the Middle Ages*, Leiden, E. J. Brill, 1954.

KERLING, N. J. M. 'Relations of English Merchants with Bergen op Zoom, 1480–1481', *Bull. Inst. Historical Studies* xxxi (1958), 130–40.

KOPPE, W. 'Revals Schiffsverkehr und Seehandel in den Jahren 1378–84', *Hans. Geschichtsbl.* lxiv (1939), 111–52.

KREKIĆ, B. *Dubrovnik et le Levant au Moyen Age*, Paris, Mouton, 1961.

KUSKE, B. 'Handel und Handelspolitik am Niederrhein vom 13 bis 16 Jahrhundert', *Hans. Geschichtsbl.* xv (1909), 301–27.

KUSKE, B. *Quellen zur Geschichte des Kölner Handels und Verkehrs im Mittelalter*, Publikationen der Gesellschaft für Rheinische Geschichtskunde xxxiii (1923–34), Bonn.

LANE, F. C. *Andrea Barbarigo: merchant of Venice 1418–1449*, Johns Hopkins University Studies in Historical and Political science, ser. 62, no. 1, Baltimore, 1944.

LANE, F. C. 'Venetian shipping during the commercial revolution',

# Bibliography

*Am. Hist. Rev.* xxxviii (1932–33), 219–39.

LANE, F. C. *Venetian Ships and Shipbuilders of the Renaissance*, Johns Hopkins University Press, 1934.

LAURENT, H. *Un Grand commerce d'exploitation au moyen âge: la draperie des Pays-Bas, en France et dans les pays Méditerranéens*, Paris, 1935.

LECHNER, G. *Die Hansischen Pfundzollisten des Jahres 1368*, Quellen und Darstellungen zur hansischen Geschichte x, 1935, Lübeck.

LESTOCQUOY, J. *Les Dynasties Bourgeoises d'Arras du XIe au XVe Siècle*, Mémoires de la Commission Départementale des Monuments Historiques du Pas-de-Calais, vol. v, fasc 1, Arras, 1945.

LEWIS, A. R. *Naval Power and Trade in the Mediterranean, A.D. 500–1100*, Princeton University Press, 1951.

LEWIS, A. R. *The Northern Seas*, Princeton University Press, 1958.

LOMBARD, M. 'La route de la Meuse et les relations lointaines des pays mosans entre le VIIIe et le XIe siècle', *L'Art Mosan*, Bibl. Gén. Ec. Prat. Htes Ets, Paris, 1953.

LOPEZ, R. S. and RAYMOND, I. W. *Medieval Trade in the Mediterranean World*, Oxford University Press, 1955.

LOPEZ, R. S. and RAYMOND, A. W. 'The Evolution of Land Transport in the Middle Ages', *Past and Present*, ix (1956), 17–29.

LÜTGE, F. 'Der Handel Nürnbergs nach dem Osten im 15/16 Jahrhundert', *Beiträge zur Wirtschaftsgesch. Nürnbergs*, Nürnberg, 1967, vol. i, 318–76.

MALLET, M. E. *The Florentine Galleys in the Fifteenth Century*, Oxford, Clarendon Press, 1967.

MALOWIST, M. 'Polish-Flemish Trade in the Middle Ages', *Baltic and Scandinavian Countries*, iv (1938), 1–9.

MOLLAT, M. *Le Commerce maritime Normand à la fin du moyen âge*, Paris, Librairie Plon, 1952.

NAUDÉ, W. *Die Getreidehandelspolitik der europäischen Staaten vom 13 bis zum 18 Jahrhundert (Acta Borussica, vol. i)*, Berlin, 1896.

*Rec. Soc. Jean Bodin*, vol. v, *La Foire*, Brussels, 1953.

ORIGO, I. *The Merchant of Prato*, Knopf, 1957.

RENOUARD, Y. 'La consommation des grands vins de Bourbonnais et de Bourgogne à la cour pontificale d'Avignon', *Ann. Bourgogne* xxiv (1952), 221–44.

RENOUARD, Y. 'Le grand commerce du vin au moyen âge', *Etudes d'Histoire Médiévale*, Paris, SEVPEN, 1968, 235–48.

RENOUARD, Y. 'Les Cahorsins, hommes d'affaires français du XIIIe siècle', *Trans. Roy. Hist. Soc.*, xi (1961), 43–67.

RENOUARD, Y. *Les Hommes d'affaires Italiens du moyen âge*, Paris, Armand Colin, 1949.

REYNOLDS, R. L. 'The market for northern textiles in Genoa 1179–1200', *Rev. Belge Phil. Hist.* viii (1929), 831–51.

# Bibliography

SCHAUBE, A. *Handelsgeschichte der Romanischen Völker des Mittel-meergebiets bis zum Ende der Kreuzzüge*, Munich, 1906.

SCHULTE, A., *Geschichte der grossen Ravensburger Handelsgesellschaft 1380–1530*, 4 vols, Stuttgart, 1923.

SCHULTE, A. *Geschichte des mittelalterlichen Handels und Verkehrs zwischen Westdeutschland und Italien mit Ausschluss von Vendig*, 2 vols, Leipzig, 1900.

SIMONSFELD, H. *Der Fondaco dei Tedeschi in Venedig und die deutsch-venetianischen Handelsbeziehungen*, 2 vols, Stuttgart, 1887.

STURLER, J. DE. *Les Relations politiques et les échanges commerciaux entre le Duché de Brabant et l'Angleterre au moyen âge*, Paris, 1936.

THIRIET, F. *La Romanie Vénitienne au moyen âge*, Bibliothèque des Ecoles Françaises d'Athènes et de Rome, no. 193, 1959.

USHER, A. P. *The History of the Grain Trade in France 1400–1710*, Harvard University Press, 1913.

VAN DER WEE, H. *The Growth of the Antwerp Market and the European Economy*, Université de Louvain, *Recueil de Travaux d'Histoire et de Philologie*, fasc. 28 and 29, Louvain, 1963.

VOGEL, W. 'Ein seefahrender Kaufmann um 1100', 1944. *Hans. Geschbl.* xviii (1912), 239–48.

WERVEKE, H. VAN. *Bruges et Anvers: huit siècles de commerce flamand*, Brussels, 1944.

WILKENS, H. 'Zur Geschichte des niederländischen Handels im Mittel-alter, *Hans. Geschichtsbl.* xxxv (1908), 296–356; xxxvi (1909), 123–203.

YVER, G. *Le Commerce et les marchands dans l'Italie méridionale au XIIIe et au XIVe Siècle*, Bibliothèque des Ecoles Françaises d'Athènes et de Rome, no. 88, Paris, 1903.

CHAPTER 9

## The commercial revolution

BECKER, M. B. 'Some common features of Italian urban experience', *Med. Hum.*, n.s. i (1970), 175–201.

BRAUDEL, F. 'Monnaies et civilisations: de l'or du Sudan à l'argent d'Amerique', *Ann. ESC* i (1946), 9–22.

CIPOLLA, C. M. 'Currency depreciation in medieval Europe', *Econ. Hist. Rev.* xv (1963–64), 413–22.

CIPOLLA, C. M. *Money, Prices and Civilization in the Mediterranean World*, New York, Gordian Press, 1967.

DE LA RONCIÈRE, C. M. 'Indirect taxes or "gabelles" at Florence in the fourteenth century', in *Florentine Studies*, ed. N. Rubinstein, Faber, 1968, 140–92.

EHRENBERG, R. *Capital and Finance in the Age of the Renaissance*, Cape, 1928.

EVANS, A. 'Some coinage systems of the fourteenth century', *J. Economic and Business History*, iii (1931), 481–96.

FAVREAU, R. 'Les changeurs du Royaume sous le Règne de Louis XI', *Bibl. Ec. Chartes* cxxii (1964), 216–51.

KOENIGSBERGER, H. G. 'Property and the price revolution', *Econ. Hist. Rev.*, ix (1956–67), 1–15.

LANE, F. C. 'Family partnerships and joint ventures in the Venetian republic', in *Enterprise and Secular Change*, ed. F. C. Lane and J. C. Riemersma, Homewood, Ill., Irwin, 1953, 86–101.

LANE, F. C. 'The funded debt of the Venetian Republic', *Venice and History*, Johns Hopkins University Press, 1966, 87–98.

LUZZATTO, G. 'Small and great merchants in the Italian cities of the Renaissance', *Enterprise and Secular Change*, ed. Lane (above), 41–52.

MCLAUGHLIN, T. P. 'The Teaching of the canonists on usury', *Mediaeval Studies* i (1939), 81–147; ii (1940), 1–22.

MILLER, E., WERVEKE, H. VAN, LONNROTH, E. and CIPOLLA, C. M. 'The economic policies of governments', in *Camb. Econ. Hist.*, 1963 iii, 281–429.

MISKIMIN, H. A. *Money, Prices and Foreign Exchange in Fourteenth Century France*, Yale Studies in Economics, Yale University Press, 1963.

NELSON, B. *The Idea of Usury*, Chicago University Press, 1969.

ORIGO, I. *The Merchant of Prato*, Knopf, 1957.

POSTAN, M. M. 'Italy and the economic development of England in the Middle Ages', *J. Econ. Hist*, xi (1951), 339–46.

ROOVER, R. DE. 'The commercial revolution of the thirteenth century', *Enterprise and Secular Change*, ed. Lane (above), 80–5.

ROOVER, R. DE. 'The concept of the just price: theory and economic policy', *J. Econ. Hist.* xviii (1958), 418–38.

ROOVER, R. DE. *L'Evolution de la Lettre de Change: XIVe–XVIIIe siècles*, Ec. Prat. Htes. Ets., 6e section, Affaires et Gens d'Affaires, Paris, 1953.

ROOVER, R. DE. *Money, Banking and Credit in Medieval Bruges*, Cambridge, Mass., Mediaeval Academy of America, 1948.

ROOVER, R. DE. 'The organization of trade', in *Camb. Econ. Hist.*, 1963, iii, 42–118.

ROOVER, R. DE. *The Rise and Decline of the Medici Bank 1397–1494*, New York, Norton, 1966.

ROOVER, R. DE. *San Bernardino of Siena and Sant' Antonino of Florence*, The Kress Library of Business and Economics, Harvard University, no. 19, Harvard University Press, 1967.

ROOVER, R. DE. 'What is dry exchange? A contribution to the study of English mercantilism', *J. Pol. Econ.* lii (1944), 250–66.

SPUFFORD, P. *Monetary Problems and Policies in the Burgundian Netherlands 1433–1496*, Leiden, E. J. Brill, 1970.

USHER, A. P. *The Early History of Deposit Banking in Mediterranean Europe*, Harvard University Press, 1943.

USHER, A. P. 'The origins of banking: the primitive bank of deposit, 1200–1600', *Enterprise and Secular Change*, ed. Lane (above), 262–91.

WILSON, T. *A Discourse upon Usury*, with historical introduction by R. H. Tawney, Bell, 1925.

CHAPTER 10

# The late Middle Ages

ABEL, W. *Die Wüstungen des ausgehenden Mittelalters*, 2nd edn, Stuttgart, Gustav Fischer Verlag, 1955.

ABEL, W. 'Wüstungen und Preisfall im spätmittelalterlichen Europa', *Jahr. Nat-ökon. Stat.* clxv (1953), 380–427.

ASTON, M. *The Fifteenth Century*, Thames & Hudson, 1968.

BRIDBURY, A. R. *Economic Growth: England in the Later Middle Ages*, Allen & Unwin, 1962.

BRUCKER, G. A. 'The Ciompi revolution', in *Florentine Studies*, ed. N. Rubinstein, Faber, 1968.

CHAMBERS, D. S. *The Imperial Age of Venice, 1380–1580*, Thames & Hudson, 1970.

CIPOLLA, C. M. 'The trends in Italian economic history in the later Middle Ages', *Econ. Hist. Rev.*, ii (1949–50), 181–4.

CIPOLLA, C. M. 'Economic depression of the Renaissance?', *Econ. Hist. Rev.* xvi (1963–64), 519–24.

HERLIHY, D. 'Santa Maria Impruneta: a rural commune in the late Middle Ages', *Florentine Studies*, ed. N. Rubinstein, Faber, 1968, 242–76.

KOSMINSKY, E. A. 'Peut-on considerer le XIV et le XV siècles comme l'époque de la décadence de l'économie européenne?' *Stud. On. A. Sapori*, Milan, Istituto Editoriale Cisalpino, 1957, i, 551–69.

LEWIS, P. S. *Later Medieval France: the polity*, Macmillan, 1968.

LOPEZ, R. S. 'Hard times and investment in culture', in *The Renaissance: medieval or modern*, ed. K. H. Dannenfeldt, D. C. Heath, 1959, 50–61.

LOPEZ, R. S. and MISKIMIN, H. A. 'The economic depression of the Renaissance', *Econ. Hist. Rev.* xiv (1962), 408–26.

LUCAS, H. S. *The Low Countries and the Hundred Years' War, 1326–1347*, University of Michigan Press, 1929.

LÜTGE, F. 'Das 14/15 Jahrhundert in der Sozial- und Wirtschaftsgeschichte', *Jahr. Nat-ökon. Stat.* clxii (1950), 161–213.

MALOWIST, M. 'The problem of the inequality of economic development in Europe in the later Middle Ages', *Econ. Hist. Rev.*, xix (1966), 15–28.

MIANI, G. 'L'économie lombarde aux XIVe et XVe siècles: une exception à la règle?', *Ann. ESC* xix (1964), 569–79.

MISKIMIN, H. A. *The Economy of Early Renaissance Europe, 1300–1460*, Prentice-Hall, 1969.

MOLHO, A. *Social and Economic Foundations of the Italian Renaissance*, Wiley, 1969.

NEF, J. U. 'The genesis of industrialism and of modern science', in *Essays in Honor of Conyers Read*, ed. Norton Downs, University of Chicago Press, 1953, 200–69.

PERROY, E. 'A l'origine d'une économie contractée: les crises du XIV siècle', *Ann. ESC* iv (1949), 167–82.

PERROY, E. 'Wage labour in France in the later Middle Ages', *Econ. Hist. Rev.*, viii (1955–56), 232–9.

POSTAN, M. M. 'The fifteenth century', *Econ. Hist. Rev.*, ix (1938–39), 160–7.

ROOVER, R. DE. 'Labour conditions in Florence around 1400: theory, policy and reality', in *Florentine Studies*, ed. N. Rubinstein, Faber, 1968, 277–313.

SAPORI, ARMANDO. 'The culture of the medieval Italian merchant', *Enterprise and Secular Change*, ed. F. C. Lane and J. C. Riemersma, Homewood, Ill., Irwin, 1953, 53–65.

VILAR, P. 'Le declin catalan du bas moyen âge', *Estudios de Historia Moderna*, vi (1956–59), 3–68.

VAN DER WEE, H. *The Growth of the Antwerp Market and the European Economy*, Recueil de Travaux d'Histoire et de Philologie, 4e série, fasc. 29, Louvain, 1963.

WALEY, D. *Later Medieval Europe*, Longmans, 1964.

WERVEKE, H. VAN. 'Essor et declin de la Flandre', *Stud. On. Gino Luzzatto*, Milan, Dott. A. Giuffré, 1949, 152–60.

# Index

545

# Index

# Index

# Index

# Index